ELEVENTH EDITION

APPLYING ETHICS

A Text with Readings

JULIE C. VAN CAMP
California State University
Long Beach

JEFFREY OLEN
Regis University
Colorado Springs

VINCENT BARRY
Bakersfield College

CENGAGE
Learning·

Australia • Brazil • Japan • Korea • Mexico • Singapore • Spain • United Kingdom • United States

CENGAGE
Learning·

**Applying Ethics: A Text with Readings,
Eleventh Edition**
Julie C. Van Camp, Jeffrey Olen,
Vincent Barry

Product Director: Suzanne Jeans

Product Manager: Debra Matteson

Content Developer: Florence Kilgo

Content Coordinator: Joshua Duncan

Media Developer: Christine Biagetti

Marketing Development Manager:
  Shanna Shelton

Content Project Manager: Alison Eigel Zade

Art Director: Kristina Mose-Libon, PMG

Manufacturing Planner: Sandee Milewski

Rights Acquisition Specialist:
  Shalice Shah-Caldwell

Production Service & Compositor: diacriTech

Cover Designer: PreMediaGlobal

Cover Image: ©steve kitching/Photos.com

For product information and technology assistance, contact us at
Cengage Learning Customer & Sales Support, 1-800-354-9706

For permission to use material from this text or product,
submit all requests online at **www.cengage.com/permissions**.
Further permissions questions can be emailed to
permissionrequest@cengage.com.

Library of Congress Control Number: 2013954886

ISBN-13: 978-1-285-19677-0

ISBN-10: 1-285-19677-5

Cengage Learning
20 Channel Center Street
Boston, MA 02210
USA

Cengage Learning is a leading provider of customized learning solutions with
office locations around the globe, including Singapore, the United Kingdom,
Australia, Mexico, Brazil and Japan. Locate your local office at
www.cengage.com/global

Cengage Learning products are represented in Canada by
Nelson Education, Ltd.

For your course and learning solutions, visit **www.cengage.com**

Purchase any of our products at your local college store or at our preferred
online store **www.cengagebrain.com**

Instructors: Please visit **login.cengage.com** and log in to access
instructor-specific resources.

Printed in the United States of America
2 3 4 5 6   25 24 23 22 21

To My Students—
J.C.V.C

To Jane Cullen—
J.O.

To Jim Wilson—
V.B.

CONTENTS

PREFACE

FOR MOST STUDENTS taking applied ethics, it will be their first—and maybe only—philosophy course. They may have thought and argued about topics such as abortion and the death penalty, welfare and affirmative action, but they enter the classroom with little experience in moral philosophy or critical thinking. Nor do they always have a firm handle on the legal, scientific, and other information relevant to the issues they'll be discussing. Throughout the eleven editions of *Applying Ethics,* the book's goal has been to meet these students' needs. *Applying Ethics* is, as the subtitle says, a text with readings, providing a variety of features to help students and their instructors approach the most significant moral controversies of the day.

The book contains two distinct parts. Part 1, "Moral Reasoning," provides the philosophical background that many readers will find helpful. The first chapter deals with moral reasons and principles, drawing on the views of such philosophers as Aristotle, Kant, Mill, Plato, and Held. It also includes discussions of ethical relativism and what it means to think morally. The second chapter is an introduction to critical thinking, with particular emphasis on the evaluation of moral arguments.

The chapters in Part 2, "Issues," begin with introductory essays by the book's authors. Each lays out the relevant moral issues and background material. Next come pro and con arguments on the chapter's central dispute, written in colloquial "point–counterpoint" style. After that come four readings, each preceded by head notes summarizing the main points and followed by questions for analysis. And then, to provoke further class discussion, each chapter ends with four Case Presentations.

NEW FEATURES

1. Updates of Chapter 1, including a new reading by Plato.
2. Updates of Chapter 3, including two new readings: Margaret A. Farley, "Framework for a Sexual Ethic: Just Sex" and Ann Ferguson, "Gay Marriage: An American and Feminist Dilemma," and new information on the latest U.S. Supreme Court decisions.
3. Updates of Chapter 4, including a new reading: Bertha Alvarez Manninen, "Expanding the Discussion about Fetal Life within Prochoice Advocacy."

4. Updates of Chapter 5, including a new reading: J. David Velleman, "Against the Right to Die."

5. Updates of Chapter 6, including a new reading on synthetic biology by the Presidential Commission for the Study of Bioethical Issues and updated information on stem cell research.

6. Updates of Chapter 7, including updated information on the abolition of the death penalty in several states and the increased rate of execution of women.

7. Updates of Chapter 8, including updated information on efforts to combat terrorism and the use of drones.

8. Updates of Chapter 9, including a new reading: Peter Singer, "Global Poverty: What Are Our Obligations."

9. Updates of Chapter 10, including a new reading: Elizabeth Anderson, "Affirmative Action Is About Helping All of Us" and a new case study on *Fisher v. University of Texas.*

10. Updates of Chapter 11, including updated information on climate change.

11. Updates of Chapter 12, including a new reading: Eugene H. Spafford, "Are Computer Hacker Break-ins Ethical?" and censorship issues on Twitter.

12. Several case presentations from previous editions are available on the Cengage website.

ACKNOWLEDGMENTS

As a teacher who used this book for many years, I have long been grateful for the work of Vincent Barry, who produced the first two editions alone, and Jeffrey Olen, who joined him as coauthor. Ken King was the Wadsworth philosophy editor for the first four editions, followed by Tammy Goldfield, Peter Adams, Steve Wainwright, Worth Hawes, Joann Kozyrev, and Debra Matteson. I also greatly appreciate the many helpful suggestions from reviewers over the years on successive editions.

I have been honored to join such an exceptional team for the eighth, ninth, tenth, and now eleventh editions, and I hope this new one lives up to the expectations of our most important readers, our students.

Julie C. Van Camp

Moral Reasoning

CHAPTER ONE

Moral Reasons

- **Moral Reasoning**
- **Individual Morality and Social Morality**
- **Ethical Relativism**
- **Principles of Individual Morality**
- **Principles of Social Morality**
- **Summary and Conclusions**

ARISTOTLE **Moral Virtue**
IMMANUEL KANT **Respect for Persons**
JOHN STUART MILL **Utilitarianism**
PLATO **Justice as a Virtue**
VIRGINIA HELD **The Ethics of Care**

WHEN WE ACT, we act for reasons. We eat breakfast because we are hungry or because it gives us the energy we need to get through the morning. We read a book because we want to be entertained or because we want to learn something. We buy a car because it's reliable, fun to drive, or affordable.

At any one time, we might—and usually do—have many reasons to do all sorts of things. Most of what we do we do for more than one reason. We buy a car because it's reliable *and* fun to drive and affordable, and we read a book because it's entertaining *and* informative.

But not all of our relevant reasons support the same course of action when we choose to do something. Often, we find ourselves faced with conflicting reasons, reasons both to do and not to do something. In addition to our reasons *for* eating breakfast, we might have reasons for *not* eating it. We might be in a hurry, or we might be trying to lose weight.

When our reasons lead us in different directions like that, we must decide which direction to take. Although we can make our decision in a purely arbitrary way—by flipping a coin, perhaps—the rational way to proceed is to weigh the conflicting reasons and ask ourselves which of the conflicting reasons are the best reasons. If we are lucky, we will answer the question correctly. That is, we will choose the best thing to do, the right course of action. We will do what we ought to do under the circumstances. If we are unlucky, we will choose the wrong course of action. We will do what we ought not to do.

Of course, whether we choose correctly is not merely a matter of luck. If it were, rational deliberation would be no more trustworthy than the flip of a coin. Whether we choose correctly is also a matter of how well informed we are, how carefully we reason, how accurately we gauge the pros and cons of the alternatives, how exhaustive our deliberations are. Thus, we can minimize the element of luck when buying a car by test-driving various models, by reading reports in *Car and Driver* and *Consumer Reports,* and by giving careful attention to our own needs and preferences. Do we really need a car with this much power? Does appearance matter that much to us? Can we afford all of these options?

We can also minimize the element of luck by making sure that we reason in a reliable way. In the next chapter, we will take a careful look at what makes reasoning reliable. For the rest of this chapter, though, we concentrate on a particular kind of reasoning—moral reasoning.

MORAL REASONING

To reason morally is not to reason in a certain way. Rather, it is to consider certain kinds of reasons—moral reasons. It is to try to arrive at the best moral reasons for acting, to choose the morally right course of action, to do what we morally ought to do.

There are, after all, many different ways in which an action can be right or wrong. An artist who puts the right finishing touches on a painting does what is aesthetically right. An investor who buys and sells stock at the right times does what is financially right. Someone who gives up smoking cigarettes does what is right for her health. And someone who returns a found wallet does what is morally right. In the first case, we have an action supported by the best aesthetic reasons. In the second, one supported by the best financial reasons. In the third, one supported by the best health-related reasons. In the fourth, one supported by the best moral reasons.

Sometimes an action will be right in one way but wrong in another. That is, the best reasons of one kind will support it, while the best reasons of another kind will support something else. Reasons of self-interest, for example, might lead us to conclude that we ought to keep a found wallet. Moral reasons, on the other hand, lead us to conclude that we ought to return it. In cases like that, we must decide which kind of reason is best. We must decide what we ought to do, all things considered.

When we make these all-things-considered judgments, we generally do so based on what matters to us most. Some people are willing to risk their health because they enjoy smoking; others are not. Some people are willing to forego a higher paying job for a more pleasant one; others are not. Some people are willing to set aside their self-interest to do what is morally right; others are not.

Although we generally give people a lot of leeway in determining what most matters to them, we do expect them to give moral reasons high priority. And when the moral stakes are very high, we expect people to give moral reasons top priority. We expect them to realize that the morally right course of action is the best course of action—what they ought to do, all things considered.

These are not unreasonable expectations. If we are to live together in society, we must cooperate with one another. And if we are to cooperate with one another, we must trust one another. And we cannot trust people who treat honesty, good faith, and loyalty lightly.

INDIVIDUAL MORALITY AND SOCIAL MORALITY

Honesty, good faith, and loyalty are important considerations of *individual* morality. When each of us, as individuals, must decide what to do, we must, if we are to decide morally, consider whether we are being honest or dishonest, faithful to our commitments to others or unfaithful to them, loyal to those who deserve our loyalty or disloyal to them. The roles that such considerations play in our lives are crucial to our understanding of ourselves as moral people. And the roles that they play in the lives of others are crucial to our moral judgments of both them and their actions.

Because the topics discussed in Part 2 of this book concern the morality of various kinds of actions, considerations of individual morality will play an important role in those discussions. But so will moral considerations of another kind—*social* morality. In discussing issues such as abortion, we will be concerned not only with whether it is moral for an individual woman to have an abortion in various kinds of circumstances, but also with how society as a whole should deal with abortion.

The two concerns are related, of course, but as we shall see, answering the first does not necessarily settle the second. Rape and armed robbery are obviously immoral, and even rational rapists and armed robbers, we can safely suppose, understand why we require laws forbidding such behavior and why we are perfectly justified in locking up people who disobey them. But no rational person believes that every immoral act should be punishable by imprisonment or even made illegal. Who would want to prosecute everyone who cheats in a "friendly" game of tennis?

Also, we might have good reason to want society to regulate various kinds of behavior that do not violate any considerations of individual morality. Many people feel, for instance, that a mature, psychologically sound adult does nothing immoral by enjoying pornography in the privacy of his or her home, but these same people might also feel that pornography presents serious social dangers and should be curbed or outlawed.

Obviously, what we need are some general principles of social morality to guide us when we ask ourselves how society ought to deal with morally important social issues. And just as obviously, we need some general principles of individual morality to guide us when we ask ourselves how individuals ought to act in particular situations.

But before we take a look at various principles of individual and social morality, we should take a look at another issue, the issue of ethical relativism.

ETHICAL RELATIVISM

Ethical relativism is the view that moral truths are not absolutely true but true relative to a particular society or individual. According to an ethical relativist, whether an action is right or wrong depends on the moral norms of society or the moral commitments of the individual, and no absolute standard exists by which differing rules or commitments can be judged. So what's morally right in one society may be morally wrong in another, and what's morally right for Mary might be morally wrong for John.

As this description suggests, there are two forms of relativism—**cultural relativism** and **individual relativism.** According to the cultural relativist, the rightness or wrongness of an action depends on society's norms. According to the individual relativist, the rightness or wrongness of an action depends on the individual's own commitments.

The appeal of ethical relativism rests on two points. First, different societies often do have different moral norms, and individuals often do have different moral commitments. Second, there seems to be no decisive way to settle moral disputes as there are decisive ways to settle many other kinds of disputes. If two individuals or societies differ radically about right and wrong, there seem to be no tests or experiments we can run to confirm the views of one or the other.

Both kinds of relativism exist in varying degrees. Someone can be a relativist about some matters—sexual morality, for instance—but a nonrelativist about others—slavery, for instance. Someone can also be a cultural relativist about some matters and an individual relativist about others or both a cultural and individual relativist about all moral matters. Relativism can also come in more or less sophisticated versions. In the least sophisticated versions, arguing about abortion, affirmative action, or any other issue we address in Part 2 is like arguing about whether chocolate tastes better than vanilla. In other words, morality is merely a matter of taste or custom; and one taste or custom is as good as another, whether the taste is for slavery or brightly colored clothes, for theft or science fiction. In the more sophisticated versions of relativism, morality is much more complicated; and arguments about the issues in Part 2 concern much more than individual taste or social custom, leading to the conclusion that some tastes or customs are decidedly worse than others.

Relativism is, of course, a controversial view. Opponents argue that variation in moral commitments does not prove that moral truth is relative any more than variation in scientific belief proves that scientific truth is relative. They also argue that the difficulty of deciding moral disputes can be dispelled by a deeper understanding of morality. Although we cannot go through all the arguments for and against the many forms of relativism here, we should note a few points that pertain to the rest of the book.

First of all, even if it turns out that some form of relativism is true, that does not mean we cannot criticize the norms of our society or the moral commitments of others. Morality is not, as the least sophisticated forms of relativism would have it, merely an arbitrary matter of taste, like the preference for vanilla over chocolate, nor is it merely a matter of custom, like Fourth of July fireworks. As will be stressed throughout this book, we have the norms and commitments we do for *reasons,* and because they govern the most important areas of our lives, it is important that we examine these reasons carefully. Perhaps some of our moral commitments rest on false beliefs. Perhaps some rest on outmoded assumptions about what makes for a harmonious or desirable society. Perhaps some are inconsistent with other more deeply held moral commitments, such as fairness. Perhaps we neglected important considerations when we first arrived at some of our moral commitments.

The discovery of such flaws in our moral reasoning has led us to abandon a variety of practices, from racial segregation to involuntary medical treatment. As we shall see, many people feel that similar flaws undercut our justification of other practices—abortion, for instance, or treatment of animals, or capital punishment. And whether we feel that our conceptions of fairness and a desirable society are absolutely valid or only relatively valid, we can—and must, if we are to consider our society a good one—test our practices against them.

PRINCIPLES OF INDIVIDUAL MORALITY

It is easy to think of morality as a system of rules—some telling us not to do certain things, like cheat, lie, break promises, steal, rape, and kill, and others telling us to do certain things, like help others in need, pay our debts, and be loyal to friends and family. But why do we have these rules and not others?

The quick answer is that these are the rules we were taught. And there is no arguing with that answer. Moral rules are the rules accepted by the members of a given society, the rules we agree to follow and expect others to follow, in large part because we were taught to do so. But if we look at morality in only that way, we do both morality and ourselves a disservice. We do morality a disservice by making it look arbitrary. We are in effect saying that we have the moral rules we do because we have the moral rules we do. And we do ourselves a disservice by making ourselves look like mindless followers of arbitrary rules.

But moral rules are not arbitrary. We have the rules we do for good reason. And we are not mindless followers of them. We accept them because we understand that we have them for good reason. And when we feel that reason requires us to change them, we do just that.

Consider one timely example of moral change. Not too long ago, women were expected to live their lives within narrowly defined roles. It was considered their duty to stay home with their children, their obligation to see to various household tasks, and while men might be praised for helping out every now and then, they were not morally required to do so. They were morally required to be the family breadwinner, and women were morally required not to take jobs from other family breadwinners.

All that has changed, of course—or is at least in the process of changing. Many women and an increasing number of men have come to doubt the acceptability of such rules. And what makes them unacceptable is that they are now seen as violating some general moral *principles*—the principle of fairness, most notably. Women do not believe it fair that their lives are so restricted, and many men have come to agree.

What this example shows is that morality is not merely a matter of rules but also of principles—general standards for evaluating conduct, standards that we apply to all behavior and rules.

This point can be made in another way. No moral rule is exceptionless. Sometimes we are morally justified in breaking a promise. Sometimes we are morally justified in failing to help someone in need. Consider how easy it is to find yourself in a situation in which you must break a promise to Mary to help John or must fail to help John to keep your promise to Mary. Unless we allow that the two rules have exceptions and one of them applies here, we are left with a morally immovable object and a morally irresistible force—that is, a morally impossible situation. To resolve the dilemma, we must recognize that one of the rules takes precedence in this particular case and that we are dealing with a legitimate exception to the other. How do we decide which takes precedence? By appealing to some general moral principle.

There is also one more thing that shows the importance of moral principles. The debates of Part 2 of this book are, in part, about what moral rules we should adopt. Should we adopt a rule that forbids us to give terminally ill patients in great pain a lethal injection if they request it? Should we adopt a rule that permits us to do so? Or should we adopt a rule that requires us to do so? Should we adopt a rule forbidding all abortions, some abortions, or no abortions? If suitable answers are to be found, we must appeal to moral principles.

The Principle of Utility

One of the best known general moral principles is closely associated with a number of moral philosophers, most notably the British philosopher John Stuart Mill (1806–1873). It is known as both the **principle of utility** and the **greatest happiness principle.** It tells us to produce the greatest balance of happiness over unhappiness, making sure that we give equal consideration to the happiness and unhappiness of everyone who stands to be affected by our actions.

The principle of utility can be applied in two different ways. The first is to apply it to individual *acts*. How are we to do that? Well, we might ask ourselves every time we act which of the options open to us will maximize happiness, but Mill did not recommend that procedure because it would be much too time consuming. Since we know that lying and stealing and cheating will rarely maximize happiness when everyone is taken equally into account, the sensible thing to do is avoid such behavior without worrying about the principle of utility.

But we sometimes have reason to believe that what usually maximizes happiness might not. Remember the example in which you cannot both keep your promise to Mary and help John. Although keeping promises usually maximizes happiness and helping others usually maximizes happiness, in this case, one will not. That's when Mill tells us to appeal to the principle of utility before we act.

The second way is to apply the principle to *rules* rather than to acts. Following this method, we appeal to the principle of utility only when we are considering which moral rules we should adopt. We ask ourselves which of the alternatives will maximize happiness if generally followed by the members of our society. Would a moral rule permitting mercy killing maximize happiness, or would one forbidding it? Whichever one would, that's the rule we ought to adopt.

The principle of utility is certainly a reasonable moral principle, whether applied to acts or rules. How our behavior affects others should be of moral concern to us. Moreover, we want our moral rules to make our society a good society, and it is hard to argue against the claim that a happy society is better than an unhappy society. So it is not surprising that utilitarian considerations play an important role in the moral reasoning of many individuals. Nor is it surprising that they play an important role in many of the arguments of Part 2.

Still, most people believe that it would be a mistake to make the principle of utility the final arbiter of *all* moral decisions. Suppose Bill borrows $10 from Carol on the condition that he pay her back tomorrow. Doesn't that create an obligation to her? And since it does, does Bill have the moral right to neglect that obligation merely because he can maximize happiness by doing something else with the money?

That's one reason for recognizing limits to the principle. Another is that it is a very demanding principle. Very rarely, after all, do most of us take into equal account everybody's happiness before we act. Often, we think that our own happiness and the happiness of people who most matter to us should take precedence. That's why we sometimes splurge on presents for our families, even though we might create greater happiness by spending our money on the poor instead. Although we might agree that it would be commendable to do otherwise, it hardly seems *wrong* to splurge on the people we love.

Even when applied to rules rather than acts, the principle of utility seems to have its limitations. Although we want our moral rules to create happiness and avoid unhappiness, we don't want them to do only that. We also want them to be fair. And we sometimes find that the principle of utility justifies unfair rules. For example, we can easily imagine rules allowing researchers to experiment on selectively chosen human beings. Such rules might very well create the greatest balance of happiness over unhappiness but still be morally unacceptable—because the chosen few would be involuntary subjects or because they would have to be "sacrificed" during the experiments. Although the medical knowledge gained might benefit the rest of us so enormously that it outweighs the harm to the subjects, it is unfair of us to benefit at their expense in that way.

So the principle of utility cannot be, as Mill thought, the one fundamental moral principle that underlies all of morality. But the effect of our actions and moral rules on the happiness and unhappiness of people remains an important moral consideration all the same.

Fairness

Fairness, we just saw, often plays a crucial role in moral reasoning. But as we shall see in Part 2, it's not always easy to know what the fairest thing to do is. The problem will be especially acute when we discuss affirmative action, an issue in which different but equally important notions of fairness lead to different resolutions. We can't look at all the conceptions of fairness that come into play in moral reasoning here—some are better considered in Part 2 and some in connection with principles of social morality—but we can look at some.

The Golden Rule

Many people take the golden rule to be the best standard of fairness. Certainly, it is a principle that most of us learned very early in our moral education and one that plays a very large role in our moral lives. But applying it is not as simple a matter as most people think.

For most of us, to do unto others as we would have them do unto us is to do much more than we are inclined to do. Even more important, it is to do much more than we think we ought to do. Most of us would be very pleased if utter strangers walked up to us and gave us wads of $100 bills, for example. Yet we do not think that we ought to do the same for others.

The reason we rarely think of such things when we think of the golden rule is that we usually apply it in the context of other moral rules and principles. That is, we don't necessarily think that we ought to act toward others as we would *like* them to act toward us so much as we think that we ought to act toward others as they *ought* to act toward us. If we are to act morally, we must follow the same moral rules in our dealings with others that we expect them to follow in their dealings with us.

When we look at the golden rule that way, we recognize that none of us is a special case. The same moral standards apply to all of us. That is indeed an important thing to recognize if we are to reason morally, but it doesn't always tell us what those standards are.

The negative version of the golden rule gives us more help here. The negative version tells us *not* to treat others as we would *not* have them treat us. That is certainly one reason we find a moral rule allowing experimentation on unwilling subjects morally unacceptable. We would not have somebody experiment on us against our will.

But even the negative version requires a context of other rules and principles for its application because not all of us find the same treatment unacceptable. Consider one common example. Some people prefer to be lied to rather than face unpleasant truths, while others insist on the truth come what may (a fact that physicians are probably most aware of). But that does not mean that the people who don't want to hear the truth should withhold it from those who do.

Respect for Persons

Why shouldn't people who want the truth withheld from them withhold it from others who don't? The answer is simple. In such cases, they should respect the wishes of others. How the other person feels about being lied to matters more than how the would-be liar feels.

More generally, we should always treat other people with respect, and many moral philosophers take **respect for persons** to be *the* fundamental moral principle. The kind of respect they have in mind should not be confused with the kind of respect exemplified by calling people by their appropriate titles. It is a special kind of respect, often called Kantian respect, after the German philosopher Immanuel Kant (1724–1804). Kantian respect is captured by this moral principle: Never use other people merely as a means to your own ends. The reading "Respect for Persons," included here, discusses this in more detail.

Be sure to notice the word "merely" in the principle. It makes a crucial difference, telling us when it is moral to use another person for our own ends and when it is not. It tells us that it is moral to use a bank teller to cash our checks, a waiter to bring our food, a mechanic to fix our cars, and an accountant to prepare our tax forms. Why are they and other like examples moral? Because the people involved are not *merely* serving our own ends. They are serving their own ends as well. They are, among other things, earning their food and rent money.

For an example of using others merely as a means to our own ends, we can return to an earlier one. To experiment on unwilling subjects is a perfect illustration. To do that is to give no consideration to the subjects' ends. It is to treat them as mere things that exist for our own ends, not as persons who have their own ends in life.

Put another way, respect for persons is intimately connected to the recognition that persons are *autonomous* beings. Our behavior is the product of our choices, and our choices are the product of what we take to be the best reasons for acting. And that is what makes us autonomous. We have our own goals and aspirations, we are capable of evaluating and weighing them against one another, we can reject or change them as we see fit, and we can determine how best to achieve those goals and then act accordingly.

To respect persons, then, is to recognize them as autonomous beings and treat them accordingly. It is to recognize that they have their own reasons for acting and to give those reasons the same respect we feel our own reasons warrant from others. And forcing someone to be a subject in a medical experiment is an obvious case of failing to respect his or her autonomy. So is any kind of coercion—from extortion and armed robbery to slavery and murder.

Many other cases are less obvious. Lying is one. When John lies to Maria, he is trying to manipulate her. His goal is to get her to act as he wants her to act, not as she would act if she knew the truth. Withholding information is another. If Maria wants to borrow John's car for purposes he doesn't approve of, she violates Kantian respect by not telling him. She is manipulating him. And the same is true of making commitments we have no intention of honoring.

Does that mean we should never lie, withhold information, or break a promise? Kant thought we should never lie, but we needn't agree with him. Not only do we find white lies permissible, but we also think it right to lie in some cases if there is no other way to prevent someone from doing serious harm. Respect for persons certainly justifies the moral rule "Don't lie," but it needn't lead to the conclusion that lying to save an innocent life isn't a legitimate exception. The important thing about respect for persons is that it cannot justify lying merely for our own convenience or merely to maximize happiness.

If we want to know what does count as a legitimate exception, probably the best thing to do is apply the following test. Imagine that a group of reasonable people is trying to decide what rules they ought to follow and that the rules they pick will include a list of all the exceptions. If it seems likely that they would freely agree to the proposed exception, then we may consider it legitimate.

Many moral philosophers like that test because it manifests Kantian respect. To apply it is to treat others as they would agree to be treated if it were up to them to participate in the making of our moral rules. And to treat them that way is to recognize them as autonomous beings.

Kantian respect is a very powerful notion. It can explain why various kinds of behavior are wrong and why others are right. Also, it is a very reasonable thing to accept as a general moral principle. But many people believe that it's not powerful enough. Since animals are not autonomous beings, it provides no guidelines for our treatment of them. The same can be said about fetuses. Also, Kantian respect seems to permit a variety of practices that many people consider immoral, like homosexuality among consenting adults or giving lethal injections to terminally ill patients who ask for them.

Whether these practices are immoral is, of course, a matter of great controversy, which is why we will look at them in Part 2. Still, the fact that they are controversial shows that many people adhere to other moral principles. Respect for persons may give us an excellent handle on fairness, but like the principle of utility, it may not be our only fundamental moral principle.

Proper Human Excellences

The moral principles we have looked at so far focus on an individual's obligations to others. They provide general guidelines for how we ought to act toward one another. But ethical thought has also paid close attention to another aspect of human life—the human good. Philosophers who pursue this line of thought do not focus on obligations but on character traits and activities that are distinctively human and, when taken together, constitute the good life for human beings. According to this approach to ethics, there are certain excellences uniquely proper to human life, and the full moral life involves the development of these excellences.

Before considering what these excellences might be, let's look at why this line of thought is so appealing. A good place to start is with the ancient Greek philosopher

Aristotle (384–322 B.C.E.), included in the readings here. As Aristotle pointed out, human artifacts have distinctive purposes. The purpose of a pen is to write; of a lamp, to give light; of a knife, to cut. And knowing the purpose of any artifact, we also know how to tell whether it is a good or bad one. A knife with a strong blade is better than one with a weak blade. So is a knife with a handle that gives us a sure, comfortable grip better than one with a handle that does not. Thus, a strong blade and a sure, comfortable grip can be called excellences proper to a knife.

Similar remarks hold for human activities—from performing surgery to playing basketball. Each has its own purpose (or purposes), and there are corresponding excellences appropriate to engaging in each of them. Good basketball players are able to shoot, pass, rebound, and make it difficult for opponents to shoot, pass, and rebound; various physical and mental skills, plus proper conditioning, will help them do just those things.

Of course, not all of us are basketball players—or surgeons, welders, attorneys, or lifeguards, for that matter. So the distinctive excellences proper to those roles need not concern us. But some excellences are proper to all of these roles, and those that are, such as concentration and pride in our work, should concern us. Even more important, we are sons or daughters, friends, neighbors, co-workers, and citizens, and we are—or are likely to be—lovers, spouses, parents, and grandparents. And the excellences proper to these roles—loyalty, generosity, honesty, kindness, and the like—are proper to us all. They are, that is, proper human excellences, which are often called **virtues.**

Are there proper human excellences apart from our social roles? Aristotle thought so. He believed that there are natural purposes as well as social purposes. To him, everything in nature has a natural purpose or goal—from the acorn, whose natural purpose is to become an oak tree, to the human being. The human being's natural purpose is *eudaimonia*, a Greek word usually translated as "happiness" but better understood as total well-being. It is what all of us naturally strive for.

Aristotle believed that a good part of *eudaimonia* is fulfilling our social roles, but far from all of it. We are not, after all, just social animals (or as he put it, political animals). We are also rational animals. Indeed, our ability to reason as we do is, he thought, the trait that best defines us. So an essential part of *eudaimonia* must consist in the proper use of reason. And that means that we must live well-ordered lives, lives not given to extremes. We should not let courage turn to foolhardiness or generosity turn to extravagance. Nor should we let our emotions run away with us. We should display them only when appropriate, and then only to the appropriate degree.

To avoid extremes is the key to what Aristotle called practical wisdom, which is one of the two kinds of wisdom that humans are capable of. The other is the wisdom that comes from contemplating the world in which we live. It is a deep understanding of the world, and like practical wisdom, it too is a proper human excellence. We cannot achieve total well-being without it.

Aristotle's concern with contemplation takes us far from the issues of Part 2, but his other points do have relevance for us. For one thing, many of the issues we'll be discussing relate directly to various social roles and the excellences proper to them. Is it the proper role of healthcare professionals actively and intentionally to bring about the death of a terminally ill patient? To treat a baby born three months premature one way and a fetus of six months another?

These issues also touch on the more general human excellences. Thus, we will consider compassion for the dying, respect for nature, mercy for those convicted of capital crimes, understanding toward pregnant women, and concern for fetuses.

Moreover, virtue and the notion of a well-ordered life play a large role in the discussion of sexual morality. The Catholic thinker Thomas Aquinas (1225–1274) is most important here. Taking his cue from Aristotle's view on purpose in nature, he argued that our sexual organs have as their natural purpose procreation, and any sexual activity that is not open to that end is disordered and immoral. Catholic thinking since Aquinas has continued to emphasize that purpose, but it has also emphasized another proper purpose of human sexuality—the expression of fully human love and dignity. According to this line of thought, sex that is not such an expression, including all sex outside of marriage, is disordered and immoral.

The Catholic position is, of course, highly controversial. So, for that matter, is Aristotle's view that there are natural purposes in addition to social ones. But those controversies are matters for Part 2. For now, the important point is this: Ethical thinking includes consideration of human virtues as well as of obligations to others. And in asking what moral rules to adopt, we must ask ourselves what kind of people we should be and how we should live our lives.

The Will of God

To many people, religious belief provides the final word on moral questions. And because the issues we'll be looking at later have been addressed by religious traditions of all kinds, many people rely on their religious belief for guidance. It is not surprising, then, that much of the popular debate that we find in such places as the letter-to-the-editor sections of local newspapers is filled with appeals to the will of God.

Why give God the final word in these matters? Two possibilities come readily to mind. The first is that God is the ultimate source of morality. God made the universe and put human beings in it for some purpose, and whether we act rightly or wrongly depends on how well we pursue that purpose. In other words, there are both moral laws and physical laws, and God is the author of both.

That was the view of Thomas Aquinas, who referred to the system of divine moral laws as **natural law.** Unlike the conventional laws enacted by legislatures, the natural law, according to Aquinas, is embedded in nature, just as natural purposes are embedded in nature. It is also embedded in human reason. So the natural law is not only the law of God but the law of reason as well. And by turning our reason to moral matters, Aquinas said, we can know such basic moral truths as "Thou shalt not kill" as surely as we know that two plus two equals four.

According to the other possibility, God is not so much the source of morality as the best authority on morality. What makes God the best authority depends on how we think of morality. Some people think of morality as a collection of moral facts, much as they think of science as a collection of scientific facts. And God, being all knowing, knows both kinds of facts. Others think of morality in a different way. To them, the right thing to do is what an ideal observer would consider the best thing to do—an ideal observer being someone who is fully informed about the case at hand and totally impartial. And God alone is in that position.

Reliance on God does raise some problems, though. Can we really be certain what God wants us to do? Different religious traditions do give conflicting answers to various moral questions, and even within any given religious tradition, we can often find conflicting answers. Moreover, we should not forget agnostics and atheists, nor should we forget religious individuals who, for one reason or another, sincerely believe that they must look to their own consciences for the ultimate answers to moral questions.

Such considerations needn't lead to disrespect for religious belief, of course, any more than they need lead to the conclusion that religious people should disregard religious belief when making moral decisions. But they do show the limitations of religious belief for purposes of moral argument.

As we shall see in the next chapter, a good argument goes from statements accepted as true to a conclusion well supported by those statements. If the initial statements are not accepted by our opponents, our arguments will have no force. Also, the better our justification for accepting those initial statements as true, the better the argument. And given the role that faith plays in religious belief, statements about God can have less independent justification than the conclusions they are asked to support.

It is for those reasons, more than antipathy toward religious belief, that moral philosophers addressing a varied audience concentrate on arguments that do not rely on statements about God's will. And it is for the same reasons that this book will do the same.

References to natural law, on the other hand, will appear in Part 2, since philosophers from the time of Aristotle to the present have argued that human behavior can be divided into the natural and unnatural without reliance on the will of God.

PRINCIPLES OF SOCIAL MORALITY

So far, we have been concerned with how individuals ought to act. Our focus has been on the moral principles that guide individuals when they must determine what they, and others, ought to do.

But we act collectively as well as individually. Most important for our purposes, we act as a municipality, as a state, as a nation. We enact laws, we imprison, fine, and execute people, we enter into treaties and wage war. And collective action, like individual action, can be moral or immoral. Whether it is one or the other, like individual action, depends on how well it is supported by moral principles.

As we shall see, the relevant principles are often the same. Individually and collectively, we should be concerned with human happiness, so the principle of utility is an important principle of social morality. Individually and collectively, we should be concerned with fairness, so respect for persons too is an important principle of social morality. And when we act collectively, we care about what kind of society we should be as much as we care about what kind of individuals we should be when we act individually.

But collective action does pose one special difficulty. When Congress acts, the United States acts, but many U.S. citizens will invariably disagree with how Congress acts, including some members of Congress itself. Their disagreement notwithstanding, they are bound by the acts of Congress. They must pay taxes for purposes they find abhorrent, they must submit to regulations they find offensive, and they must give up freedoms they hold dear—that, or face fine or imprisonment. Governments, even democratic governments like our own, are inherently coercive. That is the special difficulty, and it is why we need additional principles of social morality.

Social Justice

If we ask ourselves what kind of society we should be, the natural answer is this: a just society. Candidates on the campaign trail may disagree on all sorts of issues, but none will speak out in favor of injustice. Many will speak out in favor of positions that others consider unjust, but they will argue in turn that our own positions are the unjust ones. We disagree about what justice requires, but not that we are morally required to be just.

In other words, the issue of social justice—what makes a society a just one—is a very controversial matter. People of good will who share the same principles of individual morality—people who are fair, loyal, honest, faithful, and kind—have great difficulty agreeing on principles of social justice.

That difficulty is due largely to the difficulty noted just before. Government action is coercive action. All of us are in principle against coercion, but we also recognize the occasional need for it. Unfortunately, we don't always recognize it on the same occasions. A look at some important principles of social justice will explain why.

Individual Rights

The Bill of Rights explicitly guarantees us a number of individual freedoms—freedoms of speech, press, religion, and assembly, for example. As part of our Constitution, these guarantees are part of the fundamental law of the land, as are the Bill of Rights' guarantees of a fair trial and its protection against unreasonable search and seizure.

Although these guarantees are set forth in plain enough English, many people of good will disagree about how they should be interpreted. That our guarantee of a free press allows us to criticize government policies is not a matter of controversy. That it allows us to print and sell hard-core pornography is. When such controversies arise, they are settled by the courts, which are the ultimate legal arbiters of how these guarantees are to be understood.

The courts also serve as the ultimate legal arbiters in controversies about implicit constitutional guarantees. The right to privacy, to pick an example that will concern us in Part 2, is not explicitly mentioned in the Bill of Rights or anywhere else in the Constitution. Still, the courts have held that it is a constitutionally protected one.

If enough of us disagree with the courts, we can amend the Constitution. But barring such amendments, the decisions of the courts remain the law of the land. They set the legal limits on what kinds of individual behavior the various levels of government can regulate and on the ways it can regulate them. Even if we doubt that a woman has a moral right to abort a fetus in the early months of her pregnancy, we cannot doubt, as matters now stand, that she has the legal right to do so.

But ought she have that legal right? Ought consenting adults have the legal right to engage in private homosexual acts? Ought we grant pornography the same protections as weekly newsmagazines? What legal rights should we grant? And why?

Natural Rights

One historically important answer to these questions is this: We ought to have the legal right to do whatever we have the natural right to do because no government can justly violate our natural rights. That answer was powerfully advanced by the English philosopher John Locke (1632–1704) and echoed by Thomas Jefferson in the Declaration of Independence. Among its most recent champions was the American philosopher Robert Nozick (1938–2002).

Natural rights are rights that all of us are born with. They belong to us by virtue of the fact that we are human beings, and no one has the right to interfere with our exercise of them. Locke and Nozick list them as life, liberty, and property; Jefferson as life, liberty, and the pursuit of happiness. Because no one can interfere with the exercise of our natural rights, we cannot interfere with anyone else's. And that places the only legitimate limits on our exercise of those rights. Our right to swing our arms, the popular saying has it, stops at someone else's nose. But as long as no one's nose (or property, for that matter) is in the way, we are free to swing.

Even the government, according to natural rights theorists, has no right to interfere. The reason is simple. The government derives its rightful powers from the governed, and the governed cannot transfer to the government any rights they do not have by nature. Since all of us have the right to protect our natural rights, we can transfer the right to protect our lives, liberty, and property to the government. Since none of us has the right to interfere with anyone else's natural rights, we cannot transfer any such right to the government. A just society can have police forces, then, but it cannot tell us what we can and cannot read. It can imprison thieves and rapists, but it cannot imprison its peaceful critics.

These restrictions on government action are more severe than they might at first seem. They leave much behavior—even immoral behavior—free of government interference. The 1964 Civil Rights Act forbidding racial discrimination in privately owned places of public accommodation such as theaters and restaurants is, on this view, an unjust law. Since no one has a natural right to enter anyone's property against the owner's wishes, racial exclusion is an exercise of natural property rights that the government cannot interfere with. It goes without saying, then, that this view would not endorse government-mandated affirmative-action programs, one of the topics to be considered in Part 2. Nor would it endorse government payments to the poor, another topic we will consider. Since no one has the natural right to force others to give to the poor, we cannot transfer that right to the government.

Mutual Agreement behind the Veil of Ignorance

Where do natural rights come from? How do we get them? Locke and Jefferson thought them God given, but few philosophers today are willing to argue that way.

John Rawls (1921–2002), another American philosopher, takes a different approach to individual rights. Instead of saying that a just society is one that protects but does not interfere with natural rights, he says that the individual rights we ought to have are those that a just society would give us. His claim that justice should be the most important virtue of social institutions echoes Plato's views on justice over two thousand years earlier, although Rawls develops that principle in far more detail.

What is a just society, according to Rawls? A society in which no one has an unfair advantage over others. And how do we ensure that no one has an unfair advantage over others? By adopting fundamental principles of social justice that pass the following test: They must be principles that we would rationally agree upon behind the **veil of ignorance.** And what, finally, is it to be behind the veil of ignorance? It is to know how the principles would shape society but not to know what particular positions each of us would have in that society.

The reason that test would work, Rawls says, is that rational people would not agree to live in any unjust society if they did not know whether they would be the ones who would be unfairly taken advantage of. They would not, for example, be willing to institute slavery if they didn't know whether they'd be slave or master. Anything they would agree to behind the veil of ignorance, therefore, must be just.

What they would agree to are the following two principles:

The Equality Principle Every person has a right to the greatest basic freedom compatible with equal freedom for all. That is, there must be equal freedom for all, and if freedom can be increased without violating that requirement, it must be.

The Difference Principle All social and economic inequalities must meet two requirements. First, they must be to everyone's advantage, including the people at the bottom. It is, for example, to the advantage of everyone that surgeons make more money than unskilled workers. Everyone, including unskilled workers, benefits by having enough surgeons, and financial rewards help guarantee that enough people will pay the cost in time and money of going through medical school. Second, the inequalities must be attached to positions open to all. If surgeons are to be paid more than unskilled workers, then no one can be excluded from becoming a surgeon because of, say, race or sex.

The first principle gives us many freedoms covered by Locke's and Nozick's natural rights, including speech, press, religion, assembly, and more generally, the freedom to do as we please as long as we do not interfere with the rights of others.

The second principle, on the other hand, gives us many individual rights that are not among Locke's and Nozick's natural rights. In doing so, it places some important restrictions on Locke's and Nozick's natural rights—most important, on property rights. For example, the difference principle gives people at the bottom of the social-economic ladder the right to a minimum level of income. If their income falls below that level, the government has the obligation to supplement it with money collected through taxes. And that, from the viewpoint of natural rights advocates, is an unjust restriction on other people's property rights. The government is taking money that they earned so it can help the poor rather than letting them spend it as they see fit.

Equality

Another central principle of social justice is equality. A society in which all citizens are not treated equally can hardly be considered a just one. On that we all agree, just as we all agree that we ought to be a just society. But we do not all agree on what equal treatment requires of us any more than we all agree on what justice requires of us.

Consider equal treatment under the law, for example. To many people, equal treatment under the law is merely a procedural matter. As long as each of us is treated according to the same legal procedures, we are granted equal treatment under the law. Thus, what matters in criminal trials, say, is that all defendants are allowed full exercise of their rights, including their rights to counsel, to subpoena witnesses, to cross-examination, and to a jury of their peers. To others, equal treatment under the law means much more. If, for example, juries are more likely to apply the death penalty in cases where the victim is white than in cases where the victim is black, then equal treatment under the law is denied in capital cases, regardless of procedural guarantees.

Similar difficulties muddle the issue of equal opportunity. To some people, equal opportunity means lack of discrimination: As long as employers and universities choose employees and students on the basis of merit, not on the basis of sex or race, equal opportunity is secured. To others, equal opportunity requires affirmative action. Given the history of oppression against blacks, they argue, mere lack of discrimination cannot secure equal opportunity. Others go even further. Can we really believe, they ask, that the son of a millionaire and the daughter of a welfare recipient begin life with equal advantages? How many of you have enjoyed the same opportunities in life as George W. Bush? Can we really believe that differences in natural endowment make no difference to opportunity? How many of you have enjoyed the same opportunities as Michael Jordan or Julia Roberts?

People who argue that way generally conclude that equal treatment requires equality of results. Given that we cannot start out equally, there can be no real equal opportunity. The just thing to do, then, is see that society's wealth is distributed equally. Or they might reach a variation of that conclusion, arguing instead that the just thing to do is see that society's wealth is distributed according to need. Rawls, as we saw, argues in favor of equal distribution, except when it is in everyone's interest that some people have more. The German philosopher Karl Marx (1818–1883) famously advanced another principle: From each according to his abilities, to each according to his needs.

The General Welfare

The doctrine of natural rights greatly influenced the American Founding Fathers. Its influence appears not only in the Declaration of Independence but also in the Bill of Rights. The preamble to the Constitution shows another concern of the Founding Fathers—the general welfare—which brings us to another important principle of social morality: The different levels of government should promote the general welfare, or as it is often put, the common good, or the public interest.

Thus, we have come to expect our governments to do much in the promotion of the general welfare. We expect public schools and libraries, public funding of highways and medical research, zoning ordinances that guarantee us livable neighborhoods, laws protecting our rivers and air, and much else that is no longer controversial.

Much else that governments do to promote the general welfare is controversial. So is much else that various people propose that our governments do to promote it. Sometimes the controversy is merely over practical considerations, as when we debate whether one policy or another will better increase worker productivity. Often, though, the controversy is over profoundly moral considerations, as when we debate the issues of Part 2 of this book.

One particularly profound moral consideration concerns the general welfare itself. Many people of good will differ over what constitutes the general welfare. Another concerns how far the government can rightly go in promoting it. Many people of good will also differ about the proper limits of government action.

Public Decency and Morality

To most people, the general welfare includes a healthy moral environment. Part of a healthy moral environment is public decency. Some things—like sex between married people—are obviously moral in private but generally considered indecent in public thoroughfares. Other things—like drinking a few Scotches too many—are less obviously moral in private (here reasonable people will differ) and also considered indecent in public thoroughfares. Thus, we have laws against indecent exposure and drunk and disorderly conduct, laws that most people agree promote the general welfare.

More controversially, some people feel that the general welfare requires more and that a healthy moral environment includes more than public decency. They feel that it includes various restrictions on private behavior too. Homosexual acts between consenting adults constitute one area of private behavior that has been illegal in many jurisdictions. Another involves pornography. In some jurisdictions, certain films cannot be shown in theaters even if minors are kept out and billboards visible to the passing public are not themselves pornographic.

What principles do proponents of these restrictions appeal to? The following three are most important.

The Principle of Paternalism John Stuart Mill distinguished what he called self-regarding virtues and vices from other-regarding virtues and vices. Gluttony is an example of a self-regarding vice. Although overeating might cause direct harm to ourselves, it does not cause direct harm to others. A propensity to settle disagreements by beating up those who disagree with us, on the other hand, is an other-regarding vice. It does cause direct harm to others.

The legitimacy of laws forbidding assault and battery is not to be disputed. And the same goes for many similar laws involving other-regarding vices. But when we turn to self-regarding vices, the legitimacy of laws involving them is often disputed. People who steal from us, extort money from us, or rape us violate our most cherished rights, and it is the job of government to protect those rights. Gluttons do not violate our rights. Nor do homosexuals or pornography watchers. If homosexuality and pornography viewing are vices (and reasonable people disagree), they do not on the face of it seem to be other-regarding vices.

Some people justify restrictions on such behavior by appealing to a principle of paternalism: Just as parents are justified in preventing their children from harming themselves, so are governments justified in preventing their citizens from harming themselves. And if homosexuality and pornography cause us moral harm, governments should outlaw them. Otherwise, they do not promote the general welfare.

Protecting the Public Morality Mill's distinction between self-regarding and other-regarding vices rests on the presence or absence of direct harm to others. Many self-regarding vices, though, can and do cause *indirect* harm to others. A glutton can eat himself into a fatal heart attack, for example, and then his wife and children will suffer.

The courts have made similar claims about the indirect harm that can result from homosexuality and pornography. Sometimes, the harm they refer to is moral harm. If society tolerates behavior it considers immoral, that behavior may spread. And that means that people who engage in that behavior may be causing indirect moral harm to others.

Moreover, the indirect moral harm may come to minors as well as adults. Even if pornography is limited by law to adults only, minors will always find a way to view it. Just as legal drinking ages don't prevent minors from drinking their parents' liquor or getting adults to buy it for them, so do laws prohibiting sales of pornography to minors fail to prevent minors from looking at their parents' pornography or getting adults to buy it for them.

Whether or not the behavior does spread to minors, courts have repeatedly held that governments do have a legitimate interest in protecting the public morality, and that their legitimate interest in doing so does justify prohibiting behavior that many of us would consider self-regarding.

Preventing Indirect Social Costs The glutton who eats himself into a fatal heart attack may end up harming more than just his wife and children. His death may have social costs as well, especially if his family is forced to go on welfare. Indeed, many self-regarding vices have social costs. Smoking-related illnesses exact enormous costs in lost work hours, medical care, and insurance premiums. So do injuries resulting from failure to use automobile seat belts.

Much debate over the issues of Part 2 also involves the social costs of private behavior. Many people have expressed concern about the long-term effects of legal tolerance of homosexuality. How will it affect society's family structure? And what changes will that lead to in other areas of society? Will legal recognition of same-sex marriage lead to a deterioration of the sanctity of traditional marriage among heterosexuals?

Many other people reject the claim that such considerations can justify restrictions on private behavior. Many more reject the principle of paternalism and the principle of protecting the public morality. To them, such principles of collective action lead to unacceptable limits on individual freedom. Some worry that these principles, carried to their extremes, would lead to the outlawing of everything bad for us, including ice cream and other foods high in cholesterol. Others have even stronger objections. Their concern is that such considerations are in principle unacceptable.

People like Nozick would rule them out on the grounds of natural right. If our natural right to liberty is to count for anything, it must include the right to decide for ourselves what is morally harmful to us. Others would rule them out on different grounds. To them, the basic issue is that we live in a free society. In a free society, the general welfare is not to be advanced at the cost of individual freedoms that cause direct harm to nobody else. The government has an obligation to prevent violence toward women, but in a free society, it should fulfill that obligation by educating its citizens and punishing offenders—not by restricting the legitimate freedoms of nonoffenders.

Pluralism and Freedom

In the previous section, we looked at reasons in favor of government action. It's now time to look at reasons against government action. All can be seen as arguments in favor of individual freedom. They can also be seen as arguments in favor of **pluralism.**

A pluralistic society is a society with many independent centers of power, a society in which no one institution has unlimited power over the others. The more independent and varied the institutions of society are, the more pluralistic the society; the more limits that are placed on the most powerful institution of society, the more pluralistic the society.

In our society, of course, the federal government is the most powerful institution. Among the independent centers of power are the family, the press, religions, business and labor organizations, private (and perhaps even public) universities, and the like. And to the extent that the government allows these other institutions to pursue their own ends in their own ways, the more pluralistic our own society.

Although pluralism is not highly valued in all societies (the People's Republic of China and Iran, for example), it is highly valued in our own. The Founding Fathers, in placing limits on the powers of the federal government, sought to protect pluralism. And the frequent calls we hear to limit governmental interference in matters best left to the family, or the medical professions, or any other institutions are calls to protect or advance pluralism.

Individual Freedom

One reason for valuing pluralism is its close connection to individual freedom. The connection is twofold.

First, to allow institutions to pursue their own ends in their own ways is, more often than not, to allow individuals to pursue their own ends in their own ways. If the government leaves certain areas of concern to the family, it leaves them to individual family members. If it allows research decisions to be made by the scientific community, it allows them to be made by individual scientists. And the less it interferes with media organizations, the less it interferes with individual journalists.

Second, the more independent centers of power there are and the more independent they are permitted to be, the more bulwarks there are against government restrictions on individual freedom. A free press protects the freedoms of all of us, not just of journalists. Independent universities, hospitals, and businesses protect the freedom to choose among varied alternatives of all of us, not just the freedoms of professors, physicians, and managers.

To be sure, independent institutions can also threaten our freedoms. Businesses with monopoly powers, for instance, can greatly restrict our freedom of choice in the marketplace. They can also threaten vital public goods such as clean air and water. So we cannot allow them to be unbridled centers of power, any more than we can allow the government to be one. Nor can we give parents unbridled power over their children or hospitals unbridled power over their patients.

How and where to set these limits fuel many of the controversies of Part 2. Is the joint decision to withhold treatment from defective newborns within the proper bounds of parents and physicians? Should private businesses be free to pursue affirmative action, should they be forced to pursue it, or should they be barred from doing so?

How we answer such questions depends on a number of factors, some specific to each issue and others relating to the general principles we've been examining. Fairness, of course, is an important factor. So is the matter of individual rights. But where fairness should lead us and what rights are at stake are not always clear. What is fair to the minority woman might not be fair to the white male. And the question of what rights we ought to extend to a newborn child or fetus is far from settled.

The general welfare is also an important factor. It can, after all, be harmed by government action as well as advanced by government action. So far, we have looked only at ways in which government action can advance it. But pluralists are equally concerned about the ways government action can harm it.

The Social Utility of Pluralism

For Locke, Jefferson, and Nozick, the individual freedoms that rightfully belong to us are matters of natural right, and they need no further justification than that. For Rawls, the individual freedoms that rightfully belong to us are the ones we would agree to under ideal conditions of fairness. For Mill, the individual freedoms that rightfully belong to us are the ones that will maximize human happiness.

Mill felt very strongly that the only freedom that will not maximize human happiness is the freedom to harm others. He felt that other-regarding vices fall under the legitimate control of governments, but not self-regarding ones. Many of his arguments for this claim center on specific individual freedoms, and it would take us far beyond our purposes here to look at all of them. But two general arguments are very important for us.

The first is one we often hear in political debates: Individuals are in a better position to know what makes them happy than paternalistic governments are. Individuals will make mistakes from time to time, but so will governments. The important point is that individuals will make them less frequently. For one thing, we know ourselves better than our governments know us. For another, each of us is different, and it is extremely unlikely that one judgment about self-regarding behavior made for all individuals in society will promote individual happiness as efficiently as individual judgments made by each of us.

The second deals directly with the link between public morality and the general welfare. According to Mill, the best way to live our lives must always remain an open question. Nobody can now know for certain that particular ways of life are the best ways of life. If we outlaw certain kinds of self-regarding behavior, Mill said, we cut off moral experimentation that might help us discover better ways of life. And even if we can be fairly certain that some ways of life are not good ones, we will not maximize happiness by outlawing them. Bad ways of life may still have some good in them. Also, the rest of us can always learn from bad examples, even if what we learn is only to have greater confidence in the goodness of our own ways of life. A docile citizenry, one that does what it is told rather than what it thinks best, is not a citizenry likely to maximize happiness. Nor, those who agree with Mill might add, are docile hospitals, universities, or media organizations likely to maximize happiness.

SUMMARY AND CONCLUSIONS

We have looked at a variety of general moral principles in this chapter, some primarily concerned with individual morality and others with social morality. In doing so, we have also looked at the most important considerations we can bring to bear when deciding how we should act, whether individually or collectively. Among them are human happiness, fairness, justice, individual rights, equality, individual freedom, and the general welfare.

What conclusions can we draw from our discussions? Perhaps the most obvious conclusion is that moral questions can be very difficult questions. One moral principle can lead us to one answer, while another equally important moral principle can lead us to another answer. Thus, we may very well be stuck with some very hard choices—between respecting individual freedoms and promoting the general welfare, for example. Also, we may very well find that the same moral principle leads us to different answers. In cases like that, we will find ourselves stuck with hard choices of another kind—between being fair to one group or another, for example, or between protecting one individual's rights or another's.

The existence of such moral dilemmas often leads to a kind of moral skepticism, the view that our answers to moral questions are opinions, not knowledge. Whether that view is correct is a much too complicated matter to deal with here. But even if it is correct, it does not mean that we should give up trying to answer moral questions. They remain very important questions. The answers we eventually decide on will have great impact on the kind of society we are and on the lives of all of us who live in it. We have a responsibility to deal with these questions as best we can, even if we cannot be sure that our answers represent knowledge.

And even if our answers are opinions, not all opinions are equal. At the beginning of a baseball season, nobody can know who will win the World Series, but that doesn't mean that we can't distinguish good picks from bad picks. Few of you can know which career choice will work out best for you, but that doesn't mean that any opinion on the matter is as good as any other. Similarly, perhaps none of us can know whether a woman really has a moral right to an abortion or whether justice really requires affirmative action, but that doesn't mean that we can't distinguish better and worse ways of dealing with those issues.

Basing our judgments on moral principle is one thing we must do if we are to deal with these issues well. But we must also do something else. We must make sure that our debates on these issues are thoughtful, careful, and well reasoned. The combination of good moral principles and faulty reasoning guarantees very little. In this chapter, we look at the principles; in the next, we will look at reasoning.

Moral Virtue

ARISTOTLE

The following selection is from Books One and Two of Aristotle's *Nichomachean Ethics*. In Book One, Aristotle argues that the highest human good is *eudaimonia* (total well-being, or happiness). It is, he says, our only self-sufficient goal and the ultimate goal of all human action. He then argues that human happiness is determined by the proper function of humans, which he defines as "an activity of the soul or a course of action in accordance with reason." Thus, a happy individual is one who lives in accordance with reason, and each individual should develop virtues (character traits or dispositions) that lead to this goal. Because human reason is both practical and intellectual, human virtues come in two kinds, moral and intellectual.

In Book Two, Aristotle turns to a discussion of the moral virtues. After stressing the importance of childhood training and self-discipline in the development of moral virtues, he proceeds to define the nature of moral virtue. Moral virtue is, he concludes, a "mean" between the vices of deficiency and excess; that is, virtue is a form of moderation, a midpoint between two extremes. Courage, for example, is a midpoint between cowardice and foolhardiness. Friendliness is a midpoint between flattery and surliness.

BOOK ONE

Chapter I

It is thought that every activity, artistic or scientific, in fact every deliberate action or pursuit, has for its object the attainment of some good. We may therefore assent to the view which has been expressed that 'the good' is 'that at which all things aim.'[1] Since modes of action involving the prac- tised hand and the instructed brain are numerous, the number of their ends is proportionately large. For instance, the end of medical science is health; of military science, victory; of economic science, wealth. All skills of that kind which come under a single 'faculty'—a skill in making bridles or any other part of a horse's gear comes under the faculty or art of horsemanship, while horsemanship itself and every branch of military practice comes

From *The Ethics of Aristotle*, translated by A. K. Thomson, George Allen &Unwin Ltd. Reprinted by permission.

under the art of war, and in like manner other arts and techniques are subordinate to yet others—in all these the ends of the master arts are to be preferred to those of the subordinate skills, for it is the former that provide the motive for pursuing the latter.[2]

Chapter IV

To resume. Since every activity involving some acquired skill or some moral decision aims at some good, what do we take to be the end of politics—what is the supreme good attainable in our actions? Well, so far as the name goes there is pretty general agreement. 'It is happiness,' say both intellectuals and the unsophisticated, meaning by 'happiness' living well or faring well. But when it comes to saying in what happiness consists, opinions differ and the account given by the generality of mankind is not at all like that given by the philosophers. The masses take it to be something plain and tangible, like pleasure or money or social standing. Some maintain that it is one of these, some that it is another, and the same man will change his opinion about it more than once. When he has caught an illness he will say that it is health, and when he is hard up he will say that it is money. Conscious that they are out of their depths in such discussions, most people are impressed by anyone who pontificates and says something that is over their heads. Now it would no doubt be a waste of time to examine all these opinions; enough if we consider those which are most in evidence or have something to be said for them. Among these we shall have to discuss the view held by some that, over and above particular goods like those I have just mentioned, there is another which is good in itself and the cause of whatever goodness there is in all these others....

Chapter V

Let us return from this digression.—There is a general assumption that the manner of a man's life is a clue to what he on reflection regards as the good—in other words happiness. Persons of low tastes (always in the majority) hold that it is pleasure. Accordingly they ask for nothing better than the sort of life which consists in having a good time. (I have in mind the three well-known types of life—that just mentioned, that of the man of affairs, that of the philosophic student.) The utter vulgarity of the herd of men comes out in their preference for the sort of existence a cow leads. Their view would hardly get a respectful hearing, were it not that those who occupy great positions sympathize with a monster of sensuality like Sardanapalus. The gentleman, however, and the man of affairs identify the good with honour, which may fairly be described as the end which men pursue in political or public life. Yet honour is surely too superficial a thing to be the good we are seeking. Honour depends more on those who confer than on him who receives it, and we cannot but feel that the good is something personal and almost inseparable from its possessor. Again, why do men seek honour? Surely in order to confirm the favourable opinion they have formed of themselves. It is at all events by intelligent men who know them personally that they seek to be honoured. And for what? For their moral qualities. The inference is clear; public men prefer virtue to honour. It might therefore seem reasonable to suppose that virtue rather than honour is the end pursued in the life of the public servant. But clearly even virtue cannot be quite the end. It is possible, most people think, to possess virtue while you are asleep, to possess it without acting under its influence during any portion of one's life. Besides, the virtuous man may meet with the most atrocious luck or ill-treatment; and nobody, who was not arguing for argument's sake, would maintain that a man with an existence of that sort was 'happy.'[3] The third type of life is the 'contemplative,' and this we shall discuss later.

As for the life of the business man, it does not give him much freedom of action. Besides, wealth obviously is not the good we seek, for the sole purpose it serves is to provide the means of getting something else. So far as that goes, the ends we have already mentioned would have a better title to be considered the good, for they are desired on their own account. But in fact even their claim must be disallowed. We may say that they have furnished the ground for many arguments, and leave the matter at that.

Chapter VII

From this digression we may return to the good which is the object of our search. What is it? The question must be asked because good seems to vary with the art or pursuit in which it appears. It is one thing in medicine and another in strategy, and so in the other branches of human skill. We must enquire, then, what is the good which is the end common to all of them. Shall we say it is that for the sake of which everything else is done? In medicine this is health, in military science victory, in architecture a building, and so on—different ends in different arts; every consciously directed activity has an end for the sake of which everything that it does is done. This end may be described as its good. Consequently, if there be some one thing which is the end of all things consciously done, this will be the doable good; or, if there be more than one end, then it will be all of these. Thus the ground on which our argument proceeds is shifted, but the conclusion arrived at is the same.

I must try, however, to make my meaning clearer.

In our actions we aim at more ends than one—that seems to be certain—but, since we choose some (wealth, for example, or flutes and tools or instruments generally) as means to something else, it is clear that not all of them are ends in the full sense of the word, whereas the good, that is the supreme good, is surely such an end. Assuming then that there is some one thing which alone is an end beyond which there are no further ends, we may call *that* the good of which we are in search. If there be more than one such final end, the good will be that end which has the highest degree of finality. An object pursued for its own sake possesses a higher degree of finality than one pursued with an eye to something else. A corollary to that is that a thing which is never chosen as a means to some remoter object has a higher degree of finality than things which are chosen both as ends in themselves and as means to such ends. We may conclude, then, that something which is always chosen for its own sake and never for the sake of something else is without qualification a final end.

Now happiness more than anything else appears to be just such an end, for we always choose it for its own sake and never for the sake of some other thing. It is different with honour, pleasure, intelligence and good qualities generally. We choose them indeed for their own sake in the sense that we should be glad to have them irrespective of any advantage which might accrue from them. But we also choose them for the sake of our happiness in the belief that they will be instrumental in promoting that. On the other hand nobody chooses happiness as a means of achieving them or anything else whatsoever than just happiness.

The same conclusion would seem to follow from another consideration. It is a generally accepted view that the final good is self-sufficient. By 'self-sufficient' is meant not what is sufficient for oneself living the life of a solitary but includes parents, wife and children, friends and fellow-citizens in general. For man is a social animal.[4] A self-sufficient thing, then, we take to be one which on its own footing tends to make life desirable and lacking in nothing. And we regard happiness as such a thing. Add to this that we regard it as the most desirable of all things without having it counted in with some other desirable thing. For, if such an addition were possible, clearly we should regard it as more desirable when even the smallest advantage was added to it. For the result would be an increase in the number of advantages, and the larger sum of advantages is preferable to the smaller.

Happiness then, the end to which all our conscious acts are directed, is found to be something final and self-sufficient.

But no doubt people will say, 'To call happiness the highest good is a truism. We want a more distinct account of what it is.' We might arrive at this if we could grasp what is meant by the 'function' of a human being. If we take a flautist or a sculptor or any craftsman—in fact any class of men at all who have some special job or profession—we find that his special talent and excellence comes out in that job, and this is his function. The same thing will be true of man simply as man—that is of course if 'man' does have a function. But is it likely that joiners and shoemakers have certain functions or specialized activities, while man as such has none but has been left by Nature a functionless being? Seeing that eye and hand and foot and every one of our members has some obvious function, must we not believe that in like manner a human being has a function over and above these particular functions? Then what exactly is it? The mere act of living is not peculiar to man—we find it even in the vegetable kingdom—and what we are looking for is something peculiar to him. We must therefore exclude from our definition the life that manifests itself in mere nurture and growth. A step higher should come the life that is confined to experiencing sensations. But that we see is shared by horses, cows and the brute creation as a whole. We are left, then, with a life concerning which we can make two statements. First, it belongs to the rational part of man. Secondly, it finds expression in actions. The rational part may be either active or passive: passive in so far as it follows the dictates of reason, active in so far as it possesses and exercises the power of reasoning. A similar distinction can be drawn within the rational life; that is to say, the reasonable element in it may be active or passive. Let us take it that what we are concerned with here is the reasoning power in action, for it will be generally allowed that when we speak of 'reasoning' we really mean *exercising* our reasoning faculties. (This seems the more correct use of the word.) Now let us assume for the moment the truth of the following propositions. (*a*) The function of a man is the exercise of his non-corporeal faculties or 'soul' in accordance with, or at least not divorced from, a rational principle. (*b*) The function of an individual and of a *good* individual in the same class—a harp player, for example, and a good harp player, and so through the classes—is generically the same, except that we must add superiority in accomplishment to the function, the function of the harp player being merely to play on the harp, while the function of the good harp player is to play on it well. (*c*) The function of man is a certain form of life, namely an activity of the soul exercised in combination with a rational principle or reasonable ground of action. (*d*) The function of a good man is to exert such activity well. (*e*) A function is performed well when performed in accordance with the excellence proper to it.—If these assumptions are granted, we conclude that the good for man is 'an activity of soul in accordance with goodness' or (on the supposition that

there may be more than one form of goodness) 'in accordance with the best and most complete form of goodness.'

There is another condition of happiness; it cannot be achieved in less than a complete lifetime. One swallow does not make a summer; neither does one fine day. And one day, or indeed any brief period of felicity, does not make a man entirely and perfectly happy....

BOOK TWO
Chapter I

Virtue, then, is of two kinds, intellectual and moral. Of these the intellectual is in the main indebted to teaching for its production and growth, and this calls for time and experience. Moral goodness, on the other hand, is the child of habit, from which it has got its very name, ethics being derived from *ethos*, "habit," by a slight alteration in the quantity of the *e*. This is an indication that none of the moral virtues is implanted in us by nature, since nothing that nature creates can be taught by habit to change the direction of its development. For instance a stone, the natural tendency of which is to fall down, could never, however often you threw it up in the air, be trained to go in that direction. No more can you train fire to burn downwards. Nothing in fact, if the law of its being is to behave in one way, can be habituated to behave in another. The moral virtues, then, are produced in us neither *by* Nature nor *against* Nature. Nature, indeed, prepares in us the ground for their reception, but their complete formation is the product of habit.

Consider again these powers or faculties with which Nature endows us. We acquire the ability to use them before we do use them. The senses provide us with a good illustration of this truth. We have not acquired the sense of sight from repeated acts of seeing, or the sense of hearing from repeated acts of hearing. It is the other way round. We had these senses before we used them; we did not acquire them as a result of using them. But the moral virtues we do acquire by first exercising them. The same is true of the arts and crafts in general. The craftsman has to learn how to make things, but he learns in the process of making them. So men become builders by building, harp players by playing the harp. By a similar process we become just by performing just actions, temperate by performing temperate actions, brave by performing brave actions. Look at what happens in political societies—it confirms our view. We find legislators seeking to make good men of their fellows by making good behaviour habitual with them. That is the aim of every lawgiver, and when he is unable to carry it out effectively, he is a failure; nay, success or failure in this is what makes the difference between a good constitution and a bad.

Again, the creation and the destruction of any virtue are effected by identical causes and identical means; and this may be said, too, of every art. It is as a result of playing the harp that harpers become good or bad in their art. The same is true of builders and all other craftsmen. Men will become good builders as a result of building well, and bad builders as a result of building badly. Otherwise what would be the use of having anyone to teach a trade? Craftsmen would all be born either good or bad. Now this holds also of the virtues. It is in the course of our dealings with our fellow-men that we become just or unjust. It is our behaviour in a crisis and our habitual reactions to danger that make us brave or cowardly, as it may be. So with our desires and passions. Some men are made temperate and gentle, others profligate and passionate, the former by conducting themselves in one way, the latter by conducting themselves in another, in situations in which their feelings are involved. We may sum it all up in the generalization, "Like activities produce like dispositions." This makes it our duty to see that our activities have the right character, since the differences of quality in them are repeated in the dispositions that follow in their train. So it is a matter of real importance whether our early education confirms us in one set of habits or another. It would be nearer the truth to say that it makes a very great difference indeed, in fact all the difference in the world.

Chapter II

Since the branch of philosophy on which we are at present engaged differs from the others in not being a subject of merely intellectual interest— I mean we are not concerned to know what goodness essentially is, but how we are to become good men, for this alone gives the study its practical value—we must apply our minds to the solution of the problems of conduct. For, as I remarked, it is our actions that determine our dispositions.

Now that when we act we should do so according to the right principle, is common ground and I propose to take it as a basis of discussion.[5] But we must begin with the admission that any theory of conduct must be content with an outline without much precision in details. We noted this when I said at the beginning of our discussion of this part of our subject that the measure of exactness of statement in any field of study must be determined by the nature of the matter studied. Now matters of conduct and considerations of what is to our advantage have no fixity about them any more than matters affecting our health. And if this be true of moral philosophy as a whole, it is still more true that the discussion of particular problems in ethics admits of no exactitude. For they do not fall under any science or professional tradition, but those who are following some line of conduct are forced in every collocation of circumstances to think out for themselves what is suited to these circumstances, just as doctors and navigators have to do in their different *métiers*. We can do no more than give our arguments, inexact as they necessarily are, such support as is available.

Let us begin with the following observation. It is in the nature of moral qualities that they can be destroyed by deficiency on the one hand and excess on the other. We can see this in the instances of bodily health and strength.[6] Physical strength is destroyed by too much and also by too little exercise. Similarly health is ruined by eating and drinking either too much or too little, while it is produced, increased and preserved by taking the right quantity of drink and victuals. Well, it is the same with temperance, courage, and the other virtues. The man who shuns and fears everything and can stand up to nothing becomes a coward. The man who is afraid of nothing at all, but marches up to every danger, becomes foolhardy. In the same way the man who indulges in every pleasure without refraining from a single one becomes incontinent. If, on the other hand, a man behaves like the Boor in comedy and turns his back on every pleasure, he will find his sensibilities becoming blunted. So also temperance and courage are destroyed both by excess and deficiency, and they are kept alive by observance of the mean.

Let us go back to our statement that the virtues are produced and fostered as a result, and by the agency, of actions of the same quality as effect their destruction. It is also true that after the virtues have been formed they find expression in actions of that kind. We may see this in a concrete instance—bodily strength. It results from taking plenty of nourishment and going in for hard training, and it is the strong man who is best fitted to cope with such conditions. So with the virtues. It is by refraining from pleasures that we become temperate, and it is when we have become temperate that we are most able to abstain from pleasures. Or take courage. It is by habituating ourselves to make light of alarming situations and to confront them that we become brave, and it is when we have become brave that we shall be most able to face an alarming situation.

Chapter III

We may use the pleasure (or pain) that accompanies the exercise of our dispositions as an index of how far they have established themselves. A man is temperate who abstaining from bodily pleasures finds this abstinence pleasant; if he finds it irksome, he is intemperate. Again, it is the man who encounters danger gladly, or at least without painful sensations, who is brave; the man who has these sensations is a coward. In a word, moral virtue has to do with pains and pleasures. There are a number of reasons for believing this. (1) Pleasure has a way of making us do what is disgraceful; pain deters us from doing what is right and fine. Hence the importance—I quote Plato—of having been brought up to find pleasure and pain in the right things. True education is just such a training. (2) The virtues operate with actions and emotions, each of which is accompanied by pleasure or pain. This is only another way of saying that virtue has to do with pleasures and pains. (3) Pain is used as an instrument of punishment. For in her remedies Nature works by opposites, and pain can be remedial. (4) When any disposition finds its complete

expression it is, as we noted, in dealing with just those things by which it is its nature to be made better or worse, and which constitute the sphere of its operations. (5) Now when men become bad it is under the influence of pleasures and pains when they seek the wrong ones among them, or seek them at the wrong time, or in the wrong manner, or in any of the wrong forms which such offenses may take; and in seeking the wrong pleasures and pains they shun the right. This has led some thinkers to identify the moral virtues with conditions of the soul in which passion is eliminated or reduced to a minimum. But this is to make too absolute a statement—it needs to be qualified by adding that such a condition must be attained "in the right manner and at the right time" together with the other modifying circumstances.

So far, then, we have got this result. Moral goodness is a quality disposing us to act in the best way when we are dealing with pleasures and pains, while vice is one which leads us to act in the worst way when we deal with them.

The point may be brought out more clearly by some other considerations. There are three kinds of things that determine our choice in all our actions—the morally fine, the expedient, the pleasant; the three that we shun—the base, the harmful, the painful. Now in his dealings with all of these it is the good man who is most likely to go right, and the bad man who tends to go wrong, and that most notably in the matter of pleasure. The sensation of pleasure is felt by us in common with all animals, accompanying everything we choose, for even the fine and the expedient have a pleasurable effect upon us. (6) The capacity for experiencing pleasure has grown in us from infancy as part of our general development, and human life, being dyed in grain with it, receives therefrom a colour hard to scrape off. (7) Pleasure and pain are also the standards by which with greater or less strictness we regulate our considered actions. Since to feel pleasure and pain rightly or wrongly is an important factor in human behaviour, it follows that we are primarily concerned with these sensations. (8) Heraclitus says it is hard to fight against anger, but it is harder still to fight against pleasure. Yet to grapple with the harder has always been the business, as of art, so of goodness, success in a task being proportionate to its difficulty. This gives us another reason for believing that morality and statesmanship must concentrate on pleasures and pains, seeing it is the man who deals rightly with them who will be good, and the man who deals with them wrongly who will be bad.

Here, then, are our conclusions. (a) Virtue is concerned with pains and pleasures. (b) The actions which produce virtue are identical in character with those which increase it. (c) These actions differently performed destroy it. (d) The actions which produced it are identical with those in which it finds expression.

Chapter IV

A difficulty, however, may be raised as to what we mean when we say that we must perform just actions if we are to become just, and temperate actions if we are to be temperate. It may be argued that, if I do what is just and temperate, I am just and temperate already, exactly as, if I spell words or play music correctly, I must already be literate or musical. This I take to be a false analogy, even in the arts. It is possible to spell a word right by accident or because somebody tips you the answer. But you will be a scholar only if your spelling is done as a scholar does it, that is thanks to the scholarship in your own mind. Nor will the suggested analogy with the arts bear scrutiny. A work of art is good or bad in itself—let it possess a certain quality, and that is all we ask of it. But virtuous actions are not done in a virtuous—a just or temperate—way merely because *they* have the appropriate quality. The *doer* must be in a certain frame of mind when he does them. Three conditions are involved. (1) The agent must act in full consciousness of what he is doing. (2) He must "will" his action, and will it for its own sake. (3) The act must proceed from a fixed and unchangeable disposition. Now these requirements, if we except mere knowledge, are not counted among the necessary qualifications of an artist. For the acquisition of virtue, on the other hand, knowledge is of little or no value, but the other requirements are of immense, of sovran, importance, since it is the repeated performance

of just and temperate actions that produces virtue. Actions, to be sure, are *called* just and temperate when they are such as a just or temperate man would do. But the doer is just or temperate not because he does such things but when he does them in the way of just and temperate persons. It is therefore quite fair to say that a man becomes just by the performance of just, and temperate by the performance of temperate, actions; nor is there the smallest likelihood of a man's becoming good by any other course of conduct. It is not, however, a popular line to take, most men preferring theory to practice under the impression that arguing about morals proves them to be philosophers, and that in this way they will turn out to be fine characters. Herein they resemble invalids, who listen carefully to all the doctor says but do not carry out a single one of his orders. The bodies of such people will never respond to treatment—nor will the souls of such "philosophers."

Chapter V

We now come to the formal definition of virtue. Note first, however, that the human soul is conditioned in three ways. It may have (1) feelings, (2) capacities, (3) dispositions; so virtue must be one of these three. By "feelings" I mean desire, anger, fear, daring, envy, gratification, friendliness, hatred, longing, jealousy, pity and in general all states of mind that are attended by pleasure or pain. By "capacities" I mean those faculties in virtue of which we may be described as capable of the feelings in question—anger, for instance, or pain, or pity. By "dispositions" I mean states of mind in virtue of which we are well or ill disposed in respect of the feelings concerned. We have, for instance, a bad disposition where angry feelings are concerned if we are disposed to become excessively or insufficiently angry, and a good disposition in this respect if we consistently feel the due amount of anger, which comes between these extremes. So with the other feelings.

Now, neither the virtues nor the vices are feelings. We are not spoken of as good or bad in respect of our feelings but of our virtues and vices. Neither are we praised or blamed for the way we feel. A man is not praised for being frightened or angry, nor is he blamed just for being angry; it is for being angry in a particular way. But we *are* praised and blamed for our virtues and vices. Again, feeling angry or frightened is something we can't help, but our virtues are in a manner expressions of our will; at any rate there is an element of will in their formation. Finally, we are said to be "moved" when our feelings are affected, but when it is a question of moral goodness or badness we are not said to be "moved" but to be "disposed" in a particular way. A similar line of reasoning will prove that the virtues and vices are not capacities either. We are not spoken of as good or bad, nor are we praised or blamed, merely because we are *capable* of feeling. Again, what capacities we have, we have by nature; but it is not nature that makes us good or bad.... So, if the virtues are neither feelings nor capacities, it remains that they must be dispositions....

Chapter VI

It is not, however, enough to give this account of the *genus* of virtue—that it is a disposition; we must describe its *species*. Let us begin, then, with this proposition. Excellence of whatever kind affects that of which it is the excellence in two ways. (1) It produces a good state in it. (2) It enables it to perform its function well. Take eyesight. The goodness of your eye is not only that which makes your eye good, it is also that which makes it function well. Or take the case of a horse. The goodness of a horse makes him a good horse, but it also makes him good at running, carrying a rider and facing the enemy. Our proposition, then, seems to be true, and it enables us to say that virtue in a man will be the disposition which (a) makes him a good man, (b) enables him to perform his function well. We have already touched on this point, but more light will be thrown upon it if we consider what is the specific nature of virtue.

In anything continuous and divisible it is possible to take the half, or more than the half, or less than the half. Now these parts may be larger, smaller and equal either in relation to the thing divided or in relation to us. The equal part may be described as a mean between too much and too little. By the mean of the thing I understand a point equidistant from the extremes; and this is

one and the same for everybody. Let me give an illustration. Ten, let us say, is "many" and two is "few" of something. We get the mean of the thing if we take six;[7] that is, six exceeds and is exceeded by an equal number. This is the rule which gives us the arithmetical mean. But such a method will not give us the mean in relation to ourselves. Let ten pounds of food be a large, and two pounds a small, allowance for an athlete. It does not follow that the trainer will prescribe six pounds. That might be a large or it might be a small allowance for the particular athlete who is to get it. It would be little for Milo but a lot for a man who has just begun his training.[8] It is the same in all walks of life. The man who knows his business avoids both too much and too little. It is the mean he seeks and adopts—not the mean of the thing but the relative mean.

Every form, then, of applied knowledge, when it performs its function well, looks to the mean and works to the standard set by that. It is because people feel this that they apply the *cliché*, "You couldn't add anything to it or take anything from it" to an artistic masterpiece, the implication being that too much and too little alike destroy perfection, while the mean preserves it. Now if this be so, and if it be true, as we say, that good craftsmen work to the standard of the mean, then, since goodness like nature is more exact and of a higher character than any art, it follows that goodness is the quality that hits the mean. By "goodness" I mean goodness of moral character, since it is moral goodness that deals with feelings and actions, and it is in them that we find excess, deficiency and a mean. It is possible, for example, to experience fear, boldness, desire, anger, pity, and pleasures and pains generally, too much or too little or to the right amount. If we feel them too much or too little, we are wrong. But to have these feelings at the right times on the right occasions toward the right people for the right motive and in the right way is to have them in the right measure, that is somewhere between the extremes; and this is what characterizes goodness. The same may be said of the mean and extremes in actions. Now it is in the field of actions and feelings that goodness operates; in them we find excess, deficiency and, between them, the mean, the first two being wrong, the mean right and praised as such.[9]

Goodness, then, is a mean condition in the sense that it aims at and hits the mean.

Consider, too, that it is possible to go wrong in more ways than one. (In Pythagorean terminology evil is a form of the Unlimited, good of the Limited.) But there is only one way of being right. That is why going wrong is easy, and going right difficult; it is easy to miss the bull's eye and difficult to hit it. Here, then, is another explanation of why the too much and the too little are connected with evil and the mean with good. As the poet says,

Goodness is one, evil is multiform.

We may now define virtue as a disposition of the soul in which, when it has to choose among actions and feelings, it observes the mean relative to us, this being determined by such a rule or principle as would take shape in the mind of a man of sense or practical wisdom. We call it a mean condition as lying between two forms of badness, one being excess and the other deficiency; and also for this reason, that, whereas badness either falls short of or exceeds the right measure in feelings and actions, virtue discovers the mean and deliberately chooses it. Thus, looked at from the point of view of its essence as embodied in its definition, virtue no doubt is a mean; judged by the standard of what is right and best, it is an extreme.

But choice of a mean is not possible in every action or every feeling. The very names of some have an immediate connotation of evil. Such are malice, shamelessness, envy among feelings, and among actions adultery, theft, murder. All these and more like them have a bad name as being evil in themselves; it is not merely the excess or deficiency of them that we censure. In their case, then it is impossible to act rightly; whatever we do is wrong. Nor do circumstances make any difference in the rightness or wrongness of them. When a man commits adultery there is no point in asking whether it is with the right woman or at the right time or in the right way, for to do anything like that is simply wrong. It would amount to claiming that there is a mean and excess and defect in unjust or cowardly or intemperate actions. If such a thing were possible, we should find ourselves with a mean quantity of excess, a mean of deficiency, an

excess of excess and a deficiency of deficiency. But just as in temperance and justice there can be no mean or excess or deficiency, because the mean in a sense *is* an extreme, so there can be no mean or excess or deficiency in those vicious actions—however done, they are wrong. Putting the matter into general language, we may say that there is no mean in the extremes, and no extreme in the mean, to be observed by anybody.

Chapter VII

But a generalization of this kind is not enough; we must show that our definition fits particular cases. When we are discussing actions particular statements come nearer the heart of the matter, though general statements cover a wider field. The reason is that human behaviour consists in the performance of particular acts, and our theories must be brought into harmony with them.

You see here a diagram of the virtues. Let us take our particular instances from that.

In the section confined to the feelings inspired by danger you will observe that the mean state is "courage." Of those who go to extremes in one direction or the other the man who shows an excess of fearlessness has no name to describe him,[10] the man who exceeds in confidence or daring is called "rash" or "foolhardy," the man who shows an excess of fear and a deficiency of confidence is called a "coward." In the pleasures and pains—though not all pleasures and pains, especially pains—the virtue which observes the mean is "temperance," the excess is the vice of "intemperance." Persons defective in the power to enjoy pleasures are a somewhat rare class, and so have not had a name assigned to them: suppose we call them "unimpressionable." Coming to the giving and acquiring of money, we find that the mean is "liberality," the excess "prodigality," the deficiency "meanness." But here we meet a complication. The prodigal man and the mean man exceed and fall short in opposite ways. The prodigal exceeds in giving and falls short in getting money, whereas the mean man exceeds in getting and falls short in giving it away. Of course this is but a summary account of the matter—a bare outline. But it meets our immediate requirements. Later on these types of character will be more accurately delineated.

But there are other dispositions which declare themselves in the way they deal with money. One is "lordliness" or "magnificence," which differs from liberality in that the lordly man deals in large sums, the liberal man in small. Magnificence is the mean state here, the excess is "bad taste" or "vulgarity," the defect is "shabbiness." These are not the same as the excess and defect on either side of liberality. How they differ is a point which will be discussed later. In the matter of honour the mean is "proper pride," the excess "vanity," the defect "poor-spiritedness." And just as liberality differs, as I said, from magnificence in being concerned with small sums of money, so there is a state related to proper pride in the same way, being concerned with small honours, while pride is concerned with great. For it is possible to aspire to small honours in the right way, or to a greater or less extent than is right. The man who has this aspiration to excess is called "ambitious"; if he does not cherish it enough, he is "unambitious"; but the man who has it to the right extent—that is, strikes the mean—has no special designation. This is true also of the corresponding dispositions with one exception, that of the ambitious man, which is called "ambitiousness." This will explain why each of the extreme characters stakes out a claim in the middle region. Indeed we ourselves call the character between the extremes sometimes "ambitious" and sometimes "unambitious." That is proved by our sometimes praising a man for being ambitious and sometimes for being unambitious. The reason will appear later. In the meantime let us continue our discussion of the remaining virtues and vices, following the method already laid down.

Let us next take anger. Here too we find excess, deficiency and the mean. Hardly one of the states of mind involved has a special name; but, since we call the man who attains the mean in this sphere "gentle," we may call his disposition "gentleness." Of the extremes the man who is angry overmuch may be called "irascible," and his vice "irascibility" while the man who reacts too feebly to anger may be called "poor-spirited" and his disposition "poor-spiritedness."

There are, in addition to those we have named, three other modes of observing the mean which in some ways resemble and in other ways differ from one another. They are all concerned with what we do and say in social intercourse, but they differ in this respect, that one is concerned with truthfulness in such intercourse, the other two with the agreeable, one of these two with the agreeable in amusement, the other with the agreeable element in every relation of life. About these two, then, we must say a word, in order that we may more fully convince ourselves that in all things the mean is to be commended, while the extremes are neither commendable nor right but reprehensible. I am afraid most of these too are nameless; but, as in the other cases, we must try to coin names for them in the interests of clearness and to make it easy to follow the argument. Well then, as regards veracity, the character who aims at the mean may be called "truthful" and what he aims at "truthfulness." Pretending, when it goes too far, is "boastfulness" and the man who shows it is a "boaster" or "braggart." If it takes the form of understatement, the pretense is called "irony" and the man who shows it "ironical." In agreeableness in social amusement the man who hits the mean is "witty" and what characterizes him is "wittiness." The excess is "buffoonery" and the man who exhibits that is a "buffoon." The opposite of the buffoon is the "boor" and his characteristic is "boorishness." In the other sphere of the agreeable—the general business of life— the person who is agreeable in the right way is "friendly" and his disposition "friendliness." The man who makes himself too agreeable, supposing him to have no ulterior object, is "obsequious"; if he has such an object, he is a "flatterer." The man who is deficient in this quality and takes every opportunity of making himself disagreeable may be called "peevish" or "sulky" or "surly."

Even when feelings and emotional states are involved one notes that mean conditions exist. And here also, it would be agreed, we may find one man observing the mean and another going beyond it, for instance the "shamefaced" man, who is put out of countenance by anything. Or a man may fall short here of the due mean. Thus anyone who is deficient in a sense of shame, or has none at all, is called "shameless." The man who avoids both extremes is "modest," and him we praise. For, while modesty is not a form of goodness, it is praised; it and the modest man. Then there is "righteous indignation." This is felt by anyone who strikes the mean between "envy" and "malice," by which last word I mean a pleased feeling at the misfortunes of other people. These are emotions concerned with the pains and pleasures we feel at the fortunes of our neighbours. The man who feels righteous indignation is pained by undeserved good fortune; but the envious man goes beyond that and is pained at anybody's success. The malicious man, on the other hand, is so far from being pained by the misfortunes of another that he is actually tickled by them....

Chapter IX

I have said enough to show that moral excellence is a mean, and I have shown in what sense it is so. It is, namely, a mean between two forms of badness, one of excess and the other of defect, and is so described because it aims at hitting the mean point in feelings and in actions. This makes virtue hard of achievement, because finding the middle point is never easy. It is not everybody, for instance, who can find the center of a circle—that calls for a geometrician. Thus, too, it is easy to fly into a passion—anybody can do that—but to be angry with the right person and to the right extent and at the right time and with the right object and in the right way—that is not easy, and it is not everyone who can do it. This is equally true of giving or spending money. Hence we infer that to do these things properly is rare, laudable and fine....

NOTES

1. It is of course obvious that to a certain extent they do not all aim at the same thing, for in some cases the end will be an activity, in others the product which goes beyond the actual activity. In the arts which aim at results of this kind the results or products are intrinsically superior to the activities.
2. It makes no difference if the ends of the activities are the activities themselves or something over and above these, as in the case of the sciences I have mentioned.
3. I am absolved from a more detailed discussion of this point by the full treatment it has received in current literature.
4. Of course we must draw the line somewhere. For, if we stretch it to include ancestors and descendants and friends' friends, there will be no end to it. But there will be another opportunity of considering this point.
5. There will be an opportunity later of considering what is meant by this formula, in particular what is meant by "the right principle" and how, in its ethical aspect, it is related to the moral virtues.
6. If we are to illustrate the material, it must be by concrete images.
7. $6 - 2 = 10 - 6$
8. What applies to gymnastics applies also to running and wrestling.
9. Being right or successful and being praised are both indicative of excellence.
10. We shall often have to make similar admissions.

♛ QUESTIONS FOR ANALYSIS

1. What is the nature of "happiness"? How much weight should we give to the varying opinions of different people about the nature of happiness?
2. How is happiness different from honor, pleasure, intelligence, and good qualities generally? What does Aristotle mean in claiming that happiness is final and self-sufficient?
3. Do you agree with Aristotle that a complete lifetime is required to achieve happiness?
4. According to Aristotle, moral qualities can be destroyed by both excess and deficiency. What examples does he give? What other examples might he have used?
5. What connections does Aristotle make between virtue and pleasure? What roles do pleasure and pain play in moral education?
6. Whether an action is virtuous, Aristotle says, depends on both the action and the doer's frame of mind. Why? What must the frame of mind be?
7. Why does Aristotle call goodness a mean? In what sense does goodness aim at and hit the mean? Can you think of virtues that are not aptly described as means?

Respect for Persons

IMMANUEL KANT

In these selections from the *Fundamental Principles of the Metaphysics of Morals,* Immanuel Kant develops his principle of respect for persons. He explains his concept of the categorical imperative, which he contrasts with hypothetical imperatives. Hypothetical imperatives are conditional commands. They are commands we have reason to follow if they serve some desire of ours. According to Kant, all imperatives except the supreme principle of morality are hypothetical. For example, "Be at the theater at eight" is conditional on our desire to see the movie from the beginning. A categorical imperative, on the other hand, is a command that applies to all rational beings *independent* of their desires. It is a command that reason tells us to follow no matter what. Because its authority does not depend on subjective factors, Kant considers it an objective law of reason. Because it applies to all of us, he calls it a universal practical law for all rational beings. And because this universal law has its source in our own capacity to reason, he calls us *legislators* of the universal law.

Although Kant says there is only one categorical imperative, he offers three formulations. The first is "[N]ever act in such a way that I could not also will that my maxim should be a universal law." By maxim, he means the principle on which a person's decision to act is made. To use one of Kant's own examples, someone who borrows money with no intention of repaying it would be acting on the maxim, "Whenever I need money I'll borrow it and promise to repay it though I know I never will." That maxim could never be a universal law, he says, because under those conditions, no one would believe promises any more and the institution of promising would self-destruct.

The third formulation is similar to the first, though Kant does not state it in the form of an imperative. It is "the idea of the will of every rational being as making universal law."

Kant's second formulation is "Act so that you treat humanity, whether in your own person or in that of another, as an end and never as a means only." Human beings, he says, have unconditional worth; that is, we do not consider our own existence to be a means to some further end but we consider it to be an end in itself. Therefore, we should not treat one another merely as a means to some further end. He then discusses the inherent worth and dignity of persons. Because we are subject only to the laws of our own reason, he says, we are autonomous beings. And our autonomy gives us a dignity and worth beyond all price. Because of our priceless dignity and worth, all persons are worthy of respect.

FIRST SECTION

...Nothing can possibly be conceived in the world, or even out of it, which can be called good, without qualification, except a good will. Intelligence, wit, judgment, and the other talents of the mind, however they may be named, or courage, resolution, perseverance, as qualities of temperament, are undoubtedly good and desirable in many respects; but these gifts of nature may also become extremely bad and mischievous if the will which is to make use of them, and which, therefore, constitutes what is

Derived from a translation by Thomas Kingsmill Abbott in 1895 of Kant's *Fundamental Principles of the Metaphysics of Morals* (1785).

called character, is not good. It is the same with the gifts of fortune. Power, riches, honor, even health, and the general well-being and contentment with one's condition which is called happiness, inspire pride, and often presumption, if there is not a good will to correct the influence of these on the mind, and with this also to rectify the whole principle of acting and adapt it to its end. The sight of a being who is not adorned with a single feature of a pure and good will, enjoying unbroken prosperity, can never give pleasure to an impartial rational spectator. Thus a good will appears to constitute the indispensable condition even of being worthy of happiness....

A good will is good not because of what it performs or effects, not by its aptness for the attainment of some proposed end, but simply by virtue of the volition; that is, it is good in itself, and considered by itself is to be esteemed much higher than all that can be brought about by it in favor of any inclination, nay even of the sum total of all inclinations. Even if it should happen that, owing to special disfavor of fortune, or the stingy provision of a step-motherly nature, this will should wholly lack power to accomplish its purpose, if with its greatest efforts it should yet achieve nothing, and there should remain only the good will (not, to be sure, a mere wish, but the summoning of all means in our power), then, like a jewel, it would still shine by its own light, as a thing which has its whole value in itself. Its usefulness or fruitlessness can neither add nor take away anything from this value. It would be, as it were, only the setting to enable us to handle it more conveniently in common commerce, or to attract to it the attention of those who are not yet connoisseurs, but not to recommend it to true connoisseurs, or to determine its value....

Thus the moral worth of an action does not lie in the effect expected from it, nor in any principle of action which requires to borrow its motive from this expected effect. For all these effects—agreeableness of one's condition and even the promotion of the happiness of others—could have been also brought about by other causes, so that for this there would have been no need of the will of a rational being; whereas it is in this

alone that the supreme and unconditional good can be found. The pre-eminent good which we call moral can therefore consist in nothing else than the conception of law in itself, which certainly is only possible in a rational being, in so far as this conception, and not the expected effect, determines the will. This is a good which is already present in the person who acts accordingly, and we have not to wait for it to appear first in the result.

But what sort of law can that be, the conception of which must determine the will, even without paying any regard to the effect expected from it, in order that this will may be called good absolutely and without qualification? As I have deprived the will of every impulse which could arise to it from obedience to any law, there remains nothing but the universal conformity of its actions to law in general, which alone is to serve the will as a principle, i.e., I am never to act otherwise than so that I could also will that my maxim should become a universal law. Here, now, it is the simple conformity to law in general, without assuming any particular law applicable to certain actions, that serves the will as its principle and must so serve it, if duty is not to be a vain delusion and a chimerical notion. The common reason of men in its practical judgments perfectly coincides with this and always has in view the principle here suggested.

Let the question be, for example: May I when in distress make a promise with the intention not to keep it? I readily distinguish here between the two significations which the question may have: Whether it is prudent, or whether it is right, to make a false promise? The former may undoubtedly of be the case. I see clearly indeed that it is not enough to extricate myself from a present difficulty by means of this subterfuge, but it must be well considered whether there may not hereafter spring from this lie much greater inconvenience than that from which I now free myself, and as, with all my supposed cunning, the consequences cannot be so easily foreseen but that credit once lost may be much more injurious to me than any mischief which I seek to avoid at present, it should be considered whether it would not be more prudent to act herein according to a universal maxim and to make it a habit to promise nothing except with the intention of keeping it. But it is soon clear to me that such a maxim will still only be based on the fear of consequences.

Now it is a wholly different thing to be truthful from duty and to be so from apprehension of injurious consequences. In the first case, the very notion of the action already implies a law for me; in the second case, I must first look about elsewhere to see what results may be combined with it which would affect myself. For to deviate from the principle of duty is beyond all doubt wicked; but to be unfaithful to my maxim of prudence may often be very advantageous to me, although to abide by it is certainly safer. The shortest way, however, and an unerring one, to discover the answer to this question whether a lying promise is consistent with duty, is to ask myself, "Should I be content that my maxim (to extricate myself from difficulty by a false promise) should hold good as a universal law, for myself as well as for others?" and should I be able to say to myself, "Every one may make a deceitful promise when he finds himself in a difficulty from which he cannot otherwise extricate himself?" Then I presently become aware that while I can will the lie, I can by no means will that lying should be a universal law. For with such a law there would be no promises at all, since it would be in vain to allege my intention in regard to my future actions to those who would not believe this allegation, or if they over hastily did so would pay me back in my own coin. Hence my maxim, as soon as it should be made a universal law, would necessarily destroy itself.

I do not, therefore, need any far-reaching penetration to discern what I have to do in order that my will may be morally good. Inexperienced in the course of the world, incapable of being prepared for all its contingencies, I only ask myself: Canst thou also will that thy maxim should be a universal law? If not, then it must be rejected, and that not because of a disadvantage accruing from it to myself or even to others, but because it cannot enter as a principle into a possible universal legislation, and reason extorts from me immediate respect for such legislation. I do not indeed as yet discern on what this respect is based (this the philosopher may inquire), but at least I understand this, that it is an estimation of the worth which far outweighs all worth of what is recommended by inclination, and that the necessity of acting from pure respect for the practical law is what constitutes duty, to which every other motive must give place, because it is the condition of a will being good in itself, and the worth of such a will is above everything.

SECOND SECTION

Everything in nature works according to laws. Rational beings alone have the faculty of acting according to the conception of laws, that is according to principles, i.e., have a will. Since the deduction of actions from principles requires reason, the will is nothing but practical reason....

The conception of an objective principle, in so far as it is obligatory for a will, is called a command (of reason), and the formula of the command is called an *imperative*.

All imperatives are expressed by the word ought or shall, and thereby indicate the relation of an objective law of reason to a will, which from its subjective constitution is not necessarily determined by it (an obligation). They say that something would be good to do or to forbear, but they say it to a will which does not always do a thing because it is conceived to be good to do it. That is practically good, however, which determines the will by means of the conceptions of reason, and consequently not from subjective causes, but objectively, that is on principles which are valid for every rational being as such. It is distinguished from the pleasant, as that which influences the will only by means of sensation from merely subjective causes, valid only for the sense of this or that one, and not as a principle of reason, which holds for every one....

Now all imperatives command either *hypothetically* or *categorically*. The former represent the practical necessity of a possible action as means to something else that is willed (or at least which one might possibly will). The *categorical imperative* would be that which represented an action as necessary of itself without reference to another end, i.e., as objectively necessary.

Since every practical law represents a possible action as good and, on this account, for a subject who is practically determinable by reason, necessary, all imperatives are formulae determining an action which is necessary according to the principle of a will good in some respects. If now the action is good only as a means to something else, then the imperative is hypothetical; if it is conceived as good in itself and consequently as being necessarily the principle of a will which of itself conforms to reason, then it is categorical....

Finally, there is an imperative which commands a certain conduct immediately, without having as its condition any other purpose to be attained by it. This imperative is categorical. It concerns not the matter of the action, or its intended result, but its form and the principle of which it is itself a result; and what is essentially good in it consists in the mental disposition, let the consequence be what it may. This imperative may be called that of morality....

When I conceive a hypothetical imperative, in general I do not know beforehand what it will contain until I am given the condition. But when I conceive a categorical imperative, I know at once what it contains. For as the imperative contains besides the law only the necessity that the maxims shall conform to this law, while the law contains no conditions restricting it, there remains nothing but the general statement that the maxim of the action should conform to a universal law, and it is this conformity alone that the imperative properly represents as necessary.

There is therefore but one categorical imperative, namely, this: Act only on that maxim whereby you can at the same time will that it should become a universal law.

Now if all imperatives of duty can be deduced from this one imperative as from their principle, then, although it should remain undecided what is called duty is not merely a vain notion, yet at least we shall be able to show what we understand by it and what this notion means.

Since the universality of the law according to which effects are produced constitutes what is properly called nature in the most general sense (as to form), i.e., the existence of things so far as it is determined by general laws, the imperative of duty may be expressed thus: Act as if the maxim of your action were to become by your will a universal law of nature....

Supposing, however, that there were something whose existence has in itself an absolute worth, something which, being an end in itself, could be a source of definite laws; then in this and this alone would lie the source of a possible categorical imperative, i.e., a practical law.

Now I say: man and generally any rational being exists as an end in himself, not merely as a means to be arbitrarily used by this or that will, but in all his actions, whether they concern himself or other rational beings, must be always regarded at the same time as an end. All objects of the inclinations have only a conditional worth, for if the inclinations and the wants founded on them did not exist, then their object would be without value. But the inclinations, themselves being sources of want, are so far from having an absolute worth for which they should be desired that on the contrary it must be the universal wish of every rational being to be wholly free from them. Thus the worth of any object which is to be acquired by our action is always conditional. Beings whose existence depends not on our will but on nature's, have nevertheless, if they are irrational beings, only a relative value as means, and are therefore called things; rational beings, on the contrary, are called *persons*, because their very nature points them out as ends in themselves, that is as something which must not be used merely as means, and so far therefore restricts freedom of action (and is an object of respect). These, therefore, are not merely subjective ends whose existence has a worth for us as an effect of our action, but objective ends, that is, things whose existence is an end in itself; an end moreover for which no other can be substituted, which they should subserve merely as means, for otherwise nothing whatever would possess absolute worth; but if all worth were conditioned and therefore contingent, then there would be no supreme practical principle of reason whatever.

If then there is a supreme practical principle or, in respect of the human will, a categorical imperative, it must be one which, being drawn from the conception of that which is necessarily an end for everyone because it is an end in itself, constitutes an objective principle of will, and can therefore serve as a universal practical law. The foundation of this principle is: rational nature exists as an end in itself. Man necessarily conceives his own existence as being so; so far then this is a subjective principle of human actions. But every other rational being regards its existence similarly, just on the same rational principle that holds for me: so that it is at the same time an objective principle, from which as a supreme practical law all laws of the will must be capable of being deduced. Accordingly the practical imperative will be as follows: So act as to treat humanity, whether in your own person or in that of any other, in every case as an end, never as means only....

Looking back now on all previous attempts to discover the principle of morality, we need not wonder why they all failed. It was seen that man was bound to laws by duty, but it was not observed that the laws to which he is subject are only those of his own giving, though at the same time they are universal, and that he is only bound to act in conformity with his own will; a will, however, which is designed by nature to give universal laws. For when one has conceived man only as subject to a law (no matter what), then this law required some interest, either by way of attraction or constraint, since it did not originate as a law from his own will, but this will was according to a law obliged by something else to act in a certain manner. Now by this necessary consequence all the labor spent in finding a supreme principle of duty was irrevocably lost. For men never elicited duty, but only a necessity of acting from a certain interest. Whether this interest was private or otherwise, in any case the imperative must be conditional and could not by any means be capable of being a moral command. I will therefore call this the principle of *autonomy* of the will, in contrast with every other which I accordingly reckon as heteronomy.

The conception of the will of every rational being as one which must consider itself as giving in all the maxims of its will universal laws, so as to judge itself and its actions from this point of view; this conception leads to another which depends on it and is very fruitful, namely that of a *kingdom of ends*.

By a kingdom I understand the union of different rational beings in a system by common laws. Now since it is by laws that ends are determined as regards their universal validity, hence, if we abstract from the personal differences of rational beings and likewise from all the content of their private ends, we shall be able to conceive all ends combined in a systematic whole (including both rational beings as ends in themselves, and also the special ends which each may propose to himself), that is to say, we can conceive a kingdom of ends, which on the preceding principles is possible.

For all rational beings come under the law that each of them must treat itself and all others never merely as means, but in every case at the same time as ends in themselves. Hence results a systematic union of rational being by common objective laws, i.e., a kingdom which may be called a kingdom of ends, since what these laws have in view is just the relation of these beings to one another as ends and means. It is certainly only an ideal.

A rational being belongs as a member to the kingdom of ends when, although giving universal laws in it, he is also himself subject to these laws. He belongs to it as sovereign when, while giving laws, he is not subject to the will of any other.

A rational being must always regard himself as giving laws either as member or as sovereign in a kingdom of ends which is rendered possible by the freedom of will. He cannot, however, maintain the latter position merely by the maxims of his will, but only in case he is a completely independent being without wants and with unrestricted power adequate to his will.

Morality consists then in the reference of all action to the legislation which alone can render a kingdom of ends possible. This legislation must be capable of existing in every rational being and of emanating from his will, so that the principle of this will is never to act on any maxim which could not without contradiction be also a universal law and, accordingly, always so to act that the will could at the same time regard itself as giving in its maxims universal laws. If now the maxims of rational beings are not by their own nature coincident with this objective principle, then the necessity of acting on it is called practical necessitation, i.e., duty. Duty does not apply to the sovereign in the kingdom of ends, but it does to every member of it and to all in the same degree.

The practical necessity of acting on this principle, i.e., duty, does not rest at all on feelings, impulses, or inclinations, but solely on the relation of rational beings to one another, a relation in which the will of a rational being must always be regarded as legislative, since otherwise it could not be conceived as an end in itself. Reason then refers every maxim of the will, regarding it as legislating universally, to every other will and also to every action towards oneself; and this not on account of any other practical motive or any future advantage, but from the idea of the dignity of a rational being, obeying no law but that which he himself also gives.

In the kingdom of ends everything has either value or dignity. Whatever has a value can be replaced by something else which is equivalent; whatever, on the other hand, is above all value, and therefore admits of no equivalent, has a dignity.

Whatever has reference to the general inclinations and wants of mankind has a market value; whatever, without presupposing a want, corresponds to a certain taste, that is to a satisfaction in the mere purposeless play of our faculties, has a fancy value; but that which constitutes the condition under which alone anything can be an end in itself, this has not merely a relative worth, i.e., value, but an intrinsic worth, that is, dignity.

Now morality is the condition under which alone a rational being can be an end in himself, since by this alone is it possible that he should be a legislating member in the kingdom of ends. Thus morality, and humanity as capable of it, is that which alone has dignity. Skill and diligence in labor have a market value; wit, lively imagination, and humor, have fancy value; on the other hand, fidelity to promises, benevolence from principle (not from instinct), have an intrinsic worth. Neither nature nor art contains anything which in default

of these it could put in their place, for their worth consists not in the effects which spring from them, not in the use and advantage which they secure, but in the disposition of mind, that is, the maxims of the will which are ready to manifest themselves in such actions, even though they should not have the desired effect. These actions also need no recommendation from any subjective taste or sentiment, that they may be looked on with immediate favor and satisfaction: they need no immediate propensity or feeling for them; they exhibit the will that performs them as an object of an immediate respect, and nothing but reason is required to impose them on the will; not to flatter it into them, which, in the case of duties, would be a contradiction. This estimation therefore shows that the worth of such a disposition is dignity, and places it infinitely above all value, with which it cannot for a moment be brought into comparison or competition without as it were violating its sanctity.

What then is it which justifies virtue or the morally good disposition, in making such lofty claims? It is nothing less than the privilege it secures to the rational being of participating in the giving of universal laws, by which it qualifies him to be a member of a possible kingdom of ends, a privilege to which he was already destined by his own nature as being an end in himself and, on that account, legislating in the kingdom of ends; free as regards all laws of physical nature, and obeying those only which he himself gives, and by which his maxims can belong to a system of universal law, to which at the same time he submits himself. For nothing has any worth except what the law assigns it. Now the legislation itself which assigns the worth of everything must for that very reason possess dignity, that is an unconditional incomparable worth; and the word respect alone supplies a becoming expression for the esteem which a rational being must have for it. Autonomy then is the basis of the dignity of human and of every rational nature....

⚜ QUESTIONS FOR ANALYSIS

1. Why is "good will" considered good without qualification? How is it different from other good things?
2. How is a categorical imperative different from a hypothetical imperative? How do categorical imperatives get their authority? What does Kant

   mean in saying that all rational beings are "legislators" of universal law?
3. How would Kant evaluate this maxim: "I will keep my promises only when it is my own personal best interest"?

4. What does Kant mean by "absolute worth"? Why do persons, but not things, have absolute worth?

5. What does it mean to treat a person as a thing rather than as an end in itself? What examples can you think of?

6. According to Kant, human autonomy lies in the fact that we are subject to the moral law of our own will, not a moral law from an external source. What does it mean to be subject to a law of our own will? Why does our subjection to it make us autonomous?

7. What is the importance of Kant's distinction between value and dignity? Why does he say that human autonomy is the basis of human dignity?

8. What does Kant mean by a "kingdom of ends"? What role does the concept play in his moral thought?

Utilitarianism

JOHN STUART MILL

In the following selection from *Utilitarianism,* John Stuart Mill argues that the principle of utility, or the greatest happiness principle—choose the action that creates the greatest happiness for all concerned—is the foundation of all morality. All other moral principles, he says, are "secondary principles," which we adopt because following them will help us maximize happiness. Because he takes the principle of utility to be fundamental, he calls his view utilitarianism.

After defining *happiness* as "pleasure and the absence of pain," Mill distinguishes higher—distinctively human—pleasures from lower—animal—pleasures. The rest of the selection is devoted to defending utilitarianism from various objections, the most notable being that it amounts to expediency and selfishness.

The creed which accepts as the foundation of morals Utility, or the Greatest Happiness Principle, holds that actions are right in proportion as they tend to promote happiness, wrong as they tend to produce the reverse of happiness. By happiness is intended pleasure and the absence of pain; by unhappiness, pain and the privation of pleasure. To give a clear view of the moral standard set up by the theory, much more requires to be said, in particular, what things it includes in the ideas of pain and pleasure and to what extent this is left an open question. But these supplementary explanations do not affect the theory of life on which this theory of morality is grounded—namely, that pleasure and freedom from pain are the only things desirable as ends, and that all desirable things (which are as numerous in the utilitarian as in any other scheme) are desirable either for the pleasure inherent in themselves or as means to the promotion of pleasure and the prevention of pain.

Now, such a theory of life excites in many minds, and among them in some of the most estimable in feeling and purpose, inveterate dislike. To suppose that life has (as they express it) no higher end than pleasure—no better and nobler object of desire and pursuit—they designate as utterly mean and groveling, as a doctrine worthy only of swine, to whom the followers of Epicurus were, at a very early period, contemptuously likened; and modern holders of the doctrine are occasionally made the subject of equally polite comparisons by its German, French, and English assailants.

When thus attacked, the Epicureans have always answered that it is not they, but their accusers who represent human nature in a degrading light, since the accusation supposes human beings

From John Stuart Mill, *Utilitarianism* (1863).

to be capable of no pleasures except those of which swine are capable. If this supposition were true, the charge could not be gainsaid, but would then be no longer an imputation; for if the sources of pleasure were precisely the same to human beings and to swine, the rule of life which is good enough for the one would be good enough for the other. The comparison of the Epicurean life to that of beasts is felt as degrading precisely because a beast's pleasures do not satisfy a human being's conceptions of happiness. Human beings have faculties more elevated than the animal appetites and, when once made conscious of them, do not regard anything as happiness which does not include their gratification. I do not, indeed, consider the Epicureans to have been by any means faultless in drawing out their scheme of consequences from the utilitarian principle. To do this in any sufficient manner, many Stoic, as well as Christian, elements require to be included. But there is no known Epicurean theory of life which does not assign to the pleasures of the intellect, of the feelings and imagination, and of the moral sentiments a much higher value as pleasures than to those of mere sensation.

It must be admitted, however, that utilitarian writers in general have placed the superiority of mental over bodily pleasures chiefly in the greater permanency, safety, uncostliness, etc., of the former—that is, in their circumstantial advantages rather than in their intrinsic nature. And on all these points, utilitarians have fully proved their case; but they might have taken the other and, as it may be called, higher ground with entire consistency. It is quite compatible with the principle of utility to recognize the fact that some *kinds* of pleasure are more desirable and more valuable than others. It would be absurd that while, in estimating all other things, quality is considered as well as quantity, the estimation of pleasures should be supposed to depend on quantity alone.

If I am asked what I mean by difference of quality in pleasures or what makes one pleasure more valuable than another, merely as a pleasure, except its being greater in amount, there is but one possible answer. Of two pleasures, if there be one to which all or almost all who have experience of both give a decided preference, irrespective of any feeling of moral obligation to prefer it,

that is the more desirable pleasure. If one of the two is, by those who are competently acquainted with both, placed so far above the other that they prefer it, even though knowing it to be attended with a greater amount of discontent, and would not resign it for any quantity of the other pleasure of which their nature is capable, we are justified in ascribing to the preferred enjoyment a superiority in quality so far outweighing quantity as to render it, in comparison, of small account.

Now, it is an unquestionable fact that those who are equally acquainted with and equally capable of appreciating and enjoying both do give a most marked preference to the manner of existence which employs their higher faculties. Few human creatures would consent to be changed into any of the lower animals for a promise of the fullest allowance of a beast's pleasures; no intelligent human being would consent to be a fool, no instructed person would be an ignoramus, no person of feeling and conscience would be selfish and base, even though they should be persuaded that the fool, the dunce, or the rascal is better satisfied with his lot than they are with theirs. They would not resign what they possess more than he for the most complete satisfaction of all the desires which they have in common with him….

I must again repeat what the assailants of utilitarianism seldom have the justice to acknowledge, that the happiness which forms the utilitarian standard of what is right in conduct is not the agent's own happiness, but that of all concerned. As between his own happiness and that of others, utilitarianism requires him to be as strictly impartial as a disinterested and benevolent spectator. In the golden rule of Jesus of Nazareth, we read the complete spirit of the ethics of utility. To do as you would be done by and to love your neighbor as yourself constitute the ideal perfection of utilitarian morality. As the means of making the nearest approach to this ideal, utility would enjoin first that laws and social arrangements should place the happiness, or (as speaking practically it may be called) the interest, of every individual as nearly as possible in harmony with the interest of the whole; and secondly, that education and opinion, which have so vast a power over human character, should so use that power as to establish in the mind of every individual an indissoluble association between his own happiness and the good of the whole—especially between his own happiness and the practice of such modes of conduct, negative and positive, as regard for the universal happiness prescribes, so that not only he may be unable to conceive the possibility of happiness to himself consistently with conduct opposed to the general good, but also that a direct impulse to promote the general good may be in every individual one of the habitual motives of action and the sentiments connected therewith may fill a large and prominent place in every human being's sentient existence. If the impugners of the utilitarian morality represented it to their own minds in this its true character, I know not what recommendation possessed by any other morality they could possibly affirm to be wanting to it, what more beautiful or more exalted developments of human nature any other ethical system can be supposed to foster, or what springs of action, not accessible to the utilitarian, such systems rely on for giving effect to their mandates.

The objectors to utilitarianism cannot always be charged with representing it in a discreditable light. On the contrary, those among them who entertain anything like a just idea of its disinterested character sometimes find fault with its standard as being too high for humanity. They say it is exacting too much to require that people shall always act from the inducement of promoting the general interests of society. But this is to mistake the very meaning of a standard of morals and confound the rule of action with the motive of it. It is the business of ethics to tell us what are our duties or by what test we may know them; but no system of ethics requires that the sole motive of all we do shall be a feeling of duty: on the contrary, ninety-nine hundredths of all our actions are done from other motives, and rightly so done, if the rule of duty does not condemn them. It is the more unjust to utilitarianism that this particular misapprehension should be made a ground of objection to it, inasmuch as utilitarian moralists have gone beyond almost all others in affirming that the motive has nothing to do with the morality of the action, though much with the worth of the agent. He who saves a fellow creature from drowning does what is morally right, whether his motive be duty or the hope of being paid for his trouble; he who betrays the friend that trusts him is guilty of a crime, even if his object be to serve another friend to whom he is under greater obligations. But to speak only of actions done from the motive of duty, and in direct obedience to principle: it is a misapprehension of the utilitarian mode of thought to conceive it as implying that people should fix their minds upon so wide a generality as the world or society at large. The great majority of good actions are intended not for the benefit of the world, but for that of individuals, of which the good of the world is made up; and the thoughts of the most virtuous man need not on these occasions travel beyond the particular persons concerned, except so far as is necessary to assure himself that in benefiting them he is not violating the rights, that is the legitimate and authorized expectations, of anyone else. The multiplication of happiness is, according to the utilitarian ethics, the object of virtue: the occasions on which any person (except one in a thousand) has it in his power to do this on an extended scale, in other words to be a public benefactor, are but exceptional; and on these occasions alone is he called on to consider public utility; in every other case, private utility, the interest or happiness of some few persons, is all he has to attend to. Those alone the influence of whose actions extends to society in general need concern themselves habitually about so large an object. In the case of abstinences, indeed—of things which people forbear to do from moral considerations, though the consequences in the particular case might be beneficial—it would be unworthy of an intelligent agent not to be consciously aware that the action is of a class which, if practiced generally, would be generally injurious, and that this is the ground of the obligation to abstain from it. The amount of regard for the public interest implied in this recognition is no greater than is demanded by every system of morals, for they all enjoin to abstain from whatever is manifestly pernicious to society....

Again, Utility is often summarily stigmatized as an immoral doctrine by giving it the name of Expediency and taking advantage of the popular use of that term to contrast it with Principle. But the Expedient, in the sense in which it is opposed to the Right, generally means that which is expedient for the particular interest of the agent himself, as when a minister sacrifices the interests of his country to keep himself in place. When it means anything better than this, it means that which is expedient for some immediate object, some temporary purpose, but which violates a rule whose observance is expedient in a much higher degree. The Expedient, in this sense, instead of being the same thing as the useful, is a branch of the hurtful.

Thus, it would often be expedient, for the purpose of getting over some momentary embarrassment, or attaining some object immediately useful to ourselves or others, to tell a lie. But inasmuch as the cultivation in ourselves of a sensitive feeling on the subject of veracity is one of the most useful, and the enfeeblement of that feeling one of the most hurtful, things to which our conduct can be instrumental; and inasmuch as any, even unintentional, deviation from truth does that much toward weakening the trustworthiness of human assertion, which is not only the principal support of all present social well-being, but the insufficiency of which does more than any one thing that can be named to keep back civilization, virtue, everything on which human happiness on the largest scale depends—we feel that the violation, for a present advantage, of a rule of such transcendent expediency is not expedient and that he, who for the sake of a convenience to himself or to some other individual, does what depends on him to deprive mankind of the good, and inflict upon them the evil, involved in the greater or less reliance which they can place in each other's word, acts the part of one of their worst enemies.

Yet, that even this rule, sacred as it is, admits of possible exceptions is acknowledged by all moralists, the chief of which is when the withholding of some fact (as of information from a malefactor or of bad news from a person dangerously ill) would save an individual (especially an individual other than oneself) from great and unmerited evil, and when the withholding can only be effected by denial. But in order that the exception may not extend itself beyond the need and may have the least possible effect in weakening reliance on veracity, it ought to be recognized and, if possible, its limits defined; and if the principle of utility is good for anything, it must be good for weighing these conflicting utilities

against one another and marking out the region within which one or the other preponderates.

Again, defenders of utility often find themselves called upon to reply to such objections as this—that there is not time, previous to action, for calculating and weighing the effects of any line of conduct on the general happiness. This is exactly as if anyone were to say that it is impossible to guide our conduct by Christianity because there is not time, on every occasion on which anything has to be done, to read through the Old and New Testaments. The answer to the objection is that there has been ample time, namely, the whole past duration of the human species. During all that time, mankind have been learning by experience the tendencies of actions, on which experience all the prudence, as well as all the morality of life, are dependent. People talk as if the commencement of this course of experience had hitherto been put off, and as if, at the moment when some man feels tempted to meddle with the property or life of another, he had to begin considering for the first time whether murder and theft are injurious to human happiness. Even then, I do not think that he would find the question very puzzling; but, at all events, the matter is now done to his hand. It is truly a whimsical supposition that if mankind were agreed in considering utility to be the test of morality, they would remain without any agreement as to what is useful and would take no measures for having their notions on the subject taught to the young and enforced by law and opinion. There is no difficulty in proving any ethical standard whatever to work ill, if we suppose universal idiocy to be conjoined with it; but on any hypothesis short of that, mankind must by this time have acquired positive beliefs as to the effects of some actions on their happiness; and the beliefs which have thus come down are the rules of morality for the multitude, and for the philosopher until he has succeeded in finding better.

That philosophers might easily do this, even now, on many subjects; that the received code of ethics is by no means of divine right; and that mankind have still much to learn as to the effects of actions on the general happiness—I admit, or, rather, earnestly maintain. The corollaries from the principle of utility, like the precepts of every practical art, admit of indefinite improvement, and, in a progressive state of the human mind, their improvement is perpetually going on. But to consider the rules of morality as improvable is one thing; to pass over the intermediate generalizations entirely, and endeavor to test each individual action directly by the first principle, is another. It is a strange notion that the acknowledgment of a first principle is inconsistent with the admission of secondary ones. To inform a traveler respecting the place of his ultimate destination is not to forbid the use of landmarks and direction-posts on the way. The proposition that happiness is the end and aim of morality does not mean that no road ought to be laid down to that goal or that persons going thither should not be advised to take one direction, rather than another. Men really ought to leave off talking a kind of nonsense on this subject, which they would neither talk nor listen to on other matters of practical concernment. Nobody argues that the art of navigation is not founded on astronomy because sailors cannot wait to calculate the Nautical Almanack. Being rational creatures, they go to sea with it ready calculated; and all rational creatures go out upon the sea of life with their minds made up on the common questions of right and wrong, as well as on many of the far more difficult questions of wise and foolish. And this, as long as foresight is a human quality, it is to be presumed they will continue to do. Whatever we adopt as the fundamental principle of morality, we require subordinate principles to apply it by; the impossibility of doing without them, being common to all systems, can afford no argument against any one in particular; but gravely to argue as if no such secondary principles could be had, and as if mankind had remained till now, and always remain, without drawing any general conclusions from the experience of human life, is as high a pitch, I think, as absurdity has ever reached in philosophical controversy.

The remainder of the stock arguments against utilitarianism mostly consist in laying to its charge the common infirmities of human nature and the general difficulties which embarrass conscientious persons in shaping their course through life. We are told that a utilitarian will be apt to make his own particular case an exception to moral rules and, when under temptation, will see a utility in the breach of a rule greater than he will see in its observance. But is utility the only creed which is able to furnish us with excuses for evildoing and means of cheating our own conscience? They are afforded in abundance by all doctrines which recognize as a fact in morals the existence of conflicting considerations, which all doctrines do that have been believed by sane persons. It is not the fault of any creed, but of the complicated nature of human affairs, that rules of conduct cannot be so framed as to require no exceptions and that hardly any kind of action can safely be laid down as either always obligatory or always condemnable. There is no ethical creed which does not temper the rigidity of its laws by giving a certain latitude, under the moral responsibility of the agent, for accommodation to peculiarities of circumstances; and under every creed, at the opening thus made, self-deception and dishonest casuistry get in. There exists no moral system under which there do not arise unequivocal cases of conflicting obligation. These are the real difficulties, the knotty points both in the theory of ethics and in the conscientious guidance of personal conduct. They are overcome practically with greater or with less success according to the intellect and virtue of the individual; but it can hardly be pretended that anyone will be the less qualified for dealing with them from possessing an ultimate standard to which conflicting rights and duties can be referred. If utility is the ultimate source of moral obligations, utility may be invoked to decide between them when their demands are incompatible. Though the application of the standard may be difficult, it is better than none at all: while in other systems the moral laws all claiming independent authority, there is no common umpire entitled to interfere between them; their claims to precedence one over another rest on little better than sophistry, and unless determined, as they generally are, by the unacknowledged influence of considerations of utility, afford a free scope for the action of personal desires and partialities. We must remember that only in these cases of conflict between secondary principles is it requisite that first principles should be appealed to. There is no case of moral obligation in which some secondary principle is not involved; and, if only one, there can seldombe any real doubt which one it is in the mind of any person by whom the principle itself is recognized.

---

1. How does Mill distinguish higher and lower pleasures? What test does he propose?
2. According to Mill, utilitarianism and the golden rule are both in the same spirit. Why? Do you agree? Why or why not?
3. What is the importance of Mill's distinction between private and public utility? What criticism is it intended to disarm?
4. Mill says that we need appeal directly to the greatest happiness principle only when secondary principles conflict. Why?
5. Mill's ethical view is often called hedonistic because it considers pleasure to be the only good desirable in itself. Can you think of goods that are desirable independent of any pleasure they might give?

Justice as a Virtue

PLATO

In *The Republic*, Plato (427-347 B.C.E.) discusses whether justice is best understood as a virtue of a good city or of good individuals. He shows that, in many ways, they are inseparable, as understanding the virtue of individuals helps us understand virtue in cities. The excerpts here are from Book II, which asks whether it is always better to be just than unjust, and Book IV, which argues that justice is a personal virtue as well as a virtue of the state. In later Books, Plato defends his characterizations of the good city and offers proofs that being just is better than being unjust.

Plato wrote in a style called "dialogues," in which Socrates (his own teacher) discusses ideas with several other persons. This technique is designed to draw out knowledge by asking questions and examining the proposed answers. In these passages, Socrates is the narrator, reporting on his discussions with several other people.

IS IT BETTER TO BE JUST THAN UNJUST? (BOOK II)

...Glaucon: Socrates, do you wish really to persuade us, or only to seem to have persuaded us, that to be just is always better than to be unjust?

I should wish really to persuade you, I replied, if I could.

Then you certainly have not succeeded. Let me ask you now: How would you arrange goods—are there not some which we welcome for their own sakes, and independently of their consequences, as, for example, harmless pleasures and enjoyments, which delight us at the time, although nothing follows from them?

I agree in thinking that there is such a class, I replied.

Is there not also a second class of goods, such as knowledge, sight, health, which are desirable not only in themselves, but also for their results?

Certainly, I said.

And would you not recognize a third class, such as gymnastic, and the care of the sick, and the physician's art; also the various ways of money-making—these do us good but we regard them as disagreeable; and no one would choose them

---

Derived from a translation by Benjamin Jowett in 1892 of Plato's *The Republic*.

for their own sakes, but only for the sake of some reward or result which flows from them?

There is, I said, this third class also. But why do you ask?

Because I want to know in which of the three classes you would place justice?

In the highest class, I replied, among those goods which he who would be happy desires both for their own sake and for the sake of their results....

[J]ustice, which is the subject of our enquiry, is, as you know, sometimes spoken of as the virtue of an individual, and sometimes as the virtue of a State.

True, he replied.

And is not a State larger than an individual?

It is.

Then in the larger the quantity of justice is likely to be larger and more easily discernible. I propose therefore that we enquire into the nature of justice and injustice, first as they appear in the State, and secondly in the individual, proceeding from the greater to the lesser and comparing them.

That, he said, is an excellent proposal.

And if we imagine the State in process of creation, we shall see the justice and injustice of the State in process of creation also.

I dare say.

When the State is completed there may be a hope that the object of our search will be more easily discovered.

Yes, far more easily.

But ought we to attempt to construct one? I said; for to do so, as I am inclined to think, will be a very serious task. Reflect therefore.... A State, I said, arises, as I conceive, out of the needs of mankind; no one is self-sufficing, but all of us have many wants. Can any other origin of a State be imagined?

There can be no other.

Then, as we have many wants, and many persons are needed to supply them, one takes a helper for one purpose and another for another; and when these partners and helpers are gathered together in one habitation the body of inhabitants is termed a State....

JUSTICE AS A VIRTUE FOR THE INDIVIDUAL AND THE STATE (BOOK IV)

...[O]ur aim in founding the State was not the disproportionate happiness of anyone class, but the greatest happiness of the whole; we thought that in a State which is ordered with a view to the good of the whole we should be most likely to find justice and in the ill-ordered State injustice: and, having found them, we might then decide which of the two is the happier. At present, I take it, we are fashioning the happy State, not piecemeal, or with a view of making a few happy citizens, but as a whole; and by-and-by we will proceed to view the opposite kind of State....

[W]hen the guardians of the laws and of the government are only seeming and not real guardians, then see how they turn the State upside down; and on the other hand they alone have the power of giving order and happiness to the State. We mean our guardians to be true saviors and not the destroyers of the State, whereas our opponent is thinking of peasants at a festival, who are enjoying a life of revelry, not of citizens who are doing their duty to the State. But, if so, we mean different things, and he is speaking of something which is not a State. And therefore we must consider whether in appointing our guardians we would look to their greatest happiness individually, or whether this principle of happiness does not rather reside in the State as a whole. But if the latter be the truth, then the guardians and auxiliaries, and all others equally with them, must be compelled or induced to do their own work in the best way. And thus the whole State will grow up in a noble order, and the several classes will receive the proportion of happiness which nature assigns to them.

... And so, I said, we may consider three out of the four virtues to have been discovered in our State [temperance, courage, wisdom]. The last of those qualities which make a state virtuous must be justice, if we only knew what that was.

... [T]he original principle which we were always laying down as the foundation of the State, that one man should practice one thing only, the thing to which his nature was best adapted;—now justice is this principle or a part of it.

Yes, we often said that one man should do one thing only.

Further, we affirmed that justice was doing one's own business, and not being a busybody; we said so again and again, and many others have said the same to us.

Yes, we said so.

Then to do one's own business in a certain way may be assumed to be justice. Can you tell me whence I derive this inference?

I cannot, but I should like to be told.

Because I think that this is the only virtue which remains in the State when the other virtues of temperance and courage and wisdom are abstracted; and, that this is the ultimate cause and condition of the existence of all of them, and while remaining in them is also their preservative; and we were saying that if the three were discovered by us, justice would be the fourth or remaining one.

That follows of necessity.

If we are asked to determine which of these four qualities by its presence contributes most to the excellence of the State, whether the agreement of rulers and subjects, or the preservation in the soldiers of the opinion which the law ordains about the true nature of dangers, or wisdom and watchfulness in the rulers, or whether this other which I am mentioning, and which is found in children and women, slave and freeman, artisan, ruler, subject,—the quality, I mean, of everyone doing his own work, and not being a busybody, would claim the palm—the question is not so easily answered.

Certainly, he replied, there would be a difficulty in saying which.

Then the power of each individual in the State to do his own work appears to compete with the other political virtues, wisdom, temperance, courage.

Yes, he said.

And the virtue which enters into this competition is justice?

Exactly.

Let us look at the question from another point of view: Are not the rulers in a State those to whom you would entrust the office of determining suits at law?

Certainly.

And are suits decided on any other ground but that a man may neither take what is another's, nor be deprived of what is his own?

Yes; that is their principle.

Which is a just principle?

Yes.

Then on this view also justice will be admitted to be the having and doing what is a man's own, and belongs to him?

Very true....

We will not, I said, be over-positive as yet; but if, on trial, this conception of justice be verified in the individual as well as in the State, there will be no longer any room for doubt; if it be not verified, we must have a fresh enquiry. First let us complete the old investigation, which we began, as you remember, under the impression that, if we could previously examine justice on the larger scale, there would be less difficulty in discerning her in the individual. That larger example appeared to be the State, and accordingly we constructed as good a one as we could, knowing well that in the good State justice would be found. Let the discovery which we made be now applied to the individual—if they agree, we shall be satisfied; or, if there be a difference in the individual, we will come back to the State and have another trial of the theory. The friction of the two when rubbed together may possibly strike a light in which justice will shine forth, and the vision which is then revealed we will fix in our souls.

That will be in regular course; let us do as you say.

I proceeded to ask: When two things, a greater and less, are called by the same name, are they like or unlike in so far as they are called the same?

Like, he replied.

The just man then, if we regard the idea of justice only, will be like the just State?

He will.

And a State was thought by us to be just when the three classes in the State severally did their own business; and also thought to be temperate and valiant and wise by reason of certain other affections and qualities of these same classes?

True, he said.

And so of the individual; we may assume that he has the same three principles in his own soul which are found in the State; and he may be rightly described in the same terms, because he is affected in the same manner?

Certainly, he said....

And is justice dimmer in the individual, and is her form different, or is she the same which we found her to be in the State?

There is no difference in my opinion, he said....

And the reason is that each part of him is doing its own business, whether in ruling or being ruled?

Exactly so.

Are you satisfied then that the quality which makes such men and such states is justice, or do you hope to discover some other?

Not I, indeed....

But in reality justice was such as we were describing, being concerned however, not with the outward man, but with the inward, which is the true self and concernment of man: for the just man does not permit the several elements within him to interfere with one another, or any of them to do the work of others,—he sets in order his own

inner life, and is his own master and his own law, and at peace with himself; and when he has bound together the three principles within him, which may be compared to the higher, lower, and middle notes of the scale, and the intermediate intervals—when he has bound all these together, and is no longer many, but has become one entirely temperate and perfectly adjusted nature, then he proceeds to act, if he has to act, whether in a matter of property, or in the treatment of the body, or in some affair of politics or private business; always thinking and calling that which preserves and co-operates with this harmonious condition, just and good action, and the knowledge which presides over it, wisdom, and that which at any time impairs this condition, he will call unjust action, and the opinion which presides over it ignorance.

You have said the exact truth, Socrates.

Very good; and if we were to affirm that we had discovered the just man and the just State, and the nature of justice in each of them, we should not be telling a falsehood?

Most certainly not.

☙ QUESTIONS FOR ANALYSIS

1. Do you agree that justice is desired both for its own sake and for the sake of its results? What would be examples of results that justice might produce?
2. Do you believe that it is better to be just than unjust? What is your reasoning to reach this conclusion?
3. What does Socrates mean when he says the state arises out of the needs of the mankind?
4. What constitutes the greatest happiness for all in the creation of the State?
5. What are the four virtues of the State? What is the relationship of justice to the other virtues?
6. What is the relationship of justice in the individual and justice in the state?

The Ethics of Care

VIRGINIA HELD

A Distinguished Professor at the City University of New York Graduate School, Virginia Held also has taught at Hunter College, Hamilton College, Dartmouth College, and Barnard College. She is widely recognized for her pioneering work in feminist philosophy, especially feminist ethics.

From Virginia Held, *The Ethics of Care: Personal, Political, and Global*, pp. 9-15, Oxford University Press (2006). Reprinted by permission of Oxford University Press, Inc.

The excerpt here from her book *The Ethics of Care: Personal, Political, and Global* develops ideas that have been presented by several feminist philosophers in recent decades on "care ethics," including those of Carol Gilligan, Eva Kittay, Nel Noddings and Sara Ruddick. This feminist approach to ethics rejects a traditional emphasis on rational persons entering into contracts, a paradigm which assumes a male model of behavior. Instead, it focuses on a paradigm of a mother-child relationship that is positive and constructive, seeking consensus and community.

FEATURES OF THE ETHICS OF CARE

Some advocates of the ethics of care resist generalizing this approach into something that can be fitted into the form of a moral theory. They see it as a mosaic of insights and value the way it is sensitive to contextual nuance and particular narratives rather than making the abstract and universal claims of more familiar moral theories. Still, I think one can discern among various versions of the ethics of care a number of major features.

First, the central focus of the ethics of care is on the compelling moral salience of attending to and meeting the needs of the particular others for whom we take responsibility. Caring for one's child, for instance, may well and defensibly be at the forefront of a person's moral concerns. The ethics of care recognizes that human beings are dependent for many years of their lives, that the moral claim of those dependent on us for the care they need is pressing, and that there are highly important moral aspects in developing the relations of caring that enable human beings to live and progress. All persons need care for at least their early years. Prospects for human progress and flourishing hinge fundamentally on the care that those needing it receive, and the ethics of care stresses the moral force of the responsibility to respond to the needs of the dependent. Many persons will become ill and dependent for some periods of their later lives, including in frail old age, and some who are permanently disabled will need care the whole of their lives. Moralities built on the image of the independent, autonomous, rational individual largely overlook the reality of human dependence and the morality for which it calls. The ethics of care attends to this central concern of human life and delineates the moral values involved. It refuses to relegate care to a realm "outside morality." How caring for particular others should be reconciled with the claims of, for instance, universal justice is an issue that needs to be addressed. But the ethics of care starts with the moral claims of particular others, for instance, of one's child, whose claims can be compelling regardless of universal principles.

Second, in the epistemological process of trying to understand what morality would recommend and what it would be morally best for us to do and to be, the ethics of care values emotion rather than rejects it. Not all emotion is valued, of course, but in contrast with the dominant rationalist approaches, such emotions as sympathy, empathy, sensitivity, and responsiveness are seen as the kind of moral emotions that need to be cultivated not only to help in the implementation of the dictates of reason but to better ascertain what morality recommends. Even anger may be a component of the moral indignation that should be felt when people are treated unjustly or inhumanely, and it may contribute to (rather than interfere with) an appropriate interpretation of the moral wrong. This is not to say that raw emotion can be a guide to morality; feelings need to be reflected on and educated. But from the care perspective, moral inquiries that rely entirely on reason and rationalistic deductions or calculations are seen as deficient.

The emotions that are typically considered and rejected in rationalistic moral theories are the egoistic feelings that undermine universal moral norms, the favoritism that interferes with impartiality, and the aggressive and vengeful impulses for which morality is to provide restraints. The ethics of care, in contrast, typically appreciates the emotions and relational capabilities that enable morally concerned persons in actual interpersonal contexts to understand what would be best. Since even the helpful emotions can often become misguided or worse—as when excessive empathy with others leads to a wrongful degree of self-denial or when benevolent concern crosses over into controlling domination—we need an *ethics* of care, not just care itself. The various aspects and expressions of care and caring relations need to be subjected to moral scrutiny and *evaluated,* not just observed and described.

Third, the ethics of care rejects the view of the dominant moral theories that the more abstract the reasoning about a moral problem the better because the more likely to avoid bias and arbitrariness, the more nearly to achieve impartiality. The ethics of care respects rather than removes itself from the claims of particular others with whom we share actual relationships. It calls into question the universalistic and abstract rules of the dominant theories. When the latter consider such actual relations as between a parent and child, if they say anything about them at all, they may see them as permitted and cultivating them a preference that a person may have. Or they may recognize a universal obligation for all parents to care for their children. But they do not permit actual relations ever to take priority over the requirements of impartiality....

The ethics of care may seek to limit the applicability of universal rules to certain domains where they are more appropriate, like the domain of law, and resist their extension to other domains. Such rules may simply be inappropriate in, for instance, the contexts of family and friendship, yet relations in these domains should certainly be *evaluated,* not merely described, hence morality should not be limited to abstract rules. We should be able to give moral guidance concerning actual relations that are trusting, considerate, and caring and concerning those that are not.

Dominant moral theories tend to interpret moral problems as if they were conflicts between egoistic individual interests on the one hand, and universal moral principles on the other. The extremes of "selfish individual" and "humanity" are recognized, but what lies between these is often overlooked. The ethics of care, in contrast, focuses especially on the area between these extremes. Those who conscientiously care for others are not seeking primarily to further their own *individual* interests; their interests are intertwined with the persons they care for. Neither are they acting for the sake of *all others* or *humanity in general;* they seek instead to preserve or promote an actual human relation between themselves and *particular others.* Persons in caring relations are acting for self-and-other together. Their characteristic stance is neither egoistic nor altruistic; these are the options in a conflictual situation, but the well-being of a caring relation involves the cooperative well-being of those in the relation and the well-being of the relation itself.

In trying to overcome the attitudes and problems of tribalism and religious intolerance, dominant moralities have tended to assimilate the domains of family and friendship to the tribal, or to a source of the unfair favoring of one's own. Or they have seen the attachments people have in these areas as among the nonmoral private preferences people are permitted to pursue if restrained by impartial moral norms. The ethics of care recognizes the *moral* value and importance of relations of family and friendship and the need for *moral* guidance in these domains to understand how existing relations should often be changed and new ones developed. Having grasped the value of caring relations in such contexts as these more personal ones, the ethics of care then often examines social and political arrangements in the light of these values. In its more developed forms, the ethics of care as a feminist ethic offers suggestions for the radical transformation of society. It demands not just equality for women in existing structures of society but equal consideration for the experience that reveals the values, importance, and moral significance, of caring.

A fourth characteristic of the ethics of care is that like much feminist thought in many areas, it reconceptualizes traditional notions about the public and the private. The traditional view, built into the dominant moral theories, is that the household is a private sphere beyond politics into which government, based on consent, should not intrude. Feminists have shown how the greater social, political, economic, and cultural power of men has structured this "private" sphere to the disadvantage of women and children, rendering them vulnerable to domestic violence without outside interference, often leaving women economically dependent on men and subject to a highly inequitable division of labor in the family. The law has not hesitated to intervene into women's private decisions concerning reproduction but has been highly reluctant to intrude on men's exercise of coercive power within the "castles" of their homes.

Dominant moral theories have seen "public" life as relevant to morality while missing the moral significance of the "private" domains of family and friendship. Thus the dominant theories have assumed that morality should be sought for unrelated, independent, and mutually indifferent individuals assumed to be equal. They have posited an abstract, fully rational "agent as such" from which to construct morality, while missing the moral issues that arise between interconnected persons in the contexts of family, friendship, and social groups. In the context of the family, it is typical for relations to be between persons with highly unequal power who did not choose the ties and obligations in which they find themselves enmeshed. For instance, no child can choose her parents yet she may well have obligations to care for them. Relations of this kind are standardly noncontractual, and conceptualizing them as contractual would often undermine or at least obscure the trust on which their worth depends. The ethics of care addresses rather than neglects moral issues arising in relations among the unequal and dependent, relations that are often laden with emotion and involuntary, and then notices how often these attributes apply not only in the household but in the wider society as well. For instance, persons do not choose which gender, racial, class, ethnic, religious, national, or cultural groups to be brought up in, yet these sorts of ties may be important aspects of who they are and how their experience can contribute to moral understanding.

A fifth characteristic of the ethics of care is the conception of persons with which it begins. … The ethics of care usually works with a conception of persons as relational, rather than as the self-sufficient independent individuals of the dominant moral theories. The dominant theories can be interpreted as importing into moral theory a concept of the person developed primarily for liberal political and economic theory, seeing the person as a rational, autonomous agent, or a self-interested individual.…

The ethics of care, in contrast, characteristically sees persons as relational and interdependent, morally and epistemologically. Every person starts out as a child dependent on those providing us care, and we remain interdependent with others in thoroughly fundamental ways throughout our lives. That we can think and act as if we were independent depends on a network of social relations making it possible for us to do so. And our relations are part of what constitute our identity. This is not to say that we cannot become autonomous; feminists have done much interesting work developing an alternative conception of autonomy in place of the liberal individualist one. Feminists have much experience rejecting or reconstituting relational ties that are oppressive. But it means that from the perspective of an ethics of care, to construct morality *as if* we were Robinson Crusoes, or, to use Hobbes's image, mushrooms sprung from nowhere, is misleading.…

Not only does the liberal individualist conception of the person foster a false picture of society and the persons in it, it is, from the perspective of the ethics of care, impoverished also as an ideal. The ethics of care values the ties we have with particular other persons and the actual relationships that partly constitute our identity. Although persons often may and should reshape their relations with others—distancing themselves from some persons and groups and developing or strengthening ties with others—the autonomy sought within the ethics of care is a capacity to reshape and cultivate new relations, not to ever more closely resemble the unencumbered abstract rational self of liberal political and moral theories. Those motivated by the ethics of care would seek to become more admirable relational persons in better caring relations.…

The conception of the person adopted by the dominant moral theories provides moralities at best suitable for legal, political, and economic interactions between relative strangers, once adequate trust exists for them to form a political entity. The ethics of care is, instead, hospitable to the relatedness of persons. It sees many of our responsibilities as not freely entered into but presented to us by the accidents of our embeddedness in familial and social and historical contexts. It often calls on us to *take* responsibility, while liberal individualist morality focuses on how we should leave each other alone. The view of persons as embedded and encumbered seems fundamental to much feminist thinking about morality and especially to the ethics of care....

⚜ QUESTIONS FOR ANALYSIS

1. What is the central focus of the ethics of care, according to Held?
2. What is the role of emotion in the ethics of care, and how does it contrast with dominant rationalist approaches in ethics?
3. What are the problems with the universalistic and abstract rules of the dominant approaches to ethics?
4. How does the ethics of care address the extremes of the "selfish individual" and "humanity"?
5. How does the conception of the person contrast with the more traditional view of persons as self-sufficient independent individuals?

CHAPTER TWO

Good Reasoning

- **Arguments**
- **Evaluating Moral Arguments**
- **Summary and Conclusions**

NOT ALL OPINIONS are equal, the first chapter concluded, and we looked at a few examples that seemed to show that some opinions are indeed better than others. However, we did not explain *why* some opinions are better than others.

Of course, given the nature of the examples, explanation might have seemed unnecessary. Let's go back to two of them. If any opinion about the best career for Mary is to be a good one, it must be based on some obvious factors—what she likes to do, what she's good at, availability of jobs, where she would like to live, and so on. Any opinion that ignores these factors is not one that will have much value to her. Similarly, any worthwhile opinion at the beginning of the baseball season regarding the outcome of the World Series must be based on equally obvious factors, like pitching and hitting.

The same can be said about any opinion. If it is to be a good one, it must be well grounded. It must be supported by good reasons. And the better the support, the better the opinion, whether it's a scientific opinion or a moral one, an opinion about what's wrong with your car, or an opinion about what's wrong with something you did. To be sure, an opinion that is not well grounded may turn out to be correct. Even the most ignorant of ignoramuses are right sometimes. But when they are, it is a matter of pure luck. Their opinions are not to be trusted in the future because they are not arrived at in a reliable way.

What makes an opinion well grounded? Well, one obvious consideration is knowledge. The more relevant details we know about a particular matter, the better grounded our opinions will be. Be sure to notice the word *relevant*. It is most important, particularly when we deal with moral problems. In fact, one of the biggest difficulties we will encounter in our dealings with the issues of Part 2 is trying to decide what the relevant details are.

Another thing is logic. A well-supported opinion is logically arrived at. It comes at the end of a reliable pattern of reasoning. Or as philosophers often put it, it is the conclusion of a strong *argument*.

ARGUMENTS

To philosophers, scientists, attorneys, and others who engage in intellectual debate, an **argument** is a collection of statements. One of the statements is the conclusion. The other statements are called *premises, reasons, evidence, supporting statements,* or *grounds.* Whatever we call them, the important point is this: Their purpose is to show that the conclusion is true or that it is reasonable to accept the conclusion as true.

Much of Part 2 will be devoted to arguments for and against various positions. And much of your task in reading Part 2 will be to do your best to evaluate these arguments. That is, you will have to decide whether the arguments for or against particular positions are the better ones. And to do that, you will have to ask yourself a variety of questions: Are the supporting statements true? If so, do they really lend support to the conclusions, or are they irrelevant to the conclusions? Are the patterns of reasoning followed by these arguments reliable ones? Has anything of importance been left out of these arguments?

In the rest of this chapter, we give you some help in answering these questions. But first, we must distinguish two kinds of argument.

Deductive Arguments

Consider the following two sentences:

1. If Clint Eastwood is a bulldog, then he has four legs.
2. Clint Eastwood is a bulldog.

Chances are, you know what comes next:

3. Therefore, Clint Eastwood has four legs.

How did you know that? Not because of anything you know about Clint Eastwood. People may have different opinions about his movies, but all of us agree that he has only two legs. Nor does your knowledge of bulldogs make a difference. Suppose the first sentence had been "If Clint Eastwood is a bulldog, then he has eight legs." Then you would have drawn a different conclusion: "Therefore, Clint Eastwood has eight legs."

What makes the difference is your knowledge of a rule of **deductive logic**, as follows:

1. If A, then B.
2. A.
3. Therefore, B.

That rule is called a **truth-preserving rule.** To say that the rule is truth preserving is to say that whenever you follow it, if the first two statements (called the **premises**) are true, the conclusion will also be true. Truth-preserving rules are also called *valid rules,* and any argument that follows only valid rules is called a **valid deductive argument.**

The notion of a valid deductive argument will prove to be very useful. Even more important is the notion of a **sound deductive argument.** To be sound, an argument must pass two tests: first, it must be valid, and second, all of its premises must be true. A valid argument with false premises may or may not have a true conclusion, but the conclusion of a sound argument must be true. In other words, if we can assure ourselves that all the premises of an argument are true, and if we can also assure ourselves that the argument follows only valid deductive rules, then we can assure ourselves that the conclusion must be true.

There are many valid rules of deductive reasoning, far too many to go into here. Fortunately, we do not need to know all of them to decide whether an argument is valid. Instead, we can use a simple method for detecting invalidity. That method is known as the method of **counterexample.** Consider the following argument, which many people mistakenly think is valid:

1. If John took a shower, then he got wet.
2. John didn't take a shower.
3. Therefore, John didn't get wet.

That argument follows this rule:

1. If A, then B.
2. A is not true.
3. Therefore, B is not true.

And we can show that *that* rule is not truth preserving by giving a counterexample to the rule. To do that, we find an argument that has true premises, follows the same rule, but has a false conclusion. If we can do that, the rule is certainly not truth preserving. For instance,

1. If Rin Tin Tin had been a collie, then he'd have been a dog.
2. Rin Tin Tin was not a collie.
3. Therefore, Rin Tin Tin was not a dog.

Here's another example of an invalid argument:

1. Some baseball players are left-handed.
2. Some baseball players are pitchers.
3. Therefore, some pitchers are left-handed.

If you don't believe that the argument is invalid, consider this counterexample:

1. Some animals are human.
2. Some animals are fish.
3. Therefore, some fish are human.

And here, finally, is another:

1. All ravens are black.
2. A dove is not a raven.
3. Therefore, a dove is not black.

And here is a counterexample:

1. All ravens are black.
2. A panther is not a raven.
3. Therefore, a panther is not black.

In each of the preceding cases, we provided a counterexample by constructing an entirely new argument. Sometimes you may find it easier just to ask a few questions about the original argument. Take the argument that concluded that John didn't get wet (because he didn't take a shower). What if he'd taken a bath instead? Or take the argument that concluded that some pitchers are left-handed (because some baseball players are pitchers and some are left-handed). What if all the left-handed players are outfielders? Or take the last one. What if there are black doves?

Fortunately, you will not come upon many invalid arguments in the readings in Part 2. Unfortunately, you *will* come across many invalid arguments in other discussions of the same issues—perhaps even in class discussions—so recognizing one when you see it is an important skill.

What you are more likely to come across in the readings in Part 2 are valid but *unsound* arguments. So you must be careful to ask whether the premises are true when you evaluate the arguments you encounter.

Inductive Arguments

Most ordinary reasoning is not deductive. The supporting statements, if true, do not guarantee the truth of the conclusion. Rather, they establish that it is more reasonable than not to accept the conclusion. That is, they establish that the conclusion is likely to be true. Arguments of that kind are called **inductive arguments.** The supporting statements of inductive arguments are called *reasons, evidence,* or *grounds* instead of premises, and a good inductive argument is called a **warranted argument** instead of a sound one.

When we reason from cause to effect or from effect to cause, we generally reason inductively. If, for example, we hear a loud bang outside, we would most likely conclude that a car had just backfired. Although other explanations are possible—somebody might have shot her neighbor, say—in most neighborhoods, a backfiring car is the most probable one. Since our evidence does admit of other possibilities, though, we cannot say that we reasoned deductively. Similarly, when we put a pot of water on the stove and come back later expecting the water to be boiling, we are also reasoning inductively. Various factors may have kept the water from boiling—the gas might have been turned off, for instance—but more likely than not, the water is boiling.

Most generalizations are also examples of inductive reasoning. We examine a sample taken from a larger population, notice some features shared by a certain percentage of our sample, and then conclude that the same—or nearly the same—pattern occurs in the population at large. Thus, from a sample of green and only green emeralds, we conclude that all emeralds are green, and from a sample of Nielsen families, we conclude that more viewers watch NFL football games than NBA basketball games. These generalizations are reliable, but they are not arrived at by deductive reasoning. Because there is always some probability—however small—that the larger population does not match the sample, such reasoning is inductive.

Although inductive reasoning does not have rules in the same way that deductive reasoning does, we use a variety of criteria to evaluate inductive arguments. For our purposes, the most important are those that concern *causal* generalizations because those are the kinds of arguments that will be most prominent in Part 2.

Consider this argument:

1. John takes two aspirin tablets every day.
2. John never has a cold.
3. Therefore, aspirin prevents colds.

There is much, of course, that is wrong with that argument. Two flaws are most obvious. First, a sample of one is hardly large enough to support a generalization about all human beings. Second, no care has been taken to rule out other explanations of John's good fortune. Thus, the following are important criteria for evaluating causal generalizations. First, the sample must be large enough to support the generalization. Second, it must also be representative of the larger population that's being generalized about.

Third, to help rule out other explanations, there must be a *control group*—another sample as much like the original sample (called the *experimental group*) as possible except that its members are not exposed to the factor being tested. If we are testing to see whether aspirin prevents colds, for example, we will want to study two groups, one that takes aspirin daily and one that does not. Only after the control group and the experimental group have been compared are we entitled to make our causal generalization.

But even then, we must be careful. Statistical links are not the same as causal links. Two factors may be associated without one being the cause of the other. Sneezing and coughing often go together, but one does not cause the other. Rather, both have a common cause—often a flu virus. So even after a statistical link has been established, further experiments may be necessary to establish a causal link.

To be sure, few people are ever in a position to carry out such experiments. For most of us, inductive reasoning is far less formal. We do not have the statistical techniques to evaluate the reliability of our samples, nor do we have the time and money to design and carry out tests on experimental and control groups. That's why we must rely on people who do—scientists—before we can say that a causal generalization has been established. This does not mean, however, that we can't reach reasonable conclusions before science has spoken. We can. Indeed, often we must. But when doing so, we must remember two points.

First, we must keep in mind that the more closely our reasoning resembles the scientist's, the better it is. The more numerous and representative the cases we have to generalize from, the better our evidence and the more reasonable our conclusion. And the more justified we are in ruling out other causes, the more reasonable our conclusion.

Second, no matter how reasonable our conclusion may be, we are not entitled to claim that we've established it. Inductive reasoning, unlike deductive reasoning, cannot be neatly divided into the sound and the unsound. Although it *can* be divided into the warranted and the unwarranted, warrant admits of degrees. One sound deductive argument is as conclusive as another. One warranted inductive argument is not as conclusive as another. Our confidence in our conclusions, then, should be no greater than the degree of our warrant. And as long as our inductive reasoning is informal, our degree of warrant requires a corresponding degree of humility.

Moral Arguments

A familiar position on abortion is that abortion is wrong except to save the life of the mother, and a common justification for that position is that taking an innocent life is wrong except to save a life. Proponents of broad abortion rights, on the other hand, often support their views by claiming that women have the right to control their own bodies as long as they don't harm anyone else. Like all the moral arguments we will come across in Part 2, each proceeds from a general moral principle (the first about taking an innocent life, the second about a woman's rights over her body) to a moral conclusion about a particular issue (the morality of abortion). The best way to examine such arguments is to treat them as abbreviated deductive arguments. We do that by supplying additional premises that make the arguments valid.

Consider the first argument. We are given only one premise:

1. Taking an innocent life is wrong except to save a life.

One premise that must be added is the following:

2. Abortion is the taking of an innocent life.

Together, those premises lead to:

3. Therefore, abortion is wrong except to save a life.

Though that is an important conclusion of the argument, it is only an *intermediate* conclusion. To get to the *final* conclusion, we must add another premise:

4. The only life that can be saved by an abortion is the mother's.

From that premise and the intermediate conclusion, we get the final conclusion:

5. Therefore, abortion is wrong except to save the life of the mother.

Because the preceding argument reaches an intermediate conclusion, it is a two-step argument. Multiple-step arguments are not unusual in moral debates. In fact, the opposing argument, once the missing premises are added, turns out to be a three-step argument because it goes through two intermediate conclusions, one at line three and the other at line five:

1. Women have the right to control their own bodies as long as they don't harm another person.
2. A woman's right to control her body includes the right to have any medical procedure she and her doctor choose.
3. Therefore, a woman has a right to any medical procedure she and her doctor choose as long as it doesn't harm another person.
4. An abortion is a medical procedure.
5. Therefore, a woman has a right to an abortion as long as it doesn't harm another person.
6. An abortion hurts nothing but the fetus, which is not a person.
7. Therefore, women have the right to an abortion.

Both of these arguments are valid, but since they reach opposite conclusions, they cannot both be sound. At least one of them must have at least one false premise. And that is why it is useful for us to treat moral arguments as deductive. If we do so, they become much easier to evaluate. We can lay out opposing arguments in a clear fashion, make sure that we understand the reasoning behind each one, isolate all of the premises, and then examine the premises of each to see whether they are true. The ones with true premises, or with premises more likely to be true, are the ones we should accept.

EVALUATING MORAL ARGUMENTS

Once again, one of your main tasks in dealing with the issues of Part 2 will be to evaluate arguments in favor of opposing positions. As we just saw, that task breaks down into two subtasks. The first is to try to reconstruct each argument as a valid deductive argument. The second is to examine the premises to see if they are true. Let's begin our discussion of these two tasks by looking at an example.

A Sample Evaluation

A common argument in favor of legalized abortion is often put this way: Catholics and fundamentalist Christians have no right to turn their religious beliefs into law. That is a very short argument. If we are to try to turn it into a valid argument, we must ask ourselves what premises are *assumed* by the argument but not explicitly stated by it. That is, we must ask what premises we should *add* to make the argument valid.

One way we can make it valid is by adding only one premise. Then the argument would go like this:

1. Catholics and fundamentalist Christians have no right to turn their religious beliefs into law.
2. That abortions should be banned is a religious belief of Catholics and fundamentalist Christians.
3. Therefore, Catholics and fundamentalist Christians have no right to make abortions illegal.

That is a valid argument, to be sure, but it's not very convincing as it stands. After all, why should we pick on Catholics and fundamentalist Christians? Do Presbyterians have the right to turn their religious beliefs into law? Quakers? Jews? Also, the conclusion is a very weak one. It claims that two groups have no right to make abortion illegal but not that nobody has the right to make abortion illegal.

So let's try another approach.

1. No religious group has the right to turn its religious beliefs into law.
2. Opponents of abortion are trying to turn their religious beliefs into law.
3. Therefore, opponents of abortion have no right to make abortion illegal.

That's a little better. At least it doesn't pick on two religious groups unfairly. Still, the premises are not very plausible. The trouble with the first is that *many* religious beliefs have been turned into law, often rightfully. Religious beliefs against murder, armed robbery, and rape come most readily to mind. The trouble with the second is that many opponents of abortion oppose it for nonreligious reasons. If the argument is to have any force, then, further changes must be made.

For example,

1. If there are no good nonreligious reasons for turning some group's religious beliefs into law, then nobody has the right to turn those beliefs into law.
2. That abortion should be banned is a religious belief of some groups.
3. Therefore, if there are no good nonreligious reasons for making abortion illegal, nobody has the right to make it illegal.
4. There are no good nonreligious reasons for making abortion illegal.
5. Therefore, nobody has the right to make abortion illegal.

Is that much better? Not really. For one thing, item four is not obviously true. Indeed, whether it *is* true is precisely what the debate over abortion is all about. For another thing, what the argument now boils down to is this:

1. If there are no good reasons to make abortion illegal, it should be legal.
2. There are no good reasons to make abortion illegal.
3. Therefore, abortion should be legal.

And that is not much of an argument at all. Granted, it is certainly valid, but until we have an argument in favor of premise two, opponents of abortion have no reason to take it seriously.

Reconstructing Arguments

What we did in the previous section is not nearly as difficult as it might first appear. All it takes is a little common sense plus the knowledge of a few valid rules of deductive logic. And those few rules are also common sense. One, which we already looked at in our Clint Eastwood example, is:

1. If A, then B.
2. A.
3. Therefore, B.

That is a rule that all of you already knew. No doubt you know the others as well. For example:

1. Either John is home or he's at the library.
2. He's not home.
3. Therefore, what?

The answer, obviously, is that he's at the library. And the rule is:

1. A or B.
2. A is not true.
3. Therefore, B.

Here's another:

1. If Mary is home, she's in the den.
2. She's not in the den.
3. Therefore, what?

The answer here is that she's not home. And the rule is:

1. If A, then B.
2. B is not true.
3. Therefore, A is not true.

There are only three others you need to know (and no doubt already know), and they are equally matters of common sense. Examples are:

1. All dogs are mammals.
2. Lassie is a dog.
3. Therefore, Lassie is a mammal.

And:

1. All dogs are mammals.
2. My parrot is not a mammal.
3. Therefore, my parrot is not a dog.

And:

1. No pigs can fly.
2. Robins can fly.
3. Therefore, robins aren't pigs.

And the rules are:

1. All A is B.
2. C is A.
3. Therefore, C is B.

And:

1. All A is B.
2. C is not B.
3. Therefore, C is not A.

And:

1. No A is B.
2. C is B.
3. Therefore, C is not A.

Armed with these commonsense rules, you will be able to turn any logical moral argument into a valid deductive argument. That is, as long as the argument doesn't depend on any invalid rules, you can do what we did in the previous section. For example, we often hear that homosexuality is wrong because it's unnatural. That claim is really an abbreviated argument, as follows:

1. Anything unnatural is morally wrong.
2. Homosexuality is unnatural.
3. Therefore, homosexuality is morally wrong.

Of course, few people actually put it that way. The first premise is generally left unsaid, but common sense tells us that something like the first premise is required if the argument is to be valid. Along the same lines, common sense tells us that something must be added when people claim that capital punishment is wrong because it does not deter crime any better than life imprisonment does. When we add what is needed, we get:

1. If one punishment is more severe than another, it is wrong to impose the more severe one if it is not a better deterrent than the less severe one.
2. Capital punishment is more severe than life imprisonment.
3. Therefore, it is wrong to impose capital punishment if it is not a better deterrent than life imprisonment.
4. Capital punishment is not a better deterrent than life imprisonment.
5. Therefore, it is wrong to impose capital punishment.

How do we know which premises to add? There is no precise formula that anybody can give, but we can provide some general directions. First, we must choose premises that can be used with valid deductive rules. When we look at the claim that homosexuality is wrong because it's unnatural, for instance, we know that the conclusion is "Homosexuality is wrong" and that one premise is "Homosexuality is unnatural." What we need, then, is a premise like "If anything is unnatural, it's wrong," or "All unnatural behavior is wrong."

Second, we must make sure that our added premises are *general* enough to look like real moral principles, not prejudices. That is why we put "anything" and "all unnatural behavior" in the above premises, not "homosexuality" and "all homosexual acts." If we make the premise read "If homosexuality is unnatural, then it's wrong," somebody could justifiably ask us "Why just homosexuality?" That's why we changed "Catholics and fundamentalist Christians" to "religious groups" in an earlier example. In moral arguments, we must appeal to moral principles, and the more general a statement is, the more like a genuine moral principle and the less like an expression of prejudice it is.

Third, we must add *enough* premises to make the argument valid. That requirement is not just a matter of logic. If we are to evaluate an argument adequately, we must be able to examine all of its premises. And if we don't have enough premises to make the argument valid, we are lacking at least one assumed premise.

Fourth, we must use a little **charity**, even if we don't agree with the argument's conclusion. We must allow our opponents the best arguments we can if we are to give them a fair hearing. This means that we must do our best to give them *plausible* premises. A few pages back, for example, we looked at the claim that a woman has the right to an abortion because she has the right to control her own body. One of the premises we added was "A woman's right to control her own body includes the right to have any medical procedure she and her doctor choose." Now that may or may not be true, but it is certainly plausible. On the other hand, the following premise is most certainly not: "A woman's right to control her body includes the right to murder her children." Granted, many abortion foes believe that pro-choice advocates are claiming that, but it is most unfair to make it a premise in their arguments.

Fifth, we must do our best to make sure that the premises we add are *faithful* to the beliefs of the person putting forth the argument. Although we cannot always be sure on this point, there are ways to increase our confidence. If we add a premise that is inconsistent with sentences that appear elsewhere in the reading, we have probably failed. Of course, sometimes people are inconsistent, but if it is possible to read them in a way that makes them consistent, we should do so. (That, of course, is required of us by the principle of charity.)

Also, arguers often give us hints of their broader commitments. In arguing against abortion, for example, some philosophers make it clear that they agree with much of traditional Catholic theology, although they attempt to rest their arguments on purely secular grounds. We should not supply anti-Catholic premises to such philosophers.

Sixth, we must be careful not to beg any questions. To *beg a question* is to assume what you are trying to prove, and a **question-begging argument** is one that contains the conclusion as one of its premises. Sometimes that cannot be helped. If John says that he believes Mary because she's honest, and he knows she's honest because she told him so, and he believed her because she's honest, there is not much we can do to save his argument. On the other hand, we are not forced to beg any questions when reconstructing the pro-choice argument based on a woman's right to control her own body. In that case, we should not add the following:

1. A woman's right to control her body includes the right to do anything moral.
2. Abortions are moral.
3. Therefore, a woman has the right to an abortion.

Although premise two is not precisely the same as the conclusion, it is certainly close enough to qualify as question begging.

Seventh, we must be careful not to *equivocate*. That is, we must not allow the argument to turn on different meanings of the same word. For example, the word *unnatural* can mean either "perverse" or "out of the ordinary." Many things, like writing poetry or skydiving, are unnatural in the second sense of the word but not the first. Anyone who argues that skydiving is out of the ordinary, and therefore unnatural, and therefore perverse is guilty of equivocating. Of course, sometimes the arguments we are trying to reconstruct *will* turn on equivocations. Some arguments against homosexuality, for example, may turn on an equivocation on *natural* much like the one we just looked at. In those cases, we have no choice but to give up. An argument that turns on an equivocation is not a valid one, and we cannot make it valid without creating an entirely different argument.

Examining Premises

Once we have a valid argument before us, we must next ask whether it is a sound argument. The first premises to look at are the general ones because they are most likely to be questionable. Although many statements with words like *all* and *every* and *any* and *no* are true, many others are not.

Consider the general statements that appear in our pro- and anti-abortion arguments, for example. Is it really true that a woman's right to control her own body includes the right to have *any* medical procedure she and her doctor choose? What about experimental procedures that have not been approved for the general public? Or procedures that have been outlawed because they are ineffective or dangerous?

Similarly, is it really true that taking an innocent life is *always* wrong except to save another life? (The word *always* did not appear in the premise of our argument, but as in many general statements, the general word is assumed. With a sentence like "Dogs are mammals," or even "A dog is a mammal," we should understand it as being about all dogs unless we are told otherwise.) Judith Jarvis Thomson, in her defense of abortion that appears in Part 2, doesn't think so, and she provides examples to back up her point.

Thomson's examples are meant to be *counterexamples* to the generalization in the anti-abortion argument, just as the examples of unapproved medical procedures were offered as counterexamples to the generalization in the pro-abortion argument. That is, they are meant to be examples in which the generalization breaks down.

If the proposed counterexamples are genuine counterexamples, we may still be able to save the premise in a slightly altered form. Suppose we grant that a woman does not have the right to an unapproved medical procedure. All we have to do is add the phrase "medically approved" to that premise and other premises in which it is now needed to make the argument valid. The additions will not harm the argument because most abortions are medically approved.

On the other hand, the counterexamples may be decisive. That is, there may be no way to alter the premise without destroying the argument. Whether Thomson's counterexamples are decisive is not for us to decide now, but we can look at another case in which counterexamples are decisive. Take this argument:

1. Lying is wrong.
2. Telling a friend that her ugly baby is cute is lying.
3. Therefore, telling a friend that her ugly baby is cute is wrong.

Most of us agree that white lies are genuine counterexamples to the first premise. Honesty is commendable, but not when it causes our friends great hurt and the lie is an innocuous one. But once we change the first premise to exempt white lies, the argument falls apart.

One way to challenge a general premise, then, is to find a decisive counterexample. Another way is to question the assumptions it rests on. Many people, for example, take issue with premise six of the pro-abortion argument, which says that a fetus is not a person (or no fetus is a person, or all fetuses are not persons). They cannot point to a counterexample that abortion proponents will accept because the view that fetuses are not persons is based on certain assumptions about what it is to be a person—and those assumptions rule out all fetuses. What abortion opponents must do, then, is challenge the assumptions. That is, they must show that the other side is wrong about what it is to be a person and that a proper understanding would show that all or most or some fetuses are persons.

Very often, the challenged assumptions will be moral assumptions. An argument may conclude that something is right because it is justified by the principle of utility, say. Someone who disagrees with the argument, on the other hand, might feel that respect for persons must take precedence in this instance. Another argument may conclude that justice requires us to do one thing, while someone who disagrees might feel that justice requires us to do something else.

Such disagreements are, of course, very hard to settle. They often boil down to what philosophers call conflicting **moral intuitions.** By moral intuition, we do not mean some mysterious sixth sense for divining moral truths. Rather, we mean only a moral conviction arrived at after careful consideration of the relevant facts—a conviction that strikes us as right but not provable. But even though they are not provable, moral intuitions can be challenged, discussed, and even changed on reasonable grounds.

The idea is to think of a variety of cases—some ordinary, some a bit fanciful—and see if consideration of these cases has any effect on our intuitions. What these cases add is new relevant information. Many of our moral intuitions, after all, are based on a small sample of possible cases. Some of them may be generalizations we've arrived at a little too quickly. Often, we can benefit by opening them up to some careful scrutiny. So when you come across arguments that rest on moral assumptions that conflict with your intuitions, it is best to examine both the assumptions and your intuitions as carefully as possible.

Other general statements that require careful scrutiny are **causal generalizations.** Although many causal generalizations are extremely well established—friction causes heat, for example—many others are controversial at best. Among the most controversial are those that some readings in Part 2 rely on—about the deterrent effects of capital punishment or the effects of various social programs on the poor. Most of us have our own opinions on these matters, but more often than not, they are based on what we take to be common sense rather than on well-designed studies.

By well-designed studies, of course, we mean studies with large representative samples and adequate controls. Sometimes such studies exist, but they are inconclusive. Sometimes different studies on the same issue will come to conflicting conclusions. Sometimes they just don't exist. How, then, can we evaluate causal generalizations under such conditions?

First, see how they are supported. Often, they are supported by *analogies.* Many opponents of mercy killing and abortion sometimes draw analogies between those practices and what went on in Nazi death camps. When faced with such analogies, we must ask in what ways they hold up and in what ways they do not. Are there relevant differences that suggest that the compared practices will have different effects? Are there better analogies than the ones being drawn?

Causal claims might also be supported by an argument called the *slippery slope* argument. The idea here is that what at first looks like one small step is just the beginning of a series of small steps that will be difficult or impossible to stop after we've taken the first one. Some have argued that administering lethal injections to pain-wracked terminally ill patients who ask for them is the beginning of such a slippery slope—and that at the bottom we will find ourselves ordering the deaths of undesirables as a matter of social policy.

Whether such theorists are right about that is again something that is not for us to decide here. But as a general rule, we should scrutinize such arguments carefully. Not all slopes are as slippery as they first appear. Perhaps there are very good reasons for taking the first step and very good reasons for not taking the second. Perhaps there are principled reasons for digging in our heels somewhere along the way and nothing to stop us from doing so.

Also, causal generalizations might be "supported" by a kind of *hand waving.* That is, the argument might boil down to a nonargument, something like "Everybody knows that..." To be sure, there are many things that everybody *does* know, and things that everybody knows are the best premises for an argument we can find. But we must be careful, especially when dealing with causal generalizations, and even more especially when dealing with causal generalizations about human behavior, to ask whether *anybody,* let alone everybody, really knows that they're true.

Moreover, the mere fact that we don't know that they're false is insufficient support for them. The proper response to ignorance is to try to learn more. If we must decide what to do before we can learn more, we must do the same kind of calculating that's required whenever we try to make a rational decision under conditions of uncertainty. That is, we must ask ourselves what we stand to gain and lose by acting on a belief we don't know to be true. (For an example of this kind of reasoning, see Ernest van den Haag's defense of capital punishment in Part 2.)

Finally, causal generalizations might be supported by inductive arguments based on things we *do* know. Because these arguments will not support their conclusions as strongly as well-designed studies can, they must be approached very carefully. At best, they can establish their conclusions as reasonable, perhaps even more reasonable than their competitors, given what we now know. But what we now know, we must remember, is incomplete. That is why well-designed studies are so important. They fill in the many gaps in current knowledge, and once those gaps are filled, we may find that what was once the most reasonable conclusion is false.

Two other kinds of general premises deserve consideration here. These are generalizations about the arguer's supporters and opponents. For example, you may come across the claim that social scientists agree that such and such is true. To make the argument valid, you must add a premise like "Whatever social scientists agree on is true," or the weaker "If social scientists agree on something, we should accept it as true." You might also hear someone argue that you should not accept opponents' arguments because the opponents are untrustworthy for one reason or another. Then you must add a premise like "Arguments by untrustworthy people are unsound."

The first two of these premises appeal to the *authority* of social scientists. Are they true? Not as they now stand. On the other hand, this variation probably is: "If social scientists agree on a generalization about human behavior that is based on strong research, we should accept it as true." Of course, not being social scientists ourselves, we cannot adequately evaluate their research, but if social scientists at respectable universities claim that their agreement is based on strong research, we are certainly justified in believing them. If their agreement is just a widely shared hunch, however, then their authority is lessened. And if their agreement is on a matter other than human behavior—if it is on the best brand of toothpaste, say—then their authority evaporates.

The third of the three premises, about untrustworthy opponents, is an example of an ***ad hominem* argument** (from the Latin phrase meaning "to the man"). Like appeals to authority, they may or may not be acceptable. The premise at hand is not. Granted, untrustworthy people often do present unsound arguments, but as long as they do present arguments, we should evaluate those arguments, not the arguers. (Even paranoids have enemies, as the saying has it.) On the other hand, when someone offers us nothing better than an unsupported claim rather than an argument, all we can go on is the trustworthiness of the person making the offer.

Trying Alternative Premises

In the previous sections, we saw that we sometimes have to change an argument's premise. Often, the reason is that the premise is questionable or downright false. Why change it rather than just reject the argument? The principle of charity gives us one answer. But we are interested in more than just fairness to our opponents. We are also interested in solving moral problems, and that interest should lead us to consider the strongest arguments possible.

For example, let's return to our argument against capital punishment. The first premise read:

1. If one punishment is more severe than another, it is wrong to impose the more severe one if it is not a better deterrent than the less severe one.

There seem to be many counterexamples to that statement. Is the threat of a ten-year prison term a greater deterrent than the threat of a nine-year prison term? Is the threat of life imprisonment a greater deterrent than the threat of a thirty-year prison term? Although we can't be absolutely sure about the answers to these questions, the more plausible answer is no. Still, we see nothing wrong in giving some people thirty-year sentences and others life sentences.

More generally, though, we can say this: Deterrence is not the only consideration in determining a just sentence. Another is our concern to protect other people from individuals convicted of serious crimes. Still another is our feeling that the severity of the punishment should reflect the severity of the crime. Presumably, people who argue against capital punishment on the grounds that it does not deter know that. So we might recast the premise this way:

1. If two punishments equally reflect the severity of the crime and offer equal protection from the convicted criminal, it is wrong to impose the more severe one if it is not a better deterrent.

Notice how this procedure helps us focus on the important issues. By exposing points that the argument takes for granted, it allows us to evaluate them as well as the points it does not take for granted. Now we must add new premises—that life imprisonment protects others from convicted criminals as well as capital punishment protects them, and that life imprisonment reflects the severity of capital crimes as adequately as capital punishment does. And we must then evaluate them.

Moreover, we might want to evaluate the new version of the first premise. Why, we might ask, must punishment *always* reflect the severity of the crime? If we really believe that it must, shouldn't we have even more awful punishments than we now have? If a man brutally rapes and tortures a half dozen women before killing them, does that mean we should subject him to something equally horrible? Or should we recognize instead that there are moral limits to the severity of punishment regardless of other factors, and maybe those limits mean we should stop short of capital punishment?

In short, trying new premises helps us do more than just evaluate arguments. It helps us think clearly and thoroughly about the problems at hand.

Another example also helps show this. Sometimes we should try new premises because the ones we first added are not the only reasonable possibilities. That reason applies to one of the premises in the pro-abortion argument we looked at:

2. A woman's right to control her body includes the right to have any medically approved medical procedure she and her doctor choose.

Perhaps people who defend the right to an abortion on the grounds of a woman's right to control her own body mean something else, like:

3. A woman's right to control her body includes the right not to have her body used for purposes she does not want it used for.

In that case, we get a new intermediate conclusion:

4. A woman has the right not to have her body used for purposes she does not want it used for as long as she does not harm another person.

Then we add this premise:

5. A woman carrying an unwanted fetus is having her body used for purposes she does not want it used for.

And then we get this intermediate conclusion:

6. Therefore, a woman has the right not to carry an unwanted fetus as long as she does not harm another person.

Whether this version or the original version of the argument is sound is, once again, not to be decided here. But looking at both can be important. Judith Jarvis Thomson's article, for example, focuses on the new interpretation of a woman's right to control her own body, not the original one, and it might make an important difference. The reason it might is that Thomson believes a woman has the right not to have her body used in a way she doesn't want it to be used even in some cases where an innocent person *is* harmed, even fatally. Thus, she defends a woman's right to have an abortion without the premise that fetuses are not persons.

Questions of Relevance

Whether a premise is really relevant to the moral issue at hand is, of course, an important matter. Much of the advice for evaluating arguments that we've been looking at has been closely connected to the question of relevance.

Most important has been the advice about supplying and evaluating implicit general premises. If the implicit general premise turns out to be false, that is often because an explicit premise is irrelevant. To pick an obvious example, remember the implicit premise in our sample *ad hominem* argument: Arguments by untrustworthy people are unsound. Any premise that requires a general premise like that is irrelevant. That is why we need not, in general, pay any attention to *ad hominem* arguments. It is also why the arguments we will find in the readings in Part 2 will not depend on many of the emotion-laden phrases we often find in the letters columns of local newspapers, phrases like "bra burners," "Bible thumpers," "secular humanists," "bleeding hearts," and "ultra-rightists."

Irrelevancies that are intended to distract our attention from the real issues are known as **red herrings.** Because red herrings often involve appeals to our emotions, many textbooks caution their readers to be extremely wary of emotional appeals. This is good advice, if not taken too far—especially in moral arguments. When emotion takes us where reason does not, appeals to emotion are certainly out of order. On the other hand, appeals to emotion are unavoidable in moral debate. Any argument in favor of voluntary euthanasia, for example, must appeal to our sympathy for pain-wracked terminally ill patients. Any argument in favor of capital punishment must appeal to our fear and loathing of brutal murderers. Such appeals will be there even if unintended. Important moral issues are emotional ones, and there is no getting around it.

But if we cannot totally separate emotion from moral argument, we can still question particular connections in particular cases. Are our emotions being whipped up by flamboyant language? By questionable claims? By sentimental anecdotes that are unrepresentative of most relevant cases? Is our attention being diverted from relevant facts? From important moral considerations like individual rights and obligations? If so, we are being victimized by red herrings.

We must also take care not to be victimized by another kind of irrelevance—the *straw man.* Sustained arguments for a position usually include criticisms of opposing arguments. If the opposing arguments are faithfully rendered, all is as it should be. But if they are unfaithfully rendered, the arguer is attacking a straw man. And whatever defects the straw man may have, they are irrelevant to what really matters—the opponent's real arguments. So one question you must always be careful to ask is this: Is *that* what the people on the other side are *really* saying?

Fallacies

A **fallacy** is an unreliable means of arguing that does not provide good reason for accepting the argument's conclusion. **Formal fallacies** are invalid deductive rules like those we looked at in the beginning of this chapter. **Informal fallacies**, on the other hand, are a mixed bag of unreliable strategies that people commonly tend to use. In general, informal fallacies arise in arguments that rely on hidden premises that are false or irrelevant or otherwise suspect. Although we did not introduce the term earlier, we did look at various informal fallacies when we discussed how to supply and evaluate missing premises. Here, for convenience, is a list of those informal fallacies with brief definitions and examples.

Ad Hominem Argument

An attack on the opponent rather than the opponent's argument. Name calling and casting doubt on an opponent's character are the most common but not the only forms. For example, to say that men have no rightful say in abortion disputes would be to commit this fallacy. The same goes for saying that a fur seller's arguments against animal rights aren't worth hearing.

Faulty Analogy

A misuse of an **argument by analogy**, which is an argument that two things that are alike in some respects must be alike in other respects. Suppose, for example, someone notes that tigers and hard-core pornography are alike in that both can be harmful to children. This is true, as far as it goes, even if the types of harm are quite different. But if he then goes on to conclude that pornography must be controlled in the same way as tigers—banned from private homes, say—he has carried the analogy too far. For one thing, there are constitutional protections regarding expression but none regarding the ownership of dangerous animals. For another, there are less drastic ways of protecting children from pornography than banning it from private homes.

Questionable Authority

Supporting a conclusion by depending on the judgment of someone who is not a reliable authority on the subject at hand. Citing horror stories from supermarket tabloids to back up a point—unless it's a point about the tabloids themselves, of course—is an obvious example. The same could be said about most postings on Internet bulletin boards or an athlete's paid endorsement of cereal.

Begging the Question

Assuming as a premise what you want to prove. If, for example, someone claims that all opponents of affirmative action are racist and then defends the point by saying, "If they weren't racist, they wouldn't oppose it," that person is begging the question.

Equivocation

Implicit reliance on two different meanings of the same word to reach a conclusion. For example, it's been said on occasion that the preamble to the Declaration of Independence does not apply to women because it says "all men are created equal" rather than "all humans" or "all persons." But the word *men* in the document refers to both male and female humans, not just to males.

Hand Waving

Claiming that something is true (or false) because everyone knows so. A classic case of hand waving is the following: "We don't need evidence to prove that capital punishment is a better deterrent to crime than life imprisonment. Everyone knows it—it's just common sense."

Hasty Generalization

Reaching a general conclusion from a sample that is biased or too small. Some abortion opponents, for example, have argued that women who have abortions suffer great psychological trauma but defend their assertion by pointing to only a few isolated cases.

Appeal to Ignorance

Arguing that a claim is true (or false) because we have no evidence proving otherwise. Arguing that global warming is (or is not) a compelling threat because nobody's proved that it isn't (or is) exemplifies such an appeal.

Post Hoc, Ergo Propter Hoc ("after this, therefore because of this")

Claiming that one thing is caused by another because it follows the other. Politicians, for example, like to take credit for every good thing that happens after they take office, when it's not always clear that their policies are responsible.

Red Herring

An irrelevant issue introduced to distract attention from the issue at hand. Suppose, for example, someone presents an argument in favor of increasing welfare benefits to families with children, and you respond by saying, "Look at all the babies dying in abortion clinics. If you really cared about children, you'd be doing something about that." However sincere your convictions, you'd be committing this fallacy.

Slippery Slope

Assuming that an action will lead to an unwanted outcome as the result of many small steps that will inevitably follow. Whether such an assumption is a fallacy depends on your justification for making it. For an obvious example of when it would be a fallacy, imagine someone arguing that having sex with someone you don't plan to marry will eventually lead you to become a streetwalker—because it's one small step to having sex with someone you don't love, and another small step to having sex with multiple partners, and another small step to accepting expensive gifts for sex, and another small step to soliciting sex for money on the street.

Straw Man

A distortion of an opponent's actual position. This is a very common tactic that can be found in any controversy that arouses passion. In environmental debates, for example, we often hear it from both sides. Someone will argue that a proposed regulation is too expensive and will be met by the charge that he or she advocates the poisoning of children. Or someone will argue for better protection of endangered species and will be told he or she is saying owls matter more than people.

Although it is useful to keep these fallacies in mind, we should also point out that wrongly accusing an opponent of committing a fallacy can itself be considered a fallacy. For example, the fact that an opponent appeals to an authority does not automatically mean she has committed a fallacy. Many appeals to authority are justified. What matters is whether the alleged authority is a good authority on the topic at hand. Similarly, whether someone commits a fallacy by drawing an analogy depends on how strong the analogy is. For a third example, whether a claim that one thing causes another is a post hoc fallacy depends on the supporting evidence. When tobacco company executives argue that scientists have established only a statistical link between smoking and cancer, not a causal link, they are the ones who commit the fallacy.

SUMMARY AND CONCLUSIONS

In a play by the seventeenth-century French playwright Molière, the main character is delighted to learn that he has been speaking prose for as long as he has been talking. One thing you might have learned during the course of this chapter is that you have been reasoning logically for as long as you have been thinking. But some people speak better prose than others, and some people reason more logically than others. In each case, what often makes the difference is a bit of reflection on what distinguishes good prose or logical reasoning, followed by a little practice.

This chapter has picked out some of the features that distinguish logical reasoning, and it has applied them to various moral arguments. So should you apply them to the moral arguments of Part 2. If you do, you will provide yourself with more than just a little practice. Before we turn to Part 2, though, we should make a few final remarks.

First, don't be intimidated by the task of evaluating arguments. You don't have to write out every argument and then rewrite it every time you think of an alternative missing premise. All you have to do is *think* as you read or listen. And that holds not just for the readings in Part 2 but for any argument you encounter—in a newspaper, a conversation, another course, or anyplace else. Passive reading or listening is never good reading or listening, especially when the writer or speaker is trying to convince you of something.

Second, the techniques for evaluating arguments we have looked at are intended not only for other people's arguments but for our own, too. Whenever we arrive at a conclusion, we do so for reasons, and our reasons may be good or bad, better or worse. It is important, then, that we challenge ourselves as well as others.

Third, this is a book in applied ethics, as its title makes clear. Although every textbook is (or at least should be) an exercise in applied logic (as well as applied prose), our basic concern is to come to grips with some important moral problems. And that means you should apply the material in *both* chapters of Part 1 to the material in Part 2. We want our moral conclusions to be based on both our most general moral principles and good reasoning.

Because this chapter has said little about those principles so far, it should close by tying them to what it has said. Each of the sample moral arguments we looked at contained at least one moral principle—about a woman's rights, the taking of innocent life, or the justification of punishment, to mention just three. Some were more general than others, but none was as general as the principle of utility, say, or respect for persons. This does not mean, though, that these most general principles have no important work to do in moral arguments. Why not?

For one thing, the less general principles are based on the most general ones. We accept them because we believe the most general ones require us to accept them. If we think that some kinds of punishment are unjustified, it's because we think them unfair or inconsistent with respect for persons or because we think they will not maximize utility. Also, if we think that there are legitimate exceptions to the less general principles, it's because we think that the most general ones require the exceptions. Thus, we justify white lies, for example, because a principle more general than honesty—the principle of utility, say—requires it. So these most general principles did play an important role in our sample arguments, even though we did not make them explicit.

Sometimes, however, they *must* be made explicit. That happens when a less general principle, or a proposed exception to a less general principle, is controversial. When that does happen, we need an argument for the principle or its proposed exception, and that will take us back to the most general principles. We will have to ask whether any of our most general principles support the controversial premise. If they don't, we can reject it. If they do, then we will have to ask whether any of our other most general principles give a conflicting answer. If they don't do that, we can accept the premise. If they do, we will have to ask which of the conflicting principles should take precedence.

That last question is a particularly difficult one to answer, and moral problems that turn on it are particularly difficult to resolve to everyone's satisfaction. Men and women of good will may, in the end, come to different resolutions because they cannot agree on which principle takes precedence. Not surprisingly, many of the problems of Part 2 turn on precisely that question, which is why they are still with us. But difficult is not the same as impossible, which is why many similar problems are no longer with us.

If we were writing this book thirty years ago, we might have included a chapter on civil disobedience—we might have looked at arguments for and against the view that people have the moral right to protest laws they consider unjust by peacefully and publicly violating those laws. Also, our chapter on discrimination would have been very different. Instead of looking at arguments for and against affirmative action, we might very well have been considering whether private employers have the right to discriminate *against* minorities and women. Today, such chapters would be unthinkable. The extraordinarily powerful moral arguments of people such as Martin Luther King, Jr., have made them unthinkable. Perhaps in another thirty years, we will be able to make the same statement about some of the chapters in the book you are now reading.

Issues

CHAPTER THREE

Sexual Morality

- **The Traditional View**
- **The Libertarian View**
- **Treating Sex Differently**
- **Arguments for Sexual Libertarianism**
- **Arguments against Sexual Libertarianism**

THE VATICAN   **Declaration on Certain Questions Concerning Sexual Ethics**
MARGARET A. FARLEY   **Framework for a Sexual Ethics: Just Sex**
THOMAS A. MAPPES   **Sexual Morality and the Concept of Using Another Person**
ANN FERGUSON   **Gay Marriage: An American and Feminist Dilemma**

CASE PRESENTATIONS: • *Disease v. Promiscuity?* • Lawrence v. Texas: *Private Rights and Public Morality* • Goodridge v. Dept. of Public Health: *A Right of Gay Marriage* • *A Slippery Slope to Polygamy?*

DURING THE 1960S and 1970s, the United States was abuzz with talk of the "new morality" and the "sexual revolution." Almost everywhere, people were discussing singles bars, casual sex, one-night stands, open marriage, unwed motherhood, creative divorce, cohabitation, group sex, teen sex, and sexual preference. Traditional sexual morality was breaking or had already broken down.

To traditionalists, the changes were at best disturbing and at worst alarming. They worried about the future of their children, of the family, and of society. What they saw when they looked around was moral decline. To those caught up in the revolution, on the other hand, the changes were liberating. When they looked around, they saw new options, new freedoms, new manners of expression, and fulfillment.

Many of you are likely to take the sexual revolution as much for granted as you take the American Revolution. Some of you may even wonder what all the fuss was about. Others may think of the old morality as quaint. You might ask: Were women really supposed to remain virgins until marriage? Did people really think that living together was immoral? Could a talented and beautiful movie star like Ingrid Bergman really be run out of Hollywood for having an affair with a married man? Did parents and universities really insist on separate dorms for male and female students?

Of course, others of you do not take the new morality for granted. Some of you probably agree totally with the traditionalists, despite the pressures you might feel from your peers. Some of you probably accept parts of the new morality but not other parts. Perhaps you believe in nonmarital sex but feel that the people involved should love each other. Perhaps you find nothing wrong with premarital sex but draw the line at adultery. Perhaps you accept total freedom when it comes to heterosexual sex but believe that homosexuality is immoral.

Such differences show that the victory of the sexual revolution was not total. Moreover, certain trends in today's world suggest that we may be in store for some counterrevolutionary changes. The risk of AIDS and other sexually transmitted diseases seems to be affecting the sexual behavior of both heterosexuals and homosexuals. The large number of teenage pregnancies is also causing doubts about the new morality. And some feminists have begun calling for a "new celibacy."

For these reasons and others, debate about sexual morality continues. The issues involved are many and complex. The best place to start, no doubt, is with the two extreme positions: the traditional and the libertarian.

THE TRADITIONAL VIEW

The traditional view can be put quite simply: All sex outside marriage is wrong. Although people have held the traditional view for a variety of reasons, its most influential line of defense comes from the Roman Catholic church.

As we saw in Part 1, Catholic moral teaching was greatly influenced by Aristotle, the ancient Greek philosopher whose ideas were incorporated into church doctrine by the medieval thinker St. Thomas Aquinas. Four of Aristotle's ideas are particularly important here. First, everything in nature has a purpose. Second, everything in nature has an essential nature—certain features that constitute its defining features. Third, everything in nature has its proper good. Fourth, something's natural purpose, its essential nature, and its proper good are intimately related.

That the Roman Catholic church believes that the natural purpose of sex is reproduction is well known. Equally well known is one consequence that the church draws from that belief—that artificial means of birth control are immoral. Less well known are other, related beliefs that are also directly related to sexual morality. These beliefs are spelled out in the Vatican's 1976 "Declaration on Certain Questions Concerning Sexual Ethics," excerpts from which are included in this chapter.

There, the authors stress what they take to be an essential characteristic of human beings—the ability to engage in fully human love, which includes genuine caring, sincerity, respect, commitment, and fidelity. Moreover, the declaration argues, fully human love does not stop at romantic love; it naturally evolves into parental love. That is, true human love is made complete by love for the children produced by that love. These facts about human sexuality are what set it apart from mere animal sexuality. They are also what make it more valuable. Equally important, they are what give human sex and sexual relationships their special dignity.

To engage in sex without love, then, or to engage in sex not open to the possibility of procreation, is to engage in sex that violates our essential nature and dignity. And because to violate our essential nature and dignity is to turn away from the proper human good, to engage in sex without love or sex not open to procreation is to engage in wrongful sex. This does not mean, however, that unmarried sex with love and without contraception is moral in the church's view. Given the changeableness of human desire and commitment, we need added guarantees of sincerity and fidelity. And only marriage can provide those guarantees.

THE LIBERTARIAN VIEW

According to the libertarian view, sex is an activity like any other—tennis, say, or conversation or studying—and what determines whether any sexual act is moral or immoral is no different from what determines whether any other act is moral or immoral. As long as the act involves no dishonesty, exploitation, or coercion, and as long as it does not violate any obligations to others, it is not immoral.

Consider premarital sex. Many things can make it immoral. If John tells Mary that he loves her and wants to take her home to meet his parents and she goes to bed with him as a result, John acts immorally if he doesn't mean what he tells her. If Mary has a venereal disease and does not warn John ahead of time, then she acts immorally. If John tries to coerce Mary into performing sexual acts she dislikes, then he acts immorally. But if neither of them is looking for anything more than a one-night stand, and if neither holds back any important information, and if neither resorts to any coercion or breaks any promise, and if neither violates any obligation to a third person, then neither does anything wrong.

Of course, we are assuming here that both John and Mary are adults. Children are incapable of the kind of informed consent required to ensure that they are not being exploited. But there are other things we need not assume. For example, we need not assume that the adults involved are of different sexes. Whatever holds for John and Mary also holds for John and Bill or for Jane and Mary. Nor need we assume that only *two* adults are involved. Group sex that violates none of our conditions is perfectly acceptable to the libertarian. Furthermore, we need not even assume that John and Mary are not close relatives, like brother and sister. Even incest is acceptable to the libertarian, as long as there is no dishonesty, coercion, or exploitation and as long as reliable means of contraception are used.

Similar remarks hold for adultery. Even though marriage involves the promise of fidelity, husbands and wives are perfectly free to release each other from their vows, just as we are all free to release one another from any other promise. If a married couple agrees that both members would be happier if they could have extramarital affairs, then they are morally free to do so—provided, of course, that they do not keep their marriage a secret from sexual partners who do not wish to have affairs with married people.

Arguments in favor of **sexual libertarianism** are basically of the "why not" sort. Why *shouldn't* sex be treated like any other activity? Why should we consider it moral to play tennis with somebody we don't love but immoral to have sex with somebody we don't love? Why should we consider it moral to eat lunch with somebody of the same sex but immoral to have sex with that very same person? Why should we be permitted to go to a movie purely for pleasure but not have sex purely for pleasure? What's so different about sex that it requires such special rules? Why can't sexual morality be determined by the same general moral principles—the principle of utility, respect for persons, the golden rule, and so forth—that determine right and wrong in the rest of our lives?

TREATING SEX DIFFERENTLY

We have already looked at one answer to the libertarian's questions, the one offered by the Vatican. Not surprisingly, sexual libertarians reject it. Many of their reasons for rejecting it will become apparent throughout this chapter, but for now, let's just mention one. Libertarians generally feel that it is up to each individual to determine his or her own good. Human dignity lies in our capacity to pursue our own good as we see fit—provided we do not interfere with another person's pursuit of his or her own good—not in adhering to any particular sexual morality. Sex between consenting adults is a private matter, and private matters are matters of individual conscience.

Many other answers to the libertarians' arguments focus on the social context of sex. The sex lives of any particular individuals may be private, but the widespread adoption of any particular sexual morality can have far-reaching social ramifications. Let's look at several of these issues.

Venereal Diseases and AIDS

Gonorrhea, syphilis, and other venereal diseases are familiar hazards of sex. Although some can be extremely serious—even fatal—if left untreated, they *are* treatable. Because they are, fear of contracting them rarely interferes with most people's sex lives. When genital herpes burst on the scene in the seventies, however, fear did begin to play a role in many people's sexual decisions. Although not as dangerous as syphilis, herpes is a chronic condition.

In the eighties, a new and far more dangerous threat appeared—AIDS (acquired immune deficiency syndrome). There is no known cure for AIDS, nor has a vaccine been developed to prevent its spread, and that leaves its victims with the hopeless prospect of a protracted, agonizing death and leaves potential victims with a terrifying question mark. AIDS "cocktail" medications have prolonged the lives and improved the quality of life for many, but they are not cures, they are not effective for everyone, and they can cause many debilitating side effects.

Although there is much controversy over how AIDS is transmitted, five means of transmission are well established: anal sex, vaginal sex, intravenous needles and syringes, blood transfusions, and pregnancy. (Other feared possibilities, like "deep" kissing and eating utensils, have not been established as means of transmitting the disease.) Because of the controversy over transmission of AIDS, there is a corresponding controversy over its potential victims. Historically, the groups facing the highest risk in the United States have been male homosexuals, intravenous drug users, hemophiliacs, the sex partners of members of these three groups, and children of women at risk when pregnant.

AIDS has already taken a terrible toll among the homosexual population. According to the Centers for Disease Control and Prevention, homosexual sex between men accounted for two-thirds of new HIV/AIDS cases diagnosed in the United States in 2010, the most recent year for which data are available. Heterosexual sex continues as a significant source of new cases, as does injection drug use either from direct transmission through needles or from sex with a drug user. As of 2009, well over one million persons in the United States are estimated to be infected with HIV, with 18 percent of those undiagnosed. The highest rate of new infections in 2010 was with individuals aged 25–34 (31% of all new infections), with the rate for individuals 13–24 at 26 percent of all new infections. The most rapid rate of increase in infection in recent years has been among young women and women of color, but this rate of new infection dropped by 21 percent in 2010 compared with 2008. Whether AIDS can or cannot be spread by casual contact and whether all of us or only those of us in high-risk groups need be immediately concerned for our own safety, AIDS does raise serious concerns about sexual morality. Given what we do know, sexual promiscuity— both heterosexual and homosexual—increases the risk of AIDS, not only to ourselves, but to our partners and future children.

At the minimum, then, people who cannot be certain about their sexual partners should engage in "safe" sex. That is, they should use condoms. Even libertarians can agree on that point. Other people go further. Some argue that the threat of AIDS should cause us to return to traditional sexual morality. Others claim that we need not go that far. Perhaps we should retreat from promiscuity, they say, but monogamous relationships among unmarried people can be just as safe as among married people. Still others claim that the threat of AIDS does not even require monogamy, as long as we do not engage in sex with people in high-risk groups.

Threats to the Family

One of the most alarming trends in recent decades was the sharp rise in single-parent households. Although different people find different aspects of the trend alarming, one concern is shared by all. Most single parents are women, and single women and their children are often poor. As much as 40 percent of the homeless population in the nation consists of children. Most are with single mothers, although economic difficulties also account for a recent surge in homeless families.

That many single parents are teenagers is another concern shared by all. Whether they are forced to drop out of school or manage to continue their educations, teenage motherhood places a great burden on them, their children, and society. A promising trend was reported by the Centers for Disease Control in 2013. The rate of teenage births from 2007 to 2011 dropped by 30 percent. Experts in this field attribute better education with credit for this decline, although they also cite the difficult economy during those years, which discouraged many from having children.

The causes of single parenthood are complex. Any list of contributing factors would have to include a variety of social conditions, including, most notably, poverty. Researchers have found clear evidence that more education correlates strongly with the postponement of childbearing. But nothing can be more evident than this: no sex, no children. Another point is equally evident: the fewer the divorces, the fewer the single parents. And it is these two points that critics of sexual libertarianism stress.

Regarding the first, they say that the spread of the sexual revolution from adults to teenagers was inevitable. When unmarried rock stars and other teen heroes openly live together and have children, when the media are filled with representations of casual sex, how can teenagers not be affected? And given their lack of maturity and responsibility, the normal confusions of adolescence, and various pressures that many teens feel, how could we have expected anything less than an explosion of teen pregnancies?

The connection between the sexual revolution and divorce may seem more tenuous, but to some people, it is no less real. If sex outside marriage is freely available and without moral stigma, if sexual adventure and variety are prized at least as much as monogamy, if love and commitment are no longer seen as natural accompaniments to sex, then marital ties inevitably weaken.

What makes sex different, according to this line of argument, then, is the intimate connection between sexual behavior and the health of the family, plus the social costs that the decline of the family entails. If sexual morality concerned only the individuals involved in any particular sexual act, then perhaps we could treat sex like tennis. But it doesn't, so we can't.

Personal Fulfillment

For those of us with no aspirations to be Roger Federer or Venus Williams, tennis is little more than an enjoyable game, a pleasant way to get fresh air and exercise, or a welcome opportunity for camaraderie. Even if such things are important to us, and even if tennis is our favorite way to get them, the role of tennis in our lives remains relatively limited.

Can we say the same about sex? Hardly. For one thing, there is a strong biological component to our sexual lives. Thus, both biological and behavioral scientists talk of sex *drives* as well as desires. For another, sexual development cannot be separated from psychological development. How we learn to deal with our sexuality is crucial to the kind of person we become, and our sexual identity is a critical feature of our personal identity. For yet another, our sexual relationships are among the most powerful and influential relationships we can have.

Critics of sexual libertarianism often charge that to treat sex like any other activity is to miss everything that is important about sex and its role in our lives. In particular, it is to ignore its importance to personal growth and fulfillment. Any sexual morality must take account of that fact. Such critics don't necessarily call for a return to traditional morality, but they do insist that we view sex as more than merely a pleasant activity. What we should do is ask ourselves questions like these: Does our sex life contribute to our sense of worth and dignity? Is it consistent with our most important goals in life? Does it reflect the kind of person we most want to be? Is it the sex life of a mature, well-adjusted person? Does it help us develop or maintain the character traits that most matter to us? Does it enhance our lives as much as it might? Does it help us build the kind of relationships we most value?

To ask such questions is to steer a middle course between the sexual traditionalist and the sexual libertarian. The questions are, after all, very much in the spirit of the Vatican declaration. The concerns they raise—fundamental values, personal dignity and fulfillment, the quality of our lives and relationships—are the same. But unlike the authors of the declaration, many people who insist that we ask these questions do not assume that our answers must follow any particular line. In that respect, they are more like the libertarians. For example, they allow that many people engaged in loving homosexual relationships can answer yes to all these questions. So can many unmarried heterosexuals with active sex lives.

People who support this way of treating sex, then, are like the traditionalists in that they do not treat sex like any other activity, but they are like the libertarians in that they make room for a variety of personal decisions about sex.

The Naturalness Argument

Another line of attack against sexual libertarianism also shares certain features with the Vatican declaration. According to this line, sex organs and sexual activity are natural phenomena, and like any other natural phenomenon, they have their own natural manifestations and purposes. In that case, we can distinguish natural from unnatural sex and natural from unnatural use of our sex organs. And because what is natural is moral and what is unnatural is immoral, we can distinguish moral from immoral sex.

Although the Vatican declaration applies this reasoning to a variety of sexual behaviors—masturbation and the use of contraception, for instance, as well as homosexuality—many people confine it to homosexuality alone.

What is it that makes homosexuality unnatural? Various answers are given. Homosexual behavior violates the laws of nature, some people say. Or it is an abnormal occurrence in nature. Or it involves an unnatural use of sex organs.

Libertarian Objections

Many libertarians share some of the concerns we have just looked at. They do not, however, conclude that these concerns justify a retreat from full sexual freedom. Sexual libertarians do not advocate moral irresponsibility, they say, but only sexual freedom. And sexual libertarianism can be just as morally responsible as sexual traditionalism.

Consider the AIDS threat. Certainly, libertarians say, we all have an obligation to avoid behavior that might cause us to become carriers of the virus and pass it on to others. And just as certainly, that obligation involves taking necessary precautions like using condoms when we cannot be sure about our sexual partners. But as long as we do take such necessary precautions, we have no obligation to turn to chastity or heterosexual monogamy.

As for teen pregnancy and single parenthood, sexual libertarians argue that the blame for these problems does not rest with them. As long as they behave responsibly, they cannot be held accountable for the irresponsibility of others. Nor should they be morally required to restrict their sex lives. The solution to such social problems lies in education, easy access to birth control counseling, and social programs to alleviate poverty and hopelessness—not in the restriction of sexual freedom.

Libertarians also point out that about half of all women and children experiencing homelessness are fleeing domestic violence. As many of those relationships were traditional marriages, there must be other explanations for this homelessness and poverty than the availability of sex outside marriage. Perhaps women are less likely now to tolerate domestic violence and instead seek other options.

What about personal fulfillment? Many libertarians might well agree with many of the remarks in that argument, as long as each individual is free to supply his or her own answers to the recommended questions. Others, though, might wonder why sex need be taken so seriously. If Jane is satisfied enough with her life, even though she takes a very casual approach to sex, why should she feel any more pressure to involve herself in any soul searching about sex than about any other aspect of her life? No doubt sex and sexual relationships are very important to many people, but if other people feel differently, who's to say they shouldn't?

Finally, there is the naturalness argument. Here, libertarians remain totally unimpressed. Does homosexuality really violate the laws of nature? No, because *nothing* can violate the laws of nature. Natural laws are not like criminal laws. They describe how the world actually works. They do not tell us how we ought to behave. Everything that happens, then, must be in accord with natural law. Is homosexuality an abnormal occurrence in nature? Perhaps, but that does not make it immoral. After all, great genius, great basketball talent, and great musical ability are even more abnormal, but we prize them when they occur, not condemn them. Does homosexuality involve the unnatural use of our sex organs? Again, perhaps, but how does that differ from using our ears for holding earrings, our eyes for giving playful winks, or our thumbs for hitching rides?

Advocates of **marriage** for homosexual couples also point out that many of those relationships are as stable as heterosexual marriages, even though the unions are not traditional relationships. These advocates suggest that the values of traditional marriages are highly regarded in these **relationships** and should be encouraged, regardless of the sexual preference of the couple. Many of these couples also adopt children who are otherwise difficult to place, including the children of drug addicts and AIDS-infected babies. Thus, they promote traditional family values, even though they are outside the definition of a traditional heterosexual marriage.

ARGUMENTS FOR SEXUAL LIBERTARIANISM

1. *Sex is a private matter.*
   POINT: "Whatever goes on between consenting adults in private is nobody's business but their own, and that holds as much for sex as for anything else. Why should anybody even care whether Mary has fifteen lovers or none, whether Jack prefers sex with Bill to sex with Jane, or whether married couples like to 'swing' with other married couples? Just because you personally disapprove of such things doesn't make them wrong. We all have the right to live our lives as we see fit as long as we don't interfere with the rights of others to live their lives as they see fit. Promiscuous people, homosexuals, and swingers don't tell you how to live your life. Don't tell them how to live theirs."

   COUNTERPOINT: "Sex isn't nearly as private as you think. All of society is affected by the sexual revolution you're so fond of. Who do you think has to pick up the tab for all the illegitimate children your libertarianism is giving us? The taxpayers. And who has to pick up the tab for AIDS research? The taxpayers. And who has to live with all the abortion mills, the fear of AIDS, and the worry over how all of this free sex will affect our children? All of us."

2. *You can't turn the clock back on the sexual revolution.*
   POINT: "Whether you approve of what's happened to sexual morality or not, one thing's certain: You can't turn the clock back. Once people get a taste of freedom—sexual or any other kind—they don't want to give it up. Do you really think that sexually active unmarried people are going to turn to celibacy, or that homosexuals are going to deny their sexual identity and pretend to be something they're not, or that married couples who feel that open marriage works better for them than fidelity are going to settle for fidelity? Let's face it. Human nature just doesn't work that way."

   COUNTERPOINT: "Maybe not, but that doesn't make the sexual revolution right. The whole point of morality is to curb some of the excesses of human nature, to try to get people to exercise their freedoms responsibly. Besides, nobody expects to turn everything around overnight. The point is to insist that certain behavior is wrong, to make young people understand the proper place of sex in their lives, and to get them to make responsible choices about sex. It'll take some time, but eventually the changes can come."

3. *Curbing sexual freedom is unfair.*
   POINT: "You're neglecting an important point here—fairness. The crux of the issue isn't just that people don't want to turn back the clock but that it's

unfair to make them turn it back. You're comfortable with your traditional morality, but to other people, it can be a straitjacket. For them, it's impossible to live fulfilling lives under those conditions. The worst victims, of course, would be the homosexuals. What are they supposed to do—live a heterosexual life or give up sex and love altogether? But they wouldn't be the only victims. Some people are totally unsuited to marriage. Others are totally unsuited to monogamy. They have as much right to fulfilling sex lives as you do."

COUNTERPOINT: "Nobody has the right to seek fulfillment immorally. And there's nothing unfair about making people turn away from immoral behavior. I'm not denying that traditional sexual morality is more demanding for some people than it is for others, but that doesn't make it any different from any other area of moral concern. Pathological liars and kleptomaniacs have a harder time doing right than the rest of us do, but our sympathy for them can't lead us to approve of their lies and thefts. The same holds for homosexuals. We can sympathize, but we can't condone."

4. *Traditional sexual morality is hypocritical.*

POINT: "What you're really calling for is a return to hypocrisy. Let's all pretend to be faithful heterosexual monogamists while we do whatever we feel like doing on the sly. Adultery, premarital sex, promiscuity, and homosexuality aren't new, you know. The only thing that's changed is that people are more honest about them now. And that's a change for the good."

COUNTERPOINT: "Adultery, premarital sex, promiscuity, and homosexuality may not be new, but they're sure a lot more prevalent than they used to be. And you can thank your precious honesty for that. Once people start being proud about things like that, once they start going public about them, it has to start affecting other people's behavior. They start thinking, 'If it's good enough for Dick and Jane, maybe I should give it a try.' In other words, a little bit of hypocrisy is a good thing. You don't want armed robbers telling their kids there's nothing wrong with armed robbery, do you? Well, I don't want unwed mothers telling their kids there's nothing wrong with premarital sex."

ARGUMENTS AGAINST SEXUAL LIBERTARIANISM

1. *Sexual libertarianism undermines public morality.*

POINT: "Morality is like law. Once you encourage disrespect for a particular law, you encourage disrespect for all laws. And once you encourage disrespect for sexual morality, you encourage disrespect for all of morality. That's why it's no surprise that the sexual revolution brought with it an explosion of pornography and abortion. It's also why I wouldn't be surprised to learn that people don't care as much about loyalty and honesty as they used to. After all, a large part of your revolution is that marriage vows don't have to mean anything."

COUNTERPOINT: "Sexual libertarianism isn't about disrespect for morality. It's about moral change. If you want to talk about disrespect for morality, the real culprit is your traditional sexual morality. That's a morality that people won't adhere to, and a morality like that is bound to breed disrespect. And don't confuse sexual libertarianism with disloyalty and dishonesty. A husband and wife who agree that affairs with other people will make their marriage better aren't being disloyal to each other—and they're certainly not being dishonest."

2. *Sex without love is empty.*

POINT: "One of the biggest problems with your view is that it erases the connection between sex and love. Even you have to admit that sex with someone you love is better than sex with someone you don't love. With someone you love, sex isn't mere empty pleasure. It's communication, it's sharing, it's an expression of affection and care. It *means* something. The sex that you advocate means nothing at all. It's sterile, and it adds nothing of worth to our lives. What you're really doing is reducing human sexuality to animal sexuality. We might as well be rabbits, according to you. But we're not rabbits, and because we're not, loveless sex can't possibly satisfy us or be fulfilling for us."

COUNTERPOINT: "First of all, I'm not advocating any kind of sex. All I'm advocating is people's moral right to engage in the kinds of sex they prefer as long as they don't hurt anyone. Second, who are you to declare that the kind of sex you prefer is the best kind of sex for anyone else? Third, even if you're right—even if loving sex is better than loveless sex—what morally important difference does that make? Some cars are better than others, but there's nothing immoral about driving the inferior ones. Or to pick an even closer analogy, celebrating good news with someone you love is probably better than celebrating good news with someone you don't love, but nobody's going to say you're doing wrong if you do celebrate good news with someone you don't love."

3. *Sexual libertarianism undermines marriage.*

POINT: "If society adopts your position, we might as well forget about the institution of marriage. Unmarried people will have no good reason to get married because sex will be freely available. Even having children won't count as a good reason any more, as it becomes more and more acceptable to be an unmarried parent. And married people will have little reason to stay married. After all, once marital fidelity goes, there goes the most important bond between husband and wife. And even if some kind of bond remains, how can it stand up against the constant temptations that married people will face? Or the jealousies? Or the insecurities?"

COUNTERPOINT: "Aren't you being a little too cynical? People get married for lots of reasons other than sex, and they stay married because of a variety of bonds and intimacies. I'm not going to deny that sexual libertarianism can have some negative effects on marriage, but I *am* going to deny that the effects are all negative. For one thing, people with sexual experience before marriage are less likely to confuse sex with love, and that makes it less likely that they'll choose their spouses unwisely. For another, they're less likely to feel they've missed something before getting married, and that should help protect them from temptation. And for still another, some marriages actually gain from being open to extramarital affairs. If married people feel the need for sexual variety, the possibility of having an open marriage can remove a reason for divorce."

4. *Sexual libertarianism is turning society upside down.*

   POINT: "Your views have led to a number of crazy consequences. I'm not just talking about such tragedies as teen mothers, but things like the gay rights movement. First we have homosexuals demanding the right to teach in elementary schools, then we have homosexual couples demanding the right to adopt children, then we have them demanding that homosexual 'spouses' be included in family medical plans and the like. I have no idea where all this is ultimately heading, but it's certainly not in the right direction. We can't let children grow up believing that homosexuality is just another lifestyle, and we can't have society treating homosexual relationships like real marriages. No society can survive that."

   COUNTERPOINT: "Why not? If homosexuality isn't immoral to begin with, what's wrong with giving homosexuals the same rights as heterosexuals? If you're afraid that we'd end up raising an entire generation of homosexual children, you're just being unrealistic. Besides, you're mixing up two different issues. Whether homosexuality is moral is one thing. Whether homosexual relationships should have the same legal status as heterosexual marriages is another."

Declaration on Certain Questions Concerning Sexual Ethics

THE VATICAN

This declaration, approved by Pope Paul VI, was issued in 1975 in response to "the growing difficulties experienced by the faithful in obtaining knowledge of wholesome moral teaching, especially in sexual matters, and of the growing difficulties experienced by pastors in expounding this teaching effectively." The teachings of the Catholic Church rely on natural law, which provides objective standards based in human nature for how people should behave. Natural law, articulated by St. Thomas Aquinas, provides a major basis for ethical reasoning today for many people.

This excerpt explains how values are innate in human nature and how human reason, as well as divine revelation, should be used to recognize and develop those values. While understanding that the conditions of life are ever-changing, this Declaration insists that values are immutable and do not change.

Premarital sex is wrong, even among those with a firm intention to marry. This position is supported not just by appeals to scripture, but also appeals to experience, reflection, history, and human dignity. Having children outside of marriage is also considered immoral, as it deprives children of the stable environment they deserve in a marriage.

Although the Declaration urges that homosexuals be treated with "understanding," it concludes that homosexual acts are "intrinsically disordered" and can never be approved of. Masturbation is also condemned as "a grave moral disorder."

I

According to contemporary scientific research, the human person is so profoundly affected by sexuality that it must be considered as one of the factors which give to each individual's life the principal traits that distinguish it. In fact it is from sex that the human person receives the characteristics which, on the biological, psychological and spiritual levels, make that person a man or a woman, and thereby largely condition his or her progress towards maturity and insertion into society. Hence sexual matters, as is obvious to everyone, today constitute a theme frequently and openly dealt with in books, reviews, magazines and other means of social communication.

In the present period, the corruption of morals has increased, and one of the most serious indications of this corruption is the unbridled exaltation of sex. Moreover, through the means of social communication and through public entertainment this corruption has reached the point of invading the field of education and of infecting the general mentality.

In this context certain educators, teachers and moralists have been able to contribute to a better understanding and integration into life of the values proper to each of the sexes; on the other hand there are those who have put forward concepts and modes of behavior which are contrary to the true moral exigencies of the human person. Some members of the latter group have even gone so far as to favor a licentious hedonism.

As a result, in the course of a few years, teachings, moral criteria and modes of living hitherto faithfully preserved have been very much unsettled, even among Christians. There are many people today who, being confronted with widespread opinions opposed to the teaching which they received from the Church, have come to wonder what must still hold as true.

II

The Church cannot remain indifferent to this confusion of minds and relaxation of morals. It is a question, in fact, of a matter which is of the utmost importance both for the personal lives of Christians and for the social life of our time.[1]...

III

The people of our time are more and more convinced that the human person's dignity and vocation demand that they should discover, by the light of their own intelligence, the values innate in their nature, that they should ceaselessly develop these values and realize them in their lives, in order to achieve an ever greater development.

In moral matters man cannot make value judgments according to his personal whim: "In the depths of his conscience, man detects a law which he does not impose on himself, but which holds him to obedience.... For man has in his heart a law written by God. To obey it is the very dignity of man; according to it he will be judged."[2]

Moreover, through His revelation God has made known to us Christians His plan of salvation, and He has held up to us Christ, the Savior and Sanctifier, in His teaching and example, as the supreme and immutable Law of life: "I am the light of the world; anyone who follows Me will not be walking in the dark, he will have the light of life."[3]

Therefore there can be no true promotion of man's dignity unless the essential order of his nature is respected. Of course, in the history of civilization many of the concrete conditions and needs of human life have changed and will continue to change. But all evolution of morals and every type of life must be kept within the limits imposed by the immutable principles based upon every human person's constitutive elements and essential relations—elements and relations which transcend historical contingency.

These fundamental principles, which can be grasped by reason, are contained in "the Divine Law—eternal, objective and universal—whereby God orders, directs and governs the entire universe and all the ways of the human community, by a plan conceived in wisdom and love. Man has been made by God to participate in this law, with the result that, under the gentle disposition of Divine Providence, he can come to perceive ever increasingly the unchanging truth."[4] This Divine Law is accessible to our minds.

IV

Hence, those many people are in error who today assert that one can find neither in human nature nor in the revealed law any absolute and immutable norm to serve for particular actions other than the one which expresses itself in the general law of charity and respect for human dignity. As a proof of their assertion they put forward the view that so-called norms of the natural law or precepts of Sacred Scripture are to be regarded only as given expressions of a form of particular culture at a certain moment of history.

But in fact, Divine Revelation and, in its own proper order, philosophical wisdom, emphasize the authentic exigencies of human nature. They thereby necessarily manifest the existence of immutable laws inscribed in the constitutive elements of human nature and which are revealed to be identical in all beings endowed with reason....

V

Since sexual ethics concern fundamental values of human and Christian life, this general teaching equally applies to sexual ethics. In this domain there exist principles and norms which the Church has always unhesitatingly transmitted as part of her teaching, however much the opinions and morals of the world may have been opposed to them. These principles and norms in no way owe their origin to a certain type of culture, but rather to knowledge of the Divine Law and of human nature. They therefore cannot be considered as having become out of date or doubtful under the pretext that a new cultural situation has arisen.

It is these principles which inspired the exhortations and directives given by the Second Vatican Council for an education and an organization of social life taking account of the equal dignity of man and woman while respecting their difference.[5]

Speaking of "the sexual nature of man and the human faculty of procreation," the Council noted that they "wonderfully exceed the dispositions of lower forms of life."[6] It then took particular care to expound the principles and criteria which concern human sexuality in marriage, and which are based upon the finality of the specific function of sexuality.

In this regard the Council declares that the moral goodness of the acts proper to conjugal life, acts which are ordered according to true human dignity, "does not depend solely on sincere intentions or on an evaluation of motives. It must be determined by objective standards. These, based on the nature of the human person and his acts, preserve the full sense of mutual self-giving and human procreation in the context of true love."[7]

These final words briefly sum up the Council's teaching—more fully expounded in an earlier part of the same Constitution[8]—on the finality of the sexual act and on the principal criterion of its morality: it is respect for its finality that ensures the moral goodness of this act.

This same principle, which the Church holds from Divine Revelation and from her authentic interpretation of the natural law, is also the basis of her traditional doctrine, which states that the use of the sexual function has its true meaning and moral rectitude only in true marriage.[9]

VI

It is not the purpose of the present Declaration to deal with all the abuses of the sexual faculty, nor with all the elements involved in the practice of chastity. Its object is rather to repeat the Church's doctrine on certain particular points, in view of the urgent need to oppose serious errors and widespread aberrant modes of behavior.

VII

Today there are many who vindicate the right to sexual union before marriage, at least in those cases where a firm intention to marry and an affection which is already in some way conjugal in the psychology of the subjects require this completion, which they judge to be connatural. This is especially the case when the celebration of the marriage is impeded by circumstances or when this intimate relationship seems necessary in order for love to be preserved.

This opinion is contrary to Christian doctrine, which states that every genital act must be within the framework of marriage. However firm the intention of those who practice such premature sexual relations may be, the fact remains that these relations cannot ensure, in sincerity and fidelity, the interpersonal relationship between a man and a woman, nor especially can they protect this relationship from whims and caprices. Now it is a stable union that Jesus willed, and He restored its original requirement, beginning with the sexual difference. "Have you not read that the Creator from the beginning made them male and female and that He said: This is why a man must leave father and mother, and cling to his wife, and the two become one body? They are no longer two, therefore, but one body. So then, what God has united, man must not divide."[10]...

This is what the Church has always understood and taught,[11] and she finds a profound agreement with her doctrine in men's reflection and in the lessons of history.

Experience teaches us that love must find its safeguard in the stability of marriage, if sexual intercourse is truly to respond to the requirements of its own finality and to those of human dignity. These requirements call for a conjugal contract sanctioned and guaranteed by society—a contract which establishes a state of life of capital importance both for the exclusive union of the man and the woman and for the good of their family and of the human community. Most often, in fact, premarital relations exclude the possibility of children. What is represented to be conjugal love is not able, as it absolutely should be, to develop into paternal and maternal love. Or, if it does happen to do so, this will be to the detriment of the children, who will be deprived of the stable environment in which they ought to develop in order to find in it the way and the means of their insertion into society as a whole.

The consent given by people who wish to be united in marriage must therefore be manifested externally and in a manner which makes it valid in the eyes of society. As far as the faithful are concerned, their consent to the setting up of a community of conjugal life must be expressed according to the laws of the Church. It is a consent which makes their marriage a Sacrament of Christ.

VIII

At the present time there are those who, basing themselves on observations in the psychological order, have begun to judge indulgently, and even to excuse completely, homosexual relations between certain people....

A distinction is drawn, and it seems with some reason, between homosexuals whose tendency comes from a false education, from a lack of normal sexual development, from habit, from bad example, or from other similar causes, and is transitory or at least not incurable; and homosexuals who are definitively such because of some kind of innate instinct or a pathological constitution judged to be incurable.

In regard to this second category of subjects, some people conclude that their tendency is so natural that it justifies in their case homosexual relations within a sincere communion of life and love analogous to marriage, in so far as such homosexuals feel incapable of enduring a solitary life.

In the pastoral field, these homosexuals must certainly be treated with understanding and sustained in the hope of overcoming their personal difficulties and their inability to fit into society. Their culpability will be judged with prudence.

But no pastoral method can be employed which would give moral justification to these acts on the grounds that they would be consonant with the condition of such people. For according to the objective moral order, homosexual relations are acts which lack an essential and indispensable finality. In Sacred Scripture they are condemned as a serious depravity and even presented as the sad consequence of rejecting God.[12] This judgment of Scripture does not of course permit us to conclude that all those who suffer from this anomaly are personally responsible for it, but it does attest to the fact that homosexual acts are intrinsically disordered and can in no case be approved of.

IX

The traditional Catholic doctrine that masturbation constitutes a grave moral disorder is often called into doubt or expressly denied today. It is said that psychology and sociology show that it is a normal phenomenon of sexual development, especially among the young. It is stated that there is real and serious fault only in the measure that the subject deliberately indulges in solitary pleasure closed in on self ("ipsation"), because in this case the act would indeed be radically opposed to the loving communion between persons of different sex which some hold is what is principally sought in the use of the sexual faculty.

This opinion is contradictory to the teaching and pastoral practice of the Catholic Church. Whatever the force of certain arguments of a biological and philosophical nature, which have sometimes been used by theologians, in fact both the Magisterium of the Church—in the course of a constant tradition—and the moral sense of the faithful have declared without hesitation that masturbation is an intrinsically and seriously disordered act.[13] The main reason is that, whatever the motive for acting this way, the deliberate use of the sexual faculty outside normal conjugal relations essentially contradicts the finality of the faculty. For it lacks the sexual relationship called for by the moral order, namely the relationship which realizes "the full sense of mutual self-giving and human procreation in the context of true love."[14]

All deliberate exercise of sexuality must be reserved to this regular relationship. Even if it cannot be proved that Scripture condemns this sin by name, the tradition of the Church has rightly understood it to be condemned in the New Testament when the latter speaks of "impurity," "unchasteness" and other vices contrary to chastity and continence.

Sociological surveys are able to show the frequency of this disorder according to the places, populations or circumstances studied. In this way facts are discovered, but facts do not constitute a criterion for judging the moral value of human acts.[15] The frequency of the phenomenon in question is certainly to be linked with man's innate weakness following original sin; but it is also to be linked with the loss of sense of God, with the corruption of morals engendered by the commercialization of vice, with the unrestrained licentiousness of so many public entertainments and publications, as well as with the neglect of modesty, which is the guardian of chastity.

On the subject of masturbation modern psychology provides much valid and useful information for formulating a more equitable judgment on moral responsibility and for orienting pastoral action. Psychology helps one to see how the immaturity of adolescence (which can sometimes persist after that age), psychological imbalance or habit can influence behavior, diminishing the deliberate character of the act and bringing about a situation whereby subjectively there may not always be serious fault. But in general, the absence of serious responsibility must not be presumed; this would be to misunderstand people's moral capacity.

In the pastoral ministry, in order to form an adequate judgment in concrete cases, the habitual behavior of people will be considered in its totality, not only with regard to the individual's practice of charity and of justice but also with regard to the individual's care in observing the particular precepts of chastity. In particular, one will have to examine whether the individual is using the necessary means, both natural and supernatural, which Christian asceticism from its long experience recommends for overcoming the passions and progressing in virtue....

NOTES

1. Cf. Second Vatican Ecumenical Council, Constitution on the Church in the Modern World *"Gaudium et Spes,"* 47 AAS 58 (1966), p. 1067.

2. *"Gaudium et Spes,"* 16 AAS 58 (1966), p. 1037.

3. *Jn* 8:12.

4. Second Vatican Ecumenical Council, Declaration *"Dignitatis Humanae,"* 3 AAS 58 (1996), p. 931.

5. Cf. Second Vatican Ecumenical Council, Declaration *"Gravissimum Educationis,"* 1, 8: AAS 58 (1966), pp. 729–730; 734–736 *"Gaudium et Spes,"* 29, 60, 67 AAS 58 (1966), pp. 1048–1049, 1080–1081, 1088–1089.

6. *"Gaudium et Spes,"* 51 AAS 58 (1966), pp. 1072.

7. *Ibid:* cf also 49 loc cit, pp. 1069–1070.

8. *Ibid*, 49, 50 loc cit, pp. 1069–1072.

9. The present Declaration does not go into further detail regarding the norms of sexual life within marriage; these norms have been clearly taught in the encyclical letter *"Casti Connubii"* and *"Humanae Vitae."*

10. Cf. *Mt* 19:4–6.

11. Cf. Innocent IV, letter *"Sub catholica professione,"* March 6th, 1254, DS 835; Pius II, *"Propos damn in Ep Cum sicut accepimus."* Nov 13th, 1459, DS 1367; decrees of the Holy Office, Sept 24th, 1665, DS 2045; March 2nd, 1679, DS 2148 Pius XI, encyclical letter *"Casti Connubii,"* Dec 31st, 1930 AAS 22 (1930), pp. 558–559.

12. *Rom* 1:24–27 "That is why God left them to their filthy enjoyments and the practices with which they dishonor their own bodies since they have given up Divine truth for a lie and have worshipped and served creatures instead of the Creator, Who is blessed forever. Amen! That is why God has abandoned them to degrading passions; why their women have turned from natural intercourse to unnatural practices and why their menfolk have given up natural intercourse to be consumed with passion for each other, men doing shameless things with men and getting an appropriate reward for their perversion" See also what St. Paul says of *"masculorum concubitores"* in I *Cor* 6:10; I *Tim* 1:10.

13. Cf. Leo IX, letter *"Ad splendidum nitentis,"* in the year 1054 DS 687–688, decree of the Holy Office, March 2nd, 1679: DS 2149; Pius XII, *"Allocutio,"* Oct 8th, 1953 AAS 45 (1953), pp. 677–678; May 19th, 1956 AAS 48 (1956), pp. 472–473.

14. *"Gaudium et Spes,"* 51 AAS 58 (1966), p. 1072.

15. "… it [sic] sociological surveys are useful for better discovering the thought patterns of the people of a particular place, the anxieties and needs of those to whom we proclaim the word of God, and also the opposition made to it by modern reasoning through the widespread notion that outside science there exists no legitimate form of knowledge, still the conclusions drawn from such surveys could not of themselves constitute a determining criterion of truth," Paul VI, apostolic exhortation *"Quinque iam anni."* Dec 8th 1970, AAS 63 (1971), p. 102.

☖ QUESTIONS FOR ANALYSIS

1. This Vatican document expresses concern about the corruption of morals in contemporary times. What influences have caused this corruption, according to the Declaration? Does this corruption and those influences continue today? Are there additional sources of corruption and influence that impact morals today?

2. The analysis depends on recognizing and understanding the essential nature of persons. For those who do not adhere to this particular religious tradition, can this essential nature be identified through human reasoning alone, without appeal to revelations of sacred texts? Is this likely to result in the same conclusions by everyone?

3. What reasons does the Declaration provide against premarital sex? Are these persuasive today? Are these reasons also persuasive in arguing that having children outside marriage is immoral?

4. What reasons are provided for concluding that homosexual acts are "intrinsically disordered and can in no case be approved of"?

5. What is the main reason provided for the view that masturbation is a "grave moral disorder"? Is this persuasive reasoning for those who do not share the theological views of the Catholic Church?

6. What roles are recognized in this Declaration as appropriate for scientific work in biology, psychology, and sociology? Should additional or conflicting conclusions be drawn from this scientific work?

Framework for a Sexual Ethic: Just Sex

MARGARET A. FARLEY

Margaret A. Farley was a professor at Yale University Divinity School for thirty-six years, until she retired in 2007 as the Gilbert L. Stark Professor Emerita of Christian Ethics. She served as President of the Society of Christian Ethics and the Catholic Theological Society of America, as well as receiving numerous honorary degrees and other honors during her career. A member of the Religious Sisters of Mercy, she has published over 100 articles and chapters of books, as well as seven books.

The excerpts below are from her most recent book, *Just Love: A Framework for Christian Sexual Ethics* (2006). In developing her theory of justice and fairness in sexual relationships, she draws widely from contemporary work in science, theology, and biblical analyses, as well as extensive reliance on western philosophers from Immanuel Kant, Thomas Aquinas, Augustine, Aristotle, and John Stuart Mill to Michel Foucault, Catherine MacKinnon, Martha Nussbaum, and Annette Baier.

Farley understands "justice" in what she calls "the classic fundamental 'formal' meaning: to render to each her or his due." From this she develops a basic ethical principal: "Persons and groups of persons ought to be affirmed according to their concrete reality, actual and potential." Justice in loving, she argues, depends on the concrete reality of persons, "their needs, capacities, relational claims, vulnerability, possibilities." She emphasizes two features of personhood: autonomy and relationality. Her development of the concept of a person is strongly reminiscent of Kant, as "terminal centers, ends in ourselves, because in some way we both transcend ourselves and yet belong to ourselves." Her norms for "just sex" are: (1) Do No Unjust Harm, (2) Free Consent, (3) Mutuality, (4) Equality, (5) Commitment, (6) Fruitfulness, and (7) Social Justice.

Farley applies her principles and norms to a wide range of contemporary issues in human sexuality. The excerpts below address many of the issues in the 1975 Declaration which appears in this text.

SEXUAL RELATIONS WITH ONESELF

Most of the justice norms that I have delineated in this chapter derive at least in part from "relationality," one of the basic obligating features of human persons. The norms as I have presented them are clearly relevant to sexual relationships between persons, but it is not so clear how this justice ethic relates to sexual relations with one's self. I do not thereby want to dismiss the importance of questions about "self-pleasuring" (or masturbation), especially since general perceptions and attitudes regarding this form of sexual expression have changed radically in the latter part of the twentieth century. Perhaps the most important insight we need in this regard is that it, like other sexual activities, needs to be moved out of the realm of taboo morality.

Through centuries of Western thought masturbation was judged to be not only an immoral sexual practice, but one that should be particularly repugnant to human individuals and the human community. As Immanuel Kant insisted, it places humans "below the level of animals." Christian traditions looked upon it as the "solitary sin," "onanism," "self-abuse," and judged it harshly until the twentieth century, although perhaps not so harshly in every prior century. Traditions of professional medical opinion undergirded and joined in the negative judgments made by religious authorities. Although there are theologians and church traditions that continue to consider masturbation immoral, many others (most, as far as I can tell, along with most medical practitioners) do not assess it in this manner anymore. Masturbation is more likely to be considered morally neutral, which could mean that it is either good or bad, depending on the circumstances and the individual. It could also mean that, while the practice may raise psychological questions (if it becomes obsessive, for example), it usually does not raise any moral questions at all.

Ever since the Kinsey studies, it has been impossible to claim with any credibility that masturbation is a practice of only a very few, or that past dire predictions about dangerous physical or psychological injury from the practice are accurate. Anecdotal reports today tend to show that any evil or injury involved is the result of misinformation, unsubstantiated myths, and experiences of defilement and guilt in what is perceived to be the breaking of religious or cultural taboos. It is surely the case that many women, following the "our bodies our selves" movement in the fourth quarter of the twentieth century, have found great good in self-pleasuring—perhaps especially in the discovery of their own possibilities for pleasure—something many had not experienced or even known about in their ordinary sexual relations with husbands or lovers. In this way, it could be said that masturbation actually serves relationships rather than hindering them.

My final observation is, then, that the norms of justice as I have presented them would seem to apply to the choice of sexual self-pleasuring only insofar as this activity may help or harm, only insofar as it supports or limits, well-being and liberty of spirit. This remains largely an empirical question, not a moral one....

SAME-SEX RELATIONSHIPS

... an ethic applicable to and illuminative of same-sex relationships is based on an obligation to respect persons. To respect persons requires respecting their autonomy and their relationality— their capacity for relationships through knowledge and love. Since autonomy and relationality combine to make human persons ends in themselves, the first requirement in the sexual; sphere as in any other spheres of human life is the requirement not to harm persons unjustly—whether they happen to be heterosexual or gay or lesbian.

Essential to relation to persons as ends in themselves, especially when their embodied selves are what is at stake, is a minimum but absolute requirement for the free consent of sexual partners. Everything that is ruled out for heterosexual relationships—rape, violence, harmful use of power, seduction and manipulation of individuals who have limited capacities of choice by reason of immaturity, intellectual disability, or special dependency—is ruled out for same-sex relationships as well. Derivatively, truth-telling is required in same-sex relationships as well as an intent to keep any promises made.

In order to respect the relationality of homosexual persons, same-sex relationships ought also to be characterized by a significant degree of mutuality—of desire, action, and response. Similarly, reasonable equality is required in order to make free choice possible and to introduce an important qualification to mutuality. In addition, some form of commitment is expected and required by a Christian same-sex ethic, as is some form of fruitfulness. These latter two norms bear further consideration as they characterize same-sex relationships.

Many gay men and lesbians, like many heterosexual men and women, not only desire but consider necessary some form of commitment to relationships in which they are sexually active. Commitment today, of course, has become problematic, as much for homosexuals as for heterosexuals. If it is seen as a shutting down of one's life, a dampening of the possibilities of sexual expression, or as something that is almost impossible in today's world, it can hardly take the form of an obligation for sexual relationships. Moreover, if it is construed in terms identified with traditional forms of heterosexual marriage, with accompanying concerns for the procreation and rearing of children and for the domestication of sexuality, it can hardly be what gays and lesbians are obligated to embrace. Culturally conditioned expectations regarding gender roles, and assumed inequality in the power relations intrinsic to marriage, are not what either homosexuals or many heterosexuals find tolerable or just.

Yet commitment in sexual relationships that are just need not stifle either life or sexual love and desire; it may instead nurture, sustain, anchor, and transform sexuality. Its aim, at least, is to give a future to love and to a shared life, holding in continually ratified free choice what is otherwise fleeting and fragile. Commitment, or especially frameworks for commitment, are means, not ends in themselves. But they are means to the affirmation of persons as ends in themselves and the endurance of love that is an end in itself for those who want their relationships to hold. At its best, this is why the Christian community still recognizes commitment at the heart of an ethic for sexual activities and relationships. It prevents the use of sexual partners as mere means (for sustaining one's sexual desire and providing sexual pleasure), and it offers the possibility for the integration of sexuality into the whole of one's loves and one's life. It alone offers the possibility of sexuality as expression of transcendent embodiment in the highest forms of friendship.

Fruitfulness as a norm for sexual relations need not ... refer only to the conceiving of children. It can refer to multiple forms of fruitfulness

in love of others, care for others, making the world a better place for others than just the "two of us." It is the opposite of the sterility of an *égoism à deux* [selfishness of two, to the exclusion of all around them]. For those who object to same-sex relationships because they cannot be procreative, their objections represent either a failure of imagination or a narrowness of experience that disallows an appreciation of all the ways in which humans bring life into the world, and all the ways that the world needs new life from those to whom the gift of love has been given. In the Christian community, the gift of love constitutes a calling, and it is a divine gift and divine call to lesbians and gay men, as it is to heterosexual women and men. Hence fruitfulness is both an obligation and an appeal, a requirement and a graced opportunity....

Presently one of the most urgent issues before the U.S. public is marriage for same-sex partners—that is, the granting of social recognition and legal standing to unions between lesbians and gays comparable to unions between heterosexuals. This issue in some ways focuses the difficulties entailed in achieving respect for homosexual persons and for their incorporation into the ordinary life of the churches, while at the same time denying them communal and societal supports that are available to heterosexuals. The major argument against same-sex marriage has tended to be that it will weaken support for traditional heterosexual marriage and traditional notions of family. It is difficult to make sense of this reasoning, especially since the churches do not mount campaigns against laws that recognize divorce—arguably a greater threat to heterosexual marriage than gay marriages might be. A more persuasive position is that the possibility of gay marriage would actually reinforce the value of commitment for heterosexuals as well as homosexuals....

⚜ QUESTIONS FOR ANALYSIS

1. Why does Farley conclude that "self-pleasuring" is an empirical question, not a moral one? Why is the late twentieth century view held by many so different from those earlier in history? What factors seem to have led to this change in attitude?

2. Farley relies heavily on Kantian reasoning. Find specific passages and languages that seem to be drawn from Kant's approach to ethics and consider whether this reasoning is sound in this context. Can her conclusions be justified solely through

Kantian reasoning without the additional appeal to Christianity, regardless of one's religious views?

3. Along with affirmative arguments in support of same-sex marriage, Farley addresses common objections, including the lack of traditional procreation and supposed threats to traditional heterosexual marriage. How does she answer those objections? Are they persuasive answers?

4. Both the Vatican document and this excerpt by Farley appeal to scientific knowledge, yet they arrive at very different conclusions on these social issues. What role should science play in tackling these issues? What does science contribute? What are its limitations?

Sexual Morality and the Concept of Using Another Person

THOMAS A. MAPPES

Thomas A. Mappes is Professor Emeritus of Philosophy at Frostburg State University in Maryland, where he taught from 1973–2007. He received his Ph.D. in philosophy from Georgetown University and specializes in ethics, biomedical ethics, philosophy of law, and modern philosophy.

Mappes proposes that sexual morality be analyzed in the term of Kant's principle that persons should be respected as ends in themselves and should never be used merely as a means to someone else's end. In developing his position, Mappes relies on the concept of "voluntary informed consent" to identify when people are not being used merely as a means. This consent requirement is violated in situations where there is deception or dishonesty of various kinds. Mappes's reliance on Kantian principles of autonomy and self-determination constitutes a very different approach to analyzing sexual morality from traditional views drawn from natural law.

The central tenet of *conventional* sexual morality is that nonmarital sex is immoral. A somewhat less restrictive sexual ethic holds that *sex without love* is immoral. If neither of these positions is philosophically defensible, and I would content that neither is, it does not follow that there are no substantive moral restrictions on human sexual interaction. *Any* human interaction, including sexual interaction, may be judged morally objectionable to the extent that it transgresses a justified moral rule or principle. The way to construct a detailed account of sexual morality, it would seem, is simply to work out the implications of relevant moral rules or principles in the area of human sexual interaction.

As one important step in the direction of such an account, I will attempt to work out the implications of an especially relevant moral principle, the principle that it is wrong for one person to use another person. However ambiguous the expression "using another person" may seem to be, there is a determinate and clearly specifiable sense according to which using another person is morally objectionable. Once this morally significant sense of "using another person" is identified and explicated, the concept of using another person can play an important role in the articulation of a defensible account of sexual morality.

Reprinted from Thomas A. Mappes and Jane Zembaty, eds., *Social Ethics: Morality and Social Policy*, 7th ed. New York: McGraw-Hill, 2007. Pp. 169–183. Reprinted with permission of the author. © 1985 by Thomas A. Mappes.

THE MORALLY SIGNIFICANT SENSE OF "USING ANOTHER PERSON"

Historically, the concept of using another person is associated with the ethical system of Immanuel Kant. According to a fundamental Kantian principle, it is morally wrong for A to use B *merely as a means* (to achieve A's ends). Kant's principle does not rule out A using as a means, only A using B *merely* as a means, that is, in a way incompatible with respect for B as a person. In the ordinary course of life, it is surely unavoidable (and morally unproblematic) that each of us in numerous ways uses others as a means to achieve our various ends. A college teacher uses students as a means to achieve his or her livelihood. A college student uses instructors as a means of gaining knowledge and skills. Such human interactions, presumably based on the voluntary participation of the respective parties, are quite compatible with the idea of respect for persons. But respect for persons entails that each of us recognize the rightful authority of other persons (as rational beings) to conduct their individual lives as they see fit. We may legitimately recruit others to participate in the satisfaction of our personal ends, but they are used merely as a means whenever we undermine the voluntary or informed character of their consent to interact with us in some desired way. A coerces B at knife point to hand over $200. A uses B merely as a means. If A had requested of B a gift of $200, leaving B free to determine whether or not to make that gift, A would have proceeded in a manner compatible with respect for B as a person. C deceptively rolls back the odometer of a car and thereby manipulates D's decision to buy the car. C uses D merely as a means.

On the basis of these considerations, I would suggest that the morally significant sense of "using another person" is best understood by reference to the notion of *voluntary informed consent*. More specifically, A immorally uses B if and only if A intentionally acts in a way that violates the requirement that B's involvement with A's ends be based on B's voluntary informed consent. If this account is correct, using another person (in the morally significant sense) can arise in at least two important ways: via *coercion*, which is antithetical to voluntary consent, and via *deception*, which undermines the informed character of voluntary consent....

DECEPTION AND SEXUAL MORALITY

... I will now apply this account to the area of human sexual interaction and explore its implications. For economy of expression in what follows, "using" (and its cognates) is to be understood as referring only to the morally significant sense.

If we presume a state of affairs in which A desires some form of sexual interaction with B, we can say that this desired form of sexual interaction with B is A's end. Thus A sexually uses if and only if A intentionally acts in a way that violates the requirement that B's sexual interaction with A be based on B's voluntary informed consent. It seems clear then that A may sexually use B in at least two distinctive ways, (1) via coercion and (2) via deception. However, before proceeding to discuss deception and then the more problematic case of coercion, one important point must be made. In emphasizing the centrality of coercion and deception as mechanisms for the sexual using of another person, I have in mind sexual interaction with a fully competent adult partner. We should also want to say, I think, that sexual interaction with a child inescapably involves the sexual using of another person. Even if a child "consents" to sexual interaction, he or she is, strictly speaking, incapable of *informed* consent. It's a matter of being *incompetent* to give consent. Similarly to the extent that a mentally retarded person is rightly considered incompetent, sexual interaction with such a person amounts to the sexual using of that person, unless someone empowered to give "proxy consent" has done so. (In certain circumstances, sexual involvement might be in the best interests of a mentally retarded person.) We can also visualize the case of an otherwise fully competent adult temporarily disordered by drugs or alcohol. To the extent that such a person is rightly regarded as temporarily incompetent, winning his or her "consent" to sexual interaction could culminate in the sexual using of that person.

There are a host of clear cases in which one person sexually uses another precisely because the former employs deception in a way that undermines the informed character of the latter's consent to sexual interaction. Consider this example. One person, A, has decided, as a matter of personal prudence based on past experience, not to become sexually involved outside the confines of a loving relationship. Another person, B, strongly desires a sexual relationship with A but does not love A. B, aware of A's unwillingness to engage in sex without love, professes love for A, thereby hoping to win A's consent to a sexual relationship. B's ploy is successful; A consents. When the smoke clears and A becomes aware of B's deception, it would be both appropriate and natural for A to complain, "I've been used."

In the same vein, here are some other examples. (1) Mr. A is aware that Ms. B will consent to sexual involvement only on the understanding that in time the two will be married. Mr. A has no intention of marrying Ms. B but says that he will. (2) Ms. C has herpes and is well aware that Mr. D will never consent to sex if he knows of her condition. When asked by Mr. D, Ms. C denies that she has herpes. (3) Mr. E knows that Ms. F will not consent to sexual intercourse in the absence of responsible birth control measures. Mr. E tells Ms. F that he has had a vasectomy, which is not the case. (4) Ms. G knows that Mr. H would not consent to sexual involvement with a married woman. Ms. G is married but tells Mr. H that she is single. (5) Ms. I is well aware that Ms. J is interested in a stable lesbian relationship and will not consent to become sexually involved with someone who is bisexual. Ms. I tells Ms. J that she is exclusively homosexual, whereas the truth is that she is bisexual.

If one person's consent to sex is predicated on false beliefs that have been intentionally and deceptively inculcated by one's sexual partner in an effort to win the former's consent, the resulting sexual interaction involves one person sexually using another. In each of the above cases, one person explicitly *lies* to another. False information is intentionally conveyed to win consent to sexual interactions, and the end result is the sexual using of another person.

As noted earlier, however, lying is not the only form of deception. Under certain circumstances, the simple withholding of information can be considered a form of deception. Accordingly, it is possible to sexually use another person not only by (deceptively) lying about relevant facts but also by (deceptively) not disclosing relevant facts. If A has good reason to believe that B would refuse to consent to sexual interaction should B become aware of certain factual information, and if A withholds disclosure of this information in order to enhance the possibility of gaining B's consent, then, if B does consent, A sexually uses B via deception. One example will suffice. Suppose that Mr. A meets Ms. B in a singles bar. Mr. A realizes immediately that Ms. B is the sister of Ms. C, a woman that Mr. A has been sexually involved with for a long time. Mr. A, knowing that it is very unlikely that Ms. B will consent to sexual interaction if she becomes aware of Mr. A's involvement with her sister, decides not to disclose this information. If Ms. B eventually consents to sexual interaction, since her consent is the product of Mr. A's deception, it is rightly thought that she has been sexually used by him.

COERCION AND SEXUAL MORALITY

We have considered the case of deception. The present task is to consider the more difficult case of coercion. Whereas deception functions to undermine the *informed* character of voluntary consent (to sexual interaction), coercion either obliterates consent entirely (the case of occurrent coercion) or undermines the voluntariness of consent (the case of dispositional coercion).

Forcible rape is the most conspicuous, and most brutal, way of sexually using another person via coercion.[1] Forcible rape may involve either occurrent coercion or dispositional coersion. A man who rapes a woman by the employment of sheer physical force, by simply overpowering her, employs occurrent coercion. There is literally no sexual *interaction* in such a case; only the rapist performs an action. In no sense does the woman consent to or participate in sexual activity. She has no choice in what takes place, or rather, physical force results in her choice being simply beside the point. The employment of occurrent coercion for the purpose of rape "objectifies" the victim in the strongest sense of that term. She is treated like a physical object. One does not interact with physical objects; one acts upon them. In a perfectly ordinary (not the morally significant) sense of the term, we "use" physical objects. But when the victim of rape is treated as if she were a physical object, there we have one of the most vivid examples of the immoral using of another person.

Frequently, forcible rape involves not occurrent coercion (or not *only* occurrent coercion) but dispositional coercion.[2] In dispositional coercion, the relevant factor is not physical force but the threat of harm. The rapist threatens his victim with immediate and serious bodily harm. For example, a man threatens to kill or beat a woman if she resists his sexual demands. She "consents," that is, she submits to his demands. He may demand only passive participation (simply not struggling against him) or he may demand some measure of active participation. Rape that employs dispositional coercion is surely just as wrong as rape that employs occurrent coercion, but there is a notable difference in the mechanism by which the rapist uses his victim in the two cases. With occurrent coercion, the victim's consent is entirely bypassed. With dispositional coercion, the victim's consent is not bypassed. It is coerced. Dispositional coercion undermines the *voluntariness* of consent. With occurrent coercion, the victim's consent is entirely bypassed. The rapist, by employing the threat of immediate and serious bodily harm, may succeed in bending the victim's will. He may gain the victim's "consent." But he uses another person precisely because consent is coerced.

The relevance of occurrent coercion is limited to the case of forcible rape. Dispositional coercion, a notion that also plays an indispensable role in an overall account of forcible rape, now becomes our central concern. Although the threat of immediate and serious bodily harm stands out as the most brutal way of coercing consent to sexual interaction, we must not neglect the employment of other kinds of threats to this same end. There are numerous ways in which one person can effectively harm,

and thus effectively threaten, another. Accordingly, for example, consent to sexual interaction might be coerced by threatening to damage someone's reputation. If a person consents to sexual interaction to avoid a threatened harm, then that person has been sexually used (via dispositional coercion). In the face of a threat, of course, it remains possible that a person will refuse to comply with another's sexual demands. It is probably best to describe this sort of situation as a case not of coercion, which entails the *successful* use of threats to gain compliance, but of *attempted* coercion. Of course, the moral fault of an individual emerges with the *attempt* to coerce. A person who attempts murder is morally blameworthy even if the attempt fails. The same is true for someone who fails in an effort to coerce consent to sexual interaction.

Consider now each of the following cases:

Case 1 Mr. Supervisor makes a series of increasingly less subtle sexual overtures to Ms. Employee. These advances are consistently and firmly rejected by Ms. Employee. Eventually, Mr. Supervisor makes it clear that the granting of "sexual favors" is a condition of her continued employment.

Case 2 Ms. Debtor borrowed a substantial sum of money from Mr. Creditor, on the understanding that she would pay it back within one year. In the meantime, Ms. Debtor has become sexually attracted to Mr. Creditor, but he does not share her interest. At the end of the one-year period, Mr. Creditor asks Ms. Debtor to return the money. She says she will be happy to return the money so long as he consents to sexual interaction with her.

Case 3 Mr. Theatergoer has two tickets to the most talked-about play of the season. He is introduced to a woman whom he finds sexually attractive and who shares his interest in the theater. In the course of their conversation, she expresses disappointment that the play everyone is talking about is sold out; she would love to see it. At this point, Mr. Theatergoer suggests that she be his guest at the theater. "Oh, by the way," he says, "I always expect sex from my dates."

Case 4 Ms. Jetsetter is planning a trip to Europe. She has been trying for some time to develop a sexual relationship with a man who has shown little interest in her. She knows, however, that he has always wanted to go to Europe and that it is only lack of money that has deterred him. Ms. Jetsetter proposes that he come along as her traveling companion, all expenses paid, on the express understanding that sex is part of the arrangement.

Cases 1 and 2 involve attempts to sexually use another person whereas cases 3 and 4 do not. To see why this is so, it is essential to introduce a distinction between two kinds of proposals, viz., the distinction between *threats* and *offers*.[3] The logical form of a threat differs from the logical form of an offer in the following way. Threat: "If you *do not* do what I am proposing you do, I will bring about an *undesirable consequence* for you." Offer: "If you *do* what I am proposing you do, I will bring about a *desirable consequence* for you." The person who makes a threat attempts to gain compliance by attaching an undesirable consequence to the alternative of noncompliance. This person attempts to coerce consent. The person who makes an offer attempts to gain compliance by attaching a desirable consequence to the alternative of compliance. This person attempts not to coerce but to *induce* consent.

Since threats are morally problematic in a way that offers are not, it is not uncommon for threats to be advanced in the language of offers. Threats are represented as if they were offers. An armed assailant might say, "I'm going to make you an *offer*. If you give me your money, I will allow you to go on living." Though this proposal on the surface has the logical form of an offer, it is in reality a threat. The underlying sense of the proposal is this: "If you do not give me your money, I will kill you." If, in a given case, it is initially unclear whether a certain proposal is to count as a threat or an offer, ask the following question. Does the proposal in question have the effect of making a person *worse off upon noncompliance*? The recipient of an offer, upon noncompliance, *is not worse off* than he or she was before the offer. In contrast, the recipient of a threat, upon noncompliance, *is worse off* than he or she was before the threat. Since the "offer" of our armed assailant has the effect, upon compliance, of rendering its recipient worse off (relative to the preproposal situation of the recipient), the recipient is faced with a threat, not an offer.

The most obvious way for a coercer to attach an undesirable consequence to the path of noncompliance is by threatening to render the victim of coercion materially worse off than he or she has heretofore been. Thus a person is threatened with loss of life, bodily injury, damage to property, damage to reputation, etc. It is important to realize, however, that a person can also be effectively coerced by being threatened with the withholding of something (in some cases, what we would call a "benefit") to which the person is entitled. Suppose that A is mired in quicksand and is slowly but surely approaching death. When B happens along, A cries out to B for assistance. All B need do is throw A a rope. B is quite willing to accommodate A, "provided you pay me $100,000 over the next ten years." Is B making A an offer? Hardly! B, we must presume, stands under a moral obligation to come to the aid of a person in serious distress, at least when such assistance entails no significant risk, sacrifice of time, etc. A is entitled to B's assistance. Thus, in reality, B attaches an undesirable consequence to A's noncompliance with the proposal that A pay B $100,000. A is undoubtedly better off that B has happened along, but A is not rendered better off *by B's proposal*. Before B's proposal, A was legitimately expected assistance from B, "no strings attached." In attaching a very unwelcome string, B's proposal effectively renders A worse off. What B proposes, then, is not an offer of assistance. Rather, B threatens A with the withholding of something (assistance) that A is entitled to have from B…

With the distinction between threats and offers clearly in view, it now becomes clear why cases 1 and 2 do indeed involve attempts to sexually use another person whereas cases 3 and 4 do not. Cases 1 and 2 embody threats, whereas cases 3 and 4 embody offers. In case 1, Mr. Supervisor proposes sexual interaction with Ms. Employee and, in an effort to gain compliance, threatens her with the loss of her job. Mr. Supervisor thereby attaches an undesirable consequence to one of Ms. Employee's alternatives, the path of noncompliance. Typical of the threat situation, Mr. Supervisor's proposal has the effect of rendering Ms. Employee worse off upon noncompliance. Mr. Supervisor is attempting via (dispositional) coercion to sexually use Ms. Employee. The situation in case 2 is similar. Ms. Debtor, as *she* might be inclined to say, "offers" to pay Mr. Creditor the money she owes him if he consents to sexual interaction with her. In reality, Ms. Debtor is threatening Mr. Creditor, attempting to coerce his consent to sexual interaction, attempting to sexually use him. Though Mr. Creditor is not now in possession of the money Ms. Debtor owes him, he is *entitled* to receive it from her at this time. She threatens to deprive him of something to which he is entitled. Clearly, her proposal has the effect of rendering him worse off upon noncompliance. Before her proposal, he had the legitimate expectation, "no strings attached," of receiving the money in question.

Cases 3 and 4 embody offers; neither involves an attempt to sexually use another person. Mr. Theatergoer simply provides an inducement for the woman he has just met to accept his proposal of sexual interaction. He offers her the opportunity to see the play that everyone is talking about. In attaching a desirable consequence to the alternative of compliance, Mr. Theatergoer in no way threatens or attempts to coerce his potential companion. Typical of the offer situation, his proposal does not have the effect of rendering her worse off upon noncompliance. She now has a new opportunity; if she chooses to forgo this opportunity, she is no worse off. The situation in case 4 is similar. Ms. Jetsetter provides an inducement for a man that she is interested in to accept her proposal of sexual involvement. She offers him the opportunity to see Europe, without expense, as her traveling companion. Before Ms. Jetsetter's proposal, he had no prospect of a European trip. If he chooses to reject her proposal, he is no worse off than he has heretofore been. Ms. Jetsetter's proposal

embodies an offer, not a threat. She cannot be accused of attempting to sexually use her potential traveling companion.

Consider now two further cases, 5 and 6, each of which develops in the following way. Professor Highstatus, a man of high academic accomplishment, is sexually attracted to a student in one of his classes. He is very anxious to secure her consent to sexual interaction. Ms. Student, confused and unsettled by his sexual advances, has begun to practice "avoidance behavior." To the extent that it is possible, she goes out of her way to avoid him.

Case 5 Professor Highstatus tells Ms. Student that, though her work is such as to entitle her to a grade of B in the class, she will be assigned a D unless she consents to sexual interaction.

Case 6 Professor Highstatus tells Ms. Student that, though her work is such as to entitle her to a grade of B, she will be assigned an A if she consents to sexual interaction.

It is clear that case 5 involves an attempt to sexually use another person. Case 6, however, at least at face value, does not. In case 5, Professor Highstatus *threatens* to deprive Ms. Student of the grade she deserves. In case 6, he *offers* to assign her a grade that is higher than she deserves. In case 5, Ms. Student would be worse off upon noncompliance with Professor Highstatus's, proposal. In case 6, she would not be worse off upon noncompliance with his proposal. In saying that case 6 does not involve an attempt to sexually use another person, it is not being asserted that Professor Highstatus is acting in a morally legitimate fashion. In offering a student a higher grade than she deserves, he is guilty of abusing his institutional authority. He is under an obligation to assign the grades that students earn, as defined by the relevant course standards. In case 6, Professor Highstatus is undoubtedly acting in a morally reprehensible way, but in contrast to case 5, where it is fair to say that he both abuses his institutional authority *and* attempts to sexually use another person, we can plausibly say that in case 6 his moral failure is limited to abuse of his institutional authority.

There remains, however, a suspicion that case 6 might after all embody an attempt to sexually use another person. There is no question that the literal content of what Professor Highstatus conveys to Ms. Student has the logical form of an offer and not a threat. Still, is it not the case that Ms. Student may very well feel threatened? Professor Highstatus, in an effort to secure consent to sexual interaction, has announced that he will assign Ms. Student a higher grade than she deserves. Can she really turn him down without substantial risk? Is he not likely to retaliate? If she spurns him, will he not lower her grade or otherwise make it harder for her to succeed in her academic program? He does, after all, have power over her. Will he use it to her detriment? Surely he is not above abusing his institutional authority to achieve his ends; this much is abundantly clear from his willingness to assign a grade higher than a student deserves.

Is Professor Highstatus naive to the threat that Ms. Student may find implicit in the situation? Perhaps. In such a case, if Ms. Student reluctantly consents to sexual interaction, we may be inclined to say that he has *unwittingly* used her. More likely, Professor Highstatus is well aware of the way in which Ms. Student will perceive his proposal. He knows that threats need not be verbally expressed. Indeed, it may even be the case that he consciously exploits his underground reputation. "Everyone knows what happens to the women who reject Professor Highstatus's little offers." To the extent, then, that Professor Highstatus intends to convey a threat in case 6, he is attempting via coercion to sexually use another person....

THE IDEA OF A COERCIVE OFFER

In section III, I have sketched an overall account of sexually using another person *via coercion*. In this section, I will consider the need for modifications or extensions of the suggested account. As before, certain case studies will serve as points of departure.

Case 7 Ms. Starlet, a glamorous, wealthy and highly successful model, wants nothing more than to become a movie superstar. Mr. Moviemogul, a famous producer, is very taken with Ms. Starlet's beauty. He invites her to come to his office for a screen test. After the screen test, Mr. Moviemogul tells Ms. Starlet that he is prepared to make her a star, on the condition that she agree to sexual involvement with him. Ms. Starlet finds Mr. Moviemogul personally repugnant; she is not at all sexually attracted to him. With great reluctance, she agrees to his proposal.

Has Mr. Moviemogul sexually used Ms. Starlet? No. He has made her an offer that she has accepted, however reluctantly. The situation would be quite different if it were plausible to believe that she was, before acceptance of his proposal, *entitled* to his efforts to make her a star. Then we could read case 7 as amounting to his threatening to deprive her of something to which she was entitled. But what conceivable grounds could be found for the claim that Mr. Moviemogul, before Ms. Starlet's acceptance of his proposal, is under an obligation to make her a star? He does not threaten her; he makes her an offer. Even if there are other good grounds for morally condemning his action, it is a mistake to think that he is guilty of coercing consent.

But some would assert that Mr. Moviemogul's offer, on the grounds that it confronts Ms. Starlet with an overwhelming inducement, is simply an exercise of a coercive offer. The more general claim at issue is that offers are coercive precisely inasmuch as they are extremely enticing or seductive. Though there is an important reality associated with the notion of a coercive offer, a reality that must shortly be confronted, we ought not embrace the view that an offer is coercive merely because it is extremely enticing or seductive.... Though it is surely not true that the extremely enticing character of an offer is sufficient to make it coercive, we need not reach the conclusion that no sense can be made out of the notion of a coercive offer. Indeed, there is an important social reality that the notion of a coercive offer appears to capture, and insight into this reality can be gained by simply taking note of the sort of case that most draws us to the language of "coercive offer." Is it not a case in which the recipient of an offer is in circumstances of genuine need, and acceptance of the offer seems to present the only realistic possibility for alleviating the need? Assuming that this sort of case is the heart of the matter, it seems that we cannot avoid introducing some sort of distinction between *genuine needs* and *mere wants*. Though the philosophical difficulties involved in drawing this distinction are not insignificant, I nevertheless claim that we will not achieve any clarity about the notion of a coercive offer, at least in this context, except in reference to it. Whatever puzzlement we may feel with regard to the host of borderline cases that can be advanced, it is nevertheless true, for example, that I *genuinely need* food and that I *merely want* a backyard tennis court. In the same spirit, I think it can be acknowledged by all that Ms. Starlet, though she *wants* very much to be a star, does not in any relevant sense *need* to be a star. Accordingly, there is little plausibility in thinking that Mr. Moviemogul makes her a coercive offer. The following case, in contrast, can more plausibly be thought to embody a coercive offer.

> **Case 8** Mr. Troubled is a young widower who is raising his three children. He lives in a small town and believes that it is important for him to stay there so that his children continue to have the emotional support of other family members. But economic times are tough. Mr. Troubled has been laid off from his job and has not been able to find another. His unemployment benefits have ceased and his relatives are in no position to help him financially. If he is unable to come up with the money for his mortgage payments, he will lose his rather modest house. Ms. Opportunistic lives in the same town. Since shortly after the death of Mr. Troubled's wife, she has consistently made sexual overtures in his direction. Mr. Troubled, for his part, does not care for Ms. Opportunistic and has made it clear to her that he is not interested in sexual involvement with her. She, however, is well aware of his present difficulties. To win his consent to a sexual affair, Ms. Opportunistic offers to make

mortgage payments for Mr. Troubled on a continuing basis.

Is Ms. Opportunistic attempting to sexually use Mr. Troubled? The correct answer is yes, even though we must first accept the conclusion that her proposal embodies an offer and not a threat. If Ms. Opportunistic were threatening Mr. Troubled, her proposal would have the effect of rendering him worse off upon noncompliance. But this is not the case. If he rejects her proposal, his situation will not worsen; he will simply remain, as before, in circumstances of extreme need. It might be objected at this point that Ms. Opportunistic does in fact threaten Mr. Troubled. She threatens to deprive him of something to which he is entitled, namely, the alleviation of a genuine need. But this approach is defensible only if, before acceptance of her proposal, he is entitled to have his needs alleviated *by her*. And whatever Mr. Troubled and his children are entitled to from their society as a whole—they are perhaps slipping through the "social safety net"—it cannot be plausibly maintained that Mr. Troubled is entitled to have his mortgage payments made *by Ms. Opportunistic*.

Yet, though she does not threaten him, she is attempting to sexually use him. How can this conclusion be reconciled with our overall account of sexually using another person? First of all, I want to suggest that nothing hangs on whether or not we decide to call Ms. Opportunistic's offer "coercive." More important than the label "coercive offer" is an appreciation of the social reality that inclines us to consider the label appropriate. The label most forcefully asserts itself when we reflect on what Mr. Troubled is likely to say after accepting the offer. "I really had no choice." "I didn't want to accept her offer but what could I do? I have my children to think about." Both Mr. Troubled and Ms. Starlet (in our previous case) *reluctantly* consented to sexual interaction, but I think it can be agreed that Ms. Starlet had a choice in a way that Mr. Troubled did not. Mr. Troubled's choice was *severely constrained by his needs*, whereas Ms. Starlet's was not. As for Ms. Opportunistic, it seems that we might describe her approach as in some sense exploiting or taking advantage of Mr. Troubled's desperate situation. It is not so much, as we would say in the case of threats, that she coerces him or his consent, but rather that she achieves her aim of winning consent by taking advantage of the fact that he is already "under coercion," that is, his choice is severely constrained by his need. If we choose to describe what has taken place as a "coercive offer," we should remember that Mr. Troubled is "coerced" (constrained) by his own need or perhaps by preexisting factors in his situation rather than by Ms. Opportunistic or her offer.

Since it is not quite right to say that Ms. Opportunistic is attempting to coerce Mr. Troubled, even if we are prepared to embrace the label "coercive offer," we cannot simply say, as we would say in the case of threats, that she is attempting to sexually use him via coercion. The proper account of the way in which Ms. Opportunistic attempts to sexually use Mr. Troubled is somewhat different. Let us say simply that she attempts to sexually use him *by taking advantage of his desperate situation*. The sense behind this distinctive way of sexually using someone is that a person's choice situation can sometimes be subject to such severe prior constraints that the possibility of *voluntary* consent to sexual interaction is precluded. A advances an offer calculated to gain B's reluctant consent to sexual interaction by confronting B, who has no apparent way of alleviating a genuine need, with an opportunity to do so, but makes this opportunity contingent upon consent to sexual interaction. In such a case, should we not say simply that B's need, when coupled with a lack of viable alternatives, results in B being incapable of *voluntarily* accepting A's offer? Thus A, in making an offer which B "cannot refuse," although not

coercing B, nevertheless does intentionally act in a way that violates the requirement that B's sexual interaction with A be based upon B's voluntary informed consent. Thus A sexually uses B.

The central claim of this paper is that A sexually uses B if and only if A intentionally acts in a way that violates the requirement that B's sexual interaction with A be based on B's voluntary informed consent. Clearly, deception and coercion are important mechanisms whereby sexual using takes place. But consideration of case 8 has led us to the identification of yet another mechanism. In summary, then, limiting attention to cases of sexual interaction with a fully competent adult partner, A can sexually use B not only (1) by deceiving B or (2) by coercing B but also (3) by taking advantage of B's desperate situation.

NOTES

1. Statutory rape, sexual relations with a person under the legal age of consent, can also be construed as the sexual using of another person. In contrast to forcible rape, however, statutory rape need not involve coercion. The victim of statutory rape may freely "consent" to sexual interaction but, at least in the eyes of the law, is deemed incompetent to consent.

2. A man wrestles a woman to the ground. She is the victim of occurrent coercion. He threatens to beat her unless she submits to his sexual demands. Now she becomes the victim of dispositional coercion.

3. My account of this distinction largely derives from Robert Nozick, "Coercion," in Sidney Morgenbesser, Patrick Suppes, and Morton White, eds., *Philosophy, Science, and Method* (New York: St. Martin's Press, 1969), pp. 440–472, and from Michael D. Bayles, "Coercive Offers and Public Benefits," *The Personalist* 55, no. 2 (Spring 1974), 139–144.

☙ QUESTIONS FOR ANALYSIS

1. What is the concept of "voluntary informed consent" in sexual relationships? Does it adequately mark out ethical and unethical conduct in those relationships?

2. How does deception destroy the possibility of voluntary informed consent?

3. What is the difference between a threat and an offer? How does it impact voluntary informed consent?

4. What is "dispositional coercion" and "occurrent coercion"?

5. Mappes does not explicitly address marriage, adultery, premarital sex, homosexuality, or masturbation.

Does his Kantian approach provide a useful alternative for analyzing sexual morality? If you find it lacking, what additional ethical principles would you propose for developing an ethical standards for sexual conduct?

6. Is prostitution immoral under Mappes's analytical framework?

Gay Marriage: An American and Feminist Dilemma

ANN FERGUSON

Ann Ferguson is Professor Emerita of Philosophy and Women's Studies at the University of Massachusetts, Amherst, where she taught courses on feminist theory, philosophy of gender and sexuality, and Foucault. She has published numerous articles and several books of feminist philosophy.

In the excerpts below, she examines arguments in support of marriage equality, but she goes on to ask whether feminists should support the tradition of marriage in any form, whether heterosexual or homosexual.

Gay marriage highlights a contradiction in American national identity: if gay marriage is supported, the normative status of the heterosexual nuclear family is undermined, while if not, the civil rights of homosexuals are undermined. This essay discusses the feminist dilemma of whether to support gay marriage to promote these individual civil rights or whether to critique marriage as a part of the patriarchal system that oppresses women.

Marriage is supposed to be the private institution that establishes kinship relations in the family. As such, we should see it as a contract chosen in the private arena. Nonetheless, marriage is regulated by the state, and the campaign to change the requirements of legal marriage to allow gays and lesbians to marry created the greatest controversy among all the public policy questions raised in the last U.S. presidential election. Why are there such hoopla and public scrutiny and dismay over the question of what contracts individuals wish to sign about their sexual, intimate, and economic commitments to each other?

One answer is that the authority of the state and its laws rests on the imaginary identification of each member of society to other members as a part of a national identity. Disagreements about the content of this national identity have been particularly virulent recently as a result of the civil rights movements initiated in the 1960s and 1970s for racial minorities, women, and lesbians, gays, and queers. The right-wing backlash against social justice identity politics has intensified around the gay marriage debate. The national identity, the "American way of life," is portrayed as so dependent on our intimate sexual and reproductive choices that private life must be made a public political issue, and wrong choices here are seen to undermine our national identity. Those supporting right-wing "family values" from the Reagan era forward have perpetuated the fantasy that the patriarchal heterosexual family, where abortion never occurs, is basic for a healthy national identity, and that allowing single motherhood, lesbian and gay marriage, and reproductive choice will

"Gay Marriage: An American and Feminist Dilemma," *Hypatia* vol. 22, No. 1 (winter 2007), 39–57. Copyright 2007.

lead to chaos and disorder that will weaken our nation (Berlant 1997).

But the situation is more complicated: our national identity is both heterosexual-family-oriented and individualistic; so, in this sense, there is a conflict of values that gay marriage brings to the fore. Supporting individualism, U.S. national identity prides itself on civil rights for all adults, including minorities—we are, we proudly remind ourselves, a nation of immigrants—thus we advocate individual freedom and pluralism in the choice of lifestyles. So, one common argument for gay marriage is that government denial of the legal right to gay marriage deprives gays and lesbians of access to the social sanction and status that marriage confers, and hence to full adulthood, rights to familial or joint property and inheritance rights, and full citizenship (Rauch 1997).

As a means to defend individualism in the form of freedom of religion and of values, as well as to prevent religious wars involving attempts to set up a state church, the Bill of Rights of the U.S. Constitution advocates the separation of church and state. Refusing the right to gay marriage because of the so-called sanctity of marriage, a religious concept, would seem to deprive the sexual minority of the freedom to be free to marry if they choose a lifestyle not sanctioned by many religious denominations, and hence imposes the religious view that marriage should be a heterosexual privilege.[1]

Why have modern nation-states like the United States continued to deny lesbians and gays full citizenship in this matter? Feminist legal scholars such as Drucilla Cornell (1998) have argued that one basic function of the family law of modern nation-states contradicts lesbian and gay marriage and family rights, and hence full citizenship. This is that such nations, including the United States, have assumed the prerogative to control biological reproduction through institutionalizing and preserving the patriarchal heterosexual nuclear family. Privileging this institution requires the continued outlawing of gay and lesbian claims to marriage and adoption rights. The issue of gay marriage thus highlights a contradiction in the American national identity: if gay marriage is supported, then the normative status of the heterosexual nuclear family is undermined, while if gay marriage is disallowed, then the individual freedom and civil rights of homosexuals are undermined. Whatever way we resolve it, *if* we can find a way to resolve it, the national identity will have to change. This is what I see as the general American dilemma of gay marriage.

There is also a feminist dilemma concerning gay marriage. On the one hand, feminists have critiqued traditional marriage as part of the institutional system that oppresses women and perpetuates male domination. On the other hand, feminists have supported rights to reproductive choice and sexual freedom. Gay marriage would seem to be a way to support such rights. But in supporting it, feminists seem also to be supporting that very institution, marriage, of which many are still leery because of women's persistent inequality within it. For example, in her critique of marriage, Claudia Card (1997) dwells on the problem battered women have in escaping from abusive marriages due to the persistent social and economic inequalities of women.

My questions about these dilemmas that gay marriage poses are, first, from a perspective defending the civil liberties and rights of sexual minorities: what would it take to redefine our national identity in order to legalize gay marriage? Second, would this be a major step toward civil equality and freedom for lesbians and gays? And, third, should feminists who have challenged the institution of marriage altogether support the legalization of gay marriage, even though doing so would seem to promote an institution that is oppressive to women in general?

I will argue that the national political imaginary can only be reformed to include gay marriage as an option if *other* radical revisions are made to our national identity that move us away from the neo-conservative Right's exclusive focus on the ownership society and toward a caring society. This means that queers, gays and lesbians, and our allies must make coalitions with others to expand the entitlements of the welfare state to include everyone, whether or not they are married, employed, or well off. Second, the reformist gay strategy, to use gay marriage as a wedge for undermining homophobia, is not likely to succeed in many states because of the tenacity of a heteronormative understanding of family as key to the nation's health. The larger feminist and lesbigay political project we embrace must create alliances with heterosexuals and bisexuals to support our own *chosen kinship* relations as a part of a set of *radical democratic family values* in opposition to authoritarian traditional family models. We must expose the contradiction in the *Griswold vs. Connecticut* case, in which the U.S. Supreme Court found that married couples had the right to use birth control, yet still upheld the state's interest in protecting the monogamous, heterosexual family because of its implications for reproduction—in other words, you can have your individual rights in your bedroom, but only if Big Brother is allowed to watch to ensure you are supporting the national imaginary of the heterosexual nuclear family.

PROBLEMS OF CHOSEN KINSHIP

In *Undoing Gender*, Judith Butler defines kinship as "a set of practices that institutes relationships of various kinds which negotiate the reproduction of life and the demands of death" (2004, 102). Based on this definition, kinship practices, she suggests, are "those that emerge to address fundamental forms of human dependency, which may include birth, child rearing, relations of emotional dependency and support, generational ties, illness, dying, and death (to name a few)" (103). Kinship, then, is an ongoing sphere of social life, which the state does not fully regulate. Kinship is important to people's emotional lives even as it has become less central for organizing the economy with the rise of capitalism and the split between public commodity production and the private household (Rubin 1975). Many authors have documented how kinship relations operate outside the state, even though the state divides them into "legitimate" and "illegitimate" forms. Stigmatized and oppressed communities, such as African Americans under slavery,

where master-slave offspring were not accorded legitimacy, developed their own chosen kinship relations, such as common-law marriages and interracial marriages, that the state did not acknowledge. Indeed, in the South, interracial marriages were illegal until 1972. Because of the violence of slavery, its forcible separation of kin, and the later migrations it caused, the African-American community has developed its own forms of socially chosen kinship, such as "othermothers," that is, nonbiological chosen kin roles of communal parenting adopted by close women friends (Collins 2000; Stack 1974). Various forms of godparenting and "*comadre*" kin-like chosen obligations arose in Latin American countries like Mexico and in immigrant communities like Latino, Italian, and Irish communities (Behar 1993). Kath Weston has documented lesbian and gay nonmarital kinship relations through her ethnographies of lesbians and gays. The well-known documentary *Paris is Burning* features African-American "houses" of drag queens and transgendered people, each with their own chosen "mother" of the "tribal" or house "line" (Butler 1993; hooks 1992).

But queer chosen kin networks like those mentioned above only partially protect their members from heterosexual normativity and homophobia. Let me discuss my own experience. I am a bisexual lesbian with an adopted daughter, formerly married to the adoptive father of my daughter. My daughter chose my lesbian partner of many years to be the godmother of my granddaughter when she was born. I think she did this as a way of choosing and acknowledging a kin relation for my partner that she could not (yet) obtain through legal marriage. I was happy for my partner to be given a kin status by my daughter, although "godmother" is not an active category in my secular WASP community. It supported the impetus for my partner to form committed caring relationships with my daughter and granddaughter, and to take on the attendant duties and privileges implied. I also took full advantage of being a grandmother to see my granddaughter every week and often overnight on weekends. My partner, though not living with me, was often present during these weekends, so my granddaughter learned to think of us as a couple.

Last year, my son-in-law, a Muslim in a fundamentalist mosque, discovered that my partner and I are a lesbian couple. He subsequently persuaded my daughter, who converted to Islam on her marriage, that lesbian sexuality is opposed to their religion, and therefore we should not have kin status or grandparent visitation rights. What makes the situation even more ironic is that my son-in-law is only the stepfather of my oldest granddaughter; yet in his chosen kin role, as a patriarch in his religious tradition, he has the heterosexual and masculinist privilege to declare my kin relation to my granddaughter illegitimate, and he has persuaded my daughter that his claims to full parental rights trump any rights that my partner or I formerly had.

Would gay marriage cure this heterosexist deprivation of kin privileges? As of May 17, 2004, we do have gay marriage in Massachusetts, where I live. But it is clear that our legal and social situation vis-à-vis my granddaughter and daughter would not improve if my partner and I were to marry. Grandparents, whether married or not, do not have legal rights to visitation privileges with grandchildren, unless they have been chief custodial parent for a certain length of time.

In this and other cases of queer chosen kinship, no legal changes by themselves to the structure of marriage will remove the stigma of violating the heterosexual normativity required for legitimate kinship. Only a pluralist culture that accepts the sexual rights of those who deviate from the heterosexual norm will do this. My situation used to be quasi-legitimate as an adoptive, married mother and grandmother. It was only "quasi" however because, according to my son-in-law, I was never a "real" mother but only an adoptive one. In any case, my sexuality, now out of the closet, is considered a sin that makes me queer enough to deprive me of those visitation rights I used to have. And my partner, whose chosen kinship status was conveyed on her by the consent of my daughter, has now had that kinship status removed, divorced from her as it

were, without either her or my granddaughter's consent.[2]

THE NATIONAL IDENTITY AND ITS GENDER AND SEXUAL SYMBOLIC

My partner and I and our chosen kin relationships do not fit into the national sexual imaginary of the United States at this time. We are thus the noncitizens, the abject Other that has to be constantly repressed to maintain the national ideal. The national imaginary of the United States, like most other nations in the world, is based on a heterosexual norm of the rights and obligations of its citizens, and this, in turn, is based on the institution of the heterosexual family with its kinship ties legalized by marriage. The heterosexual family is key for two reasons. First, it organizes obligations for the consequences of biological reproduction and creates legitimate kinship. Second, it perpetuates the traditional sexual division of labor in which the father and husband acts as male protector, head of household, and potential citizen soldier, and the mother and wife acts as primary caregiver, nurturer, and wifely dependent protected by and subordinate to the husband and father. In this heterosexual norm and ideal, men are seen as the primary citizens because of their role as citizen soldiers and primary breadwinners, while women are seen as subordinate, or secondary, citizens because they are perceived as the dependent property of the men who protect them. Women thus symbolically best fulfill their obligations to the nation-state by reproducing and mothering children so that the nation has a future generation (Wilton 1995)....

FEMINIST CRITIQUES OF MARRIAGE

Three core values—equality, freedom, and committed caring relationships—are sometimes seen to be in conflict in the debate about gay marriage. Conservatives often paint feminists, lesbians, and gays as selfish individuals who advocate their own equality with men or with heterosexuals, and their own individual freedom, yet who eschew the caring relationships of the traditional heterosexual family. So, one question we need to consider is whether gay marriage is a goal that will co-opt us into supporting an institution, marriage, that will continue to oppress women....

Feminists have attacked the assumptions behind the ideal of the heterosexual, gender-role-differentiated family in several ways. Liberal feminists like Betty Friedan (1963) argued that the male breadwinner/female housewife model of family deprives women of the possibility of equality with men that, in turn, requires their freedom to have a paid career and develop independence from men. Radical feminists argue that women should have the right to choose to remain single, not to become mothers, or to be lesbians—and all of these choices undermine the heterosexual, procreative, gender-differentiated family model, and marriages premised on this model.

Some radical feminists have taken this opposition to the traditional family model further to critique any participation by feminists in marriage at all. Early-twentieth-century radical feminist and socialist/anarchist Emma Goldman wrote in 1910 and 1911 in her essays "The Traffic in Women" and "Marriage and Love" (Goldman 1969) that marriage oppresses women because it is primarily an economic arrangement that makes women dependent on men. Goldman described marriage as only one step up from prostitution: whereas in marriage a woman is only dependent on one man, in prostitution she is dependent on many men. Furthermore, Goldman believed that marriage undermines the conditions for love, which ought to be free of economic constraints and not regulated by the state. She went so far as to argue that free motherhood could only be single motherhood, where a mother's relation to her child is not dependent on a love or economic relation with its father, whether in a free union or in marriage. One can see why conservatives both when she was writing and today, almost one hundred years later, would panic at this position. Indeed, Goldman's positions on marriage, sexuality, and other social issues were so radical for her time that she was ultimately deported from the United States....

In contrast to the radical feminist rejection of marriage as an institution necessarily oppressive to women, many contemporary liberal feminists assume a reform position on marriage; that is, they support the choice to marry on the understanding that women and men can conduct their marriages in nontraditional ways that will eventually undermine patriarchal aspects of the traditional model. A feminist nontraditional marriage minimizes or eliminates gender-differentiated roles in hopes of creating the conditions for gender equality between husband and wife and equal freedom for each partner. A nontraditional marriage can even be an open marriage if both partners agree; that is, each partner has the freedom to engage in nonmonogamous relationships as long as they don't take priority over the central marriage bond. In the ideal feminist heterosexual marriage, both partners share equally in the unpaid work of childcare and domestic labor in the home and both equally are breadwinners, hopefully with chosen careers.

Marriage-reform liberal feminists tend to agree that there is a core truth behind the conservative emphasis on family values: there is great value in the committed, caring relationships marriage can foster, whether or not children are a part of the family. They might even agree that the traditional heterosexual extended and nuclear family kin models have been the key institutions in the past that provided the necessary material basis, kinship networks, and social identification for the caring work and the caring relations they preserve. But they would disagree with conservatives that married heterosexual family and kinship structures are the *only* way to guarantee such caring relations, or that caring relations must be structured by a gender division of labor into caretakers and caregivers. Thus, they would challenge the conservative view that defense of women's and gay rights necessarily undermines committed caring relationships, although it certainly is at odds with the imaginary ideology of the patriarchal and hierarchical daddy-mommy-children family....

In my view, the question before us is not whether the U.S. states that have passed defense of marriage acts which exclude lesbians and gays are correct or whether we should resist the current right-wing agenda to pass an amendment to the U.S. Constitution. I would agree with Drucilla Cornell (1998) that we need to broaden the U.S. political imaginary in a pluralist way that would permit all of us, including lesbians, gays, transgendered, and intersexed persons, the right to represent our sexuate beings (Luce Irigaray initiated the concept of the sexuate being, 1975/1985) in ways that we individually choose. Such a self-representation ought to be able to be expressed by gender and sexual minorities in any institution open to heterosexuals; hence, if marriage continues as an institution of self-representation, lesbians and gays ought to have the right to participate in it.[3]

I would argue that the debate between radical lesbian and marriage reform feminists as to whether to espouse lesbian and gay marriage is based on a false dichotomy: that of reform versus revolution. The "reject marriage for moral revolution" view assumes an essentialist understanding of marriage as an institution with specific social functions, such as organizing and regulating kinship relations and reproduction, perpetuating patriarchy by perpetuating an exploitative sexual division of labor, and upholding a certain sort of heterosexual normativity by stigmatizing nonheterosexual, nonmonogamous relationships.

But marriage is neither an institution with an essential meaning or function, nor an institution that can be reformed in all contexts, so the "reform or revolution" dichotomy is overly simplistic. Rather, whether marriage is reformable in a feminist direction in a particular context depends on the other resources available to women through the legal system, as well as their options in the economic system, and their social and citizen status. As it is presently embedded in these other institutions, marriage can be seen to be *morally risky* (Ferguson 1998). Calling the institution morally risky means that individuals are morally permitted to engage in it through their own choice, but that supporting it or expanding it will not automatically lead to a morally desirable state of affairs, and engaging in it may indeed lead to a worse situation in certain contexts. The point is that the unequal salaries of men and women because of the gender division of wage labor, the second-shift problems of unpaid housework and childcare for working women because of the gendered division of household labor, and the lack of automatic state welfare supports for single mothers in the United States make marriage, whether heterosexual or homosexual, an institution that continues to perpetuate gender inequality and lack of freedom for women.

In sum, marriage today is not what I would call a morally safe or morally basic institution for feminists. It cannot be assumed to promote equality, freedom, and caring among those who engage in it. Nonetheless, we have strong reasons in the present context to think we should not simply reject marriage and hope it withers away, but instead should attempt to reform it as a better way to achieve these feminist goals....

In conclusion, we should defend gay marriage as the formal right to access a basic citizen right that if denied keeps lesbians and gays in the position of abject Other. Marrying for some is a way to confirm social standing for their same-sex bodily desires and relational commitments to a loved other. This should be available as an option in the construction of chosen and free social kinship relations. But we must defend a broader vision of queer relational rights for both straights and gays, centered in an ideal of democratic family and chosen kin relationships free of normative prohibitions by the state.

NOTES

1. Religious advocates of gay marriage believe in a broader scope for marriage as a religious sacrament, and under this auspice, Unitarian and other progressive Protestant denominations have been performing gay marriage ceremonies for years, while being unable to legalize these ceremonies. Gay marriage advocates, whether religious or not, have claimed that there should be no religious litmus test for who is entitled to civil marriage.

2. Two years farther along in this struggle for legitimacy, the intervention of my ninety-four-year-old mother, who argued to my daughter and husband that the grandchildren should be allowed access to their grandmother and partner regularly, has resulted in an uneasy truce in which we can petition for a few hours' visit every month. Such visits

can be granted on whim and only if the children are chaperoned by my daughter to guard against any "improper influence" by us.

3. One of the transformative goals of feminists and lesbigay advocates should be to promote the conditions for autonomy, or self-conscious agency (in this sense of freedom), for everyone, particularly women in relation to men, but also for other oppressed groups, for example, racial minorities in relation to whites, working-class folk in relation to the middle class and the wealthy, and lesbians and gays in relation to heterosexuals. A relational understanding of subjectivity makes it clear that a person's ability to interpret and rearticulate their goals and identity is partially dependent on the social recognition of others through whom their identities are defined (Benjamin 1995; Butler 2004). How one understands one's social identity as a woman depends on how *woman* is defined in relation to *man*. Thus one's freedom to interpret and redefine that identity depends in part on other women and men giving one the acknowledgment and social space to do so. Drucilla Cornell (1998, 8) defends gay marriage and other lesbian and gay rights on the ground that everyone should have the legal and socially recognized right to be accepted as the source of meaning, to frame our own ideal in the imaginary domain of our sexuate being.

REFERENCES

Behar, Ruth. 1993. *Translated woman: Crossing the border with Esperanza's story.* Boston: Beacon.

Benjamin, Jessica. 1995. *Like subjects, love objects: Essays on recognition and sexual difference.* New Haven, Conn.: Yale University Press.

Benston, Margaret. 1969. "The political economy of women's liberation." *Monthly Review* 21 (2).

Berlant, Lauren. 1997. *The Queen of America goes to Washington city: Essays on sex and citizenship.* Durham, N.C.: Duke University Press.

Brown, Wendy. 1997. *States of injury: Power and freedom in late modernity.* Princeton, N.J.: Princeton University Press.

Butler, Judith. 1993. *Bodies that matter: On the discursive limits of "sex."* New York: Routledge.

Butler, Judith. 2004. *Undoing gender.* New York: Routledge.

Card, Claudia. 1997. "Against marriage." *In Same sex,* ed. Corvino.

Collins, Patricia Hill. 2000. *Black feminist thought: Knowledge, consciousness, and the politics of empowerment.* New York: Routledge.

Cornell, Drucilla. 1998. *At the heart of freedom.* Princeton, N.J.: Princeton University Press.

Corvino, John ed. 1997. *Same sex: Debating the ethics, science, and culture of homosexuality.* Lanham, Md.: Rowman & Littlefield.

Dornbush, Sanford, and MyraStrober, eds. 1988. *Feminism, children, and the new families.* New York: Guilford.

Feinberg, Leslie. 1993. *Stone butch blues.* Ithaca, N.Y.: Firebrand.

Ferguson, Ann. 1998. "Prostitution as a morally risky practice." In *Daring to be good: Essays in feminist ethico-politics,* ed. Bat-Ami Bar On and Ann Ferguson. New York: Routledge.

Ferguson, Ann. 2006. "Socialist feminism, cooperatives, and the right to care." In *Beyond global capitalism: Socialist visions of a possible future,* ed. Anatole Anton and Richard Schmitt. Boston: Lexington Press.

Fraser, Nancy. 1997. *Justice interruptus: Critical reflections on the "postsocialist" condition.* New York: Routledge.

Friedan, Betty. 1963. *The feminine mystique.* New York: Dell.

Goldman, Emma. 1969. *Anarchism and other essays.* New York: Dover.

hooks, bell. 1992. "Is Paris burning?" In *Black looks: Race and representation.* Boston: South End.

Irigaray, Luce. 1975/1985. *This sex which is not one.* Trans. Catherine Porter. Ithaca, N.Y.: Cornell University Press.

Lakoff, George. 2004. "What's in a word?" Alternet. http://www.alternet.org/members/story.html StoryID=17876 (accessed February 17, 2004).

Rauch, Jonathan. 1997. "Who needs marriage?" In *Same sex,* ed. Corvino.

Rubin, Gayle. 1975. "The traffic in women." In *Toward an anthropology of women,* ed. Rayna Reiter. New York: Monthly Review Press.

Stack, Carol. 1974. *All our kin.* New York: Harper and Row.

Sullivan, Andrew ed. 2004. *Same-sex marriage pro and con: A reader.* New York: Vintage/Random.

Wardle, Lynn D., Mark Strasser, William C. Duncan, and David Orgon Coolidge, eds. *Marriage and same-sex unions: A debate.* London: Praeger.

Weston, Kath. 1991. *Families we choose.* New York: Columbia University Press.

Wilton, Tamsin. 1995. *Lesbian studies: Setting an agenda.* London: Routledge.

👑 QUESTIONS FOR ANALYSIS

1. What are the tensions in our "national identity" that underlie current debates about gay marriage, according to Ferguson? How is this identity evolving through time and generations? How does that evolution impact national acceptance of marriage equality?

2. What competing rights are at stake in the national debate over marriage equality? How can these disagreements be resolved in the future?

3. What does Ferguson consider to be the "feminist dilemma" with regard to gay marriage?

4. What are "kinship" and "kin networks"? What role do they play in Ferguson's analysis?

5. How do you understand the core values of equality, freedom, and committed caring relationships? Do you consider them in conflict in the debate over marriage equality? In what ways do they conflict?

6. How does Ferguson understand the institution of marriage? What does she propose we do in reconsidering our understanding of the institution?

CASE PRESENTATION

Disease v. Promiscuity?

On June 29, 2006, the Advisory Committee on Immunization Practices (ACIP) of the Centers for Disease Control announced its recommendation that a new vaccine protecting women from the human papillomavirus (HPV) be given routinely to girls aged eleven to twelve years. It noted that the vaccine was most effective before any sexual activity, which might expose girls and women to the virus. They also recommended that girls and women aged thirteen to twenty-six be given the vaccine.

Scientists have long known that two types of HPV cause 70 percent of all cervical cancer, a disease that causes 3700 deaths each year in the United States and is the second leading cause of cancer death of women in the United States. Unlike most cancers, the clear causal link between the virus and the cancer makes this a highly preventable disease with a vaccine against the virus.

It is estimated that at least half of the U.S. adult population has been infected with HPV, the most widespread sexually transmitted disease (STD) in the United States, even though most of those cases will not lead to cervical cancer. Currently, the Pap test provides early-detection testing for adult women, but this test is not readily available to many women, and it detects abnormalities in the cervix after they have already developed. The vaccine would prevent most of those abnormalities from ever developing, but only if the vaccine were administered before any exposure to the virus.

In 2013, researchers at the Oklahoma City Veterans Affairs Medical Center released the results of a study about the prevalence of HPV-caused cancers. They found a significant increase in these cancers from 1978 to 2007, before the release of the new vaccine. The vaccine would prevent about 75 percent of the 27,900 cases of cervical, vulvar, vaginal, anal, penile, and head and neck cancers every year caused by the HPV virus.

The National Organization for Women notes that women's-health advocates have urged that all girls be vaccinated. The organization Advocates for Youth urges that the vaccine be included in all school vaccination programs, with an "opt-out" option for parents who object to the vaccine for their daughters.

However, representatives of the Family Research Council, a conservative Christian advocacy organization, have expressed concern about the message that vaccination would convey to young girls as a license to engage in premarital sex. The FRC urges abstinence until marriage as the best protection against all sexually transmitted diseases. Although it does not officially object to voluntary vaccination, the FRC opposes making the vaccine mandatory by state and local governments or school boards.

The National Vaccine Information Center also opposes the CDC action, stating that the safety of the vaccine has not been satisfactorily demonstrated. The NVIC was founded in 1982 by parents of children who had been injured by various vaccines.

As of 2013, according to the National Conference of State Legislatures, 21 states have enacted legislation either requiring the vaccine for girls or providing funding and education about the importance of the vaccine. Several states and cities now provide free vaccines for all girls under 18. Several additional state legislatures are considering the enactment of similar legislation.

1. Should access to this vaccine be restricted, so as to avoid sending a message to young girls that sex is safe? Should it be available only through private physicians, not public school districts? Should public tax funds be used to pay for this vaccine, when some traditionalists believe it immorally encourages promiscuity?

2. Is vaccination likely to lead to greater promiscuity and to the failure of "abstinence only" education campaigns? Should the government require that everyone receiving the vaccine be urged to practice abstinence as a better form of prevention?

3. Some traditionalists lamented the advent of the birth control pill in the 1960s, maintaining that it removed a strong deterrent to sex outside of marriage—namely, unwanted pregnancies. The advent of incurable and often fatal STDs, such as herpes and HIV/AIDS, led many to restrain their sexual activity for fear of disease, and traditionalists seem to have gathered momentum in this environment for their "abstinence only" message. Although vaccines have not yet been developed for herpes or AIDS, scientists are attempting to develop such vaccines. Would they be likely to encourage more promiscuity, as some fear the HPV vaccine will do? Would it be better for the government to spend more funds on encouragement of abstinence and less on scientific research to develop such vaccines against STDs?

CASE PRESENTATION

Lawrence v. Texas: *Private Rights and Public Morality*

This 2003 U.S. Supreme Court decision overturned the 1986 decision *Bowers v. Hardwick*, which had held that private homosexual conduct among consenting adults was not protected under the U.S. Constitution.

The *Lawrence* decision has assumed increasing importance in recognizing the rights of consenting homosexuals in the continuing debate over marriage equality.

MAJORITY OPINION (WRITTEN BY JUSTICE KENNEDY)

Liberty protects the person from unwarranted government intrusions into a dwelling or other private places. In our tradition the State is not omnipresent in the home. And there are other spheres of our lives and existence, outside the home, where the State should not be a dominant presence. Freedom extends beyond spatial bounds. Liberty presumes an autonomy of self that includes freedom of thought, belief, expression, and certain intimate conduct. The instant case involves liberty of the person both in its spatial and more transcendent dimensions.

The question before the Court is the validity of a Texas statute making it a crime for two persons of the same sex to engage in certain intimate sexual conduct. … The applicable state law … provides: "A person commits an offense if he engages in deviate sexual intercourse with another individual of the same sex."

The statute defines "[d]eviate sexual intercourse" as follows:

"(A) any contact between any part of the genitals of one person and the mouth or anus of another person; or

"(B) the penetration of the genitals or the anus of another person with an object." …

We conclude the case should be resolved by determining whether the petitioners were free as adults to engage in the private conduct in the exercise of their liberty under the Due Process Clause of the Fourteenth Amendment to the Constitution. For this inquiry we deem it necessary to reconsider the Court's holding in *Bowers*.

… The Court began its substantive discussion in *Bowers* as follows: "The issue presented is whether the Federal Constitution confers a fundamental right upon homosexuals to engage in sodomy and hence invalidates the laws of the many States that still make such conduct illegal and have done so for a very long time." … That statement, we now conclude, discloses the Court's own failure to appreciate the extent of the liberty at stake. To say that the issue in *Bowers* was simply the right to engage in certain sexual conduct demeans the claim the individual put forward, just as it would demean a married couple were it to be said marriage is simply about the right to have sexual intercourse. The laws involved in *Bowers* and here are, to be sure, statutes that purport to do no more than prohibit a particular sexual act. Their penalties and purposes, though, have more far-reaching consequences, touching upon the most private human conduct, sexual behavior, and in the most private of places, the home. The statutes do seek to control a personal relationship that, whether or not entitled to formal recognition in the law, is within the liberty of persons to choose without being punished as criminals.

This, as a general rule, should counsel against attempts by the State, or a court, to define the meaning of the relationship or to set its boundaries absent injury to a person or abuse of an institution the law protects. It suffices for us to acknowledge that adults may choose to enter upon this relationship in the confines of their homes and their own private lives and still retain their dignity as free persons. When sexuality finds overt expression in intimate conduct with another person, the conduct can be but one element in a personal bond that is more enduring. The liberty protected by the Constitution allows homosexual persons the right to make this choice.

… It must be acknowledged, of course, that the Court in *Bowers* was making the broader point that for centuries there have been powerful voices to condemn homosexual conduct as immoral. The condemnation has been shaped by religious beliefs, conceptions of right and acceptable behavior, and respect for the traditional family. For many persons these are not trivial concerns but profound and deep convictions accepted as ethical and moral principles to which they aspire and which thus determine the course of their lives. These considerations do not answer the question before us, however. The issue is whether the majority may use the power of the State to enforce these views on the whole society through operation of the criminal law.…

… Equality of treatment and the due process right to demand respect for conduct protected by the substantive guarantee of liberty are linked in important respects, and a decision on the latter point advances both interests. If protected conduct is made criminal and the law which does so remains unexamined for its substantive validity, its stigma might remain even if it were not enforceable as drawn for equal protection reasons. When homosexual conduct is made criminal by the law of the State, that declaration in and of itself is an invitation to subject homosexual persons to discrimination both in the public and in the private spheres. The central holding of *Bowers* has been brought in question by this case, and it should be addressed. Its continuance as precedent demeans the lives of homosexual persons.…

… *Bowers* was not correct when it was decided, and it is not correct today. It ought not to remain binding precedent. *Bowers v. Hardwick* should be and now is overruled.

The present case does not involve minors. It does not involve persons who might be injured or coerced or who are situated in relationships where consent might not easily be refused. It does not involve public conduct or prostitution. It does not involve whether the government must give formal recognition to any relationship that homosexual persons seek to enter. The case does involve two adults who, with full and mutual consent from each other, engaged in sexual practices common to a homosexual lifestyle. The petitioners are entitled to respect for their private lives. The State cannot demean their existence or control their destiny by making their private sexual conduct a crime. Their right to liberty under the Due Process Clause gives them the full right to engage in their conduct without intervention of the government.… The Texas statute furthers no legitimate state interest which can justify its intrusion into the personal and private life of the individual.

Had those who drew and ratified the Due Process Clauses of the Fifth Amendment or the Fourteenth Amendment known the components of liberty in its manifold possibilities, they might have been more specific. They did not presume to have this insight. They knew times can blind us to certain truths and later generations can see that laws once thought necessary and proper in fact serve only to oppress. As the Constitution endures, persons in every generation can invoke its principles in their own search for greater freedom.…

Justice Scalia, dissenting

… The Texas statute undeniably seeks to further the belief of its citizens that certain forms of sexual behavior are "immoral and unacceptable,"… the same interest furthered by criminal laws against fornication, bigamy, adultery, adult incest, bestiality, and obscenity. *Bowers* held that this was a legitimate state interest. The Court today reaches the opposite conclusion. The Texas statute, it says, "furthers no legitimate state interest which can justify its intrusion into the personal and private life of the individual,".… The Court embraces instead Justice Stevens' declaration in his *Bowers* dissent, that "the fact that the governing majority in a State has traditionally viewed a particular practice as immoral is not a sufficient reason for upholding a law prohibiting the practice,".… This effectively decrees the end of all morals legislation. If, as the Court asserts, the promotion of majoritarian sexual morality is not even a legitimate state interest, none of the above-mentioned laws can survive rational-basis review.…

One of the most revealing statements in today's opinion is the Court's grim warning that the criminalization of homosexual conduct is "an invitation to subject homosexual persons to discrimination both in the public and in the private spheres." … It is clear from this that the Court has taken sides in the culture war, departing from its role of assuring, as neutral observer, that the democratic rules of engagement are observed. Many Americans do not want persons who openly engage in homosexual conduct as partners in their business, as scoutmasters for their children, as teachers in their children's schools, or as boarders in their home. They view this as protecting themselves and their families from a lifestyle that they believe to be immoral and destructive. The Court views it as "discrimination" which it is the function of our judgments to deter….

One of the benefits of leaving regulation of this matter to the people rather than to the courts is that the people, unlike judges, need not carry things to their logical conclusion. The people may feel that their disapprobation of homosexual conduct is strong enough to disallow homosexual marriage, but not strong enough to criminalize private homosexual acts—and may legislate accordingly. The Court today pretends that it possesses a similar freedom of action, so that we need not fear judicial imposition of homosexual marriage, as has recently occurred in Canada (in a decision that the Canadian Government has chosen not to appeal).… At the end of its opinion—after having laid waste the foundations of our rational-basis jurisprudence—the Court says that the present case "does not involve whether the government must give formal recognition to any relationship that homosexual persons seek to enter." … Do not believe it.… Today's opinion dismantles the structure of constitutional law that has permitted a distinction to be made between heterosexual and homosexual unions, insofar as formal recognition in marriage is concerned. If moral disapprobation of homosexual conduct is "no legitimate state interest" for purposes of proscribing that conduct,…; and if, as the Court coos (casting aside all pretense of neutrality), "[w]hen sexuality finds overt expression in intimate conduct with another person, the conduct can be but one element in a personal bond that is more enduring," …; what justification could there possibly be for denying the benefits of marriage to homosexual couples exercising "[t]he liberty protected by the Constitution,"… Surely not the encouragement of procreation, since the sterile and the elderly are allowed to marry. This case "does not involve" the issue of homosexual marriage only if one entertains the belief that principle and logic have nothing to do with the decisions of this Court. Many will hope that, as the Court comfortingly assures us, this is so.…

⚜ QUESTIONS FOR ANALYSIS

1. Has the majority opinion struck the right balance between the appropriate roles of the law and of private morality? Is there any immoral behavior that should still be illegal, even if society's concerns originated in moral prohibitions?
2. Under the reasoning of the majority opinion here, should the criminal laws on fornication, bigamy, adultery, adult incest, bestiality, and obscenity also be struck down? If not, what considerations can you cite to support the continuation of those laws?
3. Does Justice Scalia engage in "slippery slope" reasoning?
4. Does the majority opinion provide a compelling basis for eventually holding that homosexual "marriage" is a constitutional right, despite the court's insistence that it has not? Is Justice Scalia right to be concerned that the reasoning of the majority makes it inevitable that homosexual "marriage" will eventually be found to be a constitutional right?
5. How would the Vatican, Farley, Mappes, and Ferguson, respectively, critique *Lawrence v. Texas*?

CASE PRESENTATION

Goodridge v. Dept. of Public Health: *A Right of Gay Marriage*

In 2004 the Supreme Court of Massachusetts, in a 4–3 decision, held that homosexuals had the same rights under state law to the benefits of marriage as heterosexuals. Although this decision applies only to Massachusetts, its reasoning anticipates many of the arguments presented in other states giving rights of marriage equality to homosexuals.

MAJORITY OPINION (WRITTEN BY CHIEF JUDGE MARSHALL)

Marriage is a vital social institution. The exclusive commitment of two individuals to each other nurtures love and mutual support; it brings stability to our society. For those who choose to marry, and for their children, marriage provides an abundance of legal, financial, and social benefits. In return it imposes weighty legal, financial, and social obligations. The question before us is whether, consistent with the Massachusetts Constitution, the Commonwealth may deny the protections, benefits, and obligations conferred by civil marriage to two individuals of the same sex who wish to marry. We conclude that it may not. The Massachusetts Constitution affirms the dignity and equality of all individuals. It forbids the creation of second-class citizens. In reaching our conclusion we have given full deference to the arguments made by the Commonwealth. But it has failed to identify any constitutionally adequate reason for denying civil marriage to same-sex couples.

We are mindful that our decision marks a change in the history of our marriage law. Many people hold deep-seated religious, moral, and ethical convictions that marriage should be limited to the union of one man and one woman, and that homosexual conduct is immoral. Many hold equally strong religious, moral, and ethical convictions that same-sex couples are entitled to be married, and that homosexual persons should be treated no differently than their heterosexual neighbors. Neither view answers the question before us. Our concern is with the Massachusetts Constitution as a charter of governance for every person properly within its reach....

Whether the Commonwealth may use its formidable regulatory authority to bar same-sex couples from civil marriage is a question not previously addressed by a Massachusetts appellate court. It is a question the United States Supreme Court left open as a matter of Federal law in Lawrence ... where it was not an issue. ... The Massachusetts Constitution is, if anything, more protective of individual liberty and equality than the Federal Constitution; it may demand broader protection for fundamental rights; and it is less tolerant of government intrusion into the protected spheres of private life.

Barred access to the protections, benefits, and obligations of civil marriage, a person who enters into an intimate, exclusive union with another of the same sex is arbitrarily deprived of membership in one of our community's most rewarding and cherished institutions. That exclusion is incompatible with the constitutional

principles of respect for individual autonomy and equality under law....

The plaintiffs include business executives, lawyers, an investment banker, educators, therapists, and a computer engineer. Many are active in church, community, and school groups. They have employed such legal means as are available to them—for example, joint adoption, powers of attorney, and joint ownership of real property—to secure aspects of their relationships. Each plaintiff attests a desire to marry his or her partner in order to affirm publicly their commitment to each other and to secure the legal protections and benefits afforded to married couples and their children....

The plaintiffs' claim that the marriage restriction violates the Massachusetts Constitution can be analyzed in two ways. Does it offend the Constitution's guarantees of equality before the law? Or do the liberty and due process provisions of the Massachusetts Constitution secure the plaintiffs' right to marry their chosen partner? In matters implicating marriage, family life, and the upbringing of children, the two constitutional concepts frequently overlap, as they do here....

We begin by considering the nature of civil marriage itself. Simply put, the government creates civil marriage. In Massachusetts, civil marriage is, and since pre-Colonial days has been, precisely what its name implies: a wholly secular institution.... No religious ceremony has ever been required to validate a Massachusetts marriage....

Without the right to marry—or more properly, the right to choose to marry—one is excluded from the full range of human experience and denied full protection of the laws for one's "avowed commitment to an intimate and lasting human relationship." ... Because civil marriage is central to the lives of individuals and the welfare of the community, our laws assiduously protect the individual's right to marry against undue government incursion....

For decades, indeed centuries, in much of this country (including Massachusetts) no lawful marriage was possible between white and black Americans. That long history availed not when the Supreme Court of California held in 1948 that a legislative prohibition against interracial marriage violated the due process and equality guarantees of the Fourteenth Amendment, ... or when, nineteen years later, the United States Supreme Court also held that a statutory bar to interracial marriage violated the Fourteenth Amendment.... As both [decisions] make clear, the right to marry means little if it does not include the right to marry the person of one's choice, subject to appropriate government restrictions in the interests of public health, safety, and welfare....

The individual liberty and equality safeguards of the Massachusetts Constitution protect both "freedom from" unwarranted government intrusion into protected spheres of life and "freedom to" partake in benefits created by the State for the common good…. Both freedoms are involved here. Whether and whom to marry, how to express sexual intimacy, and whether and how to establish a family—these are among the most basic of every individual's liberty and due process rights…. And central to personal freedom and security is the assurance that the laws will apply equally to persons in similar situations…. The liberty interest in choosing whether and whom to marry would be hollow if the Commonwealth could, without sufficient justification, foreclose an individual from freely choosing the person with whom to share an exclusive commitment in the unique institution of civil marriage….

Our laws of civil marriage do not privilege procreative heterosexual intercourse between married people above every other form of adult intimacy and every other means of creating a family…. Fertility is not a condition of marriage, nor is it grounds for divorce. People who have never consummated their marriage, and never plan to, may be and stay married…. People who cannot stir from their deathbed may marry…. While it is certainly true that many, perhaps most, married couples have children together (assisted or unassisted), it is the exclusive and permanent commitment of the marriage partners to one another, not the begetting of children, that is the *sine qua non* of civil marriage….

No one disputes that the plaintiff couples are families, that many are parents, and that the children they are raising, like all children, need and should have the fullest opportunity to grow up in a secure, protected family unit. Similarly, no one disputes that, under the rubric of marriage, the State provides a cornucopia of substantial benefits to married parents and their children….

In this case, we are confronted with an entire, sizeable class of parents raising children who have absolutely no access to civil marriage and its protections because they are forbidden from procuring a marriage license. It cannot be rational under our laws, and indeed it is not permitted, to penalize children by depriving them of State benefits because the State disapproves of their parents' sexual orientation….

An absolute statutory ban on same-sex marriage bears no rational relationship to the goal of economy. First, the department's conclusory generalization—that same-sex couples are less financially dependent on each other than opposite-sex couples—ignores that many same-sex couples, such as many of the plaintiffs in this case, have children and other dependents (here, aged parents) in their care. The department does not contend, nor could it, that these dependents are less needy or deserving than the dependents of married couples. Second, Massachusetts marriage laws do not condition receipt of public and private financial benefits to married individuals on a demonstration of financial dependence on each other; the benefits are available to married couples regardless of whether they mingle their finances or actually depend on each other for support….

We also reject the argument suggested by the department, and elaborated by some amici, that expanding the institution of civil marriage in Massachusetts to include same-sex couples will lead to interstate conflict. We would not presume to dictate how another State should respond to today's decision. But neither should considerations of comity prevent us from according Massachusetts residents the full measure of protection available under the Massachusetts Constitution. The genius of our Federal system is that each State's Constitution has vitality specific to its own traditions, and that, subject to the minimum requirements of the Fourteenth Amendment, each State is free to address difficult issues of individual liberty in the manner its own Constitution demands….

Here, no one argues that striking down the marriage laws is an appropriate form of relief. Eliminating civil marriage would be wholly inconsistent with the Legislature's deep commitment to fostering stable families and would dismantle a vital organizing principle of our society….

We construe civil marriage to mean the voluntary union of two persons as spouses, to the exclusion of all others. This reformulation redresses the plaintiffs' constitutional injury and furthers the aim of marriage to promote stable, exclusive relationships. It advances the two legitimate State interests the department has identified: providing a stable setting for child rearing and conserving State resources. It leaves intact the Legislature's broad discretion to regulate marriage….

We declare that barring an individual from the protections, benefits, and obligations of civil marriage solely because that person would marry a person of the same sex violates the Massachusetts Constitution….

* * *

Recognition of marriage equality has moved rapidly since the *Goodman* decision. As of June 2013, twelve states and the District of Columbia permit same-sex marriage, either due to legislation or state court decisions. The U.S. Supreme Court issued two important decisions in June 2013, but neither recognized marriage equality as a right under the Federal constitution. Groups opposed to same-sex marriage promise to again introduce an amendment to the Federal constitution that would ban it, but this has been introduced in the past and has never achieved the necessary two-thirds majority of both the House and the Senate. Groups supporting same-sex marriage hope that the Supreme Court will some day recognize this as a Federal right under the Constitution, protected by Equal Protection and Due Process, as they once recognized a right to interracial marriage. But it is likely that such a decision, should it ever be issued, will be several years in the future.

Even so, the two 2013 decisions have been hailed by civil rights activists as very important decisions. *United States v. Windsor* struck down as unconstitutional the Federal "Defense of Marriage Act" (DOMA), which Congress had passed in 1996. DOMA said that in all Federal laws and regulations, only marriages between one man and one woman would be recognized. This restriction impacted over 1000 Federal laws in which marital status was relevant, from Social Security benefits to Federal estate and personal income taxes, even when a state government had established the same-sex marriage. In striking down this provision, Justice Kennedy, writing for the 5-4 majority, said:

> The liberty protected by the Fifth Amendment's Due Process Clause contains within it the prohibition against denying to any person the equal protection of the laws.... While the Fifth Amendment itself withdraws from Government the power to degrade or demean in the way this law does, the equal protection guarantee of the Fourteenth Amendment makes that Fifth Amendment right all the more specific and all the better understood and preserved.

> The class to which DOMA directs its restrictions and restraints are those persons who are joined in same-sex marriages made lawful by the State. DOMA singles out a class of persons deemed by a State entitled to recognition and protection to enhance their own liberty. It imposes a disability on the class by refusing to acknowledge a status the State finds to be dignified and proper. DOMA instructs all federal officials, and indeed all persons with whom same-sex couples interact, including their own children, that their marriage is less worthy than the marriages of others. The federal statute is invalid, for no legitimate purpose overcomes the purpose and effect to disparage and to injure those whom the State, by its marriage laws, sought to protect in personhood and dignity. By seeking to displace this protection and treating those persons as living in marriages less respected than others, the federal statute is in violation of the Fifth Amendment. This opinion and its holding are confined to those lawful marriages.

This federal recognition only applies to those states which recognize same-sex marriage. Further, the Court left in place another provision of DOMA which says that no state is required to recognize the same-sex marriages of another state.

In another decision in June 2013, the Court let stand a decision of a Federal district court which struck down California's so-called "Prop 8." Like DOMA, Prop 8 had said that only marriages between one man and one woman would be recognized by the state. The district court had struck that down on the grounds that it denied equal protection to same-sex marriages. So Prop 8 is now invalidated and same-sex marriage is again permitted in the state of California.

☙ QUESTIONS FOR ANALYSIS

1. Arguments against the morality of homosexuality sometimes appeal to the "unnaturalness" of these relationships. Should the inability of gay or lesbian couples to procreate in the traditional way support a prohibition on their marriage or civil union? How should we determine what counts as "natural" for these purposes?

2. Justice Scalia, in his dissent in *Lawrence*, claimed that decision set the groundwork for claims of a right to homosexual marriage in later decisions. Does the *Goodridge* decision here vindicate his worry? Could an argument for a right to homosexual marriage be made without appealing to the principles of *Lawrence*?

3. Should courts always defer to the moral preferences of the majority? Or do they have an obligation to uphold individual civil liberties, even if the rights claimed are unpopular with the majority?

4. In February 2012, the legislature in New Jersey approved same-sex marriage, but the law was vetoed by Governor Chris Christie. The Governor said that this decision should be decided by all voters in a referendum. Should civil rights always be decided by voters in a referendum? Do you believe a majority of voters would approve of the civil rights important to you, whether interracial marriage, school desegregation, or other issues?

CASE PRESENTATION

A Slippery Slope to Polygamy?

In Justice Scalia's dissent in *Lawrence*, he warned that the majority opinion set the stage for striking down other laws that banned behavior most consider immoral, including bigamy. In the few years since he wrote those words, several legal challenges have been made in Utah to that state's laws prohibiting polygamy, although none has succeeded to date.

The territory of Utah made several unsuccessful attempts to achieve statehood in the nineteenth century, but these attempts were rebuffed, in large measure, because of the practice of polygamy in the Church of Jesus Christ of Latter-Day Saints, the Mormons. LDS doctrine at the time claimed that it was "the duty of male members" of the church to practice polygamy. In 1862, President Abraham Lincoln signed legislation banning bigamy in the territories. The law was upheld in 1879 in a U.S. Supreme Court decision, *Reynolds v. United States*, a decision that has never been overturned. That Court said that a right of religious freedom in the First Amendment to the Constitution did not invalidate the ban on bigamy. The Court noted that polygamy had long been considered an "odious" practice in the Western world, although it was accepted in some areas of Asia and Africa. It also noted approvingly an argument that the real "innocent victims" of polygamy are the "pure-minded women" and "innocent children" who are the "sufferers" of this practice.

Utah finally achieved statehood in 1896, but only after including a ban on polygamy in its state constitution and a policy change by the Mormon church that it no longer advocated polygamy. But even today, break-away groups claiming allegiance to the original Mormon teaching practice polygamy in Utah and other western states. In 2004, a trio sued in Federal court, claiming their rights were violated when the Salt Lake County Clerk denied them a marriage license. The case was dismissed, noting that the *Lawrence* decision protected, at most, the private sexual practices of consenting adults but did not require the state to issue a marriage license. Another case was brought in the Utah State Supreme Court in 2006 challenging the state law prohibiting polygamy and arguing that the *Lawrence* decision should be considered precedent for a liberty right to engage in polygamy.

In March 2006, HBO launched an original series called "Big Love," in which a fictional Salt Lake City businessman in contemporary Utah is a polygamist with three wives. The show includes a disclaimer: "According to a joint report issued by the Utah and Arizona attorney generals' offices, July 2005, 'Approximately 20,000 to 40,000 or more people currently practice polygamy in the United States.' The Mormon Church officially banned the practice of polygamy in 1890." News reports at the time of the premiere indicated considerable concern in Utah that the series would revive old stereotypes about their Church. An anti-polygamy group called "Tapestry Against Polygamy" has argued that the practice exploits women and children, and it helps women in such illegal marriages to escape.

👑 QUESTIONS FOR ANALYSIS

1. Does the reasoning of the Massachusetts Supreme Court granting a right of gay marriage also support a right to polygamous marriage?
2. Can gay marriage be distinguished from polygamous marriage in analyzing human rights to liberty and privacy?
3. Is it possible for women to freely consent to a polygamous marriage with one man? Are women and children the victims of these arrangements, as the *Reynolds* court said over a century ago?
4. Would you support polygamous marriage if both men and women had an equal right to multiple spouses?
5. Is polygamous marriage any more or less "natural" than homosexual marriage? What do you understand "natural" to mean for these purposes?

CHAPTER FOUR

Abortion

- **Biological Background**
- **The Moral Problem**
- **The Ontological Status of the Fetus**
- **The Moral Status of the Fetus**
- **Pro-Life Arguments (against Abortion)**
- **Pro-Choice Arguments (for Abortion)**

DONALD MARQUIS **Why Abortion Is Immoral**

JUDITH JARVIS THOMSON **A Defense of Abortion**

MARY ANNE WARREN **On the Moral and Legal Status of Abortion**

BERTHA ALVAREZ MANNINEN **Expanding the Discussion about Fetal Life within Prochoice Advocacy**

CASE PRESENTATIONS: • *Conceived in Violence, Born in Hate* • *Death in Pensacola* • *The Fight for Martina Greywind's Baby* • *Sex Selection Abortions*

JANE ROE WAS an unmarried pregnant woman who wished to have an abortion, an intentional termination of a pregnancy by inducing the loss of the fetus. But Ms. Roe lived in Texas, where statutes forbade abortion except to save the life of the mother. So she went to court to prove that the statutes were unconstitutional.

The three-judge district court ruled that Jane Roe had reason to sue, that the Texas criminal abortion statutes were void on their face, and most important, that the right to choose whether to have children was protected by the right to privacy implicit in several amendments to the U.S. Constitution. Even though the word "privacy" does not appear in the Constitution, the court reasoned that privacy rights they had earlier recognized to use contraception and to permit interracial marriage extended to a right to choose whether or not to have children. Since the district court denied a number of other aspects of the suit, the case went to the U.S. Supreme Court. On January 22, 1973, in the now famous *Roe v. Wade* decision (410 U.S. 113), the Supreme Court affirmed the district court's judgment.

Expressing the views of seven members of the Court, Justice Blackmun pointed out that the right to privacy applies to a woman's decision on whether to terminate her pregnancy but that her right to terminate is not absolute. Her right may be limited by the state's legitimate interests in safeguarding the woman's health, in maintaining proper medical standards, and in protecting human life. Blackmun went on to point out that fetuses are not included within the definition of *person* as used in the Fourteenth Amendment. Most important, he indicated that prior to the end of the first trimester of pregnancy, the state may not interfere with or regulate an attending physician's decision, reached in consultation with the patient, that the patient's pregnancy should be terminated. After the first trimester and until the fetus is viable, the state may regulate the abortion procedure only for the health of the mother. After the fetus becomes viable, the state may prohibit all abortions except those necessary to preserve the health or life of the mother.

In dissenting, Justices White and Rehnquist said that nothing in the language or history of the U.S. Constitution supported the Court's judgment and that the Court had simply manufactured a new constitutional right for pregnant women. The abortion issue, they said, should have been left with the people and the political processes they had devised to govern their affairs.

So for the time being at least, the question of a woman's constitutional right to an abortion has been legally resolved. But the issue is hardly settled. Since the *Roe* decision, a number of anti-abortion movements have surfaced, and many state legislatures have passed restrictive abortion laws, some designed to narrow abortion rights and discourage abortions, others designed to challenge *Roe v. Wade* in the courts in the hope that it will be overturned.

In an important case decided July 3, 1989, *Webster v. Reproductive Health Services* (492 U.S. 490), the U.S. Supreme Court upheld a Missouri law that declared in its preamble that the "life of each human being begins at conception." The Court considered this statement to be only a "value judgment favoring childbirth over abortion" and said they would not rule on its constitutionality or unconstitutionality. The law also requires physicians to conduct viability tests on the fetuses of women twenty weeks pregnant and prohibits the use of public funds, employees, and facilities to perform, assist, or counsel abortions not necessary to save the mother's life. Moreover, four justices indicated a willingness to overturn the *Roe* decision. Since then, the Court has upheld state laws requiring parental consent for abortions on minors.

The Court's most significant decision on abortion since *Webster* was *Planned Parenthood v. Casey* (505 U.S. 833), announced June 29, 1992. The issue in this case was a Pennsylvania law regulating abortions. The Court again upheld the right to abortion by a 5–4 majority, citing this as a fundamental "liberty" right, a word that does appear in the Constitution, even though the word "privacy" does not. It also upheld two of the law's restrictions. The first requires a twenty-four hour waiting period following a mandatory presentation intended to dissuade the woman from having an abortion. The second requires teenagers to have the consent of a parent or a judge. Also upheld were two other provisions: one specifying medical emergencies that exempt a woman from the restrictions, the other requiring clinics and doctors to provide the state with statistical reports on abortions performed. One other requirement, that married women first tell their husbands, was struck down as placing an "undue burden" on them.

Also significant was the Court's *Stenberg v. Carhart* decision (530 U.S. 914), announced June 28, 2000. At issue was a Nebraska law banning in all circumstances except to save the woman's life a rare but highly controversial abortion technique called *evacuation and extraction* (D&X). The law did not use that term, however. Instead, it referred to the procedure with the term commonly used by abortion opponents, "partial birth abortion," which the law defined as "deliberately and intentionally delivering into the vagina a living unborn child, or a substantial portion thereof, for the purpose of performing a procedure that the person performing such procedure knows will kill the unborn child." The majority opinion cited two chief reasons for declaring the law unconstitutional. First, the law allowed no exception to preserve the woman's health. Second, the law's definition of "partial birth abortion" was broad enough to cover another abortion procedure, the one most commonly used in the second trimester (*dilation and evacuation*, or D&E). In doing so, it placed an "undue burden on a woman's right to terminate her pregnancy before viability."

Three years after this decision, the U.S. Congress passed, and President George W. Bush signed into law, a Federal ban very similar to the Nebraska ban struck down in the *Carhart* decision. This Federal law was upheld on April 18, 2007, in a 5–4 decision by the U.S. Supreme Court in *Gonzalez v. Carhart* (550 U.S. 124), even though it does not include a health exception for the mother. The Court reasoned that the law bans only one procedure, which is not medically necessary.

Although these decisions focused on late-term abortions, this type of abortion, according to the Guttmacher Institute, constitutes only 1.2 percent of the actual number of abortions in this country. Sixty-two percent of abortions occur earlier than nine weeks and 88 percent occur in the first twelve weeks of pregnancy.

In the next section, we will explain these and other abortion procedures. For now, it's enough to say that abortion opponents are drafting new laws prohibiting D&X that are designed to withstand the Court's objections. We should also stress that the fight to overturn *Roe v. Wade*, whether through a constitutional amendment or sympathetic appointments to the Supreme Court, continues, as do efforts in state legislatures to shut down abortion clinics. Thus, abortion remains a live and controversial issue, both morally and legally.

Some say an abortion is right if (1) it is therapeutic—that is, if it is necessary to preserve the physical or mental health of the woman; (2) it prevents the birth of a child with a severe disability; or (3) it ends a pregnancy resulting from some criminal act of sexual intercourse, most notably, rape or incest. Others say that all abortions are immoral, even to save the life of the mother. Even among the strongest pro-choice supporters, virtually no one argues that abortion should be permitted in the last trimester for no reason at all.

It also should be noted that some people believe that abortion is morally wrong, but that it should be legal so others can make that moral choice for themselves. To evaluate such claims, it is helpful to know some biological background and to consider what sort of entities the unborn are and whether they have rights.

BIOLOGICAL BACKGROUND

Because most of the controversy surrounding the abortion issue concerns precisely when a human individual or "person" is considered to exist, it is important to have some background about the development of the human fetus and familiarity with the terms that designate the various developmental stages. Conception or fertilization occurs when a female germ cell, or *ovum*, is penetrated by a male germ cell, or *spermatozoon*. The result is a single cell containing a full genetic code of forty-six chromosomes, called the *zygote*. The zygote then journeys down the fallopian tube, which carries ova from the ovary to the uterus. This passage generally takes two or three days. During the journey, the zygote begins a process of cellular division that increases its size. Occasionally, the zygote ends its journey in the fallopian tube, where it continues to develop. Because the tube is so narrow, such a pregnancy generally must be terminated by surgery.

When the multicell zygote reaches the uterus, it floats free in the intrauterine fluid and develops into what is termed a *blastocyst*, a ball of cells surrounding a fluid-filled cavity. By the end of the second week, the blastocyst implants itself in the uterine wall. From the end of the second week until the end of the eighth week, the unborn entity is termed an *embryo*. In the interim (four to five weeks), organ systems begin to develop, and the embryo takes on distinctly human external features.

The eighth week is important in the biological development and in a discussion of abortion because it is then that brain activity generally becomes detectable. From this point until birth, the embryo is termed a *fetus*, although in common parlance *fetus* is used to designate the unborn entity at whatever stage.

Two other terms that designate events in fetal development are worth noting because they sometimes arise in abortion discussions. One is *quickening*, which refers to when the mother begins to feel the movements of the fetus. This occurs somewhere between the thirteenth and twentieth weeks. The second term is *viability*, the point at which the fetus is capable of surviving outside the womb. The fetus ordinarily reaches viability around the twenty-fourth week. Generally, then, events during pregnancy unfold as follows:

Developmental Timetable

zygote: first through third day

blastocyst: second day through second week

embryo: third week through eighth week

fetus: ninth week until birth

quickening: thirteenth week through twentieth week

viability: around twenty-fourth week

Should the unborn entity be terminated at any point in this timetable, an abortion is said to occur. Thus, *abortion simply refers to the termination of a pregnancy.*

Abortions can happen for a number of reasons. Sometimes the abortion occurs "spontaneously" because of internal biochemical factors or because of an injury to the woman. Such spontaneous abortions are ordinarily termed *miscarriages.* These generally involve no moral issues.

Abortions also can result directly from human intervention, which can occur in a variety of ways. Sometimes it happens very early, as when a woman takes a drug such as the "morning-after pill" to prevent the blastocyst from implanting in the uterine wall.

Subsequent intervention during the first trimester (through the twelfth week) usually takes the form of *vacuum aspiration*. In this procedure, the narrow opening of the uterus, the cervix, is dilated, and a small vacuum tube is inserted into the uterus to evacuate its contents through suction.

The most common abortion procedure after the twelfth week is dilation and evacuation. This procedure also involves dilation of the cervix, but the doctor uses surgical instruments, rather than a vacuum tube, to empty the uterus. How this procedure is performed depends on how advanced the pregnancy is. Up to week fifteen, fetal tissue is easily broken, so a spoon-shaped instrument known as a curette is used to scrape the uterine walls to make sure that no fetal tissue remains. After week fifteen, the fetus is generally too large to pass through the cervix, and its bones, having become more rigid, are less likely to break off. In that case, the evacuation requires that the fetus be dismembered after it has been partially pulled through the cervix.

After week sixteen, at the earliest, two other variants of D&E may be used. In the first, known as *intact D&E*, the skull of the fetus is collapsed by a sharp instrument before the entire fetus is pulled through the cervix. In the second, the position of the fetus is reversed to the breech position (feet first) and the skull is collapsed after the fetal body is pulled through the cervix. This procedure, dilation and extraction, was the one that Nebraska attempted to ban.

Before the widespread use of D&E in second trimester abortions, the most common method in use was *saline injection*, in which salt water is injected into the uterus to induce a miscarriage. The change to D&E came about because it is safer for the woman's health. Similarly, intact D&E is considered safer after the sixteenth week of pregnancy, and in a few rare cases—although there is some dispute among doctors— D&X is considered even safer.

Finally, there is one other form of abortion to consider, *mifepristone*, or RU-486, the abortion pill. Mifepristone works by blocking the action of progesterone, a steroid hormone needed to maintain a pregnancy. Approved first by France and China in 1988, and by thirteen other countries since, it did not receive approval in the United States until September 28, 2000, when the Food and Drug Administration (FDA) declared it safe and effective. Abortion by mifepristone is a three-step process. First, the woman takes the drug in her doctor's office. Second, she returns within thirty-six or forty-eight hours to take another drug, misoprostal, which forces the uterus to contract and expel the fetus. Third, she returns to the doctor's office two weeks later to make sure the pregnancy is terminated and her uterus is free of the fetal tissue.

In approving mifepristone, the FDA issued a number of restrictions. Most important, the drug cannot be used after the seventh week following the woman's last menstrual period. As 62 percent of all abortions are performed before the ninth week, this method is potentially very significant in reducing the need for surgical abortions. Plan B, the "morning after" emergency contraception, is not an abortion. It is now available without a prescription. The medical advisory panel at the Food and Drug Administration concluded that it could be taken with minimal risk, far less than the risk of an unwanted pregnancy or abortion.

THE MORAL PROBLEM

The key moral problem of abortion is: Under what conditions, if any, is abortion morally justifiable? In answer to this question, three positions are broadly identifiable.

(1) The so-called conservative view holds that abortion is never morally justifiable or, at most, justifiable only when the abortion is necessary to save the mother's life. This view is commonly associated with Roman Catholics, although they are certainly not the only persons who espouse it. (2) The so-called liberal view holds that abortion is always morally justifiable, regardless of the reasons or the time in fetal development, although it is rare to find persons who support third-semester abortions unless the life or health of the mother is in danger. (3) The so-called intermediate or moderate views consider abortion morally acceptable up to a certain point in fetal development and/or claim that some reasons, not all, provide a sufficient justification for abortion.

While there is no consensus on the moral acceptability of abortion, there is agreement that any answer to the question depends on one's view of what sort of entities fetuses are and whether such entities have rights. These two important problems generally are referred to as the ontological and moral status of the fetus.

THE ONTOLOGICAL STATUS OF THE FETUS

In philosophy, the term **ontology** refers to the theory and nature of being and existence. When we speak of the **ontological** status of the fetus, we mean the kind of entity the fetus is. Determining the ontological status of fetuses bears directly on the issue of fetal rights and, subsequently, on permissible treatment of the fetus.

Actually, the problem of ontological status embraces a number of questions, such as: (1) whether the fetus is an individual organism; (2) whether the fetus is biologically a human being; (3) whether the fetus is psychologically a human being; (4) whether the fetus is a person.[1] Presumably, to affirm question two is to attribute more significant status to the fetus than to affirm question one, and to affirm question three is to assign even greater status. To affirm question four, that the fetus is a person, probably is to assign the most significant status to the fetus, although this, as well as the other presumptions, depends on the precise meaning of the concepts involved.

Complicating the question of the fetus's ontological status is the meaning of the expression *human life*. The concept of "human life" can be used in at least two different ways. On the one hand, it can refer to *biological* human life—that is, to a set of biological characteristics that distinguish the human species from other nonhuman species. In this sense, "human life" may be coextensive with "individual organism" as in question one. On the other hand, "human life" may refer to *psychological* human life—that is, to life that is characterized by the properties that are distinctly human. Among these properties might be the abilities to use symbols, to think, and to imagine. Abortion discussions can easily founder when these distinctions are not made. For example, many who would agree that abortion involves the taking of human life in the biological sense would deny that it involves taking human life in the psychological sense. Moreover, they might see nothing immoral about taking life exclusively in the biological sense, although they would consider taking life in the psychological sense morally unacceptable. Thus, they find nothing morally objectionable about abortion. Of course, at the root of this judgment is an assumption about the meaning of *human life*.

Intertwined with one's concept of human life is one's concept of "personhood." The concept of personhood may or may not differ from either the biological or the psychological sense of "human life." Some would argue that to be a person is simply to have the biological and/or psychological properties that make an organism human. However, others would propose additional conditions for personhood, such as consciousness, self-consciousness, rationality, even the capacities for communication and moral judgment. In this view, an entity must satisfy some or all of these criteria, even additional ones, to be a person. Still other theorists would extend the concept of personhood to include properties bestowed by human evaluation, in addition to the factual properties possessed by a person. Thus, they might argue that a person must be the bearer of legal rights and social responsibilities, and must be capable of being assigned moral responsibility, of being praised or blamed.

---

[1]Tom L. Beauchamp and Le Roy Waiters, *Contemporary Issues in Bioethics* (Belmont, Calif.: Dickenson, 1978), p. 188.

Clearly, the conditions that one believes are necessary for "person" status directly affect the ontological status of the fetus. For example, if the condition is only of an elementary biological nature, then the fetus can more easily qualify as a person than if the conditions include a list of factual properties. Further, if personhood must be analyzable in terms of properties bestowed by human evaluation, it becomes substantially more difficult for the fetus to qualify as a person. It is worth noting that the U.S. Supreme Court has never stated its view of when "personhood" occurs.

In the final analysis, the ontological status of fetuses remains an open issue. But some viewpoint ultimately underpins any position on the morality of abortion. Whether conservative, liberal, or moderate, one must be prepared eventually to defend one's view of the ontological status of fetuses.

When Ontological Status Is Attained

Further complicating the problem of the ontological status is the question of when in fetal development the fetus gains full ontological status. Whether one claims the fetus is an individual organism, a biological human being, a psychological human being, or a full-fledged person, one must specify at what point in its biological development the fetus attains this status. It is one thing to say what status the fetus has; it is another to say *when* it has attained such status. A judgment about when the fetus has the status bears as directly on abortion views as does a judgment of the status itself.

We can identify a number of positions on when status is attained. An extreme conservative position would argue that the fetus has full ontological status from conception; at the time of conception, the fetus must be regarded as an individual person. In direct contrast to this view is the extreme liberal position, which holds that the fetus never achieves ontological status.

Viewing these as polar positions, we can identify a cluster of moderate views that fall between them. In every instance, the moderate view tries to pinpoint full ontological status somewhere between conception and birth. For example, some draw the line when brain activity is first present; others draw it at quickening; still others draw the line at viability.

Continuing progress in medicine has made these determinations increasingly difficult. With extraordinary medical support, very premature infants can be kept alive, challenging traditional views of what counts as viability. Some believe viability should be measured by an ability to live outside the womb without any medical intervention. Others believe newborn infants meet the test of viability even with the support of incubators, transfusions, and increasingly sophisticated medical assistance.

Medical advances have also challenged our definition of death, the cessation of the life of a person. Where cessation of a heartbeat once counted as death, the advent of heart transplants and mechanical hearts forced a change. Persons are now considered legally dead when all brain wave activity ceases. Some moderate abortion advocates suggest that the start of brain activity in a fetus should be the decisive point at which the fetus becomes a person and thus has the rights of persons. But there is disagreement about the extent of brain activity that would be required for such a test of personhood. And abortion foes say that the potential of a fetus for the development of brain activity—something a deceased person no longer has—makes the end of the life of a person irrelevant for determining the start of the life of a person.

THE MORAL STATUS OF THE FETUS

The issue of moral status of the fetus is generally, but not always, discussed in terms of the fetus's rights. What rights, if any, does it have? Any position on abortion must at some point address this question, and all seriously argued positions do, at least by implication.

Various views on the moral status of the fetus are currently circulating. Each view can be associated with one or another of the views on the fetus's ontological status. For example, claiming that the fetus has full ontological status at conception, the extreme conservative view also holds that it has full moral status at the same stage. From the moment of conception on, the unborn entity enjoys the same rights we attribute to any adult human. In this view, abortion would be a case of denying the unborn the right to life. Therefore, abortion could never be undertaken without reasons sufficient to override the unborn's claim to life. In other words, only conditions that would justify the killing of an adult human—for example, self-defense—would morally justify an abortion.

Liberals similarly derive their view of moral status from their theory of ontological status. The extreme liberal view would deny the fetus any moral status. In this view, abortion is not considered comparable to killing an adult person. Indeed, abortion may be viewed as removing a mass of organic material, not unlike an appendectomy. Its removal raises no serious moral problems. A somewhat less liberal view, while granting the fetus ontological status as being biologically human, claims it is not human in any significant moral sense and thus has no significant rights.

Likewise, moderates would assign moral status to the fetus at the point that the entity attained full ontological status. If brain activity is taken as the point of ontological status, for example, then abortions conducted before that time would not raise serious moral questions; those conducted subsequent to that development would. Currently, viability seems to be an especially popular point at which to assign ontological status. And so, many moderate theorists today insist that abortion raises significant moral questions only *after* the fetus has attained viability. This view is reflected in some of the opinions delivered by the U.S. Supreme Court. As 88 percent of all abortions occur during the first 12 weeks, according to the respected Guttmacher Institute, the precise time a brain becomes functioning or of viability is significant for the moral questions of major concern to such moderates.

It is important to note that granting the fetus moral status does not at all deny moral status to the woman. Indeed, the question of whose rights should take precedence when a conflict develops raises thorny questions, especially for conservatives and moderates. For example, while granting the fetus full moral status, some conservatives nonetheless approve of therapeutic abortions—abortions performed to save the woman's life or to correct some life-threatening condition. These are often viewed as cases of self-defense or justifiable homicide. Since self-defense and justifiable homicide commonly are considered acceptable grounds for killing an adult person, they are also taken as moral justification for killing a fetus. But other conservatives disapprove of even therapeutic abortions.

Similarly, while moderates grant the fetus moral status at some point in development, they too must arbitrate cases of conflicting rights. They must determine just what conditions are sufficient for allowing the woman's right to override the fetus's right to life. Here the whole gamut of conditions involving the pregnancy must be evaluated, including rape, incest, fetal deformity, and of course, physical or psychological harm to the woman.

Moral Implications

Determining the moral status of the fetus, then, is directly related to determining when the fetus is actually a person. There is no question that even at the zygote stage, and from then on, the fetus is at least potentially a person (until it becomes actually so). At whatever point it becomes a person, we face a set of serious moral issues regarding abortion, among which are

1. Does the fetus have a right to be carried to full term?
2. Under what circumstances, if ever, can we take an innocent human life?
3. Is any other right more important than the right to life—for example, the woman's right to privacy and liberty, the woman's right not to be forced to carry a child that will make it impossible for her to have children in the future, or the woman's right not to carry the child of her rapist or her father or brother?
4. If the woman's life is in danger because of the pregnancy, how do we decide whose right prevails?

If, as is the case at present, we can't agree at what point the fetus becomes a person, we're confronted with another set of problems.

1. Can we morally disregard the possibility that the fetus may be actually a person (or may not)? If we do, does that imply, at best, an indifference to an important moral value? And is not such an attitude of not caring about a moral value itself morally questionable at least?
2. Can we ever act morally on a doubt—for example, a doubt about our obligation, the morally relevant facts, the morally correct means? How are we to resolve our doubt?
3. If reasonable people in the country hold irreconcilable moral and religious views on an issue such as abortion, is it appropriate for the government to "take sides" by forcing everyone to accept one of those views, whether through legislation or court decisions?

Abortion has been one of the most polarizing issues in the public arena for many decades. President Barack Obama, in his speech at Notre Dame University on May 17, 2009, summed up the difficulties of ever reaching a resolution acceptable to most Americans.

> … As citizens of a vibrant and varied democracy, how do we engage in vigorous debate? How does each of us remain firm in our principles, and fight for what we consider right, without … demonizing those with just as strongly held convictions on the other side?
>
> And of course, nowhere do these questions come up more powerfully than on the issue of abortion.
>
> As I considered the controversy surrounding my visit here, I was reminded of an encounter I had during my Senate campaign, one that I describe in a book I wrote called "The Audacity of Hope." A few days after I won the Democratic nomination, I received an e-mail from a doctor who told me that while he voted for me in the Illinois primary, he had a serious concern that might prevent him from voting for me in the general election. He described himself as a Christian who was strongly pro-life—but that was not what was preventing him potentially from voting for me.
>
> What bothered the doctor was an entry that my campaign staff had posted on my website—an entry that said I would fight "right-wing ideologues

who want to take away a woman's right to choose." The doctor said he had assumed I was a reasonable person, he supported my policy initiatives to help the poor and to lift up our educational system, but that if I truly believed that every pro-life individual was simply an ideologue who wanted to inflict suffering on women, then I was not very reasonable. He wrote, "I do not ask at this point that you oppose abortion, only that you speak about this issue in fair-minded words." Fair-minded words.

After I read the doctor's letter, I wrote back to him and I thanked him. And I didn't change my underlying position, but I did tell my staff to change the words on my website. And I said a prayer that night that I might extend the same presumption of good faith to others that the doctor had extended to me. Because when we do that—when we open up our hearts and our minds to those who may not think precisely like we do or believe precisely what we believe—that's when we discover at least the possibility of common ground.

That's when we begin to say, "Maybe we won't agree on abortion, but we can still agree that this heart-wrenching decision for any woman is not made casually, it has both moral and spiritual dimensions."

So let us work together to reduce the number of women seeking abortions, let's reduce unintended pregnancies. Let's make adoption more available. Let's provide care and support for women who do carry their children to term. Let's honor the conscience of those who disagree with abortion, and draft a sensible conscience clause, and make sure that all of our health care policies are grounded not only in sound science, but also in clear ethics, as well as respect for the equality of women. Those are things we can do.

Now, understand…, I do not suggest that the debate surrounding abortion can or should go away. Because no matter how much we may want to fudge it—indeed, while we know that the views of most Americans on the subject are complex and even contradictory—the fact is that at some level, the views of the two camps are irreconcilable. Each side will continue to make its case to the public with passion and conviction. But surely we can do so without reducing those with differing views to caricature….

(The full text of the president's speech can be obtained at: http://www.whitehouse.gov/the_press_office/Remarks-by-the-President-at-Notre-Dame-Commencement/)

PRO-LIFE ARGUMENTS (AGAINST ABORTION)

1. *Abortion is murder.*

    POINT: "The simple fact of the matter is that abortion is murder. What you call a 'fetus' is an unborn baby, a human being, and an abortion is nothing but the deliberate killing of that human being."

    COUNTERPOINT: "Murder is the deliberate killing of a human person, and though a fetus is certainly a human *something*, it's hardly a person. In the earliest stages, it's nothing but a mass of cells. Even in later stages, when it begins to biologically resemble a human person, it still doesn't have anything remotely resembling a human life. It has no hopes, no plans, no concept of self, no stake in its own future. Sentimentalize it all you like, you still can't put a fetus ahead of the woman who carries it."

2. *Abortion sets a dangerous precedent.*

   POINT: "Anything that leads to disrespect for human life is wrong. Anything that leads to a casual attitude toward human life is wrong. Whatever else you say about abortion, it certainly leads to disrespect for and a casual attitude toward human life. And that doesn't just hold for abortions of convenience or for sex selection. It holds for therapeutic abortions and abortions of deformed fetuses as well. Once we decide that some human lives can be destroyed because they're inconvenient or not worth living, what's to stop us from killing individuals with severe disabilities, dysfunctions, senility, and mentally illness?"

   COUNTERPOINT: "Abortion has been legal in this country for more than two decades, and we haven't started to slide down any slippery slopes because of it yet. To the contrary, in 1990 Congress passed, and the president signed, a landmark civil rights act for individuals with handicaps. We both know that abortion is a distinct issue from the treatment of various groups in society, and each has to be decided on its own merits."

3. *Abortion involves psychological risks to the woman.*

   POINT: "A woman and the child she's carrying are as close to each other as any two humans can get. And I don't just mean biologically close but emotionally and psychologically close as well. Just ask any mother. A woman who intentionally harms her unborn child violates the deepest levels of her unconscious needs and desires, and she's bound to pay a psychological price for it. Plenty already have, as both psychologists and women who've had abortions can tell you."

   COUNTERPOINT: "Many women, maybe even most, do want to carry their fetuses to term. And no doubt there are some women who do carry emotional scars from their abortions. But the vast majority of women who had abortions seem to have come through them quite well. The psychological portrait you paint of women and the deepest levels of their unconscious is nothing but a stereotype. And your desire to protect them from their considered decisions concerning what's best for them is insulting paternalism."

4. *Alternatives to abortion are available.*

   POINT: "You abortion rights advocates make it sound as though abortion is the only alternative to rearing an unwanted child. But it's not. Countless couples and individuals are dying to have children but can't. Because of all the abortion mills throughout the country, many of them can't even adopt a healthy infant. So adoption is one alternative to abortion. Even in cases of infants with severe deformities, there are alternatives. If no one wants to adopt them, there are plenty of agencies and institutions to take care of them."

   COUNTERPOINT: "Why should a woman be treated as a breeding animal for childless couples? The mere fact that other people want her child doesn't mean she has to face the health risks and discomforts of pregnancy for them. It's her body, after all. Besides, the anguish of giving up a child carried to term can be much worse than aborting a fetus. And as for infants with severe deformities, what kind of favor are you doing them by sentencing them to miserable lives in institutions?"

5. *Women must be responsible for their sexual activity.*

POINT: "No woman *has* to get pregnant. There are plenty of readily available contraceptives on the market. If a woman doesn't take advantage of them, it's her own fault and she has to take responsibility for her carelessness. To condone abortion is to condone her own irresponsibility. Even worse, it's to condone the killing of innocent life as an after-the-fact form of birth control."

COUNTERPOINT: "First of all, no form of birth control is 100 percent effective, except abstinence. To say that every unwanted pregnancy is the result of carelessness is like saying that every driver struck by another car is at fault. But even if the woman was careless, that doesn't affect her right to have an abortion any more than careless driving affects the driver's right to medical treatment. To deny her that right is to engage in vindictiveness, not to uphold any principle of responsibility."

PRO-CHOICE ARGUMENTS (FOR ABORTION)

1. *Women have rights over their own bodies.*

POINT: "An unwanted pregnancy is an invasion of the woman's body, and to force a woman to carry a fetus to term is to force her to use her body for purposes she doesn't want to use it for. So the real issue here is whether women have the right to control their own bodies, whether they have the right to avail themselves of a simple, safe medical procedure to allow themselves to live their lives as they choose. Clearly the answer has to be yes. It's as fundamental a right as I can think of."

COUNTERPOINT: "No right is absolute. My right to swing my fist stops at your nose. My right to say whatever I please stops at yelling 'fire!' in a crowded theater. Similarly, a woman's right to control her own body stops at taking the life of her unborn child. All your talk of 'invasion' and 'simple medical procedures' obscures the plain fact that once a woman conceives a child she's responsible for it. And that responsibility overrides her right to control her own body."

2. *Unwanted pregnancies carry physical and emotional burdens.*

POINT: "Pregnancy isn't easy for women. Apart from the morning sickness, the back pains, the pain of childbirth, and a host of other discomforts in normal pregnancies, the possibility of unforeseen complications poses a real risk to their physical health and sometimes even their lives. To demand that a woman face all that in an unwanted pregnancy is to demand too much. And the unreasonable demands don't even stop there. Unwanted pregnancies carry emotional burdens as well as physical ones. Pregnancy can be a significant interruption in a woman's life, and motherhood can bring a serious disruption of her hopes and plans. Reproductive freedom isn't just a slogan. It's a matter of allowing a woman to control her own destiny."

COUNTERPOINT: "Yes, pregnancy can be difficult, and though I don't want to sound unsympathetic to pregnant women, I still have to insist that the woman isn't the only one involved here. Against the back pains, hemorrhoids, and varicose veins you have to balance the life of her child, which has to count for more. And as for the disruption of her hopes and plans, nobody says she has to rear the child. Don't forget—there's always adoption. The only place you may have a point is when it comes to serious risk to the woman's life. But to justify abortion for *every* woman on the grounds that she *might* face that risk is preposterous. Modern medicine has come too far for that."

3. *The alternative to legal abortion is back alley abortion.*

    POINT: "You may think that the burdens of unwanted pregnancy are minor, but many women don't. If safe, legal abortions aren't available to them, they'll resort to unsafe, illegal abortions. And if the past is any guide, that means serious infections in many cases and in some cases even death, especially for poor women who won't be able to afford anything but back alley abortions."

    COUNTERPOINT: "Now you're confusing the issue. Whatever problems there may be in enforcing abortion laws is one issue. Whether abortion is moral or immoral is another. Enforcement problems might provide a reason not to ban abortions, but they certainly don't make abortions morally right. Then again, enforcement problems don't even provide a very good reason against banning abortions. As unfortunate as back alley abortions are for both the mothers and their unborn children, legalization encourages abortions; and if they're banned, there will be fewer of them."

4. *The woman counts more than the fetus.*

    POINT: "Everything you say is based on a single assumption—that the fetus counts as much as or even more than the woman. But that can't be true. A woman is a full-fledged person. She has real desires and fears, real aspirations and memories. She's connected to the world through her family and friends. She cares about her life and her future. At the very most, a fetus has only the potential for all that. And though I'm not saying the fetus's potential counts for nothing, I am saying an actual full human life out in the world has to count more than a potential full human life in the womb."

    COUNTERPOINT: "Your distinction between an actual human life and a potential one just doesn't hold up. The difference between the mother and her unborn child isn't a matter of kind but of degree. Human life begins at conception. At that moment, we don't have a potential human life but a developing one. And who's to say that the more developed human life counts for more than the less developed one? If a woman doesn't count more than a ten-year-old, and if neither counts more than a two-year-old, why should any one of them count more than an unborn human life?"

Why Abortion Is Immoral

DONALD MARQUIS

Donald Marquis is a professor of philosophy at the University of Kansas, where he has taught since 1967. He received a B.A. in Anatomy and Physiology and a Ph.D. in Philosophy from Indiana University. Marquis has published extensively on issues in medical ethics. In these excerpts from his widely discussed essay "Why Abortion Is Immoral", he argues that killing a

Don Marquis, "Why Abortion Is Immoral." *The Journal of Philosophy* 86:4 (April 1989), 183–202. Reprinted by permission of *The Journal of Philosophy*, and the author.

fetus is just as immoral as killing an adult human being. In both situations, they are deprived of all value of their future. However, he concludes that contraception is not wrong, under his analysis, as it does not deny something a human future of value.

The view that abortion is, with rare exceptions, seriously immoral has received little support in the recent philosophical literature. No doubt most philosophers affiliated with secular institutions of higher education believe that the anti-abortion position is either a symptom of irrational religious dogma or a conclusion generated by seriously confused philosophical argument. The purpose of this essay is to undermine this general belief. This essay sets out an argument that purports to show, as well as any argument in ethics can show, that abortion is, except possibly in rare cases, seriously immoral, that it is in the same moral category as killing an innocent adult human being.

The argument is based on a major assumption. Many of the most insightful and careful writers on the ethics of abortion … believe that whether or not abortion is morally permissible stands or falls on whether or not a fetus is the sort of being whose life it is seriously wrong to end. The argument of this essay will assume, but not argue, that they are correct.[1]

Also, this essay will neglect issues of great importance to a complete ethics of abortion. Some anti-abortionists will allow that certain abortions, such as abortion before implantation or abortion when the life of a woman is threatened by a pregnancy or abortion after rape, may be morally permissible. This essay will not explore the casuistry of these hard cases. The purpose of this essay is to develop a general argument for the claim that the overwhelming majority of deliberate abortions are seriously immoral.

… A necessary condition of resolving the abortion controversy is a … theoretical account of the wrongness of killing. After all, if we merely believe, but do not understand, why killing adult human beings such as ourselves is wrong, how could we conceivably show that abortion is either immoral or permissible?…

In order to develop such an account, we can start from the following unproblematic assumption concerning our own case: it is wrong to kill *us*. Why is it wrong? Some answers can be easily eliminated. It might be said that what makes killing us wrong is that a killing brutalizes the one who kills. But the brutalization consists of being inured to the performance of an act that is hideously immoral; hence, the brutalization does not explain the immorality. It might be said that what makes killing us wrong is the great loss others would experience due to our absence. Although such hubris is understandable, such an explanation does not account for the wrongness of killing hermits, or those whose lives are relatively independent and whose friends find it easy to make new friends.

A more obvious answer is better. What primarily makes killing wrong is neither its effect on the murderer nor its effect on the victim's friends and relatives, but its effect on the victim. The loss of one's life is one of the greatest losses one can suffer. The loss of one's life deprives one of all the experiences, activities, projects, and enjoyments that would otherwise have constituted one's future. Therefore, killing someone is wrong, primarily because the killing inflicts (one of) the greatest possible losses on the victim. To describe this as the loss of life can be misleading, however. The change in my biological state does not by itself make killing me wrong. The effect of the loss of my biological life is the loss to me of all those activities, projects, experiences, and enjoyments which would otherwise have constituted my future personal life. These activities, projects, experiences, and enjoyments are either valuable for their own sakes or are means to something else that is valuable for its own sake. Some parts of my future are not valued by me now, but will come to be valued by me as I grow older and as my values and capacities change. When I am killed, I am deprived both of what I now value which would have been part of my future personal life, but also what I would come to value. Therefore, when I die, I am deprived of all of the value of my future. Inflicting this loss on me is ultimately what makes killing me wrong. This being the case, it would seem that what makes killing *any* adult human being prima facie seriously wrong is the loss of his or her future.[2]

How should this rudimentary theory of the wrongness of killing be evaluated? It cannot be faulted for deriving an 'ought' from an 'is', for it does not. The analysis assumes that killing me (or you, reader) is prima facie seriously wrong. The point of the analysis is to establish which natural property ultimately explains the wrongness of the killing, given that it is wrong. A natural property will ultimately explain the wrongness of killing, only if (1) the explanation fits with our intuitions about the matter and (2) there is no other natural property that provides the basis for a better explanation of the wrongness of killing. This analysis rests on the intuition that what makes killing a particular human or animal wrong is what it does to that particular human or animal. What makes killing wrong is some natural effect or other of the killing. Some would deny this. For instance, a divine-command theorist in ethics would deny it. Surely this denial is, however, one of those features of divine-command theory which renders it so implausible.

The claim that what makes killing wrong is the loss of the victim's future is directly supported by two considerations. In the first place, this theory explains why we regard killing as one of the worst of crimes. Killing is especially wrong, because it deprives the victim of more than perhaps any other crime. In the second place, people with AIDS or cancer who know they are dying believe, of course, that dying is a very bad thing for them. They believe that the loss of a future to them that they would otherwise have experienced is what makes their premature death a very bad thing for them. A better theory of the wrongness of killing would require a different natural property associated with killing which better fits with the attitudes of the dying. What could it be?

The view that what makes killing wrong is the loss to the victim of the value of the victim's future gains additional support when some of its implications are examined. In the first place, it is incompatible with the view that it is wrong to kill only beings who are biologically human. It is possible that there exists a different species from another planet whose members have a future like ours. Since having a future like that is what makes killing someone wrong, this theory entails that it would be wrong to kill members of such a species. Hence, this theory is opposed to the claim that only life that is biologically human has great moral worth, a claim which many anti-abortionists have seemed to adopt. This opposition, which this theory has in common with personhood theories, seems to be a merit of the theory.

In the second place, the claim that the loss of one's future is the wrong-making feature of one's being killed entails the possibility that the futures of some actual nonhuman mammals on our own planet are sufficiently like ours that it is seriously wrong to kill them also. Whether some animals do have the same right to life as human beings depends on adding to the account of the wrongness of killing some additional account of just what it is about my future or the futures of other adult human beings which makes it wrong to kill us. No such additional account will be offered in this essay. Undoubtedly, the provision of such an account would be a very difficult matter. Undoubtedly, any such account would be quite controversial. Hence, it surely should not reflect badly on this sketch of an elementary theory of the wrongness of killing that it is indeterminate with respect to some very difficult issues regarding animal rights.

In the third place, the claim that the loss of one's future is the wrong-making feature of one's being killed does not entail, as sanctity of human life theories do, that active euthanasia is wrong. Persons who are severely and incurably ill, who face a future of pain and despair, and who wish to die will not have suffered a loss if they are killed. It is, strictly speaking, the value of a human's future which makes killing wrong in this theory. This being so, killing does not necessarily wrong some persons who are sick and dying. Of course, there may be other reasons for a prohibition of active euthanasia, but that is another matter. Sanctity-of-human-life theories seem to hold that active euthanasia is seriously wrong even in an individual case where there seems to be good reason for it independently of public policy considerations. This consequence is most implausible, and it is a plus for the claim that the loss of a future of value is what makes killing wrong that it does not share this consequence.

In the fourth place, the account of the wrongness of killing defended in this essay does straightforwardly entail that it is prima facie seriously wrong to kill children and infants, for we do presume that they have futures of value. Since we do believe that it is wrong to kill defenseless little babies, it is important that a theory of the wrongness of killing easily account for this. Personhood theories of the wrongness of killing, on the other hand, cannot straightforwardly account for the wrongness of killing infants and young children. Hence, such theories must add special ad hoc accounts of the wrongness of killing the young. The plausibility of such ad hoc theories seems to be a function of how desperately one wants such theories to work. The claim that the primary wrong-making feature of a killing is the loss to the victim of the value of its future accounts for the wrongness of killing young children and infants directly; it makes the wrongness of such acts as obvious as we actually think it is. This is a further merit of this theory. Accordingly, it seems that this value of a future-like-ours theory of the wrongness of killing shares strengths of both sanctity-of-life and personhood accounts while avoiding weaknesses of both. In addition, it meshes with a central intuition concerning what makes killing wrong.

The claim that the primary wrong-making feature of a killing is the loss to the victim of the value of its future has obvious consequences for the ethics of abortion. The future of a standard fetus includes a set of experiences, projects, activities, and such which are identical with the futures of adult human beings and are identical with the futures of young children. Since the reason that is sufficient to explain why it is wrong to kill human beings after the time of birth is a reason that also applies to fetuses, it follows that abortion is prima facie seriously morally wrong.

This argument does not rely on the invalid inference that, since it is wrong to kill persons, it is wrong to kill potential persons also. The category that is morally central to this analysis is the category of having a valuable future like ours; it is not the category of personhood. The argument to the conclusion that abortion is prima facie seriously morally wrong proceeded independently of the notion of person or potential person or any equivalent. Someone may wish to start with this analysis in terms of the value of a human future, conclude that abortion is, except perhaps in rare circumstances, seriously morally wrong, infer that fetuses have the right to life, and then call fetuses "persons" as a result of their having the right to life. Clearly, in this case, the category of person is being used to state the *conclusion* of the analysis rather than to generate the *argument* of the analysis.

The structure of this anti-abortion argument can be both illuminated and defended by comparing it to what appears to be the best argument for the wrongness of the wanton infliction of pain on animals. This latter argument is based on the assumption that it is prima facie wrong to inflict pain on me (or you, reader). What is the natural property associated with the infliction of pain which makes such infliction wrong? The obvious answer seems to be that the infliction of pain causes suffering and that suffering is a misfortune. The suffering caused by the infliction of pain is what makes the wanton infliction of pain on me wrong. The wanton infliction of pain on other adult humans causes suffering. The wanton infliction of pain on animals causes suffering. Since causing suffering is what makes the wanton infliction of pain wrong and since the wanton infliction of pain on animals causes suffering, it follows that the wanton infliction of pain on animals is wrong.

This argument for the wrongness of the wanton infliction of pain on animals shares a number of structural features with the argument for the serious prima facie wrongness of abortion. Both arguments start with an obvious assumption concerning what it is wrong to do to me (or you, reader). Both then look for the characteristic or the consequence of the wrong action which makes the action wrong. Both recognize that the wrong-making feature of these immoral actions is a property of actions sometimes directed at individuals other than postnatal human beings. If the structure of the argument for the wrongness of the wanton infliction of pain on animals is sound, then the structure of the argument for the prima facie serious wrongness of abortion is also sound, for the structure of the two arguments is the same. The structure common to both is the key to the explanation of how the wrongness of abortion can be demonstrated without recourse to the category of person. In neither argument is that category crucial....

Of course, this value of a future-like-ours argument, if sound, shows only that abortion is prima facie wrong, not that it is wrong in any and all circumstances. Since the loss of the future to a standard fetus, if killed, is, however, at least as great a loss as the loss of the future to a standard adult human being who is killed, abortion, like ordinary killing, could be justified only by the most compelling reasons. The loss of one's life is almost the greatest misfortune that can happen to one. Presumably abortion could be justified in some circumstances, only if the loss consequent on failing to abort would be at least as great. Accordingly, morally permissible abortions will be rare indeed unless, perhaps, they occur so early in pregnancy that a fetus is not yet definitely an individual. Hence, this argument should be taken as showing that abortion is presumptively very seriously wrong, where the presumption is very strong—as strong as the presumption that killing another adult human being is wrong....

In this essay, it has been argued that the correct ethic of the wrongness of killing can be extended to fetal life and used to show that there is a strong presumption that any abortion is morally impermissible. If the ethic of killing adopted here entails, however, that contraception is also seriously immoral, then there would appear to be a difficulty with the analysis of this essay.

But this analysis does not entail that contraception is wrong. Of course, contraception prevents the actualization of a possible future of value. Hence, it follows from the claim that futures of value should be maximized that contraception is prima facie immoral. This obligation to maximize does not exist, however; furthermore, nothing in the ethics of killing in this paper entails that it does. The ethics of killing in this essay would entail that

contraception is wrong only if something were denied a human future of value by contraception. Nothing at all is denied such a future by contraception, however.

Candidates for a subject of harm by contraception fall into four categories: (1) some sperm or other, (2) some ovum or other, (3) a sperm and an ovum separately, and (4) a sperm and an ovum together. Assigning the harm to some sperm is utterly arbitrary, for no reason can be given for making a sperm the subject of harm rather than an ovum. Assigning the harm to some ovum is utterly arbitrary, for no reason can be given for making an ovum the subject of harm rather than a sperm. One might attempt to avoid these problems by insisting that contraception deprives both the sperm and the ovum separately of a valuable future like ours. On this alternative, too many futures are lost. Contraception was supposed to be wrong, because it deprived us of one future of value, not two. One might attempt to avoid this problem by holding that contraception deprives the combination of sperm and ovum of a valuable future like ours. But here the definite article misleads. At the time of contraception, there are hundreds of millions of sperm, one (released) ovum and millions of possible combinations of all of these. There is no actual combination at all. Is the subject of the loss to be a merely possible combination? Which one? This alternative does not yield an actual subject of harm either. Accordingly, the immorality of contraception is not entailed by the loss of a future-like-ours argument simply because there is no nonarbitrarily identifiable subject of the loss in the case of contraception....

The purpose of this essay has been to set out an argument for the serious presumptive wrongness of abortion subject to the assumption that the moral permissibility of abortion stands or falls on the moral status of the fetus. Since a fetus possesses a property, the possession of which in adult human beings is sufficient to make killing an adult human being wrong, abortion is wrong. This way of dealing with the problem of abortion seems superior to other approaches to the ethics of abortion, because it rests on an ethics of killing which is close to self-evident, because the crucial morally relevant property clearly applies to fetuses, and because the argument avoids the usual equivocations on 'human life', 'human being', or 'person'. The argument rests neither on religious claims nor on Papal dogma. It is not subject to the objection of "speciesism." Its soundness is compatible with the moral permissibility of euthanasia and contraception. It deals with our intuitions concerning young children.

Finally, this analysis can be viewed as resolving a standard problem—indeed, *the* standard problem—concerning the ethics of abortion. Clearly, it is wrong to kill adult human beings. Clearly, it is not wrong to end the life of some arbitrarily chosen single human cell. Fetuses seem to be like arbitrarily chosen human cells in some respects and like adult humans in other respects. The problem of the ethics of abortion is the problem of determining the fetal property that settles this moral controversy. The thesis of this essay is that the problem of the ethics of abortion, so understood, is solvable.

NOTES

1. Judith Jarvis Thomson has rejected this assumption in a famous essay, "A Defense of Abortion," *Philosophy and Public Affairs* 1:1 (1971), 47–66.
2. I have been most influenced on this matter by Jonathan Glover, *Causing Death and Saving Lives* (New York: Penguin, 1977), ch. 3; and Robert Young, "What Is So Wrong with Killing People?" *Philosophy* 1.IV, 210 (1979): 515–528.

⚜ QUESTIONS FOR ANALYSIS

1. Marquis assumes that fetuses and adult human beings are indistinguishable with respect to "the moral value of their lives." Does he provide any arguments in support of this view? What objections might be raised?
2. Does Marquis make any exceptions in his argument for the immorality of abortion? Are there circumstances when an abortion might not be immoral?
3. Marquis rests much of his account on the wrongness of killing in general. How does he present that argument? What is most important in understanding the wrongness of killing in general?
4. What role does the loss of one's future play in Marquis' reasoning? What is lost of importance for him?
5. How does Marquis reason that contraception is not wrong, even though he acknowledges that it prevents the actualization of a possible future of value?

A Defense of Abortion

JUDITH JARVIS THOMSON

Judith Jarvis Thomson, Professor Emeritus of Philosophy, Massachusetts Institute of Technology, wrote this essay in 1971, two years before the Supreme Court decision in *Roe v. Wade*. It has since become a classic in the literature of abortion.

What makes her treatment of the pro-choice position unique is that it begins by conceding, for the sake of argument, that the fetus is a person from the moment of conception. This

From Judith Jarvis Thomson, "A Defense of Abortion." *Philosophy & Public Affairs*, 1, no. 1 (Fall 1971). Copyright © 1971 by Princeton University Press. Reprinted by permission of Blackwell Publishing Ltd. Ms. Thomson acknowledges her indebtedness to James Thomson for discussion, criticism, and many helpful suggestions.

concession is significant because, as Thomson points out, most opposition to abortion builds on the assumption that the fetus has person status and rights from the moment of conception.

Thomson focuses her essay on an important question: Granted that the fetus is a person from the moment of conception, does it necessarily follow that abortion is always wrong? She thinks not. Relying primarily on a series of analogies, she attacks the argument that the immorality of abortion is entailed by the premise that asserts the person status of the fetus.

Toward the end of her essay, Thomson admits that anti-abortionists might object that the immorality of abortion follows not so much from the fact that the fetus is a person as from the special relationship between the fetus and the mother. Thus, anti-abortionists claim that the fetus is a person for whom the woman has a unique kind of responsibility because she is the mother.

In responding to this claim, Thomson argues that we have no responsibility for another person unless we have assumed it. If parents do not take any birth control measures, if they do not elect an abortion, if they choose to take the child home with them from the hospital, then certainly, they have a responsibility to and for the child. For they then have assumed responsibility, implicitly and explicitly, in all their actions. But if a couple has taken measures to prevent conception, this implies quite the opposite of any "special responsibility" for the unintended and unwanted fetus. Thus, in Thomson's view, the woman has no special responsibility to the fetus simply because of a biological relationship.

Ironically, as Thomson points out, many pro-choice advocates object to her argument for a couple of reasons. First, while Thomson argues that abortion is not impermissible, she does not think it is always permissible. There may be times, for example, when carrying the child to term requires only minimal inconvenience; in such cases, the woman would be required by "Minimally Decent Samaritanism" to have the child. Those supporting abortion on demand object to such a limitation of choice.

Second, while Thomson, like act utilitarians, would sanction some acts of abortion, she is not arguing for the right to kill the unborn child. That is, removing a nonviable fetus from the mother's body and thereby guaranteeing its death is not the same as removing a viable fetus from the mother's body and then killing it. In Thomson's view, the former may be permissible; the latter never is. Again, some pro-choice advocates object to this limitation of choice.

Most opposition to abortion relies on the premise that the fetus is a human being, a person, from the moment of conception. The premise is argued for, but, as I think, not well. Take, for example, the most common argument. We are asked to notice that the development of a human being from conception through birth into childhood is continuous; then it is said that to draw a line, to choose a point in this development and say "before this point the thing is not a person, after this point it is a person" is to make an arbitrary choice, a choice for which in the nature of things no good reason can be given. It is concluded that the fetus is, or anyway that we had better say it is, a person from the moment of conception. But this conclusion does not follow. Similar things might be said about the development of an acorn into an oak tree, and it does not follow that acorns are oak trees, or that we had better say they are. Arguments of this form are sometimes called "slippery slope arguments"—the phrase is perhaps self-explanatory—and it is dismaying that opponents of abortion rely on them so heavily and uncritically.

I am inclined to agree, however, that the prospects for "drawing a line" in the development of the fetus look dim. I am inclined to think also that we shall probably have to agree that the fetus has already become a human person well before birth. Indeed, it comes as a surprise when one first learns how early in its life it begins to acquire human characteristics. By the tenth week, for example, it already has a face, arms and legs, fingers and toes; it has internal organs, and brain activity is detectable.[1] On the other hand, I think that the premise is false, that the fetus is not a person from the moment of conception. A newly fertilized ovum, a newly implanted clump of cells, is no more a person than an acorn is an oak tree. But I shall not discuss any of this. For it seems to me to be of great interest to ask what happens if, for the sake of argument, we allow the premise. How, precisely, are we supposed to get from there to the conclusion that abortion is morally impermissible? Opponents of abortion commonly spend most of their time establishing that the fetus is a person, and hardly any time explaining the step from there to the impermissibility of abortion. Perhaps they think the step too simple and obvious to require much comment. Or perhaps instead they are simply being economical in argument. Many of those who defend abortion rely on the premise that the fetus is not a person, but only a bit of tissue that will become a person at birth; and why pay out more arguments than you have to? Whatever the explanation, I suggest that the step they take is neither easy nor obvious, that it calls for closer examination than it is commonly given, and that when we do give it this closer examination we shall feel inclined to reject it.

I propose, then, that we grant that the fetus is a person from the moment of conception. How does the argument go from here? Something like this, I take it. Every person has a right to life. So the fetus has a right to life. No doubt the mother has a right to decide what shall happen in and to her body; everyone would grant that. But surely a person's right to life is stronger and more stringent than the mother's right to decide what happens in and to her body, and so outweighs it. So the fetus may not be killed; an abortion may not be performed.

It sounds plausible. But now let me ask you to imagine this. You wake up in the morning and find yourself back to back in bed with an unconscious violinist. A famous unconscious violinist. He has been found to have a fatal kidney ailment, and the Society of Music Lovers has canvassed all the available medical records and found that you alone have the right blood type to help. They have therefore kidnapped you, and last night the violinist's circulatory system was plugged into yours, so that your kidneys can be used to extract poisons from his blood as well as your own. The director of the hospital now tells you, "Look, we're sorry the Society of Music Lovers did this to you—we would never have permitted it if we had known. But still, they did it, and the violinist now is plugged into you. To unplug you would be to kill him. But never mind, it's only for nine months. By then he will have recovered from his ailment, and can safely be unplugged from you." Is it morally incumbent on you to accede to this situation? No doubt it would be very nice of you if you did, a great kindness. But do you *have* to accede to it? What if it were not nine months, but nine years? Or longer still? What if the director of the hospital says, "Tough luck, I agree, but you've now got to stay in bed, with the violinist plugged into you, for the rest of your life. Because remember this. All persons have a right to life, and violinists are persons. Granted you have a right to decide what happens in and to your body, but a person's right to life outweighs your right to decide what happens in and to your body. So you cannot ever be unplugged from him." I imagine you would regard this as outrageous, which suggests that something really is wrong with that plausible-sounding argument I mentioned a moment ago.

In this case, of course, you were kidnapped; you didn't volunteer for the operation that plugged the violinist into your kidneys. Can those who oppose abortion on the ground I mentioned make an exception for a pregnancy due to rape? Certainly. They can say that persons have a right to life only if they didn't come into existence because of rape; or they can say that all persons have a right to life, but that some have less of a right to life than others, in particular, that those who came into existence because of rape have less. But these statements have a rather unpleasant sound. Surely the question of whether you have a right to life at all, or how much of it you have, shouldn't turn on the question of whether or not you are the product of a rape. And in fact the people who oppose abortion on the ground I mentioned do not make this distinction, and hence do not make an exception in the case of rape.

Nor do they make an exception for a case in which the mother has to spend the nine months of her pregnancy in bed. They would agree that would be a great pity, and hard on the mother; but all the same, all persons have a right to life, the fetus is a person, and so on. I suspect, in fact, that they would not make an exception for a case in which, miraculously enough, the pregnancy went on for nine years, or even the rest of the mother's life.

Some won't even make an exception for a case in which continuation of the pregnancy is likely to shorten the mother's life; they regard abortion as impermissible even to save the mother's life. Such cases are nowadays very rare, and many opponents of abortion do not accept this extreme view. All the same, it is a good place to begin: A number of points of interest come out in respect to it.

1. Let us call the view that abortion is impermissible even to save the mother's life "the extreme view." I want to suggest first that it does not issue from the argument I mentioned earlier without the addition of some fairly powerful premises. Suppose a woman has become pregnant, and now learns that she has a cardiac condition such that she will die if she carries the baby to term. What may be done for her? The fetus, being a person, has a right to life, but as the mother is a person too, so has she a right to life. Presumably they have an equal right to life. How is it supposed to come out that an abortion may not be performed? If mother and child have an equal right to life, shouldn't we perhaps flip a coin? Or should we add to the mother's right to life her right to decide what happens in and to her body, which everybody seems to be ready to grant—the sum of her rights now outweighing the fetus' right to life?

The most familiar argument here is the following. We are told that performing the abortion would be directly killing[2] the child, whereas doing nothing would not be killing the mother, but only letting her die. Moreover, in killing the child, one would be killing an innocent person, for the child has committed no crime, and is not aiming at his mother's death. And then there are a variety of ways in which this might be continued. (1) But as directly killing an innocent person is always and absolutely impermissible, an abortion may not be performed. Or, (2) as directly killing an innocent person is murder, and murder is always and absolutely impermissible, an abortion may not be performed.[3] Or, (3) as one's duty to refrain from directly killing an innocent person is more stringent than one's duty to keep a person from dying, an abortion may not be

performed. Or, (4) if one's only options are directly killing an innocent person or letting a person die, one must prefer letting the person die, and thus an abortion may not be performed.[4]

Some people seem to have thought that these are not further premises which must be added if the conclusion is to be reached, but that they follow from the very fact that an innocent person has a right to life.[5] But this seems to me to be a mistake, and perhaps the simplest way to show this is to bring out that while we must certainly grant that innocent persons have a right to life, the theses in (1) through (4) are all false. Take (2), for example. If directly killing an innocent person is murder, and thus is impermissible, then the mother's directly killing the innocent person inside her is murder, and thus is impermissible. But it cannot seriously be thought to be murder if the mother performs an abortion on herself to save her life. It cannot seriously be said that she *must* refrain, that she *must* sit passively by and wait for her death. Let us look again at the case of you and the violinist. There you are, in bed with the violinist, and the director of the hospital says to you, "It's all most distressing, and I deeply sympathize, but you see this is putting an additional strain on your kidneys, and you'll be dead within the month. But you *have* to stay where you are all the same. Because unplugging you would be directly killing an innocent violinist, and that's murder, and that's impermissible." If anything in the world is true, it is that you do not commit murder, you do not do what is impermissible, if you reach around to your back and unplug yourself from that violinist to save your life.

The main focus of attention in writings on abortion has been on what a third party may or may not do in answer to a request from a woman for an abortion. This is in a way understandable. Things being as they are, there isn't much a woman can safely do to abort herself. So the question asked is what a third party may do, and what the mother may do, if it is mentioned at all, is deduced, almost as an afterthought, from what it is concluded that third parties may do. But it seems to me that to treat the matter in this way is to refuse to grant to the mother that very status of person which is so firmly insisted on for the fetus. For we cannot simply read off what a person may do from what a third party may do. Suppose you find yourself trapped in a tiny house with a growing child. I mean a very tiny house, and a rapidly growing child—you are already up against the wall of the house and in a few minutes you'll be crushed to death. The child on the other hand won't be crushed to death; if nothing is done to stop him from growing he'll be hurt, but in the end he'll simply burst open the house and walk out a free man. Now I could well understand it if a bystander were to say, "There's nothing we can do for you. We cannot choose between your life and his, we cannot be the ones to decide who is to live, we cannot intervene." But it cannot be concluded that you too can do nothing, that you cannot attack it to save your life. However innocent the child may be, you do not have to wait passively while it crushes you to death. Perhaps a pregnant woman is vaguely felt to have the status of house, to which we don't allow the right of self-defense. But if the woman houses the child, it should be remembered that she is a person who houses it.

I should perhaps stop to say explicitly that I am not claiming that people have a right to do anything whatever to save their lives. I think, rather, that there are drastic limits to the right of self defense. If someone threatens you with death unless you torture someone else to death, I think you have not the right, even to save your life, to do so. But the case under consideration here is very different. In our case there are only two people involved, one whose life is threatened, and one who threatens it. Both are innocent: The one who is threatened is not threatened because of any fault, the one who threatens does not threaten because of any fault. For this reason we may feel that we bystanders cannot intervene. But the person threatened can.

In sum, a woman surely can defend her life against the threat to it posed by the unborn child, even if doing so involves its death. And this shows not merely that the theses in (1) through (4) are false; it shows also that the extreme view of abortion is false, and so we need not canvass any other possible ways of arriving at it from the argument I mentioned at the outset.

2. The extreme view could of course be weakened to say that while abortion is permissible to save the mother's life, it may not be performed by a third party, but only by the mother herself. But this cannot be right either. For what we have to keep in mind is that the mother and the unborn child are not like two tenants in a small house which has, by an unfortunate mistake, been rented to both: The mother *owns* the house. The fact that she does adds to the offensiveness of deducing that the mother can do nothing from the supposition that third parties can do nothing. But it does more than this: It casts a bright light on the supposition that third parties can do nothing. Certainly it lets us see that a third party who says "I cannot choose between you" is fooling himself if he thinks this is impartiality. If Jones has found and fastened on a certain coat, which he needs to keep him from freezing, but which Smith also needs to keep him from freezing, then it is not impartiality that says "I cannot choose between you" when Smith owns the coat. Women have said again and again "This body is *my* body!" and they have reason to feel angry, reason to feel that it has been like shouting into the wind. Smith, after all, is hardly likely to bless us if we say to him, "Of course it's your coat, anybody would grant that it is. But no one may choose between you and Jones who is to have it."

We should really ask what it is that says "no one may choose" in the face of the fact that the body that houses the child is the mother's body. It may be simply a failure to appreciate this fact. But it may be something more interesting, namely the sense that one has a right to refuse to lay hands on people, even where it would be just and fair to do so, even where justice seems to require that somebody do so. Thus justice might call for somebody to get Smith's coat back from Jones, and yet you have a right to refuse to be the one to lay hands on Jones, a right to refuse to do physical violence to him. This, I think, must be granted. But then what should be said is not "no one may choose," but only "*I* cannot choose," and indeed not even this, but "*I* will not *act*," leaving it open that somebody else can or should, and in particular that anyone in a position of authority, with the job of securing people's rights, both can and should. So this is no difficulty. I have not been arguing that any given third party must accede to the mother's request that he perform an abortion to save her life, but only that he may.

I suppose that in some views of human life the mother's body is only on loan to her, the loan not being one which gives her any prior claim to it. One who held this view might well think it impartiality to say "I cannot choose." But I shall simply ignore this possibility. My own view is that if a human being has any just, prior claim to anything at all, he has a just, prior claim to his own body. And perhaps this needn't be argued for here anyway, since, as I mentioned, the arguments against abortion we are looking at do grant that the woman has a right to decide what happens in and to her body.

But although they do grant it, I have tried to show that they do not take seriously what is done in granting it. I suggest the same thing will reappear even more clearly when we turn away from cases in which the mother's life is at stake, and attend, as I propose we now do, to the vastly more common cases in which a woman wants an abortion for some less weighty reason than preserving her own life.

3. Where the mother's life is not at stake, the argument I mentioned at the outset seems to have a much stronger pull. "Everyone has a right to life, so the unborn person has a right to life." And isn't the child's right to life weightier than anything other than the mother's own right to life, which she might put forward as ground for an abortion?

This argument treats the right to life as if it were unproblematic. It is not, and this seems to me to be precisely the source of the mistake.

For we should now, at long last, ask what it comes to, to have a right to life. In some views having a right to life includes having a right to be given at least the bare minimum one needs for continued life. But suppose that what in fact is the bare minimum a man needs for continued life is something he has no right at all to be given? If I am sick unto death, and the only thing that will save my life is the touch of Henry Fonda's cool hand on my fevered brow, then all the same, I have no right to be given the touch of Henry Fonda's cool hand on my fevered brow. It would be frightfully nice of him to fly in from the West Coast to provide it. It would be less nice, though no doubt well meant, if my friends flew out to the West Coast and carried Henry Fonda back with them. But I have no right at all against anybody that he

should do this for me. Or again, to return to the story I told earlier, the fact that for continued life that violinist needs the continued use of your kidneys does not establish that he has a right to be given the continued use of your kidneys. He certainly has no right against you that *you* should give him continued use of your kidneys. For nobody has any right to use your kidneys unless you give him such a right; and nobody has the right against you that you shall give him this right—if you do allow him to go on using your kidneys, this is a kindness on your part, and not something he can claim from you as his due. Nor has he any right against anybody else that *they* should give him continued use of your kidneys. Certainly he had no right against the Society of Music Lovers that they should plug him into you in the first place. And if you now start to unplug yourself, having learned that you will otherwise have to spend nine years in bed with him, there is nobody in the world who must try to prevent you, in order to see to it that he is given something he has a right to be given.

Some people are rather stricter about the right to life. In their view, it does not include the right to be given anything, but amounts to, and only to, the right not to be killed by anybody. But here a related difficulty arises. If everybody is to refrain from killing that violinist, then everybody must refrain from doing a great many different sorts of things. Everybody must refrain from slitting his throat, everybody must refrain from shooting him and everybody must refrain from unplugging you from him. But does he have a right against everybody that they shall refrain from unplugging you from him? To refrain from doing this is to allow him to continue to use your kidneys. It could be argued that he has a right against us that we should allow him to continue to use your kidneys. That is, while he had no right against us that we should give him the use of your kidneys, it might be argued that he anyway has a right against us that we shall not now intervene and deprive him of the use of your kidneys. I shall come back to third-party interventions later. But certainly the violinist has no right against you that *you* shall allow him to continue to use your kidneys. As I said, if you do allow him to use them, it is a kindness on your part, and not something you owe him.

The difficulty I point to here is not peculiar to the right of life. It reappears in connection with all the other natural rights; and it is something which an adequate account of rights must deal with. For present purposes it is enough just to draw attention to it. But I would stress that I am not arguing that people do not have a right to life—quite to the contrary, it seems to me that the primary control we must place on the acceptability of an account of rights is that it should turn out in that account to be a truth that all persons have a right to life. I am arguing only that having a right to life does not guarantee having either a right to be given the use of or a right to be allowed continued use of another person's body—even if one needs it for life itself. So the right to life will not serve the opponents of abortion in the very simple and clear way in which they seem to have thought it would.

4. There is another way to bring out the difficulty. In the most ordinary sort of case, to deprive someone of what he has a right to is to treat him unjustly. Suppose a boy and his small brother are jointly given a box of chocolates for Christmas. If the older boy takes the box and refuses to give his brother any of the chocolates, he is unjust to him, for the brother has been given a right to half of them. But suppose that, having learned that otherwise it means nine years in bed with that violinist, you unplug yourself from him. You surely are not being unjust to him, for you gave him no right to use your kidneys, and no one else can have given him any such right. But we have to notice that in unplugging yourself, you are killing him; and violinists, like everybody else, have a right to life, and thus in the view we were considering just now, the right not to be killed. So here you do what he supposedly has a right you shall not do, but you do not act unjustly to him in doing it.

The emendation which may be made at this point is this: The right to life consists not in the right not to be killed, but rather in the right not to be killed unjustly. This runs a risk of circularity, but never mind: It would enable us to square the fact that the violinist has a right to life with the fact that you do not act unjustly toward him in unplugging yourself, thereby killing him. For if you do not kill him unjustly, you do not violate his right to life, and so it is no wonder you do him no injustice.

But if this emendation is accepted, the gap in the argument against abortion stares us plainly in the face: It is by no means enough to show that the fetus is a person, and to remind us that all persons have a right to life—we need to be shown also that killing the fetus violates its right to life, that abortion is unjust killing. And is it?

I suppose we may take it as a datum that in the case of pregnancy due to rape the mother has not given the unborn person a right to the use of her body for food and shelter. Indeed, in what pregnancy should it be supposed that the mother has given the unborn person such a right? It is not as if there were unborn persons drifting about the world, to whom a woman who wants a child says "I invite you in."

But it might be argued that there are other ways one can have acquired a right to the use of another person's body than by having been invited to use it by that person. Suppose a woman voluntarily indulges in intercourse, knowing of the chance it will issue in pregnancy, and then she does become pregnant; is she not in part responsible for the presence, in fact the very existence, of the unborn person inside? No doubt she did not invite it in. But doesn't her partial responsibility for its being there itself give it a right to the use of her body?[6] If so, then her aborting it would be more like the boy's taking away the chocolates, and less like your unplugging yourself from the violinist—doing so would be depriving it of what it does have a right to, and thus would be doing it an injustice.

And then, too, it might be asked whether or not she can kill it even to save her own life: If she voluntarily called it into existence, how can she now kill it, even in self-defense?

The first thing to be said about this is that it is something new. Opponents of abortion have been so concerned to make out the independence of the fetus, in order to establish that it has a right to life, just as its mother does, that they have tended to overlook the possible support they might gain from making out that the fetus is *dependent* on the mother, in order to establish that she has a special kind of responsibility for it, a responsibility that gives it rights against her which are not possessed by any independent person—such as an ailing violinist who is a stranger to her.

On the other hand, this argument would give the unborn person a right to its mother's body only if her pregnancy resulted from a voluntary act, undertaken in full knowledge of the chance a pregnancy might result from it. It would leave out entirely the unborn person whose existence is due to rape. Pending the availability of some further argument, then, we would be left with the conclusion that unborn persons whose existence is due to rape have no right to the use of their mothers' bodies, and thus that aborting them is not depriving them of anything they have a right to and hence is not unjust killing.

And we should also notice that it is not at all plain that this argument really does go even as far as it purports to. For there are cases and cases, and the details make a difference. If the room is stuffy, and I therefore open a window to air it, and a burglar climbs in, it would be absurd to say, "Ah, now he can stay, she's given him a right to the use of her house—for she is partially responsible for his presence there, having voluntarily done what enabled him to get in, in full knowledge that there are such things as burglars, and that burglars burgle." It would be still more absurd to say this if I had had bars installed outside my windows, precisely to prevent burglars from getting in, and a burglar got in only because of a defect in the bars. It remains equally absurd if we imagine it is not a burglar who climbs in, but an innocent person who blunders or falls in. Again, suppose it were like this: People seeds drift about in the air like pollen, and if you open your windows, one may drift in and take root in your carpets or upholstery. You don't want children, so you fix up your windows with fine mesh screens, the very best you can buy. As can happen, however, and on very, very rare occasions does happen, one of the screens is defective; and a seed drifts in and takes root. Does the person plant who now develops have a right to the use of your house? Surely not—despite the fact that you voluntarily opened your windows, you knowingly kept carpets and upholstered furniture, and you knew that screens were sometimes defective. Someone may argue that you are responsible for its rooting, that it does have a right to your house, because after all you could have lived out your life with bare floors and furniture, or with sealed windows and doors. But this won't do—for by the same token anyone can avoid a pregnancy due to rape by having a hysterectomy, or anyway by never leaving home without a (reliable) army.

It seems to me that the argument we are looking at can establish at most that there are *some* cases in which the unborn person has a right to the use of its mother's body, and therefore *some* cases in which abortion is unjust killing. There is room for much discussion and argument as to precisely which, if any. But I think we should sidestep this issue and leave it open, for at any rate the argument certainly does not establish that all abortion is unjust killing.

5. There is room for yet another argument here, however. We surely must grant that there may be cases in which it would be morally indecent to detach a person from your body at the cost of his life. Suppose you learn that what the violinist needs is not nine years of your life, but only one hour: All you need do to save his life is spend one hour in that bed with him. Suppose also that letting him use your kidneys for that one hour would not affect your health in the slightest. Admittedly you were kidnapped. Admittedly you did not give anyone permission to plug him into you. Nevertheless it seems to me plain you *ought* to allow him to use your kidneys for that hour—it would be indecent to refuse.

Again, suppose pregnancy lasted only an hour, and constituted no threat to life or death [sic]. And suppose that a woman becomes pregnant as a result of rape. Admittedly she did not voluntarily do anything to bring about the existence of a child. Admittedly she did nothing at all which would give the unborn person a right to the use of her body. All the same it might well be said, as in the newly emended violinist story, that she *ought* to allow it to remain for that hour that it would be indecent in her to refuse.

Now some people are inclined to use the term "right" in such a way that it follows from the fact that you ought to allow a person to use your body for the hour he needs, that he has a right to use your body for the hour he needs, even though he has not been given that right by any person or act. They may say that it follows also that if you refuse, you act unjustly toward him. This use of the term is perhaps so common that it cannot be called wrong; nevertheless it seems to me to be an unfortunate loosening of what we would do better to keep a tight rein on. Suppose that box of chocolates I mentioned earlier had not been given to both boys jointly, but was given only to the older boy. There he sits, stolidly eating his way through the box, his small brother watching enviously. Here we are likely to say "You ought not to be so mean. You ought to give your brother some of those chocolates." My own view is that it just does not follow from the truth of this that the brother has any right to any of the chocolates. If the boy refuses to give his brother any, he is greedy, stingy, callous—but not unjust. I suppose that the people I have in mind will say it does follow that the brother has a right to some of the chocolates, and thus that the boy does act unjustly if he refuses to give his brother any. But the effect of saying this is to obscure what we should keep distinct, namely the difference between the boy's refusal in this case and the boy's refusal in the earlier case, in which the box was given to both boys jointly, and in which the small brother thus had what was from any point of view clear title to half.

A further objection to so using the term "right" that from the fact that A ought to do a thing for B, it follows that B has a right against A that A do it for him, is that it is going to make the question of whether or not a man has a right to a thing turn on how easy it is to provide him with it; and this seems not merely unfortunate, but morally unacceptable. Take the case of Henry Fonda again. I said earlier that I had no right to the touch of his cool hand on my fevered brow, even though I needed it to save my life. I said it would be frightfully nice of him to fly in from the West Coast to provide me with it, but that I had no right against him that he should do so. But suppose he isn't on the West Coast. Suppose he has only to walk across the room, place a hand briefly on my brow—and lo, my life is saved. Then surely he ought to do it, it would be indecent to refuse. Is it to be said, "Ah, well, it follows that in this case she has a right to the touch of his hand on her brow, and so it would be an injustice in him

to refuse"? So that I have a right to it when it is easy for him to provide it, though no right when it's hard? It's rather a shocking idea that anyone's rights should fade away and disappear as it gets harder and harder to accord them to him.

So my own view is that even though you ought to let the violinist use your kidneys for the one hour he needs, we should not conclude that he has a right to do so—we should say that if you refuse, you are, like the boy who owns all the chocolates and will give none away, self-centered and callous, indecent in fact, but not unjust. And similarly, that even supposing a case in which a woman pregnant due to rape ought to allow the unborn person to use her body for the hour he needs, we should not conclude that he has a right to do so; we should conclude that she is self-centered, callous, indecent, but not unjust, if she refuses. The complaints are no less grave; they are just different. However, there is no need to insist on this point. If anyone does wish to deduce "he has a right" from "you ought," then all the same he must surely grant that there are cases in which it is not morally required of you that you allow that violinist to use your kidneys, and in which he does not have a right to use them, and in which you do not do him an injustice if you refuse. And so also for mother and unborn child. Except in such cases as the unborn person has a right to demand it—and we were leaving open the possibility that there may be such cases—nobody is morally *required* to make large sacrifices, of health, of all other interests and concerns, of all other duties and commitments, for nine years, or even for nine months, in order to keep another person alive.

6. We have in fact to distinguish between the two kinds of Samaritan: the Good Samaritan and what we might call the Minimally Decent Samaritan. The story of the Good Samaritan, you will remember, goes like this:

> A certain man went down from Jerusalem to Jericho, and fell among thieves, which stripped him of his raiment, and wounded him, and departed, leaving him half dead.
>
> And by chance there came down a certain priest that way; and when he saw him, he passed by on the other side.

And likewise a Levite, when he was at the place, came and looked on him, and passed by on the other side.

But a certain Samaritan, as he journeyed, came where he was; and when he saw him he had compassion on him.

And went to him, and bound up his wounds, pouring in oil and wine, and set him on his own beast, and brought him to an inn, and took care of him.

And on the morrow, when he departed, he took out two pence, and gave them to the host, and said unto him, "Take care of him; and whatsoever thou spendest more, when I come again, I will repay thee."

(Luke 10:30–35)

The Good Samaritan went out of his way, at some cost to himself, to help one in need of it. We are not told what the options were, that is, whether or not the priest and the Levite could have helped by doing less than the Good Samaritan did, but assuming they could have, then the fact they did nothing at all shows they were not even Minimally Decent Samaritans, not because they were not Samaritans, but because they were not even minimally decent.

These things are a matter of degree, of course, but there is a difference, and it comes out perhaps most clearly in the story of Kitty Genovese, who, as you will remember, was murdered while thirty-eight people watched or listened, and did nothing at all to help her. A Good Samaritan would have rushed out to give direct assistance against the murderer. Or perhaps we had better allow that it would have been a Splendid Samaritan who did this, on the ground that it would have involved a risk of death for himself. But the thirty-eight not only did not do this, they did not even trouble to pick up a phone to call the police. Minimally Decent Samaritanism would call for doing at least that, and their not having done it was monstrous.

After telling the story of the Good Samaritan, Jesus said, "Go, and do thou likewise." Perhaps he meant that we are morally required to act as the Good Samaritan did. Perhaps he was urging people to do more than is morally required of them. At all events it seems plain that it was not morally required of any of the thirty-eight that he rush out to give direct assistance at the risk of his own life, and that it is not morally required of anyone that he give long stretches of his life—nine years or nine months—to sustaining the life of a person who has no special right (we were leaving open the possibility of this) to demand it.

Indeed, with one rather striking class of exceptions, no one in any country in the world is *legally* required to do anywhere near as much as this for anyone else. The class of exceptions is obvious. My main concern here is not the state of the law in respect to abortion, but it is worth drawing attention to the fact that in no state in this country is any man compelled by law to be even a Minimally Decent Samaritan to any person; there is no law under which charges could be brought against the thirty-eight who stood by while Kitty Genovese died. By contrast, in most states in this country women are compelled by law to be not merely Minimally Decent Samaritans, but Good Samaritans to unborn persons inside them. This doesn't by itself settle anything one way or the other, because it may well be argued that there should be laws in this country—as there are in many European countries—compelling at least Minimally Decent Samaritanism.[7] But it does show that there is a gross injustice in the existing state of the law. And it shows also that the groups currently working against liberalization of abortion laws, in fact working toward having it declared unconstitutional for a state to permit abortion, had better start working for the adoption of Good Samaritan laws generally, or earn the charge that they are acting in bad faith.

I should think, myself, that Minimally Decent Samaritan laws would be one thing, Good Samaritan laws quite another, and in fact highly improper. But we are not here concerned with the law. What we should ask is not whether anybody should be compelled by law to be a Good Samaritan, but whether we must accede to a situation in which somebody is being compelled—by nature, perhaps—to be a Good Samaritan. We have, in other words, to look now at third-party interventions. I have been arguing that no person is morally required to make large sacrifices to sustain the life of another who has no right to demand them, and this even where the sacrifices do not include life itself; we are not morally required to be Good Samaritans or anyway Very Good Samaritans to one another. But what if a man cannot extricate himself from such a situation? What if he appeals to us to extricate him? It seems to me plain that there are cases in which we can, cases in which a Good Samaritan would extricate him. There you are, you were kidnapped, and nine years in bed with that violinist lie ahead of you. You have your own life to lead. You are sorry, but you simply cannot see giving up so much of your life to the sustaining of his. You cannot extricate yourself, and ask us to do so. I should have thought that—in light of his having no right to the use of your body—it was obvious that we do not have to accede to your being forced to give up so much. We can do what you ask. There is no injustice to the violinist in our doing so.

7. Following the lead of the opponents of abortion, I have throughout been speaking of the fetus merely as a person, and what I have been asking is whether or not the argument we began with, which proceeds only from the fetus' being a person, really does establish its conclusion. I have argued that it does not.

But of course there are arguments and arguments, and it may be said that I have simply fastened on the wrong one. It may be said that what is important is not merely the fact that the fetus is a person, but that it is a person for whom the woman has a special kind of responsibility issuing from the fact that she is its mother. And it might be argued that all my analogies are therefore irrelevant—for you do not have that special kind of responsibility for that violinist, Henry Fonda does not have that special kind of responsibility for me. And our attention might be drawn to the fact that men and women both *are* compelled by law to provide support for their children.

I have in effect dealt (briefly) with this argument in section 4 above; but a (still briefer) recapitulation now may be in order. Surely we do not have any such "special responsibility" for a person unless we have assumed it, explicitly or implicitly. If a set of parents do not try to prevent pregnancy, do not obtain an abortion, but rather take it home with them, then they have assumed responsibility for it, they have given it rights, and they cannot *now* withdraw support from it at the cost of its life because

they now find it difficult to go on providing for it. But if they have taken all reasonable precautions against having a child, they do not simply by virtue of their biological relationship to the child who comes into existence have a special responsibility for it. They may wish to assume responsibility for it, or they may not wish to. And I am suggesting that if assuming responsibility for it would require large sacrifices, then they may refuse. A Good Samaritan would not refuse—or anyway, a Splendid Samaritan, if the sacrifices that had to be made were enormous. But then so would a Good Samaritan assume responsibility for that violinist; so would Henry Fonda, if he is a Good Samaritan, fly in from the West Coast and assume responsibility for me.

8. My argument will be found unsatisfactory on two counts by many of those who want to regard abortion as morally permissible. First, while I do argue that abortion is not impermissible, I do not argue that it is always permissible. There may well be cases in which carrying the child to term requires only Minimally Decent Samaritanism of the mother, and this is a standard we must not fall below. I am inclined to think it a merit of my account precisely that it does *not* give a general yes or a general no. It allows for and supports our sense that, for example, a sick and desperately frightened fourteen-year-old schoolgirl, pregnant due to rape, may of course choose abortion, and that any law which rules this out is an insane law. And it also allows for and supports our sense that in other cases resort to abortion is even positively indecent. It would be indecent in the woman to request an abortion, and indecent in a doctor to perform it, if she is in her seventh month, and wants the abortion just to avoid the nuisance of postponing a trip abroad. The very fact that the arguments I have been drawing attention to treat all cases of abortion, or even all cases of abortion in which the mother's life is not at stake, as morally on a par ought to have made them suspect at the outset.

Secondly, while I am arguing for the permissibility of abortion in some cases, I am not arguing for the right to secure the death of the unborn child. It is easy to confuse these two things in that up to a certain point in the life of the fetus it is not able to survive outside the mother's body; hence removing it from her body guarantees its death.

But they are importantly different. I have argued that you are not morally required to spend nine months in bed, sustaining the life of that violinist; but to say this is by no means to say that if, when you unplug yourself, there is a miracle and he survives, you then have a right to turn around and slit his throat. You may detach yourself even if this costs him his life; you have no right to be guaranteed his death, by some other means, if unplugging yourself does not kill him. There are some people who will feel dissatisfied by this feature of my argument. A woman may be utterly devastated by the thought of a child, a bit of herself, put out for adoption and never seen or heard of again. She may therefore want not merely that the child be detached from her, but more, that it die. Some opponents of abortion are inclined to regard this as beneath contempt—thereby showing insensitivity to what is surely a powerful source of despair. All the same, I agree that the desire for the child's death is not one which anybody may gratify, should it turn out to be possible to detach the child alive.

At this place, however, it should be remembered that we have only been pretending throughout that the fetus is a human being from the moment of conception. A very early abortion is surely not the killing of a person, and so is not dealt with by anything I have said here.

NOTES

1. Daniel Callahan, *Abortion: Law, Choice and Morality* (New York, 1970), p. 373. This book gives a fascinating survey of the available information on abortion. The Jewish tradition in David M. Feldman, *Birth Control in Jewish Law* (New York, 1963), part 5; the Catholic tradition in John T. Noonan, Jr., "An Almost Absolute Value in History" in *The Morality of Abortion*, ed. John T. Noonan, Jr. (Cambridge, Mass., 1970).

2. The term "direct" in the arguments I refer to is a technical one. Roughly, what is meant by "direct killing" is either killing as an end in itself, or killing as a means to some end, for example, the end of saving someone else's life. See note 5 on the next page, for an example of its use.

3. *Cf. Encyclical Letter of Pope Pius XI on Christian Marriage*, St. Paul Editions (Boston, n.d.), p. 32: "However much we may pity the mother whose health and even life is gravely imperiled in the performance of the duty allotted to her by nature, nevertheless what could ever be a sufficient reason for excusing in any way the direct murder of the innocent? This is precisely what we are dealing with here." Noonan (*The Morality of Abortion*, p. 43) reads this as follows: "What cause can ever avail to excuse in any way the direct killing of the innocent? For it is a question of that."

4. The thesis in (4) is in an interesting way weaker than those in (1), (2), and (3): They rule out abortion even in cases in which both mother *and* child will die if the abortion is not performed. By contrast, one who held the view expressed in (4) could consistently say that one needn't prefer letting two persons die to killing one.

5. Cf. the following passage from Pius XII, *Address to the Italian Catholic Society of Midwives*: "The baby in the maternal breast has the right to life immediately from God.—Hence there is no man, no human authority, no science, no medical, eugenic, social, economic or moral 'indication' which can establish or grant a valid juridical ground for a direct deliberate disposition of an innocent human life, that is a disposition which looks to its destruction either as an end or as a means to another end perhaps in itself not illicit.—The baby, still not born, is a man in the same degree and for the same reason as the mother" (quoted in Noonan, *The Morality of Abortion*, p. 45).

6. The need for a discussion of this argument was brought home to me by members of the Society for Ethical and Legal Philosophy, to whom this paper was originally presented.

7. For a discussion of the difficulties involved, and a survey of the European experience with such laws, see *The Good Samaritan and the Law*, ed. James M. Ratcliffe (New York, 1966).

☫ QUESTIONS FOR ANALYSIS

1. Does the belief that abortion is always impermissible necessarily result from the argument that the unborn is a person from the moment of conception? If not, what additional premises are necessary?

2. Why does Thomson conclude that "a woman surely can defend her life against the threat to it posed by the unborn child, even if doing so involves its death"?

3. How does Thomson answer the claim that the fetus's right to life weighs more (in the moral sense) than anything other than the mother's own right to life?

4. Does Thomson feel that there may be cases in which it would be wrong for a woman to have an abortion? Explain.

5. Distinguish between a "Good Samaritan" and a "Minimally Decent Samaritan."

On the Moral and Legal Status of Abortion

MARY ANNE WARREN

Mary Anne Warren (1946–2010) was a professor emerita of philosophy, San Francisco State University. In this extreme liberal position on abortion, she challenges both John T. Noonan and Judith Jarvis Thomson. Against Thomson, she argues that the ontological status of the fetus is crucial to any discussion of the morality of abortion. If the fetus is a person with full moral rights, there are many situations—more than Thomson allows—in which abortion is not morally justified. Thomson's example of a woman involuntarily tied to a famous violinist to save his life has little in common with most pregnancies, she argues. It justifies abortion in the case of rape but not in the normal case of unwanted pregnancy, in which the woman bears at least some responsibility for her plight.

Against Noonan, she argues that the fetus is not a person. Her argument relies on a distinction between two senses of "human," the biological sense and the moral sense. Noonan shows that a fetus is human in the former sense but not the latter. And Warren argues, the fetus is not human in the moral sense. To support this claim, she gives five criteria for being a person and argues that the fetus meets none of them. She also argues that being a potential person does not give the fetus rights against the rights of the woman carrying it.

In a postscript added after publication, Warren addresses the issue of infanticide. Her arguments in favor of abortion rights do not support a right to kill newborn babies.

We will be concerned with both the moral status of abortion, which for our purposes we may define as the act which a woman performs in voluntarily terminating, or allowing another person to terminate, her pregnancy, and the legal status which is appropriate for this act. I will argue that, while it is not possible to produce a satisfactory defense of a woman's right to obtain an abortion without showing that a fetus is not a human being, in the morally relevant sense of that term, we ought not to conclude that the difficulties involved in determining whether or not a fetus is human make it impossible to produce any satisfactory solution to the problem of the moral status of abortion. For it is possible to show that, on the basis of intuitions which we may expect even the opponents of abortion to share, a fetus is not a person, and hence not the sort of entity to which it is proper to ascribe full moral rights.

From "On the Moral and Legal Status of Abortion," *The Monist* (January 1973). Copyright ©, 1973 *The Monist: An International Quarterly Journal of General Philosophical Inquiry*, Open Court Publishing Company, Chicago, Illinois. Reprinted by permission. "Postscript on Infanticide," in *Today's Moral Problems*, edited by Richard Wasserstrom (1979), pp. 135–136.

Of course, while some philosophers would deny the possibility of any such proof,[1] others will deny that there is any need for it, since the moral permissibility of abortion appears to them to be too obvious to require proof. But the inadequacy of this attitude should be evident from the fact that both the friends and the foes of abortion consider their position to be morally self-evident. Because pro-abortionists have never adequately come to grips with the conceptual issues surrounding abortion, most, if not all, of the arguments which they advance in opposition to laws restricting access to abortion fail to refute or even weaken the traditional antiabortion argument, i.e., that a fetus is a human being, and therefore abortion is murder.

These arguments are typically of one of two sorts. Either they point to the terrible side effects of the restrictive laws, e.g., the deaths due to illegal abortions, and the fact that it is poor women who suffer the most as a result of these laws, or else they state that to deny a woman access to abortion is to deprive her of her right to control her own body. Unfortunately, however, the fact that restricting access to abortion has tragic side effects does not, in itself, show that the restrictions are unjustified, since murder is wrong regardless of the consequences of prohibiting it; and the appeal to the right to control one's body, which is generally construed as a property right, is at best a rather feeble argument for the permissibility of abortion. Mere ownership does not give me the right to kill innocent people whom I find on my property, and indeed I am apt to be held responsible if such people injure themselves while on my property. It is equally unclear that I have any moral right to expel an innocent person from my property when I know that doing so will result in his death.

Furthermore, it is probably inappropriate to describe a woman's body as her property, since it seems natural to hold that a person is something distinct from her property, but not from her body. Even those who would object to the identification of a person with his body, or with the conjunction of his body and his mind, must admit that it would be very odd to describe, say, breaking a leg, as damaging one's property, and much more appropriate to describe it as injuring one*self*. Thus

it is probably a mistake to argue that the right to obtain an abortion is in any way derived from the right to own and regulate property.

But however we wish to construe the right to abortion, we cannot hope to convince those who consider abortion a form of murder of the existence of any such right unless we are able to produce a clear and convincing refutation of the traditional antiabortion argument, and this has not, to my knowledge, been done. With respect to the two most vital issues which that argument involves, i.e., the humanity of the fetus and its implication for the moral status of abortion, confusion has prevailed on both sides of the dispute.

Thus, both pro-abortionists and antiabortionists have tended to abstract the question of whether abortion is wrong to that of whether it is wrong to destroy a fetus, just as though the rights of another person were not necessarily involved. This mistaken abstraction has led to the almost universal assumption that if a fetus is a human being, with a right to life, then it follows immediately that abortion is wrong (except perhaps when necessary to save the woman's life), and that it ought to be prohibited. It has also been generally assumed that unless the question about the status of the fetus is answered, the moral status of abortion cannot possibly be determined.... John Noonan is correct in saying that "the fundamental question in the long history of abortion is, How do you determine the humanity of a being?"[2] He summarizes his own antiabortion argument, which is a version of the official position of the Catholic Church, as follows:

> ... it is wrong to kill humans, however poor, weak, defenseless, and lacking in opportunity to develop their potential they may be. It is therefore morally wrong to kill Biafrans. Similarly, it is morally wrong to kill embryos.[3]

Noonan bases his claim that fetuses are human upon what he calls the theologians' criterion of humanity: that whoever is conceived of human beings is human. But although he argues at length for the appropriateness of this criterion, he never questions the assumption that if a fetus is human then abortion is wrong for exactly the same reason that murder is wrong.

Judith Thomson is, in fact, the only writer I am aware of who has seriously questioned this assumption; she has argued that, even if we grant the anti-abortionist his claim that a fetus is a human being, with the same right to life as any other human being, we can still demonstrate that, in at least some and perhaps most cases, a woman is under no moral obligation to complete an unwanted pregnancy.[4] Her argument is worth examining, since if it holds up it may enable us to establish the moral permissibility of abortion without becoming involved in problems about what entitles an entity to be considered human, and accorded full moral rights. To be able to do this would be a great gain in the power and simplicity of the proabortion position, since, although I will argue that these problems can be solved at least as decisively as can any other moral problem, we should certainly be pleased to be able to avoid having to solve them as part of the justification of abortion.

On the other hand, even if Thomson's argument does not hold up, her insight, i.e., that it requires *argument* to show that if fetuses are human then abortion is properly classified as murder, is an extremely valuable one. The assumption she attacks is particularly invidious, for it amounts to the decision that it is appropriate, in deciding the moral status of abortion, to leave the rights of the pregnant woman out of consideration entirely, except possibly when her life is threatened. Obviously, this will not do; determining what moral rights, if any, a fetus possesses is only the first step in determining the moral status of abortion. Step two, which is at least equally essential, is finding a just solution to the conflict between whatever rights the fetus may have, and the rights of the woman who is unwillingly pregnant. While the historical error has been to pay far too little attention to the second step, Ms. Thomson's suggestion is that if we look at the second step first we may find that a woman has a right to obtain an abortion *regardless* of what rights the fetus has.

Our own inquiry will also have two stages. In Section I, we will consider whether or not it is possible to establish that abortion is morally permissible even on the assumption that a fetus is an entity with a full-fledged right to life. I will argue that in fact this cannot be established, at least not with the conclusiveness which is essential to our hopes of convincing those who are skeptical about the morality of abortion, and that we therefore cannot avoid dealing with the question of whether or not a fetus really does have the same right to life as a (more fully developed) human being.

In Section II, I will propose an answer to this question, namely, that a fetus cannot be considered a member of the moral community, the set of beings with full and equal moral rights, for the simple reason that it is not a person, and that it is personhood, and not genetic humanity, i.e., humanity as defined by Noonan, which is the basis for membership in this community. I will argue that a fetus, whatever its stage of development, satisfies none of the basic criteria of personhood, and is not even enough *like* a person to be accorded even some of the same rights on the basis of this resemblance. Nor, as we will see, is a fetus's *potential* personhood a threat to the morality of abortion, since, whatever the rights of potential people may be, they are invariably overridden in any conflict with the moral rights of actual people.

I

We turn now to Professor Thomson's case for the claim that even if a fetus has full moral rights, abortion is still morally permissible, at least sometimes, and for some reasons other than to save the woman's life. Her argument is based upon a clever, but I think faulty, analogy. She asks us to picture ourselves waking up one day, in bed with a famous violinist. Imagine that you have been kidnapped, and your bloodstream hooked up to that of the violinist, who happens to have an ailment which will certainly kill him unless he is permitted to share your kidneys for a period of nine months. No one else can save him, since you alone have the right type of blood. He will be unconscious all that time, and you will have to stay in bed with him, but after the nine months are over he may be unplugged, completely cured, that is, provided that you have cooperated.

Now then, she continues, what are your obligations in this situation? The antiabortionist, if he is consistent, will have to say that you are obligated to stay in bed with the violinist: for all people have a right to life, and violinists are people, and therefore it would be murder for you to disconnect yourself from him and let him die. But this is outrageous, and so there must be something wrong with the same argument when it is applied to abortion. It would certainly be commendable of you to agree to save the violinist, but it is absurd to suggest that your refusal to do so would be murder. His right to life does not obligate you to do whatever is required to keep him alive; nor does it justify anyone else in forcing you to do so. A law which required you to stay in bed with the violinist would clearly be an unjust law, since it is no proper function of the law to force unwilling people to make huge sacrifices for the sake of other people toward whom they have no such prior obligation.

Thomson concludes that, if this analogy is an apt one, then we can grant the antiabortionist his claim that a fetus is a human being, and still hold that it is at least sometimes the case that a pregnant woman has the right to refuse to be a Good Samaritan towards the fetus, i.e., to obtain an abortion. For there is a great gap between the claim that X has a right to life, and the claim that Y is obligated to do whatever is necessary to keep X alive, let alone that he ought to be forced to do so. It is Y's duty to keep X alive only if he has somehow contracted a *special* obligation to do so; and a woman who is unwillingly pregnant, e.g., who was raped, has done nothing which obligates her to make the enormous sacrifice which is necessary to preserve the conceptus.

This argument is initially quite plausible, and in the extreme case of pregnancy due to rape is probably conclusive. Difficulties arise, however, when we try to specify more exactly the range of cases in which abortion is clearly justifiable even on the assumption that the fetus is human. Professor Thomson considers it a virtue of her argument that it does not enable us to conclude that abortion is *always* permissible. It would, she says, be "indecent" for a woman in her seventh month to obtain an abortion just to avoid having to postpone a trip to Europe. On the other hand, her argument enables us to see that "a sick and desperately frightened schoolgirl pregnant due to

rape may *of course* choose abortion, and that any law which rules this out is an insane law" (p. 65). So far, so good; but what are we to say about the woman who becomes pregnant not through rape but as a result of her own carelessness, or because of contraceptive failure, or who gets pregnant intentionally and then changes her mind about wanting a child? With respect to such cases, the violinist analogy is of much less use to the defender of the woman's right to obtain an abortion.

Indeed, the choice of a pregnancy due to rape, as an example of a case in which abortion is permissible even if a fetus is considered a human being, is extremely significant; for it is only in the case of pregnancy due to rape that the woman's situation is adequately analogous to the violinist case for our intuitions about the latter to transfer convincingly. The crucial difference between a pregnancy due to rape and the *normal* case of an unwanted pregnancy is that in the normal case we cannot claim that the woman is in no way responsible for her predicament; she could have remained chaste, or taken her pills more faithfully, or abstained on dangerous days, and so on. If, on the other hand, you are kidnapped by strangers, and hooked up to a strange violinist, then you are free of any shred of responsibility for the situation, on the basis of which it could be argued that you are obligated to keep the violinist alive. Only when her pregnancy is due to rape is a woman clearly just as nonresponsible.[5]

Consequently, there is room for the antiabortionist to argue that in the normal case of unwanted pregnancy a woman has, by her own actions, assumed responsibility for the fetus. For if X behaves in a way which he could have avoided, and which he knows involves, let us say, a 1 percent chance of bringing into existence a human being, with a right to life, and does so knowing that if this should happen then that human being will perish unless X does certain things to keep him alive, then it is by no means clear that when it does happen X is free of any obligation to what he knew in advance would be required to keep that human being alive.

The plausibility of such an argument is enough to show that the Thomson analogy can provide a clear and persuasive defense of a woman's right to obtain an abortion only with respect to those cases in which the woman is in no way responsible for her pregnancy, e.g., where it is due to rape. In all other cases, we would almost certainly conclude that it was necessary to look carefully at the particular circumstances in order to determine the extent of the woman's responsibility, and hence the extent of her obligation. This is an extremely unsatisfactory outcome, from the viewpoint of the opponents of restrictive abortion laws, most of whom are convinced that a woman has a right to obtain an abortion regardless of how and why she got pregnant.

Of course a supporter of the violinist analogy might point out that it is absurd to suggest that forgetting her pill one day might be sufficient to obligate a woman to complete an unwanted pregnancy. And indeed it *is* absurd to suggest this. As we will see, the moral right to obtain an abortion is not in the least dependent upon the extent to which the woman is responsible for her pregnancy. But unfortunately, once we allow the assumption that a fetus has full moral rights, we cannot avoid taking this absurd suggestion seriously. Perhaps we can make this point more clear by altering the violinist story just enough to make it more analogous to a normal unwanted pregnancy and less to a pregnancy due to rape, and then seeing whether it is still obvious that you are not obligated to stay in bed with the fellow.

Suppose, then, that violinists are peculiarly prone to the sort of illness the only cure for which is the use of someone else's bloodstream for nine months, and that because of this there has been formed a society of music lovers who agree that whenever a violinist is stricken they will draw lots and the loser will, by some means, be made the one and only person capable of saving him. Now then, would you be obligated to cooperate in curing the violinist if you had voluntarily joined this society, knowing the possible consequences, and then your name had been drawn and you had been kidnapped? Admittedly, you did not promise ahead of time that you would, but you did deliberately place yourself in a position in which it might happen that a human life would be lost if you did not. Surely this is at least a prima facie reason for supposing that you have an obligation to stay in bed with the violinist. Suppose that you

had gotten your name drawn deliberately; surely *that* would be quite a strong reason for thinking that you had such an obligation.

It might be suggested that there is one important disanalogy between the modified violinist case and the case of an unwanted pregnancy, which makes the woman's responsibility significantly less, namely, the fact that the fetus *comes into existence* as the result of the woman's actions. This fact might give her a right to refuse to keep it alive, whereas she would not have had this right had it existed previously, independently, and then as a result of her actions become dependent upon her for its survival.

My own intuition, however, is that X has no more right to bring into existence, either deliberately or as a foreseeable result of actions he could have avoided, a being with full moral rights (Y), and then refuse to do what he knew beforehand would be required to keep that being alive, than he has to enter into an agreement with an existing person, whereby he may be called upon to save that person's life, and then refuse to do so when so called upon. Thus, X's responsibility for Y's existence does not seem to lessen his obligation to keep Y alive, if he is also responsible for Y's being in a situation in which only he can save him.

Whether or not this intuition is entirely correct, it brings us back once again to the conclusion that once we allow the assumption that a fetus has full moral rights it becomes an extremely complex and difficult question whether and when abortion is justifiable. Thus the Thomson analogy cannot help us produce a clear and persuasive proof of the moral permissibility of abortion. Nor will the opponents of the restrictive laws thank us for anything less; for their conviction (for the most part) is that abortion is obviously *not* a morally serious and extremely unfortunate, even though sometimes justified, act comparable to killing in self-defense or to letting the violinist die, but rather is closer to being a morally neutral act, like cutting one's hair.

The basis of this conviction, I believe, is the realization that a fetus is not a person, and thus does not have a full-fledged right to life. Perhaps the reason why this claim has been so inadequately defended is that it seems self-evident to those who accept it. And so it is, insofar as it follows from what I take to be perfectly obvious claims about the nature of personhood and about the proper grounds for ascribing moral rights, claims which ought, indeed, to be obvious to both the friends and foes of abortion. Nevertheless, it is worth examining these claims, and showing how they demonstrate the moral innocuousness of abortion, since this apparently has not been adequately done before.

II

The question which we must answer in order to produce a satisfactory solution to the problem of the moral status of abortion is this: How are we to define the moral community, the set of beings with full and equal moral rights, such that we can decide whether a human fetus is a member of this community or not? What sort of entity, exactly, has the inalienable rights to life, liberty, and the pursuit of happiness? Jefferson attributed these rights to all *men*, and it may or may not be fair to suggest that he intended to attribute them *only* to men. Perhaps he ought to have attributed them to all human beings. If so, then we arrive, first, at Noonan's problem of defining what makes a being human, and, second, at the equally vital question which Noonan does not consider; namely, What reason is there for identifying the moral community with the set of all human beings, in whatever way we have chosen to define that term?

1. On the Definition of "Human"

One reason why this vital second question is so frequently overlooked in the debate over the moral status of abortion is that the term "human" has two distinct, but not often distinguished, senses. This fact results in a slide of meaning, which serves to conceal the fallaciousness of the traditional argument that since (1) it is wrong to kill innocent human beings, and (2) fetuses are innocent human beings, then (3) it is wrong to kill fetuses. For if "human" is used in the same sense in both (1) and (2) then, whichever of the two senses is meant, one of these premises is question-begging. And if it is used in two different senses then of course the conclusion doesn't follow.

Thus, (1) is a self-evident moral truth,[6] and avoids begging the question about abortion only if "human being" is used to mean something like "a full-fledged member of the moral community." (It may or may not also be meant to refer exclusively to members of the species *Homo Sapiens*.) *We may call this the moral* sense of "human." It is not to be confused with what we will call the *genetic* sense, i.e., the sense in which *any* member of the species is a human being, and no member of any other species could be. If (1) is acceptable only if the moral sense is intended, (2) is non-question-begging only if what is intended is the genetic sense.

In "Deciding Who Is Human," Noonan argues for the classification of fetuses with human beings by pointing to the presence of the full genetic code, and the potential capacity for rational thought (p. 135). It is clear that what he needs to show, for his version of the traditional argument to be valid, is that fetuses are human in the moral sense, the sense in which it is analytically true that all human beings have full moral rights. But, in the absence of any argument showing that whatever is genetically human is also morally human, and he gives none, nothing more than genetic humanity can be demonstrated by the presence of the human genetic code. And, as we will see, the *potential* capacity for rational thought can at most show that an entity has the potential for *becoming* human in the moral sense.

2. Defining the Moral Community

Can it be established that genetic humanity is sufficient for moral humanity? I think that there are very good reasons for not defining the moral community in this way. I would like to suggest an alternative way of defining the moral community, which I will argue for only to the extent of explaining why it is, or should be, self-evident. The suggestion is simply that the moral community consists of all and only *people*, rather than all and only human beings;[7] and probably the best way of demonstrating its self-evidence is by considering the concept of personhood, to see what sorts of entity are and are not persons, and what the decision that a being is or is not a person implies about its moral rights.

What characteristics entitle an entity to be considered a person? This is obviously not the place to attempt a complete analysis of the concept of personhood, but we do not need such a fully adequate analysis just to determine whether and why a fetus is or isn't a person. All we need is a rough and approximate list of the most basic criteria of personhood, and some idea of which, or how many, of these an entity must satisfy in order to properly be considered a person.

In searching for such criteria, it is useful to look beyond the set of people with whom we are acquainted, and ask how we would decide whether a totally alien being was a person or not. (For we have no right to assume that genetic humanity is necessary for personhood.) Imagine a space traveler who lands on an unknown planet and encounters a race of beings utterly unlike any he has ever seen or heard of. If he wants to be sure of behaving morally toward these beings, he has to somehow decide whether they are people, and hence have full moral rights, or whether they are the sort of thing which he need not feel guilty about treating as, for example, a source of food.

How should he go about making this decision? If he has some anthropological background, he might look for such things as religion, art, and the manufacturing of tools, weapons, or shelters, since these factors have been used to distinguish our human from our prehuman ancestors, in what seems to be closer to the moral than the genetic sense of "human." And no doubt he would be right to consider the presence of such factors as good evidence that the alien beings were people, and morally human. It would, however, be overly anthropocentric of him to take the absence of these things as adequate evidence that they were not, since we can imagine people who have progressed beyond, or evolved without ever developing, these cultural characteristics.

I suggest that the traits which are most central to the concept of personhood, or humanity in the moral sense, are, very roughly, the following:

1. consciousness (of objects and events external and/or internal to the being), and in particular the capacity to feel pain;
2. reasoning (the *developed* capacity to solve new and relatively complex problems);
3. self-motivated activity (activity which is relatively independent of either genetic or direct external control);
4. the capacity to communicate, by whatever means, messages of an indefinite variety of types, that is, not just with an indefinite number of possible contents, but on indefinitely many possible topics;
5. the presence of self-concepts, and self-awareness, either individual or racial, or both.

Admittedly, there are apt to be a great many problems involved in formulating precise definitions of these criteria, let alone in developing universally valid behavioral criteria for deciding when they apply. But I will assume that both we and our explorer know approximately what (1)–(5) mean, and that he is also able to determine whether or not they apply. How, then, should he use his findings to decide whether or not the alien beings are people? We needn't suppose that an entity must have *all* of these attributes to be properly considered a person; (1) and (2) alone may well be sufficient for personhood, and quite probably (1)–(3) are sufficient. Neither do we need to insist that any one of these criteria is *necessary* for personhood, although once again (1) and (2) look like fairly good candidates for necessary conditions, as does (3), if "activity" is construed so as to include the activity of reasoning.

All we need to claim, to demonstrate that a fetus is not a person, is that any being which satisfies *none* of (1)–(5) is certainly not a person. I consider this claim to be so obvious that I think anyone who denied it, and claimed that a being which satisfied none of (1)–(5) was a person all the same, would thereby demonstrate that he had no notion at all of what a person is—perhaps because he had confused the concept of a person with that of genetic humanity. If the opponents of abortion were to deny the appropriateness of these five criteria, I do not know what further arguments would convince them. We would probably have to admit that our conceptual schemes are indeed irreconcilably different, and that our dispute could not be settled objectively.

I do not expect this to happen, however, since I think that the concept of a person is one which is very nearly universal (to people), and that it is common to both pro-abortionists and anti-abortionists, even though neither group has fully realized the relevance of this concept to the resolution of their dispute. Furthermore, I think that on reflection even the antiabortionists ought to agree not only that (1)–(5) are central to the concept of personhood, but also that it is apart of this concept that all and only people have full moral rights. The concept of a person is in part a moral concept; once we have admitted that X is a person we have recognized, even if we have not agreed to respect, X's right to be treated as a member of the moral community. It is true that the claim that X is a *human being* is more commonly voiced as part of an appeal to treat X decently than is the claim that X is a person, but this is either because "human being" is here used in the sense which implies personhood, or because the genetic and moral senses of "human" have been confused.

Note if (1)–(5) are indeed the primary criteria of personhood, then it is clear that genetic humanity is neither necessary nor sufficient for establishing that an entity is a person. Some human beings are not people, and there may be people who are not human beings. A man or woman whose consciousness has been permanently obliterated but who remains alive is a human being which is no longer a person; defective human beings, with no appreciable mental capacity, are not and presumably never will be people; and a fetus is a human being which is not yet a person, and which therefore cannot coherently be said to have full moral rights. Citizens of the next century should be prepared to recognize highly advanced, self-aware robots or computers, should such be developed, and intelligent inhabitants of other worlds, should such be found, as people in the fullest sense, and to respect their moral rights. But to ascribe full moral rights to an entity which is not a person is as absurd as to ascribe moral obligations and responsibilities to such an entity.

3. Fetal Development and the Right to Life

Two problems arise in the application of these suggestions for the definition of the moral community to the determination of the precise moral status of a human fetus. Given that the paradigm example of a person is a normal adult human being, then (1) How like this paradigm, in particular how far advanced since conception, does a human being need to be before it begins to have a right to life by virtue, not of being fully a person as of yet, but of being *like* a person? and (2) To what extent, if any, does the fact that a fetus has the *potential* for becoming a person endow it with some of the same rights? Each of these questions requires some comment.

In answering the first question, we need not attempt a detailed consideration of the moral rights of organisms which are not developed enough, aware enough, intelligent enough, etc., to be considered people, but which resemble people in some respects. It does seem reasonable to suggest that the more like a person, in the relevant respects, a being is, the stronger is the case for regarding it as having a right to life, and indeed the stronger its right to life is. Thus we ought to take seriously the suggestion that, insofar as "the human individual develops biologically in a continuous fashion ... the rights of a human person might develop in the same way."[8] But we must keep in mind that the attributes which are relevant in determining whether or not an entity is enough like a person to be regarded as having some of the same moral rights are no different from those which are relevant to determining whether or not it is a fully a person—i.e., are no different from (1)–(5)—and that being genetically human, or having recognizably human facial and other physical features, or detectable brain activity, or the capacity to survive outside the uterus, is simply not among these relevant attributes.

Thus it is clear that even though a seven- or eight-month fetus has features which make it apt to arouse in us almost the same powerful protective instinct as is commonly aroused by a small infant, nevertheless it is not significantly more personlike than is a very small embryo. It is *somewhat* more personlike; it can apparently feel and respond to pain, and it may even have a rudimentary form of consciousness, insofar as its brain is quite active. Nevertheless, it seems safe to say that it is not fully conscious, in the way that an infant of a few months is, and that it cannot reason, or communicate messages of indefinitely many sorts, does not engage in self-motivated activity, and has no self-awareness. Thus, in the *relevant* respects, a fetus, even a fully developed one, is considerably less personlike than is the average mature mammal, indeed the average fish. And I think that a rational person must conclude that if the right to life of a fetus is to be based upon its resemblance to a person, then it cannot be said to have any more right to life than, let us say, a newborn guppy (which also seems to be capable of feeling pain), and that right of that magnitude could never override a woman's right to obtain an abortion, at any stage of her pregnancy.

There may, of course, be other arguments in favor of placing legal limits upon the stage of pregnancy in which an abortion may be performed. Given the relative safety of the new techniques of artificially inducing labor during the third trimester, the danger to the woman's life or health is no longer such an argument. Neither is the fact that people tend to respond to the thought of abortion in the later stages of pregnancy with emotional repulsion, since mere emotional responses cannot take the place of moral reasoning in determining what ought to be permitted. Nor, finally, is the frequently heard argument that legalizing abortion, especially late in the pregnancy, may erode the level of respect for human life, leading, perhaps, to an increase in unjustified euthanasia and other crimes. For this threat, if it is a threat, can be better met by educating people to the kinds of moral distinctions which we are making here than by limiting access to abortion (which limitation may, in its disregard for the rights of women, be just as damaging to the level of respect for human rights).

Thus, since the fact that even a fully developed fetus is not personlike enough to have any significant right to life on the basis of its personlikeness shows that no legal restrictions upon the stage of pregnancy in which an abortion may be performed can be justified on the grounds that we should protect the rights of the older fetus; and since there is no other apparent justification for such restrictions, we may conclude that they are entirely unjustified. Whether or not it would be *indecent* (whatever that means) for a woman in her seventh month to obtain an abortion just to avoid having to postpone

a trip to Europe, it would not, in itself, be *immoral*, and therefore it ought to be permitted.

4. Potential Personhood and Right to Life

We have seen that a fetus does not resemble a person in any way which can support the claim that it has even some of the same rights. But what about its *potential*, the fact that if nurtured and allowed to develop naturally it will very probably become a person? Doesn't that alone give it at least some right to life? It is hard to deny that the fact that an entity is a potential person is a strong prima facie reason for not destroying it; but we need not conclude from this that a potential person has a right to life, by virtue of that potential. It may be that our feeling that it is better, other things being equal, not to destroy a potential person is better explained by the fact that potential people are still (felt to be) an invaluable resource, not to be lightly squandered. Surely, if every speck of dust were a potential person, we would be much less apt to conclude that every potential person has a right to become actual.

Still, we do not need to insist that a potential person has no right to life whatever. There may well be something immoral, and not just imprudent, about wantonly destroying potential people, when doing so isn't necessary to protect anyone's rights. But even if a potential person does have some prima facie right to life, such a right could not possibly outweigh the right of a woman to obtain an abortion, since the rights of any actual person invariably outweigh those of any potential person, whenever the two conflict. Since this may not be immediately obvious in the case of a human fetus, let us look at another case.

Suppose that our space explorer falls into the hand of an alien culture, whose scientists decide to create a few hundred thousand or more human beings, by breaking his body into its component cells, and using these to create fully developed human beings, with, of course, his genetic code. We may imagine that each of these newly created men will have all of the original man's abilities, skills, knowledge, and so on, and also have an individual self-concept, in short that each of them will be a bona fide (though hardly unique) person. Imagine that the whole project will take only seconds, and that its chances of success are extremely high, and that our explorer knows all of this, and also knows that these people will be treated fairly. I maintain that in such a situation he would have every right to escape if he could, and thus to deprive all of these potential people of their potential lives; for his right to life outweighs all of theirs together, in spite of the fact that they are all genetically human, all innocent, and all have a very high probability of becoming people very soon, if only he refrains from acting.

Indeed, I think he would have a right to escape even if it were not his life which the alien scientists planned to take, but only a year of his freedom, or indeed, only a day. Nor would he be obligated to stay if he had gotten captured (thus bringing all these people-potentials into existence) because of his own carelessness, or even if he had done so deliberately, knowing the consequences. Regardless of how he got captured, he is not morally obligated to remain in captivity for *any* period of time for the sake of permitting any number of potential people to come into actuality, so great is the margin by which one actual person's right to liberty outweighs whatever right to life even a hundred thousand potential people have. And it seems reasonable to conclude that the rights of a woman will outweigh by a similar margin whatever right to life a fetus may have by virtue of its potential personhood.

Thus, neither a fetus's resemblance to a person, nor its potential for becoming a person provides any basis whatever for the claim that it has any significant right to life. Consequently, a woman's right to protect her health, happiness, freedom, and even her life,[9] by terminating an unwanted pregnancy, will always override whatever right to life may be appropriate to ascribe to a fetus, even a fully developed one. And thus, in the absence of any overwhelming social need for every possible child, the laws which restrict the right to obtain an abortion, or limit the period of pregnancy during which an abortion may be performed, are a wholly unjustified violation of a woman's most basic moral and constitutional rights.[10]....

POSTSCRIPT ON INFANTICIDE

Since the publication of this article, many people have written to point out that my argument appears to justify not only abortion, but infanticide as well. For a newborn infant is not significantly more personlike than an advanced fetus, and consequently it would seem that if the destruction of the latter is permissible so too must be that of the former. Inasmuch as most people, regardless of how they feel about the morality of abortion, consider infanticide a form of murder, this might appear to represent a serious flaw in my argument.

Now, if I am right in holding that it is only people who have a full-fledged right to life, and who can be murdered, and if the criteria of personhood are as I have described them, then it obviously follows that killing newborn infants isn't murder. It does *not* follow, however, that infanticide is permissible, for two reasons. In the first place, it would be wrong, at least in this country and in this period of history, and other things being equal, to kill a newborn infant, because even if its parents do not want it and would not suffer from its destruction, there are other people who would like to have it, and would, in all probability, be deprived of a great deal of pleasure by its destruction. Thus, infanticide is wrong for reasons analogous to those which make it wrong to wantonly destroy natural resources, or great works of art.

Second, most people, at least in this country, value infants and would much prefer that they be preserved, even if foster parents are not immediately available. Most of us would rather be taxed to support orphanages than allow unwanted infants to be destroyed. So long as there are people who want an infant preserved, and who are willing and able to provide the means of caring for it, under reasonably humane conditions, it is, *ceteris parabis*, wrong to destroy it.

But, it might be replied, if this argument shows that infanticide is wrong, at least at this time and in this country, doesn't it also show that abortion is wrong? After all, many people value fetuses, are disturbed by their destruction, and would much prefer that they be preserved, even at some cost to themselves. Furthermore, as a potential source of pleasure to some foster family, a fetus is just as valuable as an infant. There is, however, a crucial difference between the two cases: so long as the fetus is unborn, its preservation, contrary to the wishes of the pregnant woman, violates her rights to freedom, happiness, and self-determination. Her rights override the rights of those who would like the fetus preserved, just as if someone's life or limb is threatened by a wild animal, his right to protect himself by destroying the animal overrides the rights of those who would prefer that the animal not be harmed.

The minute the infant is born, however, its preservation no longer violates any of its mother's rights, even if she wants it destroyed, because she is free to put it up for adoption. Consequently, while the moment of birth does not mark any sharp discontinuity in the degree to which an infant possesses the right to life, it does mark the end of its mother's right to determine its fate. Indeed, if abortion could be performed without killing the fetus, she would never possess the right to have the fetus destroyed, for the same reasons that she has no right to have an infant destroyed.

On the other hand, it follows from my argument that when an unwanted or defective infant is born into a society which cannot afford and/ or is not willing to care for it, then its destruction is permissible. This conclusion will, no doubt, strike many people as heartless and immoral; but remember that the very existence of people who feel this way, and who are willing and able to provide care for unwanted infants, is reason enough to conclude that they should be preserved.

NOTES

1. For example, Roger Wertheimer, who in "Understanding the Abortion Argument" (*Philosophy and Public Affairs*, 1, no. 1 [Fall, 1971], 67–95,) argues that the problem of the moral status of abortion is insoluble, in that the dispute over the status of the fetus is not a question of fact at all, but only a question of how one responds to the facts.

2. John Noonan, "Abortion and the Catholic Church: A Summary History," *Natural Law Forum*, 12 (1967); 125.

3. John Noonan, "Deciding Who Is Human," *Natural Law Forum*, 13 (1968), 134.

4. "A Defense of Abortion."

5. We may safely ignore the fact that she might have avoided getting raped, e.g., by carrying a gun, since by similar means you might likewise have avoided getting kidnapped, and in neither case does the victim's failure to take all possible precautions against a highly unlikely event (as opposed to reasonable precautions against a rather likely event) mean that he is morally responsible for what happens.

6. Of course, the principle that it is (always) wrong to kill innocent human beings is in need of many other modifications, e.g., that it may be permissible to do so to save a greater number of other innocent human beings, but we may safely ignore these complications here.

7. From here on, we will use "human" to mean genetically human, since the moral sense seems closely connected to, and perhaps derived from, the assumption that genetic humanity is sufficient for membership in the moral community.

8. Thomas L. Hayes, "A Biological View," *Commonweal*, 85 (March 17, 1967), 677–78; quoted by Daniel Callahan, in *Abortion, Law, Choice, and Morality* (London: Macmillan & Co., 1970).

9. That is, insofar as the death rate, for the woman, is higher for childbirth than for early abortion.

10. My thanks to the following people, who were kind enough to read and criticize an earlier version of this paper: Herbert Gold, Gene Glass, Anne Lauterbach, Judith Thomson, Mary Mothersill, and Timothy Binkley.

☙ QUESTIONS FOR ANALYSIS

1. Is Warren's objection to Thomson's analogy of the woman tied up against her will well taken?

2. According to Warren, Noonan makes no case for the position that whatever is genetically human is morally human. Do you agree? If so, what kind of case can be made?

3. Why does Warren discount the claim that being a potential person gives the fetus rights against the mother?

4. Because the fetus has no rights against the woman carrying it, Warren says, there is nothing immoral about having a late-term abortion in order to take

a European vacation. Is this step warranted? Are there moral considerations she neglects?

5. Warren likens the moral reasons for not killing an infant to the moral reasons for not destroying a work of art. How persuasive is this analogy?

6. Do you agree with Warren's criteria for being human in the moral sense?

Expanding the Discussion about Fetal Life within Prochoice Advocacy

BERTHA ALVAREZ MANNINEN

An associate professor of philosophy at the New College of Interdisciplinary Arts and Sciences, Arizona State University, Bertha Alvarez Manninen has published numerous articles in bioethics with a goal of finding balance and compromise in such contemporary controversies as abortion, stem cell research, and euthanasia.

In this essay, she argues that pro-choice advocates can consistently hold that fetuses possess some degree of value while also insisting that women have the right to decide whether to continue a pregnancy. She acknowledges that this sounds like "having your cake and eating it too," but she believes this can be accomplished, even in today's heated discussions over abortion rights.

Introduction

For the first six years I taught Applied Ethics, I assigned Mary Anne Warren's "On the Moral and Legal Status of Abortion" as a partial representation of the prochoice perspective. Within the last two years, however, I have ceased assigning the article because I noticed that many students respond aggressively to it. Particularly, they recoiled at Warren's statement that human fetuses are equal in moral status and value to a newborn guppy, and that, for those who support abortion choice, abortion is a morally innocuous act comparable to obtaining a haircut (Warren 1973, 52–58). Repeatedly I would hear from my students that Warren's position regarding the value of fetal life, one that derided it in a seemingly callous manner, was sufficient for deterring them from self-identifying as prochoice advocates … even though they actually did believe in abortion choice.

Warren's flippancy toward fetal life can be seen in the writings of other members of the prochoice community. In her book *Why I Am An Abortion Doctor*, Dr. Suzanne Poppema, although providing an excellent perspective on the need to retain access to safe and legal abortion, consistently refers to fetal life in less than respectful ways. She tells a story of a plumber who is called to her clinic to install a disposal system in order to reduce large pieces of postabortion embryonic and fetal remains. The plumber, realizing what the disposal system would be used for, starts to sob and refuses to continue the installation process. Poppema derides the plumber's reaction, referring to the "spectacle of a plumber on his knees sobbing about a garbage disposal" as reminiscent of a "dark comic opera" (Poppema 1996, 165). Throughout her book she calls the embryonic and fetal remains simply "tissue," and regards the disposal of embryonic and fetal life as no

---

Bertha Alvarez Manninen, "The Value of Choice and the Choice to Value: Expanding the Discussion about Fetal Life within Prochoice Advocacy," *Hypatia* 28:3 (Summer 2013), 662–683.

more significant than the disposal of any other postsurgical tissue.

In yet another example, in her book *Breaking the Abortion Deadlock*, Eileen McDonagh argues in favor of abortion rights by construing the fetus as, essentially, an aggressive intruder whose removal warrants lethal violence. She argues that all cases of compelled pregnancy are morally akin to rape and kidnapping, since the fetus intrudes upon the body of the woman without her consent (McDonagh 1996, 75, 89, and 169). Although McDonagh explicitly acknowledges that the fetus is not a moral agent, and so is not intending to intrude on or harm the woman in any way, she still continually refers to it in language that paints the fetus as, essentially, a tiny rapist who coerces a woman into pregnancy.

The reason I have highlighted these three writers is not to claim that their respective positions are typical of those of prochoice supporters. Indeed, there are feminist prochoice advocates who, while fervently arguing in favor of abortion rights, also express care about the welfare of fetal life. For example, Linda Francke's *The Ambivalence of Abortion* begins with her writing about her own abortion experience, and how it deepened her view of the moral ambiguity that may accompany exercising the choice she had fought so hard to protect. In response to her husband's attempt at comfort, telling her that an early embryo is "not a life … it's a bunch of cells smaller than my fingernail," Francke thinks to herself: "any woman who has had children knows that certain feeling in her taut, swollen breasts, and the slight but constant ache in her uterus signals the arrival of life. Though I would march myself into blisters for a woman's right to exercise the option of motherhood, I discovered there in the waiting room that I was not the modern woman I thought I was" (Francke 1978, 5). Prochoice philosopher Margaret Olivia Little also advocates marrying prochoice advocacy with a respect for fetal life, even if one ultimately does not believe that the fetus is a person with full moral rights and moral status. She writes that "burgeoning human life, we might put it, is respect-worthy. Abortion involves loss. Not just loss of the hope that various parties might have invested, but loss of

something valuable in its own right" (Little 2002, 581). Many women who choose abortion, Little continues, do so not because they do not respect human life, or because they assign no value to the role of motherhood; the contrary is very often the case. Many women who opt for abortion do so precisely because they understand and appreciate that gestation will not just yield a baby, rather it will yield their baby; gestation and birthing turns one into a mother. Many women have a precise idea of what it means to be a good mother, and they are honest that, at the present time, they fall short of that ideal. Consequently, a woman aborts, not because she does not respect fetal life, but because she understands that gestation "is likely to reshape her heart and soul, transferring her into a mother emotionally, not just officially; and it is precisely that transformation that she does not want to undergo. It is because continuing pregnancy brings with it this new identity and, likely, relationship, then, that many feel it legitimate to decline" (582).

Many other feminist writers acknowledge the moral ambiguity that may accompany a particular exercise of abortion choice, even if they ultimately argue in favor of women possessing this right.[1] Likewise, many members of the prochoice community do not regard fetal life as having any value at all. Both kinds of individuals make up abortion rights supporters, but my concern is that it is the position of the latter group that is sometimes regarded as the official face of prochoice advocacy, and that it is, in part, this "face" that is leading to our losing the public relations battle in the United States. This concern stems from over ten years of discussing abortion ethics with students, colleagues, and many individuals in the general public, in addition to how I have seen prochoice advocacy portrayed in the media. Francke's reflections on her abortion experience tacitly illustrate that even she regarded her concern with fetal life as being at odds with her feminism and prochoice advocacy. As I will illustrate below, voices within the younger generation of prochoice advocacy wish to frame abortion as an ambiguous moral issue that moves beyond the question of just whether women have a right to obtain one. Therefore, it is incumbent upon abortion rights supporters to advocate a shift in emphasis so that our position is no longer perceived as inherently incompatible with expressing respect for fetal life, and is one that demonstrates a fuller respect for the women who must make decisions regarding that life.

A complete understanding of why so many prochoice advocates may reject the position that fetal life has value requires knowledge and appreciation of the climate of women's lives in the past, and the extent to which women's bodies and reproduction were "owned" by men. The feminist movement arose as a reactionary response to a society that denied women personhood and individuality, and cashed out their moral worth in direct proportion to their efficacy as wives and mothers. Given this, it is understandable why women might have wanted to disassociate themselves from the fetus, so that they could affirm their own separateness, and claiming that the fetus is just a "clump of cells" or mere "tissue" may be an example of this dissociation. Indeed, the fact that the younger generation of prochoice advocates wants to do more to include the fetus in abortion rights discourse illustrates that they are far removed from the concerns and oppression suffered by the generations of women before them. That is, they feel comfortable talking about the fetus in moral terms because fetuses are no longer necessarily symbolic of the predestined role of women as mothers and homemakers.

Prochoice Stereotypes and the Need to Combat Them

In 2005, prochoice advocate Frances Kissling, the former president of Catholics for a Free Choice, challenged prochoice advocates to begin viewing the fetus as a being with some degree of intrinsic worth. To refuse to do so, she argued, paints a picture of prochoice advocacy as hardened or callous toward fetal life:

> I am deeply struck by the number of thoughtful, progressive people who have been turned off to the prochoice movement by the lack of adequate and clear expressions of respect for fetal life…. There is a strong distaste of the prochoice community in many facets of society because of the inability or unwillingness to acknowledge one iota of value in fetal life. (Kissling 2005)

Kissling seems to conclude that there is something intrinsic about prochoice advocacy that results in a "hardening of the heart" in regard to fetal life, and her evidence for this is that many individuals, including those who are sympathetic to the view that women possess abortion rights, perceive prochoice advocates in this way. This conclusion, of course, does not follow—we cannot conclude that belief x is intrinsic to position y simply because many individuals believe that it is. However, Kissling's conclusion is one that is shared by many individuals, including many young women who make up the new generation of abortion rights supporters.

Consider the words of Heidi, a young woman who obtained an abortion and, while supporting abortion choice for other women, is hesitant to self-identify as a prochoice advocate:

> Heidi also feels alienation from reproductive rights activists, whom she feels treat abortion too casually. She says, "I find myself not being a great supporter of the pro-choice movement. When I ask myself why that is, since I believe in the right to choose, what comes back as my answer is that it is something you are killing." Heidi laments that so much of the pro-choice side "tries to pretend that's not true." (Kushner 1997, 148)

Even though Heidi shared the core belief of the prochoice movement that women have a right to decide whether they will continue a pregnancy, she did not want to be labeled "prochoice" because she did not want to be associated with views that she regarded as intrinsic to the position: that the taking of fetal life is of little or no consequence.

A recent article in Newsweek entitled "Remember Roe!" tells about how women of the post-Roe generation have become lax in defending abortion rights, mostly because they take them for granted. Young members of NARAL Pro-Choice America don't "view abortion as an imperiled right in need of defenders." Moreover, "young voters flat-out disapproved of a woman's abortion, called her actions immoral, yet maintained that the government had absolutely no right to intervene" (Kliff 2010). Another poll finds that although 52% of young people agree that abortion should remain legal in all or most cases, "legalities aside, 59% believe abortion is morally wrong." One telling finding is that "[f]or millennials, three-quarters said they identified with the term pro-choice, while 65% said they could also be described as pro-life" (Rovner 2011). In other words, the younger generation holds complex and nuanced views regarding abortion; although most of them support keeping abortion legal, they also recognize that there is a moral dimension to abortion that expands beyond the issue of legalities. According to one young prochoice woman: "I only get mad when [a friend] tries telling me, 'It is nothing, oh well, it is just an abortion.' 'It wasn't the abortion itself that seemed to trouble the woman; rather, it was her friend's nonchalance. 'Even if it was like nothing,' the woman told NARAL, 'it was something'" (Kliff 2010).

What we can conclude from all this is that a stereotype of prochoice advocacy exists that paints abortion rights supporters as callous toward fetal life and unwilling to acknowledge the moral ambiguities of abortion. Antichoice advocates have seized upon this stereotype, and have used it to advance their cause. As Kathleen McDonnell notes:

> Abortion rights, and, indeed, feminism itself had come to be identified in the popular mind with an anti-family, anti-child mentality that had little respect for traditional values and cultural traditions. The opponents of feminism and abortion attempted to capitalize on this: feminists, they said, see children as mere inconveniences, obstacles to career fulfillment; pro-abortionists, they said, have no respect for the value of life and, even worse, want to impose their lack of values on the rest of society. (McDonnell 1984, 68)

Francke's and Little's respective citations illustrate that this view of prochoice advocacy is indeed a stereotype—there are prochoice feminists, academics, and even women who themselves have obtained abortions who deeply grapple with the moral ambiguity of abortion. From where, then, does this pervasive stereotype come? To be sure, there are prochoice advocates who do not regard abortion as a moral issue, and who disagree that fetal life is valuable and worthy of some degree of protection. But given that there is disagreement among prochoice advocates concerning this issue, why isn't this disagreement more showcased, and why has the

pendulum swung in favor of representing prochoice advocacy in the spirit of Warren, rather than in the spirit of Francke or Little? Much of it can be attributed to the pervasive distortion of the prochoice view from the rhetoric of some antichoice advocates themselves. But prochoice supporters are also to blame, for we have allowed this misrepresentation of our position to go largely unchecked.

Reading about the experiences of women who obtain abortions reveals that regarding the fetus as a subject of little value does not reflect the phenomenology of pregnancy or abortion for many women. Consider these two examples:

> The whole handling of the abortion issue is wrong. You don't toss [the fetus] in the garbage. I mean, I've had an abortion, it was an incredibly painful experience. I didn't toss it in the garbage. And I find it really distressing to hear it referred to in that way. (Cannold 1998, 36)
>
> I desperately wanted a feminist article, pamphlet, speech, anything that would let me have both the abortion and my own ambivalence.... I wanted to deal with the moral balance sheet of abortion, not to have to deny that one existed for me. Instead people kept telling me I was misguided, brainwashed by the patriarchy. They patiently explained that the fetus was just a bunch of cells. (Van Gelder 1978, 66–67)

This last citation reveals a need many women have that it seems the prochoice community is failing to meet. When prochoice supporters dismiss fetal life as being no more valuable than a "clump of cells," we do a disservice to the many women who obtain abortions but who, nevertheless, feel quite strongly that there is a moral dimension to their action that they wish to openly discuss. Even in the immediate aftermath of an abortion, a woman can feel some degree of sadness. Bobbie Jeanne Kennedy, an abortion nurse, writes about dealing with the emotional reactions of postabortive women. She tells the story of a woman who "reached out her beautifully delicate young hand, gently touched the cheek of her newly aborted tiny fetus and said 'I'm sorry, baby'" (Kennedy 1988, 1067). Another woman obtained an abortion after her fetus was diagnosed with a deformity: "The woman said: 'I don't want to deny that this baby existed.' She gave it a name, had a funeral for it, and buried it in the family plot alongside her grandmother" (1068). Discussing this moral dimension does not entail regretting the abortion, or even feeling that the choice to abort in a particular circumstance is wrong. Also, the reactions of the above-cited women should not be taken as evidence for what some antichoice advocates call "Post-Abortion Syndrome," a kind of posttraumatic stress disorder that they argue is intrinsic to abortion choice (see, for example, Reardon 1987). There is no evidence such a condition exists; although some women (but certainly not all) may feel sadness in the aftermath of an abortion, emotions of sadness are not equivalent to a clinical or pathological disease.[2] What these women pine for is acknowledgment of their emotions, and they desire to ground their abortion decision not via a dismissal of the worth of fetal life, but, rather, by acknowledging its value and still defending abortion rights through this lens. As is illustrated in "Remember Roe!" and in Heidi's comment, it is the perception of prochoice advocates as having "hardened hearts" that has resulted in some women turning their backs on the prochoice movement. Indeed, as a result of her conversation with the younger members of NARAL, pollster Anna Greenberg has concluded that the prochoice community needs to start "an open discussion about the moral, ethical, and emotional complexity of abortion that would be more likely to resonate with young Americans" (Kliff 2010).

Most antichoice advocates also hold a highly negative view of prochoice advocacy. Writing about the experiences and activities of antichoice advocates, Carol J. C. Maxwell reports the following words from an interviewee: "I think that we do not value people and we do not value ourselves.... That's part of why we have all these women killing their kids" (Maxwell 2002, 141). Similarly, some maintain that women who abort must think it permissible to kill anyone who is unwanted (98). According to Faye Ginsburg in her book *Contested Lives*, antichoice women regard women who abort as callous, materialistic, and uncaring (Ginsburg 1998, 185). Many antichoice supporters take these views and use them to gain political influence for restrictive abortion laws. For example,

Kristi Burton, sponsor of 2008's Personhood Amendment in Colorado (which, had it passed, would have granted embryos and fetuses the legal status of persons from fertilization), argued in favor of passing the amendment by stating that abortion rights have resulted in the cheapening of the value of life, and that it is only through granting fetuses the status of persons that society can "restore the dignity and respect unborn children have lost" (Ertelt 2008). For all these reasons, in the general reluctance to openly discuss abortion as a hard moral question, or acknowledge the value of fetal life, the prochoice position has suffered. As McDonnell writes:

> the feminist tendency has been to sidestep the entire moral discussion of abortion, either because we didn't see it as relevant to our concerns or because, though we may have been uncomfortable with the "clump of tissue" argument, we couldn't see anything else that didn't pose a threat to our basic position that women must control their own bodies. Consequently, we have largely abdicated any role in the moral discussion of abortion, and Right-to-Life ideology has filled the vacuum. (McDonnell 1984, 47)

There are two interconnected reasons, then, why prochoice feminists should strive to move away from Warren-like views regarding the value of fetal life.[3] First, because many pregnant women do view fetal life as valuable, even though some may nevertheless opt for abortion, regarding fetal life in a disparaging manner is insensitive to their views and alienates them from the prochoice community. Second, the younger prochoice generation is hungry for a discussion of the moral complexities of abortion, one that includes a discussion of the moral value of the fetus that moves beyond regarding it as mere "tissue." The prochoice community must work toward satiating this hunger.

Meeting Kissling's Challenge

In this section I will outline three ways prochoice advocates can meet Kissling's challenge by doing more to acknowledge the moral complexities, and at times ambiguities, of abortion. Weaving these suggestions into prochoice ideology can help soften the view of prochoice advocacy as necessarily callous toward fetal life, and to respect the women who regard abortion as a choice they indeed ought to possess, but one that carries with it serious moral dimensions. This, in turn, will allow us to begin the conversation in which it seems the younger generation of prochoice supporters is eager to partake.

Abortion, Decency, and Virtue

In Judith Jarvis Thomson's "A Defense of Abortion," she argues that, in terms of maintaining a pro-abortion-rights stance, it matters not whether the fetus is regarded as a person with rights equal to that of any extra-uterine person. Because no person's right to life entails that another person can be compelled to use her body for continued sustenance, the fetus cannot be given this right over the woman either. Thomson's argument is regarded as a seminal defense of abortion rights, but it has also been met with much criticism (see, for example, Wilcox 1989; Beckwith 1992; and Kaczor 2011, among many others). Yet although she spends the bulk of her essay arguing in favor of abortion rights, there is one aspect of her argument that is often overlooked. Although she argues that abortions are never unjust, she does argue that there are some abortions that are indecent. Although she never defines what she means by an "indecent" abortion, she does give an example of what such an abortion would look like: "It would be indecent in the woman to request an abortion, and indecent in a doctor to perform it, if she is in her seventh month, and wants the abortion just to avoid the nuisance of postponing a trip abroad" (Thomson 1971, 65). She also lumps "indecency" together with other displays of nonvirtuous character traits, such as self-centeredness and callousness (61). Therefore, Thomson seems to be arguing that although a woman is always within her moral rights to obtain an abortion, some reasons for doing so do not reflect a good character.

Rosalind Hursthouse develops this position in her article "Virtue Theory and Abortion." She argues that, from a virtue ethics perspective, although it may be the case that women possess a right to abort, this does not exhaust the moral dimensions of the matter. According to Hursthouse, we must ask the further, complex, question: are women using their abortion rights well?

> [I]n exercising a moral right I can do something cruel or callous, or selfish, light-minded, self-righteous, stupid, inconsiderate, disloyal, dishonest—that is, act viciously. Love and friendship do not survive their parties' constantly insisting on their rights, nor do people live well when they think that getting what they have a right to is of preeminent importance; they harm others, and they harm themselves. (Hursthouse 1991, 235)

Hursthouse spends the rest of her article detailing the difference between a vicious and a nonvicious/virtuous abortion. Because of her adherence to virtue theory, this will be determined largely by whether the woman in question was manifesting a virtuous or vicious character when coming to her decision to abort. As an example of an abortion that would betray a less-than-virtuous character, Hursthouse cites aborting for the sake of avoiding one's responsibilities in exchange for "'having a good time,' or for the pursuit of some false vision of ideals of freedom or self-realization" (242). Hursthouse also offers a criticism of Warren's disparaging view of fetal life.

> The fact that the premature termination of a pregnancy is, in some sense, the cutting off of a new human life, and thereby, like the procreation of a new human life, connects with all our thoughts about human life and death, parenthood, and family relationships, must make it a serious matter. To disregard this fact about it, to think of abortion as nothing but the killing of something that does not matter, or as nothing but the exercise of some right or rights one has, or as the incidental means to some desirable states of affairs, is to do something callous and light-minded, the sort of thing that no virtuous or wise person would do. (237–38)

Yet she also argues that some abortions do not reflect a vicious character; that, indeed, some abortions can be obtained for reasons that manifest virtues such as responsibility and care:

> Consider, for instance, a woman who has already had several children and fears that to have another will seriously affect her capacity to be a good mother to the ones she has—she does not show a lack of

appreciation of the intrinsic value of being a parent by opting for abortion. Nor does a woman who has been a good mother and is approaching the age at which she may be looking forward to being a good grandmother. Nor does a woman who discovers that her pregnancy may well kill her. Nor, necessarily, does a woman who has decided to lead a life centered around some other worthwhile activity or activities with which mother-hood would compete ... (241)

Hursthouse is not arguing, then, that women should not have a right to an abortion. Rather, what she is maintaining is that we extend the conversation beyond the question of rights. With all our rights there are responsible and irresponsible, callous and caring, ways of exercising them. Although some prochoice advocates may recoil at the thought of subjecting the abortion right to this analysis, it seems that, in light of the above-mentioned desire to have this conversation by prochoice supporters themselves, we have come to a point where it is essential to start doing so.

Leslie Cannold's research, featured in her book *The Abortion Myth*, illustrates that there are many prochoice women who already make judgments about particular abortion decisions in a manner similar to that of Hursthouse and Thomson:

> Almost all the women I interviewed saw the abortion issue as revolving around the pregnant woman's decision-making process. An abortion decision that did not reflect a woman's "feelings" and "love" for her could-be child and other significant people in her life, and that was not motivated by care and protective concern for all those she loves, was just plain wrong. (Cannold 1998, xix–xx)

In her interviews with the young women who support abortion choice, Cannold notes that they were eager to move beyond the discussion of abortion qua rights and more toward discussion of the morality of individual abortion choices; a "morally right" abortion is one that displays certain virtues: responsibility, caring, compassion, and respect for fetal life (17). As an illustration of this, Cannold asks many of the women to give their thoughts on what is known as "abortion doping": the rumored practice among Olympian female runners to deliberately become pregnant in order to abort right before a competition; the added hormones

produced by the recently terminated pregnancy are said to enhance performance. According to Cannold, the "vast majority of women found the idea of using pregnancy as a means to another end completely repugnant." One prochoice woman, Carey, chastised anyone who participated in abortion doping for failing to "'honor' pregnancy as 'the phenomenal creation of life'" (91). Another prochoice woman, Frances, maintained that what's wrong about abortion doping is that it leaves out "the 'emotional' and 'spiritual' aspects of the pregnancy ..." (91). Notice that what is being judged is not the act of abortion itself, but rather the motivations for the abortion, or what traits of character were being expressed by women who engage in abortion doping. Whereas an abortion obtained for reasons having to do with caring for dependents, out of respect for the value of motherhood (and perhaps being honest about one's inability to fulfill the requirements of motherhood to a particular fetus at a particular time), and even out of love for the fetus, would be considered acceptable, aborting for reasons such as abortion doping, or for the sake of "having a good time" would be considered morally repugnant. These women never contested the right to an abortion, but the reasons for which one exercises that right can be subject to moral scrutiny.

From this we can conclude that the newer generation of prochoice women are already having these discussions among themselves, and that, in general, the prochoice community must keep up with these women by taking up the discussion as an important aspect of prochoice ideology. The new questions that need to be asked are: "Are there irresponsible pregnancies? Which reasons for having an abortion are bad ones? Even if women have a right to choose abortion, is it always right for them to do so? Why, after all this time, have these questions never been answered, and so rarely been asked?" (Cannold 1998, 17). Even NARAL President Nancy Keenan has noticed the need to engage in this discussion: "Our reluctance to address the moral complexity of this debate is no longer serving our cause or our country well. In our silence, we have ceded moral ground" (Kliff 2010).

No doubt some antichoice advocates will attempt to usurp the discussion as evidence that even prochoice advocates recognize the moral wrongness of abortion, but this is why it is critical that prochoice advocates have this discussion on their own terms. Moreover, acknowledging that there is a moral dimension to abortion beyond the subject of rights recognizes what so many pro- and antichoice women already believe: that fetal life has value, and that, therefore, there has to be a framework for determining what constitutes a morally acceptable reason for taking that life. This, of course, needs much more development than I can provide here, but expanding upon Hursthouse's use of virtue ethics provides a promising way.

Caring for Women Who Grieve

As mentioned above, the evidence strongly suggests that there is no such thing as Post-Abortion Syndrome. Most women typically handle their decision to abort well; there is even evidence that some women who choose abortion see it as an overall positive life experience (see, for example, Zabin et al. 1989 and Warren et al. 2010). However, there are women who do experience postabortion maladjustment. Some risk factors include events that occur after the abortion, perceived lack of support for the abortion decision, ambivalence concerning the decision to abort, compromised coping capacities in general, quality of relationship with male partner, and feeling coerced into the abortion (see, for example, Adler et al. 1990; Major and Cozzarelli 1992; Major et al. 1997). Moreover, many women who experience psychiatric disorders after an abortion likely suffered from psychiatric disorders before the abortion as well (Major et al. 2008, 89). Consequently, it is "likely that psychological maladjustment occurring subsequent to an abortion frequently is misattributed to the abortion experience, whereas it may be more indicative of adjustment problems present prior to pregnancy" (Major and Cozzarelli 1992, 136).[4] However, this is not to say that there aren't women who feel some degree of sadness, sorrow, or feelings of loss after an abortion, for "[a]bortion is an experience often hallmarked by ambivalence, and a mix of positive and negative emotions is to be expected" (Major et al. 2008, 885).

Ambivalent postabortion feelings are sometimes not taken very seriously, even by members of the prochoice community. In her book, Cannold writes about the reaction of a prochoice colleague when she shared her research findings that many women who abort do indeed regard the fetus as a valuable entity worthy of respect: "When I pointed out to him how women's views and experiences repeatedly contradicted established moral thought on abortion he replied: 'Well, who cares what women think? That they think it doesn't make it right'" (Cannold 1998, xxxi). Consider Heather's experiences after her abortion; she writes that she felt "angry at the feminist movement, which I am whole-heartedly a part of. I didn't expect such an emotional experience.... I felt betrayed that abortion was made to look like an easy decision, and it wasn't for me. I had carefully weighed it all out. It was still the right decision at the time. But I still had to cry, to grieve the loss of this potential child, and the loss of my pregnant state" (Banoit 1983, 21). Another woman, Naomi, writes that "[t]he women I talked to weren't all that supportive of my feelings. In fact some of them were cruel, telling me not to be so upset. After all, I had chosen this" (20). Another woman is hesitant to express sadness over an abortion precisely because she fears being regarded as traitorous to the feminist movement: "[t]here seemed to be this unspoken rule that a good feminist isn't supposed to grieve" (McDonnell 1984, 34). When Ava Torre-Bueno, a head counselor at San Diego's Planned Parenthood for twenty years, tried to get Planned Parenthood to help market her book *Peace After Abortion*, she was denounced by the director as being a "dupe of the antis" (Bazelon 2007). Torre-Bueno is an ardent prochoice advocate who firmly maintains that there is no such condition as Post-Abortion Syndrome (Torre-Bueno 1997, 78). Nevertheless, she legitimizes postabortion grief (4–7) and argues that the prochoice community should as well: "what you hear in the movement is 'Let's not make noise about this' and 'Most women are fine, I'm sure you will be too.' And that is unfair" (Bazelon 2007).

What can prochoice advocates do to support these women? One pivotal step is to ensure excellent pre-abortion counseling that would be sensitive to the abovementioned markers for postabortion maladjustment. One example of stellar pre-abortion counseling can be found in Dr. Susan Wicklund's book *This Common Secret*, which chronicles her decades-long experiences as an abortion provider. In her practice, she offers extensive pre-abortion counseling, where she insists on ensuring that the woman is acting out of her own volition. If there seems to be any hesitation regarding the extent to which a woman is certain of her decision to abort, Wicklund refuses to perform the procedure. In one example, she sends a prospective patient away twice because of her ambivalence, performing the abortion only after she is sure that her uncertainty has abated. The patient thanks Wicklund for her patience, admitting to her that "I'd have been a wreck if you had done the abortion the first time I came in" (Wicklund and Kesselheim 2007, 100).

Counseling sessions at Wicklund's practice often last hours before the abortion is performed to ensure the woman's emotional stability and, most important, to make certain that the decision to abort is entirely autonomous (Wicklund and Kesselheim 2007, 98). Her methods are the epitome of what prochoice philosophy ought to be. Despite what some antichoice advocates may believe, being prochoice is not about pushing or touting abortion as the best option for all women facing an unplanned pregnancy. Being prochoice is about three things: one, ensuring that women have access to safe and legal abortion if they so choose; two, ensuring that a woman's choice to abort really is a genuine choice of her own accord and free will; and three, respecting and supporting any choice that a woman makes in regard to her pregnancy, whether that be abortion, adoption, or parenting.

Excellent pre-abortion counseling must be accompanied by excellent postabortion counseling as well. Rachel Needle and Lenore Walker's book *Abortion Counseling* illustrates effective postabortion counseling techniques. One case study involves a woman, Laura, who felt sadness, loss, and guilt after her abortion. Her counselor writes:

> The most important thing for me to do when Laura came back to my office was to be empathic and allow her to express her feelings of guilt and sadness. I gave Laura permission to cry. We then

began to explore her decision to have an abortion. Laura had a long list of reasons why having the abortion was the right thing for her to do. I reinforced her decision, by reflecting back her reasons that helped her make the decision to terminate the pregnancy.... Being empathic, listening, and helping Laura reflect on her decision proved helpful to her. (Needle and Walker 2008, 134)

Similar examples abound throughout the book, but the common denominator is that, in all cases where women express postabortion grief or sorrow, the therapist creates a "safe, compassionate, nonjudgmental and trusting environment" (Needle and Walker 2008, 135) for the patient. One important thing to note is how the use of dismissive language to refer to the fetus may have an adverse affect on a woman's postabortion coping abilities. Torre-Bueno notes that one of her patients had lingering sorrow after an abortion partly because "[s]he couldn't grieve for them earlier because she had no one to support her in thinking of them as babies or children she had lost" (Torre-Bueno 1997, 23). The employees at another abortion clinic justify their use of the term "baby" to describe fetuses given similar concerns: "if the woman who is choosing abortion experiences this as a baby, how are we helping her deal with her decision if we tell her she is wrong?" (Ludlow 2008, 43).

Finally, postabortion counseling services should provide, for the women who desire them, postabortion rituals designed to help women deal with any negative feelings they may be experiencing. Torre-Bueno's book describes many different kinds of postabortion rituals, some as simple as "lighting candles on the anniversary of your abortion, or the date you would have delivered if you hadn't had the abortion" as a way of working through grief (Torre-Bueno 1997, 23). A prochoice grieving ritual should affirm the validity of a woman's decision to abort, both by acknowledging the reasons she aborted as well as the difficulties she may have experienced in reaching that decision. Moreover, the ritual should serve as an open forum to allow women to express any and all emotions that come with her abortion, from sorrow to relief or any feelings in between, and allow her an opportunity to say goodbye to the fetus.[5] Finally, the ritual should acknowledge that fetal death is of some consequence; that the very reason a ritual is desired, and that abortion can be painful, is because the destruction of fetal life is so very unlike the destruction of any other part of a woman's body. Prochoice advocates consistently (and correctly) argue that abortion is never an easy decision for women, that they typically make the decision carefully and responsibly. The likely reason for this is that women who abort typically understand the significance of their decision precisely because they understand that aborting a fetus is not like removing any other organic material from one's body. That is, women do not typically experience pregnancy and abortion as a form of "disembodiment, of separation of woman from fetus, of mother from child. These are the experiences that speak to the complexity of abortion as it is lived by women rather than as it is expounded by activists" (Ludlow 2008, 44).

Reducing Abortions

Although prochoice advocates need to continue fighting for a woman's right to safe and legal abortion, they should also make it an important part of prochoice advocacy that abortion is a right that is exercised with less frequency. Adopting this secondary goal helps to draw a distinction between being "prochoice" and being "proabortion"; a distinction that is often collapsed. The term "proabortion" denotes someone who encourages abortion, who celebrates abortion, who desires to see women choose abortion over other options. I know of no prochoice advocate who meets this definition.

There are, essentially, two ways to reduce abortion rates: one, via the prevention of unplanned pregnancies and two, via changing certain aspects of society so that women aren't coerced into choosing abortion because they fear having a child will force them to compromise other worthwhile goals. Achieving the first goal is rather straightforward—various studies have confirmed that an essential component to reducing unplanned pregnancies is to increase access to effective contraception, in addition to comprehensive sex education that ensures its correct and consistent use

(see, for example, Bongaarts and Westoff 2000; Deschner and Cohen 2003). The second part of the abortion-reducing equation is more difficult to achieve. The reality facing single young women if they decide to bring an unplanned pregnancy to term is stark enough to understand why so many decide to abort. Women who live below the poverty line are about four times as likely to obtain an abortion when compared to women who live 300% above the poverty level (Jones, Darroch, and Henshaw 2002). On average, single women have higher poverty rates than single men, a phenomenon described by Diana Pearce as "the feminization of poverty" (Pearce 1978, 28–36; see also Casper, McLanahan, and Garfinkel 1994; Pressman 2002).

Children born to unwed teenage mothers, and the mothers themselves, face a host of difficulties, including an increased risk of failure in school, of poverty, and even of incidences of physical and mental illness (American Academy of Child and Adolescent Psychiatry 2004). One of the most prevalent reasons women choose abortion is financial difficulty (see, for example, Finer et al. 2005; Jones, Finer, and Singh 2008). This should concern prochoice advocates because aborting for such reasons compromises genuine choice. As McDonnell writes:

> If poverty is the reason she is terminating the pregnancy, if in fact she wants the child but cannot afford to have it, she is actually being coerced into an abortion. She does not, in fact, have a choice at all.... Feminists should make our position clear that when we talk about the "right to choose," we are not talking about women having abortions solely because they can't afford the child. Obviously, if we are going to work for choice in our reproductive lives, we also have to work to bring about the conditions—social, economic, cultural—that will make it a real possibility. (McDonnell 1984, 71)

Tellingly, the countries with the fewest incidences of abortion are the ones that have implemented comprehensive sex education programs and access to contraception, in addition to offering social support programs that provide a financial safety net for their citizens and residents. The Netherlands, for example, has one of the lowest rates of abortion in the world (7 for every 1,000 women). It also provides:

> a range of what sociologists call "social" and what reproductive health advocates call "human" rights: the right to housing, healthcare, and a minimum income. Not only do such rights ensure access, if need be, to free contraceptive and abortion services, government support makes coming of age less perilous for both teenagers and parents. This might make the prospect of sex derailing a child less haunting. Ironically, the very lack of such rights and high rates of childhood poverty in the U.S. contribute to high rates of births among teenagers. Without adequate support systems or education and job opportunities, young people are simply more likely to start parenthood early in life. (Schalet 2010, 20)

There is evidence that providing assistance in the form of financial help, childcare services, and medical services results in decreased abortion rates (Reid 2010). In addition to providing postnatal medical support, which eases the economic hardship that comes with raising a child, easy access to medical care means easy access to effective contraception, which, in turn, reduces the need to seek abortions in the first place. Joseph Wright, writing on behalf of the group Catholics in Alliance for the Common Good, issued a report on the various studies that illustrate the socioeconomic factors that influence many women's decision to abort. Because he represents a Catholic organization, Wright makes it clear that he is in favor of restrictive abortion laws; however, he also argues that, if the goal is to reduce abortion, criminalizing it without offering concurrent social support will be ineffective. Rather, a genuine effort to reduce abortions would include implementing social policies that would offer prenatal and postnatal care, nutritional care for both mother and child, as well as pediatric care for the child, quality and affordable childcare so that young parents can either complete their education or obtain full-time work, and support for victims of sexual and physical abuse (Wright 2008).

In reference to the impact financial assistance has on the decision to abort, Wright notes that "[i]n states where families typically have higher incomes, there may be less economic pressure to end a pregnancy through abortion because the cost of caring for a child constitutes a smaller share of the typical family's income" (Wright 2008). In reference to the correlation between increased financial assistance to poor families and reduced abortion rates, Wright reports that an increase of $100 per person in the form of child-centered welfare "was correlated with a decrease in the abortion rate of about 20% … approximately 195,000 abortions per year" (Wright 2008). Increasing poverty by 3.8% increased the rate of abortion by 10% (90,000 more abortions per year). In terms of employment, increasing male employment by 4% is correlated with a 21% drop in abortion rates, whereas increasing female employment by 4% is correlated with a 17% increase in abortion rates. Wright argues this increase may be related to a lack of affordable and quality childcare (Wright 2008). What seems to be effective in reducing abortion rates is not simply criminalizing abortions (research illustrates that countries with restrictive abortion laws nevertheless have high incidences of abortion) (Deschner and Cohen 2003, 7). Rather, what is effective is support for families once the infant is born: commitment to nutritional and health care, quality childcare, and access to education or work programs designed to help single mothers overcome poverty.

For those whose political theory regards the state as having an important role in social welfare, advocating for this particular instance of social welfare should be regarded as a core component of their position on abortion.[6] In addition to fostering genuine choice, this helps meet Kissling's challenge because it illustrates that not even prochoice advocates see abortion as an innocuous action; rather, that they see it as a choice that, ideally, fewer and fewer women would have to make. Of course, this will not eliminate abortions—contraception will occasionally fail, even with perfect use, and some women simply do not want to be mothers, neither at the time of their unplanned pregnancy nor ever. Moreover, as long as sexual violence exists against women, abortion access is needed for the women who cannot bring themselves to gestate after being victimized.

Why Endorsing Abortion Rights and Fetal Value Are Not Mutually Exclusive

If successful, Thomson's argument illustrates that granting fetuses the status of persons is not sufficient for justifying a ban on abortion. Even if we grant the fetus all the rights of any extra-uterine person, this does not entail that abortions are impermissible, since no extra-uterine person has a right to use the body of another for sustenance. But Thomson's argument may serve a secondary function as well: if successful, it allows us to simultaneously express respect for fetal life while maintaining that women have a right to an abortion. As much as we can feel for the life of patients in need of organ transplants, we cannot force otherwise healthy persons to donate nonvital organs to save the sick. This does not mean that the lives of these patients have no value; rather what it means is that no matter how valuable they are, this value cannot be used as grounds to infringe upon the rights of other persons. Similarly, we can argue that being prochoice need not entail a wanton disregard of fetal life, but, rather, an acknowledgment that, like all persons, pregnant women have a right to decide if they want to use their bodies to sustain another.

Even if Thomson's argument is rejected, however, there are other avenues open to those who wish to simultaneously endorse abortion rights and respect for fetal life. As mentioned above, we can appeal to Hursthouse's use of virtue ethics to distinguish between supporting a right to x, without always endorsing how that right is exercised. Drawing this distinction allows one to argue that there are really two pertinent questions in abortion rights discourse: 1. Do women have a right to obtain abortions? 2. Are all exercises of this right virtuous ones? One can answer the first question in the affirmative, while admitting that in some cases the second can be answered in the negative. The reason we may sometimes frown upon certain justifications for obtaining an abortion is that it does involve the death of a being that has moral value, and the death of that being should be regarded with respect rather than flippancy (the latter, for

example, is certainly the way the death of the fetus is regarded in cases of abortion doping).

A third way is to deny that human fetuses are persons who have interests, and therefore are not rights-bearers (so that killing them does not violate a right to life), but still maintain that they are valuable beings in virtue of their status as nascent human life. A way to understand this perspective is to consider our treatment of nonhuman animals; although they are not typically considered persons with a right to life (euthanizing an animal, for example, is not considered homicide), many would agree that they should be treated humanely and with respect in virtue of their sentient nature, and that they should not be unjustifiably or wantonly killed, even if, ultimately, their deaths are not tantamount to murder. Similarly, one can argue, because embryos and early fetuses lack certain morally relevant traits (for example, embryos and early fetuses are nonsentient and lack the capacity for conscious awareness), killing them is not tantamount to murder. Yet because they are living members of the species *Homo sapiens* and because they are potential persons, they possess morally relevant traits that render them worthy of some degree of respect, and their deaths ought not to be taken lightly. This, for example, is the position of Ronald Dworkin, who spends most of his book *Life's Dominion* defending the right to an abortion on the grounds that early to mid-term fetuses lack interests due to their lack of sentience and consciousness. Nevertheless, he still regards an abortion as "a waste of a human life and is, therefore, in itself, a bad thing to happen, a shame" (Dworkin 1993, 84). In other words, one can simultaneously deny that fetuses possesses moral status and rights equal to those of persons (because they lack certain morally relevant traits), but also deny that they are completely devoid of value altogether (because they possess other morally relevant traits).

These are brief sketches of possible ways a prochoice advocate can simultaneously endorse abortion rights and embrace the value of fetal life. All deserve more elaboration than I can offer here, and none are devoid of difficulties. What I want to show is that we do not have to completely erase the fetus from moral consideration in order to defend abortion rights. The stereotype that prochoice advocacy inevitably entails the dehumanization of the fetus does not advance the prochoice position in the eyes of American society. Prochoice advocates must do more to combat this stereotype, and we must do more to broaden our arguments in favor of abortion rights in a way that is open to respecting fetal life. Given the constant onslaught of restrictive abortion laws, prochoice advocacy cannot afford to be reduced or erased from public discourse. Fetal life matters to many women, including women who abort and who defend the right to abortion. Prochoice discourse could become stronger if we "embraced discussion and images of the fetus and honest stories of the full range—from joy to grief—of women's relationships to their fetuses and emotional responses to abortion" (Ludlow 2008, 46).

To trivialize fetal life is to dismiss the phenomenology of pregnancy and abortions for many women. It is to be dismissive not just of nascent human life, but of the very women whose rights we fight so vehemently to defend and whose support we may stand to lose.

NOTES

Many thanks to Nina Anton, Jackie Gately (Arizona State University), Kate Padgett Walsh (Iowa State University), and Michelle Beer (Florida International University), for their help with earlier drafts and incarnations of this paper. Also, thank you to Ann Cudd, Asia Ferrin, and to the anonymous *Hypatia* reviewers for all their comments, suggestions, and patience. Finally, as always, thank you to my husband Tuomas Manninen and our daughter Michelle for their support and love.

I would like to dedicate this paper to Professors Jack and Melissa Mulder (Hope College). Although we share differing views on abortion, they have helped me realize the need that exists for prochoice and prolife advocates to dialogue about the difficult issues that are present on both sides of the abortion debate, and the need that exists to take each other's concerns more seriously.

1. See, for example, the writings of Naomi Wolf, Linda Bird Francke, Sue Nathanson, Leslie Cannold, Laurie Shrage, Monica Casper, Christine Overall, Margaret Olivia Little, Kathleen McDonnell, Lynn Morgan, Rayna Rapp, Faye Ginsburg, Linda Layne, Rachel Roth, Barbara Katz Rothman, among many others.

2. Some examples of studies that conclude there is no such condition as Post-Abortion Syndrome: Buckels 1982; Adler et al. 1990; Dagg 1991; Stotland 1991; Major and Cozzarelli 1992; Wilmouth et al. 1992; Gilchrist et al. 1995; Major et al. 2000; Needle and Walker 2008; Major et al. 2009; and Munk-Olsen et al. 2011.

3. It should be noted that Warren later softened her view regarding the moral status of the fetus, and was willing to grant it some degree of moral status after the fetus has acquired sentience. However, until her death she still held to a generally prochoice position. See Warren 1997 for her updated arguments.

4. One noteworthy consequence of these predictors of abortion maladjustment is that parental and spousal notification laws may serve to work against a woman's mental well-being. If a woman perceives her parents or partner as being supportive of her decision to abort, she will likely voluntarily inform them of her decision. A woman who typically refuses to reveal this information to her parents or partner does so because she likely feels they will be unsupportive, or that they will attempt to thwart the abortion. Consequently, laws that require her to do so will likely put her in a situation of perceived lack of support, which, in turn, may serve to retard her postabortion emotional adjustment.

5. I should emphasize here that I am not condemning women who fail to grieve after an abortion. Women who grieve should be allowed to do so, but that is not to say that women must grieve, or that they are morally remiss if they fail to do so. In 2000, a postabortion telephone counseling service called "Exhale" opened its doors for any woman, partners, family, or friends who wish to talk about any difficulties they are facing after an abortion. Their mission statement reads: "Exhale creates a social climate where each person's unique experience with abortion is supported, respected and free from stigma." Although founded by women who have procured abortions, Exhale counselors do not describe themselves as either "prochoice" or

"prolife," but, rather, "provoice." The popularity of Exhale points to a need for their services, and prochoice advocates should make it a priority, as an essential aspect of prochoice advocacy, to help meet the needs of these women.

6. Thank you to my anonymous *Hypatia* reviewer for this wording.

REFERENCES

Adler, Nancy, Henry P. David, Brenda Major, Susan Roth, Nancy Russo, and Gail Wyatt. 1990. Psychological responses after abortion. *Science* 248 (4951): 41-44.

American Academy of Child and Adolescent Psychiatry. 2004. When children have children. http://www.aacap.org/cs/root/facts_for_families/when_children_have_children (accessed November 12, 2011).

Banoit, Cecilia. 1983. The right to grieve: Two women talk about their abortions. *Healthsharing: A Woman's Health Quarterly* 5 (1): 19-26.

Bazelon, Emily. 2007. Is there a post-abortion syndrome? *The New York Times,* January 21. http://www.nytimes.com/2007/01/21/magazine/21abortion.t.html?_r=1&pagewanted=print (accessed November 12, 2011).

Beckwith, Francis. 1992. Personal bodily rights, abortion, and unplugging the violinist. *International Philosophical Quarterly* 32 (1): 105-18.

Buckels, Nancy. 1982. Abortion: A technique for working through grief. *Journal of American College Health Association* 30 (4): 18-19.

Cannold, Leslie. 1998. *The abortion myth: Feminism, morality, and the hard choices women make.* Hanover, N.H.: Wesleyan University Press.

Casper, Lynn, Sara S. McLanahan, and Irwin Garfinkel. 1994. The gender–poverty gap: What we can learn from other countries. *American Sociological Review* 59 (4): 594-605.

Dagg, Paul K. B.. 1991. The psychological sequelae of therapeutic abortions—denied and completed. *American Journal of Psychiatry* 148 (5): 578-85.

Deschner, Amy, and Susan Cohen. 2003. Contraceptive use is key to reducing abortion worldwide. *The Guttmacher Report on Public Policy* 6 (4): 7-10.

Dworkin, Ronald. 1993. *Life's dominion: Argument about abortion, euthanasia, and individual freedom.* New York: Random House.

Ertelt, Steven. 2008. Colorado Abortion-Personhood Amendment Gets OK from Top Pro-Life Group.

http://www.lifenews.com/2008/08/06/state-3430/ (accessed March 20, 2012).

Francke, Linda. 1978. *The ambivalence of abortion.* New York: Random House.

Finer, Lawrence B., Lori F. Finer, Lindsay Frohwirth, A. Dauphinee, Sushella Singh, and Ann M. Moore. 2005. Reasons U.S. women have abortions: Quantitative and qualitative perspectives. *Perspectives on Sexual and Reproductive Health* 37 (3): 110-18.

Gilchrist, A. C., P. C. Hannaford, P. Frank, and C. R. Kay. 1995. Termination of pregnancy and psychiatric morbidity. *British Journal of Psychiatry* 167 (2): 243-48.

Ginsburg, Faye. 1998. *Contested lives: The abortion debate in an American community.* Los Angeles: University of California Press.

Hursthouse, Rosalind. 1991. Virtue theory and abortion. *Philosophy and Public Affairs* 20 (3): 223-46.

Jones, Rachel, Lawrence B. Finer, and Susheela Singh. 2008. Characteristics of U.S. abortion patients. http://www.guttmacher.org/pubs/US-Abortion-Patients.pdf (accessed November 21, 2011).

Jones, Rachel, Jacqueline Darroch, and Stanley K. Henshaw. 2002. Patterns in the socioeconomic characteristics of women obtaining abortion in 2000–2001. *Perspectives on Sexual and Reproductive Health* 34 (5): 226-35.

Kaczor, Christopher. 2011. *The ethics of abortion: Women's rights, human life, and the question of justice.* New York: Routledge.

Kennedy, Bobbie Jeanne. 1988. I'm sorry baby. *American Journal of Nursing* 88 (8): 1067-69.

Kissling, Frances. 2005. Is there life after Roe?: How to think about the fetus. *Conscience: The News Journal of Catholic Opinion.* http://www.catholicsforchoice.org/conscience/archives/c2004win_lifeafterroe.asp (accessed January 5, 2012).

Kliff, Sarah. 2010. Remember Roe! How can the next generation defend abortion rights when they don't think abortion rights need defending? *Newsweek,* April 29.

Kushner, Eve. 1997. *Experiencing abortion: A weaving of women's words.* New York: Harrington Park Press.

Little, Margaret Olivia. 2002. The morality of abortion. In *Ethical issues in modern medicine,* ed. Bonnie Steinbock, John Arras and Alex John London. New York: McGraw Hill.

Ludlow, Jeannie. 2008. Sometimes, it's a child and a choice: Toward an embodied abortion praxis. *Feminism Formations* 20 (1): 26-50.

Major, Brenda, and Catherine Cozzarelli. 1992. Psychosocial predictors of adjustment to abortion. *Journal of Social Issues* 48 (3): 121-42.

Major, Brenda, Josephine Zubek, M. Lynne Cooper, Catherine Cozzarelli, and Caroline Richards. 1997. Mixed messages: Implications of social conflict and social support within close relationships for adjustment to a stressful life event. *Journal of Personality and Social Psychology* 72 (6): 1349-63.

Major, Brenda, Mark Appelbaum, Linda Beckman, Mary Ann Dutton, Nancy Felipe Russo, and Carolyn West. 2009. Abortion and mental health—evaluating the evidence. *American Psychologist* 64 (9): 863-90.

Major, Brenda, Catherine Cozzarelli, M. Lynne Cooper, Josephine Zubek, Caroline Richards, Michael Wilhite, and Richard Gramzow. 2000. Psychological response of women after first–trimester abortion. *Archives of General Psychiatry* 57: 777-78.

Major, Brenda, Mark Applebaum, Linda Beckman, Mary Ann Dutton, Nancy Felipe Russo, and Carolyn West. 2008. *Report of the APA task force on mental health and abortion.* http://www.apa.org/pi/wpo/mental-health-abortion-report.pdf (accessed November 21, 2011).

Maxwell, Carol. 2002. *Pro-life activists in America.* New York: Cambridge University Press.

McDonagh, Eileen. 1996. *Breaking the abortion deadlock: From choice to consent.* New York: Oxford University Press.

McDonnell, Kathleen. 1984. *Not an easy choice: A feminist re-examines abortion.* Toronto: The Women's Press.

Munk-Olsen, Trine, Thomas Munk Laursen, Carsten B. Pedersen, Øjvind Lidegaard, and Preben Bo Mortensen. 2011. Induced first-trimester abortion and risk of mental disorder. *New England Journal of Medicine* 364 (4): 332-38.

Needle, Rachel, and Lenore Walker. 2008. *Abortion counseling: A clinician's guide to psychology, legislation, politics, and competency.* New York: Springer Publishing Company.

Pearce, Diana. 1978. The feminization of poverty: Women, work, and welfare. *Urban and Social Change Review* 11 (1–2): 28-36.

Poppema, Suzanne. 1996. *Why I am an abortion doctor.* New York: Prometheus Books.

Pressman, Steven. 2002. Explaining the gender poverty gap in developed and transitional economies. *Journal of Economic Issues* 36 (1): 17-40.

Reardon, David. 1987. *Aborted women: Silent no more.* Westchester, Ill.: Crossway Books.

Reid, T. R. 2010. Universal healthcare tends to cut abortion rate. *The Washington Post*, March 14. http://www.washingtonpost.com/wpdyn/content/article/2010/03/12/AR2010031202287.html (accessed November 12, 2011).

Rovner, Julie 2011. Poll: Generation Y divided on abortion, like their parents. http://www.npr.org/blogs/health/2011/06/09/137079714/poll-generation-y-supports-gay-marriage-but-is-divided-on-abortion?sc=fb&cc=fp (accessed November 21, 2011).

Schalet, Amy. 2010. Sex, love, and autonomy in the teenage sleepover. *Contexts* 9 (3): 16-21.

Stotland, Nada, ed. 1991. *Psychiatric aspects of abortion.* Washington, D.C.: American Psychiatric Press.

Thomson, Judith Jarvis. 1971. A defense of abortion. *Philosophy and Public Affairs* 1 (1): 47-66.

Torre-Bueno, Ava. 1997. *Peace after abortion.* San Diego: Pimpernel Press.

Van Gelder, Linsy. 1978. Cracking the women's movement protection game. *Ms. Magazine*, December.

Warren, Jocelyn T., S. Marie Harvey, and Jillian T. Henderson. 2010. Do depression and low self-esteem follow abortion among adolescents? Evidence from a national study. *Perspectives on Sexual and Reproductive Health* 42 (4): 230-35.

Warren, Mary Anne. 1973. On the moral and legal status of abortion. *The Monist* 57 (1): 43-61.

Warren, Mary Anne. 1997. *Moral status: Obligations to persons and other living things.* New York: Oxford University Press.

Wicklund, Sue, and Alan Kesselheim. 2007. *This common secret: My journey as an abortion doctor.* New York: Perseus Books.

Wilcox, John. 1989. Nature as demonic in Thomson's defense of abortion. *New Scholasticism* 63 (4): 463-84.

Wilmouth, Gregory, Martin de Alteriis, and Danielle Bussell. 1992. Prevalence of psychological risks following legal abortion in the U.S.: Limits of the evidence. *Journal of Social Issues* 48 (3): 37-66.

Wright, Joseph. 2008. Reducing abortion in America: The effect of socioeconomic factors. http://www.catholicsinalliance.org/files/CACG_Final.pdf (accessed November 12, 2011).

Zabin, L. S., M. B. Hirsch, and M. R. Emerson. 1989. When urban adolescents choose abortion: Effects on education, psychological status, and subsequent pregnancy. *Family Planning Perspective* 21 (6): 248-55.

⚜ QUESTIONS FOR ANALYSIS

1. What are examples of prochoice stereotypes of concern to Manninen? Are there others you can think of that are not included here? Has she fairly characterized these stereotypes?
2. What aspects of Thomson's article (included in this anthology) does Manninen find helpful to her goal of highlighting the moral issues in abortion?
3. In urging appropriate counseling for women who grieve after an abortion, how does Manninen reconcile her recognition of this grief with a prochoice position?
4. What are the two major ways in which abortions can be dramatically reduced, according to Manninen?
5. How does Manninen argue that abortion rights and fetal value are not mutually exclusive?

CASE PRESENTATION

Conceived in Violence, Born in Hate[1]

Shortly after returning home, a twenty-seven-year-old mother was gagged, tied up, and raped by a 220-pound guard from a nearby Air Force base who had forced his way into her home. The woman received medical treatment at a hospital and from her own physician. Nevertheless, the episode had left her pregnant.

Not wanting the child, the woman sought an abortion. Although the state's abortion law was, at the time (1955), one of the least restrictive, no hospital in her state would permit her to have an abortion.

Unable to afford to travel abroad for a legal abortion, the woman and her husband were left with two choices: a clandestine illegal abortion or having the baby. Deeply religious and law abiding, the couple chose to carry the baby to term.

During her pregnancy, the woman admitted to hating the fetus she was carrying and to eagerly awaiting the time she would be rid of it. "Thus the child, conceived in violence and born in hatred, came into the world."[2]

Many politicians otherwise opposed to abortion have typically supported an exemption for pregnancies caused by rape or incest. In the 2012 political campaign, however, the Republican Party adopted a national platform opposing all abortions, with no exemptions. Several prominent candidates emphasized this position in their campaigns. One losing Senate candidate in Indiana said that rape was "God's plan." Another losing candidate, this one in Missouri, said that no rape exception was needed, as women's bodies "have a way of shutting down" after a rape and avoiding pregnancy. These remarks, and many others, have reignited the debate over whether abortion should be permitted after rape or incest, even if banned in other circumstances.

⚜ QUESTIONS FOR ANALYSIS

1. Do you think abortion should or should not be legal when the pregnancy results from rape? Regardless of whether it's legal, is it moral? If one opposes all abortion on the grounds that fetuses are persons from the moment of conception, is it possible to consistently defend an exception for pregnancies resulting from rape?
2. The traditional Roman Catholic position on abortion rests on the assumption that the unborn is a person from conception. Since the fetus is an innocent person, even when a pregnancy is due to rape or incest, the fetus may not be held accountable and made to suffer through its death. According to Roman Catholicism, then, a *direct* abortion is never morally justifiable. (Although the fetus may never be deliberately killed, it may be allowed to die as a consequence of an action that is intended to save the life of the mother, such as the removal of a malignant uterus.) By this account, an abortion in the preceding case would be immoral. Evaluate this position.

3. Christian moralist Joseph Fletcher has written: "No unwanted and unintended baby should ever be born."[3] Do you think such a rule would produce the greatest social benefit?
4. Do you think Rawls's first principle of social justice has any relevance to the abortion issue?

[1]Reported in Burton M. Leiser, *Liberty, Justice, and Morals: Contemporary Value Conflicts* (New York: Macmillan, 1973), p. 96.
[2]Leiser, *Liberty, Justice, and Morals*, p. 96.
[3]Joseph Fletcher, *Situation Ethics: The New Morality* (Philadelphia: Westminster Press, 1966), p. 39.

CASE PRESENTATION

Death in Pensacola

Paul J. Hill was a former Presbyterian minister who had been divested by the Orthodox Presbyterian Church. Among the reasons for his divestiture were his many quarrels with the church over abortion. Hill was strongly anti-abortion, the church moderately pro-choice. After his divestiture, he moved to Pensacola, Florida, where he became active in the pro-life movement, founding a group he called Defensive Action and leading protests at the city's two abortion clinics. One of those clinics made front-page headlines throughout the country in March 1993, when abortion doctor David Gunn was shot and killed outside it by an anti-abortion assailant. The killing, in turn, made Hill a national figure. Appearing on such talk shows as *Donahue* and *Sonya Live*, he approved of the murder as biblically justified homicide and advocated more of the same. Then, in July of the following year, he apparently put his theology into practice. Shot dead outside the city's other abortion clinic were Dr. John Britton and clinic volunteer James Barrett. Barrett's wife, June, also a volunteer, survived her wounds. Prosecutors charged Hill with the shootings the following day.

As newspaper reports over the following days made clear, Barrett was an improbable martyr for the pro-choice movement. Unlike Dr. Gunn, who had been an abortion rights advocate, he personally opposed abortions and frequently tried to discourage his patients from having them. Still, in the face of death threats and considerable harassment, he continued to work at the clinic. He wore a bullet-proof vest to and from the clinic as a precaution but refused offers of police protection.

Operation Rescue and other pro-life groups denounced the killings. President Clinton ordered federal marshals to stand guard at abortion clinics throughout the country three days after the killings occurred. During Dr. Britton's funeral, a small group of abortion opponents demonstrated outside the church. Said one demonstrator, "May he rot in hell."

Paul Hill was executed by the state of Florida on September 3, 2003. His last words before his death included, "If you believe abortion is a lethal force, you should oppose the force and do what you have to do to stop it."

QUESTIONS FOR ANALYSIS

1. Many abortion rights activists blame anti-abortion rhetoric for contributing to violence at clinics, even if the rhetoric comes from peaceful protestors. The rhetoric they have in mind includes calling abortion doctors murderers and comparing abortion to the Nazi holocaust of the Jews. Do you agree?
2. Hill and other extreme abortion foes consider abortion the moral equivalent of killing school children. What do you consider the proper level of protest for people who genuinely feel that way?

What steps do you think they can justifiably take to prevent abortions?

3. The year 1994 saw the introduction of three significant legal obstacles to anti-abortion demonstrators. In one, the U.S. Supreme Court ruled that clinics can sue groups like Operation Rescue, which systematically attempt to shut clinics down, under the federal racketeering law. In another, the Court ruled that restricting peaceful demonstrators to a distance from which they cannot block

access to a clinic is constitutional. In the third, Congress passed the Access to Clinic Entrances Act, making interference with a woman's right to enter a clinic a federal crime. Do such measures unfairly restrict free speech and assembly rights? Should tougher measures be enacted? Do abortion opponents have the moral right to defy the restrictions as an act of civil disobedience?

4. During the 1992 Democratic Convention in New York City that nominated Bill Clinton for president, abortion foe Harley David Belew was arrested after trying to give the nominee a plastic bag containing a fetus. In Oslo, Norway, almost two years later, thieves stole the famous Edvard Munch painting, *The Scream*, from the National Art Museum and offered to return it if the national television station aired *The Silent Scream*, an anti-abortion film. (Though the station refused, the painting was recovered.) Are such novel but illegal protests justifiable?

CASE PRESENTATION

The Fight for Martina Greywind's Baby

By the young age of twenty-eight years, Martina Greywind had already carried and delivered six children. All had been taken away from her on the grounds that she was an unfit mother. Now she was again pregnant. She was also a penniless street person and a paint-fume addict.

While serving a brief sentence in a Fargo, North Dakota, jail for sniffing paint, she met a group of prisoners doing time for an altogether different offense. Members of an anti-abortion organization called Lambs of Christ, they had come to Fargo to shut down the state's only abortion clinic. Greywind told them of her pregnancy and her plans for abortion. Seeking to change her mind, they made this offer: If she did not abort, they would give her $10,000 plus food and shelter and medical care. Greywind went ahead with the abortion anyway, after the Lamb of Christ members found five couples who were willing to adopt her baby.

Why did she reject the offer? According to those who made it, she was coerced by local prosecutors. Because her paint sniffing had continued during the pregnancy, she faced charges of reckless endangerment of a fetus; the only way to get the charges dropped was to abort. They supported their accusation by claiming she told them in jail that she didn't want the abortion. Greywind did not comment on the claim.

After the abortion, the Lamb of Christ members made another accusation. The state, they said, had violated a state law prohibiting the use of public funds for abortions when it drove Greywind in a state vehicle from a mental hospital to the clinic, a distance of 100 miles.

QUESTIONS FOR ANALYSIS

1. Should Greywind have had the abortion?
2. Abortion rights activists try to frame the abortion debate as a matter of choice. Did Greywind have a real choice or was she coerced?
3. Do laws against reckless endangerment of a fetus promote abortion?
4. Were the Lambs of Christ members trying to help Greywind or merely using her in their anti-abortion crusade?

CASE PRESENTATION

Sex-Selection Abortions

The availability in recent decades of ultrasound technology makes it possible to identify the sex of a fetus in the early months of a pregnancy. The sex can be identified with near certainty at twenty weeks, though some technicians claim reliable identification as early as eleven weeks in the pregnancy. Newer, more invasive genetic testing can identify the sex of the fetus even earlier.

One result is the now-widespread practice of aborting fetuses of a gender undesirable in the minds of the parents. In the nation of India, even though using ultrasound for this purpose was made illegal in 1994, no criminal charges have been reported for violation of this law. Public health experts note that in 2001, only 927 females per 1,000 males were born in India, reflecting the widespread preference for sons. Daughters are considered a liability, for example, because of the requirement that when they marry, their parents provide a dowry to the husband and his family.

Sex-selection abortions also appear to be common in China, where the population control programs of the government limit each couple to one child, and parents typically prefer a son to a daughter. After decades of this practice, one consequence is the difficulty men have in finding a wife, as the proportion of women in the population declines. Although some provinces in China have attempted to ban this use of abortions, their efforts appear no more successful than similar laws in India.

Sex-selection abortions are currently banned in Canada, the United Kingdom, Germany, and France. Sex-selection abortions are currently banned in four states (Arizona, Illinois, Oklahoma, and Pennsylvania) and nine more states were considering such bans in 2013. In May 2012, the U.S. House of Representatives defeated the Prenatal Nondiscrimination Act, which the bill's sponsor, Congressman Trent Franks (R-AZ), said would end the "war on unborn little girls." Opponents of the bill, including President Obama, said it would violate women's right to privacy.

The American Society for Reproductive Medicine (ASRM) has noted that sex-selection procedures might reinforce gender bias in society and encourage other forms of genetic engineering to produce so-called designer babies.

One challenge in moral reasoning is whether a pregnant woman should have to give a reason for an abortion that others find morally acceptable, so long as she otherwise conforms with the law. The principle of moral autonomy in medicine suggests that each patient, including a pregnant woman, should be able to make her own decisions in seeking or refusing a medical procedure, regardless of whether others consider those decisions appropriate.

Feminist philosopher Mary V. Rorty, a clinical professor at the Stanford Center for Biomedical Ethics, has noted the dilemma here for feminists. Whereas they might applaud autonomy for women in deciding whether to have an abortion, they also are alarmed at the devaluation of the worth of women reflected in the practice of aborting female fetuses in preference for male children.

QUESTIONS FOR ANALYSIS

1. Assuming an abortion otherwise complies with American law, is it ethical for a woman to terminate a pregnancy simply because she does not like the sex of the fetus? Should she have to defend this decision to someone else, perhaps a medical review board, before the abortion would be performed?

2. If the ban on sex-selection abortions were adopted in the United States, might this be a slippery slope toward banning other elective abortions or requiring approval by a medical review board for the reasons for the abortion? Should women have to give a reason why they want an abortion? Who should decide what constitutes a "good" reason and what a "bad" reason? Would such a review process threaten the autonomy of women to make their own decisions concerning abortion? Would such review constitute an "undue burden" on women, which the U.S. Supreme Court has recognized as an unconstitutional barrier to abortion rights?

3. Some disability rights advocates are alarmed that it is permissible in this country to abort a child because prenatal testing determines that it will be born with serious physical defects, such as Down's syndrome. These advocates believe the practice devalues living persons with those conditions. Should feminists be alarmed that sex-selection abortions that terminate female fetuses devalue the status of women in the society?

CHAPTER FIVE

Euthanasia

- **Personhood**
- **Death**
- **Ordinary vs. Extraordinary Treatment**
- **Killing vs. Allowing to Die**
- **Meaning of *Euthanasia*: Narrow vs. Broad Interpretations**
- **Voluntary vs. Nonvoluntary Euthanasia**
- **Assisted Suicide**
- **The Right to Refuse Treatment**
- **Defective Newborns**
- **Arguments for Voluntary (Active) Euthanasia**
- **Arguments against Voluntary (Active) Euthanasia**

DAN W. BROCK   **Voluntary Active Euthanasia**

J. DAVID VELLEMAN   **Against the Right to Die**

JAMES RACHELS   **Active and Passive Euthanasia**

SUSAN M. WOLF   **Gender, Feminism, and Death: Physician-Assisted Suicide and Euthanasia**

CASE PRESENTATIONS: • *"I Did It Because I Loved My Son"* • *"A Choice Central to Personal Dignity"* • *Legalized Assisted Suicide and Decriminalized Euthanasia* • *Terri Schiavo: Voluntary Euthanasia or Murder?*

THE CASE OF KAREN ANN Quinlan has probably done more than any other in recent decades to rivet public attention on the legal and moral aspects of euthanasia, which generally refers to the act of painlessly putting to death a person suffering from a terminal or incurable disease or condition. On the night of April 15, 1975, for reasons still unclear, Karen Ann Quinlan ceased breathing for at least two fifteen-minute periods. Failing to respond to mouth-to-mouth resuscitation by friends, she was taken by ambulance to Newton Memorial Hospital in New Jersey. She had a temperature of 100 degrees, her pupils were unreactive, and she did not respond even to deep pain. Physicians who examined her characterized Karen as being in a "chronic, persistent, vegetative state," and later it was judged that no form of treatment could restore her to cognitive life. Her father, Joseph Quinlan, asked to be appointed her legal guardian with the expressed purpose of discontinuing the use of the respirator by which Karen was being sustained. Eventually, the Supreme Court of New Jersey granted the request. The respirator was turned off. However, Karen Ann Quinlan remained alive but comatose until June 11, 1985, when she died at the age of thirty-one. Although widely publicized, the Quinlan case is by no means the only one that has raised questions concerning euthanasia.

In fact, improvements in biomedical technology have made euthanasia an issue that more and more individuals and institutions must confront and that society must address. Respirators, artificial kidneys, intravenous feeding, new drugs—all have made it possible to sustain an individual's life artificially—that is, long after the individual has lost the capacity to sustain life independently. In cases like Quinlan's, individuals have fallen into a state of irreversible coma, what some health professionals term a vegetative state. In other instances, such as after severe accidents or with congenital brain disease, the individual's consciousness has been so dulled and the personality has so deteriorated that he or she lacks the capacity for development and growth. In still other cases, such as with terminal cancer, individuals vacillate between agonizing pain and a drug-induced stupor, with no possibility of ever again enjoying life. Not too long ago, "nature would have taken its course"; such patients would have died. Today, we have the technological capacity to keep them alive artificially. Should we? Or at least in some instances, are we justified in not doing this and even obliged not to?

As with abortion, euthanasia raises two basic moral issues that must be distinguished. The first deals with the morality of euthanasia itself; the second concerns the morality of euthanasia legislation. We consider both issues in this chapter.

Before discussing the arguments related to these issues, we must clarify a number of concepts central to euthanasia. Among them are the meanings of *personhood* and *death,* the difference between "ordinary" and "extraordinary" treatment, the distinctions between "killing" and "allowing to die," the various meanings of *euthanasia,* and the difference between "voluntary" and "nonvoluntary" euthanasia.

PERSONHOOD

The question of personhood bears as much on euthanasia as on abortion debates. What conditions should be used as the criteria of personhood? Can an entity be considered a **person** merely because it possesses certain biological properties? Or should other factors be introduced, such as consciousness, self-consciousness, rationality, and the capacities for communication and moral judgment? If personhood is just an elementary biological matter, then patients like Karen Ann Quinlan can qualify as persons more easily than if personhood depends on a complex list of psychosocial factors.

But "person" is not necessarily synonymous with the biological category "*homo sapiens.*" It includes, for many, the concept of a functioning brain or mind. From a religious perspective, personhood denotes the possession of a soul. For some it is a moral concept identifying an entity that is autonomous and should be treated with dignity and respect. Personhood is also a legal concept recognizing status under the U.S. Constitution, a status granted to newly freed slaves after the U.S. Civil War by the Fourteenth Amendment. Just as much of the abortion debate involves determinations of when we first become a "person" (whether at conception or at birth or at the point of viability or the point of having a functioning brain; see Chapter 4), the point at which we cease to be a person is important in sorting through the euthanasia issues.

In part, the significance of the personhood issue lies in the assignment of basic patient rights; once the criteria for personhood are established, those qualifying presumably enjoy the same general rights as any other patient. Conversely, for those who do not qualify and have no reasonable chance of ever qualifying, the rights issue is far less problematic. This doesn't mean that a death decision necessarily follows when an entity is determined to be a nonperson. But it does mean that whatever may be inherently objectionable about allowing or causing a person to die dissolves because the entity is no longer a person. So the concept of personhood bears directly on a death decision.

DEATH

Related to personhood is the conceptual issue of death. To get some idea of the complexities enshrouding the concept of death, consider this episode, which is based on an actual case.[1]

A terrible auto accident has occurred. One of the cars was occupied by a husband and wife. Authorities on the scene pronounce the man dead and rush the unconscious woman to a hospital, where she spends the next seventeen days in a coma due to severe brain damage. On the morning of the eighteenth day, she dies. Some time afterward, a relative contesting the couple's estate claims that the two people died simultaneously. Did they?

Not too long ago, legal and medical experts would have said yes. But when this case went to the Supreme Court of Arkansas in 1958, the court ruled that since the woman was breathing after the accident, she was alive, even though unconscious. The court relied on the time-honored definition of death as "the cessation of life; the ceasing to exist; defined by physicians as a total stoppage of the circulation of blood and a cessation of the animal and vital functions consequent thereon, such as respiration, pulsation, etc."[2] By this definition, death occurs if and only if there is a total cessation of respiration and blood flow.

Using heart-lung functioning as a criterion for death served well enough until recent developments in biomedical technology made it questionable. One of these developments is the increasing and widespread use of devices that can sustain respiration and heartbeat indefinitely, even when there is no brain activity. If the traditional heart-lung criterion is applied in cases like the preceding, then these individuals are technically still alive. Yet to many—including relatives of the comatose and those who must treat them—such people are, for all intents and purposes, dead.

To address these concerns, a model statute for determination of death was proposed in 1981 by the National Conference of Commissioners on Uniform State Laws, in consultation with the American Medical Association and the American Bar Association. The uniform statute, which has been adopted by forty-three U.S. states and territories, is as follows:

> An Individual who has sustained either (1) irreversible cessation of circulatory and respiratory functions, or (2) irreversible cessation of all functions of the entire brain, including the brain stem, is dead. A determination of death must be made in accordance with accepted medical standards.

---

[1] *Smith v. Smith*, 229 Arkansas 579, 3175. W. 2d. 275 (1958).
[2] *Black's Law Dictionary*, 4th ed. (St. Paul, Minn.: West Publishing), 1951, p. 488.

All fifty states now recognize brain death as the principal test of death.

Another development that has cast doubt on the traditional definition of death is the need for still-viable organs in transplant surgery. In general, a transplant is most successful if the organs are removed immediately after death. Thus, there is intense pressure on transplant teams to harvest organs as soon as possible. The moral implications of this pressure are serious, as we'll see shortly.

But these developments are only part of what makes the whole issue of defining death so nettlesome. Also relevant are three distinct categories of concerns that can be identified in any discussion of death: the philosophical, the physiological, and the methodical.

Philosophical Concerns

The philosophical level refers to one's basic concept of death, which inevitably springs from some view of what it means to be human. For example, if we believe it is the capacity to think and reason that makes one a human, we will likely associate the loss of personhood with the loss of rationality. If we consider consciousness as the defining characteristic, we will be more inclined to consider a person to have lost that status when a number of characteristics such as the capacities to remember, enjoy, worry, and will are gone. Although the absence of rational or experimental capacities would not necessarily define death, it would dispose us toward such a definition, since we are already disposed to accept the absence of personhood in the absence of those criteria. So there is interplay between our concepts of personhood and death.

Physiological Concerns

These concerns are related to the functioning of specific body systems or organs. The traditional physiological standard for recognizing death has been irreversible loss of circulatory and respiratory functions. This was the so-called "common law" definition of "death" used in the 1958 Arkansas decision and *Black's Law Dictionary*. The more recent uniform statute includes that definition but also includes a standard focused on the central nervous system—the brain and spinal cord. Specifically, these standards are the irreversible loss of reflex activity mediated through the brain or spinal cord, electrical activity in the cerebral neocortex, and/or cerebral blood flow. Whether traditional or recent, these physiological standards can be used individually or in combination. The significance of the physiological category in death decisions is that a patient declared alive by one set of criteria might be ruled dead by another. If a patient is considered dead, obviously euthanasia becomes academic; if the person is considered alive, euthanasia is a real concern.

Methodical Concerns

This category refers to specific means for determining physiological standards. The method used to determine traditional heart-lung standards has been taking the pulse or reading an electrocardiogram or both. For the central nervous system, electroencephalographs can be used to measure electrical activity in the neocortex, and radioactive tracers can be injected into the circulatory system for detecting cerebral blood flow.

Moral Implications

What makes defining death so important in discussions of euthanasia and the general study of bioethics is the interplay between definitional and moral considerations. To illustrate, suppose an attacker has clubbed a woman into a comatose condition.

She is rushed to a hospital, is determined to have suffered profound and irreversible brain damage, and is put on an artificial respirator. Efforts to identify her fail. As the team tending her debates whether to remove her from the respirator, one member, using one of the brain-death criteria, claims she is already dead. Therefore, withdrawing the respirator poses no special problems. Another member demurs. Using the heart-lung criterion, she insists that the woman is still alive and that the team has an obligation to sustain her life. What ought the team do?

One answer is, let the law decide. But some states allow either of the two alternative definitions. And even where the law is decisive, moral problems remain about the rightness of the standard itself. Beyond this, even when the law sanctions a brain-death criterion, as it now does in most states, it does not compel health professionals or anyone else to implement it. So although brain-death law may legally protect health professionals, it does not obligate them to act. Health professionals, presumably in consultation with others, must still wrestle with moral decisions in cases of irreversible coma.

Then there is the phenomenon of organ transplants, which promises to become of even greater concern as technology and techniques improve. A number of interests are identifiable in such cases. First, there are the interests of recipients, whose welfare depends on the availability of organs. Then there are the interests of health teams, who are obliged to provide adequate healthcare, which may include appropriate quality organs. There are also the interests of the donors, who may fear that their organs will be pirated prior to death or that their own healthcare providers will perform less than adequately in trying to sustain their lives. Moreover, there are the obligations of health teams to guard donors against physical violations as well as the psychological threat of violations and to guard themselves against developing a cannibalistic image. And finally, society at large must be watchful that the rights of its citizens to protection are not flouted, while at the same time ensuring that its ill citizens are not denied needed medical care and treatment, which may involve transplants.

ORDINARY vs. EXTRAORDINARY TREATMENT

A third issue that arises in euthanasia discussions involves the concept of ordinary as opposed to extraordinary treatment, terms used to differentiate two broad categories of medical intervention. Although the terms are often applied facilely, they elude hard-and-fast definition.

Moralist Paul Ramsey, for one, has applied *ordinary* to all medicines, treatments, and surgical procedures that offer a reasonable hope of benefit to the patient but do not involve excessive pain, expense, or other inconveniences. In contrast, he has identified *extraordinary* as measures that are unusual, extremely difficult, dangerous, inordinately expensive, or that offer no reasonable hope of benefit to the patient.[3]

Other theorists, philosophers, and theologians have suggested additional factors for demarcating "extraordinary" treatment, including those which are experimental, those for which the investment in costs and personnel are disproportionate to the likely results, and those for which the strain and suffering of the patient is disproportionate to the benefits. A problem for all these tests of "extraordinariness"

---

[3]Paul Ramsey, *The Patient as Person* (New Haven, Conn.: Yale University Press, 1970), pp. 122–123.

is that this is a moving target, given rapid advances in medical technology and research.

Such descriptions are useful and probably find widespread acceptance. But they do raise questions. An obvious one concerns the concepts used to define *ordinary* and *extraordinary*. What can be considered "reasonable hope of benefit to the patient"? What measures qualify as "unusual"? Ramsey mentions cost, but some would claim that cost has no place in a moral calculation. And then there is always the question of whether these criteria should be used individually or in combination; if in combination, what is the proper mix? Furthermore, patient idiosyncrasies inevitably influence a determination of ordinary and extraordinary in a particular case. For example, the use of antibiotics for a pneumonia patient undoubtedly qualifies as ordinary treatment. But does it remain ordinary treatment when the patient with pneumonia happens to have terminal cancer with metastasis to the brain and liver? The institutional setting can also affect evaluations of what constitutes ordinary and extraordinary: What is extraordinary treatment in a small community hospital could be ordinary in a large teaching hospital.[4]

The significance of trying to pin down these two concepts is that euthanasia arguments often rely on them to distinguish the permissible from the impermissible act of euthanasia. Most moralists, both religious and secular, argue that health professionals should provide ordinary treatment for the moribund but not extraordinary, which may be withheld or never started. Others insist that health professionals initiate extraordinary measures. Indeed, the medical profession itself makes similar operational distinctions in making death decisions.

KILLING vs. ALLOWING TO DIE

A fourth conceptual issue that we should try to clarify is what some consider to be the difference between killing a person and allowing a person to die. Presumably, "killing" a person refers to a definite action taken to end someone's life, as in the case of the physician who, out of mercy, injects a terminally ill patient with air or a lethal dose of a medication. Killing is an act of commission. In contrast, "allowing to die" presumably is an act of omission, whereby the steps needed to preserve someone's life simply are not taken. For example, a doctor, again out of mercy, fails to give an injection of antibiotics to a terminally ill patient who has contracted pneumonia. As a result of this omission, the patient dies.

Those making this distinction, such as the American Medical Association (AMA), say that the distinction is reasonable because in ordinary language and everyday life we distinguish between causing someone harm and permitting the harm to happen to them. If, in cases of euthanasia, the distinction is not made between killing and allowing to die, we lose the important distinction between causing someone harm and permitting that harm to happen.

Proponents also claim that the distinction acknowledges cases in which additional curative treatment would serve no purpose and in fact would interfere with a person's natural death. It recognizes that medical science will not initiate or sustain

---

[4]See A. J. Davis and M. A. Aroskar, *Ethical Dilemmas and Nursing Practice* (New York: Appleton-Century-Crofts, 1978), p. 117.

extraordinary means to preserve the life of a dying patient when such means would obviously serve no useful purpose for the patient or the patient's family.

Finally, some argue that the distinction is important in determining causation of death and ultimate responsibility. In instances where the patient dies following non-treatment, the proximate cause of death is the patient's disease, not the treatment or the person who did not provide it. If we fail to differentiate between killing and allowing to die, we blur this distinction. If allowing to die is subsumed under the category of euthanasia, then the nontreatment is the cause of the death, not the disease.

Not everyone, however, agrees that the distinction is a logical one. Some argue that withholding extraordinary treatment or suspending heroic measures in terminal cases is tantamount to the intentional termination of the life of one human being by another; that is, it is an act of killing. Thus, they claim that no logical distinction can be made between killing and allowing to die.

Whether or not the distinction between the two can be sustained logically is only one question raised by the killing vs. letting die debate. Another is the moral relevance of such a distinction. Even if the distinction is logical, does it have any bearing on the rightness or wrongness of acts commonly termed *euthanasia*?

On the one hand, for those making the distinction, allowing a patient to die under carefully circumscribed conditions could be moral. On the other hand, they seemingly would regard the killing of a patient, even out of mercy, an immoral act. But those opposing the killing–letting die distinction would not necessarily accept the close connection between killing a dying patient and an immoral act. For them, while killing is generally wrong, in some cases it may be the right thing to do. What determines the morality of killing a patient, what is of moral relevance and importance, is not the manner of causing the death but the circumstances in which the death is caused.

In summary, those distinguishing killing from allowing to die claim that the distinction is logically and morally relevant. Generally, they would condemn any act of killing a patient, while recognizing that some acts of allowing a patient to die may be moral (as, for example, in cases where life is being preserved heroically and death is imminent). In contrast are those who hold that the killing-letting die distinction is not logical and that allowing to die is in effect killing. They claim that killing a patient may be morally justifiable depending on the circumstances and not the manner in which the death is caused. The debate that surrounds the killing vs. allowing to die question is basic to the very meaning of euthanasia, a fifth conceptual issue that needs clarification.

MEANING OF *EUTHANASIA*: NARROW vs. BROAD INTERPRETATIONS

Construing euthanasia (from the Greek, meaning "good or happy death") narrowly, some philosophers have taken it to be the equivalent of killing. Since allowing someone to die does not involve killing, allowing to die would not actually be an act of euthanasia at all. By this account, then, there are acts of allowing to die, which may be moral, and acts of euthanasia, which are always wrong.

Other philosophers interpret the meaning of **euthanasia** more broadly. For them, euthanasia includes not only acts of killing but also acts of allowing to die. In other words, euthanasia can take an active or passive form. **Active** (sometimes termed positive) **euthanasia** refers to the act of painlessly putting to death persons suffering from incurable conditions or diseases. Injecting a lethal dosage of medication into a terminally ill patient would constitute active euthanasia. **Passive euthanasia,** in contrast, refers to any act of allowing a patient to die. Not providing a terminally ill patient the needed antibiotics to survive pneumonia would be an example of passive euthanasia.

It is tempting to view the debate between the narrow and the broad interpretations of euthanasia largely in terms of semantics. While the meaning of euthanasia certainly is a factor in the disagreement, the issue involves more than mere word definition.

One side, the narrow interpretation, considers killing a patient always morally wrong. Since euthanasia, by this definition, is killing a patient, euthanasia is always morally wrong. But allowing a patient to die does not involve killing a patient. Therefore, allowing a patient to die does not fall under the moral prohibition that euthanasia does; allowing a patient to die may be morally right.

The other side, the broad interpretation, considers acts of allowing patients to die acts of euthanasia, albeit passive euthanasia. They argue that if euthanasia is wrong, then so is allowing patients to die (since it is a form of euthanasia). But if allowing patients to die is not wrong, then euthanasia is not always wrong. Generally, those favoring the broad interpretation in fact claim that allowing patients to die is not always wrong and that euthanasia, therefore, may be morally justifiable. With the possible moral justifiability of euthanasia established, it is conceivable that acts of active euthanasia, as well as passive, may be moral. What determines their morality are the conditions under which the death is caused and not the manner in which it is caused. It is within these broad interpretations that the most problematic cases of death decisions fall—including the Quinlan case.

VOLUNTARY vs. NONVOLUNTARY EUTHANASIA

In addition to the preceding, there is another conceptual issue that arises in discussions of euthanasia. It concerns the difference between voluntary and nonvoluntary decisions about death.

Voluntary decisions about death refer to cases in which a competent adult patient requests or gives informed consent to a particular course of medical treatment or nontreatment. Generally speaking, informed consent exists when patients can understand what they are agreeing to and voluntarily choose it. Voluntary decisions also include cases in which persons take their own lives either directly or by refusing treatment and cases where patients deputize others to act in their behalf. For example, a woman who is terminally ill instructs her husband and family not to permit antibiotic treatment should she contract pneumonia, or not to use artificial support systems should she lapse into a coma and be unable to speak for herself. Similarly, a man requests that he be given a lethal injection after an industrial explosion has left him with third-degree burns over most of his body and no real hope of recovery. For a decision about death to be voluntary, the individual must give explicit consent.

A nonvoluntary decision about death refers to cases in which the decision is not made by the person who is to die. Such cases would include situations where, because of age, mental impairment, or unconsciousness, patients are not competent to give informed consent to life-or-death decisions and where others make the decisions for them. For example, suppose that as a result of an automobile accident, a man suffers massive and irreparable brain damage, falls into unconsciousness, and can be maintained only by artificial means. Should he regain consciousness, he would likely be little more than a vegetable. Given this prognosis, the man's family, in consultation with his physicians, decides to suspend artificial life-sustaining means and allow him to die.

In actual situations, the difference between voluntary and nonvoluntary decisions about death is not always clear. For example, take the case of a man who has heard his mother say that she would never want to be kept alive with "machines and pumps and tubes." Now that she is in fact being kept alive that way and is unable to express a life- or-death decision, the man is not sure that his mother actually would choose to be allowed to die. Similarly, a doctor might not be certain that the tormented cries of a stomach-cancer patient to be "put out of my misery" are an expression of informed consent or of profound pain and momentary despair.

The voluntary–nonvoluntary distinction is relevant to both the narrow and the broad interpretations of the meaning of euthanasia. Each interpretation seemingly distinguishes four kinds of death decisions in which the voluntary–nonvoluntary distinction plays a part. Thus, the narrow interpretation recognizes cases of:

1. Voluntary euthanasia
2. Nonvoluntary euthanasia
3. Voluntary allowing to die
4. Nonvoluntary allowing to die

By this account, the first two generally are considered immoral; instances of the second two may be moral under carefully circumscribed conditions.

Recognizing no logical or morally relevant distinction between euthanasia and allowing to die, the broad interpretation allows four forms of euthanasia:

1. Voluntary active euthanasia
2. Nonvoluntary active euthanasia
3. Voluntary passive euthanasia
4. Nonvoluntary passive euthanasia

By this account, any of these types of euthanasia may be morally justifiable under carefully circumscribed conditions.

The narrow and the broad interpretations differ sharply in their moral judgment of *deliberate* acts taken to end or shorten a patient's life—that is, acts that the narrow interpretation terms voluntary or nonvoluntary euthanasia and that the broad interpretation terms voluntary or nonvoluntary *active* euthanasia. Generally, the narrow interpretation considers such acts always morally repugnant; the broad interpretation views them as being morally justifiable under carefully circumscribed conditions.

Some discussions of euthanasia distinguish nonvoluntary euthanasia from involuntary euthanasia. Nonvoluntary in these discussions is limited to euthanasia in which the patient is not able now to make a meaningful decision about euthanasia but has previously made preferences clear to a caretaker or family member, usually through a **living will** or directive. **Involuntary euthanasia** involves a decision made by someone else that the person's life should end, even though that person has never made these preferences known to anyone. This might be a decision by a hospital ethics committee that the person should be euthanized, even though no such wishes were ever expressed by that person. In the discussion here, **nonvoluntary euthanasia** includes all situations where the decision for euthanasia is made by someone other than the patient, whether or not that patient had previously expressed a preference for this course of action.

ASSISTED SUICIDE

Closely related to the issue of euthanasia is that of **assisted suicide,** which has become one of the most debated moral and legal issues of recent years. Most of the debate centers on *physician*-assisted suicide—whether to allow doctors to assist terminally ill patients in taking their own lives, usually by prescribing a lethal dose of drugs. For all the similarities between assisted suicide and voluntary active euthanasia, there is one crucial if subtle difference: In the former, the physician does not directly cause the patient's death but enables the patient to choose the time and circumstances of his or her own death. Because of this difference, proponents of physician-assisted suicide see it as a moral solution to the problem posed by the suffering of the terminally ill. If the terminally ill have the right to end their suffering, which proponents feel they do, then they also have the right to seek their doctors' assistance. Opponents counter that the terminally ill have no right to take their own lives and that assisting in suicide is not the proper role of physicians.

The debate was sparked by Dr. Jack Kevorkian and his "suicide machine," an invention of his that enables patients to give themselves lethal injections. The Michigan doctor first provided the device in 1990 to a woman who suffered from Alzheimer's disease. Because Michigan had no law forbidding assisted suicide at the time, he was not charged. But then, after assisting in the suicides of two other women the following year, he was charged with two counts of murder, both of which a judge dismissed. These dismissals led the state's legislature to enact a temporary ban on assisted suicide. Undeterred, Kevorkian continued to make his machine available, and he was consequently charged with violating the new law. On May 3, 1994, a jury acquitted him. After the temporary ban expired, the State attempted to prosecute him for several assisted suicides, but either juries acquitted him or judges declared mistrials and charges were dropped. Another Michigan state law banning physician-assisted suicide went into effect in 1998. During an episode of "60 Minutes" on CBS, Kevorkian was shown giving a lethal injection to Thomas Youk, who had Lou Gehrig's disease. A few days later, Michigan authorities charged Kevorkian with murder. He was convicted in April 1999 and sentenced to ten to twenty-five years in prison, with eligibility for parole after six years. He was released on parole in 2007 for good behavior. Until his death in 2011 at the age of eighty-three, he continued to give speeches in defense of assisted suicide and claimed he had assisted in at least 130 deaths.

Kevorkian's persistence and legal troubles generated enormous attention and controversy, which quickly turned to action as voters in various states petitioned for ballot initiatives either to allow assisted suicide or to ban it. In states with existing legislation banning the practice, terminally ill patients went to court asking that the laws be declared unconstitutional. In June 1997, the U.S. Supreme Court upheld the constitutionality of laws in two states, Washington and New York, that ban assisted suicide (*Washington v. Glucksberg* and *Vacco v. Quill,* respectively). Then in October of that year, the Court refused to hear a challenge to an Oregon law—this one passed by voters in a 1994 ballot initiative—that legalized assisted suicide. After a legal challenge, Oregon voters passed another ballot initiative permitting assisting suicide in 1997. From 1997 to 2012, according to the Oregon Public Health Division, 1,050 people have obtained prescriptions for the Death With Dignity Act (DWDA) drugs and 673 have died from taking those medications.

In 2002, during the presidency of George W. Bush, efforts by the U.S. Department of Justice to prosecute doctors who participated in Oregon's assisted suicide program were halted by a federal court. The U.S. Supreme Court rejected a challenge to the Oregon law by the U.S. Justice Department in January 2005, in a 6–3 decision (*Gonzales v. Oregon*).

In November 2008, voters in the state of Washington passed the "Death With Dignity" proposition, a state measure similar to Oregon's, to permit assisted suicide. Patients must have a terminal disease and have less than six months to live. Doctors are permitted to prescribe life-ending medication under the new law. Various safeguards include proof of voluntary consent by the patient and concurrence from a second physician. In May 2013, Vermont became the third state to pass a Death with Dignity Act. Over two-thirds of the states have laws expressly prohibiting assisted suicide.

So far, attempts to pass a ban on assisted suicide by the U.S. Congress have failed. Thus, the issue is left to the states for now. The terminally ill have no constitutional right to commit suicide, but states may allow them to do so with the assistance of their doctors.

THE RIGHT TO REFUSE TREATMENT

Though the right to refuse medical treatment has long been widely recognized, and though many state courts (as in the Karen Ann Quinlan case) have upheld the right of family members to refuse life-preserving treatment, it was not until the summer of 1990 that the U.S. Supreme Court, in *Cruzan v. Missouri Health Services*, recognized the right of a competent patient to refuse life-preserving medical treatment, including artificial (nonoral) delivery of nutrition and water. The court also ruled that when the patient is not competent to make the decision, it may be made by a surrogate acting according to the patient's wishes.

Thus, the court established a constitutional basis for voluntary passive euthanasia (or allowing to die) in some cases. But the court also ruled that states may require clear and convincing evidence that the surrogate is in fact acting in accordance with the patient's wishes. The case was returned to the Missouri trial court to hear additional evidence of her intent. This court held that there was sufficient clear and convincing evidence to remove the feeding tube, which was done on December 14, 1990. Nancy Cruzan died eleven days later.

One consequence of the ruling is the legal validity of *living wills,* documents that direct physicians not to apply artificial means of preserving life. A model living will, Directive to Physicians, was created by the California legislature in 1977 as part of the state's Natural Death Act (see Figure 5.1). Living wills have long been advocated by many Americans, including those who advocate not only the right to refuse treatment but also a broader right, the right to die, which also includes the right to voluntary active euthanasia. That broader right has not been recognized by the courts, and most current controversy surrounding euthanasia concerns whether it should be.

DEFECTIVE NEWBORNS

The legal and moral questions of refusing treatment become more complicated in cases of newborns with defects, babies born with serious birth defects, such as

DIRECTIVE TO PHYSICIANS

Directive made this _____ day of _____ (month, year).

I, _____ being of sound mind, willfully and voluntarily make known my desire that my life shall not be artificially prolonged under the circumstances set forth below, do hereby declare:

1. If at any time I should have an incurable injury, disease, or illness certified to be a terminal condition by two physicians, and where the application of life-sustaining procedures would serve only to artificially prolong the moment of my death and where my physician determines that my death is imminent whether or not life-sustaining procedures are utilized, I direct that such procedures be withheld or withdrawn, and that I be permitted to die naturally.

2. In the absence of my ability to give directions regarding the use of such life-sustaining procedures, it is my intention that this directive shall be honored by my family and physician(s) as the final expression of my legal right to refuse medical or surgical treatment and accept the consequences from such refusal.

3. If I have been diagnosed as pregnant and that diagnosis is known to my physician, this directive shall have no force or effect during the course of my pregnancy.

4. I have been diagnosed and notified at least 14 days ago as having a terminal condition by_____, M.D., whose address is _____and whose telephone number is _____. I understand that if I have not filled in the physician's name and address, it shall be presumed that I did not have a terminal condition when I made out this directive.

5. This directive shall have no force or effect five years from the date filled in above.

6. I understand the full import of this directive and I am emotionally and mentally competent to make this directive.

Signed_____

City, County and State of Residence_____

The declarant has been personally known to me and I believe him or her to be of sound mind.

Witness_____

Witness_____

FIGURE 5.1 Model Living Will (California Natural Death Act)

Tay-Sachs, a fatal degenerative disease; Down's syndrome, which manifests itself in mental retardation and various physical abnormalities; and duodenal atresia, in which the upper part of the small intestine, the duodenum, is closed off, therefore preventing the passage and digestion of food. (Although duodenal atresia can usually be treated through surgery, it often is accompanied by other serious birth defects.)

One complication concerns the treatment in question. Allowing defective newborns to die often includes the withholding of ordinary treatment, such as simple nourishment. Another concerns the defects themselves. Although some birth defects, such as anencephalus (the partial or total absence of the brain), guarantee a life in a vegetative state, children with others, such as Down's syndrome, often lead meaningful, if limited, lives.

It is possible to identify three broad positions on the moral acceptability of allowing defective newborns to die. Underpinning each are controversial value assumptions.

The first and most permissive position is that allowing seriously defective newborns to die is morally permissible not only when there is no significant potential for meaningful human existence but also when the emotional or financial hardship of caring for the child would place a grave burden on the family. Adherents to this view argue their case on the grounds that newborns are not yet persons, which, as we saw in Chapter 4, is a controversial assumption.

The second position is that it is permissible only if there is no significant potential for meaningful human existence. Clearly implied here is a quality-of-life judgment, which often elicits debate. Should we make such judgments? And if so, what should count as a meaningful human existence? The degree of retardation associated with Down's syndrome, for example, can vary widely. At what point can we separate a meaningful from a meaningless human existence?

The third position asserts that it is never morally permissible to allow a defective newborn to die. Stated more cautiously, it is never moral to withhold from a defective newborn any treatment that would be provided to a normal one. The clear implication here is that the defective infant has full personhood and must be treated accordingly. Just as clearly, this view rejects any quality-of-life or cost factors in determining the acceptability of allowing a defective infant to die. Like the other positions, this one is fraught with debatable value judgments, and in cases of duodenal atresia, it ignores that normal infants would not require corrective surgery to digest food.

It is quite apparent, then, that whether cases involve defective newborns or adults who are terminally ill, the central moral question concerns the acceptability of a death decision and subsequent action. But there are additional moral problems relating to death decisions in the institutional setting that are worth considering.

ARGUMENTS FOR VOLUNTARY (ACTIVE) EUTHANASIA

1. *Individuals have the right to decide about their own lives and deaths.*
   POINT: "What more basic right is there than the right of terminally ill patients to control the circumstances of their own deaths? To decide whether they'll spend their last days in great pain or not, hooked up to machines or not, conscious or not, drugged to a stupor or not? If they wish to spare themselves the agony of a drawn-out death and their families the agony of watching them go through it, who are we to deny them the right to do so?"

   COUNTERPOINT: "What you're really saying is that all of us have the right to commit suicide. But we don't have that right and we shouldn't have it. It's one thing to say that we have the right to refuse medical treatment, but it's quite another to say that we have the right to decide when our lives are no longer bearable and then end them. If we follow your reasoning, we'd also have to say that the nonterminally ill have the right to determine the circumstances of their death too. After all, we're all going to die some day anyway."

2. *Denying terminally ill patients the right to die is unfair and cruel.*
   POINT: "We allow terminally ill patients to refuse life-preserving treatment out of compassion. We allow them to refuse to be hooked up to respirators or intravenous feeding tubes, to refuse treatment for pneumonia. But what can be crueler than to let suffering cancer patients starve to death or wait for pneumonia when we can end their misery immediately? Besides, denying

suffering patients the right to active euthanasia isn't fair to those who aren't on life support. Why should they be denied the right to die when it's not denied to those who are on life support?"

COUNTERPOINT: "The issue isn't the right to die but the right to refuse extraordinary means of treatment, the right of all patients, including the terminally ill, to decide that further medical treatment won't benefit them. There's also another issue at stake, the role of healthcare professionals. When they disconnect life-support systems, they're respecting the autonomy of their patients. If they give them lethal injections, they'll be committing an act of deliberately killing a fellow human being. Everyone feels compassion for these patients, but you can't justify everything in the name of compassion."

3. *The golden rule requires that we allow active euthanasia for terminally ill patients.*

POINT: "The simplest way to put the matter is like this: If you were in a terminal cancer ward and found the suffering to be more than you could bear, you'd want your doctor to give you a lethal injection if you asked for it, wouldn't you? Then how can you justify not allowing the same for others? It's a straightforward application of the golden rule. Do unto others as you would have them do unto you."

COUNTERPOINT: "For all I know, I might end up exactly as you describe, but that still doesn't change anything. Just because we *want* someone to do something for us doesn't mean that we have the *right* to have it done. And it certainly doesn't mean that others have the obligation or even the right to do it. The golden rule applies only to moral actions, and neither suicide nor deliberate killing is moral."

4. *People have a right to die with dignity.*

POINT: "Not everyone wants to spend his or her last days lying in a hospital bed wasting away to something hardly recognizable as a human being, let alone his or her former self. To constantly fight horrible pain, to be hooked up to an intravenous machine that supplies painkilling narcotics, to drift up and back between a dream state and reality, not to recognize family and friends, to waste away to nothing while dying of dehydration or starvation—to some people that's an unacceptable affront to their dignity. Out of respect for the dignity of others, we allow them to *live* with dignity. Why not allow them to *die* with dignity?"

COUNTERPOINT: "The phrase 'death with dignity' makes perfect sense when we're talking about allowing people to die a natural death instead of being kept alive against their will by artificial means. But you're talking about avoiding natural death instead of facing it. And there's nothing undignified about facing a natural death."

ARGUMENTS AGAINST VOLUNTARY (ACTIVE) EUTHANASIA

1. *Active euthanasia is the deliberate taking of a human life.*

POINT: "The deliberate killing of a human being is wrong, pure and simple, whether the person wants to die or not. And calling it 'euthanasia' doesn't change the fact that what we're talking about is the deliberate taking of a human life."

COUNTERPOINT: "Certainly, under normal circumstances, taking a human life is wrong, but we're not talking about normal circumstances. The circumstances here involve terminally ill patients who can't bear their pointless suffering. If we're willing to disconnect the life-support systems of such patients if they request it, we should be willing to give them lethal injections if they request it. In both cases, the intention is the same—to respect their wish to be put out of their misery."

2. *We can't be sure consent is voluntary.*

POINT: "We can't ever be sure consent is voluntary. In fact, the circumstances surrounding most terminally ill patients make voluntary consent impossible. Either they're in terrible pain or they're drugged. In any case, they can't be thinking clearly enough to understand the full impact of what they're consenting to. And that hardly counts as rational free choice."

COUNTERPOINT: "Maybe not, but suppose the patient requests to be euthanized before he or she reaches that point. Or suppose the family feels the patient really wants the lethal injection. We disconnect life-support systems from patients who are no longer capable of giving informed consent in those circumstances. Why not give them lethal injections in the same circumstances?"

3. *Allowing active euthanasia will lead to abuses.*

POINT: "Killing terminally ill patients who ask for it is a dangerous step. Once you accept the principle of the right to die, what stops you from extending it to the nonterminally ill? Does an athlete who becomes a quadriplegic have the right to be put out of his misery? Someone suffering from chronic depression? Severe arthritis? Alzheimer's disease? And what happens when people like that don't request lethal injections but their families do? Are we to 'euthanize' them too?"

COUNTERPOINT: "I'm not advocating a general right to die, just the right of terminally ill patients to choose the way they die. To suggest that complying with a terminally ill cancer patient's request for a lethal injection will lead to the kind of abuses you mention is to confuse distinct and separate issues. Certainly, nobody's calling for nonvoluntary euthanasia."

4. *There's always the possibility of mistaken diagnosis, a new cure, or spontaneous remission.*

POINT: "The judgment that a patient is terminally ill isn't always the last word, you know. The diagnosis may be mistaken, a new cure may come along, and cancer patients have been known to go into spontaneous remission. But death is the last word. Once you've killed a patient, he or she is beyond all hope. How would you feel if a wonder drug turned up the next day or if the doctors discovered their diagnosis was wrong?"

COUNTERPOINT: "The judgment that a patient is terminally ill may not always be the last word, but it usually is. Despite what you say, many patients are already beyond hope. No new cure is going to come along in time to save people after cancer has metastasized throughout their bodies. And to hope for spontaneous remission or mistaken diagnosis at that point is absurd. Besides, everything you say holds for passive as well as active euthanasia. When a terminally ill cancer patient comes down with pneumonia, few, if any, people are willing to treat the pneumonia in hopes of finding a wonder drug for cancer. To do so would be outright cruelty. And that's what denying a lethal injection to a patient without pneumonia amounts to—outright cruelty."

Voluntary Active Euthanasia

DAN W. BROCK

Dan W. Brock is the Frances Glessner Lee Professor of Medical Ethics in the Department of Global Health and Social Medicine, the Director of the Division of Medical Ethics at the Harvard Medical School, and the Director of the Harvard University Program in Ethics and Health. Prior to his arrival at Harvard, Professor Brock was Senior Scientist and a member of the Department of Clinical Bioethics at the National Institutes of Health. Until July 2002, he was Charles C. Tillinghast, Jr. University Professor, Professor of Philosophy and Biomedical Ethics, and Director of the Center for Biomedical Ethics at Brown University. He is the author of several books and over 150 articles in bioethics and in moral and political philosophy. He received his Ph.D. in philosophy from Columbia University.

In these excerpts, he defends the morality of voluntary active euthanasia by appealing to the value of individual self-determination or autonomy and the value of individual well-being. He addresses the reservations of physicians to participation in euthanasia by arguing that the moral goals of physicians are in fact consistent with active voluntary euthanasia.

... My concern here will be with *voluntary* euthanasia only—that is, with the case in which a clearly competent patient makes a fully voluntary and persistent request for aid in dying. Involuntary euthanasia, in which a competent patient explicitly refuses or opposes receiving euthanasia, and nonvoluntary euthanasia, in which a patient is incompetent and unable to express his or her wishes about euthanasia, will be considered here only as potential unwanted side-effects of permitting voluntary euthanasia. I emphasize as well that I am concerned with *active* euthanasia, not with-holding or withdrawing life-sustaining treatment, which some commentators characterize as "passive euthanasia." Finally, I will be concerned with euthanasia where the motive of those who perform it is to respect the wishes of the patient and to provide the patient with a "good death," though one important issue is whether a change in legal policy could restrict the performance of euthanasia to only those cases....

THE CENTRAL ETHICAL ARGUMENT FOR VOLUNTARY ACTIVE EUTHANASIA

The central ethical argument for euthanasia is familiar. It is that the very same two fundamental ethical values supporting the consensus on

From Dan W. Brock, "Voluntary Active Euthanasia," *The Hastings Center Report* 22:2 (March–April, 1992), 10–22. Reprinted by permission of John Wiley and Sons.

patient's rights to decide about life-sustaining treatment also support the ethical permissibility of euthanasia. These values are individual self-determination or autonomy and individual well-being. By self-determination as it bears on euthanasia, I mean people's interest in making important decisions about their lives for themselves according to their own values or conceptions of a good life, and in being left free to act on those decisions. Self-determination is valuable because it permits people to form and live in accordance with their own conception of a good life, at least within the bounds of justice and consistent with others doing so as well. In exercising self-determination people take responsibility for their lives and for the kinds of persons they become. A central aspect of human dignity lies in people's capacity to direct their lives in this way. The value of exercising self-determination presupposes some minimum of decision making capacities or competence, which thus limits the scope of euthanasia supported by self-determination; it cannot justifiably be administered, for example, in cases of serious dementia or treatable clinical depression.

Does the value of individual self-determination extend to the time and manner of one's death? Most people are very concerned about the nature of the last stage of their lives. This reflects not just a fear of experiencing substantial suffering when dying, but also a desire to retain dignity and control during this last period of life. Death is today increasingly preceded by a long period of significant physical and mental decline, due in part to the technological interventions of modern medicine. Many people adjust to these disabilities and find meaning and value in new activities and ways. Others find the impairments and burdens in the last stage of their lives at some point sufficiently great to make life no longer worth living. For many patients near death, maintaining the quality of one's life, avoiding great suffering, maintaining one's dignity, and insuring that others remember us as we wish them to become of paramount importance and outweigh merely extending one's life. But there is no single, objectively correct answer for everyone as to when, if at all, one's life becomes all things considered a burden and

unwanted. If self-determination is a fundamental value, then the great variability among people on this question makes it especially important that individuals control the manner, circumstances, and timing of their dying and death.

The other main value that supports euthanasia is individual well-being. It might seem that individual well-being conflicts with a person's self-determination when the person requests euthanasia. Life itself is commonly taken to be a central good for persons, often valued for its own sake, as well as necessary for pursuit of all other goods within a life. But when a competent patient decides to forgo all further life-sustaining treatment then the patient, either explicitly or implicitly, commonly decides that the best life possible for him or her with treatment is of sufficiently poor quality that it is worse than no further life at all. Life is no longer considered a benefit by the patient, but has now become a burden. The same judgment underlies a request for euthanasia: continued life is seen by the patient as no longer a benefit, but now a burden. Especially in the often severely compromised and debilitated states of many critically ill or dying patients, there is no objective standard, but only the competent patient's judgment of whether continued life is no longer a benefit.

Of course, sometimes there are conditions, such as clinical depression, that call into question whether the patient has made a competent choice, either to forgo life-sustaining treatment or to seek euthanasia, and then the patient's choice need not be evidence that continued life is no longer a benefit for him or her. Just as with decisions about treatment, a determination of incompetence can warrant not honoring the patient's choice; in the case of treatment, we then transfer decisional authority to a surrogate, though in the case of voluntary active euthanasia a determination that the patient is incompetent means that choice is not possible.

The value or right of self-determination does not entitle patients to compel physicians to act contrary to their own moral or professional values. Physicians are moral and professional agents whose own self-determination or integrity should be respected as well. If performing euthanasia became legally permissible, but conflicted with a particular physician's reasonable understanding of his or her moral or professional responsibilities, the care of a patient who requested euthanasia should be transferred to another....

Potential Good Consequences of Permitting Euthanasia

What are the likely good consequences? First, if euthanasia were permitted it would be possible to respect the self-determination of competent patients who want it, but now cannot get it because of its illegality. We simply do not know how many such patients and people there are. In the Netherlands, with a population of about 14.5 million (in 1987), estimates in a recent study were that about 1,900 cases of voluntary active euthanasia or physician-assisted suicide occur annually. No straightforward extrapolation to the United States is possible for many reasons, among them, that we do not know how many people here who want euthanasia now get it, despite its illegality. Even with better data on the number of persons who want euthanasia but cannot get it, significant moral disagreement would remain about how much weight should be given to any instance of failure to respect a person's self-determination in this way....

A second good consequence of making euthanasia legally permissible benefits a much larger group.... No doubt the vast majority of those who support this right to euthanasia will never in fact come to want euthanasia for themselves. Nevertheless, making it legally permissible would reassure many people that if they ever do want euthanasia they would be able to obtain it. This reassurance would supplement the broader control over the process of dying given by the right to decide about life-sustaining treatment....

A third good consequence of the legalization of euthanasia concerns patients whose dying is filled with severe and unrelievable pain or suffering. When there is a life-sustaining treatment that, if forgone, will lead relatively quickly to death, then doing so can bring an end to these patients' suffering without recourse to euthanasia. For patients receiving no such treatment, however, euthanasia may be the only release from their otherwise prolonged suffering and agony....

Potential Bad Consequences of Permitting Euthanasia

Some of the arguments against permitting euthanasia are aimed specifically against physicians, while others are aimed against anyone being permitted to perform it. I shall first consider one argument of the former sort. Permitting physicians to perform euthanasia, it is said, would be incompatible with their fundamental moral and professional commitment as healers to care for patients and to protect life. Moreover, if euthanasia by physicians became common, patients would come to fear that a medication was intended not to treat or care, but instead to kill, and would thus lose trust in their physicians....

If permitting physicians to kill would undermine the very "moral center" of medicine, then almost certainly physicians should not be permitted to perform euthanasia. But how persuasive is this claim? Patients should not fear, as a consequence of permitting *voluntary* active euthanasia, that their physicians will substitute a lethal injection for what patients want and believe is part of their care. If active euthanasia is restricted to cases in which it is truly voluntary, then no patient should fear getting it unless she or he has voluntarily requested it. (The fear that we might in time also come to accept nonvoluntary, or even involuntary, active euthanasia is a slippery slope worry I address below.) Patients' trust of their physicians could be increased, not eroded, by knowledge that physicians will provide aid in dying when patients seek it....

In spelling out above what I called the positive argument for voluntary active euthanasia, I suggested that two principal values—respecting patients' self-determination and promoting their well-being—underlie the consensus that competent patients, or the surrogates of incompetent patients, are entitled to refuse any life-sustaining treatment and to choose from among available alternative treatments. It is the commitment to these two values in guiding physicians' actions as healers, comforters, and protectors of their patients' lives that should be at the "moral center" of medicine, and these two values support physicians' administering euthanasia when their patients make competent requests for it.

What should not be at that moral center is a commitment to preserving patients' lives as such, without regard to whether those patients want their lives preserved or judge their preservation a benefit to them....

A second bad consequence that some foresee is that permitting euthanasia would weaken society's commitment to provide optimal care for dying patients. We live at a time in which the control of health care costs has become, and is likely to continue to be, the dominant focus of health care policy. If euthanasia is seen as a cheaper alternative to adequate care and treatment, then we might become less scrupulous about providing sometimes costly support and other services to dying patients. Particularly if our society comes to embrace deeper and more explicit rationing of health care, frail, elderly, and dying patients will need to be strong and effective advocates for their own health care and other needs, although they are hardly in a position to do this. We should do nothing to weaken their ability to obtain adequate care and services.

This second worry is difficult to assess because there is little firm evidence about the likelihood of the feared erosion in the care of dying patients. There are at least two reasons, however, for skepticism about this argument. The first is that the same worry could have been directed at recognizing patients' or surrogates' rights to forgo life-sustaining treatment, yet there is no persuasive evidence that recognizing the right to refuse treatment has caused a serious erosion in the quality of care of dying patients. The second reason for skepticism about this worry is that only a very small proportion of deaths would occur from euthanasia if it were permitted....

This final potential bad consequence is the central concern of many opponents of euthanasia and, I believe, is the most serious objection to a legal policy permitting it. According to this "slippery slope" worry, although active euthanasia may be morally permissible in cases in which it is unequivocally voluntary and the patient finds his or her condition unbearable, a legal policy permitting euthanasia would inevitably lead to active euthanasia being performed in many other cases in which it would be morally wrong. To prevent those other wrongful cases of euthanasia we should not permit even morally justified performance of it.

Slippery slope arguments of this form are problematic and difficult to evaluate. From one perspective, they are the last refuge of conservative defenders of the status quo. When all the opponent's objections to the wrongness of euthanasia itself have been met, the opponent then shifts ground and acknowledges both that it is not in itself wrong and that a legal policy which resulted only in its being performed would not be bad. Nevertheless, the opponent maintains, it should still not be permitted because doing so would result in its being performed in other cases in which it is not voluntary and would be wrong. In this argument's most extreme form, permitting euthanasia is the first and fateful step down the slippery slope to Nazism. Once on the slope we will be unable to get off.

Now it cannot be denied that it is *possible* that permitting euthanasia could have these fateful consequences, but that cannot be enough to warrant prohibiting it if it is otherwise justified. A similar *possible* slippery slope worry could have been raised to securing competent patients' rights to decide about life support, but recent history shows such a worry would have been unfounded. It must be relevant how likely it is that we will end with horrendous consequences and an unjustified practice of euthanasia. How *likely* and *widespread* would the abuses and unwarranted extensions of permitting it be? By abuses, I mean the performance of euthanasia that fails to satisfy the conditions required for voluntary active euthanasia, for example, if the patient has been subtly pressured to accept it. By unwarranted extensions of policy, I mean later changes in legal policy to permit not just voluntary euthanasia, but also euthanasia in cases in which, for example, it need not be fully voluntary. Opponents of voluntary euthanasia on slippery slope grounds have not provided the data or evidence necessary to turn their speculative concerns into well-grounded likelihoods.

It is at least clear, however, that both the character and likelihood of abuses of a legal policy permitting euthanasia depend in significant part on the procedures put in place to protect against them. I will not try to detail fully what such procedures might be, but will just give some examples of what they might include:

1. The patient should be provided with all relevant information about his or her medical condition, current prognosis, available alternative treatments, and the prognosis of each.
2. Procedures should ensure that the patient's request for euthanasia is stable or enduring (a brief waiting period could be required) and fully voluntary (an advocate for the patient might be appointed to ensure this).
3. All reasonable alternatives must have been explored for improving the patient's quality of life and relieving any pain or suffering.
4. A psychiatric evaluation should ensure that the patient's request is not the result of a treatable psychological impairment such as depression.

These examples of procedural safeguards are all designed to ensure that the patient's choice is fully informed, voluntary, and competent, and so a true exercise of self-determination. Other proposals for euthanasia would restrict its permissibility further—for example, to the terminally ill—a restriction that cannot be supported by self-determination. Such additional restrictions might, however, be justified by concern for limiting potential harms from abuse. At the same time, it is important not to impose procedural or substantive safeguards so restrictive as to make euthanasia impermissible or practically infeasible in a wide range of justified cases.

These examples of procedural safe-guards make clear that it is possible to substantially reduce, though not to eliminate, the potential for abuse of a policy permitting voluntary active euthanasia. Any legalization of the practice should be accompanied by a well-considered set of procedural safeguards together with an ongoing evaluation of its use. Introducing euthanasia into only a few states could be a form of carefully limited and controlled social experiment that would give us evidence about the benefits and harms of the practice.

☙ QUESTIONS FOR ANALYSIS

1. How does Brock understand "voluntary euthanasia"? "involuntary euthanasia"? "active euthanasia"? "passive euthanasia"?
2. What are the two fundamental ethical values that support the ethical permissibility of euthanasia, according to Brock?
3. What are the potential good consequences of permitting euthanasia?
4. What are the potential bad consequences of permitting euthanasia?
5. How does Brock attempt to reconcile the moral obligations of physicians with the moral issues raised by euthanasia? Does his attempt reasonably satisfy the concerns of physicians?
6. What is the "slippery slope" argument against euthanasia? How does Brock respond to this criticism? Do his proposed safeguards seem adequate to reassure critics of euthanasia?

Against the Right to Die

J. DAVID VELLEMAN

J. David Velleman is Professor of Philosophy at New York University. He has published extensively on bioethics, philosophy of action, and concepts of the self. He received his Ph.D. from Princeton University and previously taught for over twenty years at the University of Michigan.

In this article, originally published in 1992 and substantially revised in 2012, he challenges the arguments in favor of assisted suicide of Dan Brock (the previous article in this anthology). He questions the reliance on Kantian "dignity" and "patient autonomy," and worries that merely giving people the option of choosing euthanasia will result in unacceptable consequences, especially pressure to choose death when that might not be the best option for all.

In this paper[1] I offer an argument against establishing an institutional right to die, but I do not consider how my argument fares against countervailing considerations, and so I do not draw any final conclusion on the subject. The argument laid out in this paper has certainly inhibited me from favoring a right to die, and it has also led me to recoil from many of the arguments offered for such a right. But I am very far from an all-things—considered judgment.

My argument is addressed to a question of public policy—namely, whether the law or the canons of medical practice should include a rule requiring, under specified circumstances, that caregivers honor a patient's request to be allowed or perhaps even helped to die. This question is distinct from the question whether anyone is ever morally entitled to be allowed or helped to die. I believe that the answer to the latter question is yes, but I doubt whether our moral obligation to facilitate some people's deaths is best discharged through the establishment of an institutional right to die.

I

Although I believe in our obligation to facilitate some deaths, I want to dissociate myself from some of the arguments that are frequently offered for such an obligation. These arguments, like many arguments in medical ethics, rely on terms borrowed from Kantian moral theory—terms such as 'dignity' and 'autonomy'. Various kinds of life-preserving treatment are said to violate a patient's dignity or to detain him in an undignified state; and the patient's right of autonomy is said to require that we respect his competent and considered wishes, including a wish to die. There may or may not be some truth in each of these claims. Yet when we evaluate such claims, we must take care not to assume that terms like 'dignity' and 'autonomy' always express the same concepts, or carry the same normative force, as they do in a particular moral theory.

When Kant speaks, for example, of the dignity that belongs to persons by virtue of their rational nature, and that places them beyond all price (Kant, 1964, p. 102), he is not invoking anything that requires the ability to walk unaided, to feed oneself, or to control one's bowels. Hence the dignity invoked in discussions of medical ethics—a status supposedly threatened by physical deterioration and dependency—cannot be the status whose claim on our moral concern is so fundamental to Kantian thought. We must therefore ask whether this other sort of dignity, whatever it may be, embodies a value that's equally worthy of protection.

My worry, in particular, is that the word 'dignity' is sometimes used to dignify, so to speak, our culture's obsession with independence, physical strength, and youth. To my mind, the dignity defined by these values—a

J. David Velleman, "Against the Right to Die," 2012. This is a revised version of a paper that was originally published in *The Journal of Medicine and Philosophy* 17(6): 665–681 (1992). This revision replaces sections II and III of the original paper with a new and substantially different section II. Reprinted by permission of the author.

dignity that is ultimately incompatible with *being cared for* at all—is a dignity not worth having.[2]

I have similar worries about the values expressed by the phrase 'patient autonomy'; for there are two very different senses in which a person's autonomy can become a value for us. On the one hand, we can obey the categorical imperative, by declining to act for reasons that we could not rationally propose as valid for all rational beings, including those who are affected by our action, such as the patient. What we value in that case is the patient's *capacity* for self-determination, and we value it in a particular way—namely, by according it *respect*. We respect the patient's autonomy by regarding the necessity of sharing our reasons with him, among others, as a constraint on what decisions we permit ourselves to reach.

On the other hand, we can value the patient's autonomy by making it our goal to maximize his effective options. What we value, in that case, is not the patient's capacity but his *opportunities* for self-determination—his having choices to make and the means with which to implement them; and we value these opportunities for self-determination by regarding them as *goods*—as objects of desire and pursuit rather than respect.

These two ways of valuing autonomy are fundamentally different. Respecting people's autonomy, in the Kantian sense, is not just a matter of giving them effective options. To make our own decisions only for reasons that we could rationally share with others is not necessarily to give *them* decisions to make, nor is it to give them the means to implement their actual decisions.[3]

As with the term 'dignity', then, we must not assume that the term 'autonomy' is always being used in the sense made familiar by Kantian moral theory; and we must therefore ask ourselves what sort of autonomy is being invoked, and whether it is indeed something worthy of our moral concern. I believe that, as with the term 'dignity', the answer to the latter question may be no in some cases, including the case of the right to die.

II

Despite my qualms about the use of Kantian language to justify euthanasia, I do believe that euthanasia can be justified, and on Kantian grounds. In particular, I believe that respect for a person's dignity, properly conceived, can require us to facilitate his death when that dignity is being irremediably compromised. I also believe, however, that a person's dignity can be so compromised only by circumstances that are likely to compromise his capacity for fully rational and autonomous decisionmaking. So although I do not favor euthanizing people against their wills, of course, neither do I favor a policy of euthanizing people for the sake of deferring to their wills, since I think that people's wills are usually impaired in the circumstances required to make euthanasia permissible. The sense in which I oppose a right to die, then, is that I oppose treating euthanasia as a protected option for the patient.

One reason for my opposition is the associated belief (also Kantian) that so long as patients would be fully competent to exercise an option of being euthanized, their doing so would be immoral, in the majority of cases, because their dignity as persons would still be intact. I discuss this argument elsewhere, but I do not return to it in the present paper.[4] In this paper I discuss a second reason for opposing euthanasia as a protected option for the patient. This reason, unlike the first, is consequentialist.

What consequentialist arguments could there be against giving the option of euthanasia to patients? One argument, of course, would be that giving this option to patients, even under carefully defined conditions, would entail providing euthanasia to some patients for whom it would be a harm rather than a benefit (Kamisar, 1970). But the argument that interests me does not depend on this strategy. My consequentialist worry about the right to die is not that some patients might mistakenly choose to die when they would be better off living.

In order to demonstrate that I am not primarily worried about [a] mistaken request to die, I shall assume, from this point forward, that patients are infallible, and that euthanasia would therefore be chosen only by those for whom it would be a benefit. Even so, I believe, the establishment of a right to die would harm many patients, by increasing their autonomy in a sense that is not only un-Kantian but also very undesirable.

This belief is sometimes expressed in public debate, although it is rarely developed in any detail. Here, for example, is Yale Kamisar's argument against "Euthanasia Legislation":

> Is this the kind of choice...that we want to offer a gravely ill person? Will we not sweep up, in the process, some who are not really tired of life, but think others are tired of them; some who do not really want to die, but who feel they should not live on, because to do so when there looms the legal alternative of euthanasia is to do a selfish or a cowardly act? Will not some feel an obligation to have themselves "eliminated"...(Kamisar, 1970)?

Note that these considerations do not, strictly speaking, militate against euthanasia itself. Rather, they militate against a particular decision procedure for euthanasia—namely, the procedure of placing the choice of euthanasia in the patient's hands. What Kamisar is questioning in this particular passage is, not the practice of helping some patients to die, but rather the practice of asking them to choose whether to die. The feature of legalizedeuthanasia that troubles him is precisely its being an option offered to patients—the very feature for which it's touted, by its proponents, as an enhancement of the patients' autonomy. Kamisar's remarks thus [betray] the suspicion that this particular enhancement of one's autonomy is not to be welcomed.

But what exactly is the point of Kamisar's rhetorical questions? The whole purpose of giving people choices, surely, is to allow those choices to be determined by their reasons and preferences rather than ours. Kamisar may think that finding one's life tiresome is a good reason for dying whereas thinking that others find one tiresome is not. But if others honestly think otherwise, why should we stand in their way? Whose life is it anyway?

IV

A theoretical framework for addressing this question can be found in Thomas Schelling's book *The Strategy of Conflict* (1960), and in Gerald Dworkin's paper 'Is more choice better than less?' (1982). These authors have shown that our intuitions about the value of options are often mistaken, and their work can help us to understand the point of arguments like Kamisar's.

We are inclined to think that, unless we are likely to make mistakes about whether to exercise an option (as I am assuming we are not), the value of having the option is as high as the value of exercising it and no lower than zero. Exercising an option can of course be worse than nothing, if it causes harm. But if we are not prone to mistakes, then we will not exercise a harmful option; and we tend to think that simply *having* the unexercised option cannot be harmful. And insofar as exercising an option would make us better off than we are, having the option must have made us better off than we were before we had it—or so we tend to think.

What Schelling showed, however, is that having an option can be harmful even if we do not exercise it and—more surprisingly—even if we exercise it and gain by doing so. Schelling's examples of this phenomenon were drawn primarily from the world of negotiation, where the only way to induce one's opponent to settle for less may be by proving that one doesn't have the option of giving him more. Schelling pointed out that in such circumstances, a lack of options can be an advantage. The union leader who cannot persuade his membersship to approve a pay-cut, or the ambassador who cannot contact his head-of-state for a change of brief, negotiates from a position of strength; whereas the negotiator for whom all concessions are possible deals from weakness. If the rank-and-file give their leader the option of offering a pay-cut, then management may not settle for anything less, whereas they might have settled for less if he hadn't had the option of making the offer. The union leader will then have to decide whether to take the option and reach an agreement or to leave the option and call a strike. But no matter which of these outcomes would make him better off, choosing it will still leave him worse off than he would have been if he had never had the option at all.

Dworkin has expanded on Schelling's point by exploring other respects in which options can be undesirable. Just as options can subject one to pressure from an opponent in negotiation, for example, they can subject one to pressure from other sources as well. The night cashier in a convenience shore doesn't want the option of opening the safe—and not because he fears that he'd make mistakes about when to open it. It is precisely because the cashier would know when he'd better open the safe that his having the option would make him an attractive target for robbers; and it's because having the option would make him a target for robbers that he'd be better off without it. The cashier who finds himself opening the safe at gunpoint can consistently think that he's doing what's best while wishing that he'd never been given the option of doing it.

Options can be undesirable, then, because they subject one to various kinds of pressure; but they can be undesirable for other reasons, too. Offering someone an alternative to the status quo makes two outcomes possible for him, but neither of them is the outcome that was possible before. He can now choose the status quo or choose the alternative, but he can no longer *have* the status quo without *choosing* it. And having the status quo by default may have been what was best for him, even though choosing the status quo is now worst. If I invite you to a dinner party, I leave you the possibilities of choosing to come or choosing to stay away; but I deprive you of something that you otherwise would have had—namely, the possibility of being absent from my table by default, as you are on all other occasions. Surely, preferring to accept an invitation is consistent with wishing you had never received it. These attitudes are consistent because refusing to attend a party is a different outcome from *not* attending without having to refuse; and even if the former of these outcomes is worse than attending, the latter may still have been better. Having choices can thus deprive one of desirable outcomes whose desirability depends on their being unchosen.

The offer of an option can also be undesirable because of what it expresses. To offer a student the option of receiving remedial instruction after class is to imply that he is not keeping up. If the student needs help but doesn't know it, the offer may clue him in. But even if the student does not need any help, to begin with, the offer may so undermine his confidence that he will need help before long. In the latter case, the student may ultimately

benefit from accepting the offer, even though he would have been better off not receiving it at all.

Note that in each of these cases, a person can be harmed by having a choice even if he chooses what's best for him. Once the option of offering a concession has undermined one's bargaining position, once the option of opening the safe has made one the target of a robbery, once the invitation to a party has eliminated the possibility of absence by default, once the offer of remedial instruction has implied that one needs it—in short, once one has been offered a problematic choice—one's situation has already been altered for the worse, and choosing what's best cannot remedy the harm that one has already suffered. Choosing what's best in these cases is simply a way of cutting one's losses.

Note, finally, that we cannot always avoid burdening people with options by offering them a second-order option as to which options they are to be offered. If issuing you an invitation to dinner would put you in an awkward position, then asking you whether you want to be invited would usually do so as well; if offering you the option of remedial instruction would send you a message, then so would asking you whether you'd like that option. In order to avoid doing harm, then, we are sometimes required, not only to withhold options, but also to take the initiative for withholding them.

V

Of course, the options that I have discussed can also be unproblematic for many people in many circumstances. Sometimes one has good reason to welcome a dinner invitation or an offer of remedial instruction. Similarly, some patients will welcome the option of euthanasia, and rightly so. The problem is how to offer the option only to those patients who will have reason to welcome it. Arguments like Kamisar's are best understood, I think, as warning that the option of euthanasia may unavoidable be offered to some who will be harmed simply by having the option, even if they go on to choose what is best.

I think that the option of euthanasia may harm some patients in all of the ways canvassed above; but I will focus my attention on only a few of those ways. The most important way in which the option of euthanasia may harm patients, I think, is that it will deny them the possibility of staying alive by default.

Now, the idea of surviving by default will be anathema to existentialists, who will insist that the choice between life and death is a choice that we have to make every day, perhaps every moment.[5] Yet even if there is a deep, philosophical sense in which we do continually choose to go on living, it is not reflected in our ordinary self-understanding. That is, we do not ordinarily think of ourselves or others as continually rejecting the option of suicide and staying alive by choice. Thus, even if the option of euthanasia won't alter a patient's existential situation, it will certainly alter the way in which his situation is generally perceived. And changes in the perception of a patient's situation will be sufficient to produce many of the problems that Schelling and Dworkin have described, since those problems are often created not just by *having* options but by [*having] been seen* to have them.

Once a person is given the choice between life and death, he will rightly be perceived as the agent of his own survival. Whereas his existence is ordinarily viewed as a given for him—as a fixed condition with which he must cope—formally offering him the option of euthanasia will cause his existence thereafter to be viewed as his doing.

The problem with this perception is that if others regard you as choosing a state of affairs, they will hold you responsible for it; and if they hold you responsible for a state of affairs, they can ask you to justify it. Hence if people ever come to regard you as existing by choice, they may expect you to justify your continued existence. If your daily arrival in the office is interpreted as meaning that you have once again declined to kill yourself, you may feel obliged to arrive with an answer to the question "Why not?"

I think that our perception of one another's existence as a given is so deeply ingrained that we can hardly imagine what life would be like without it. When someone shows impatience or displeasure with us, we jokingly say "Well, excuse me for living!" But imagine that it were no joke; imagine that living were something for which one might reasonably be thought to need an excuse. The

burden of justifying one's existence might make existence unbearable—and hence unjustifiable.

VI

I assume that people care, and are right to care, about whether they can justify their choices to others. Of course, this concern can easily seem like slavishness or neurotic insecurity; but it should not be dismissed too lightly. Our ability to justify our choices to the people around us is what enables us to sustain the role of rational agent in our dealings with them; and it is therefore essential to our remaining, in their eyes, an eligible partner in cooperation and conversation, or an appropriate object of respect.

Retaining one's status as a person among others is especially important to those who are ill or infirm. I imagine that when illness or infirmity denies one the rewards of independent activity, then the rewards of personal intercourse may be all that make life worth living. To the ill or infirm, then, the ability to sustain the role of rational person may rightly seem essential to retaining what remains of value in life. Being unable to account for one's choices may seem to entail the risk of being perceived as unreasonable—as not worth reasoning with—and consequently being cut off from meaningful intercourse with others, which is life's only remaining consolation.

Forcing a patient to take responsibility for his continued existence may therefore be tantamount to confronting with the following prospect: unless he can explain, to the satisfaction of others, why he chooses to exist, his only remaining reasons for existence may vanish.

VII

Unfortunately, our culture is extremely hostile to any attempt at justifying an existence of passivity and dependence. The burden of proof will lie heavily on the patient who thinks that his terminal illness or chronic disability is not a sufficient reason for dying.

What is worse, the people with whom a patient wants to maintain intercourse, and to whom he therefore wants to justify his choices, are often in a position to incur several financial and emotional costs from any prolongation of his life. Many of the [reasons] in favor [of] his death are therefore likely to be exquisitely salient in their minds. I believe that some of these people may actively pressure the patient to exercise the option of dying. (Students who hear me say this usually object that no one would ever do such a thing. My reply is that no one would ever do such a thing as abuse his own children or parents—except that many people do).

In practice, however, friends and relatives of a patient will not have to utter a word of encouragement, much less exert any overt pressure, once the option of euthanasia is offered. For in the discussion of a subject so hedged by taboos and inhibitions, the patient will have to make some assumptions about what they think and how they feel, irrespective of what they say (See, Schelling, 1984). And the rational assumption for him to make will be that they are especially sensible of the considerations in favor of his exercising the option.

Thus, even if a patient antecedently believes that his life is worth living, he may have good reason to assume that many of the people around him do not, and that his efforts to convince them will be frustrated by prevailing opinions about lives like his, or by the biases inherent in their perspective. Indeed, he can reasonably assume that the offer of euthanasia is itself an expression of attitudes that are likely to frustrate his efforts to justify declining it. He can therefore assume that his refusal to take the option of euthanasia will threaten his standing as rational person in the eyes of friends and family, thereby threatening the very things that make his life worthwhile. This patient may rationally judge that he's better off taking the option of euthanasia, even though he would have been best off not having the option at all.

Establishing a right to die in our culture may thus be like establishing a right to duel in a culture obsessed with personal honor.[6] If someone defended the right to duel by arguing that a duel is a private transaction between consenting adults, he would have missed the point of laws against dueling. What makes it rational for someone to throw down or pick up a gauntlet may be the social costs of choosing not to, costs that result from failing to duel only if one fails to duel by choice. Such costs disappear if the choice of dueling can be removed. By eliminating the option of dueling (if we can), we eliminate the reasons that make it rational for people to duel in most cases. To restore the option of dueling would be to give people reasons for dueling that they didn't previously have. Similarly, I believe, to offer the option of dying may be to give people new reasons for dying.

VIII

Do not attempt to refute this argument against the right to die by labeling it paternalistic. The argument is not paternalistic—at last, not in any derogatory sense of the word. Paternalism, in the derogatory sense, is the policy of saving people from self-inflicted harms, by denying them options that they might exercise unwisely. Such a policy is distasteful because it expresses a lack of respect for others' ability to make their own decisions.

But my argument is not paternalistic in this sense. My reason for withholding the option of euthanasia is not that others cannot be trusted to exercise it wisely. On the contrary, I have assumed from the outset that patients will be infallible in their deliberations. What I have argued is—not that people to whom we offer the option of euthanasia might harm themselves—but rather that in offering them this option, *we* will do them harm. My argument is therefore based on a simple policy of non-malfeasance rather than on the policy of paternalism. I am arguing that we must not harm others by giving them choices, not that we must withhold the choices from them lest they harm themselves.

Of course, harming some people by giving them choices may be unavoidable if we could not withhold those choices from them without unjustly withholding the same choices from others. If a significant number of patients were both competent and morally entitled to choose euthanasia, then we might be obligated to make that option available even if, in doing so, we would inevitably give it to some who would be harmed by having it. Consider here a closely related option.[7] People are morally entitled to refuse treatment, because they are morally entitled not to be drugged, punctured, or irradiated against their wills—in short, not to be assaulted. Protecting the right not to be assaulted entails giving some patients what amounts to the option of ending their lives. And for some subset of these patients, having the option of ending their lives by refusing treatment may be just as harmful as having the option of electing active euthanasia. Nevertheless, these harms must be tolerated as an inevitable byproduct of protecting the right not to be assaulted.

Similarly, if I believed that people had a moral right to end their lives, I would not entertain consequentialist arguments against protecting that right. But I don't believe in such a moral right, for reasons to which I have briefly alluded but cannot fully expound in this essay. My willingness to entertain the arguments expounded here thus depends on reasons that are explained elsewhere.[8]

IX

I have been assuming, in deference to existentialists, that a right to die would not alter the options available to a patient but would, at most, alter the social perception of his options.

What would follow, however, if we assumed that death was not ordinarily a genuine option? In that case, offering someone the choice of euthanasia would not only cause his existence to be perceived as his responsibility; it would actually cause his existence to become his responsibility for the first time. And this new responsibility might entail new and potentially burdensome obligations.

That options can be undesirable because they entail obligations is a familiar principle in one area of everyday life—namely, the practice of offering, accepting, and declining gifts and favors. When we decline a gift or a favor that someone has spontaneously offered, we deny him an option, the option of providing us with a particular benefit. And our reason for declining is often that he could not have the option of providing the benefit without being obligated to exercise that option. Indeed, we sometimes feel obligated, on our part, to decline a benefit precisely in order to prevent someone from being obligated, on his part, to provide it.[9] We thus recognize that giving or leaving someone

the option of providing a benefit to us may be a way of harming him, by burdening him with an obligation.

When we decline a gift or favor, our would-be benefactor sometimes protests in language similar to that used by proponents of the right to die. "I know what I'm doing", he says, "and no one is twisting my arm. It's my money [or whatever], and I want you to have it". If he's unaware of the lurking allusion, he might even put it like this: "Whose money is it, anyway?"

Well, it is his money (or whatever); and we do believe that he's entitled to dispose of his money as he likes. Yet his right of personal autonomy in disposing of his money doesn't always require that we let him dispose of it on us. We are entitled—and, as I have suggested, sometimes obligated—to restrict his freedom in spending his money for our benefit, insofar as that freedom may entail burdensome obligations.

The language in which favors are declined is equally interesting as that in which they are offered. What we often say when declining a favor is, "I can't let you do that for me: it would be too much to ask". The phrase 'too much to ask' is interesting because it is used only when we haven't in fact asked for anything. Precisely because the favor in question would be too much to ask, we haven't asked for it, and now our prospective benefactor is offering it spontaneously. Why, then, do we give our reason for not having solicited the favor as a reason for declining when it's offered unsolicited?

The answer, I think, is that we recognize how little distance there is between permitting someone to do us a favor and asking him to do it. Because leaving someone the option of doing us a favor can place him under an obligation to do it, it has all the consequences of asking for the favor. To say "I'm leaving you the option of helping me but I'm not asking you to help" is to draw a distinction without a difference, since options can be just as burdensome as requests.

X

Clearly, a patient's decision to die will sometimes be a gift or a favor bestowed on loved ones whose financial or emotional resources are being drained by his condition. And clearly, death is the sort of gift that one might well want to decline, by denying others the option of giving it. Yet protections for the option of euthanasia would in effect protect the option of giving this gift, and they would there by prevent the prospective beneficiaries from declining it. Establishing a right to die would thus be tantamount to adopting the public policy that death is never too much to ask.

I don't pretend to understand fully the ethics of gifts and favors. It's one of those subjects that gets neglected in philosophical ethics, perhaps because it has more to do with the **supererogatory** than the obligatory. One question that puzzles me is whether we are permitted to restrict people's freedom to benefit us in ways that require no active participation on our part. Someone cannot successfully give us a gift, in most cases, unless we cooperate by taking it into our possession; and denying someone the option of giving us a gift usually consists of refusing to do our part in the transaction. But what about cases in which someone can do us a good turn without any cooperation from us? To what extent are we entitled to decline the favor by means of restrictions on his behavior rather than omissions in ours?

Another question, of course, is whether we wouldn't, in fact, play some part in the deaths of patients who received socially sanctioned euthanasia. Would a medically assisted or supervised death be a gift that we truly took no part in accepting? What if "we"—the intended beneficiary of the gift—were society as a whole, the body that established the right to die and trained physicians in its implementation? Surely, establishing the right to die is tantamount to saying, to those who might contemplate dying for the social good, that such favors will never be refused.

These considerations, inconclusive though they are, show how the theoretical framework developed by Schelling and Dworkin might support remarks like Kamisar's about patients' "obligation to have themselves 'eliminated'". The worry that a right to die would become an obligation to die is of a piece with other worries about euthanasia, not in itself, but as a problematic option for the patient.

XI

As I have said, I favor euthanasia in some cases. And of course, I believe that euthanasia must not be administered [to] competent patients without their consent. To that extent, I think that the option of dying will have to be presented to some patients, so that they can [receive] the benefit of a good death.

On the basis of the foregoing arguments, however, I doubt whether policymakers can formulate a general definition that distinguishes the circumstances in which the option of dying would be beneficial from those in which it would be harmful. The factors that make an option problematic are too subtle and too various to be defined in a statute or regulation. How will the option of euthanasia be perceived by the patient and his loved ones? How will it affect the relations among them? Is he likely to fear being spurned for declining the option? Would he exercise the option merely as a favor to them? And are they genuinely willing to accept that favor? Sensitivity to these and related questions could never be incorporated into an institutional rule defining conditions under which the option must be offered.

Insofar as I am swayed by the foregoing arguments, then, I am inclined to think that society should at most permit, and never require, health professionals to offer the option of euthanasia or to grant patients' requests for it. We can probably define some conditions under which the option should never be offered; but we are not in a position to define conditions under which it should always be offered; and so we can at most define a legal permission rather than a legal requirement to offer it. The resulting rule would leave caregivers free to withhold the option whenever they see fit, even if it is explicitly and spontaneously requested. And so long as caregivers are permitted to withhold the option of euthanasia, patients will not have a right to die.

XII

The foregoing arguments make me worry even about an explicitly formulated permission for the practice of euthanasia, since an explicit law or regulation to this effect would already invite patients, and hence potentially pressure them, to request that the permission be exercised in their case. I feel most comfortable with a policy of permitting euthanasia by default—that is, by a tacit failure to enforce the institutional rules that currently serve as barriers to justified euthanasia, or a gradual elimination of those rules without fanfare. The best public policy of euthanasia, I sometimes think, is no policy at all.

This suggestion will surely strike some readers as scandalous, because of the trust that it would place in the individual judgment of physicians and patients. But I suspect that to place one's life in the hands of another person, in the way that one does today when placing oneself in the care of a physician, may simply be to enter a relationship in which such trust is essential, because it cannot be replaced or even underwritten by institutional guarantees. Although I do not share the conventional view that advances in medical technology have outrun our moral understanding of how they should be applied, I am indeed tempted to think they have outrun the capacity of institutional rules to regulate their application. I am therefore tempted to think that public policy regulating the relation between physician and patient should be weak and vague by design; and that insofar as the aim of medical ethics is to strengthen or sharpen such policy, medical ethics itself is a bad idea.

NOTES

1. This is a revised version of a paper that was originally published in *The Journal of Medicine and Philosophy* (1992). That paper began as a comment of a paper by Dan Brock, presented at the Central Division of the APA in 1991. See his 'Voluntary Active Euthanasia' (Brock, 1992). I received help in writing that paper from: Dan Brock, Elizabeth Anderson, David Hills, Yale Kamisar, and Patricia White.
2. Here I echo some excellent remarks on the subject by Felicia Ackerman (Ackerman, 1990). I discuss the issue of 'dying with dignity' in (Velleman, 1999a).
3. I discuss this issue further in (Velleman, 1999b), pp. 356–58, esp. nn. 69, 72.

4. See (Velleman, 1999a).
5. The *locus classicus* for this point is of course Camus' essay 'The myth of Sisyphus' (Camus, 1959).
6. For this analogy, see (Stell, 1979). Stell argues—implausibly, in my view—that one has the right to die for the same reason that one has a right to duel.
7. The analogy is suggested, in the form of an objection to my arguments, by Dan Brock in (Brock, [1992]).
8. See my 1999a.
9. Of course, there are many other reasons for declining gifts and favors, such as pride, embarrassment, or a desire not to be in someone else's debt. My point is simply that there are cases in which these reasons are absent and a very different reason is present—names, our desire not to burden someone else with obligations.

REFERENCES

Ackerman, Felicia: 1990, 'No, thanks, I don't want to die with dignity', *Providence Journal-Bulletin*, April 19, 1990.

Brock, Dan: 1992, 'Voluntary Active Euthanasia', *Hastings Center Report* 22, pp. 10-22; reprinted in *Life and Death; Philosophical essays in biomedical ethics* (Cambridge: Cambridge University Press, 1993).

Camus, Albert: 1956, 'The myth of Sisyphus', in *The Myth of Sisyphus and Other Essays*, tr. By Justin O'Brien, Vintage Books, New York.

Dworkin, Gerald: 1982, 'Is more choice better than less?', *Midwest Studies in Philosophy* 7, pp. 47-61.

Kamisar, Yale: 1970, 'Euthanasia legislation: Some non-religious objections', in A.B. Downing (ed.), *Euthanasia and the Right to Die*, Humanities Press, New York, pp. 85-133.

Kant, I.: 1964, *Groundwork of the Metaphysic of Morals*, trans., by H.J. Paton, Harper and Row, New York.

Schelling, Thomas: 1960, *The Strategy of Conflict*, Harvard University Press, Cambridge, Massachusetts.

Schelling, Thomas: 1984, 'Strategic relationships in dying, in *Choice and Consequence*', Harvard University Press, Cambridge, Massachusetts.

Stell, Lance K.: 1979, 'Dueling and the Right to Life', *Ethics* 90, pp. 7-26.

Velleman, J. David: 1991, 'Well-being and time', *Pacific Philosophical Quarterly* 72, pp. 48-77.

Velleman, J. David: 1999a, 'A Right of Self-Termination?', *Ethics* 109, pp. 606-28.

Velleman, J. David: 1999b, 'Love as a Moral Emotion', *Ethics* 109, pp. 338-74.

☖ QUESTIONS FOR ANALYSIS

1. Why is Velleman concerned about the concept of Kantian "dignity" in discussions of assisted suicide?
2. What are Velleman's concerns with the concept of "patient autonomy"? What are the two senses in which a person's autonomy can be a value for us?
3. Under what circumstances does Velleman believe that euthanasia can be justified?
4. Why does Velleman have a problem with deferring to people's wishes regarding euthanasia?
5. Velleman switches to consequentialist reasoning in arguing that we should not defer to a patient's wishes. What consequences are of concern to him here?
6. How do Schelling and Dworkin argue that merely having an option, even if it is not exercised, can be harmful?
7. Why does Velleman insist that his argument is not paternalistic? Why does he call it a policy of "non-malfeasance"?
8. Why does Velleman conclude that euthanasia would be moral in some circumstances, but still believe it should not be the subject of legislation?
9. Why does he say that "the best public policy of euthanasia" is "no policy at all"?

Active and Passive Euthanasia

JAMES RACHELS

The traditional view is that there is an important moral difference between active and passive euthanasia. Active euthanasia involves killing and passive euthanasia letting die, and this fact has led many physicians and philosophers to reject active euthanasia as morally wrong, even while approving of passive euthanasia.

In this essay, professor of philosophy James Rachels (1941–2003) challenges both the use and moral significance of this distinction for several reasons. First, active euthanasia is in many cases more humane than passive. Second, the conventional doctrine leads to decisions concerning life and death on irrelevant grounds. Third, the doctrine rests on a distinction between killing and letting die that itself has no moral significance. Fourth, the most common arguments in favor of the doctrine are invalid. Therefore, in Rachels's view, the American Medical Association's policy statement endorsing the active–passive distinction is unwise.

The distinction between active and passive euthanasia is thought to be crucial for medical ethics. The idea is that it is permissible, at least in some cases, to withhold treatment and allow a patient to die, but it is never permissible to take any direct action designed to kill the patient. This doctrine seems to be accepted by most doctors, and it is endorsed in a statement adopted by the House of Delegates of the American Medical Association on December 4, 1973:

The intentional termination of the life of one human being by another—mercy killing—is contrary to that for which the medical profession stands and is contrary to the policy of the American Medical Association. The cessation of the employment of extraordinary means to prolong the life of the body when there is irrefutable evidence that biological death is imminent is the decision of the patient and/or his immediate family. The advice and judgment of the physician should be freely available to the patient and/or his immediate family.

James Rachels. "Active and Passive Euthanasia," *New England Journal of Medicine*, 292 (January 9, 1975), 78–80. Copyright © 1975 Massachusetts Medical Society. Reprinted with permission from Massachusetts Medical Society.

However, a strong case can be made against this doctrine. In what follows I will set out some of the relevant arguments, and urge doctors to reconsider their views on this matter.

To begin with a familiar type of situation, a patient who is dying of incurable cancer of the throat is in terrible pain, which can no longer be satisfactorily alleviated. He is certain to die within a few days, even if present treatment is continued, but he does not want to go on living for those days since the pain is unbearable. So he asks the doctor for an end to it, and his family joins in the request.

Suppose the doctor agrees to withhold treatment, as the conventional doctrine says he may. The justification for his doing so is that the patient is in terrible agony, and since he is going to die anyway, it would be wrong to prolong his suffering needlessly. But now notice this. If one simply withholds treatment, it may take the patient longer to die, and so he may suffer more than he would if more direct action were taken and a lethal injection given. This fact provides strong reason for thinking that, once the initial decision not to prolong his agony has been made, active euthanasia is actually preferable to passive euthanasia, rather than the reverse. To say otherwise is to endorse the option that leads to more suffering rather than less, and is contrary to the humanitarian impulse that prompts the decision not to prolong his life in the first place.

Part of my point is that the process of being "allowed to die" can be relatively slow and painful, whereas being given a lethal injection is relatively quick and painless. Let me give a different sort of example. In the United States about one in 600 babies is born with Down's syndrome. Most of these babies are otherwise healthy—that is, with only the usual pediatric care, they will proceed to an otherwise normal infancy. Some, however, are born with congenital defects such as intestinal obstructions that require operations if they are to live. Sometimes, the patients and the doctor will decide not to operate, and let the infant die. Anthony Shaw describes what happens then:

> ... When surgery is denied [the doctor] must try to keep the infant from suffering while natural forces sap the baby's life away. As a surgeon whose natural inclination is to use the scalpel to fight off death, standing by and watching a salvageable baby die is the most emotionally exhausting experience I know. It is easy at a conference, in a theoretical discussion, to decide that such infants should be allowed to die. It is altogether different to stand by in the nursery and watch as dehydration and infection wither a tiny being over hours and days. This is a terrible ordeal for me and the hospital staff— much more so than for the parents who never set foot in the nursery.[1]

I can understand why some people are opposed to all euthanasia, and insist that such infants must be allowed to live. I think I can also understand why other people favor destroying these babies quickly and painlessly. But why should anyone favor letting "dehydration and infection wither a tiny being over hours and days"? The doctrine that says that a baby may be allowed to dehydrate and wither, but may not be given an injection that would end its life without suffering, seems so patently cruel as to require no further refutation. The strong language is not intended to offend, but only to put the point in the clearest possible way.

My second argument is that the conventional doctrine leads to decisions concerning life and death made on irrelevant grounds.

Consider again the case of the infants with Down's syndrome who need operations for congenital defects unrelated to the syndrome to live. Sometimes, there is no operation, and the baby dies, but when there is no such defect, the baby lives on. Now, an operation such as that to remove an intestinal obstruction is not prohibitively difficult. The reason why such operations are not performed in these cases is, clearly, that the child has Down's syndrome and the parents and the doctor judge that because of that fact it is better for the child to die.

But notice that this situation is absurd, no matter what view one takes of the lives and potentials of such babies. If the life of such an infant is worth preserving, what does it matter if it needs a simple operation? Or, if one thinks it better that such a baby should not live on, what difference does it make that it happens to have an unobstructed intestinal tract? In either case, the matter of life and death is being decided on irrelevant grounds. It is the Down's syndrome, and not the intestines, that is the issue. The matter should be decided, if at all, on that basis, and not be allowed to depend on the essentially irrelevant question of whether the intestinal tract is blocked.

What makes this situation possible, of course, is the idea that when there is an intestinal blockage, one can "let the baby die," but when there is no such defect there is nothing that can be done, for one must not "kill" it. The fact that this idea leads to such results as deciding life or death on irrelevant grounds is another good reason why the doctrine should be rejected.

One reason why so many people think that there is an important moral difference between active and passive euthanasia is that they think killing someone is morally worse than letting someone die. But is it? Is killing, in itself, worse than letting die? To investigate this issue, two cases may be considered that are exactly alike except that one involves killing whereas the other involves letting someone die. Then, it can be asked whether this difference makes any difference to the moral assessments. It is important that the cases be exactly alike, except for this one difference, since otherwise one cannot be confident that it is this difference and not some other that accounts for any variation in the assessments of the two cases. So, let us consider this pair of cases:

In the first, Smith stands to gain a large inheritance if anything should happen to his six-year-old cousin. One evening while the child is taking his bath, Smith sneaks into the bathroom and drowns the child, and then arranges things so that it will look like an accident.

In the second, Jones also stands to gain if anything should happen to his six-year-old cousin. Like Smith, Jones sneaks in planning to drown the child in his bath. However, just as he enters the bathroom Jones sees the child slip and hit his head, and fall face down in the water. Jones is delighted; he stands by, ready to push the child's head back under if it is necessary, but it is not necessary. With only a little thrashing about, the child drowns all by himself, "accidentally" as Jones watches and does nothing.

Now Smith killed the child, whereas Jones "merely" let the child die. That is the only difference between them. Did either man behave better,

from a moral point of view? If the difference between killing and letting die were in itself a morally important matter, one should say that Jones's behavior was less reprehensible than Smith's. But does one really want to say that? I think not. In the first place, both men acted from the same motive, personal gain, and both had exactly the same end in view when they acted. It may be inferred from Smith's conduct that he is a bad man, although that judgment may be withdrawn or modified if certain further facts are learned about him—for example, that he is mentally deranged. But would not the very same thing be inferred about Jones from his conduct? And would not the same further considerations also be relevant to any modification of this judgment? Moreover, suppose Jones pleaded, in his own defense, "After all, I didn't do anything except just stand there and watch the child drown. I didn't kill him; I only let him die." Again, if letting die were in itself less bad than killing, this defense should have at least some weight. But it does not. Such a "defense" can only be regarded as a grotesque perversion of moral reasoning. Morally speaking, it is no defense at all.

Now, it may be pointed out, quite properly, that the cases of euthanasia with which doctors are concerned are not like this at all. They do not involve personal gain or the destruction of normal healthy children. Doctors are concerned only with cases in which the patient's life is of no further use to him, or in which the patient's life has become or will soon become a terrible burden. However, the point is the same in these cases: The bare difference between killing and letting die does not, in itself, make a moral difference. If a doctor lets a patient die, for humane reasons, he is in the same moral position as if he had given the patient a lethal injection for humane reasons. If his decision was wrong—if, for example, the patient's illness was in fact curable—the decision would be equally regrettable no matter which method was used to carry it out. And if the doctor's decision was the right one, the method used is not in itself important.

The AMA policy statement isolates the crucial issue very well: The crucial issue is "the intentional termination of the life of one human being by another." But after identifying this issue, and forbidding "mercy killing," the statement goes on to deny that the cessation of treatment is the intentional termination of a life. This is where the mistake comes in, for what is the cessation of treatment, in these circumstances, if it is not "the intentional termination of the life of one human being by another"? Of course it is exactly that, and if it were not, there would be no point to it.

Many people will find this judgment hard to accept. One reason, I think, is that it is very easy to conflate the question of whether killing is, in itself, worse than letting die, with the very different question of whether most actual cases of killing are more reprehensible than most actual cases of letting die. Most actual cases of killing are clearly terrible (think, for example, of all the murders reported in the newspapers), and one hears of such cases everyday. On the other hand, one hardly ever hears of a case of letting die, except for the actions of doctors who are motivated by humanitarian reasons. So one learns to think of killing in a much worse light than of letting die. But this does not mean that there is something about killing that makes it in itself worse than letting die, for it is not the bare difference between killing and letting die that makes the difference in these cases. Rather, the other factors—the murderer's motive of personal gain, for example, contrasted with the doctor's humanitarian motivation—account for different reactions to the different cases.

I have argued that killing is not in itself any worse than letting die; if my contention is right, it follows that active euthanasia is not any worse than passive euthanasia. What arguments can be given on the other side? The most common, I believe, is the following:

"The important difference between active and passive euthanasia is that in passive euthanasia, the doctor does not do anything to bring about the patient's death. The doctor does nothing, and the patient dies of whatever ills already afflict him. In active euthanasia, however, the doctor does something to bring about the patient's death: He kills him. The doctor who gives the patient with cancer a lethal injection has himself caused his patient's death; whereas if he merely ceases treatment, the cancer is the cause of death."

A number of points need to be made here. The first is that it is not exactly correct to say that in passive euthanasia the doctor does nothing, for he does do one thing that is very important: He lets the patient die. "Letting someone die" is certainly different, in some respects, from other types of action—mainly in that it is a kind of action that one may perform by way of not performing certain other actions. For example, one may let a patient die by way of not giving medication, just as one may insult someone by way of not shaking his hand. But for any purpose of moral assessment, it is a type of action nonetheless. The decision to let a patient die is subject to moral appraisal in the same way that a decision to kill him would be subject to moral appraisal: It may be assessed as wise or unwise, compassionate or sadistic, right or wrong. If a doctor deliberately let a patient die who was suffering from a routinely curable illness, the doctor would certainly be to blame for what he had done, just as he would be to blame if he had needlessly killed the patient. Charges against him would then be appropriate. If so, it would be no defense at all for him to insist that he didn't "do anything." He would have done something very serious indeed, for he let his patient die.

Fixing the cause of death may be very important from a legal point of view, for it may determine whether criminal charges are brought against the doctor. But I do not think that this notion can be used to show a moral difference between active and passive euthanasia. The reason why it is considered bad to be the cause of someone's death is that death is regarded as a great evil—and so it is. However, if it has been decided that euthanasia—even passive euthanasia—is desirable in a given case, it has also been decided that in this instance death is no greater an evil than the patient's continued existence. And if this is true, the usual reason for not wanting to be the cause of someone's death simply does not apply.

Finally, doctors may think that all of this is only of academic interest—the sort of thing that philosophers may worry about but that has no practical bearing on their own work. After all, doctors must be concerned about the legal consequences of what they do, and active euthanasia is clearly forbidden by the law. But even so, doctors should also be concerned with the fact that the law is forcing upon them a moral doctrine that may well be indefensible, and has a considerable effect on their practices. Of course, most doctors are not now in the position of being coerced in this matter, for they do not regard themselves as merely going along with what the law requires. Rather, in statements such as the AMA policy statement that I have quoted, they are endorsing this doctrine as a central point of medical ethics. In that statement, active euthanasia is condemned not merely as illegal but as "contrary to that for which the medical profession stands," whereas passive euthanasia is approved. However, the preceding considerations suggest that there is really no moral difference between the two, considered in themselves (there may be important moral differences in some cases in their consequences, but, as I pointed out, these differences may make active euthanasia, and not passive euthanasia, the morally preferable option). So, whereas doctors may have to discriminate between active and passive euthanasia to satisfy the law, they should not do any more than that. In particular, they should not give the distinction any added authority and weight by writing it into official statements of medical ethics.

NOTE

1. A. Shaw, "Doctor, Do We Have a Choice?" *The New York Times Magazine,* January 30, 1972, p. 54.

⚜ QUESTIONS FOR ANALYSIS

1. Early in his essay, Rachels sets up a familiar situation involving a throat-cancer patient. What is the point of the example? Do you think that suspending pain-relieving drugs is what people generally understand by "withholding treatment"?
2. Explain, through Rachels's own example of the infant with Down syndrome, why he thinks the distinction between active and passive euthanasia leads to life-or-death decisions made on irrelevant grounds.
3. Do you agree with Rachels that the cessation of treatment is tantamount to the intentional termination of life?
4. Rachels claims that killing is not necessarily any worse than allowing a person to die. What are the implications of this claim for the morality of active euthanasia?
5. Rachels believes it is inaccurate and misleading to say that a doctor who allows a patient to die does "nothing" to cause the death. Do you agree?

Gender, Feminism, and Death: Physician-Assisted Suicide and Euthanasia

SUSAN M. WOLF

Susan M. Wolf teaches at the University of Minnesota Law School, where she is the McKnight Presidential Professor of Law, Medicine and Public Policy and the Faegre Baker Daniels Professor of Law. She also is a professor of medicine in the University's Medical School and a faculty member in the University's Center for Bioethics. She received her B.A. from Princeton University and her J.D. from Yale Law School. She has published extensively in bioethics, health law, and law and science.

In these excerpts, she expresses concern that the continuing debates over the ethics of assisted suicide and euthanasia ignore the gender differences in patients. Women are at greater risk for inadequate pain relief and for depression and suicidal thoughts, all of which make them more vulnerable to pressure to request assisted suicide and euthanasia. They often come from different contexts and relationships in situations in which assisted suicide and euthanasia might be considered an option. Wolf uses methodologies from feminist thought to reexamine whether these practices should be considered ethical.

The debate in the United States over whether to legitimate physician-assisted suicide and active euthanasia has reached new levels of intensity. ... Yet the debate over whether to legitimate physician—assisted suicide and euthanasia (by which I mean active euthanasia, as opposed to the termination of life-sustaining treatment)[1] is most often about a patient who does not exist—a patient with no gender, race, or insurance status. This is the same generic patient featured in most bioethics debates. Little discussion has focused on how differences between patients might alter the equation.

Even though the debate has largely ignored this question, there is ample reason to suspect that gender, among other factors, deserves analysis. The cases prominent in the American debate mostly feature women patients. This occurs against a backdrop of a long history of cultural images revering women's sacrifice and self-sacrifice. Moreover, dimensions of health status and health care that may affect a patient's vulnerability to considering physician-assisted suicide and euthanasia— including depression, poor pain relief, and difficulty obtaining good health care—differentially plague women. And suicide patterns themselves show a strong gender effect: women less often complete suicide, but more often attempt it.[2] These and other factors raise the question of whether the dynamics surrounding physician-assisted suicide and euthanasia may vary by gender.

Indeed, it would be surprising if gender had no influence. Women in America still live in a society marred by sexism, a society that particularly disvalues women with illness, disability, or merely advanced age. It would be hard to explain if health care, suicide, and fundamental dimensions of American society showed marked differences by gender, but gender suddenly dropped out of the equation when people became desperate enough to seek a physician's help in ending their lives.

What sort of gender effects might we expect? There are four different possibilities. First, we might anticipate a higher incidence of women than men dying by physician-assisted suicide and euthanasia in this country. This is an empirical claim that we cannot yet test; we currently lack good data in the face of the illegality of the practices in most states[3] and the condemnation of the organized medical profession.[4]

There may, however, be a second gender effect. Gender differences may translate into women seeking physician-assisted suicide and euthanasia for somewhat different reasons than men. Problems we know to be correlated with gender—difficulty getting good medical care generally, poor pain relief, a higher incidence of depression, and a higher rate of poverty—may figure more prominently in women's motivation. Society's persisting sexism may figure as well. And the long history of valorizing women's self-sacrifice may be expressed in women's requesting assisted suicide or euthanasia.

The well-recognized gender differences in suicide statistics also suggest that women's requests for physician-assisted suicide and euthanasia may more often than men's requests be an effort to change an oppressive situation rather than a literal request for death. Thus some suicidologists interpret men's predominance among suicide "completers" and women's among suicide "attempters" to mean that women more often engage in suicidal behavior with a goal other than "completion."[5]

FEMINISM BIOETHICS: BEYOND REPRODUCTION edited by Susan M. Wolf (1996) Ch.10 "Gender, Feminism, and Death: Physician-Assisted Suicide and Euthanasia" by Wolf 7,150 words from pp. 282–317. By permission of Oxford University Press, USA.

The relationship between suicide and the practices of physician-assisted suicide and euthanasia itself deserves further study; not all suicides are even motivated by terminal disease or other factors relevant to the latter practices. But the marked gender differences in suicidal behavior are suggestive.

Third, gender differences may also come to the fore in physicians' decisions about whether to grant or refuse requests for assisted suicide or euthanasia. The same historical valorization of women's self-sacrifice and the same background sexism that may affect women's readiness to request may also affect physicians' responses. Physicians may be susceptible to affirming women's negative self-judgments. This might or might not result in physicians agreeing to assist; other gender-related judgments (such as that women are too emotionally labile, or that their choices should not be taken seriously) may intervene.[6] But the point is that gender may affect not just patient but physician.

Finally, gender may affect the broad public debate. The prominent U.S. cases so far and related historical imagery suggest that in debating physician-assisted suicide and euthanasia, many in our culture may envision a woman patient. Although the AIDS epidemic has called attention to physician-assisted suicide and euthanasia in men, the cases that have dominated the news accounts and scholarly journals in the recent renewal of debate have featured women patients. Thus we have reason to be concerned that at least some advocacy for these practices may build on the sense that these stories of women's deaths are somehow "right." If there is a felt correctness to these accounts, that may be playing a hidden and undesirable part in catalyzing support for the practices' legitimation.

Thus we have cause to worry whether the debate about and practice of physician-assisted suicide and euthanasia in this country are gendered in a number of respects. Serious attention to gender therefore seems essential. Before we license physicians to kill their patients or to assist patients in killing themselves, we had better understand the dynamic at work in that encounter, why the practice seems so alluring that we should court its dangers, and what dangers are likely to manifest.

After all, the consequences of permitting killing or assistance in private encounters are serious, indeed fatal. We had better understand what distinguishes this from other forms of private violence, and other relationships of asymmetrical power that result in the deaths of women. And we had better determine whether tacit assumptions about gender are influencing the enthusiasm for legalization.

Yet even that is not enough. Beyond analyzing the way gender figures in our cases, cultural imagery, and practice, we must analyze the substantive arguments. For attention to gender, in the last two decades particularly, has yielded a wealth of feminist critiques and theoretical tools that can fruitfully be brought to bear. After all, the debate over physician-assisted suicide and euthanasia revolves around precisely the kind of issues on which feminist work has focused: what it means to talk about rights of self-determination and autonomy; the reconciliation of those rights with physicians' duties of beneficence and caring; and how to place all of this in a context including the strengths and failures of families, professionals, and communities, as well as real differentials of power and resources.

The debate over physician-assisted suicide and euthanasia so starkly raises questions of rights, caring, and context that at this point it would take determination *not* to bring to bear a literature that has been devoted to understanding those notions. Indeed, the work of Lawrence Kohlberg bears witness to what an obvious candidate this debate is for such analysis.[7] It was Kohlberg's work on moral development, of course, that provoked Carol Gilligan's *In A Different Voice,* criticizing Kohlberg's vision of progressive stages in moral maturation as one that was partial and gendered.[8] Gilligan proposed that there were really two different approaches to moral problems, one that emphasized generalized rights and universal principles, and the other that instead emphasized contextualized caring and the maintenance of particular human relationships. She suggested that although women and men could use both approaches, women tended to use the latter and men the former. Both approaches, however, were important to moral maturity. Though Gilligan's and others' work on the ethics of care has been much debated and criticized, a number of bioethicists and health care professionals have found a particular pertinence to questions of physician caregiving.[9]

Embedded in Kohlberg's work, one finds proof that the euthanasia debate in particular calls for analysis in the very terms that he employs, and that Gilligan then critiques, enlarges, and reformulates. For one of the nine moral dilemmas Kohlberg used to gauge subjects' stage of moral development was a euthanasia problem. "Dilemma IV" features "a woman" with "very bad cancer" and "in terrible pain." Her physician, Dr. Jefferson, knows she has "only about six months to live." Between periods in which she is "delirious and almost crazy with pain," she asks the doctor to kill her with morphine. The question is what he should do.[10]

The euthanasia debate thus demands analysis along the care, rights, and context axes that the Kohlberg–Gilligan debate has identified.[11] Kohlberg himself used this problem to reveal how well respondents were doing in elevating general principles over the idiosyncrasies of relationship and context. It is no stretch, then, to apply the fruits of more than a decade of feminist critique....

GENDER IN CASES, IMAGES, AND PRACTICE

The tremendous upsurge in American debate over whether to legitimate physician-assisted suicide and euthanasia in recent years has been fueled by a series of cases featuring women. The case that seems to have begun this series is that of Debbie, published in 1988 by the *Journal of the American Medical Association* (*JAMA*).[12] *JAMA* published this now infamous, first-person, and anonymous account by a resident in obstetrics and gynecology of performing euthanasia. Some subsequently queried whether the account was fiction. Yet it successfully catalyzed an enormous response.

The narrator of the piece tells us that Debbie is a young woman suffering from ovarian cancer. The resident has no prior relationship with her, but is called to her bedside late one night while on call and exhausted. Entering Debbie's room, the resident finds an older woman with her, but never pauses to find out who that second woman is and what relational context Debbie acts within. Instead, the resident responds to the patient's clear discomfort and to her words. Debbie says only one sentence, "Let's get this over with." It is unclear whether she thinks the resident is there to draw blood and wants that over with, or means something else. But on the strength of that one sentence, the resident retreats to the nursing station, prepares a lethal injection, returns to the room, and administers it. The story relates this as an act of mercy under the title "It's Over, Debbie," as if in caring response to the patient's words.

The lack of relationship to the patient; the failure to attend to her own history, relationships, and resources; the failure to explore beyond the patient's presented words and engage her in conversation; the sense that the cancer diagnosis plus the patient's words demand death; and the construal of that response as an act of mercy are all themes that recur in the later cases. The equally infamous Dr. Jack Kevorkian has provided a slew of them.

They begin with Janet Adkins, a 54-year-old Oregon woman diagnosed with Alzheimer's disease.[13] Again, on the basis of almost no relationship with Ms. Adkins, on the basis of a diagnosis by exclusion that Kevorkian could not verify, prompted by a professed desire to die that is a predictable stage in response to a number of dire diagnoses, Kevorkian rigs her up to his "Mercitron" machine in a parking lot outside Detroit in what he presents as an act of mercy.

Then there is Marjorie Wantz, a 58-year-old woman without even a diagnosis.[14] Instead, she has pelvic pain whose source remains undetermined. By the time Kevorkian reaches Ms. Wantz, he is making little pretense of focusing on her needs in the context of a therapeutic relationship. Instead, he tells the press that he is determined to create a new medical specialty of "obitiatry." Ms. Wantz is among the first six potential patients with whom he is conferring. When Kevorkian presides over her death there is another woman who dies as well, Sherry Miller. Miller, 43, has multiple sclerosis. Thus neither woman is terminal.

The subsequent cases reiterate the basic themes.[15] And it is not until the ninth "patient" that Kevorkian finally presides over the death of a man.[16] By this time, published criticism of the predominance of women had begun to appear.[17]

Kevorkian's actions might be dismissed as the bizarre behavior of one man. But the public and press response has been enormous, attesting to the power of these accounts. Many people have treated these cases as important to the debate over physician-assisted suicide and euthanasia. Nor are Kevorkian's cases so aberrant—they pick up all the themes that emerge in "Debbie."...

... Prevailing values have imbued women's deaths with specific meaning. Indeed, Carol Gilligan builds on images of women's suicides and sacrifice in novels and drama, as well as on her own data, in finding a psychology and even an ethic of self-sacrifice among women. Gilligan finds one of the "conventions of femininity" to be "the moral equation of goodness with self-sacrifice."[18] "[V]irtue for women lies in self-sacrifice...."[19]

Given this history of images and the valorization of women's self-sacrifice, it should come as no surprise that the early cases dominating the debate about self-sacrifice through physician-assisted suicide and euthanasia have been cases of women. In Greek tragedy only women were candidates for sacrifice and self-sacrifice,[20] and to this day self-sacrifice is usually regarded as a feminine not masculine virtue.

This lineage has implications. It means that even while we debate physician-assisted suicide and euthanasia rationally, we may be animated by unacknowledged images that give the practices a certain gendered logic and felt correctness. In some deep way it makes sense to us to see these women dying, it seems right. It fits an old piece into a familiar, ancient puzzle. Moreover, these acts seem good; they are born of virtue. We may not recognize that the virtues in question—female sacrifice and self-sacrifice—are ones now widely questioned and deliberately rejected. Instead, our subconscious may harken back to older forms, reembracing those ancient virtues, and thus lauding these women's deaths.

Analyzing the early cases against the background of this history also suggests hidden gender dynamics to be discovered by attending to the facts found in the accounts of these cases, or more properly the facts not found. What is most important in these accounts is what is left out, how truncated they are. We see a failure to attend to the patient's context, a readiness on the part of these physicians to facilitate death, a seeming lack of concern over why these women turn to these doctors for deliverance. A clue about why we should be concerned about each of these omissions is telegraphed by data from exit polls on the day Californians defeated a referendum measure to legalize active euthanasia. Those polls showed support for the measure lowest among women, older people, Asians, and African Americans, and highest among younger men with postgraduate education and incomes over $75,000 per year.[21] The *New York Times* analysis was that people from more vulnerable groups were more worried about allowing physicians actively to take life. This may suggest concern not only that physicians may be too ready to take their lives, but also that these patients may be markedly vulnerable to seeking such relief. Why would women, in particular, feel this?

Women are at greater risk for inadequate pain relief.[22] Indeed, fear of pain is one of the reasons most frequently cited by Americans for supporting legislation to legalize euthanasia.[23] Women are also at greater risk for depression.[24] And depression appears to underlie numerous requests for physician-assisted suicide and euthanasia.[25] These factors suggest that women may be differentially driven to consider requesting both practices.

That possibility is further supported by data showing systematic problems for women in relationship to physicians. As an American Medical Association report on gender disparities recounts, women receive more care even for the same illness, but the care is generally worse. Women are less likely to receive dialysis, kidney transplants, cardiac catheterization, and diagnostic testing for lung cancer. The report urges physicians to uproot "social or cultural biases that could affect medical care" and "presumptions about the relative worth of certain social roles."[26]

This all occurs against the background of a deeply flawed health care system that ties health insurance to employment. Men are differentially represented in the ranks of those with private health insurance, women in the ranks of the others—those either on government entitlement programs or uninsured.[27] In the U.S. two-tier health care system, men dominate in the higher-quality tier, women in the lower.

Moreover, women are differentially represented among the ranks of the poor. Many may feel they lack the resources to cope with disability and disease. To cope with Alzheimer's, breast cancer, multiple sclerosis, ALS, and a host of other diseases takes resources. It takes not only the financial resource of health insurance, but also access to stable working relationships with clinicians expert in these conditions, in the psychological issues involved, and in palliative care and pain relief. It may take access to home care, eventually residential care, and rehabilitation services. These are services often hard to get even for those with adequate resources, and almost impossible for those without. And who are those without in this country? Disproportionately they are women, people of color, the elderly, and children.[28]

Women may also be driven to consider physician-assisted suicide or euthanasia out of fear of otherwise burdening their families.[29] The dynamic at work in a family in which an ill member chooses suicide or active euthanasia is worrisome. This worry should increase when it is a woman who seeks to "avoid being a burden," or otherwise solve the problem she feels she poses, by opting for her own sacrifice. The history and persistence of family patterns in this country in which women are expected to adopt self-sacrificing behavior for the sake of the family may pave the way too for the patient's request for death. Women requesting death may also be sometimes seeking something other than death. The dominance of women among those attempting but not completing suicide in this country suggests that women may differentially engage in death-seeking behavior with a goal other than death. Instead, they may be seeking to change their relationships or circumstances.[30] A psychiatrist at Harvard has speculated about why those women among Kevorkian's "patients" who were still capable of killing themselves instead sought Kevorkian's help. After all, suicide has been decriminalized in this country,

and step-by-step instructions are readily available. The psychiatrist was apparently prompted to speculate by interviewing about twenty physicians who assisted patients' deaths and discovering that two-thirds to three-quarters of the patients had been women. The psychiatrist wondered whether turning to Kevorkian was a way to seek a relationship.[31] The women also found a supposed "expert" to rely upon, someone to whom they could yield control. But then we must wonder what circumstances, what relational context, led them to this point.

What I am suggesting is that there are issues relating to gender left out of the accounts of the early prominent cases of physician-assisted suicide and euthanasia or left unexplored that may well be driving or limiting the choices of these women. I am not suggesting that we should denigrate these choices or regard them as irrational. Rather, it is the opposite—that we should assume these decisions to be rational and grounded in a context. That forces us to attend to the background failures in that context.

… In analyzing why women may request physician-assisted suicide and euthanasia, and why indeed the California polls indicate that women may feel more vulnerable to and wary of making that request, we have insights to bring to bear from other realms. Those insights render suspect an analysis that merely asserts women are choosing physician-assisted suicide and active euthanasia, without asking why they make that choice. The analogy to other forms of violence against women behind closed doors demands that we ask why the woman is there, what features of her context brought her there, and why she may feel there is no better place to be. Finally, the analogy counsels us that the patient's consent does not resolve the question of whether the physician acts properly in deliberately taking her life through physician-assisted suicide or active euthanasia. The two people are separate moral and legal agents.[32]

This leads us from consideration, of why women patients may feel vulnerable to these practices, to the question of whether physicians may be vulnerable to regarding women's requests for physician-assisted suicide and euthanasia somewhat differently from men's. There may indeed be gender-linked reasons for physicians in this country to say "yes" to women seeking assistance in suicide or active euthanasia. In assessing whether the patient's life has become "meaningless," or a "burden," or otherwise what some might regard as suitable for extinguishing at her request, it would be remarkable if the physician's background views did not come into play on what makes a woman's life meaningful or how much of a burden on her family is too much.[33]

Second, there is a dynamic many have written about operating between the powerful expert physician and the woman surrendering to his care.[34] It is no accident that bioethics has focused on the problem of physician paternalism. Instead of an egalitarianism or what Susan Sherwin calls "amicalism,"[35] we see a vertically hierarchical arrangement built on domination and subordination. When the patient is female and the doctor male, as is true in most medical encounters, the problem is likely to be exacerbated by the background realities and history of male dominance and female subjugation in the broader society. Then a set of psychological dynamics are likely to make the male physician vulnerable to acceding to the woman patient's request for active assistance in dying. These may be a complex combination of rescue fantasies[36] and the desire to annihilate. Robert Burt talks about the pervasiveness of this ambivalence, quite apart from gender: "Rules governing doctor–patient relations must rest on the premise that anyone's wish to help a desperately pained, apparently helpless person is intertwined with a wish to hurt that person, to obliterate him from sight."[37] When the physician is from a dominant social group and the patient from a subordinate one, we should expect the ambivalence to be heightened. When the "help" requested *is* obliteration, the temptation to enact both parts of the ambivalence in a single act may be great.

FEMINISM AND THE ARGUMENTS

Shifting from the images and stories that animate debate and the dynamics operating in practice to analysis of the arguments over physician-assisted suicide and euthanasia takes us further into the concerns of feminist theory. Arguments in favor of these practices have often depended on rights claims. More recently, some authors have grounded their arguments instead on ethical concepts of caring. Yet both argumentative strategies have been flawed in ways that feminist work can illuminate. What is missing is an analysis that integrates notions of physician caring with principled boundaries to physician action, while also attending to the patient's broader context and the community's wider concerns. Such an analysis would pay careful attention to the dangers posed by these practices to the historically most vulnerable populations, including women.

Advocacy of physician-assisted suicide and euthanasia has hinged to a great extent on rights claims. The argument is that the patient has a right of self-determination or autonomy that entitles her to assistance in suicide or euthanasia. The strategy is to extend the argument that self-determination entitles the patient to refuse unwanted life-sustaining treatment by maintaining that the same rationale supports patient entitlement to more active physician assistance in death. Indeed, it is sometimes argued that there is no principled difference between termination of life-sustaining treatment and the more active practices.

The narrowness and mechanical quality of this rights thinking, however, is shown by its application to the stories recounted above. That application suggests that the physicians in these stories are dealing with a simple equation: given an eligible rights bearer and her assertion of the right, the correct result is death. What makes a person an eligible rights bearer? Kevorkian seems to require neither a terminal disease nor thorough evaluation of whether the patient has non-fatal alternatives. Indeed, the Wantz case shows he does not even require a diagnosis. Nor does the Oregon physician-assisted suicide statute require evaluation or exhaustion of non-fatal alternatives; a patient could be driven by untreated pain, and still receive physician-assisted suicide. And what counts as an assertion of the right? For Debbie's doctor, merely "Let's get this over with." Disease plus demand requires death....

... Feminist critiques suggest three different sorts of problems with the rights equation offered to justify physician-assisted suicide and euthanasia. First, it ignores context, both the patient's present context and her history. The prior and surrounding failures in her intimate relationships, in her resources to cope with illness and pain, and even in the adequacy of care being offered by the very same physician fade into invisibility next to the bright light of a rights bearer and her demand. In fact, her choices may be severely constrained. Some of those constraints may even be alterable or removable. Yet attention to those dimensions of decision is discouraged by the absolutism of the equation: either she is an eligible rights bearer or not; either she has asserted her right or not. There is no room for conceding her competence and request, yet querying whether under all the circumstances her choices are so constrained and alternatives so unexplored that acceding to the request may not be the proper course. Stark examples are provided by cases in which pain or symptomatic discomfort drives a person to request assisted suicide or euthanasia, yet the pain or discomfort are treatable. A number of Kevorkian's cases raise the problem as well: Did Janet Adkins ever receive psychological support for the predictable despair and desire to die that follow dire diagnoses such as Alzheimer's? Would the cause of Marjorie Wantz's undiagnosed pelvic pain been ascertainable and even ameliorable at a better health center? In circumstances in which women and others who have traditionally lacked resources and experienced oppression are likely to have fewer options and a tougher time getting good care, mechanical application of the rights equation will authorize their deaths even when less drastic alternatives are or should be available. It will wrongly assume that all face serious illness and disability with the resources of the idealized rights bearer—a person of means untroubled by oppression. The realities of women and others whose circumstances are far from that abstraction's will be ignored.

Second, in ignoring context and relationship, the rights equation extols the vision of a rights bearer as an isolated monad and denigrates actual dependencies. Thus it may be seen as improper to ask what family, social, economic, and medical supports she is or is not getting; this insults her individual self-governance. Nor may it be seen as proper to investigate alternatives to acceding to her request for death; this too dilutes self-rule. Yet feminists have reminded us of the actual embeddedness of persons and the descriptive falseness of a vision of each as an isolated individual. In addition, they have argued normatively that a society comprised of isolated individuals, without the pervasive connections and dependencies that we see, would be undesirable.[38] Indeed, the very meaning of the patient's request for death is socially constructed; that is the point of the prior section's review of the images animating the debate. If we construe the patient's request as a rights bearer's assertion of a right and deem that sufficient grounds on which the physician may proceed, it is because we choose to regard background failures as irrelevant even if they are differentially motivating the requests of the most vulnerable. We thereby avoid real scrutiny of the social arrangements, governmental failures, and health coverage exclusions that may underlie these requests. We also ignore the fact that these patients may be seeking improved circumstances more than death. We elect a myopia that makes the patient's request and death seem proper. We construct a story that clothes the patient's terrible despair in the glorious mantle of "rights."

Formulaic application of the rights equation in this realm thus exalts an Enlightenment vision of autonomy as self-governance and the exclusion of interfering others. Yet as feminists such as Jennifer Nedelsky have argued, this is not the only vision of autonomy available.[39] She argues that a superior vision of autonomy is to be found by rejecting "the pathological conception of autonomy as boundaries against others," a conception that takes the exclusion of others from one's property as its central symbol....

In fact, there are substantial problems with grounding advocacy for the specific practices of physician-assisted suicide and euthanasia in a rights analysis, even if one accepts the general importance of rights and self-determination. I have elsewhere argued repeatedly for an absolute or near-absolute moral and legal right to be free of unwanted life-sustaining treatment.[40] Yet the negative right to be free of unwanted bodily invasion does not imply an affirmative right to obtain bodily invasion (or assistance with bodily invasion) for the purpose of ending your own life.

Moreover, the former right is clearly grounded in fundamental entitlements to liberty, bodily privacy, and freedom from unconsented touching; in contrast there is no clear "right" to kill yourself or be killed. Suicide has been widely decriminalized, but decriminalizing an act does not mean that you have a positive right to do it and to command the help of others. Indeed, if a friend were to tell me that she wished to kill herself, I would not be lauded for giving her the tools. In fact, that act of assistance has *not* been decriminalized. That continued condemnation shows that whatever my friend's relation to the act of suicide (a "liberty," "right," or neither), it does not create a right in her sufficient to command or even permit my aid.

There are even less grounds for concluding that there is a right to be killed deliberately on request, that is, for euthanasia. There are reasons why a victim's consent has traditionally been no defense to an accusation of homicide. One reason is suggested by analogy to Mill's famous argument that one cannot consent to one's own enslavement: "The reason for not interfering ... with a person's voluntary acts, is consideration for his liberty.... But by selling himself for a slave, he abdicates his liberty; he foregoes any future use of it...."[41] Similarly, acceding to a patient's request to be killed wipes out the possibility of her future exercise of her liberty. The capacity to command or permit another to take your life deliberately, then, would seem beyond the bounds of those things to which you have a right grounded in notions of liberty. We lack the capacity to bless another's enslavement of us or direct killing of us. How is this compatible then with a right to refuse life-sustaining treatment? That right is not grounded in any so-called "right to die," however frequently the phrase appears in the general press.[42] Instead, it is grounded in rights to be free of unwanted bodily invasion, rights so fundamental that they prevail even when the foreseeable consequence is likely to be death.

Finally, the rights argument in favor of physician-assisted suicide and euthanasia confuses two separate questions: what the patient may do, and what the physician may do. After all, the real question in these debates is not what patients may request or even do. It is not at all infrequent for patients to talk about suicide and request assurance that the physician will help or actively bring on death when the patient wants;[43] that is an expected part of reaction to serious disease and discomfort. The real question is what the doctor may do in response to this predictable occurrence. That question is not answered by talk of what patients may ask; patients may and should be encouraged to reveal everything on their minds. Nor is it answered by the fact that decriminalization of suicide permits the patient to take her own life. The physician and patient are separate moral agents. Those who assert that what a patient may say or do determines the same for the physician, ignore the physician's separate moral and legal agency. They also ignore the fact that she is a professional, bound to act in keeping with a professional role and obligations. They thereby avoid a necessary argument over whether the historic obligations of the physician to "do no harm" and "give no deadly drug even if asked" should be abandoned.[44] Assertion of what the patient may do does not resolve that argument.

The inadequacy of rights arguments to legitimate physician-assisted suicide and euthanasia has led to a different approach, grounded on physicians' duties of beneficence. This might seem to be quite in keeping with feminists' development of an ethics of care.[45] Yet the beneficence argument in the euthanasia context is a strange one, because it asserts that the physician's obligation to relieve suffering permits or even commands her to annihilate the person who is experiencing the suffering. Indeed, at the end of this act of beneficence, no patient is left to experience its supposed benefits. Moreover, this argument ignores widespread agreement that fears of patient addiction in these cases should be discarded, physicians may sedate to unconsciousness, and the principle of double effect permits giving pain relief and palliative care in doses that risk inducing respiratory depression and thereby hastening death. Given all of that, it is far from clear what patients remain in the category of those whose pain or discomfort can only be relieved by killing them.

Thus this argument that a physician should provide so much "care" that she kills the patient is deeply flawed.... The inadequacies of rights arguments to establish patient entitlement to assisted suicide and euthanasia are linked to the inadequacies of a "top-down" or deductive bioethics driven by principles, abstract theories, or rules. They share certain flaws: both seem overly to ignore context and the nuances of cases; their simple abstractions overlook real power differentials in society and historic subordination; and they avoid the fact that these principles, rules, abstractions, and rights are themselves a product of historically oppressive social arrangements. Similarly, the inadequacies of beneficence and compassion arguments are linked to some of the problems with a "bottom-up" or inductive bioethics built on cases, ethnography, and detailed description. In both instances it is difficult to see where the normative boundaries lie, and where to get a normative keel for the finely described ship.

What does feminism have to offer these debates? Feminists too have struggled extensively with the question of method, with how to integrate detailed attention to individual cases with rights, justice, and principles. Thus in criticizing Kohlberg and going beyond his vision of moral development, Carol Gilligan argued that human beings should be able to utilize both an ethics of justice and an ethics of care. "To understand how the tension between responsibilities and rights sustains the dialectic of human development is to see the integrity of two disparate modes of experience that are in the end connected.... In the representation of maturity, both perspectives converge...."[46] What was less clear was precisely how the two should fit together. And unfortunately for our purposes, Gilligan never took up Kohlberg's mercy killing case to illuminate a care perspective or even more importantly, how the two perspectives might properly be interwoven in that case....

Here we find the beginning of an answer to our dilemma. It appears that we must attend to both context and abstraction, peering through the lenses of both care and justice. Yet our approach to each will be affected by its mate. Our apprehension and understanding of context or cases inevitably involves categories, while our categories and principles should be refined over time to apply to some contexts and not others.[47] Similarly, our understanding of what caring requires in a particular case will grow in part from our understanding of what sort of case this is and what limits principles set to our expressions of caring; while our principles should be scrutinized and amended according to their impact on real lives, especially the lives of those historically excluded from the process of generating principles.[48]

This notion of principled caring captures the need for limits and standards, whether technically stated as principles or some other form of generalization. Those principles or generalizations will articulate limits and obligations in a provisional way, subject to reconsideration and possible amendment in light of actual cases. Both individual cases and patterns of cases may specifically reveal that generalizations we have embraced are infected by sexism or other bias, either as those generalizations are formulated or as they function in the world. Indeed, given that both medicine and bioethics are cultural practices in a society riddled by such bias and that we have only begun to look carefully for such bias in our bioethical principles and practices, we should expect to find it.

Against this background, arguments for physician-assisted suicide and euthanasia—whether grounded on rights or beneficence—are automatically suspect when they fail to attend to the vulnerability of women and other groups. If our cases, cultural images, and perhaps practice differentially feature the deaths of women, we cannot ignore that. It is one thing to argue for these practices for the patient who is not so vulnerable, the wealthy white male living on Park Avenue in Manhattan who wants to add yet another means of control to his arsenal. It is quite another to suggest that the woman of color with no health care coverage or continuous physician relationship, who is given a dire diagnosis in the city hospital's emergency room, needs then to be offered direct killing.

To institute physician-assisted suicide and euthanasia at this point in this country—in which many millions are denied the resources to cope with serious illness, in which pain relief and palliative care are by all accounts woefully mishandled, and in which we have a long way to go to make proclaimed rights to refuse life-sustaining treatment and to use advance directives working realities in clinical settings—seems, at the very least, to be premature. Were we actually to fix those other problems, we have no idea what demand would remain for these more drastic practices and in what category of patients....

The required interweaving of principles and caring, combined with attention to the heightened vulnerability of women and others, suggests that the right answer to the debate over legitimating these practices is at least "not yet" in this grossly imperfect society and perhaps a flat "no." Beneficence and caring indeed impose positive duties upon physicians, especially with patients who are suffering, despairing, or in pain. Physicians must work with these patients intensively; provide first-rate pain relief, palliative care, and symptomatic relief; and honor patients' exercise of their rights to refuse life-sustaining treatment and use advance directives. Never should the patient's illness, deterioration, or despair occasion physician abandonment. Whatever concerns the patient has should be heard and explored, including thoughts of suicide, or requests for aid or euthanasia.

Such requests should redouble the physician's efforts, prompt consultation with those more expert in pain relief or supportive care, suggest exploration of the details of the patient's circumstance, and a host of other efforts. What such requests should not do is prompt our collective legitimation of the physician's saying "yes" and actively taking the patient's life. The mandates of caring fail to bless killing the person for whom one cares. Any such practice in the United States will inevitably reflect enormous background inequities and persisting societal biases. And there are special reasons to expect gender bias to play a role.

The principles bounding medical practice are not written in stone. They are subject to reconsideration and societal renegotiation overtime. Thus the ancient prohibitions against physicians assisting suicide and performing euthanasia do not magically defeat proposals for change. (Nor

do mere assertions that "patients want it" mandate change, as I have argued above.)[49] But we ought to have compelling reasons for changing something as serious as the limits on physician killing, and to be rather confident that change will not mire physicians in a practice that is finally untenable.

By situating assisted suicide and euthanasia in a history of women's deaths, by suggesting the social meanings that over time have attached to and justified women's deaths, by revealing the background conditions that may motivate women's requests, and by stating the obvious—that medicine does not somehow sit outside society, exempt from all of this—I have argued that we cannot have that confidence. Moreover, in the real society in which we live, with its actual and for some groups fearful history, there are compelling reasons not to allow doctors to kill. We cannot ignore that such practice would allow what for now remains an elite and predominantly male profession to take the lives of the "other." We cannot explain how we will train the young physician both to care for the patient through difficult straits and to kill. We cannot protect the most vulnerable.

CONCLUSION

Some will find it puzzling that elsewhere we seek to have women's voices heard and moral agency respected, yet here I am urging that physicians not accede to the request for assisted suicide and euthanasia. Indeed, as noted above, I have elsewhere maintained that physicians must honor patients' requests to be free of unwanted life-sustaining treatment. In fact, attention to gender and feminist argument would urge some caution in both realms. As Jay Katz has suggested, any patient request or decision of consequence merits conversation and exploration.[50] And analysis by Steven Miles and Alison August suggests that gender bias may be operating in the realm of the termination of life-sustaining treatment too.[51] Yet finally there is a difference between the two domains. As I have argued above, there is a strong right to be free of unwanted bodily invasion. Indeed, for women, a long history of being harmed specifically through unwanted bodily invasion such as rape presents particularly compelling reasons for honoring a woman's refusal of invasion and effort to maintain bodily intactness. When it comes to the question of whether women's suicides should be aided, however, or whether women should be actively killed, there is no right to command physician assistance, the dangers of permitting assistance are immense, and the history of women's subordination cuts the other way. Women have historically been seen as fit objects for bodily invasion, self-sacrifice, and death at the hands of others. The task before us is to challenge all three.[52]

Certainly some women, including some feminists, will see this problem differently. That may be especially true of women who feel in control of their lives, are less subject to subordination by age or race or wealth, and seek yet another option to add to their many. I am not arguing that women should lose control of their lives and selves. Instead, I am arguing that when women request to be put to death or ask help in taking their own lives, they become part of a broader social dynamic of which we have properly learned to be extremely wary. These are fatal practices. We can no longer ignore questions of gender or the insights of feminist argument.

NOTES

1. I restrict the term "euthanasia" to active euthanasia, excluding the termination of life-sustaining treatment, which has sometimes been called "passive euthanasia." Both law and ethics now treat the termination of treatment quite differently from the way they treat active euthanasia, so to use "euthanasia" to refer to both invites confusion. See generally "Report of the Council on Ethical and Judicial Affairs of the American Medical Association," *Issues in Law & Medicine* 10 (1994): 91–97, 92.
2. See Howard I. Kushner, "Women and Suicide in Historical Perspective," in Joyce McCarl Nielsen, ed., *Feminist Research Methods: Exemplary Readings in the Social Sciences* (Boulder, CO: Westview Press, 1990), 193–206, 198–200.
3. See Alan Meisel, *The Right to Die* (New York, NY: John Wiley & Sons, 1989), 62, & *1993 Cumulative Supplement No. 2*, 50–54.
4. See Council on Ethical and Judicial Affairs, *Code of Medical Ethics: Current Opinions with Annotations* (Chicago, IL: American Medical Association,

1994), 50–51; "Report of the Board of Trustees of the American Medical Association," *Issues in Law & Medicine* 10 (1994): 81–90; "Report of the Council on Ethical and Judicial Affairs;" *Report of the Council on Ethical and Judicial Affairs of the American Medical Association: Euthanasia.*(Chicago, IL: American Medical Association, 1989). There are U.S. data on public opinion and physicians' self-reported practices. See, for example, "Report of the Board of Trustees." But the legal and ethical condemnation of physician-assisted suicide and euthanasia in the United States undoubtedly affect the self-reporting and render this a poor indicator of actual practices.
5. See generally Howard I. Kushner, "Women and Suicidal Behavior: Epidemiology, Gender, and Lethality in Historical Perspective," in Silvia Sara Canetto and David Lester, eds., *Women and Suicidal Behavior* (New York, NY: Springer, 1995).
6. Compare Jecker, "Physician-Assisted Death," 676, on reasons physicians might differentially refuse women's requests.
7. See Lawrence Kohlberg, *The Philosophy of Moral Development: Moral Stages and the Idea of Justice*, vol. I (San Francisco, CA: Harper & Row, 1981); Lawrence Kohlberg, *The Psychology of Moral Development: The Nature and Validity of Moral Stages*, vol. II (San Francisco, CA: Harper & Row, 1984).
8. See Carol Gilligan, *In A Different Voice: Psychological Theory and Women's Development* (Cambridge, MA: Harvard University Press, 1982).
9. Gilligan's work has prompted a large literature, building upon as well as criticizing her insights and methodology. See, for example, the essays collected in Larrabee, ed., *An Ethic of Care*. On attention to the ethics of care in bioethics and on feminist criticism of the ethics of care, see my Introduction to this volume.
10. See Kohlberg, *The Psychology of Moral Development*, 644–47.
11. On the Kohlberg–Gilligan debate, see generally Lawrence A. Blum, "Gilligan and Kohlberg: Implications for Moral Theory," in Larrabee, ed., *An Ethic of Care*, 49–68; Owen Flanagan and Kathryn Jackson, "Justice, Care, and Gender: The Kohlberg–Gilligan Debate Revisited," in Larrabee, ed., *An Ethic of Care*, 69–84; Seyla Benhabib, "The Generalized and the Concrete Other: The Kohlberg–Gilligan Controversy and Feminist Theory," in SeylaBenhabib and Drucilla Cornell, eds., *Feminism as Critique: On the Politics of Gender.*

(Minneapolis, MN: University of Minnesota Press, 1987), 77–95.

12. See "It's Over, Debbie," *Journal of the American Medical Association* 259 (1988): 272.

13. See Timothy Egan, "As Memory and Music Faded, Oregon Woman Chose Death," *New York Times,* June 7, 1990, p. A1; Lisa Belkin, "Doctor Tells of First Death Using His Suicide Device," *New York Times,* June 6, 1990, p. A1.

14. See "Doctor Assists in Two More Suicides in Michigan," *New York Times,* October 24, 1991, p. A1 (Wantz and Miller).

15. See "Death at Kevorkian's Side Is Ruled Homicide," *New York Times,* June 6, 1992, p. 10; "Doctor Assists in Another Suicide," *New York Times,* September 27, 1992, p. 32; "Doctor in Michigan Helps a 6th Person To Commit Suicide," *New York Times,* November 24, 1992, p. A10; "2 Commit Suicide, Aided by Michigan Doctor," *New York Times,* December 16, 1992, p. A21.

16. See "Why Dr. Kevorkian Was Called In," *New York Times,* January 25, 1993, p. A16.

17. See B. D. Colen, "Gender Question in Assisted Suicides," *Newsday,* November 25, 1992, p. 17; Ellen Goodman, "Act Now to Stop Dr. Death," *Atlanta Journal and Constitution,* May 27, 1992, p. A11.

18. Gilligan, *In A Different Voice,* 70.

19. *Ibid.,* 132.

20. Loraux in *Tragic Ways of Killing a Woman* notes the single exception of Ajax.

21. See Peter Steinfels, "Help for the Helping Hands in Death," *New York Times,* February 14, 1993, sec. 4, pp. 1, 6.

22. See Charles S. Cleeland et al., "Pain and Its Treatment in Outpatients with Metastatic Cancer," *New England Journal of Medicine* 330 (1994): 592–96.

23. See Robert J. Blendon, U. S. Szalay, and R. A. Knox, "Should Physicians Aid Their Patients in Dying?" *Journal of the American Medical Association* 267 (1992): 2658–62.

24. See William Coryell, Jean Endicott, and Martin B. Keller, "Major Depression in a Non-Clinical Sample: Demographic and Clinical Risk Factors for First Onset," *Archives of General Psychiatry* 49 (1992): 117–25.

25. See Susan D. Block and J. Andrew Billings, "Patient Requests to Hasten Death: Evaluation and Management in Terminal Care," *Archives of Internal Medicine* 154 (1994): 2039–47.

26. Council on Ethical and Judicial Affairs, American Medical Association, "Gender Disparities in Clinical Decision Making," *Journal of the American Medical Association* 266 (1991): 559–62, 561–62.

27. See Nancy S. Jecker, "Can an employer-Based Health Insurance System Be Just?" *Journal of Health Politics, Policy & Law* 18 (1993): 657–73; Employee Benefit Research Institute (EBRI), *Sources of Health Insurance and Characteristics of the Uninsured: Analysis of the March 1992 Current Population Survey,* EBRI Issue Brief No. 133 (Jan. 1993).

28. The patterns of uninsurance and underinsurance are complex. See, for example, Employee Benefit Resources Institute, *Sources of Health Insurance.* Recall that the poorest and the elderly are covered by Medicaid and Medicare, though they are subject to the gaps and deficiencies in quality of care that plague those programs.

29. Lawrence Schneiderman et al. purport to show that patients already consider burdens to others in making termination of treatment decisions, and—more importantly for this chapter—that men do so more than women. See Lawrence J. Schneiderman et al., Attitudes of Seriously Ill Patients toward Treatment that Involves High Cost and Burdens on Others," *Journal of Clinical Ethics* 5 (1994): 109–12. But Peter A. Ubel and Robert M. Arnold criticize the methodology and dispute both conclusions in "The Euthanasia Debate and Empirical Evidence: Separating Burdens to Others from One's Own Quality of Life," *Journal of Clinical Ethics* 5 (1994): 155–58.

30. See, for example, Kushner, "Women and Suicidal Behavior."

31. See Colen, "Gender Question in Assisted Suicides."

32. Another area in which we do not allow apparent patient consent or request to authorize physician acquiescence is sex between doctor and patient. Even if the patient requests sex, the physician is morally and legally bound to refuse. The considerable consensus that now exists on this, however, has been the result of a difficult uphill battle. See generally Howard Brody, *The Healer's Power* (New Haven, CT: Yale University Press, 1992), 26–27; Nanette Gartrell et al., "Psychiatrist-Patient Sexual Contact: Results of a National Survey. Part 1. Prevalence," *American Journal of Psychiatry* 143 (1986): 1126–31.

33. As noted above, though, Nancy Jecker speculates that a physician's tendency to discount women's choices may also come into play. See Jecker, "Physician-Assisted Death," 676. Compare Silvia Sara Canetto, "Elderly Women and Suicidal

Behavior," in Canetto and Lester, eds., *Women and Suicidal Behavior,* 215–33, 228, asking whether physicians are more willing to accept women's suicides.

34. See, for example, Susan Sherwin, *No Longer Patient: Feminist Ethics and Health Care* (Philadelphia, PA: Temple University Press, 1992); Barbara Ehrenreich and Deirdre English, *For Her Own Good: 150 Years of the Experts' Advice to Women* (New York, NY: Doubleday, 1978).

35. Sherwin, *No Longer Patient,* 157.

36. Compare Brody, "The Rescue Fantasy," in *The Healer's Art,* ch. 9.

37. Robert A. Burt, *Taking Care of Strangers* (New York, NY: Free Press, 1979), vi. See also Steven H. Miles, "Physicians and Their Patients' Suicides," *Journal of the American Medical Association* 271 (1994): 1786–88. I discuss the significance of the ambivalence in the euthanasia context in Wolf, "Holding the Line on Euthanasia."

38. See, for example, Naomi Scheman, "Individualism and the Objects of Psychology," in Sandra Harding and Merrill B. Hintikka, eds., *Discovering Reality: Feminist Perspectives on Epistemology, Metaphysics, Methodology, and the Philosophy of Science* (Boston, MA: D. Reidel 1983), 225–44, 240.

39. See Jennifer Nedelsky, "Reconceiving Autonomy: Sources, Thoughts and Possibilities," *Yale Journal of Law and Feminism* 1 (1989): 7–36.

40. See, for example, Susan M. Wolf, "Nancy Beth Cruzan: In No Voice At All," *Hastings Center Report* 20 (Jan.-Feb. 1990): 38–41: *Guidelines on the Termination of Life-Sustaining Treatment and the Care of the Dying* (Bloomington, IN: Indiana University Press & The Hastings Center, 1987).

41. John Stuart Mill, "On Liberty," in Marshall Cohen, ed., *The Philosophy of John Stuart Mill: Ethical, Political and Religious* (New York, NY: Random House, 1961), 185–319, 304.

42. Leon R. Kass also argues against the existence of a "right to die" in "Is There a Right to Die?" *Hastings Center Report* 23 (Jan.-Feb. 1993): 34–43.

43. The Dutch studies show that even when patients know they can get assisted suicide and euthanasia, three times more patients ask for such assurance from their physicians than actually die that way. See van der Maas et al., "Euthanasia," *Lancet,* 673.

44. On these obligations and their derivation, see Leon R. Kass, "Neither for Love nor Money: Why Doctors Must Not Kill," *The Public Interest* 94 (Winter 1989): 25–46; Tom L. Beauchamp and James F. Childress, *Principles of Biomedical* Ethics,

4th ed. (New York, NY: Oxford University Press, 1994), 189, 226–27.

45. See Leslie Bender, "A Feminist Analysis of Physician-Assisted Dying and Voluntary Active Euthanasia," *Tennessee Law Review* 59 (1992): 519–46, making a "caring" argument in favor of "physician-assisted death."

46. See Gilligan, *In A Different Voice,* 174. Lawrence Blum points out that Kohlberg himself stated that "the final, most mature stage of moral reasoning involves an 'integration of justice and care that forms a single moral principle,'" but that Kohlberg, too, never spelled out what that integration would be. See Lawrence A. Blum, "Gilligan and Kohlberg: Implications for Moral Theory," *Ethics* 98 (1988): 472–91, 482–83 (footnote with citation omitted).

47. There are significant similarities here to Henry Richardson's proposal of "specified principlism." See DeGrazia, "Moving Forward in Bioethical Theory."

48. On the importance of paying attention to who is doing the theorizing and to what end, including in feminist theorizing, see María C. Lugones and Elizabeth V. Spelman, "Have We Got a Theory for You! Feminist Theory, Cultural Imperialism and the Demand for 'The Woman's Voice,'" *Women's Studies International Forum* 6 (1983): 573–81.

49. In these two sentences, I disagree both with Kass's suggestion that the core commitments of medicine are set for all time by the ancient formulation of the doctor's role and with Brock's assertion that the core commitment of medicine is to do whatever the patient wants. See Kass, "Neither for Love Nor Money;" Dan Brock, "Voluntary Active Euthanasia," *Hastings Center Report* 22 (Mar.- Apr. 1992): 10–22.

50. See Jay Katz, *The Silent World of Doctor and Patient* (New York, NY: Free Press, 1984), 121–22.

51. See Miles and August, "Gender, Courts, and the 'Right to Die.'"

52. While a large literature analyzes the relationship between terminating life-sustaining treatment and the practices of physician-assisted suicide and euthanasia, more recently attention has turned to the relationship between those latter practices and abortion. On the question of whether respect for women's choice of abortion requires legitimation of those practices, see, for example, Seth F. Kreimer, "Does Pro-choice Mean Pro-Kevorkian? An Essay on *Roe, Casey,* and the Right to Die," *American University Law Review* 44 (1995): 803–54. Full analysis of why respect for the choice of abortion does not require

legitimation of physician-assisted suicide and euthanasia is beyond the scope of this chapter. However, the courts themselves are beginning to argue the distinction. See Compassion in Dying v. Washington, 49 F.3d 586 (9th Cir. 1995). On gender specifically, there are strong arguments that gender equity and concern for the fate of women demand respect for the abortion choice, whereas I am arguing that gender concerns cut the other way when it comes to physician-assisted suicide and euthanasia.

♔ QUESTIONS FOR ANALYSIS

1. Why should the euthanasia debate specifically include the situation of women, according to Wolf?
2. What are the gender effects we might expect in the euthanasia issues?
3. How have issues of rights, caring, and cultural context developed in feminist studies in recent decades? What role do those insights play in our understanding of euthanasia?
4. How has the image of women as emphasizing self-sacrifice influenced our understanding of actual cases of physician-assisted suicide?
5. In recent polling, which groups seems most resistant to legalizing physician-assisted suicide? How can this be explained?
6. How has the analysis of rights in the physician-assisted suicide debate been misguided? What insights does feminist theory bring to this discussion of rights?
7. How does feminist work on the ethics of care impact our analysis of assisted suicide?
8. Why does Wolf believe physicians should not grant the requests of female patients for assisted suicide?

CASE PRESENTATION

"I Did It Because I Loved My Son"

In early May 1989, Rudolfo Linares visited his son Samuel in a Chicago hospital, where the fifteen-month-old boy, partially brain dead, lay connected to a respirator. Samuel's coma had begun nine months earlier, when he'd suffocated after swallowing an uninflated balloon at a birthday party.

Along with his wife, Tamara, Rudolfo had been pleading with hospital officials to disconnect the respirator, but always to no avail. Once, in December, he disconnected it himself, but security officers reconnected it. After that, he decided to hire a lawyer to challenge the hospital in court.

Apparently, Rudolfo was growing impatient with the legal process. On this visit to the hospital, he brought a hand gun, which he used to hold off nurses, doctors, and police officers as he disconnected the respirator and held his son in his arms. Crying all the while, he sat with his son for a full forty minutes, long after hospital instruments showed that he was dead.

"I did it because I loved my son," he said.

Prosecutors immediately charged Linares with first-degree murder, but following a storm of national publicity, charges were dropped.

♔ QUESTIONS FOR ANALYSIS

1. Who should decide whether to "pull the plug" in cases like this one: the parents, the attending physician, a hospital committee, or the courts?
2. In its *Cruzan* decision, the U.S. Supreme Court ruled that states can forbid family members to refuse treatment of an incompetent patient without clear evidence that the patient, if competent, would refuse it. Should its ruling apply to patients who, like Samuel, never were competent?
3. Suppose the patient in this case had been an adult who had never expressed an opinion about refusing or accepting treatment in such circumstances. Would his family have the moral right to refuse treatment for him?
4. If hospital officials refuse to stop treatment, do family members have the moral right to take matters into their own hands, as Rudolfo Linares did?

CASE PRESENTATION

"A Choice Central to Personal Dignity"

It was the first time a law banning assisted suicide had come before a federal judge. The setting was the U.S. District Court in Seattle. The federal judge was Judge Barbara Rothstein. Three terminally ill patients seeking assistance in ending their lives, along with five doctors and an organization named Compassion in Dying, were challenging a Washington State law that forbade them to do so. Judge Rothstein's decision came May 3, 1994: The Washington law, which had been on the books for 140 years, was unconstitutional.

As noteworthy as the ruling itself was the reasoning behind it. In declaring the law in violation of the Fourteenth Amendment, Judge Rothstein cited the Supreme Court's *Planned Parenthood v. Casey* decision, which upheld a woman's right to abortion. "Like the abortion decision," she wrote, "the decision of a terminally ill patient to end his or her life 'involves the most intimate and personal choice a person can make in a lifetime,' and constitutes a 'choice central to personal dignity and autonomy.'" Drawing on these similarities, she concluded that "The suffering of a terminally ill person cannot be deemed … any less deserving of protection from unwarranted governmental interference than that of a pregnant woman."

For one of the patients, a cancer victim who had already died, the ruling came too late. The other two were now free to seek help. And Compassion in Dying, which for two years had been referring terminally ill patients to doctors for prescription drugs they could take to end their lives, was now free to act more openly. In a front-page story two days after the ruling, *The New York Times* quoted Ralph Mero, the group's director and a Unitarian minister, as follows: "Today, every time I pick up the phone, there are three more people on voice mail asking for help." The report also quoted a statement by the Roman Catholic Bishops of Washington, who said of the ruling, "It undermines the moral integrity of the medical profession, whose duty is to heal and comfort, not kill. And it tramples on our conviction that life, no matter how feeble or impaired, is a sacred gift from God."

The state appealed the decision, and three years later, in *Washington v. Glucksberg,* the U.S. Supreme Court ruled the law constitutional. The Supreme Court reached this conclusion by rejecting the claim that committing suicide was a fundamental liberty interest. It noted that the state of Washington had an "unqualified interest in the preservation of life" and also an interest in "the integrity and ethics of the medical profession." The Court was also concerned about undue coercion of vulnerable groups, especially the poor, elderly, and disabled. It also expressed concern about starting down the slippery slope from assisted suicide to voluntary and even involuntary euthanasia. The Court did, however, state that the debate about assisted suicide could continue, as it was then continuing in Oregon and elsewhere. Although the Court did not find a right to assisted suicide, neither did it say anything that would prohibit a state from passing its own laws to permit assisted suicide.

At the time of this decision (1997), Oregon was the only state with a law permitting assisted suicide. In 2008, the state of Washington adopted a similar law, which went into effect in 2009. Vermont adopted a similar law in May 2013.

This U.S. Supreme Court case was notable for another reason. For the first time ever, six distinguished philosophers of ethics and law, writing in their capacity as philosophers, submitted a "Friend of the Court Brief" arguing in support of a right of assisted suicide. The philosophers were Ronald Dworkin, Thomas Nagel, Robert Nozick, John Rawls, Thomas Scanlon, and Judith Jarvis Thomson. Although their arguments did not persuade the Court to adopt their views, this landmark brief demonstrated the importance and relevance of philosophical reasoning in many of today's most contentious public debates. A central element of their brief was analysis of the nature of "liberty."

The full text of what has come to be known as "The Philosophers' Brief" is widely available on the Web, such as at http://www.nybooks.com/articles/1237 where it appears with an additional forward by Ronald Dworkin.

⚜ QUESTIONS FOR ANALYSIS

1. Do you agree with Judge Rothstein's analogy between the decision of a pregnant woman to abort and a terminally ill patient to take his or her own life?

2. In their statement, the bishops claimed that a physician's duty is "to heal and comfort, not kill." When healing is impossible, what kind of

comfort does the patient deserve? Does it include prescribing lethal drugs when asked?

3. The American Medical Association (AMA) reaffirmed in 2005 its policy that "physician-assisted suicide is fundamentally inconsistent with the physician's professional role." This policy, which has been praised by the National Right to Life Committee, is consistent with the concern expressed by the Supreme Court that finding a right of assisted suicide might challenge the integrity of the medical profession. The AMA urges physicians to focus on more effective treatment of pain and hospice care "to alleviate the physical and emotional suffering that dying patients experience." Is this recommendation sufficient to address the concerns of the patients bringing this case? Should patients have a right of autonomy to make the decision of assisted suicide, so long as they can obtain the services of a willing physician?

4. To address the slippery slope concern, why could not the Supreme Court simply have insisted on "clear and convincing evidence" of the patient's intent, as it did in the *Cruzan* case in 1990? If that standard was sufficient for voluntary passive euthanasia, why isn't it sufficient for assisted suicide? Is a patient in extreme pain at the end of life capable of giving meaningful consent to assisted suicide?

CASE PRESENTATION

Legalized Assisted Suicide and Decriminalized Euthanasia

Fewer than three years after the U.S. Supreme Court provided a constitutional basis for voluntary passive euthanasia in the *Cruzan* decision, one European country took a much bolder step. By a vote of 91 to 45, the parliament of the Netherlands decriminalized active euthanasia and doctor-assisted suicide under a set of strict conditions. As reported by the Associated Press, these conditions are:

Voluntary Nature. The request for euthanasia must be made "entirely of the patient's own free will" and not under pressure from others.

Weighing Alternatives. The patient must be well informed and must be able to consider the alternatives.

Certain Decision. The patient must have a "lasting longing for death." Requests made on impulse or based on a temporary depression cannot be considered.

Unacceptable Suffering. "The patient must experience his or her suffering as perpetual, unbearable and hopeless." The physician must be reasonably able to conclude that the suffering experienced is unbearable.

Consultation. The doctor must consult at least one colleague who has faced the question of euthanasia before.

Reporting. A documented written report must be drawn up stating the history of the patient's illness and declaring that the rules have been met.

The vote followed what the *New York Times* called "two decades of tormented national debate." It also followed a significant increase in doctor-reported cases of active euthanasia and assisted suicide from 1990 to 1992. According to the *Times,* Dutch legal and medical experts attributed the increase to "more open discussion of the issue and a clearer agreement on the rules that protect doctors from prosecution."

Soon after the measure passed, many observers expected the Dutch parliament to go even further by legalizing active euthanasia and assisted suicide by physicians, and in 2000, that's exactly what the parliament did. The significance of that step is twofold. First, it means that Dutch physicians who help their patients die are no longer technically committing a crime. Second, these physicians are no longer accountable to a prosecutor but to a panel of medical, legal, and ethical experts.

In 1994, as we have seen, voters in Oregon took a similar step when they passed a ballot initiative legalizing doctor-assisted suicide. That measure too contains restrictions. Among the most important are these: (1) the means of assistance are limited to a prescription for a lethal dose of medication to be taken orally; (2) two doctors must determine that the patient has six months or less to live; (3) the patient must be of sound mind; (4) the patient's request must be made in writing; (5) the prescription must be written no less than fifteen days after the request; (6) the patient, not the doctor, must administer the pills.

⚜ QUESTIONS FOR ANALYSIS

1. The Dutch rules are obviously intended to prevent abuses. Are they sufficiently strict and clear? Do any of the rules seem too vague? Do any need to be made more precise?

2. As reported by the *Times,* a Dutch study found that in 1992 doctors ended the lives of a thousand patients "without an explicit recent request." In most cases, the *Times* reported, "the patient had only days or hours to live, was often in great pain, and was either in a coma or not fully conscious. In more than half the cases the patient had either talked about euthanasia to the doctor or others." Do these findings support Velleman's concerns about the absence of genuine autonomy in this decision making?

3. Nowhere do the rules say that a patient must be suffering from a terminal illness or that death must be near. Should either condition be added?

4. After the vote, one pro-life Dutch physician declared, "Today the Netherlands abolished the Hippocratic Oath." Do you agree?

5. In many areas of moral controversy—for instance, drugs and prostitution—the Netherlands has pursued a more liberal social policy than the United States. Do you think the Dutch rules for euthanasia and assisted suicide are appropriate for the United States?

6. One forceful opponent of the Oregon measure is the American Medical Association, which argues that doctors cannot reliably determine that a patient has six months or less to live. Is this a serious flaw in the law?

7. The Oregon requirement that the patient, not the doctor, administer the pills is meant to ensure that the patient's death results from suicide, not euthanasia. Is this distinction morally significant?

CASE PRESENTATION

Terri Schiavo: Voluntary Euthanasia or Murder?

On February 25, 1990, a few months before the U.S. Supreme Court announced its decision in the Nancy Cruzan case, a Florida woman named Teresa Schiavo suffered cardiac arrest and never regained consciousness. She required constant care in nursing homes and received food and hydration through tubes. In 1998 her husband Michael petitioned a Florida court to authorize termination of the life support procedures, a petition opposed by Schiavo's parents.

After a trial in 2000, the court determined by clear and convincing evidence, the standard set in the *Cruzan* decision, that she would choose to cease life-prolonging procedures if she were competent to make that decision. The court also concluded that she was in a "persistent vegetative state" with no chance of recovery, the same condition that other courts had found for Nancy Cruzan and Karen Quinlan. The parents in the Cruzan and Quinlan cases had petitioned to remove life support; in the Schiavo case, the parents opposed this removal. But otherwise, the Schiavo case was remarkably like the Cruzan case in its legal reasoning and in the physical condition of the patient. The involvement in this case of the Florida legislature and then of the U.S. Congress and the president turned the Schiavo case into a *cause célèbre* in the public eye.

The feeding tube was removed for the first time on April 24, 2001, but after another court challenge from the parents, it was reinserted two days later. After numerous court fights, it was removed a second time on October 15, 2003. Six days later, the Florida legislature passed legislation authorizing the governor to issue an executive order to reinsert the feeding tube, which was done immediately.

In 2004, the Supreme Court of Florida struck down this Florida legislation as an unconstitutional violation of the separation of powers that recognizes three branches of government—the executive, the legislative, and the judicial. The legislation, the Court said, improperly reversed a final judgment of the Florida court, and the executive order improperly delegated legislative authority to the governor. After more legal challenges from the parents, the feeding tube was removed a third time on March 18, 2005.

Three Republican members of Congress, Senate Majority Leader Bill Frist, Senator Rick Santorum, and House Majority Leader Tom Delay, then issued congressional subpoenas to both Michael and Terri Schiavo demanding that they testify before Congress, a move to force reinsertion of the feeding tube, but a Florida judge refused to let the subpoenas interfere with the Florida order.

On March 20, 2005, which was Palm Sunday, the Senate (with only three members present) passed a bill that transferred jurisdiction over the Schiavo case to the federal courts, in an attempt to remove it from the Florida courts that had ordered removal of the feeding tube. The House of Representatives passed the bill at 12:41 a.m. on March 21. President Bush signed the bill at 1:11 a.m., after flying on Air Force One to Washington from his home in Crawford, Texas, specifically to sign the bill. He issued a statement saying, "I will continue to stand on the side of those defending life for all Americans, including those with disabilities."

Although this federal law gave the federal courts authority to review the case again, all declined to hear it, including the U.S. Supreme Court. After a last-minute flurry of legal attempts to take custody of Schiavo from the hospice, she died on March 31, 2005.

Numerous public opinion polls were taken after these events. They tended to show that solid majorities (well over 50 percent), believed it was proper to have the tube removed and that even more (ranging from 70 to 80 percent in most polls) thought it had been inappropriate for Congress to intervene in this case.

⚜ QUESTIONS FOR ANALYSIS

1. Terri Schiavo had no living will to indicate her preferences for treatment. The Florida courts consistently accepted the testimony of several witnesses, including her husband, that she had made statements before the incident indicating that she would not want to be kept alive in such a condition. The parents claimed that, as a devout Roman Catholic, she would not want to violate the Church's teachings on euthanasia by refusing nutrition and hydration. Do you find this evidence satisfactory for making such an important decision?

2. Have you made statements to friends that might be used as evidence if you were to be in Schiavo's condition? Have you prepared a living will to make your preferences clear?

3. The cost of flying Air Force One to Washington is estimated at $34,000 an hour. Critics complained that President Bush could have had someone fly the bill to him in Texas for signing, but his communications director at the time said that the president was concerned that a delay of even a few hours might endanger Schiavo's life. Was this an appropriate use of the taxpayer's money?

4. Were the actions of the Congress and the president consistent with other stated goals of restricting the role of the federal judiciary, respecting states' rights, and promoting the sanctity of marriage? Were they justifiable as a way to send a strong public message of opposition to euthanasia to the American public? Should the Congress pass a law making voluntary euthanasia a crime when it involves patients in the condition of Schiavo or Cruzan, perhaps by requiring a legally valid living will before feeding tubes or respirators could be removed?

5. Public supporters of Schiavo's parents said they (the supporters) were opposing euthanasia because they supported a "culture of life." Is this opposition to euthanasia consistent with support for capital punishment?

6. Was Schiavo's death an active or a passive euthanasia? Was the removal of the feeding tube an "act" that makes this euthanasia active? Was being allowed to starve and dehydrate to death passive?

7. If Schiavo's husband had refused to give consent to insert the feeding tube the night of her injury, would that have been considered active or passive euthanasia?

8. Once the decision was made to remove the feeding tube, would it have been more humane to simply give Schiavo a lethal injection, rather than lingering for almost two weeks as she starved to death? What might James Rachels have said about this alternative?

CHAPTER SIX

Genetic Engineering, Stem Cell Research, and Human Cloning

- How Cloning Works: A Brief History
- Why Clone Humans?
- Moral and Legal Issues
- Stem Cell Research
- Arguments against Human Cloning
- Arguments for Human Cloning

MICHAEL TOOLEY   **Moral Status of Cloning Humans**

BONNIE STEINBOCK   **The Morality of Killing Human Embryos**

PRESIDENTIAL COMMISSION FOR THE STUDY OF BIOETHICAL ISSUES
The Ethics of Synthetic Biology

PAUL LAURITZEN   **Stem Cells, Biotechnology, and Human Rights: Implications for a Posthuman Future**

CASE PRESENTATIONS: • *Cloning: Recommendations of the President's Council on Bioethics* • *A Birth to Save a Life* • *Stem Cells: Presidential Policy* • *Eight Is Enough*

"GENETIC ENGINEERING" CONJURES up associations both hopeful and horrifying—from dreams that science could give us eternal youth and miracle cures for debilitating diseases to nightmares of the mass production of Hitler clones in the fictional book and film *The Boys from Brazil*. Alterations to our basic biological make-up include a wide range of technological advances, including gene therapy to alter inherited disease tendencies, in vitro fertilization, and surrogate motherhood.

Some techniques hold out the promise of breakthroughs in curing diseases and creating designer children, even if they have not yet delivered on those possibilities. Stem cell research, both on embryonic and adult stem cells, has been a source of special controversy, as has cloning, especially the possibility of cloning persons.

The term "genetic engineering" refers not only to human possibilities, but also alterations in animal and plant life. Development of grains that are tolerant of disease and drought have addressed world food shortages, but groups such as the Union of Concerned Scientists have raised concerns that some alterations in animals and plants can also be harmful to humans. Although these are important issues, in this chapter we will focus on the genetic engineering issues concerning human beings themselves, and the considerable ethical challenges they present.

These continuing public policy debates are illustrated in the nomination in July 2009 by President Barack Obama of Dr. Francis S. Collins to be the director of the National Institutes of Health. He was confirmed unanimously by the U.S. Senate in August 2009 and continues to serve during President Obama's second term. As a leading researcher in the Human Genome Project (HGP), he was Director of the National Human Genome Research Institute at NIH from 1993 to 2008. The HGP was an international collaborative effort to completely "map" the essential sequences of DNA, what scientists call "the molecular instruction book of human life." When the completion of this sequencing was announced in 2003, scientists compared its importance to the Apollo moon landing and splitting the atom.

The promise of developing breakthrough medical cures and technologies using this knowledge has been exciting, but critics charge that researchers, including Dr. Collins, have been unrealistic in their predictions of major progress in the near future and diverted resources from other promising avenues of research. Other critics of Dr. Collins have raised concerns about his very public embrace of evangelical Christianity and wonder if it is possible to reconcile his views on religion and science.[1]

We will consider here the ethical challenges presented by genetic engineering in general, as well as two of the more controversial techniques in the debate, cloning and stem cell research. Recent decades brought a number of astonishing technological developments, many of them highly controversial. Perhaps the most controversial came from the field of biotechnology, and among them, none created more controversy than the birth of a lamb named Dolly. By all outward appearances a perfectly ordinary lamb, she was the product of the first successful cloning of an adult mammal. Ian Wilmut, who headed the team of Scottish scientists that produced her, announced the feat in 1997, and a staple of fiction suddenly loomed as an imminent reality: the successful cloning of an adult human being.

Not surprisingly, people began talking in earnest about the dangers and promises this startling development raised—maybe a U.S. Olympic basketball team composed entirely of Michael Jordan clones. And in the face of such possibilities came a raft of questions: Should the technology be made available when scientists are able to extend it to human beings? If so, to whom? And what kinds of legal restrictions, if any, should we place on its availability? More generally, is there something fundamentally immoral and frightening about human cloning, or is it—like sperm donorship, in vitro fertilization, or surrogate motherhood—a benign form of reproductive technology that individuals have a moral and legal right to use?

A number of national governments took the lead in this discussion. In the United States, for example, President Bill Clinton placed an immediate ban on all federal funding for attempts to clone humans. He also asked the National Bioethics Advisory Commission (NBAC) to issue a report within ninety days on the legal and ethical issues that surround human cloning. The resulting document, citing both safety concerns and moral concerns, called for a continuation of the president's ban. It also

---

[1]See, e.g., "Pick to Lead Health Agency Draws Praise and Some Concern," The New York Times, July 9, 2009.

called on Congress to pass legislation banning all attempts to clone human beings, whether in clinical settings or research settings. The proposed legislation should, the report added, contain a "sunset clause," which would cause the ban to expire within three to five years; at some time before that point, the status of cloning technology and the ethical and social issues involved should be reevaluated.

President George W. Bush repeatedly called for a complete ban on cloning, saying, "We must not create life to destroy life. Human beings are not research material to be used in a cruel and reckless experiment." Although the House of Representatives passed the Human Cloning Prohibition Act several years ago, it was never adopted in the Senate. The Human Cloning Ban and Stem Cell Research Protection Act of 2005 was introduced in both the House and the Senate, and it passed in July 2006, after a long delay in Senate passage. On July 19, 2006, President Bush vetoed it because of his objections to stem cell research, and Congress did not have the two-thirds vote necessary to override the veto. The Act was re-introduced in 2007 and referred to congressional committees for review, but was not referred back to the Congress for a vote. Although the Federal government has yet to pass a ban on human cloning, over a dozen states have passed bans on reproductive cloning and several have passed bans on therapeutic cloning (cloning for research purposes). The United Nations has been unable to agree on a binding resolution prohibiting cloning but in 2005 adopted a nonbinding resolution urging that human cloning be banned.

On March 9, 2009, President Barack Obama issued Executive Order 13505, "Removing Barriers to Responsible Scientific Research Involving Human Stem Cells." The Executive Order states that the Secretary of Health and Human Services, through the Director of NIH, may support and conduct responsible, scientifically worthy human stem cell research, including human embryonic stem cell (HESC) research, to the extent permitted by law. The NIH was directed to issue guidelines to implement the executive order. Draft guidelines were issued on April 23, 2009. The NIH received approximately 49,000 comments from patient advocacy groups, scientists and scientific societies, academic institutions, medical organizations, religious organizations, and private citizens, as well as members of Congress. Final guidelines were published on July 6, 2009, to be implemented immediately, and are available to the public on the NIH web site: http://stemcells.nih.gov/.

Because of the safety concerns, many have supported the proposed bans, even if they did not have ethical qualms about cloning for purposes of medical research. But many of those safety concerns are being overcome. In fact, as we'll see in the next section, one of the most serious safety problems has already been overcome. The moral concerns, however, which are the subject of this chapter, will no doubt continue long after. Stem cell research involves a different set of procedures and issues, but some of the moral and legal questions are shared with human cloning. When do we become "persons" with moral rights? How can we define our personal identities in this new world of scientific technology?

HOW CLONING WORKS: A BRIEF HISTORY

A **clone** is an exact genetic copy of a molecule, cell, plant, or animal.[2] Though the term is a relatively recent one, the phenomenon itself is as old as the simplest forms

---

[2]This definition and much of what follows in this section are adapted from the second chapter of the NBAC report, Cloning Human Beings, U.S. Government, Washington, D.C., 1997.

of life; whenever single-celled organisms like bacteria reproduce by cell division, the resultant cells are natural clones of the originals. In the laboratory, the cloning of molecules and cells has been a routine part of molecular biology for decades, as when scientists regularly clone DNA fragments in recombinant DNA technology (popularly known as "genetic engineering"). Outside the laboratory, the cloning of plants—a more complex form of cloning—has been a commonplace in ordinary households for a much longer time; whenever we take a cutting of a plant, place it in water, and grow a complete new plant from it, we produce a clone of the original plant.

Animal cloning too has been around a long time. At one end of the animal kingdom—with such invertebrates as worms, for example—an organism can be divided into two parts, and each will regenerate itself into a full genetic duplicate of the original. At the other end, we have the phenomenon of identical human twins, the result of separated embryos in the womb. In both cases, we have examples of natural animal cloning.

In the laboratory, scientists have been successfully cloning animals since the early 1980s, using a technique known as *nuclear transplantation cloning*. In its earliest form, this technique involved removing the nucleus from an unfertilized egg and replacing it with the nucleus of a somatic cell from an embryo. (A **somatic cell** is any cell other than a sperm or an egg, both of which are known as **germ cells.**) The product of the transplant, an embryo, is then implanted into a female for normal gestation.

The significance of Dolly is that the somatic cell used in the transplant came from an adult animal rather than from an embryo. And what makes that difference so important is this: As cells develop and divide after fertilization, they *differentiate* into specific tissues—muscle and bone, for example. That's why embryo cells were used in the earlier cases of cloning—because they had not yet differentiated. Mature cells, on the other hand, are cells that have differentiated, and before Dolly came along, scientists didn't know if the genes of these cells could be reprogrammed to an undifferentiated state. Previous attempts had provided discouraging results. In one series of experiments, in which the nuclei of adult frog skin cells replaced the nuclei of frog eggs, only 4 percent of the embryos resulted in tadpoles, and none of the tadpoles developed into an adult frog. In another series, using cells from adult mice, no successes occurred. With the successful cloning of Dolly, however, it seemed that mature cells could indeed be reprogrammed.

Even so, some doubts remained. The lingering uncertainty centered on the source of the cells that Wilmut's team had used for the transplant: the udder of a six-year-old female sheep in the late stages of pregnancy. Breasts of pregnant mammals grow much larger in the late stages of pregnancy, and a cell taken from one may be quite unusual in a relevant way. As the scientist Stephen J. Gould put it:

> some mammary cells, though technically adult, may remain unusually labile or even "embryo-like" and thus able to proliferate rapidly to produce new breast tissue at an appropriate stage of pregnancy. Consequently, we may only be able to clone only from unusual adult cells with effectively embryonic potential and not from any stray cheek cell, hair follicle, or drop of blood that happens to fall in the clutches of a mad Xeroxer.[3]

This uncertainty was resolved almost three years later, when scientists at the University of Connecticut at Storrs and the Prefectural Cattle Breeding Development

---

[3]"Dolly's Fashion and Louis's Passion," *Natural History* vol. 106, no. 5 (June 1997): p. 21.

Institute in Japan announced that they had cloned four calves from cells scraped from the ear of a bull—cells without, to use Gould's term, "effectively embryonic potential." This development was significant for another reason as well: the number of successful clones. (Dolly had been a single success among a large number of failures. Of 277 fusions between cell and egg, only twenty-nine became embryos; of those twenty-nine, which Wilmut's team implanted into ewes, only the embryo that produced Dolly resulted in a pregnancy.) Adding to these advances, the same team announced weeks later that it had successfully cloned one of the original clones.

The next major step in animal cloning came in April 2000, when a serious obstacle, particularly important for the prospect of human cloning, was overcome. That obstacle first came to light after an examination of Dolly's chromosomes. The tips of her chromosomes, called *telomeres*, were shorter than those of a sheep produced by sexual reproduction. What was troubling about the finding is that telomeres grow shorter each time a cell divides. So the younger the animal in normal cases, the longer the telomeres; the older the animal, the shorter the telomeres. The implication, then, was that Dolly would not live as long as a sheep conceived through sexual reproduction. And the resulting implication for the ethics of human cloning was obvious. Clearly, most people thought, it would be immoral to produce a human being in that way if he or she could not live a normal human life span. But then scientists at a Massachusetts company called Advanced Cell Technology, who had produced six cloned calves, announced that the telomeres of all the clones were not shorter than normal. To the team's surprise, they were actually longer than normal, suggesting that the calves would have an unusually long life span. So one of the most prominent of the safety issues seems no longer a problem. Others, however, remain, including the dangers of genetic mutation to the clone and other biological damage.

WHY CLONE HUMANS?

Although modern cloning technology is still too young to ensure the safe cloning of humans, many researchers think that eventually it can and will be done. When scientists have the technology to accomplish something, the common line of reasoning goes, they will use it. Besides, even if most scientists oppose its use—and even if its use is outlawed in most corners of the world—all it takes is one millionaire persistent enough to find one scientist willing to clone him. But before we discuss whether scientists ought to use this technology, we should first discuss why anyone would want to.

Some reasons have nothing to do with the aim of producing a fully developed human being. For instance, many scientists (including those at Advanced Cell Technology) see great hope in using cloning to create replacement tissue—spare parts, you might say—for humans. This is not, as some have feared, a matter of keeping a mindless clone in a closet to be "harvested" for parts when needed but of producing an embryo that can be used to generate an organ for transplant. Being an exact genetic match with the host, the organ would not be rejected. For another example, cloning not aimed at producing a fully developed human being would almost certainly bring great gains in scientific knowledge—concerning cell division, say, or genetic differentiation.

But why use cloning for human reproduction? The most obvious reasons concern couples in which one or both partners are infertile. For at least some of them, cloning might be a welcome reproductive technology, a new technique for producing genetic offspring. Similarly, there are cases in which sexual reproduction carries the risk of passing on an inheritable disease, most commonly when both parties carry the same regressive gene for the disease. Also, many homosexuals see cloning as an opportunity for homosexual couples to have children. True, in all these cases, the couples have other options—adoption or sperm donorship, for example—but they may also want their children to be genetically related to at least one of them without having to introduce the genes of some unwanted third party.

Another reason is suggested by the case of Abe and Mary Ayala, a California couple who conceived a child in 1989—seventeen years after the birth of their second and presumed last child—in the hope of providing a compatible bone marrow donor for their leukemia-stricken daughter. Although the child did prove to be a compatible donor, they had no guarantee of success. With the availability of cloning, parents in similar situations could be certain of success, since the clone would be an exact genetic match of the recipient. Then there are those couples who have lost a child in a car accident, say, and want their next child to be as much like the first as possible—a later identical twin of the lost child—or couples who may want a later identical twin of someone else dear to them, such as a parent, a grandparent, or a sibling.

Still other reasons have been given for wanting to clone human beings, some more or less fanciful than others. We may want to pass on specific traits of specific people with the hope of producing another Jordan, Mozart, Gandhi, or Martin Luther King. Or vanity may be a factor in the case of people who want to see a world inhabited by genetic copies of themselves. In other cases, the motivation may be curiosity. How, some may wonder, would they (or some other individual) have turned out if born and reared in another time and environment? Pushing this kind of reasoning even further, we can imagine scientists who specialize in twin research wanting to create clones as subjects in controlled experiments.

MORAL AND LEGAL ISSUES

No doubt many of you find yourselves uncomfortable with at least some of these possibilities, maybe even repulsed by them. And in some cases, the discomfort is fully justified. Consider the last possibility we mentioned, creating clones for experimentation. Given that human clones would have claim to all the rights of any other human being, it would clearly be immoral to experiment on them without their consent. But what about the moral status of human cloning itself?

Perhaps the most important question to ask here is whether people have the moral and legal right to reproduce by any safe means available, including cloning, which may be considered a form of asexual reproduction. Do we have a fundamental right to choose whether and how to reproduce? Notwithstanding the importance of this question, how we answer it will not settle the matter by itself. Even our most fundamental rights are not absolute. Some other factor may override them. That's why we have libel laws, for example, which limit our fundamental right to free expression. Furthermore, someone might grant that we do have a fundamental right to reproduce but deny that cloning is a form of reproduction. Many critics of human cloning say just that. To them, cloning is better described as replication or manufacturing, and they insist that we do not have a right to manufacture human beings.

What if we decide that reproduction is not a fundamental right? We might still say that our general right to freedom allows us the right to take advantage of human cloning. After all, we claim all sorts of rights that are not fundamental as long as there's no rational basis for restricting them. For example, no one would claim a fundamental right to wear socks of a particular color, but what rational basis could there be for banning brown, blue, or white socks?

Other moral issues concern the possible psychological effects of human cloning. Various commentators have wondered how the later twin will feel about his or her worth and future. Will clones feel that their right to their own identity has been infringed upon? Will they feel that their futures are foreclosed, that the limitations they see in their earlier twins, whether physical or mental, unfairly narrow their own choices in life? Will they wonder if they are loved for themselves instead of being valued as a copy of someone else, that they are merely replacements for the previous twins who were really loved? And at least in the earliest cases of human clones, will they feel like freaks?

These questions concern the psychological effects on the later twins. Other questions concern the effects on humanity as a whole. How will the availability of cloning affect humankind's understanding of itself? Will we come to see people as fundamentally different once we know they can be manufactured as well as sexually conceived? Will our view of the role that sex plays in our lives fundamentally change? Will we no longer view individual humans as unique and irreplaceable?

Beyond all that, there are more practical concerns. If, for example, cloning becomes prevalent, what will that do to the genetic diversity of the human species? Or for another example, what if scientists make multiple clones of a great artist, scientist, or moral or political leader? Do we really want some "mad Xeroxer" to produce a run of thirty or more Mozarts, Einsteins, or Kings? Or to return to the fears raised by *The Boys from Brazil*, a run of thirty or more Hitlers?

Another practical issue concerns family relationships. If a woman bears her husband's clone, is he the father to the son she bears, his twin brother, or is he both? And is she both the mother of her child and his sister-in-law? Or suppose instead that she bears her own clone. Is she both mother and twin sister to the child? Then there are cases in which the cell donor is a third party—a relative, say, or some unrelated genius. As an earlier twin, would he or she be the clone's sibling? Related to these questions are questions of legal rights and responsibilities. If the donor is a third party, what responsibilities does he have for his later twin? And what rightful claims does the clone have against his earlier twin?

These last questions raise another concern about human cloning. Once cloning is made available, it will be easy to clone humans without their consent. All it will take is one stray cell, easily obtainable without the person's knowledge or consent. Many of us, presumably, will not want to be cloned. Do we have the right not to be? And if so, how can the right be enforced?

Still other moral issues are familiar from debates surrounding other topics in this book. Just as critics of homosexuality argue that homosexual behavior is immoral because it's unnatural, many opponents of human cloning claim the same about it. Unlike other forms of reproductive technology, such as in vitro fertilization, cloning takes us out of the realm of sex altogether, and that difference, opponents say, presents a fundamental break with natural reproduction. Two other issues arise from the abortion debates. To those who feel that a human embryo is a person, a morally significant being with the right to life, creating a human embryo for scientific research or the generation of organs for transplant is every bit as wrong as abortion. In both cases, they say, a human life is being destroyed. Cloning proponents, on the other hand, argue that the constitutional right to liberty comes into play here. Just as a woman's right to liberty guarantees her right to terminate a pregnancy, so does it guarantee her the right to reproduce by cloning.

STEM CELL RESEARCH

Many have heard of stem cell research because of the highly visible lobbying efforts by such people as the late Christopher Reeve, who had been paralyzed in a riding accident; Michael J. Fox, the film and television star fighting Parkinson's disease; Nancy Reagan, wife of the late President Reagan who died of Alzheimer's; and Mary Tyler Moore, the film and television star who has shared with the public her struggle with diabetes. Public opinion polls in 2012 generally showed that about three-fourths of Americans support stem cell research, as well as federal funding of that research.

The ethical issues presented by stem cell research overlap the debate over cloning, as well as other biomedical issues, especially abortion. But the issues are sufficiently distinct that many people (such as Senator Orrin Hatch, a conservative Republican from Utah) believe they can consistently oppose cloning and abortion while supporting embryonic stem cell research.

Unfortunately, these issues are sometimes blurred in the public debate, and the confusion was exacerbated by a scandal involving a leading South Korean scientist, Hwang Woo-suk, who had been hailed as a pioneer of cloning. In 2004, he announced what he claimed were breakthroughs in creating stem cells for research by cloning human embryos. A year later, he claimed that he had made stem cell lines suitable for biomedical research from the skin cells of eleven people. In December 2005, however, a whistleblower at his lab claimed that the research had been faked, a conclusion later confirmed by a panel of distinguished academic researchers. In March 2006, Hwang was fired from his university, and several researchers on his team received various punishments, including suspension and pay cuts. In May 2006, Hwang was charged by the South Korean government with fraud, embezzlement, and bioethics violations. He was convicted in 2009 of fraud and received a two-year suspended sentence. He continues to work on animal cloning but remains disgraced in his home country. Supporters of stem cell research have responded by emphasizing the importance of ethical guidelines and effective peer oversight of this type of research in the future.

Two types of stem cell research are at issue in the United States. Research using adult stem cells is widely supported, but the promise of this approach is highly debatable. The White House press office under President Bush stated that "a variety of therapeutic treatments for diseases" has been developed from adult stem cells, but this claim is widely disputed. The National Institutes of Health reports that adult stem cells in blood have been used successfully in bone marrow transplants. While embryonic stem cells can differentiate into an almost unlimited range of organs, the adult stem cells are limited to the type of organ or tissue in which they originated, which significantly limits their potential.

Embryonic stem cell research thus seems to have greater potential for finding cures for debilitating diseases, but it also raises important ethical issues. The proposal under most serious consideration would use only the 400,000 embryos that have been created during in vitro fertilization (IVF), which would otherwise be discarded anyway. Strict ethical guidelines would prohibit payment to anyone for providing these embryos, and permission would be required from the persons providing the genetic material that had created the embryos. Specifically, the only ones used would be blastocysts, which are fertilized human eggs from the second day through the second week. (See "Biological Background" in Chapter 4 on abortion for more information about these stages.) Although these blastocysts theoretically could be implanted in a woman and produce a living child, fewer than 200 such children have been produced this way. Furthermore, many blastocysts deteriorate during the freezing process and could never be used in this manner.

Critics of this type of stem cell research believe that the blatocyst is a person from the moment of conception, even in the IVF procedure and even though it has never been implanted in a womb where it might develop. Thus, these critics argue, embryonic stem cell research amounts to murder, at least to the strongest opponents. Supporters note that these blastocysts are going to be discarded anyway and would be better used to support medical research that might result in cures for the living who suffer from debilitating conditions, from spinal cord injury to Parkinson's. If critics truly believe this research is immoral, supporters ask, why don't they take steps to make IVF procedures illegal, so as to stop the destruction of hundreds of thousands of blastocysts that are routinely discarded by these fertility clinics? As recently as December 2008, the Vatican reaffirmed its opposition to all IVF (along with its opposition to contraception, abortion, and same-sex marriage), but opponents of embryonic stem cell research in the U.S. Congress have not proposed any such ban on IVF procedures.

Another dimension to this debate is whether federal funding is appropriate. Critics say that their tax dollars should not be used to support a practice they find immoral. If this is a sufficient reason to prohibit all federal funding, supporters say, then is it acceptable to use federal funds to carry out the death penalty when a substantial portion of the American public believes it to be immoral? In this system of government, majority rules in the expenditure of funds, even if many taxpayers find certain expenditures immoral.

As of 2012, six state governments (California, Connecticut, Illinois, Maryland, New Jersey, and New York) had adopted plans to use state funds to support stem cell research. Although the Federal government has awarded a billion dollars to stem cell research, most of the funding for embryonic stem cell research comes from those states. Supporters of this type of research express concern that the leading scientists in this area might migrate to countries in Europe and Asia that *are* funding this research, resulting in a serious scientific "brain drain" in this country and loss of the technological potential if and when treatments for disease are found.

ARGUMENTS AGAINST HUMAN CLONING

1. *Cloning is unfair to the clone*.
   POINT: "Imagine what it would be like to be a clone, especially if the person you were cloned from were still alive. Your whole life would be laid out

before you. You'd be able to see yourself as an adult, what you'll look like, what you'll be capable of doing and won't be capable of doing, the aches and pains and diseases you'll suffer from, the personality quirks you and others will have to put up with. And you'd know you could never grow up to be all sorts of things you might want to be because you'd see that the person you were cloned from is not capable of any of them. And that's just not fair to the clone. Every human being has a right to an open future."

COUNTERPOINT: "Sorry, but I don't see any unfairness here. First of all, we'd be two different people, just as identical twins are two different people. Genetic makeup isn't everything, you know. How we age, what abilities we have, our health and our personalities depend as much on our environment and choices as they do on our genes. Second, if there are some biological limits on what I can be and do in life, then I might as well know about them in advance. Self-knowledge is good, right? Then why not have it as soon as I can?"

2. *Cloning is dangerous.*

POINT: "But what about the dangers of cloning? If there were ever something open to the worst kinds of abuse, this is it. Think about some mad scientist intent on producing an army of clones of some ruthless killer or some other mad scientist producing a bunch of human research subjects. And think about all the people who'd be tempted to clone themselves for all the wrong reasons—out of vanity, maybe, or the desire for spare parts. And even without the abuses, there's a host of other dangers. Most important, the more popular cloning becomes, the more we'll have clones of clones of clones of clones, and once that happens, the human race will lose much of its genetic diversity. We'll be like those interbred strains of lab mice used for medical experiments."

COUNTERPOINT: "You can make up horror stories about any new technology, but that doesn't mean they'll come true. And as for people cloning themselves for the wrong reasons, so what? People have children the old-fashioned way for all sorts of reasons, many of them selfish, and nobody's trying to put an end to that. And you can't really believe cloning will come even close to driving out the old-fashioned way of making babies. People *like* the old-fashioned way. I can't imagine them giving it up. Cloning will be like all the other forms of reproductive technology—there for people who need it, but not a replacement for normal sexual reproduction."

3. *Cloning is repugnant.*

POINT: "Doesn't the idea of human cloning make you even just a little bit sick? It should, because it's repugnant, unnatural, disgusting. What we're talking about here is children with only one biological parent, children being the genetic twins of one of their parents or maybe even some stranger, children created not by a sperm and an egg but by a cheek cell nucleus and an egg. That's just not the way things ought to be."

COUNTERPOINT: "Maybe you find it repugnant, but I don't. A clone is nothing but a later identical twin, and there's nothing repugnant about it. Besides, your repugnance is morally irrelevant in any case. Personally,

I find a lot of things repugnant—certain kinds of movies and music, for example—but that doesn't give me the right to deny them to others."

ARGUMENTS FOR HUMAN CLONING

1. *People have a right to reproduce.*

   POINT: "Both morally and legally, we have the right to reproduce. Except under the most extreme situations, you wouldn't countenance forced sterilization, would you? Of course not. Nor would you countenance forced abortion, or deny sperm donorship to a woman married to an infertile man, or the opportunity to find a surrogate mother for a woman who can't bear a child herself. So how can you deny anyone the option of cloning, which is just another form of reproductive technology?"

   COUNTERPOINT: "Cloning is not just another form of reproductive technology. In fact, it's not reproduction at all, but a means of manufacturing humans, even of mass manufacturing them. No one has the right to do that. And even if you could convince me that cloning is a form of reproduction, I'd still say it's wrong because of the dangers it poses to both the clone and society."

2. *Cloning offers many benefits to individuals.*

   POINT: "First of all, you're wrong about the dangers. But even more important, you're ignoring all the benefits cloning offers—to infertile couples, couples in which both the man and the woman carry a recessive gene for the same illness, and to gay couples too, and to couples who have lost a child and would dearly love its identical twin. Not only that, but cloning can also guarantee successful matches for life-saving transplants. How can anyone be against that?"

   COUNTERPOINT: "There are alternatives to cloning, you know—sperm donorship, surrogate motherhood, adoption. Nobody has to resort to cloning to have a child. And even the last benefit you mentioned, cloning to ensure successful matches for transplants, won't be necessary. Scientists are already at work on using cloning technology to generate organs without having to bring the embryo to term, and it won't be long before they're successful. As for cloning a dead child, that's just sick. It's one thing to want another one, but to manufacture an exact replica of the dead one? How do you think the clone would feel about that?"

3. *Cloning offers many benefits to society.*

   POINT: "But what about the benefits to society? I'm thinking about two in particular. First, think of all we can learn about the respective contributions of our genes and environment to our personalities, intelligence, and skills. Research on identical twins has been of some help here, but there just aren't that many of them, and cloning can give us more twins to study. Second, there are the advantages we can get by cloning great people from a variety of fields—scientists, political leaders, artists, athletes. Wouldn't it be great to have clones of Jonas Salk working on vaccines for diseases like AIDS?"

COUNTERPOINT: "Now you're getting into *Brave New World* territory, manufacturing people to serve some preset purpose or other—scientific research or the mass production of great people. Besides, you already admitted that our choices and the environment play a big role in shaping who we are. What makes you think a Salk clone would have any interest in searching for an AIDS vaccine?"

Moral Status of Cloning Humans

MICHAEL TOOLEY

Michael Tooley is Distinguished College Professor of Philosophy at the University of Colorado, and served as President of the American Philosophical Association (Pacific Division). The following selection is the second part of a longer essay. The first part examines the safety issues of human cloning and concludes that a temporary legal ban on cloning to produce humans is fully justified. The second part examines the moral issues and reaches two major conclusions: (1) there is nothing intrinsically immoral about human cloning, and (2) it promises to be very beneficial for society.

Along the way, Tooley addresses many of the moral issues raised by cloning's opponents, from the possible psychological harm to clones to the fears raised by what he calls *Brave New World* scenarios, and he finds none of them compelling. In fact, he even argues that there is nothing morally wrong with using cloning to produce "mindless organ banks" to be harvested for transplants. Since these clones would not be persons, he contends, using them that way would not violate respect for persons.

IS IT INTRINSICALLY WRONG TO PRODUCE A PERSON BY CLONING?

Let us now turn to the question of whether the use of cloning to produce a person is, in principle, morally acceptable or not. In this section, I shall focus on the question of whether cloning, so used, is intrinsically wrong. Then, in a later section, I shall consider whether cloning to produce persons necessarily has consequences that render it morally wrong.

How might one attempt to argue that the production of persons via cloning is intrinsically wrong? Here it seems to me that Dan Brock is right when he suggests that there are basically two lines of argument that deserve examination.[1] First, there is an argument that appeals to what might initially be described as the right of a person to be a unique individual, but which, in the end, must be characterized instead as the right of a person to a genetically unique nature. Second, there is an argument that appeals to the idea that a person has a right to a future that is, in a certain sense, open.

Does a Person Have a Right to a Genetically Unique Nature?

Many people feel that being a unique individual is important, and the basic thrust of this first attempt

From *Human Cloning*, James M. Humber and Robert F. Almeder (Totowa, N.J.: Humanities Press, 1998), pp. 77–100. Copyright © 1998 by Springer Science+Business Media.

to show that cloning is intrinsically wrong involves the idea that the uniqueness of individuals would be in some way impaired by cloning. In response, I think that one might very well question whether uniqueness is important. If, for example, it turned out that there was, perhaps on some distant planet, an individual that was qualitatively identical to oneself, down to the last detail, both physical and psychological, would that really make one's own life less valuable, less worth living?

In thinking about this issue, it may be important to distinguish two different cases: first, the case in which the two lives are qualitatively identical because of the operation of deterministic causal laws; second, the case in which it just happens that both individuals are always in similar situations in which they freely decide upon the same actions, have the same thoughts and feelings, and so on. The second of these scenarios, I suggest, is not troubling. The first, on the other hand, may be. But if it is, is it because there is a person who is qualitatively indistinguishable from oneself, or, rather, because one's life is totally determined?

I am inclined to question, accordingly, the perhaps rather widely held view that uniqueness is an important part of the value of one's life. Fortunately, however, one need not settle that issue in the present context, since cloning does not, of course, produce a person who is qualitatively indistinguishable from the individual who has been cloned, for, as is shown by the case of identical twins, two individuals with the same genetic makeup, even if raised within the same family at the same time, will differ in many respects, because of the different events that make up their life histories.

How great are those differences? The result of one study was as follows:

On average, our questionnaires show that the personality traits of identical twins have a 50 percent correlation. The traits of fraternal twins, by contrast, have a correlation of 25 percent, non-twin siblings a correlation of 11 percent and strangers a correlation of close to zero.[2]

Consequently, the personality traits of an individual and his or her clone should, on average, exhibit no more that a 50 percent correlation, and presumably, the correlation will generally be even less, given that an individual and his or her clone will typically be raised at different times, and in generations that may differ quite substantially in terms of basic beliefs and fundamental values.

The present argument, accordingly, if it is to have any chance, must shift from an appeal to the claim that a person has a right to absolute uniqueness to an appeal to the very different claim that a person has a right to a genetically unique nature. How, then, does the argument fare when reformulated in that way?

An initial point worth noticing is that any appeal to a claimed right to a genetically unique nature poses a difficulty for a theist: if there is such a right, why has God created a world where identical twins can arise? But there are, of course, many features of the world that are rather surprising, if our world is one that was created by an omnipotent, omniscient, and morally perfect person, and so the theist who appeals to a right to a genetically unique nature may simply reply that the presence of twins is just another facet of the general problem of evil.

How can one approach the question of whether persons have a right to a genetically unique nature? Some writers, I think, are content to rest with a burden of proof approach. Here the idea is that, although it may be the case that many people do think that being a unique individual, in the sense of not being qualitatively identical with anyone else, is an important part of what is valuable about being a person, the idea that persons have a right to a genetically unique identity is one that, by contrast, has been introduced only recently, and so those who advance the latter claim really need to offer some reasons for thinking that it is true.

There are, however, other ways of approaching this question that involve offering positive arguments against the claim. One possibility for example, is to appeal to the intuitions that one has upon reflection. Thus, one can consider the case of identical twins, and ask oneself whether, upon reflection, one thinks that it would be prima facie wrong to reproduce if one somehow knew that doing so would result in identical twins. I think it would be surprising if many people felt that this was so.

Another way of approaching the issue is by appealing to some plausible general theory of rights. Thus, for example, I am inclined to think that rights exist when there are serious, self-regarding interests that deserve to be protected. If some such view is correct, then one can approach the question of whether persons have a right to a genetically unique nature by asking whether one has some serious, self-regarding interest that would be impaired if one were a clone. Is the latter the case? The initial reason for thinking that it is not is that the existence of a clone does not seem to impinge on a person in the same way in which being prevented from performing some action that harms no one, or being tortured, or being killed, does: A distant clone might have no impact at all upon one's life.

In response, it might be argued that, while the mere existence of a clone need have no impact on, and so need not impair in any way, one's self-regarding interests, the situation might be very different if one knew of the existence of the clone, since that knowledge might, for example, be damaging to one's sense of individuality. But why should this be so, given that individuals can differ greatly, although sharing the same genetic makeup? It seems to me that if the knowledge that a clone of oneself exists were disturbing to one, this would probably be because of the presence of some relevant, false belief, such as a belief in genetic determinism. But if this is so, then the question arises as to whether rights exist when the interests that they protect are ones that will be harmed only if the potential subjects of the harm have certain false, and presumably irrational, beliefs. My own feeling is that the responsibility for such harm is properly assigned to the individual who has acquired the irrational beliefs whose presence is necessary if there is to be any harm. Consequently, it seems to me that the actions of others should not be constrained in order to prevent such harm from occurring, and thus that there is no right that is violated in such a case.

A third way of thinking about this question of whether there is a right to a genetically unique

nature is to consider a scenario in which individuals with the same genetic makeup are very common indeed, and to consider whether such a world would, for example, be inferior to the present world. Imagine, for example, that it is the year 4004 B.C.E., and that God is contemplating creating human beings. He has already considered the idea of letting humans come into being via evolution, but has rejected that plan on the grounds that a lottery approach to such a vital matter as bringing humans into existence hardly seems appropriate. He also considers creating an original human pair that are genetically distinct, and who will then give rise to humans who will be genetically quite diverse. Upon reflection, however, that idea also seems flawed, since the random shuffling of genes will result in individuals who may be physically impaired, or disposed to unpleasant diseases, such as cancer, that will cause them enormous suffering and lead to premature deaths. In the end, accordingly, the Creator decides upon a genetic constitution with the following two properties. First, it will not lead to serious physical handicaps and diseases, and it will allow an individual, who makes wise choices, to grow in mind and spirit. Second, all of the genes involve identical alleles. God then creates one person with that genetic makeup—call her Eve—and a second individual, Adam, whose only genetic difference is that he has one X chromosome, and one Y chromosome, where Eve has two X chromosomes. The upshot will then be that when Adam and Eve reproduce, they will breed true, because of the fact that they have, aside from the one difference, the same genetic makeup, with identical alleles for every inherited character, and so all of their descendants will be genetically identical to either Adam or Eve.

How would such a world compare with the actual world? If one were choosing from behind the Rawlsian veil of ignorance, would it be rational to prefer the actual world, or the alternative world? This is not, perhaps, an easy question. But it is clear that there would be some significant pluses associated with the alternative world. First, unlike the actual world, one would be assured of a genetic makeup that would be free of dispositions to various unwelcome and life-shortening diseases, or to other debilitating conditions such as depression, schizophrenia, and so on. Secondly, inherited traits would be distributed in a perfectly equitable fashion, and no one would start out, as is the case in the actual world, severely disadvantaged, and facing an enormous uphill battle. Third, aside from the differences between men and women, everyone would be physically the same, and so people would differ only with regard to the quality of their "souls," and thus one would have a world in which judgments of people might well have a less superficial basis than is often the case in the actual world. So there would seem to be some serious reasons for preferring the alternative world over the actual world.

The third advantage just mentioned also points, of course, to an obvious practical drawback of the alternative world: knowing who was who would be a rather more difficult matter than it is in the actual world. But this problem can be dealt with by variants on the above scenario. One variant, for example, would involve having identity of genetic makeup, except regarding the genes that determine the appearance of face and hair. Then one would be able to identify individuals in just the way that one typically does in the actual world. This change would mean, of course, that one was no longer considering an alternative world in which there was widespread identity with respect to genetic makeup. Nevertheless, if this other alternative world would be preferable to the actual world, I think that it still provides an argument against the view that individuals have a right to a unique genetic makeup. For, first of all, the preferability of this other alternative world strongly suggests that genetic difference, rather than being desirable in itself, is valuable only to the extent that it is needed to facilitate the easy identification of people. Second, is it plausible to hold that, although genetic uniqueness is crucial, a very high degree of genetic similarity is not? But in the alternative world we are considering here, the degree of genetic similarity between any two individuals would be extraordinarily high. Third, the alternative world is one in which the genes that determine the initial structure of one's brain are not merely very similar, but absolutely the same in all individuals. But, then, can one plausibly hold that genetic uniqueness is morally crucial, while conceding that a world in which individuals do not differ regarding the genes that determine the initial nature of their brains might be better than the actual world?

These three considerations, I suggest, provide good reasons for holding that one cannot plausibly maintain that individuals have a right to a genetically unique nature, without also holding that the actual world is to be preferred to the alternative world just described. The identification problem can, however, also be addressed without shifting to a world where people differ genetically, since one could instead suppose that a different mechanism for identifying other people is built into human beings. God could, for example, incorporate special circuitry into the human brain, which broadcasts both one's name and appropriate identifying information about one, and which picks up the information that is broadcast by other humans within one's perceptual field. The information is then checked against a memory bank containing information about everyone one knows, and if it turns out that one is in perceptual contact with some person with whom one is acquainted, and if one would like to know who the person in question is, one would automatically find oneself in possession of the relevant information.

The result would be a world where all individuals will have exactly the same genetic makeup, aside from an X and a Y chromosome, and all of the attractive features of the original alternative world would be present, without there being any problem of determining who was who. One can then ask how this world compares with the actual world, and whether, in particular, the fact that all people in this alternative world would have essentially the same genetic makeup really seems to be, upon reflection, a reason for preferring the actual world.

The Open Future Argument

Dan Brock mentions a second argument for the view that cloning that aims at producing persons is intrinsically wrong.[3] The argument, which is based upon ideas put forward by Joel Feinberg, who speaks of a right to an open future,[4] and by

Hans Jonas, who refers to a right to ignorance of a certain sort,[5] is essentially as follows. One's genetic makeup may very well determine to some extent the possibilities that lie open to one, and so it may constrain the course of one's future life. If there is no one with the same genetic makeup, or if there is such a person, but one is unaware of the fact, or, finally, if there is such a person, but the person is either one's contemporary, or someone who is younger, then one will not be able to observe the course of the life of someone with the same genetic makeup as oneself. But what if one does know of a genetically identical person whose life precedes one's own? Then one could have knowledge that one might well view as showing that certain possibilities were not really open to one, and so one would have less of a sense of being able to choose the course of one's life.

To see why this argument is unsound, one needs to ask about the reasoning that might be involved if someone, observing the earlier life of someone with the same genetic makeup, concludes that his or her own life is subject to certain constraints. One possibility is that one may have observed someone striving very hard, over a long period of time, to achieve some goal and failing to get anywhere near it. Perhaps the earlier, genetically identical individual wanted to be the first person to run the marathon in under two hours, and after several hears of intense and well-designed training, attention to diet, and so one, never got below two and one-half hours. One would then surely be justified in viewing that particular goal as not really open to one. But would that knowledge be a bad thing, as Jonas seems to be suggesting? I would think that, on the contrary, such knowledge would be valuable, since it would make it easier for one to choose goals that one could successfully pursue.

A very different possibility is that one might observe the course of the life of the genetically identical individual, and conclude that no life significantly different from that life could really be open to one. Then one would certainly feel that one's life was constrained to a very unwelcome extent. But in drawing the conclusion that one's life could not be significantly different from that of the other individual, one would be drawing a conclusion for which there is not only no evidence, but one that there is excellent evidence against: The lives of identical twins demonstrate that very different lives indeed are possible, given the same genetic makeup.

In short, the idea that information about the life of a person genetically identical to oneself would provide grounds for concluding that only a narrow range of alternatives was open to one would only be justified if genetic determinism, or a close approximation thereto, was correct. But nothing like genetic determinism is true. This second argument for the view that cloning with the goal of producing persons is intrinsically wrong is, accordingly, unsound.

CONSIDERATIONS IN SUPPORT OF THE CLONING OF PERSONS

Whether it is desirable to produce persons by cloning depends, as we noticed earlier, upon the outcome of an issue that is not yet decided: the aging question. Here, however, I shall simply assume that it will become possible to clone an adult individual in such a way that one winds up with a cell whose chromosomes have full-length telomeres, so that the individual who results will have a normal life expectancy. Given that assumption, I want to argue that there are a number of important benefits that may result from the cloning of humans that is done with the goal of producing persons.

In setting out what I take to be benefits of cloning, I shall not address possible objections. These will be discussed, instead, under "Objections to the Cloning of Humans."

Scientific Knowledge: Psychology and the Heredity-vs.-Environment Issue

A crucial theoretical task for psychology is the construction of a satisfactory theory that will explain the acquisition of traits of character, and central to the development of such a theory is information about the extent to which various traits are inherited, or alternatively, dependent on aspects of the environment that are controllable, or, finally, dependent on factors, either in the brain or in the environment, that have a chancy quality. But such knowledge is not just theoretically crucial to psychology. Knowledge of the contributions that are, and are not, made to the individual's development by his or her genetic makeup, by the environment in which he or she is raised, and by chance events, will enable one to develop approaches to child rearing that will increase the likelihood that one can raise people with desirable traits, people who will have a better chance of realizing their potentials, and of leading happy and satisfying lives. So this knowledge is not merely of great theoretical interest: it is also potentially very beneficial to society.

In the attempt to construct an adequate theory of human development, the study of identical twins has been very important, and has generated considerable information on the nature/nurture issue. But adequate theories still seem rather remote. Cloning would provide a powerful way of speeding up scientific progress in this area, since society could produce a number of individuals with the same genetic makeup, and then choose adoptive parents who would provide those individuals with good, but significantly different environments, in which to mature.

Cloning to Benefit Society

One very familiar suggestion is that one might benefit mankind by cloning individuals who have made very significant contributions to society. In the form in which it is usually put, when it is assumed that, if, for example, one had been able to clone Albert Einstein, the result would be an individual who would also make some very significant contribution to science, the suggestion is surely unsound. In the first place, whether an individual will do highly creative work surely depends on traits whose acquisitions is a matter of the environment in which the individual is raised, rather than on being determined simply by his or her genetic makeup. But could it not be argued in response that one could control the environment as well, raising a clone of Einstein, for example, in an environment that was as close as possible to the sort of environment in which Einstein was raised? That, of course, might prove difficult. But even if it could

be done, it is not clear that it would be sufficient, because there is a second point that can be made here, namely, that great creative achievements may depend on things that are to some extent accidental, and whose occurrence is not ensured by the combination of a certain genetic makeup and a certain general sort of environment. Many great mathematicians, for example, have developed an intense interest in numbers at an early age. Is there good reason to think that, had one been able to clone Carl Friedrich Gauss, and reared that person in an environment similar to Gauss's, that person would have developed a similar interest in numbers, and gone on to achieve great things in mathematics? Or is it likely that a clone of Einstein, raised in an environment similar to that in which Einstein was raised, would have wondered, as Einstein did, what the world would look like if one could travel as fast as light, and then gone on to reflect on the issues that fascinated Einstein, and that led ultimately to the development of revolutionary theories in physics?

I think that there are, then, some serious problems with the present suggestion in the form in which it is usually put. On the other hand, I am not convinced that a slightly more modest version cannot be sustained. Consider, for example, the Polgar sisters. There we have a case in which the father of three girls succeeded in creating an environment in which all three of his daughters became very strong chess players, and one of them, Judit Polgar, is now the strongest female chess player who has ever lived. Is it not reasonable to think that if one were to make a number of clones of Judit Polgar, and then raise them in an environment very similar to that in which the Polgar sisters were raised, the result would be a number of very strong chess players?

More generally, I think it is clear that there is a strong hereditary basis for intelligence,[6] and I also believe that there is good reason for thinking that other traits that may play a crucial role in creativity, such as extreme persistence, determination, and confidence in one's own abilities, are such as are likely to be produced by the right combination of heredity and environment. So, although the chance that the clone of an outstandingly creative individual will also achieve very great things is perhaps, at least in many areas, not especially high, I think that there is reason for thinking that, given an appropriate environment, the result will be an individual who is likely to accomplish things that may benefit society in significant ways.

Happier and Healthier Individuals

A third benefit of cloning is that it should make it possible to increase the likelihood that the person that one is bringing into existence will enjoy a healthy and happy life. For, to the extent that one's genetic constitution has a bearing on how long one is likely to live, on what diseases, both physical and mental, one is likely to suffer from, and on whether one will have traits of character or temperament that make for happiness, or for unhappiness, by cloning a person who has enjoyed a very long life, who has remained mentally alert, and not fallen prey to Alzheimer's disease, who has not suffered from cancer, arthritis, heart attacks, stroke, high blood pressure, and so on, and who has exhibited no tendencies to depression, or schizophrenia, and so on, one is increasing the chances that the individual that one is producing will also enjoy a healthy and happy life.

More Satisfying Childrearing: Individuals with Desired Traits

Many couples would prefer to raise children who possess certain traits. In some cases they may want children who have a certain physical appearance. In other cases, they might like to have children who have the physical abilities that would enable them to have a better chance of performing at a high level in certain physical activities. Or they might prefer to have children who would have the intellectual capabilities that would enable them to enjoy mathematics or science. Or they might prefer to have children who possess traits that would enable them to engage in, and enjoy, various aesthetic pursuits. Some of the traits that people might like their children to have presumably have a very strong hereditary basis; others are such as a child, given both the relevant genes, and the right environment, would be very likely to acquire. To the extent that the traits in question fall into either of these categories, the production of children

via cloning would enable more couples to raise children with traits that they judge to be desirable.

More Satisfying Childrearing: Using Self-Knowledge

There is a second way in which cloning could make childrearing more satisfying, and it emerges if one looks back on one's own childhood. Most people, when they do this, remember things that they think were good, and other things that they think would have been better if they had been different. In some cases, of course, one's views may be unsound, and it may be that some of the things that one's parents did, and which one did not like, actually had good effects on one's development. On the whole, however, it seems plausible that most people have reasonably sound views on which features of the way in which they were raised had good effects overall, and which did not.

The idea, then, is that if a couple raises a child who is a clone of one of the parents, the knowledge that the relevant parent has of the way in which he or she was raised can be used to bring up the child in a way that fits better with the individual psychology of the child. In addition, given the greater psychological similarity that will exist between the child and one of his parents in such a case, the relevant parent will better be able, at any point, to appreciate how things look from the child's point of view. So it would seem that there is a good chance both that such a couple will find childrearing a more rewarding experience, and that the child will have a happier childhood through being better understood.

Infertility

Since the successful cloning that resulted in Dolly, at least one person has expressed the intention of pushing ahead with the idea of using cloning to help infertile couples. For reasons that emerged under the second heading, "Cloning in the Present Context," the idea that cloning should be so used in the near future seems morally very problematic. In principle, however, the general idea would seem to have considerable merit. One advantage, for example, as Dan Brock and others have pointed out, is that "cloning would allow women who have no ova or men who have no sperm to produce an offspring that is biologically related to them."[7] Another advantage, also noted by Brock, is that "embryos might be cloned, either by nuclear transfer or embryo splitting, in order to increase the number of embryos for implantations and improve the chances of successful conception."[8]

Children for Homosexual Couples

Many people, especially in the United States, believe that homosexuality is deeply wrong, and that homosexuals should not be allowed either to marry or to raise children. These opinions, however, would be rejected, I think, by most philosophers, who would hold, on the contrary, that homosexuality is not morally wrong, and that homosexuals should be allowed both to marry, and to raise children. Assume, for the sake of the present discussion, that the latter views are correct. Then, as Philip Kitcher and others have noted, cloning would seem to be a promising method of providing a homosexual couple with children that they could raise, since, in the case of a gay couple, each child could be a clone of one person; in the case of a lesbian couple, every child could, in a sense, be biologically connected with both people:

> A lesbian couple wishes to have a child. Because they would like the child to be biologically connected to each of them, they request that a cell nucleus from one of them be inserted into an egg from the other, and that the embryo be implanted in the uterus of the woman who donated the egg.[9]

Cloning to Save Lives

A final possibility is suggested by the well-known case of the Ayala parents in California, who decided to have another child in the hope, which turned out to be justified, that the resulting child would be able to donate bone marrow for a transplant operation that would save the life of their teenage daughter, who was suffering from leukemia. If cloning had been possible at the time, a course of action would have been available to them that unlike having another child in the normal way, would not have been chancy: If they could have cloned the child who was ill, a tissue match would have been certain.

OBJECTIONS TO THE CLONING OF HUMANS

The Cloning of Mindless Organ Banks

Certain objections to the cloning of humans to produce mindless human organisms that would serve as a source of organs for others are perfectly intelligible. If someone objects to this idea on the grounds that one is destroying a person, the concern that is being expressed here is both completely clear and serious. The same is true if the objection is, instead, that such cloning is seriously wrong, since, in preventing a human organism from developing a functioning brain, one is depriving an immaterial soul associated with the organism in question of the possibility of experiencing life in this world. And, finally, the same is also true if someone holds that such cloning would be wrong, because it involves the destruction of an active potentiality for personhood.

The problem with these objections, accordingly, is not that they are in any way incoherent. Nor is it the case that the points raised are unimportant. The problem is simply that all of these objections are, in the end, unsound, for reasons that emerged earlier. Thus, the problem with the first objection is that there are excellent reasons for holding that human embryos do not possess those capacities, such as the capacity for thought and self-consciousness, that something must have, at some point, if it is to be a person. The problem with the second objection is that there are strong reasons for holding that the ontological basis for the capacities involved in consciousness, self-consciousness, thought, and other mental processes resides in the human brain, and not in any immaterial soul. Finally, the problem with the third objection lies in the assumption that the destruction of an active potentiality for personhood is morally wrong, for that claim is, on the one hand, unsupported by any satisfactory argument, and, on the other hand, exposed to decisive objections, one of which was set out earlier.

Often, however, it seems that people who would agree that the above objections are unsound, and who, moreover, do not view abortion as morally problematic, still express uneasiness about the idea of producing mindless human organ banks. Such uneasiness is rarely articulated, however, and it usually takes the form simply of describing the idea of mindless organ banks as a ghoulish scenario. This sort of dismissal of the use of cloning to produce organ banks is very puzzling. For what we are considering here is a way in which lives can be saved, and so, if one rejects this use of cloning, one is urging a course of action that will result in the deaths of innocent people. To do this on the grounds that mindless organ banks strike one as ghoulish seems morally irresponsible in the extreme: If this use of cloning is to be rejected, serious moral argument is called for.

The Cloning of Humans to Produce Persons

Violation of Rights Objections

Some people oppose cloning that is done with the goal of producing a person, on the grounds that such cloning involves a violation of some right of the person who is produced. The most important versions of this first sort of objection are those considered earlier, namely, that there is a violation either of a person's right to be a unique individual, or, more accurately, to be a genetically unique individual, or, alternatively, of a person's right to enjoy an open future that is not constrained by knowledge of the course of the life of some individual with the same genetic makeup. But for the reasons set out earlier, neither of these objections is sound.

Brave New World Style Objections

Next, there is a type of objection that is not frequently encountered in scholarly discussions, but which is rather common in the popular press, and which involves scenarios in which human beings are cloned in large numbers to serve as slaves, or as enthusiastic soldiers in a dictator's army. Such scenarios, however, do not seem very plausible. Is it really at all likely that, were cloning to become available, society would decide that its rejection of slavery had really been a mistake? Or that a dictator who was unable to conscript a satisfactory army from the existing citizens would be able to induce people to undertake a massive cloning program, in order that, 18 years or so down the line, he would finally have the army he had always wanted?

Psychological Distress

This objection is closely related to the earlier, violation of rights objections, because the idea is that, even if cloning does not violate a person's right to be a unique individual, or to have a unique genetic makeup, or to have an open and unconstrained future, nevertheless, people who are clones may feel that their uniqueness is compromised, or that their future is constrained, and this may cause substantial psychological harm and suffering.

There are two reasons for rejecting this objection as unsound. The first arises once one asks what one is to say about the beliefs in question, that is, the belief that one's uniqueness is compromised by the existence of a clone, and the belief that one's future is constrained if one has knowledge of the existence of a clone. Both beliefs are, as we have seen, false. But, in addition, it also seems clear that such beliefs would be, in general, irrational, since it is hard to see what grounds one could have for accepting either belief, other than something like genetic determinism, against which, as we saw earlier, there is conclusive evidence.

Once it is noted that the feelings that may give rise to psychological distress are irrational, one can appeal to the point that I made earlier, when we considered the question of whether knowledge of the existence of a clone might, for example, be damaging to one's sense of individuality, and whether, if this were so, such damage would be grounds for holding that there was a corresponding right that would be violated by cloning. What I argued at that point was that harm to an individual that arises because the individual has an irrational belief has a different moral status from harm that is not dependent on the presence of an irrational belief, and that, in particular, the possibility of the former sort of harm should not be taken as morally constraining others. The responsibility for such harm should, instead, be assigned to the individual who has the irrational belief, and the only obligation that falls on others is to point out to the person in question why the belief is an irrational one.

The second reason why the present objection cannot be sustained is also connected with the fact that the feelings in question are irrational, since the irrationality of the feelings means that they would not be likely to persist for very long, once cloning had become a familiar occurrence. For example, suppose that John feels that he is no longer a unique individual, or that his future is constrained, given that he is a clone of some other individual. Mary may also be a clone of some individual, and she may point out to John that she is very different from the person with whom she is genetically identical, and that she has not been constrained by the way the other person lived her life. Will John then persist in his irrational belief? This does not really seem very likely. If so, any distress that is produced will not be such as is likely to persist for any significant period of time.

Failing to Treat Individuals as Ends in Themselves

A fourth objection is directed, not against the cloning of persons in general, but against certain cases, such as those in which parents clone a child who is suffering from some life-threatening condition, in order to produce another child who will be able to save the first child's life. The thrust of this objection is that such cases involve a failure to view individuals as ends in themselves. Thus Philip Kitcher, referring to such cases, says that "a lingering concern remains," and he goes on to ask whether such scenarios "can be reconciled with Kant's injunction to 'treat humanity, whether in your own person or in the person of another, always at the same time as an end and never simply as a means.'"[10]

What is one to say about this objection? It may be important to be explicit about what sacrifices the child who is being produced is going

to have to make to save his or her sibling. When I set out this sort of case under the subheading "Cloning to Save Lives," I assumed that what was involved was a bone marrow transplant. Kitcher, in his formulation, assumes that it will be a kidney transplant. I think that one might well be inclined to take different views of these two cases, given that, in the kidney donation case, but not the bone marrow case, the donor is making a sacrifice that may have unhappy consequences for that person in the future.

To avoid this complicated factor, let us concentrate, then, on the bone marrow case. In such a case, would there be a violation of Kant's injunction? There could be, if the parents were to abandon, or not really care for the one child, once he or she had provided bone marrow to save the life of the other child. But this, surely, would be a very unlikely occurrence. After all, the history of the human race is mostly the history of unplanned children, often born into situations in which the parents were anything but well off, and yet, typically, those children were deeply loved by their parents.

In short, though this sort of case is, by hypothesis, one in which the parents decide to have a child with a goal in mind that has nothing to do with the well being of that child, this is no reason for supposing that they are therefore likely to treat that child merely as a means, and not also as an end in itself. Indeed, surely there is good reason to think, on the contrary, that such a child will be raised in no less loving a way than is normally the case.

Interfering with Personal Autonomy

The final objection that I shall consider is also one that has been advanced by Philip Kitcher, and he puts it as follows: "If the cloning of human beings is undertaken in the hope of generating a particular kind of person, then cloning is morally repugnant. The repugnance arises not because cloning involves biological tinkering but because it interferes with human autonomy."[11]

This objection would not apply to all of the cases that I mentioned in "Considerations in

Support of the Cloning of Persons" as ones in which the cloning of a person would be justified. It does, however, apply to many of them. Is the objection sound? I cannot see that it is. First, notice that, in some cases, when one's goal is to produce "a particular kind of person," what one is aiming at is simply a person who will have certain potentialities. Parents might, for example, want to have children who are capable of enjoying intellectual pursuits. The possession of the relevant capacities does not force the children to spend their lives engaged in such pursuits, and so it is hard to see how cloning that is directed at that goal would interfere with human autonomy.

Second, consider cases in which the goal is not to produce a person who will be *capable* of doing a wider range of things, but an individual who will be *disposed* in certain directions. Perhaps it is this sort of case that Kitcher has in mind when he speaks of interfering with human autonomy. But is it really morally problematic to attempt to create persons who will be disposed in certain directions, and not in others? To answer this question, one needs to consider concrete cases, such as the sorts of cases that I mentioned earlier. Is it morally wrong, for example, to attempt to produce, via cloning, individuals who will, because of their genetic makeup, be disposed not to suffer from conditions that may cause considerable pain, such as arthritis, or from life-threatening diseases, such as cancer, high blood pressure, strokes, and heart attacks? Or to attempt to produce individuals who will have a cheerful temperament, or who will not be disposed to depression, to anxiety, to schizophrenia, or to Alzheimer's disease?

It seems unlikely that Kitcher, or others, would want to say that attempting to produce individuals who will be constitutionally disposed in the ways just indicated is a case of interfering with human autonomy. But then, what are the traits that are such that attempting to create a person with those traits is a case of interfering with human autonomy? Perhaps Kitcher, when he speaks about creating a particular kind of person, is thinking not just of any properties that persons

have, but, more narrowly, of such things as personality traits, or traits of character, or having certain interests? But again one can ask whether there is anything morally problematic about attempting to create persons with such properties. Some personality traits are desirable, and parents typically encourage their children to develop those traits. Some character traits are virtues, and others are vices, and both parents and society attempt to encourage the acquisition of the former, and to discourage the acquisition of the latter. Finally, many interests, such as music, art, mathematics, science, games, physical activities, can add greatly to the quality of one's life, and once again, parents typically expose their children to relevant activities, and help their children to achieve levels of proficiency that will enable them to enjoy those pursuits.

The upshot is that, if cloning that aimed at producing people who would be more likely to possess various personality traits, or traits of character, or who would be more likely to have certain interests, was wrong because it was a case of interfering with personal autonomy, then the childrearing practices of almost all parents would stand condemned on precisely the same grounds. But such a claim, surely, is deeply counterintuitive.

In addition, however, one need not rest content with an appeal to intuitions here. The same conclusion follows on many high-order moral theories. Suppose, for example, that one is once again behind the Rawlsian veil of ignorance, and that one is deciding among societies that differ regarding their approaches to the rearing of children. Would it be rational to choose a society in which parents did not attempt to encourage their children to develop personality traits that would contribute to the latters' happiness? Or a society in which parents did not attempt to instill in their children a disposition to act in ways that are morally right? Or one in which parents made no attempt to develop various interests in their children? It is, I suggest, hard to see how such a choice could be a rational one, given that one would be opting, it would seem, for a society in which one would be likely to have a life that, on average, would be less worth living.

I conclude, therefore, that, contrary to what Philip Kitcher has claimed, it is not true that most cloning scenarios are morally repugnant, and that, in particular, there is, in general, nothing morally problematic about aiming at creating a child with specific attributes.

CONCLUSION

In this essay, I have distinguished between two very different cases involving the cloning of a human being—one that aims at the production of mindless human organisms that are to serve as organ banks for the people who are cloned, and another that aims at the creation of persons. Regarding the former, the objections that can be advanced are just the objections that can be directed against abortion, and, for reasons that I briefly outlined above, those objections can be shown to be unsound.

Very different objections arise in the case of cloning whose aim is the production of persons. Concerning this second sort of cloning, I argued that it is important to distinguish between the question of whether such cloning is, in principle, morally acceptable, and whether it is acceptable at the present time. Regarding the latter question, I argued that the present use of cloning to produce persons would be morally problematic. By contrast, concerning the question of whether such cloning is in principle morally acceptable, I argued, first, that such cloning is not intrinsically wrong; second, that there are a number of reasons why the cloning of persons would be desirable; and, third, that the objections that have been directed against such cloning cannot be sustained.

My overall conclusion, in short, is that the cloning of human beings, both to produce mindless organ banks, and to produce persons, is both morally acceptable, in principle, and potentially very beneficial for society.

NOTES

1. Brock, D.W. (1998) Cloning human beings: an assessment of the ethical issues pro and con, in *Clones and Clones*, Nussbaum, M. C. and Sunstein, C. R., eds., Norton, New York. *See* the section entitled "Would the use of human cloning violate important human rights?"
2. Bouchard, T.J. Jr. (1997) Whenever the twain shall meet. *The Sciences* 37, 52–57.
3. Brock, D. in the section entitled "Would the use of human cloning violate important human rights?"
4. Feinberg, J. (1980) The child's right to an open future, in *Whose Child? Children's Rights, Parental Authority, and State Power*, Aiken, W. and LaFollette, H., eds., Rowan and Littlefield, Totowa, NJ.
5. Jonas, H. (1974) *Philosophical Essay: From Ancient Creed to Technological Man*, Prentice-Hall, Englewood Cliffs, NJ.
6. *See*, for example, the discussion of this issue in Bouchard, pp. 55, 56.
7. Brock, D., in the subsection entitled "Human cloning would be a new means to relieve the infertility some persons now experience."
8. *Ibid.*
9. Kitcher, P. (1998) Whose self is it, anyway? *The Sciences* 37, 58–62. It should be noted that, although Kitcher mentions this idea as initially attractive, in the end he concludes that it is problematic, for a reason that will be considered in the subsection "The Cloning of Humans to Produce Persons."
10. *Ibid.*, p. 61.
11. *Ibid.*, p. 61.

☙ QUESTIONS FOR ANALYSIS

1. Tooley asks us to compare the world as it is to an imaginary world in which God decided to make Adam and Eve genetically identical except for the Y chromosome. What is the point of this thought experiment?
2. What benefits does Tooley think cloning would bring? Are they equally beneficial?
3. Does Tooley adequately rebut the objections to human cloning? Why or why not?
4. Do you agree with Tooley that there is nothing immoral about creating mindless human clones as organ banks?

The Morality of Killing Human Embryos

BONNIE STEINBOCK

Bonnie Steinbock, a professor of philosophy at SUNY Albany and a fellow of the Hastings Center, specializes in applied ethics, especially issues of reproduction and genetics. Here she examines several ethical perspectives on the moral status of the embryos used in stem cell research. Drawing on the extensive examination of these issues in the dialogue about the morality of abortion, she concludes that the embryos used in research lack moral status and thus may be used ethically for this purpose, so long as ethical guidelines are respected and the research is only for important purposes.

Embryonic stem cell research is morally and politically controversial because the process of deriving the embryonic stem (ES) cells kills embryos. If embryos are, as some would claim, human beings like you and me, then ES cell research is clearly impermissible. If, on the other hand, the blastocysts from which embryonic stem cells are derived are not yet human beings, but rather microscopic balls of undifferentiated cells, as others maintain, then ES cell research is probably morally permissible. Whether the research can be justified depends on such issues as its cost, chance of success, and numbers likely to benefit. But this is an issue for any research project, not just ES cell research. What makes the debate over ES cell research controversial is that it, like the debate over abortion, raises "questions that politicians cannot settle: when does human life begin, and what is the moral status of the human embryo?"[1] This paper looks at several theories of moral status and their implications for embryo research.

When we ask whether a being has moral status, we are asking whether it counts or matters from the moral point of view; whether it must be considered in our moral deliberations. It seems obvious that not everything has moral status. We are not required to consider the impact of our moral decisions on mere things—for example, ordinary rocks. It seems equally obvious that paradigmatic

people—people like you and me—do have moral status. In fact, most people take it for granted that even if moral status isn't limited to people (that animals count, for example) human beings count for more. To express this in Kantian terms, humanity has a dignity and worth which separates humankind from the rest of creation. Because this view is commonplace in moral thinking and in the law, we can call it the common-sense view of moral status.

THE COMMON-SENSE VIEW: THE BIOLOGICAL HUMANITY CRITERION

The common-sense view of moral status is derived from the Judeo-Christian traditional which teaches that only human beings are created in God's image, and therefore human beings alone have this special moral status. In addition, this special moral status belongs to all human beings, regardless of race, ethnicity, nationality, or gender. We are all God's children. Compared to views that limit moral status to members of one's own group or tribe, the Judeo-Christian view is quite progressive. Theoretically (though often not in reality), it prohibits the enslaving or killing of other human beings, simply because they are "outsiders." The secular version of this view bases the unique moral

"The Morality of Killing Human Embryos," Bonnie Steinbock, *The Journal of Law, Medicine & Ethics* 34:1 (Spring 2006), pp. 26–34. Reproduced with permission of Blackwell Publishing Ltd.

status of humanity on a biological category—membership in the species *homo sapiens*.

The biological humanity criterion of moral status states that all and only human beings, members of our species, have full moral status. But even those who agree on the criterion may differ on this question: when does a human being come into existence? Sometimes this is put in a different way: when does human *life* begin? But this question, familiar from the abortion debate, poses the issue in a misleading way, because every cell in your body is both human (possessed of a human genome) and alive. Human gametes (ova and sperm) are alive, and sperm even swim. So the question, "When does human life begin?" is better understood as asking, "when does an individual human organism come into existence?"

One answer is that a human organism comes into existence at conception. Those who hold the conception view adopt the biological humanity criterion of moral status, which says that all and only human organisms have full moral status. In addition, they believe that a human organism exists at the moment of conception. Indeed, they usually hold that this is a plain matter of biological fact.

However, this is dubious, as there are biological reasons to think that the unique human organism begins to exist only some time after the beginning of fertilization. Fertilization or conception does not occur at a precise moment. It is a process taking place over hours, even days. The process of conception is not completed until syngamy, when the chromosomes from the egg and the sperm have merged, some time after the sperm has penetrated the egg. However, even syngamy may not mark the beginning of a human organism. Ron Green points out,

> biologists usually describe the cells of an organism has having the full range of cellular structure including a single cell nucleus that contains DNA within its own nuclear membrane. But at syngamy the zygote has no definitive nuclear membrane.... A distinctive diploid cell nucleus does not make its appearance until the two-cell stage, after the zygote undergoes its first cell division...[2]

Moreover, in the early stages of an embryo's life, many of its cells, or blastomers, remain "totipotent." This means that each blastomere, is undifferentiated and remains capable, if properly manipulated, of developing into a full human being. One kind of cloning—called embryo splitting or blastomere separation—is accomplished in this way. Embryo splitting also occurs naturally in the case of identical twins (or triplets). Green comments, "if biological humanness starts with the appearance of a unique diploid genome, twins and triplets are living evidence that the early embryo is not yet one human being, but a community of possibly different individuals held together by a gelatinous membrane."[3] He goes on to quote an embryology text as saying, "a genetically unique but non-individuated embryo has yet to acquire determinate individuality, a stable human identity."[4] In this view, a genuine human organism begins to exist only after twining is no longer possible: at the beginning of gastrulation when the primitive streak (the precursor of the nervous system) forms. In a pregnancy, gastrulation coincides with implantation, the imbedding of the embryo in the uterus, which occurs about fourteen days after fertilization.

The debate over when a human organism comes into existence occurs within the context of the biological humanity criterion. However, the criterion itself has been challenged.

THE PERSON VIEW

In her classic article, "On the Moral and Legal Status of Abortion,"[5] Mary Anne Warren argues that the conservative view on abortion rests on a confusion between two distinct senses of "human being." One sense is biological or genetic. It refers to the species to which an entity belongs. Human fetuses are unquestionably human in the biological sense. However, it does not follow from their genetic humanity that they are human in the other sense, the moral sense, which refers to their moral status and rights. Why should a biological category confer a special moral status? The belief that humanness does imply such a status and rights (human rights) stems from a failure to distinguish between the two senses. To avoid this confusion, Warren suggests that we reserve the term "human" for the biological or genetic sense, and use the term "person" to refer to beings who are full-fledged members of the moral community, possessed of moral rights—in particular, the right to life. This enables us to avoid begging the question in the abortion debate, for it remains an open question whether a human fetus is a person with a right to life.

Why not base moral status and moral rights on species membership? After all, all the persons we know are, in fact, members of the species *homo sapiens.* Why not use species membership as a marker for moral personhood? The reason is the arbitrariness of limiting moral status to genetic human beings. This can be seen if we imagine coming across an extraterrestrial like the eponymous character in the movie, *E.T.* If we were deciding what it would be morally permissible to do to him—say, put him in a zoo, or make him into hamburger—surely the question would not be decided by the number of chromosomes in his cells (if he even had chromosomes). His not being a member of the species *homo sapiens* would not determine his moral status. It seems likely that we would regard him as a person—a non-human person—with all the rights of any one of us.

The example of *E.T.* is meant to show that biological humanity isn't a necessary condition of full moral status. Instead, moral status is based on certain psychological characteristics, such as sentience, consciousness, self-consciousness, the ability to use language, rationality and moral agency. These characteristics are typical of members of our species, but not necessarily limited to them, as the example of *E.T.* is intended to show. Moreover, there seem to be members of our species who lack these person-making characteristics, such as anencephalic babies and patients in persistent vegetative states. They are biologically human, but not persons, and thus do not have the moral status reserved to persons.

An objection made to the person view is that, without an account of the moral relevance of person-making characteristics, it is as arbitrary as a theory based on species membership. Why should moral status and moral rights be limited to sentient, self-conscious, language-using, rational agents? Moreover, depending on how many person-making characteristics are needed for full moral status and rights, the person view appears to exclude those human beings who, due to severe developmental disabilities or mental illness or senility, or even infancy, do not have the capacity to reason or use language. It is hard to accept that human beings in these categories—who are often members of our own families—are not moral persons, with the same moral status and rights as the rest of us. Advocates of the biological humanity criterion maintain that any criterion other than genetic humanity will have this fatal flaw.

The challenge, then, is to construct a theory of moral status that is neither arbitrary (like the biological humanity criterion) nor unduly restrictive (like the person view). Moreover, the view should explain the moral relevance of its criterion for moral status.

THE INTEREST VIEW[6]

The interest view bases moral status on the possession of interests. The view derives from Joel Feinberg's "interest principle,"[7] which was intended to answer the question, what kinds of beings can logically have rights? Feinberg suggests that the answer comes from the purpose or function of rights, which is to protect the interests of the being alleged to have the rights. He usefully analogizes having an interest in something to having a "stake" in it. I am better off if the things in which I have a stake, such as my health, my career, my assets, my family flourish or prosper. Their flourishing is in my interest. Feinberg writes:

> One's interests, then, taken as a miscellaneous collection, consist of all those things in which one has a stake, whereas one's interest in the singular, one's personal interest or self-interest, consists in the harmonious advancement of one's interests in the plural. These interests.... are distinguishable components of a person's well-being: he flourishes or languishes as they flourish or languish. What promotes them is to his advantage or *in his interest*; what thwarts them is to his detriment or *against his interest*.[8]

This is not to claim a one-to-one connection between what a person desires and what is in his self-interests. I can take an interest in something (like junk food) that is not in my interest; and something can be in my interest but not be something I take an interest in (like exercise). But the reason exercise is in my interest, and junk food is not, is that exercise promotes other goals and desires of mine, such as staying healthy and alive, and eating junk food does not. If I had no desires, goals, or preferences at all, nothing would be in my interest.

Unless a being has interests and a welfare of its own, it makes no sense to ascribe rights to it. Feinberg's insight about the logical conditions of having rights can be applied more generally to having moral status. To have moral status is to count or matter, from the moral point of view. If a being has moral status, then its interests must be considered when we engage in moral deliberation. If a being has no interests, its interests cannot be considered. So the possession of interests is a necessary condition of having moral status, and I would argue that it is also a sufficient condition. That is, if a being has interests, there is no justification for ignoring those interests when making moral decisions. (It is a separate question how much weight to accord to the interests of different beings, that is, whether there are other factors that give some beings a higher moral status than others.)

The Feinbergian account of having interests as having stakes in things suggests a conceptual link between interests and consciousness. Only conscious beings—beings with some sort of mental life, however rudimentary—can have wants; only beings with wants can have a stake in anything; only beings that can have a stake in something can have interests of their own. Non-conscious beings, whether mere things (like cars and rocks and works of art) or living things without nervous systems (like plants), have no interests of their own. This is not to say that they cannot be cared for or neglected; repaired or destroyed; nourished or killed. It is rather to say that it does not matter to non-conscious beings what we do to them. We can preserve their existence, and even promote their welfare in the sense of making them better entities of a certain kind. For example, we can fertilize the roses so that they grow vigorously and bloom; we can bring in the car for regular service so that it runs beautifully. However, we cannot do these things out of concern for what matters to them, because nothing matters to them. They do not have a stake in anything, including their own existence. For this reason, I maintain that they, unlike conscious beings, do not have a welfare or sake of their own.

Some will object that we cannot base moral status on consciousness unless we have a definition of consciousness, but there does not seem to be any satisfactory, non-circular definition. Acknowledging the problem, David Boonin says, "It is tempting to say that to be conscious is to be aware of something, for example, but then awareness will surely have to be defined in terms of being in a conscious state."[9] What follows from the absence of a definition of consciousness? Not much, Boonin argues. It is not as if we had no idea what consciousness is. He writes:

> As Nagel famously put it, using an expression that has since become ubiquitous in discussions of the subject, "an organism has conscious mental states if and only if there is something that it is like to *be* that organism—something it is like for the organism." Even if this does not constitute a definition of consciousness, you do know what I am talking about when I refer to the fact that there is something that it is like to be you when you see a clear blue sky, hear a shrill scream, feel a sharp prick, or a cold wind, or a burning itch. And this is enough to make clear what is meant by the claim that there is a morally relevant difference between an organism that is conscious in this sense and an organism that is not.[10]

The morally relevant difference between conscious and non-consciousness beings is that conscious beings have interests and a welfare of their own, compounded out of those interests. Non-conscious beings do not have either of these things.

Sentience is only one form of conscious awareness, but it is a very important one. If a being is sentient, that is, it can experience treatment as painful, it has at least one interest: the interest in not experiencing pain. The fact that a being can suffer gives us a reason to treat it in certain ways, and not in other ways. It matters to sentient beings what one does to them, and this is why they have moral claims on us. To take a homely example, it is fine if a child plucks the petals off a daisy while saying "He loves me, he loves me not." It is not fine if the child recites the rhyme while pulling the legs off an insect, or the feathers off a (trapped) bird.

IMPLICATIONS OF THE INTEREST VIEW FOR EMBRYOS

Embryos are not mere things. They are alive and, under certain conditions, have the potential to become beings with interests—indeed, to become people, like you and me. But their potential to become persons does not give them the moral status or the rights of actual persons. Early embryos, indeed early-gestation fetuses, have no consciousness, no awareness, no experiences of any kind, even the most rudimentary. Without even the precursor of a nervous system, pre-implantation embryos cannot possibly have any kind of consciousness. Without consciousness, they cannot have desires; without desires, they cannot have interests. It is not wrong to kill embryos because it doesn't matter to an embryo whether it is killed or goes on living. Its continued existence is clearly not something an embryo takes an interest in, because it is impossible for a non-conscious non-sentient being to take an interest in anything. More importantly, the interest view maintains that continued existence is not in the interests of a non-sentient fetus. For continued existence to be in its interests, it would have to have a welfare of its own, compounded out of all of its interests taken together. Lacking interests, embryos do not have a welfare of their own. In this respect, they are like gametes. Gametes are alive and human, but this is not sufficient for moral status. To have moral status is to be the kind of being whose interests and welfare we moral agents are required to consider. Without interests, there is nothing to consider. This is not to say that there might not be other reasons, including moral reasons, to protect non-interested beings. It is to say that these reasons cannot stem from their own interests or welfare, since they have none. Indeed, on a plausible conception of harming as setting back a being's interests, it follows that killing non-interested beings does not harm them.[11] If this sounds odd, it is because, for *us*, being killed is ordinarily the greatest of harms. But that is because we have interests, and in particular, an interest in continuing to exist. However, if a being has no interests, death is not a harm to it, any more than being destroyed is a harm to an automobile.

Of course, embryos differ from automobiles in one very significant way: embryos are living beings with the potential to develop into human persons, just like you or me, if they are not killed. In a now-classic article, Don Marquis argues that it is wrong to kill fetuses for the very same reason that it is wrong to kill you or me: because doing so deprives them (and us) of our valuable futures. In the next section, I will assess the Valuable Futures argument and its implications for the morality of killing embryos.

MARQUIS AND THE VALUABLE FUTURES ARGUMENT

According to Marquis, both sides of the abortion debate have insurmountable problems. What is needed is a fresh start, an account of why killing is wrong in the paradigm cases in which everyone would agree that it is wrong—namely, the killing of adult human beings, like you or me. Killing adult human beings is *prima facie* wrong because killing them deprives them of their future. Marquis writes:

> The loss of one's life is one of the greatest losses one can suffer. The loss of one's life deprives one of all the experiences, activities, projects, and enjoyments that would otherwise have constituted one's future. Therefore, killing someone is wrong, primarily because the killing inflicts (one of) the greatest possible losses on the victim.... When I am killed, I am deprived both of what I now value which would have been part of my future personal life, but also what would come to value. Therefore, when I die, I am deprived of all of the value of my future. Inflicting this loss on me is ultimately what makes killing me wrong. This being the case, it would seem that what makes killing *any* adult human being *prima facie* seriously wrong is the loss of his or her future.[12]

But exactly the same is true of killing a human fetus, and so abortion is, *prima facie*, wrong. *Prima facie* because killing is wrong only if it deprives the one killed of a "valuable future" or a "future-like-ours" (FLO, as it has come to be referred to). Thus, the valuable futures argument does not imply that it is wrong to kill someone in a persistent vegetative state (PVS) because someone in PVS no longer has a valuable future. It's also consistent with voluntary euthanasia, because persons who are severely and incurably ill and who face a future of pain and despair and who wish to die will not have suffered a loss if they are killed, because the future of which they are deprived is not considered by them to be a valuable one. Equally, the aborting of fetuses with defects so severe as to prevent them having FLO might be justifiable on Marquis's account. How severe would the disabling condition have to be to make abortion morally permissible? Is it only lethal conditions (such as Tay-Sachs disease) which deprive fetuses of FLO? Or could non-lethal conditions, such as mental retardation, deprive a fetus of FLO, and thus justify abortion? Marquis does not address these sorts of questions, indeed, does not provide an account of "just what it is about my future or the futures of other adult human beings which make it wrong to kill us."[13] His aim is, rather, to show that abortion is in general a grave wrong. For most fetuses clearly do have valuable futures. If they are not aborted, they will come to have lives they will value and enjoy, just as you and I value and enjoy our lives. Therefore, abortion is seriously wrong for the same reason that killing an innocent adult human being is seriously wrong: it deprives the victim of his or her valuable future.

On the interest view, the killing of non-sentient beings is not seriously wrong because non-sentient beings are not deprived of anything they want or have a stake in by being killed. Marquis thinks that this reveals a fundamental flaw in the interest view, or indeed in any sentience-or desire-based view. First, it seems to imply that it is not wrong to kill someone in a reversible coma or even in deep and dreamless sleep. Such a person is not now conscious or sentient. If we explain the wrongness of killing him by appealing to his future conscious states, then it seems that it is equally wrong to kill a pre-conscious fetus, who will become conscious and sentient in the natural course of events, if it is not aborted. Either the interest view entails that it is morally permissible to kill temporarily comatose adults, in which case it cannot be the right view of moral status, or it must concede that it is wrong to kill fetuses, in which case it cannot be the basis for a defense of abortion. By contrast, the FLO account can explain the wrongness of killing temporarily unconscious adults; this deprives them of their valuable futures.

Second, Marquis argues, the interest view cannot explain why it is wrong to kill someone who is conscious and sentient, but who does not want to go on living. If it is the desire to go on living that makes killing someone seriously wrong, then presumably it is not wrong to kill someone who does not have the desire to go on living, due to (treatable) depression. But of course, Marquis argues, it *is* wrong, and the FLO account can explain why. A person can have a valuable future, even if, due to depression, he does not now have the desire to go on living. It would be seriously wrong to kill him and thereby to deprive him of that valuable future. (Presumably it would not be wrong to kill someone whose depression was untreatable and who faced "a future of pain and despair." At least, it would not wrong the person killed, though Marquis leaves it open that there might be other reasons why killing him would be wrong.)

The interest view is not vulnerable to these alleged counter-examples. The difference between a fetus and a temporarily comatose adult (TCA) is that a TCA has desires, including a desire to go on living, that make it seriously wrong to kill him. The same is not true of an embryo or first-trimester fetus, which has no desires at all.[14] Admittedly, a TCA does not have any conscious desires. But even while he is unconscious, he still has desires, just as he still has beliefs. David Boonin points out that not all of our beliefs are ones of which we are consciously aware: they are not all occurrent beliefs. To illustrate the dispositional nature of many of our beliefs, Boonin gives the following example. Ten minutes ago you probably were not consciously aware of believing that a triangle has three sides. Yet if I were to ask you, "how many sides does a triangle have?" you would be disposed to answer, "three." That is why it is a dispositional belief. Nevertheless, it is one of your beliefs, a belief you already have. As Boonin puts it, "you do not lose all of your beliefs each time you go to bed and then acquire a new and identical set of beliefs each time you wake up. You retain your beliefs as dispositional beliefs and occasionally have some or others as occurrent beliefs."[15]

Similarly, if you desire not to be killed, you continue to have that desire dispositionally while you are in a reversible coma. On the basis of this desire, we can ascribe to you an interest in continued existence, an interest that exerts a moral claim on the rest of us not to kill you while you are temporarily comatose. But the same cannot be said of a being, like an embryo, that has never been conscious and so has no desires, occurrent or dispositional, and hence no interests.

In a forthcoming article, "Abortion Revisited," Marquis writes, "Boonin's account of and defense of a dispositional desire strategy for dealing with the alleged temporarily unconscious adult counterexample to the present desire view seems reasonable."[16] I take this to mean that Marquis now agrees that the alleged counter-example of the temporarily comatose adult is not a problem for desire-or sentience-based accounts. But what about someone who has no desire, occurrent or dispositional, to go on living, due to severe but temporary depression? Can the interest view explain why it would be seriously wrong to kill such a person without at the same time implying that it would be seriously wrong to kill a fetus?

Boonin responds by arguing that sometimes we need to correct a person's actual desires because, due to various distorting conditions, they do not represent what the individual really wants. He writes, "... in many cases in which we believe that the present desires of others are morally significant, we distinguish between the actual content of the desire that a person has given her actual circumstances and the content the desire she actually has *would* have had if the actual desire had been formed under more ideal circumstances."[17] In the case of the depressed person who does not want

to live, it is the depression that makes him unable to think clearly and unable to enjoy his life. When he comes out of the depression, life will seem to him to be worth living again. So of course it would be seriously wrong to kill him while he is in the depressed state. As Boonin puts it, "... when someone's desires are such that they would very strongly desire that you not do something to them were they able to reflect more clearly on the question, then that counts as a very strong moral reason not to do it."[18]

Marquis thinks that the case of the depressed person ("Hans" in Boonin's example) and the fetus are analogous. If what makes killing Hans seriously wrong is that Hans would want to go on living if he were able to think clearly, then why can't we say that what makes killing the fetus wrong is that it would want to go on living, if it could think about it. This is not like saying that a rock would want to go on living if it could think about it, because unlike a rock, a fetus has a future of value, that is, a life that it will value in the future. In this respect, the fetus is just like Hans. And so Marquis writes, "Fetuses are quite different. Hypothetical desires can be attributed as easily to fetuses as to Hans."[19] However, fetuses do not have distorted desires, which need correcting in order to perceive what they really want. Preconscious fetuses do not have desires at all. It seems to me one thing to ascribe an ideal or hypothetical desire to a person whose desires have been distorted, and quite another to ascribe hypothetical desires to a being incapable of having any desires. In any event, I am not sure how much Marquis wants or needs to base his argument on the ascription of hypothetical desires to fetuses, as he has a different argument, which is not dependent on the existence of such desires. He suggests that we can "... attribute interests to a presently insentient being in virtue of its well-being at some future sentient stage of its natural history."[20] In other words, although the fetus is now unconscious and has no desires, it can still have an interest in its future, in the sense that its future is *in* its interest. The motivation for this claim is the view of the fetus as just one stage in a person's natural history. If my life and my future existence are something I value, then it is rational for me to be glad that I was not killed at an earlier stage, for example, when I was a fetus. My valuable future is its valuable future. Having that future (that is, not being killed) is as much in its interest as it is in mine. Or rather, not being killed is as much in my interest when I was a fetus as it is in my interest now.

MCMAHAN'S MIND ESSENTIALISM

So the next question is, was I ever a fetus? That may seem indisputable, given the biological facts. Everyone, surely, started life as a zygote, which developed into an embryo, which became a fetus, and then was born as a baby. However, this is exactly what Jeff McMahan wants to deny. He writes,

> … even if we grant that a new human organism begins to exist at conception, it follows from this fact that we began to exist at conception only if we are human organisms … if I am a human organism, I began to exist when this organism did. But the assumption that I am numerically identical with the organism with which (to put it as neutrally as possible) I coexist is hardly uncontroversial.[21]

McMahan thinks that the most plausible account of what I essentially am is an embodied consciousness. And if that's the case, then I never existed as a nonconscious fetus. I came into existence when my organism began to be conscious—sometime between 20 and 28 weeks of gestation.[22] Summarizing McMahan's position, David DeGrazia writes,

> … the thesis of mind essentialism implies that early fetuses, lacking minds, cannot become minded beings, since it asserts that anything that is ever minded is always minded. Thus, early abortions do not kill beings with significant moral status, making these abortions "relevantly like contraception and wholly unlike the killing of a person." The Valuable Futures Argument therefore trips on the mistaken assumption that the early fetus will develop into a minded being. Because it will not, the early fetus does not *have* a valuable future.[23]

McMahan's theory provides a neat response to Marquis—but only if one accepts his mind essentialism, and the idea that the preconscious fetus cannot develop into a conscious fetus, much less a person like you or me. That seems to me to fly in the face of the facts. It seems much more plausible to say that I was once a child, and before that an infant, and before that a fetus. Boonin, commenting on the pictures in his office of his son, Eli, at various stages after birth, says, "through all of the remarkable changes that these pictures preserve, he remains unmistakably the same little boy." He also has another picture of Eli taken 24 weeks before his birth. Boonin writes, "there is no doubt in my mind that this picture, too, shows that same little boy at a very early stage in his physical development."[24] McMahan would have to say that the sonogram is a picture of Eli's organism at a very early stage, but it is not a picture of Eli. I would say (and I assume Boonin would agree) that I am my organism, although this is not all that I am. However, to posit a "me" that is distinct from my physical self seems implausible, and the wrong way to defend abortion. Rather, I would say that when I was a fetus, it would have been permissible to abort me, because had I been aborted before I became conscious and sentient, it would not have mattered to me. It would have made no more difference to me than preventing my conception. So while I agree with Marquis that I was once a fetus, I deny that when I was a fetus, I had an interest or a stake in my valuable future. I think that when I was a mindless fetus, I had no interests at all.

IMPLICATIONS FOR BLASTOCYSTS

I began this paper with the question whether it is seriously wrong to kill embryos at the blastocyst stage. I want to suggest now that even if Marquis is right about the morality of abortion—that it's wrong to kill fetuses because they have valuable futures it is not plausible to claim that pre-implantation embryos do. For unlike a fetus, an extracorporeal embryo is not developing into someone with a valuable future. Left alone (that is, not aborted), the fetus will (most likely) develop into someone with a valuable future. But the same is just not true of an embryo, whether left-over from IVF or deliberately created for research. Left alone, an extracorporeal embryo will just die. That's not much of a valuable future.

It might be argued that the blastocyst *could* be implanted into a uterus, where it too would develop into a baby, and thus it has, hypothetically, a valuable future. Of course, this is true only of viable embryos. Non-viable embryos—embryos incapable of further development—cannot have valuable futures. Presumably, even on Marquis's view, it would be morally permissible to use non-viable embryos left over from infertility treatment in embryo research (although I do not know if the stem cells derived from non-viable embryos could be used in treating disease should ES cell therapies ever be develop).

Most opponents of ES cell research make no distinction between embryos created by IVF and embryos created by cloning. However, on the Valuable Futures approach, there might be a considerable difference. We know that it is possible, under some set of conditions, for an IVF embryo to develop into a baby. Over 35,000 babies were born in the Untied States alone in 2000 (ASRM/SART Registry 2004). By contrast, biologist Rudof Jaenisch maintains that "a cloned embryo has little, if any, potential to develop into a normal human being." He explains:

> By circumventing the normal processes of gametogenesis and fertilization, nuclear cloning prevents the proper reprogramming of the clone's genome … which is a prerequisite for the development of an embryo into a normal organism. It is unlikely that these biologic barriers to normal development can be overcome in the foreseeable future.[25]

Jaenisch hastens to point out that the embryonic stem cells derived from a cloned embryo are functionally indistinguishable from those derived from IVF embryos, making them equally useful as a source for ES cells in research or therapy.

The chance a human embryo has of developing into a normal human being is irrelevant from the perspective of the biological humanity criterion. What matters for moral status is that the embryo is a human organism (although, as we have seen, there is considerable debate about when a human organism comes into existence). On this criterion, the moral status of the embryo is determined by its genetic humanity, not what it can or cannot develop into. Marquis, however,

explicitly rejects the genetic humanity criterion, because it is hard to see why a merely biological category should make a moral difference. Clearly, he is sympathetic to this objection expressed by pro-choicers: "why, it is asked, is it any more reasonable to base a moral conclusion on the number of chromosomes in one's cells than on the color of one's skin?"[26] By contrast, on the Valuable Futures approach, the developmental potential of an embryo makes all the difference in the world, since if a cloned embryo cannot develop into someone like you or me, it cannot have FLO. Killing it does not deprive it of its valuable future, and therefore, presumably, is not seriously wrong.

This has interesting implications for the "created/spare" distinction, appealed to by the National Bioethics Advisory Commission (NBAC) in its report, *Cloning Human Beings*. According to NBAC, it would be wrong to create embryos solely for the purpose of research; to do so would be inconsistent with the respect due to embryos as a form of human life. However, it would be ethically permissible to use embryos created for reproductive purposes, which are no longer needed (so-called "spare" embryos), since these embryos would be discarded anyway. President Bush considered this argument in his August 6, 2001 address to the nation, but ultimately rejected it. He maintained that it was impermissible to kill any embryos, even those that would be discarded anyway. On the valuable futures approach, it appears that the created/spare distinction has moral relevance, though precisely opposite to that claimed by NBAC. Whereas NBAC argued that only spare embryos can be ethically used (and destroyed) in research, in the valuable futures approach, it would be morally acceptable to use cloned human embryos as sources of stem cells since they lack FLO, but unacceptable to use embryos discarded after fertility treatment, since they have FLO. They have FLO because they could be used to make babies, even if their creators do not wish to use them for this purpose. This is a rather starting implication of the Valuable Futures argument. The claim that it is morally better to use cloned embryos rather than embryos left over from infertility treatment is not one that I have seen anywhere in the Valuable Futures literature.

My own view is that we should reject the created/spare distinction, although not for the reason President Bush gave. I think that it is permissible to use human embryos in research that kills them because embryos lack moral status. In my view, it makes no difference what the source of the embryos is, whether they are created by IVF or cloned; whether they are created specifically for research purposes or are left over from infertility treatment. However, I do not think it is permissible to use embryos for frivolous or trivial purposes. I maintain that respect for human life requires that human embryos be used for morally important purposes, but that is a topic for another paper.[27]

NOTES

1. S. G. Stolberg, "Controversy Reignites Over Stem Cells and Clones," *New York Times*, December 18, 2001, at F1.
2. R. M. Green, *The Human Embryo Research Debates* (New York: Oxford University Press, 2001): at p. 28.
3. *Id.*, at p. 29.
4. See also J. A. Robertson, *Children of Choice: Freedom and the New Reproductive Technologies* (Princeton: Princeton University Press, 1994): at 251, note 13: "… recent studies suggest that a new genome is not expressed until the four-to-eight-cell stage of development." See Braude, Bolton, and Moore, "Human Gene Expression First Occurs Between the Four and Eight-Cell Stage of Preimplantation Development," *Nature* 332 (1998): at p. 459, 460.
5. M. Warren, "On the Moral and Legal Status of Abortion," *The Monist* 57, no. 1, (1973): pp. 43–61. Warren's views have changed since 1973, and her current views on moral status are given in her book, *Moral Status*. Nevertheless, her earlier article is an excellent statement of the person view, a view that many people continue to hold.
6. I develop the interest view in Chapter 1 of my book, *Life Before Birth: The Moral and Legal Status of Embryos and Fetuses* (New York: Oxford University Press, 1992).
7. J. Feinberg, "The Rights of Animals and Unborn Generations," in William. T. Blackstone, ed., *Philosophy & Environmental Crisis* (Athens: University of Georgia Press, 1974).
8. J. Feinberg, *Harm to Others* (New York: Oxford University Press, 1984.): at p. 34.
9. D. Boonin, *A Defense of Abortion* (Cambridge: Cambridge University Press, 2003): at p. 102.
10. *Id.*, at pp. 102–103, citing T. Nagel, "What is it like to be a Bat?" in T. Nagel, *Mortal Questions* (Cambridge: Cambridge University Press, 1979): at p. 166.
11. Some philosophers apparently reject the idea that harming involves the setting back or thwarting of a being's interests. See, for example, E. Harman, "The Potentiality Problem," *Philosophical Studies* 114(2003): pp. 173–198. Harman thinks that it is obvious that beings without moral status can be harmed, and gives the following example: The deprivation of light harms a weed. However, the reason why I maintain that a weed is not harmed when it killed is not that weeds lack moral status. Rather, it is that I agree with Feinberg that harming involves the setting back or thwarting of interests. Since weeds (or prize orchids, for that matter) do not have interests, they cannot be harmed, though they can be killed. To show that this is wrong, one would need to give an alternate account of harming, something Harman does not do.
12. D. Marquis, "Why Abortion Is Immoral," *The Journal of Philosophy* 86, no. 4(1989): pp. 183–202, at pp. 189–190.
13. *Id.*, at p. 191.
14. In *Life Before Birth*, I argued that sentience was unlikely until well into the second trimester. "Pain perception requires more than brain waves. It is involves the development of neural pathways and particular cortical and subcortical centers, as well as neurochemical systems associated with pain transmission. In light of this, it seems extremely unlikely that a first-trimester fetus could be sentient," B. Steinbock, *supra* note 6, at 189. This is consistent with moral recent findings of researchers on fetal pain. Vivette Glober and Nicholas Fisk write, "To experience anything, including pain, the subject needs to be conscious, and current evidence suggests that this involves activity in the cerebral cortex and possibly the thalamus. We do not know for sure when or even if the fetus becomes conscious. However, temporary thalamocortical connections start to form at about 17 weeks and become established from 26 weeks. It seems very likely that a fetus can feel pain from that stage." V. Glover and N. Fisk, *British Medical Journal* 313 (1996): 796. For this reason, Glover and Fisk suggest that more attention should be paid to pain relief during labor and delivery for the baby as well as the mother,

and that safe methods of administering analgesia to the fetus in late terminations (after 20 weeks) should be developed. At the same time, in an interview with the BBC, Dr. Glover stressed that it is incredibly unlikely that a first-trimester fetus can feel pain because there is no linking to the brain at all. Editor, "Abortion Causes Foetal Pain," *BBC News, at* <(http://news.bbc.co.uk/1/hi/health/900848.stm> (last visited December 6, 2005).

15. D. Boonin, *A Defense of Abortion* (Cambridge: Cambridge University Press, 2003): at 65–66.

16. D. Marquis, "Abortion Revisited," in B. Steinbock, ed., *The Oxford Handbook of Bioethics* (Oxford: Oxford University Press, forthcoming).

17. Boonin, *supra* note 15, at 70.

18. *Id.*, at p. 76.

19. Marquis, *supra* note 16.

20. D. Marquis, "Justifying the Rights of Pregnancy: The Interest View," Review of Bonnie Steinbock," Life Before Birth," *Criminal Justice Ethics* 13, no. 1 (1994): pp. 67–81, at 72.

21. J. McMahan, *The Ethics of Killing: Problems at the Margins of Life* (New York: Oxford University Press, 2002): at p. 4.

22. Or as early as 17 weeks, if Glover and Fisk are right, *supra* note 14.

23. D. DeGrazia, "Identity, Killing, and the Boundaries of Our Existence," *Philosophy & Public Affairs* 31, no. 4 (2003): pp. 413–442, at p. 427.

24. Boonin, *supra* note 15, at xiv.

25. R. Jaenisch, "Human Cloning–The Science and Ethics of Nuclear Transplantation," *New England Journal of Medicine* 351, no. 27 (2004): pp. 2787–2791.

26. D. Marquis, *supra* note 12, at p. 186.

27. See B. Steinbock, "Respect for Human Embryos," in P. Lauritzen, ed., *Cloning and the Future of Human Embryo Research* (New York: Oxford University Press, 2001). See also B. Steinbock, "Moral Status, Moral Value, and Human Embryos: Implications for Stem Cell Research," in B. Steinbock, ed., *The Oxford Handbook of Bioethics* (Oxford: Oxford University Press, forthcoming).

⚜ QUESTIONS FOR ANALYSIS

1. Some defenders of embryonic stem cell research argue that because most of the frozen blastocysts will be discarded anyway, it is not unethical to use them in scientific research. Of the various positions on the status of embryos surveyed in Steinbock's article, which would be supportive of this position and why? The "common-sense view," as Steinbock calls it? Warren's "person view"? Feinberg's "interest principle" The "valuable futures" argument advanced by Marquis? McMahan's "mind essentialism"?

2. How does Steinbock distinguish between the moral status of IVF embryos and embryos created by cloning? Is medical research on cloned embryos less problematic ethically than research on IVF embryos, under her analysis?

3. Steinbock suggests that destroying embryos is justified for "morally important" purposes, but not for "frivolous or trivial" ones. What might be examples of those different purposes? Should this distinction be imposed on the decision to have an abortion? That is, should a woman have to prove that her reasons were not "frivolous or trivial" before she could get an abortion?

The Ethics of Synthetic Biology

Presidential Commission for the Study of Bioethical Issues

In May 2010, the J. Craig Venter Institute announced that it had created a self-replicating synthetic genome in a bacterial cell from a different species. This achievement, the first in the

From the report, *New Directions: The Ethics of Synthetic Biology and Emerging Technologies*, Presidential Commission for the Study of Bioethical Issues, Washington, DC, December 2010. Notes are omitted from these excerpts. Those notes and the full text of the report are available at the Commission's web site: http://bioethics.gov/synthetic-biology-report.

emerging field of "synthetic biology," raised numerous ethical concerns, despite its enormous potential. The field brings together specialists from biology, engineering, computer science, and chemistry to create new organisms with unusual characteristics. Many hailed the enormous potential of this work to create clean energy sources, medical advances, pollution control, and many other exciting discoveries. Others worried that this was the first step in artificially creating life.

In response, President Barack Obama asked the Presidential Commission for the Study of Bioethical Issues, to examine this developing field and recommend appropriate action and ethical constraints. The Commission, chaired by Amy Gutmann, President of the University of Pennsylvania, issued its report in December 2010. Following are excerpts from this report, including the ethical principles developed by the Commission.

The 21st century is widely heralded as the century of biology. Building on the fundamental understanding achieved in the second half of the last century, revolutionary advances are expected to improve many aspects of our lives, from clean energy and targeted, safer medicines to new industries. Prominent among emerging technologies is "synthetic biology," which aims to apply standardized engineering techniques to biology and thereby create organisms and biological systems with novel or specialized functions to address countless needs.

The idea of managing or manipulating biology to identify or develop specific characteristics is not new. Scientists have used DNA to create genetically engineered cells and organisms for many years; the entire biotechnology industry has grown around our expanding abilities in this area. The shelves of grocery stores across the United States are stocked with genetically engineered foods. Medical testing for genetically linked diseases is widely used by people across society.

By contrast, the idea of assembling living organisms wholesale from nonliving parts has intrigued human imagination for centuries with no success outside fiction. For some, that possibility came one step closer last May with the announcement that scientists at the J. Craig Venter Institute had created the world's first self-replicating synthetic (human-made from chemical parts) genome in a bacterial cell of a different species. Intense media coverage followed, and the announcement ricocheted across the globe within hours as proponents and critics made striking claims about potential risks and benefits of this discovery and whether it amounted to an early-stage example of "creating life."…

What the Commission found is that the Venter Institute's research and synthetic biology are in the early stages of a new direction in a long continuum of research in biology and genetics. The announcement last May, although extraordinary in many ways, does not amount to creating life as either a scientific or a moral matter. The scientific evidence before the Commission showed that the research relied on an existing natural host. The technical feat of synthesizing a genome from its chemical parts so that it becomes self-replicating when inserted into a bacterial cell of another species, while a significant accomplishment, does not represent the creation of life from inorganic chemicals alone. It is an indisputable fact that the human-made genome was inserted into an already living cell. The genome that was synthesized was also a variant of the genome of an already existing species. The feat therefore does not constitute the creation of life, the likelihood of which still remains remote for the foreseeable future. What remains realistic is the expectation that over time research in synthetic biology may lead to new products for clean energy, pollution control, and more affordable agricultural products, vaccines, and other medicines. The Commission therefore focused on the measures needed to assure the public that these efforts proceed with appropriate attention to social, environmental, and ethical risks.

President Obama gave the Commission a rare and exceptional opportunity in the world of presidential bioethics commissions to be forward looking instead of reactive. We are ahead of the emerging science, and this unique opportunity underscores the need for the government to act now to ensure a regular, ongoing process of review as the science develops. The Commission calls on the government to make its efforts transparent, to monitor risks, to support (through a peer-review process) the most publicly beneficial research, and to educate and engage with the public as this field progresses. The government must regularly review risk assessment and other issues as the science of synthetic biology progresses. Only through openness and active engagement with all the relevant communities will the government ensure ongoing public support and appropriate oversight. The Commission emphasizes the need to engage the public over time through improved science education, a publicly accessible fact-checking mechanisms for prominent advances in biotechnology, and other efforts promoting clearer communication on the state of science.

BASIC ETHICAL PRINCIPLES FOR ASSESSING EMERGING TECHNOLOGIES

To reach its recommendations, the Commission identified five ethical principles relevant to considering the social implications of emerging technologies: (1) public beneficence, (2) responsible stewardship, (3) intellectual freedom and responsibility, (4) democratic deliberation, and (5) justice and fairness. The principles are intended to illuminate and guide public policy choices to ensure that new technologies, including synthetic biology, can be developed in an ethically responsible manner.

The ideal of *public beneficence* is to act to maximize public benefits and minimize public harm. This principle encompasses the duty of a society and its government to promote individual activities and institutional practices, including scientific and biomedical research, that have great potential to improve the public's well-being. Public beneficence requires that when seeking the benefits of synthetic biology, the public and its representatives be vigilant about risks and harms, standing ready to revise policies that pursue potential benefits with insufficient caution.

The principle of *responsible stewardship* reflects a shared obligation among members of the domestic and global communities to act in ways that demonstrate concern for those who are not in a position to represent themselves (e.g., children and future generations) and for the environment in which future generations will flourish or suffer. Responsible stewardship recognizes the importance of citizens and their representatives thinking and acting collectively for the betterment of all. Importantly, it calls for *prudent vigilance*, establishing processes for assessing likely benefits along with assessing safety and security risks both before and after projects are undertaken. A responsible process will continue to assess safety and security as technologies develop and diffuse into public and private sectors. It will also include mechanisms for limiting their use when necessary.

Democracies depend on *intellectual freedom* coupled with the *responsibility* of individuals and institutions to use their creative potential in morally accountable ways. Sustained and dedicated creative intellectual exploration begets much of our scientific and technological progress. While many emerging technologies raise "dual use" concerns – when new technologies intended for good may be used to cause harm – these risks alone are generally insufficient to justify limits on intellectual freedom. As a corollary to the principle of intellectual freedom and responsibility, the Commission endorses a principle of *regulatory parsimony*, recommending only as much oversight as is truly necessary to ensure justice, fairness, security, and safety while pursuing the public good. This is particularly important in emerging technologies, which by their very definition are still in formation and are not well suited for sharply specified limitations. While clear guidelines to protect biosecurity and biosafety are imperative, undue restriction may not only inhibit the distribution of new benefits, but it also may be counterproductive to security and safety by presenting researchers from developing effective safeguards.

The principle of *democratic deliberation* reflects an approach to collaborative decision making that embraces respectful debate of opposing views and active participation by citizens. It calls for individuals and their representatives to work toward agreement whenever possible and to maintain mutual respect when it is not. Public discussion and debate with open interchange among all stakeholders can promote the perceived legitimacy of outcomes, even if those outcomes are unlikely to satisfy all interested parties. An inclusive process of deliberation, informed by relevant facts and sensitive to ethical concerns, promotes an atmosphere for debate and decision making that looks for common ground wherever possible and seeks to cultivate mutual respect where irreconcilable differences remain.

The principle of *justice and fairness* releates to the distribution of benefits and burdens across society. Biotechnology and emerging technologies such as synthetic biology, for good or ill, will affect all persons. Emerging technologies like synthetic biology will have global impacts. For this reason, every nation has a responsibility to champion fair and just systems to promote wide availability of information and fairly distribute the burdens and benefits of new technologies....

RISKS AND BENEFITS

There is considerable enthusiasm among advocates of synthetic biology for the varied benefits that this emerging field may yield for individuals and communities. Some critics have expressed concern, however, that synthetic biology will only exacerbate existing disparities with regard to health, welfare, and socioeconomic status. Similar concerns are often voiced in response to other new technologies.

Much of the optimism surrounding synthetic biology stems directly from its potential to address some of the longstanding, significant problems associated with those disparities. Synthetic biology offers potential applications that may be particularly beneficial to less advantaged populations, including improved quality and access to vaccines against infectious diseases, medications, and fuel sources. A just society recognizes the value of establishing incentives to create new knowledge and to translate it into vibrant markets in ways intended to distribute benefits widely. As new tools arrive and mature, it will be important to identify strategies to responsibly ensure that communities and nations who may most immediately benefit are empowered to do so. Doing so will require ongoing review of how intellectual property and licensing arrangements can best be structured to promote both scientific innovation and the public good.

Stakeholders should work collaboratively, aiming to ensure that advances made possible by synthetic biology reach those who could benefit from them, particularly less advantaged populations. Attention to the just distribution of potential benefits is most effective when continually examined in concert with research and development activities. It encourages an awareness of the full "life cycle" of a new application of synthetic biology, from initial research through potential global implementation. This holistic perspective recognizes that decisions made even in early stages of development may have consequences – technological, economic, or practical – that can affect the eventual implementation of potential research products positively or negatively.... Research and development activities throughout synthetic biology would be well served by similar appreciation of the relationships among current activities, potential future implementation concerns, and the concepts of justice and fairness.

⚜ QUESTIONS FOR ANALYSIS

1. The Commission argues that the accomplishments of synthetic biology to date do not constitute "the creation of life." How do they make that argument? Are you convinced?

2. The Commission identifies five basic ethical principles. How would the philosophers you have studied this semester, especially Mill, Aristotle, and Kant, evaluate those principles? Would they agree with all of them? Are all five principles consistent with each philosopher's ethical theories? Would they disagree with any?

3. Are there additional ethical principles that you believe should be added to this list?

4. What are the "dual use" concerns discussed by the Commission? What are examples of possible "dual uses" of synthetic biology that would concern you?

What other examples of scientific progress have created "dual use" problems?

5. Has the Commission proposed an appropriate balance of intellectual freedom with limitations against irresponsible research and development?

6. How should the principles of justice and fairness be implemented? Are the Commission's recommendations realistic? What steps would you urge should be taken to ensure that risks are balanced with benefits?

Stem Cells, Biotechnology, and Human Rights: Implications for a Posthuman Future

PAUL LAURITZEN

Professor of theology and religious studies and formerly the director of the Program in Applied Ethics at John Carroll University in Cleveland, Paul Lauritzen has written extensively on biomedical ethics. Here he expresses concern about research on both embryonic stem cells and adult stem cells. He believes that the debate has been cast too narrowly by all sides in the same terms used in the abortion debate. Instead, we should focus on the broader implications of the morality of the commodification of human lives.

… the final stage is come when man by eugenics, by prenatal conditioning, and by an education and propaganda based on perfect applied psychology, has obtained full control over himself. Human nature will be the last part of nature to surrender to man.

—C.S. LEWIS, The Abolition of Man

This sudden shift from a belief in Nurture, in the form of social conditioning, to Nature, in the form of genetics and brain physiology is the great intellectual event, to borrow Nietzsche's term, of the late twentieth century.

—TOM WOLFE, Hooking Up

I begin with passages from this unlikely pair of authors because, although they represent somewhat different times, differ in temperament, and differ extravagantly in personal style, they share an imaginative capacity to envision the possible consequences of modern technology. The technology that occasioned Lewis's reflections—"the

aeroplane, the wireless, and the contraceptive"—may now seem quaint, but the warning he sounded about turning humans into artifacts was eerily prescient. Similarly, although he does not directly take up stem cell research, Tom Wolfe's reflections on brain imaging technology, neuropharmacology, and genomics are worth noting in relation to the future of stem cell research. In his inimitable way, Wolf summarizes one view of the implications of this technology in the title of the essay from which the above passage comes. "Sorry," he says, "but your soul just died."

The point of beginning with Lewis and Wolfe is not that I share their dire predictions about the fate to which they believe technology propels us; instead, I begin with these writers because they invite use to take an expansive view of technology. I believe that a broader perspective is needed in the ongoing public debate over stem cell research and that such a perspective is in fact beginning to emerge.[1] This is not to say that the traditional analysis that has framed much of the

Paul Lauritzen, "Stem Cells, Biotechnology, and Human Rights: Implications for a Posthuman Future," *Hastings Center Report* 35:2 (March–April 2005): 25–33. Published with permission of John Wiley & Sons, Inc.

debate—analysis of autonomy, informed consent, and commodification, for example—is unhelpful; far from it. Nevertheless, much of the debate about stem cell research has focused on the enormously divisive issue of embryo status. Indeed, the debate about stem cell research seems almost choreographed, the steps all too familiar from the dance of abortion politics. The upshot is that much of the stem cell debate has been too narrowly focused and is repetitive and rigid.[2] For that reason, I urge that we consider stem cell research together with other forms of biogenetic research and therapy. Among other things, shifting the frame of reference in this way would require us to attend much more carefully to issues raised by adult stem cell work. Thus, instead of beginning with a question about embryo status, let us start with a question that has not typically been asked: Is adult stem cell work as unproblematic as it is often assumed to be?

Francis Collins's testimony before the President's Council on Bioethics in December 2002 suggests why this may be a productive question. Collins was asked to speak about "genetic enhancements: current and future prospects," and what he said about pre-implantation genetic screening is instructive. He noted that we are now able to screen both gametes and embryos, but because gamete screening is currently limited to sorting sperm for sex selection, he did not discuss it at length. He did, however, offer an interesting observation. Focusing on gametes, he says, is useful because it "isolates you away from some of the other compelling arguments about moral status of the embryo and allows a sort of cleaner discussion about what are the social goods or evils associated with broad alterations in the sex ratio and inequities in access to that technology."[3] In other words, the ethical issues raised by pre-implantation genetic screening are not limited to those brought about by the destruction of embryos required by PGD; indeed, screening gametes also raises serious moral issues, ones that might be eclipsed if we focus exclusively on embryos.

Might we not make a similar claim about embryonic and adult stem cell research? Adult stem cell research is often thought to sidestep some of the issues raised by work on embryonic stem cell, but in fact, does it not raise many of the most pressing issues surrounding embryonic stem cell research, only in a somewhat cleaner and more direct form?

I believe it does, and that we need to attend to a whole range of issues related to embodiment, species boundaries, and human nature that are raised by recent developments in what Bruce Jennings has referred to as the "regime of biopower."[4] I will discuss two broad concerns posed by stem cell research and related biotechnological interventions. The first has to do with the prospect of transforming the contours of human life in fairly dramatic ways. The second has to do with our attitudes toward the natural world. As we move to change the meaning of human embodiment in fundamental ways, including the possibility of eroding species boundaries, we need to ask whether we are prepared to reduce the entire natural world to the status of an artifact. These concerns raise questions about the meaning of human rights in a posthuman future.

EMBODIMENT, HUMAN RIGHTS AND HUMAN NATURE

To get a sense of what kinds of issues arise when we consider changing the contours of human existence, consider the notion that there is a species-typical pattern for human life that gives a determinate shape to our lives, a shape that has normative significance. On this view, there is a natural "trajectory" to human life, a natural ebb and flow from conception to death, that has implications for developing moral and political positions across a range of social issues, from reproductive technology to physician-assisted suicide. Yet stem cell research appears to challenge the idea of a natural trajectory to human life.

For example, Catherine Waldby and Susan Squier argue that the derivation of stem cells from early embryos demonstrates that embryos do not have one developmental trajectory. According to Waldby and Squier, stem cell research reveals the plasticity of early embryonic material, and in doing so demonstrates *the perfect contingency* of any relationship between embryo and person,

[and] the non-teleological nature of the embryo's developmental pathways." Indeed, they say, this research shows "that the embryo's life is not proto-human, and that the biology and biography of human life cannot be read backwards into its moments of orgin."[5] This claim may at first appear to be about embryo status, but Waldby and Squier mean to imply much more. In effect, they reject the notion that there is a meaningful trajectory to human life. What was killed when stem cells were first derived from the inner cell mass of a blastocyst, they say, was not a person, but a "biographical idea of human life, where the narrative arc that describes identity across time has been extended to include the earliest moments of ontogeny."[6]

That much more is at stake here than whether embryos are persons is clear if we attend to those who subscribe to the notion of a trajectory of a human life. Gilbert Meilaender, for example, has argued that our attitudes toward death and dying are shaped by our conception of what it means to have a life.[7] Indeed, according to Meilaender, two views of what it means to have a life and to be a person have been at war with each other over the past thirty years, and these views underwrite sharply different positions on practically every bioethical issue. On Meilaender's view, having a life means precisely that one is following a trajectory that traces a "natural pattern" that "moves through youth and adulthood toward old age and, finally, decline and death."[8] As he puts it, "to have a life is to be *terra animata*, a living body whose natural history has a trajectory."[9] Although Meilaender develops the notion of a natural trajectory primarily to address the issue of euthanasia, not stem cell research, talk of "natural history," "natural pattern," and "natural trajectory" is also relevant to stem cell research and related technologies. These new biotechnologies might fundamentally change our views about how and even whether a human life is constrained by the natural aging process. The question these biotechnologies raise, then, is whether such a change should be resisted.

There is little doubt that Meilaender would resist significant alteration of the natural trajectory, and other members of the President's Council on Bioethics, prominently Leon Kass and Francis Fukuyama, have raised similar concerns. But while those who oppose biotechnological interventions that may change the shape of the human life cycle are sometimes lumped together as "life cycle traditionalists," it is important to note that changing the trajectory of a life raises two distinct concerns.

The first is a more or less straightforward concern about the social consequences of altering the human life cycle. This concern is nicely illustrated by Francis Fukuyama's discussion of the social implications of dramatically lengthening the human life span in his book *Our Posthuman Future*. Suppose, he says, that regenerative medicine realizes its promise and the average life span expands from seventy to 110 years or more. What social dislocations can we expect? To explore this question, Fukuyama divides an aging cohort into two categories: the first category comprises people age sixty-five up to eighty-five; the second category is age eighty-five and older. The consequences of greatly expanding membership in these categories should give us pause, Fukuyama concludes, even if older people are much more vigorous than they are today.

"For virtually all of human history up to the present," he writes,

> people's lives and identities were bound up either with reproduction—that is, having families and raising children—or with earning the resources to support themselves and their families. Family and work both enmesh individuals in a web of social obligations over which they frequently have little control and which are a source of struggle and anxiety, but also of tremendous satisfaction. Learning to meet those social obligations is a source of both morality and character.
>
> People in Categories I and II, by contrast, will have a much more attenuated relationship to both family and work. They will be beyond reproductive years, with links primarily to ancestors and descendants. Some in Category I may choose to work, but the obligation to work and the kinds of mandatory social ties that work engenders will be replaced largely by a host of elective occupations. Those in Category II will not reproduce, not work, and indeed will see a flow of resources and obligation moving one way: toward them.[10]

Other possible negative consequences include a growing burden on the environment due to overpopulation, a prolongation of adolescent immaturity, increased burdens on an already strained health care system, and other social costs.[11]

The second concern is often expressed in terms of a threat to human identity or what it means to be human, and although this concern frequently has a consequentialist cast, it comes in a largely non-consequentialist form as well. Walter Glannon has developed the most interesting form of the identity argument. According to Glannon, one direct consequence of significantly increasing the human lifespan would be to attenuate the relationship among past, present, and future mental states of a self and thus undermine the psychological grounds of personal identity. Since a sense of psychological connectedness between the present and the future is necessary to ground future-oriented desires, the inevitable erosion of a sense of connectedness that would come with a much longer life would, paradoxically, result in the extinction of the desire for a longer life. Without a reasonably strong sense of psychological connectedness to some future self, one would have little reason to take an interest in the potential projects of that person.

In Glannon's formulation, there would be biological continuity between a present and distant future self, but psychological discontinuity: "there would be a divergence of our biology from our psychology."[12] Strictly speaking, it would be more accurate (and also more helpful) to say that a new biology would result in a new psychology. And, in fact, such a formulation is more consistent with Glannon's analysis, one aspect of which involves examining the formation-storage-retrieval process by which the brain maintains the equilibrium between remembering and forgetting that is critical to psychological unity. Discussing the function of activator and blocker CREB (cyclic AMP response element binary protein), Glannon writes:

> The function of this protein suggests that the requisite unity between these states can hold only for a limited period of time. Anticipation cannot extend so far into the future that it undermines memory of the past. By the same token, there cannot be

so much stored memory of past events that it comes at the expense of our ability to anticipate and plan for the future. A break in this equilibrium would ... undermine our ability to sustain long-term projects by breaking the unity of forward-and backward-looking attitudes necessary to ground these projects.[13]

In effect, the problem with increasing the lifespan is not that it causes psychology and biology to part company. Rather, changing the biology of human aging would profoundly change human psychology.

On one level, then, Glannon's concern about using stem cell therapies to significantly increase the human lifespan is a consequentialist worry about the psychological effects on humans of dissociating the present from the distant past or remote future. According to Glannon, we cannot rationally desire to lengthen the human life span because doing so would have disastrous consequences for our ability to undertake projects, accept responsibility for our past or future actions, or indeed, even care very much about "our" future. Notice, however, that there is a corollary to Glannon's maxim, as reformulated. If a new biology gives rise to a new psychology, it also gives rise to a new ethics. Or to put the point negatively, a new biology threatens our existing ethical commitments.

It is this kind of thought that animates the opposition of the life cycle traditionalists to biotechnologies that might alter the trajectory of a human life. When Leon Kass says that "many human goods ... are inseparable from our aging bodies, from our living in time, and from the natural life cycle," he has this worry in mind.[14] It is also a central concern of *Our Posthuman Future*. Fukuyama suggests that we can grasp the threat biotechnology poses by noting pervasiveness in modern moral discourse of the language of human rights, which is effectively the only available vocabulary for discussing human goods or ends. The most persuasive account of human rights, however, is framed in relation to the notion of a stable human nature.[15] According to Fukuyama, neither a religious conception of rights nor a positivist conception is viable. But once we recognize the relationship between human rights and human nature, we can give a very precise sense to the worry that we may be heading toward a posthuman future. The fear is that biotechnology will change the species-typical characteristics shared by all humans. If that happens, and if rights are tied to a conception of human nature that is in turn rooted in a biological reality, then biotechnology threatens the very basis of human morality as we know it.

Perhaps the life cycle traditionalists put more weight on the notion of human nature than it can reasonably bear. Still, the connection between a relatively stable set of natural capacities and the claims of human rights is important. Indeed, the sharp social and political disagreements between the life cycle traditionalists and more left-leaning theorists can lead us to overlook a shared commitment to the importance of identifying a stable set of natural human capacities. For example, although Martha Nussbaum is suspicious of the language of human nature because she thinks it has been misused to defend oppressive social structures, her work both on the human capacity for care and compassion and on basic conditions of human flourishing relies centrally on the notion of natural human capacities that give rise to basic human rights.

In a recent article, "Compassion & Terror," Nussbaum discusses Euripides' play *Trojan Women*, and explores the poet's sympathetic imagining of the fate of Trojan women and children in the course of developing her own reflections on the conditions and limits of a compassionate vision.[16] Although she is ultimately concerned about engendering such a vision for Americans in the face of terror—and particularly compassion for innocent women and children far from our shores—her analysis is also thought provoking in light of the future of biomedicine.

Nussbaum notes that compassion requires a series of judgments involving another person's suffering or lack of well-being. We must judge that someone has been harmed, that the harm is serious, and that it was not deserved. Moreover, says Nussbaum, the Western tradition has stressed what could be called the "judgment of similar possibilities." In other words, "we have compassion

only insofar as we believe that the suffering person shares vulnerabilities and possibilities with us."[17]

Surely, just about every person's catalog of human vulnerabilities includes illness, old age, and death. Yet arguably stem cell research may significantly transform the "human" experience of illness and death, at least for some. If stem cell therapies were to erode the notion of human nature, such as by blurring species boundaries, might they not also erode some basic moral sensibilities? Mary Midgley, for example, has argued that the notions of both human nature and human rights are importantly tied to membership in our species because rights are "supposed to guarantee the kind of life that all specimens of *Homo sapiens* need."[18]

Although Nussbaum avoids the language of human nature, it is precisely this sort of point that she highlights when she argues that compassion requires the belief that others share vulnerabilities and possibilities with us. Indeed, like Midgley, Nussbaum ties the notion of universal human rights to important human functions and capabilities. The basic idea, she says, is to ask what constitutes the characteristic activities of human beings: "What does the human being do, characteristically, as such—and not, say, as a member of a particular group, or a particular local community?"[19] Nussbaum notes that this inquiry proceeds by examining characteristic human activities in a wide variety of settings, and that comparing and contrasting human activities with the activities of nonhuman animals is helpful. So, too, is using myths and stories to compare humans and the gods. Such an inquiry, Nussbaum insists, helps us define limits that derive from membership in the natural world. Given the way that talk about "human nature" has been used in the past to exclude groups from full membership in the human moral community, there are good reasons to be careful about it. Nevertheless, unless we maintain some sense of nature that is not culturally constructed, we have no meaningful grounds for complaining about the lack of humane treatment of others.[20]

Indeed, although Nussbaum is exquisitely attentive to the wide variety of cultural interpretations of what it means to be human, she insists that a universal notion of human rights cannot be grounded unless one attends to human biology. Nussbaum's account of the human is neither ahistorical nor a priori; it is linked to an "empirical study of a species-specific form of life."[21] She begins her account of central human capabilities with the body:

> We live all our lives in bodies of a certain sort, whose possibilities and vulnerabilities do not as such belong to one human society rather than another. These bodies, similar far more than dissimilar (given the enormous range of possibilities) are our homes, so to speak, opening certain options and denying others, giving us certain needs and also certain possibilities for excellence. The fact that any given human being might have lived anywhere and belonged to any culture is a great part of what grounds our mutual recognitions; this fact, in turn, has a great deal to do with the general humanness of the body, its great distinctness from other bodies. The experience of the body is culturally shaped, to be sure; the importance we ascribe to its various functions is also culturally shaped. But the body itself, not culturally variant in its nutritional and other related requirements, sets limits on what can be experienced and valued, ensuring a great deal of overlap.[22]

Nussbaum's work is suggestive in another way, for she also notes how anxiety about our embodied existence, and the vulnerability that bodily existence entails, may be a profound impediment to compassion. I cannot do justice to the richness of Nussbaum's account of the emotional obstacles to compassion, but one aspect of her argument is worth noting here. In addition to analyzing the emotion of compassion, Nussbaum examines shame and digust.[23] Drawing on psychological studies of these emotions, she notes that both appear to concern a sense of vulnerability that arises from the fact that we are embodied beings. A sense of inadequacy may lead to the emotion of disgust, for example, which in turn serves to distance the self from its own vulnerabilities.

The problem with this emotional dynamic is the almost universal human tendency to project features of disgust outward, onto others, as a way of shoring up one's own sense of stability and power. "Throughout history," says Nussbaum, "certain disgust properties—sliminess, bad smell, stickiness, decay, foulness—have repeatedly and monotonously been associated with, indeed projected onto, groups by reference to whom privileged groups seek to define their superior human status."[24] Whether it is Jews, women, homosexuals, untouchables, or blacks who have been labeled and treated as disgusting, the underlying anxiety appears to be "the intolerance of humanity in oneself."[25]

Of course, once we label the other as disgusting, it is difficult to see the shared vulnerability that underwrites compassion. That is why social hierarchies based on class, race, religion, ethnicity, or gender are such impediments to compassion: they lead one group to see itself as vastly superior to another group and thus erode the possibility of seeing the common humanity of the other. In such a situation, compassion easily withers. Here, then we see the danger to which Nussbaum's work draws our attention. To the degree that applications of stem cell research may erode a sense of common humanity, and to the degree that such applications may promote a social hierarchy rooted in genetics, they run the risk of blocking compassion and advancing intolerance.

Nussbaum's work identifying the judgments that underwrite compassion and tying a universalist account of rights to common human function and capabilities highlights what may be at stake with stem cell research and with a growing list of biotechnological developments that appear to destabilize the concept of human nature. It suggests why we need to think carefully about the social implications of a situation in which some humans have access to these technologies while other humans do not. At the very least, what Paul Rabinow describes as the biologicalization of identity around genetics (rather than gender and race), combined with the possibility of manipulating genetic identity for those with the money or power to do so, does not bode well for securing widespread compassion across economic or technological divides. Even more important, however, is the recognition that the very notion of human rights may ultimately rest on the idea (and what, until recently, has always been the reality) of a natural, relatively stable human condition.

THE NATURAL WORLD AND INSTRUMENTALIZATION

A second, related worry is suggested by C.S. Lewis's warning about our unchecked hubris in seeking utter control over nature. It is not only human nature that we might destabilize, but the concept of "nature" generally and the appropriate treatment of any sentient life. Moreover, given how politically charged the concept of "human nature" is, we might do well, at least initially, to think about challenges to "human nature" by attending to views about "nature" generally, or the "nature" of non-human animals, or both.

These matters are not easily considered from within the typical frame of bioethics. Because the conceptual tools available in bioethics are not well suited to the task, I wish instead to turn to the cultural space that contemporary art provides for moral reflection on social issues posed by definitions of nature.

Patricia Piccinini has explored the issues raised by contemporary biotechnology in her sculptures, photographs, and video installations.[26] Piccinini's exhibition, "Call of the Wild," which appeared at the Museum of Contemporary Art in Sidney, Australia, is like much of her work in that it demonstrates "an interest in the human form and its potential for manipulation and enhancement through bio-technological intervention."[27] Also, like her other work, this exhibition explores the relationship between human and non-human animals as it is mediated by biotechnology. One of the works in the exhibition, "Protein Lattice," is designed to provoke discussion about the possibility of using non-human animals to grow tissue and organs for transplant to humans. It takes as its point of departure the effort to grow human ears on a three-dimensional protein lattice on the back of mice. The installation is quite complex, involving television monitors on which the viewer sees rats trapped in a maze. At the same time, large images of young digitally enhanced human female models are juxtaposed with rats that have human ears on their backs. The rats surround some of the models; others serve as perches for the rats. In another work, "Still Life with Stem Cells," Piccinini presents a young girl playing with a disturbing but still oddly attractive collection of tissue and organs sculpted to look like human flesh and intended to be seen as tissue grown from stem cells.

Although Piccinini's work should certainly be taken on its own aesthetic terms, it is illuminating to think about her work in light of Kass's defense of the "wisdom of repugnance." The images in her art are simultaneously beautiful and repulsive. Indeed, the artist makes clear her own ambivalence about biotechnology and sees her work partly as a vehicle for reflecting on how human manipulation of "nature" is both inspirational and frightening.[28] Jason Scott Robert and Françoise Baylis have recently insisted that if claims about repugnance are to have moral force, then "the intuitions captured by the 'yuck' response must be clarified."[29] One strategy for seeking clarification would be to catalog our reactions to work such as Piccinini's and explore those reactions in a sustained way. For example, the contrast between the beautiful models and the ugly rodents in "Protein Lattice" invites reflection on our views of beauty in relation to what we find repulsive. Why do we recoil from hairless mice with ears gown on their backs, but not from models with breast and lip implants? Why are the mice deemed "unnatural" and repulsive, but not the contestants of the television show "Extreme Makeover," whose bodies are arguably more "unnatural" than those of the mice? Addressing questions of this sort would be a start toward the clarification Robert and Baylis seek.

Or consider the issue of crossing species boundaries as it has been depicted and explored in the "transgenic art" of Eduardo Kac.[30] Several years ago, Kac made national and international headlines with a public art installation that included "Alba, the GFP Bunny." Alba was an albino rabbit that had been genetically modified by the insertion of a gene from a jellyfish that gave it a green fluorescent protein (GFP), causing it to glow green under certain light. Transgenic art, said Kac, is "a new art form based on the use of genetic engineering to transfer natural or synthetic genes to an organism, to create unique living beings."[31]

Many people were outraged at Kac's creation, and many dismissed his work as a publicity stunt, but in fact, part of the point of the Alba project was to generate a public conversation on the cultural and ethical implications of genetic engineering. According to Kac, "the creation of a chimerical animal forces us to examine notions of normalcy, heterogeneity, purity, hybridity and otherness."[32] Kac's work invites us to reflect on the implications of turning nonhuman animals into artifacts. To be sure, we have been doing that for a very long time. Still, it is worth asking whether creating unique living beings for our amusement or philosophical edification is morally justifiable.

That sort of question may be raised regularly in the literature on animal rights, but it is rarely asked in mainstream bioethics literature. Yet Peter Singer and others are surely right that non-human animals have natural capacities and needs and that they suffer when those capacities are thwarted and their needs go unmet. If we fail to notice this suffering, one reason is that we have ceased thinking of non-human animals as sentient beings and instead see them as machine-like. We thus fail to respect non-human animals precisely because we strip them of any determinate nature that might constrain our actions.

The significance of this point to stem cell research is that it may help us to see the reductionism of much contemporary research that understands the humans body simply as material to be manipulated. Think, for example, of the metaphors that have dominated genomic research—the genome as a book or library, the mapping of the genome as conquering a wilderness—and how these metaphors encourage us to think of the body, to borrow Courtney Campbell's words, as "an exploitable natural resource whose contents are of more interest than the integrity of the whole."[33] Arguably we have lost any sense of the "integrity of the whole" in our disregard for nonhuman animals, and we may now be losing it about humans as well.[34]

MERE "NATURE"

Despite the overwhelming preoccupation with questions of embryo status, ultimately the fundamental question raised by stem cell research is not about the embryo. Instead, it is about the future toward which biotechnology beckons us. Most succinctly, the question is: Does contemporary bio-technology, including or perhaps especially stem cell research, open the door to a post human future? Waldby and Squier raise this question explicitly when they discuss the combination of genetic engineering and stem cell therapy. They suggest that xenotransplanation forces us to confront the prospect of transgressing species boundaries.[35] When a graft involves genetically engineered stem cells from another species, questions are raised not just about the ontological status of the graft recipient, but about the illnesses to which the bio-medical technology is responding. Even the line between veterinary and human medicine may be called into question. "Stream cell technologies," Waldby and Squier write, "thus challenge both the temporal and spatial boundaries of human life, both our biography and our biological niche."[36]

Regrettably, with some notable exceptions, the ethical debate about steam cell research has not taken up in a sustained way what it would mean to pursue stem cell therapies that might significantly undermine the notion of a natural human life or erode the boundary between human and non-human species.[37] Since the status of the embryo has received so much attention, questions about the implications of pursuing adult stem cell research have not been systematically asked or answered. Given the potential for alleviating human suffering embedded in the prospects of stem cell research, it is not surprising that there appears to be widespread and largely uncritical acceptance of adult stem cell work. Nevertheless, if the promise of stem cell research is as revolutionary as is often claimed, we are going to need a much more expansive discussion of both embryonic and adult stem cell work than we have had.

I began this article with a passage from C.S. Lewis's essay "The Abolition of Man," and I end with another. Lewis writes:

> Now I take it that when we understand a thing analytically and then dominate and use it for our own convenience we reduce it to the level of "Nature" in the sense that we suspend our judgments of value about it, ignore its final cause (if any), and treat it in terms of quantity. The repression of elements in what would otherwise be our total reaction to

it is sometimes very noticeable and even painful: something has to be overcome before we can cut up a dead man or a live animal in a dissecting room.[38]

Although it is perhaps justifiable to reduce the world of nature to *mere* nature, I am inclined to agree with Lewis that something is lost when we do so. Re-reading "The Abolition of Man" in the context of debates about stem cell research, I was struck by the fact that the sort of dynamic Lewis describes in his essay is very close to that recorded in Jonathan Glover's impressive work, *Humanity: A Moral History of the Twentieth Century*.[39] Glover writes that "Human responses are the core of the humanity which contrasts with inhumanity. They are widely distributed, but to identify them with humanity is only partly an empirical claim. It remains also partly an aspiration." As Glover powerfully argues, morality must be rooted in human needs and values, and these needs and values are both rooted in "human nature" and grounded in human aspiration.

As we wrestle with issues of stem cell research, we ought to be conscious of what is at stake in the possibility of redefining either our natures or our aspirations, for as Glover makes clear, the inhumanity of humans is frightening and all too familiar.

ACKNOWLEDGMENT

This essay is a substantially revised version of the report I prepared for the President's Council on Bioethics on recent literature on the ethics of stem cell research. A number of people either helped with the preparation of the report or provided feedback on an earlier draft of this work. Thanks to Christa Adams, Diana Fritz Cates, William Fitz Patrick, James L. Lissemore, Charlie Ponyik, Mary Jane Ponyik, Kristie Varga, Lisa Wells, Lee Zwanziger, and the ethics writers' group at John Carroll University. I am also grateful to the members of the President's Council for their comments on the report.

NOTES

1. See E. Parens and L.P. Knowles, "Reprogenetics and Public Policy: Reflections and Recommendations," *Hastings Center Report*, Special Supplement, 33, no. 4 (2003). See also the report of the President's Council on Bioethics, *Reproduction and Responsibility: The Regulation of New Biotechnologies*, which explores "the intersection of the technologies of assisted reproduction, human genomic knowledge and techniques, and human embryo research" (Washington, D.C.: President's Council on Bioethics, 2004).

2. For exceptions to this generalization, see R. R. Faden et al., "Public Stem Cell Banks: Considerations of Justice in Stem Cell Research and Therapy," *Hastings Center Report* 33, no. 6 (2003): pp. 13–27; H. Bok, K. E. Schill, and R. R. Faden, "Justice. Ethnicity, and Stem-Cell Banks," *The Lancet* vol. 364 (July 2004): pp. 118–21.

3. "Testimony before the Presidents Council on Bioethics" (December 13, 2002). Available at: http://www.bioethics.gov/transcripts/dec02/session5.html.

4. Jennings defines the regime of biopower as the effort to make or remake the world in the realm of the biological. In relation to medicine, it refers to technologies that promise (or have delivered) significant interventions on the human body. See B. Jennings, "The Liberalism of Life: Bioethics in the Face of Biopower," *Raritan* 22, no. 4 (spring, 2003): pp. 133–46. On the theme of understanding life forms as manufactured products, see S. Krimsky, *Biotechnics and Society: The Rise of Industrial Genetics* (New York: Praeger, 1991).

5. C. Waldby and S. Squier, "Ontogeny, Ontology, and Phylogeny: Embryonic Life and Stem Cell Technologies," *Configurations* 11, no. 1 (2003): 33. See also S. Squier, *Liminal Lives: Imagining the Human at the Frontiers of Biomedicine* (Durham, N.C.: Duke University Press, 2004).

6. Ibid, p. 36.

7. G. Meilaender, "*Terra as animate*: On Having a Life," *Hastings Center Report* 23, no. 4 (1993): pp. 25–32.

8. Ibid., p. 29.

9. Ibid., p. 31.

10. F. Fukuyama, *Our Posthuman Future* (New York: Farrar, Strous and Giroux, 2002), pp. 70–71.

11. See W. Glannon, "Extending the Human Life Span," *The Journal of Medicine and Philosophy* 27, no. 3 (2002): pp. 339–54.

12. W. Glannon, "Identity, Prudential Concern, and Extended Lives," *Bioethics* 13, no. 3 (2002): p. 276.

13. Ibid., pp. 279–80.

14. L. Kass, "Ageless Bodies, Happy Souls," *The New Atlantis* 1 (2003): p. 12.

15. For an account of human rights that disputes this claim, see M. Ignatieff, "Human Rights as Idolatry," in *Human Rights as Politics and Idolatry*, ed. A. Gutman (Princeton, N.J.: Princeton University Press, 2001)

16. M.C. Nussbaum, "Compassion and Terror," *Daedalus* 128, no. 4 (2003): pp. 10–26.

17. Ibid., 16. Diana Fritz Cates has criticized Nussbaum's account of compassion, particularly Nussbaum's insistence that compassion requires the judgment that the person suffers undeservedly. Cates notes that this condition is sharply at odds with the understanding of compassion in some Buddhist and Christian traditions. D.F. Cates, "Conceiving Emotions: Martha Nussbaum's Upheavals of Thought," *Journal of Religious Ethics* 31 (2003): pp. 325–41. Shared possibilities/vulnerabilities can still be crucial, however. Nussbaum offers a subtly different account of the importance of shared vulnerabilities in *Upheavals of Thought* (New York: Cambridge University Press, 2001). See especially pp. 315–21. Thanks to Tom Schubeck for pressing me on this point.

18. M. Midgley, "Biotechnology and Monstrosity: Why We Should Pay Attention to the 'Yuk Factor,'" *Hastings Center Report* 30, no. 5 (2000): 9. See also M. Midgley, *Animals and Why They Matter* (Athens, Ga: University of Georgia Press, 1983).

19. M.C. Nussbaum, "Human Capabilities, Female Human Beings," in *Women, Culture, and Development: A Study of Human Capabilities*, ed. M.C. Nussbaum and J. Glover (Oxford, U.K.: Clarendon Press, 1995), 72.

20. K. Soper, *What Is Nature? Culture, Politics and the Non-Human* (Cambridge, Ma.: Blackwell, 1995).

21. Ibid., p. 75.

22. Ibid., p. 76.

23. Nussbaum, *Upheavals of Thought*. See also M.C. Nussbaum, 'Secret Sewers of Vice': Disgust, Bodies, and the Law," in *The Passion of Law*, ed. S. Bandes (New York: New York University Press, 1999).

24. Nussbaum, *Upheavals of Thought*, 347.

25. Ibid., p. 350.

26. http://www.patriciapiccinini.net/, accessed December 30, 2004.

27. See R. Kent, "Fast Forward: Accelerated Evolution." Available at: http://www.patriciapiccinini.net/.

28. P. Piccinini, "Artist Statement" (1999). Available at: http://ww.patricia piccinini.net//, accessed December 30, 2004.

29. J.S. Robert and F. Baylis, "Crossing Species Boundaries," *American Journal of Bioethics* 3, no. 3 (2003): pp. 1–13.

30. For a very interesting study of nonhuman animals in postmodern art, see S. Baker, *The Postmodern Animal* (London, U.K.: Reaktion Books, 2000).

31. "GFP Bunny," July 16, 2004, http://www.ekac.org/gfpbuny.html#gfpbunnyanchor, accessed December 30, 2004.

32. E. Kac, "GFP Bunny." For a discussion of Kac's work, see *The Eighth Day: The Transgenic Art of Eduardo Kac*, ed. S. Britton and D. Collins (Tempe, Ariz.: Arizona State University, 2003).

33. C. Campbell, "Source or Resource? Human Embryo Research as an Ethical Issue," in *Cloning and the Future of Human Embryo Research*, ed. P. Lauritzen (New York: Oxford University Press, 2001), p. 44.

34. W.S. Merwin captured the danger of this kind of reductionism in a poem entitled, "Dog": "Whatever he was to guard/Is gone. Besides, his glazed eyes/ Fixed heavily ahead stare beyond you/ Noticing nothing; he does not see you. But wrong:/ Look again: it is through you/that he looks, and the danger of his eyes/Is that in them you are not there ..." in *Green with Beasts* (London, U.K.: Hart-Davis, 1956).

35. Although he is not discussing stem cell research explicitly, Paul Rabinow's discussion of technological change during the last two decades is helpful. P. Rabinow, *French DNA: Trouble in Purgatory* (Chicago, III.: The University of Chicago Press, 1999), 13. See also L. Sharp, "The Commodification of the Body and Its Parts," *Annual Review of Anthropology* 29 (2000): pp. 287–328.

36. Waldby and Squier, "Ontogeny, Ontology, and Phylogeny," p. 46.

37. Donna Haraway has argued that concerns about boundary crossing are reminiscent of racial and immigration discourses of an earlier era. "In the appeal to intrinsic natures," she writes, "I detect a mystification of kind and purity akin to the doctrines of white racial hegemony and U.S. national integrity and purpose." ("Mice into Wormholes," in *Cyborgs and Citadels*, ed. G.L. Downey and J. Dumit (Santa Fe, N.M.: School of America Research Press, 1997), p. 218).

38. C.S. Lewis, "The Abolition of Man," *The Abolition of Man* (New York: Macmillan, 1947), p. 81.

39. J. Glover, *Humanity: A Moral History of the Twentieth Century* (New Haven, Conn.: Yale University Press, 1999).

⚜ **QUESTIONS FOR ANALYSIS**

1. What does Lauritzen mean by "a meaningful trajectory to human life"? How does he believe this is altered by stem cell research of any kind? Does every improvement in medicine, nutrition, and living conditions that extends our life span alter this trajectory? How, if at all, is stem cell research different in kind, not just in degree, from the long history of improvements in human health and longevity?

2. In what way does our understanding of human rights depend on a "natural, relatively stable human condition"? How can we revise our notion of human rights to recognize genetic alterations increasingly possible through science?

3. Lauritzen laments that contemporary scientific research considers the human body "simply as material to be manipulated." In what other ways *should* we consider the human body? Do artistic creations and literary metaphors assist us in thinking more expansively about the nature of human life? How should we think about ourselves, other than as "material to be manipulated"?

4. What might a "posthuman future" be like? Assuming it might someday be possible to cross species boundaries, what would you consider your ideal form of existence?

CASE PRESENTATION

Cloning: Recommendations of the President's Council on Bioethics[1]

The prospect of human cloning has been the subject of considerable public attention and sharp moral debate, both in the United States and around the world. Since the announcement in February 1997 of the first successful cloning of a mammal (Dolly the sheep), several other species of mammals have been cloned. Although a cloned human child has yet to be born, and although the animal experiments have had low rates of success, the production of functioning mammalian cloned offspring suggests that the eventual cloning of humans must be considered a serious possibility.

The following recommendations from the President's Council on Bioethics were published in 2002 and are representative of the debates and objections raised by many over cloning. The Council had been established by President George W. Bush in November 2001 shortly after his announcement limiting stem cell research to existing cell lines. It was chaired by Leon Kass of the University of Chicago and later by Edmund Pellegrino of Georgetown University

The Council was disbanded by President Barack Obama in June 2009. All reports by the Council have been archived on a government website: http://www.bioethics.gov/. President Obama established a new Presidential Commission for the Study of Bioethical Issues on March 10, 2010.

Critics of the Bush Council complained that it was stacked with conservatives who rationalized policies developed by President Bush. Critics of President Obama's new Commission claimed that he was merely seeking to avoid criticism of his new executive order permitting expanded stem cell research, issued in March 2009. The Commission has been chaired since 2009 by Amy Gutmann, President of the University of Pennsylvania. A wide range of projects has been undertaken, including "The Ethics of Synthetic Biology and Emerging Technologies" and "Privacy and Progress in Whole Genome Sequencing."

PUBLIC POLICY OPTIONS

The Council recognizes the challenges and risks of moving from moral assessment to public policy. Reflections on the "social contract" between science and society highlight both the importance of scientific freedom and the need for boundaries. We note that other countries often treat human cloning in the context of a broad area of biomedical technology, at the intersection of reproductive technology, embryo

---

[1]This is excerpted from the executive summary of the Council's report, *Human Cloning and Human Dignity: An Ethical Inquiry*, Washington U.S. Government, 2002. Other chapters in the report include discussions of the historical, scientific, and ethical issues surrounding cloning. The full text is archived at http://bioethics.georgetown.edu/pcbe/reports/cloningreport/

research, and genetics, while the public policy debate in the United States has treated cloning largely on its own. We recognize the special difficulty in formulating sound public policy in this area, given that the two ethically distinct matters—cloning-to-produce-children and cloning-for-biomedical-research—will be mutually affected or implicated in any attempts to legislate about either. Nevertheless, our ethical and policy analysis leads us to the conclusion that some deliberate public policy at the federal level is needed in the area of human cloning.

We reviewed the following seven possible policy options and considered their relative strengths and weaknesses: (1) Professional self-regulation but no federal legislative action ("self-regulation"); (2) A ban on cloning-to-produce-children, with neither endorsement nor restriction of cloning-for-biomedical-research ("ban plus silence"); (3) A ban on cloning-to-produce-children, with regulation of the use of cloned embryos for biomedical research ("ban plus regulation"); (4) Governmental regulation, with no legislative prohibitions ("regulation of both"); (5) A ban on all human cloning, whether to produce children or for biomedical research ("ban on both"); (6) A ban on cloning-to-produce-children, with a moratorium or temporary ban on cloning-for-biomedical-research ("ban plus moratorium"); or (7) A moratorium or temporary ban on all human cloning, whether to produce children or for biomedical research ("moratorium on both").

THE COUNCIL'S POLICY RECOMMENDATIONS

Having considered the benefits and drawbacks of each of these options, and taken into account our discussions and reflections throughout this report, the Council recommends two possible policy alternatives, each supported by a portion of the Members.

Majority Recommendation: Ten Members of the Council recommend a ban on cloning-to-produce-children combined with a four-year moratorium on cloning-for-biomedical-research. We also call for a federal review of current and projected practices of human embryo research, pre-implantation genetic diagnosis, genetic modification of human embryos and gametes, and related matters, with a view to recommending and shaping ethically sound policies for the entire field. Speaking only for ourselves, those of us who support this recommendation do so for some or all of the following reasons:

- By permanently banning cloning-to-produce-children, this policy gives force to the strong ethical

verdict against cloning-to-produce-children, unanimous in this Council (and in Congress) and widely supported by the American people. And by enacting a four-year moratorium on the creation of cloned embryos, it establishes an additional safeguard not afforded by policies that would allow the production of cloned embryos to proceed without delay.

- It calls for and provides time for further democratic deliberation about cloning-for-biomedical research, a subject about which the nation is divided and where there remains great uncertainty. A national discourse on this subject has not yet taken place in full, and a moratorium, by making it impossible for either side to cling to the status-quo, would force both to make their full case before the public. By banning all cloning for a time, it allows us to seek moral consensus on whether or not we should cross a major moral boundary (creating nascent cloned human life solely for research) and prevents our crossing it without deliberate decision. It would afford time for scientific evidence, now sorely lacking, to be gathered—from animal models and other avenues of human research—that might give us a better sense of whether cloning-for-biomedical-research would work as promised, and whether other morally nonproblematic approaches might be available. It would promote a fuller and better-informed public debate. And it would show respect for the deep moral concerns of the large number of Americans who have serious ethical objections to this research.

- Some of us hold that cloning-for-biomedical-research can never be ethically pursued, and endorse a moratorium to enable us to continue to make our case in a democratic way. Others of us support the moratorium because it would provide the time and incentive required to develop a system of national regulation that might come into use if, at the end of the four-year period, the moratorium were not reinstated or made permanent. Such a system could not be developed overnight, and therefore even those who support the research but want it regulated should see that at the very least a pause is required. In the absence of a moratorium, few proponents of the research would have much incentive to institute an effective regulatory system. Moreover, the very process of proposing such regulations would clarify the moral and prudential judgments involved in deciding whether and how to proceed with this research.

- A moratorium on cloning-for-biomedical-research would enable us to consider this activity in the larger context of research and technology in the areas of developmental biology, embryo research, and genetics, and to pursue a more comprehensive federal regulatory system for setting and executing policy in the entire area.

- Finally, we believe that a moratorium, rather than a lasting ban, signals a high regard for the value of biomedical research and an enduring concern for patients and families whose suffering such research may help alleviate. It would reaffirm the principle that science can progress while upholding the community's moral norms, and would therefore reaffirm the community's moral support for science and biomedical technology.

The decision before us is of great importance. Creating cloned embryos for any purpose requires crossing a major moral boundary, with grave risks and likely harms, and once we cross it there will be no turning back. Our society should take the time to make a judgment that is well-informed and morally sound, respectful of strongly held views, and representative of the priorities and principles of the American people. We believe this ban-plus-moratorium proposal offers the best means of achieving these goals....

Minority Recommendation: Seven Members of the Council recommend a ban on cloning-to-produce-children, with regulation of the use of cloned embryos for biomedical research. Speaking only for ourselves, those of us who support this recommendation do so for some or all of the following reasons:

- By permanently banning cloning-to-produce-children, this policy gives force to the strong ethical verdict against cloning-to-produce-children, unanimous in this Council (and in Congress) and widely supported by the American people. We believe that a ban on the transfer of cloned embryos to a woman's uterus would be a sufficient and effective legal safeguard against the practice.

- It approves cloning-for-biomedical-research and permits it to proceed without substantial delay. This is the most important advantage of this proposal. The research shows great promise, and its actual value can only be determined by allowing it to go forward now. Regardless of how much time we allow it, no amount of experimentation with animal models can provide the needed understanding of human diseases. The special benefits from working with stem cells from cloned human embryos cannot be obtained using embryos obtained by IVF. We believe this research could provide relief to millions of Americans, and that the government should therefore support it, within sensible limits imposed by regulation.

- It would establish, as a condition of proceeding, the necessary regulatory protections to avoid abuses and misuses of cloned embryos. These regulations might touch on the secure handling of embryos, licensing and prior review of research projects, the protection of egg donors, and the provision of equal access to benefits.

- Some of us also believe that mechanisms to regulate cloning-for-biomedical-research should be part of a larger regulatory program governing all research involving human embryos, and that the federal government should initiate a review of present and projected practices of human embryo research, with the aim of establishing reasonable policies on the matter.

Permitting cloning-for-biomedical-research now, while governing it through a prudent and sensible regulatory regime, is the most appropriate way to allow important research to proceed while insuring that abuses are prevented. We believe that the legitimate concerns about human cloning expressed throughout this report are sufficiently addressed by this ban-plus-regulation proposal, and that the nation should affirm and support the responsible effort to find treatments and cures that might help many who are suffering ...

⚜ QUESTIONS FOR ANALYSIS

1. All members of President Bush's council agree on recommending a permanent ban on cloning-to-produce-children. Are there developments in medical research that might someday justify permitting such cloning? Are the ethical concerns about cloning-to-produce-children sufficiently strong that no scientific advances would ever justify permitting such cloning?

2. A majority of the council recommends a four-year moratorium on cloning-for-biomedical-research to allow the nation time for further deliberation on the moral issues presented by such research. What additional ethical issues should be examined in an effort to reach the moral consensus sought by these council members? As some of these members state that they do not believe

cloning-for-biomedical-research can ever be ethically pursued, is this recommendation just a stalling tactic?

3. A minority of the council recommends allowing cloning-for-biomedical-research immediately, with appropriate government regulation to avoid abuses and misuses of cloned embryos. Why is this group of council members eager to permit this research? Would government regulation be sufficient to protect against possible abuses and overcome the ethical concerns of the majority?

CASE PRESENTATION

A Birth to Save a Life

When Louise Brown, the world's first "test-tube" baby, was born in Oldham, England, she and her parents became instant international celebrities. But that was back in 1978, an entirely different era in terms of reproductive technology. Today, by contrast, in vitro fertilization is an everyday aid in helping women to conceive, not just in the industrialized West but also in such countries as Egypt, Malaysia, and Pakistan. Whether the sperm comes from the woman's husband or an anonymous donor, it is routinely joined with her egg in a laboratory, and just as routinely the newly formed embryo is implanted in the woman's womb. Rarely do these procedures make news.

But the *Washington Post* found one such case newsworthy when it reported in October 2000 that Adam Nash, a test-tube baby, had been conceived and born to save his sister's life. The sister, six-year-old Molly Nash, was born with Franconi anemia, an inherited disease that prevents the production of bone marrow cells. Children who suffer from the condition usually die from leukemia or some other complication by the age of seven, and Molly had already developed a blood condition her doctors called "pre-leukemia." The only effective treatment for Franconi anemia is a successful cell transplant.

Unlike Louise's conception, Adam's involved another, more recent technique as well: preimplantation genetic diagnosis, which allows scientists to examine the genes of an embryo before it's implanted in the womb. Fifteen embryos were created for the Nashes, and researchers at Illinois Masonic Medical Center tested each of them for two genetic traits. First, it had to be free of Franconi anemia; second, it had to be a perfect match for Molly. Two embryos passed, one was implanted, and on August 29, 2000, Adam was born in a Denver hospital, where doctors painlessly removed the needed donor cells from his umbilical cord. A month later, they were introduced into his sister's bloodstream. According to the director of medical genetics at the center that performed the tests, Molly had an 85 to 90 percent chance of being free of the disease. And in an article that appeared in the *New York Times* the following day, the doctor who performed the transplant said that Molly's blood tests had already begun to improve.

What made the story newsworthy was the Nashes' reason for using preimplantation genetic diagnosis. In previous cases, it had been used to select genes that were best for the health of the future child. In this case, it was used for Molly's benefit. That makes Adam's conception and birth the first case in which modern reproductive technology and genetic testing combined to create a suitable donor for a transplant. It will not, however, be the last. Before the story was even reported, ten other families had begun preparing for the same procedure.

Despite the procedure's promise for such families, the articles in both newspapers raised identical ethical questions. As bioethicist Jeffrey P. Kahn told the *Times*, "We've crossed the line that we really never crossed before, selecting based on characteristics that are not best for the child being born, but for somebody else." Dr. Kahn also posed a moral dilemma that goes well beyond the technologies used for the Nashes: "Nobody wants babies to be born strictly for the parts they could create, but by the same token, I don't think we're willing as a society to ask people why they're having children and to say, 'That's not a good enough reason.'"

The other ethical question concerns "designer" babies. "You could say it's like buying a new car, where you decide which package of accessories you want," said Dr. Kahn, this time speaking to the *Post*. "I suppose it's only because we don't yet have the tests that we're not having parents asking for embryos without a predisposition to homosexuality or for kids who will grow to more than six feet tall."

1. Is it morally wrong to create a child for "parts," as the Nashes did? Would it be wrong to use cloning for the same purpose?
2. Are there good and bad reasons for having children? For using reproductive technologies or the genetic testing of embryos? If so, what distinguishes the good from the bad? How closely does the distinction parallel the distinction between good and bad reasons for creating a clone?
3. What, if any, moral concerns does the prospect of choosing embryos for a variety of traits—beauty, say, or athletic ability—raise? How close are they to the moral concerns raised by cloning?

4. Earlier in this chapter, we discussed the case of Abe and Mary Ayala, who conceived and bore a child to provide a compatible donor for their leukemia-stricken daughter. Do you see any important difference between what they did and what the Nashes did?
5. For whatever reasons the Nashes and Ayalas conceived their youngest children, they ended up loving them as much as their other children. Does that make the reasons irrelevant?

CASE PRESENTATION

Stem Cells: Presidential Policy

In November 1998, a group of scientists led by James Thomson at the University of Wisconsin announced that they had created a line of stem cells out of human embryos a few days after in vitro fertilization. A panel of experts at the National Institutes of Health then developed policies for the funding of research on these embryonic stem cells. Among the requirements were that the embryos had been donated by a couple for research after fertility treatments and were no longer needed by that couple. Before these policies could be implemented, however, George W. Bush became president and came under considerable pressure to ban such research completely. He announced his policy in a televised speech on August 9, 2001.

In his speech, President Bush limited funding for research to the stem cell lines then in existence. Although he claimed that sixty stem cell lines were in existence, scientists complained that most had been mixed with blood products from rodents, making their usefulness for research doubtful. Critics of President Bush's policy also noted that he never proposed legislation banning in vitro fertilization, as it inevitably produces excess embryos that are later discarded. The strongest opponents of stem cell research objected to using even those sixty existing lines, because doing so implicitly condoned what they considered the taking of human life.

On March 9, 2009, President Barack Obama issued an Executive Order lifting the research ban imposed

by President Bush eight years earlier and directing the National Institutes of Health to issue guidelines for federal funding. Those guidelines were announced on July 6, 2009, and went into effect immediately. The following are remarks President Obama made at the signing of the new Executive Order:

Today, with the Executive Order I am about to sign, we will bring the change that so many scientists and researchers; doctors and innovators; patients and loved ones have hoped for, and fought for, these past eight years: we will lift the ban on federal funding for promising embryonic stem cell research. We will vigorously support scientists who pursue this research. And we will aim for America to lead the world in the discoveries it one day may yield.

At this moment, the full promise of stem cell research remains unknown, and it should not be overstated. But scientists believe these tiny cells may have the potential to help us understand, and possibly cure, some of our most devastating diseases and conditions. To regenerate a severed spinal cord and lift someone from a wheelchair. To spur insulin production and spare a child from a lifetime of needles. To treat Parkinson's, cancer, heart disease and others that affect millions of Americans and the people who love them.

But that potential will not reveal itself on its own. Medical miracles do not happen simply by accident. They result from painstaking and costly research—from years of lonely trial and error, much of which never bears fruit—and from a government willing to support that work. From life-saving vaccines, to pioneering cancer treatments, to the sequencing of the human genome—that is the story of scientific progress in America. When government fails to make these investments, opportunities are missed. Promising avenues go unexplored. Some of our best scientists leave for other countries that will sponsor their work. And those countries may surge ahead of ours in the advances that transform our lives.

But in recent years, when it comes to stem cell research, rather than furthering discovery, our government has forced what I believe is a false choice between sound science and moral values. In this case, I believe the two are not inconsistent. As a person of faith, I believe we are called to care for each other and work to ease human suffering. I believe we have been given the capacity and will to pursue this research—and the humanity and conscience to do so responsibly.

It is a difficult and delicate balance. Many thoughtful and decent people are conflicted about, or strongly oppose, this research. I understand their concerns, and we must respect their point of view.

But after much discussion, debate and reflection, the proper course has become clear. The majority of Americans—from across the political spectrum, and of all backgrounds and beliefs—have come to a consensus that we should pursue this research. That the potential it offers is great, and with proper guidelines and strict oversight, the perils can be avoided.

That is a conclusion with which I agree. That is why I am signing this Executive Order, and why I hope Congress will act on a bi-partisan basis to provide further support for this research. We are joined today by many leaders who have reached across the aisle to champion this cause, and I commend them for that work.

Ultimately, I cannot guarantee that we will find the treatments and cures we seek. No President can promise that. But I can promise that we will seek them—actively, responsibly, and with the urgency required to make up for lost ground. Not just by opening up this new frontier of research today, but by supporting promising research of all kinds, including groundbreaking work to convert ordinary human cells into ones that resemble embryonic stem cells.

I can also promise that we will never undertake this research lightly. We will support it only when it is both scientifically worthy and responsibly conducted. We will develop strict guidelines, which we will rigorously enforce, because we cannot ever tolerate misuse or abuse. And we will ensure that our government never opens the door to the use of cloning for human reproduction. It is dangerous, profoundly wrong, and has no place in our society, or any society.

This Order is an important step in advancing the cause of science in America. But let's be clear: promoting science isn't just about providing resources—it is also about protecting free and open inquiry. It is about letting scientists like those here today do their jobs, free from manipulation or coercion, and listening to what they tell us, even when it's inconvenient—especially when it's inconvenient. It is about ensuring that scientific data is never distorted or concealed to serve a political agenda—and that we make scientific decisions based on facts, not ideology.

By doing this, we will ensure America's continued global leadership in scientific discoveries and technological breakthroughs. That is essential not only for our economic prosperity, but for the progress of all humanity.

That is why today, I am also signing a Presidential Memorandum directing the head of the White House Office of Science and Technology Policy to develop a strategy for restoring scientific integrity to government decision making. To ensure that in this new Administration, we base our public policies on the soundest science; that we appoint scientific advisors based on their credentials and experience, not their politics or ideology; and that we are open and honest with the American people about the science behind our decisions. That is how we will harness the power of science to achieve our goals—to preserve our environment and protect our national security; to create the jobs of the future, and live longer, healthier lives.

As we restore our commitment to science, and resume funding for promising stem cell research, we owe a debt of gratitude to so many tireless advocates, some of whom are with us today, many of whom are not. Today, we honor all those whose names we don't know, who organized, and raised awareness, and kept on fighting—even when it was too late for them, or for the people they love....

There is no finish line in the work of science. The race is always with us—the urgent work of giving substance to hope and answering those many bedside prayers, of seeking a day when words like "terminal" and "incurable" are finally retired from our vocabulary.

Today, using every resource at our disposal, with renewed determination to lead the world in the discoveries of this new century, we rededicate ourselves to this work....

⚜ QUESTIONS FOR ANALYSIS

1. President Obama believes that the previous administration policy relied on a "false choice between sound science and moral values." How does he believe these can be reconciled?
2. He promises to develop "strict guidelines" to ensure that the research is "both scientifically worthy and responsibly conducted." What might be examples of guidelines for conducting responsible research?
3. What are his goals for "restoring scientific integrity to government decision making"?
4. He also cites possible economic benefits from this line of scientific research. Is this consequentialist reasoning appropriate in an area of such serious ethical concern? Does this approach amount to the view that the end justifies the means?
5. Does his statement here adequately recognize the moral concerns voiced by others in this public debate?

CASE PRESENTATION

Eight Is Enough

In January 2009 in Los Angeles, a woman named Nadya Suleman gave birth to octuplets conceived through in vitro fertilization. Dubbed "Octomom" by pundits and comics, she already had six other children, also conceived with in vitro fertilization, for a total of fourteen children. The hospital where the babies were born, a Kaiser Permanente facility, applied to the state's Medi-Cal assistance program to cover the medical expenses. Suleman told reporters that she was not "on welfare," but it was later disclosed that she was receiving food stamps and Social Security disability payments for two of her older children. She also told various reporters that she hoped to support herself on student loans while she returned to school to earn a degree in counseling. In 2013, Los Angeles county commenced an investigation that she had received over $200,000 in income (mainly from pornography and stripping), while receiving over $60,000 in public benefits. The medical license of her fertility specialist, Dr. Michael Kamrava, was revoked in 2011, but he is fighting to regain it.

QUESTIONS FOR ANALYSIS

1. Should society somehow regulate in vitro fertilization to prevent future occurrences of such multiple births? What would those regulations be like and how would they be enforced? Should regulations be imposed on patients? doctors? others?
2. What ethical obligations did the doctor have to Suleman when performing the in vitro fertilization? What were his obligations to the children? to the taxpayers of California?
3. What ethical obligations do would-be IVF parents have to the children they wish to have through this method?
4. What obligations does society have to the children, now that they have been born?
5. Are episodes like the Suleman births an argument for making all IVF illegal?

CHAPTER SEVEN

Capital Punishment

- **The Nature and Definition of Punishment**
- **The Moral Acceptability of Punishment**
- **Aims of Punishment**
- *Retentionist* and *Abolitionist* **Defined**
- **Capital Punishment as Deterrent**
- **Abolitionist Arguments (against Capital Punishment)**
- **Retentionist Arguments (for Capital Punishment)**

JOHN STUART MILL **Speech in Favor of Capital Punishment**
IGOR PRIMORATZ **A Life for a Life**
ERNEST VAN DEN HAAG **On Deterrence and the Death Penalty**
HUGO ADAM BEDAU **Capital Punishment and Social Defense**

CASE PRESENTATIONS: • *Karla Faye Tucker and Stanley "Tookie" Williams: Rehabilitation on Death Row?* • *A Failed Experiment?* • *Warren McClesky* • *Punishing Child Rapists*

LATE ON THE NIGHT of October 4, 1983, in Huntsville, Texas, convicted killer J. D. Autry was taken from his death-row cell in the penitentiary and strapped to a wheeled cot. Intravenous tubes were connected to both arms, ready to administer a dose of poison.

Outside, a crowd shouted "Kill him, kill him, kill him!" whenever television lights were turned on.

In Washington, Supreme Court Justice Byron White waited for a last-minute application for a stay of execution. The application, written on three sheets of a yellow pad, made a new argument related to another case due to be heard by the Court. Shortly after midnight, White granted the stay. The intravenous tubes were disconnected, the straps unbuckled. Autry was returned to his cell. Only in March of 1984 was the execution carried out.

The U.S. Supreme Court decision that paved the way for Autry's execution was *Gregg v. Georgia* (1976). In an earlier decision, *Furman v. Georgia* (1972), the Court had ruled that capital punishment as then administered was cruel and unusual punishment and therefore unconstitutional. The issue in that case was *standardless discretion*—the freedom of a jury (or in some cases, a judge) to use its own discretion in determining a sentence without explicit legal standards to guide its decision. In their attempts to get around the decision, some states passed laws making the death penalty mandatory for certain crimes, while others enacted legal standards to guide the discretion of the sentencing jury or judge. In *Woodson v. North Carolina* (1976), the Supreme Court ruled laws of the first type unconstitutional. In *Gregg v. Georgia*, it upheld laws of the second type for the crime of murder.

Since that decision, capital punishment has withstood another major legal challenge—*McClesky v. Kemp* (1987). In that case, the Supreme Court ruled against Warren McClesky, a black man who had been sentenced to death for killing a white policeman. McClesky argued that the imposition of the death penalty was unconstitutionally affected by racial bias, and in support of his claim, he offered studies showing that convicted killers of white victims were more likely to receive the death penalty than were convicted killers of black victims. Although the Court did not dispute the studies, it rejected his argument. With almost 1,900 convicted killers waiting on death row, the constitutionality of the death penalty was upheld by a 5 to 4 majority.

The application of the death penalty has been narrowed, however. In 2002, in *Atkins v. Virginia*, the U.S. Supreme Court held that execution of people with mental retardation violated the constitutional protection against cruel and unusual punishment. This decision reversed a 1989 decision, *Perry v. Lynaugh*, which said that executing mentally retarded individuals did not violate the Constitution. In the *Atkins* decision, the Court said that executing people mentally retarded does not meet the deterrent nor the retributive purpose of the death penalty. They also noted a growing national consensus that executing mentally retarded people is wrong. Of the thirty-eight states that permitted capital punishment in 2002, eighteen had banned execution of mentally retarded people.

In 2005, the U.S. Supreme Court, in a 5–4 decision, abolished capital punishment for juvenile offenders in *Roper v. Simmons*. Twenty states had permitted the death penalty for offenders younger than eighteen. The decision canceled the sentences for seventy-two other juveniles then on death row, including twenty-nine awaiting execution in Texas. As recently as 1989, the Court had upheld the death penalty for offenders who were at least sixteen. In announcing the decision, Justice Anthony Kennedy said it reflected "evolving standards of decency that mark the progress of a maturing society." The dissenters said that such policies should be left to the discretion of state legislatures.

Scientific developments, especially DNA testing, have further complicated public debate over the appropriateness of the death penalty. In 2000, the governor of Illinois announced a moratorium on executions, as DNA testing had shown that thirteen people on death row were innocent. Maryland instituted a temporary moratorium, but it was lifted in 2003. (Illinois abolished the death penalty entirely in 2011 and Maryland abolished it in 2013.) Congress passed the Innocence Protection Act of 2004 to help pay the costs of post-conviction DNA testing. Since the advent of DNA testing of evidence, over 140 prisoners on death row in the United States have been freed when the tests proved they were innocent, according to the Death Penalty Information Center.

Economic woes in the states have led several state legislatures to consider abolishing the death penalty to save money, opting instead for life without parole. Although it might seem counterintuitive, life imprisonment is much cheaper as a form of punishment than execution. John Van de Kamp, attorney general of California from 1983–1991 and a death penalty supporter, has argued that the death penalty will cost the state $1 billion over the next five years. The additional expenses come from extra court costs for hearings and appeals, legal defense costs, and confinement on death row.[1] Since 1995, when thirty-eight states had the death penalty, six states have abolished it (Connecticut, Illinois, Maryland, New Jersey, New Mexico, and New York).

Another complication in administering the death penalty is the growing shortage of drugs to use for lethal injections, which most states now prefer as it seems more "humane." The last U.S. manufacturer of one of the drugs previously used has stopped all production and European manufacturers refuse to import it to the United States, as European nations typically object to the death penalty. States are now looking for alternative drugs that can be used for executions. Although support for the death penalty has declined slightly in the United States, recent polls indicate that more than half the population still supports it. More than 1000 prisoners have been executed since the 1976 *Gregg v. Georgia* decision. Internationally, however, support for capital punishment has been steadily declining. It has been abolished in Canada, Mexico, Russia, South Africa, and most industrialized nations. Amnesty International claims that more than half the nations in the world have abolished the death penalty in law or in practice. Nearly all the executions on the planet are carried out by four nations: China, Iran, Saudi Arabia, and the United States.

The death penalty is a form of punishment. Consequently, one's view of the morality of the death penalty usually is influenced by one's view of punishment generally. So the specific moral question under discussion in this chapter is: Is capital punishment ever a justifiable form of punishment?

THE NATURE AND DEFINITION OF PUNISHMENT

Generally, philosophers discuss punishment in terms of five elements. For something to be punishment, it must (1) involve pain, (2) be administered for an offense against a law or rule, (3) be administered to someone who has been judged guilty of an offense, (4) be imposed by someone other than the offender, and (5) be imposed by rightful authority. Whether a punishment is commensurate with an offense, whether it is fair and equitable—these are very important moral and legal questions. But they must be distinguished from the question of what punishment is.

1. *Punishment must involve pain, harm, or some other consequence normally considered unpleasant.* Typically, this is a deprivation of a freedom to which a person otherwise has a right. For example, if convicted robbers were sentenced to "five to twenty" in a Beverly Hills country club, this would not be considered punishment, since ordinarily it would not involve pain or other unpleasant consequences (unless the robbers had to pick up the tab). If they were sentenced to have their hands cut off, this could constitute punishment, though draconian by many people's standards.
2. *The punishment must be administered for an offense against a law or rule.* While punishment involves pain, obviously not all pain involves punishment. If robbers break into your house and steal your stereo, they are not "punishing" you, even though their action satisfies element one. Although it caused you pain, their action is not taken to punish an offense against a law or rule. However,

---

[1]John Van de Kamp, "We can't afford the death penalty," *Los Angeles Times*, June 10, 2009.

should the robbers subsequently be sent to prison for the crime, then that action would be administered for breaking a law and thus satisfy element two.

3. ***The punishment must be administered to someone who has been judged guilty of an offense***. Suppose the robbers are apprehended and imprisoned, although never judged guilty of the robbery. This would not be considered punishment. However, if they are imprisoned after their conviction for stealing your stereo, then they are being punished.

4. ***The punishment must be imposed by someone other than the offender***. It is true that people sometimes speak of "punishing themselves" for a transgression. This, however, is not punishment in the strict sense but a self-imposed act of atonement. Suffering from a twinge of conscience as they listen to the latest Willie Nelson album on your stereo, the robbers decide to "punish" themselves by listening to Robert Goulet, whom they detest, for two hours each day for a year. Properly speaking, this would not be punishment, although it might qualify as masochism.

5. ***The punishment must be imposed by rightful authority***. In a strictly legal sense, "rightful authority" would be that constituted by a legal system against whom the offense is committed. In the case of the robbers, "rightful authority" would likely be a court judge and jury. In a less legal sense, the authority might be a parent, a teacher, or some official who has a right to harm a person in a particular way for having done something or failed to do something.

These five elements, then, generally constitute the nature of punishment. Combining them produces a useful definition of punishment. Thus, a punishment is harm inflicted by a rightful authority on a person who has been judged to have violated a law or rule.[2] The punishments listed here are primarily punishments in our legal system. Punishments can also exists in a non-legal system, as when a parent disciplines a child, but many of these characteristics would be analogous to those in the legal system.

THE MORAL ACCEPTABILITY OF PUNISHMENT

Is punishment ever morally acceptable? This may seem a foolish question to ask, because it is hard to imagine society functioning without an established legal system of punishment. In fact, philosophers generally agree that punishment is morally acceptable. They, like most others, view punishment as a part of the rule and law necessary to minimize the occurrence of forbidden acts. In short, law without punishment is toothless.

Still, there are people who do not share this view. They argue that society should be restructured so that a legal system of punishment is unnecessary. Just how this can or should be done remains problematic. The method most often proposed involves some form of therapeutic treatment or behavior modification for antisocial behavior rather than a traditional form of punishment. Among the most morally controversial procedures for modifying undesirable social behavior are those associated with some startling advances in biomedicine. Such cases rarely can be resolved by a simple appeal to the individual's right to obtain appropriate treatment on request, and they are even less likely to be resolved by an appeal to society's right to order such treatment.

Consider one case provided by a leading research scientist in the field, Dr. J. R. Delgado. A number of years ago, Delgado recalls, an attractive twenty-four-year-old

[2]See Burton M. Leiser, *Liberty, Justice, and Morals* (New York: Macmillan, 1973), pp. 195–197.

woman of average intelligence and education and a long record of arrests for disorderly conduct approached him and his associates. The patient explained that she had been repeatedly involved in bar brawls in which she would entice men to fight over her. Having spent a number of years in jail and mental institutions, the woman expressed a strong desire but inability to change her behavior. Because past psychological therapy had proved ineffective, both she and her mother urgently requested that some sort of brain surgery be performed to control her antisocial and destructive behavior.

As Delgado said: "They asked specifically that electrodes be implanted to orient a possible electrocoagulation of a limited cerebral area; and if that wasn't possible, they wanted a lobotomy."[3]

At that time, medical knowledge could not determine whether such procedures could help resolve the woman's problem, so the physicians rejected surgical intervention. When Delgado and his colleagues explained their decision to the woman and her mother, the two reacted with disappointment and anxiety: "What is the future? Only jail or the hospital?"[4]

What is the future, indeed? The day could very well come when such therapeutic treatment renders traditional kinds of punishment obsolete, perhaps barbaric. But even then, pressing moral questions will remain concerning society's right to alter an individual's personality against his or her will. For now, most agree that punishment is a morally acceptable practice. What they do not agree on, however, is the aim of punishment.

AIMS OF PUNISHMENT

The aims of punishment can be divided into two categories: (1) in terms of giving people what they deserve or (2) in terms of its desirable consequences. The first category includes retributive theories of punishment; the second includes preventive, deterrent, and reformative theories.

Retribution

The term **retribution** refers to punishment given in return for some wrong done. This view of punishment holds that we should punish people simply because they deserve it. Traditionally, retributive theorists have considered punishment a principle of justice, often referred to as retributory justice, whereby offenders are made to suffer in kind for the harm they have caused others. Arguments in favor of capital punishment commonly make this point.

But another version of retribution associates punishment not with revenge but with respect for persons, both noncriminals and criminals. Proponents of this theory argue that robbers, for example, like everyone else in society, ought to live under the same limitations of freedom. When robbers steal your stereo, they are taking unfair advantage of you, disrupting the balance of equal limitations. When the state subsequently punishes them, the punishment is viewed as an attempt to restore this disrupted balance, to reaffirm society's commitment to fair treatment for all. This version of retribution focuses on the noncriminal generally and the victim in particular, claiming that respect for the parties who abide by society's limitations requires punishment of those who flout those limitations.

---

[3]J. R. Delgado, *Physical Control of the Mind: Toward a Psycho-Civilized Society* (New York: Harper & Row, 1969), p. 85.
[4]Ibid.

The other side of the respect–retribution theory concerns respect for the offender. Proponents of retribution sometimes argue that failure to punish is tantamount to treating offenders with disrespect because it denies them autonomy and responsibility for their actions. Showing respect entails giving people what they deserve, whether that be reward or punishment. To deny praise to a deserving person is disrespectful.

By the same token, to deny punishment to a deserving person is equally disrespectful. Both views of respect–retribution can be used in defense of capital punishment.

Prevention

The prevention view of punishment holds that we should punish to ensure that offenders do not repeat their offense and so further injure society. Thus, robbers should be punished, perhaps imprisoned, so that they will not steal anything else. Prevention is one of the most common justifications for capital punishment.

Deterrence

The **deterrence** view holds that we should punish to discourage others from committing similar offenses. Like the prevention theory, it aims to minimize the crime rate. Thus, when other potential thieves see that the robber has been punished for the crime, they will be less likely to steal. Deterrence is perhaps the most common argument made on behalf of capital punishment and thus is the one that those against capital punishment often focus on. For the moment, we will simply observe that if a punishment is to function effectively as a deterrent, it must be severe enough to be undesirable, and just as important, it must be known and certain. Thus, potential offenders must be aware of the kind and severity of the punishment that awaits them, and they must be convinced that they will receive it if they commit the offense.

Reform

The reform theory holds that one should punish to induce people to conform to standards of behavior they have tended to ignore or violate. The idea is that people will emerge from punishment better than they were before, insofar as they will be less likely to breach conventional standards of behavior.

Although rehabilitation often accompanies reform, the aims of each are different. Rehabilitation aims not to punish but to offer the offenders opportunities to find a useful place in society on release from prison. Modern penal institutions attempt to accomplish this goal by providing various recreational, educational, and vocational services for prisoners.

It's important to keep in mind that the aforementioned aims of punishment are not mutually exclusive. It's possible for more than one purpose of punishment to be morally legitimate. In fact, perhaps all four, in varying degrees, might be called for.

RETENTIONIST AND *ABOLITIONIST* DEFINED

Having briefly examined some aspects of punishment, including its nature and definition, its moral acceptability, and its aims, let us now turn to the particular form of punishment that is the topic of this chapter: capital punishment. The central moral question that concerns us is: Is capital punishment ever a justifiable form of punishment?

Those who support retaining or reinstituting capital punishment can be termed **retentionists.** Retentionists are not agreed that all the arguments supporting capital punishment are acceptable or on the conditions under which capital punishment should be imposed. But they do agree that capital punishment is at least sometimes morally justifiable. Those who oppose capital punishment are commonly termed **abolitionists.** Like retentionists, abolitionists disagree among themselves about which arguments against capital punishment are acceptable. But all abolitionists share the belief that capital punishment is never morally justifiable.

One common argument enlisted by both retentionists and abolitionists concerns capital punishment as a deterrent. As we'll see, retentionists sometimes claim that capital punishment deters potential murderers and therefore should be kept. For their part, some abolitionists claim that capital punishment does not serve as a deterrent and offer this—usually with other reasons—for abolishing the death penalty. Because the deterrent argument figures so prominently in capital punishment debates, we should inspect it before beginning this chapter's dialogues.

CAPITAL PUNISHMENT AS DETERRENT

Does capital punishment succeed in deterring potential murderers? At first glance, the answer seems to be a resounding yes. After all, virtually everyone seems deterred from lawbreaking by relatively mild intimidation—for example, being towed away for illegal parking or losing one's driver's license for recklessness. How much more, common sense suggests, must potential murderers be intimidated by the threat of their own death at the executioner's hand. In this instance, however, common sense misleads by failing to recognize that murderers differ from the rest of us in important respects.

First, there's the large category of murderers who kill in a fit of rage or passion. A barroom brawl escalates and one man kills another; in a gang fight, a member of one group kills a member of another, perhaps to save face or avenge a harm; in a family quarrel, a person kills a relative when things get out of hand. The list goes on and on. Such murders, of which there are many, are committed not with forethought of the consequences but in a moment of white-hot anger. Hence, not even the death penalty is likely to deter these murderers. (In fact, in instances of gang killings, it might have the opposite effect: In risking their own lives at the hands of the state, killers might feel they're proving their mettle or giving ultimate evidence of gang loyalty.)

Then there's the category of so-called professional criminals, those who deliberately calculate when, where, and how to commit crimes. It's not at all clear that this type of criminal is deterred by the death penalty. In fact, if professional criminals perceive the likely punishment for nonhomicidal crimes (e.g., robbery, burglary, rape, and so forth) as overly severe, they might be encouraged to kill their victims and witnesses rather than risk getting caught: Killing these people greatly increases the criminals' chances of getting away with their crimes, and so they may not in the least be deterred by the threat of the death penalty.

Besides these kinds of potential murderers are those who seemingly have a death wish. The annals of psychiatry are replete with cases of people so emotionally disturbed that they kill to win the death penalty and end their tortured existence. In effect, their murderous acts are expressions of suicidal impulses. Since they lack the nerve to kill themselves, they want someone else to do it for them—in this case, the state.

But what about cases of so-called normal, nonsuicidal persons who carefully weigh the risks before killing? Are these potential murderers deterred by the death penalty? Even here, the deterrent effect of capital punishment is by no means obvious or certain. What's required is a determination of how many, if any, calculating potential murderers (a small class to begin with) who are not deterred by the threat of life imprisonment would be deterred by the threat of death. Even if such a determination is possible, it's not obvious or certain that there would be any such people at all or much more than a small number annually.

A further complication in assessing the death penalty as deterrent relates not to factual questions such as the preceding but to the moral and legal costs of deterrence. Some claim there's a basic incompatibility between the deterrent efficacy of the death penalty and due process, which refers to a constitutionally guaranteed, specific, systematic procedure of appeal. The death penalty can be deterrent, the argument goes, only if due process is sacrificed. Conversely, due process can govern the inflicting of capital punishment but at the cost of deterrence. When human life is at issue—as of course it is in capital punishment cases—the courts have been understandably scrupulous in reviewing cases for error and ensuring that basic rights have been respected. The consequences of this process of rigorous judicial review are quite apparent: increasing delays of execution, an ever-increasing percentage of those convicted who are never executed, and large numbers of convictions overturned. When fully exercised, the right of appeal can lead to costly, protracted litigation, in which a criminal's fate may hinge as much on the quality of legal representation as on any other factor. Given the delay between murder and the death penalty, and the uncertainty that a death sentence will ever be carried out, one wonders about the death penalty's deterrent effect. On the other hand, to ensure swiftness and certainty mocks one of the most cherished ideals of our system of justice: due process.

Currently, the consensus among social scientists is that no statistical studies on the deterrent effect of capital punishment yield a conclusive answer. We simply don't know whether the threat of death deters people from killing. Given this picture, some argue that since there is a moral presumption against the taking of life, the burden of proving capital punishment is a deterrent should fall on those who advocate the taking of life in the form of capital punishment. But by the same token, one could contend that abolitionists should bear the burden of proof: Since we don't know for sure whether the death penalty is a deterrent, we should give the benefit of doubt to the lives of potential victims of murderers rather than to the murderers. This tack is especially forceful when applied to measures intended to reserve the death penalty for the intentional killings of law enforcement agents and others who need special protection, which they might get from the threat of the death penalty.

ABOLITIONIST ARGUMENTS (AGAINST CAPITAL PUNISHMENT)

1. *Every human life has dignity and worth.*
   POINT: "Capital punishment is nothing more than legalized cold-blooded murder. Whatever crime a person has committed, he or she is still a human being, and every human life has inherent dignity and worth. Don't get me wrong—I'm not advocating leniency toward vicious murderers. We have to protect ourselves from them, and we have to send a clear signal to other would-be murderers that society will not tolerate heinous crime. But life imprisonment without the possibility of parole is sufficient punishment

and deterrent. To strap a fellow human being into a chair and give a lethal dose of gas, a lethal jolt of electricity, or a lethal injection is unworthy of a civilized society. Capital punishment should have gone the way of legalized torture and mutilation years ago. It too is 'cruel and unusual punishment,' and like them it's morally unacceptable in today's world."

COUNTERPOINT: "I have no quarrel with a general commitment to respect for human life, but imposing the death penalty on depraved murderers who have no respect for human life themselves is the strongest commitment to that principle a society can make. First-degree murder is the ultimate crime, and anyone who commits it deserves to pay the ultimate price. As for capital punishment being 'cruel and unusual' in today's world, whether a punishment falls into that category depends on prevailing moral standards. And as long as democratically elected legislatures are willing to enact it and citizen juries are willing to impose it, it can hardly be considered cruel and unusual."

2. *Capital punishment is imposed with class and racial bias.*
   POINT: "Statistics show two very disturbing facts about the way capital punishment is imposed in our society. First, the poor, the underprivileged, and members of minority groups are far more likely to be executed than the rich, the influential, and whites. Second, the death penalty is far more likely to be imposed when the victim is white than when the victim is the member of a minority group. Regardless of your high-minded principles, capital punishment shows at best a respect for affluent white life, not human life in general. Because its implementation is patently discriminatory and therefore unjust, it must be stopped."

   COUNTERPOINT: "Though the bias you mention is indeed unjust, it's irrelevant to the morality of capital punishment. After all, the same charges have often been made against our criminal justice systems in general. Of course, such bias should be rooted out wherever it exists; and of course, comparable crimes should bring the same punishment. But whether capital punishment is justified for the worst of crimes is one issue. Whether it's currently implemented in a justifiable way is another."

3. *The innocent may die.*
   POINT: "The innocent are often convicted of crimes. As tragic as that is when the sentence is a prison term, the tragedy is far worse when the sentence is death. In the former case, society can at least make *some* reparation for time unjustly served, but no fact is more obvious than the fact that nothing can be done for the dead. To execute even one innocent person is inexcusable, and there's no way in the world that we can rule that possibility out without abolishing the death penalty."

   COUNTERPOINT: "I can't deny that the execution of an innocent human being is a terrible tragedy. Nor can I deny that the possibility will always be there. That's why we require such safeguards as the automatic right of appeal after capital convictions. But given these safeguards, the possibility remains extremely slim. And as unfortunate as that slim risk is, like many other unfortunate risks, it's one worth taking. The thousands of murders committed in the United States each year require us to take it."

4. *Capital punishment compromises the judicial system.*

    POINT: "Capital punishment compromises our judicial system in two ways. First, though the point of capital punishment is to present a tough stance against crime, it sometimes has the opposite effect. Juries have been known to strain the evidence to convict defendants of lesser charges—or even to acquit them—when a conviction of first-degree murder carries a mandatory death sentence. Second, cases of capital punishment invariably involve years of costly appeals. Not only does that delay justice, but it also subjects the victims' families, as well as the convicts', to years of cruel and unusual punishment."

    COUNTERPOINT: "Again, the problem isn't capital punishment itself but the way it's implemented. And again, the answer is to improve the judicial system, not to abolish the death penalty. We need greater care in jury selection and a more efficient appeals process. What we don't need is to keep vicious murderers alive as wards of the state."

RETENTIONIST ARGUMENTS (FOR CAPITAL PUNISHMENT)

1. *Capital punishment deters crime.*

    POINT: "Simple common sense tells us that capital punishment is a more powerful deterrent against crime than prison. The more severe the punishment, the greater the risk to the would-be criminal; and the greater the risk, the more reason not to commit the crime. I'm not saying that every would-be killer is rational enough to weigh the pros and cons before deciding whether to kill, but it certainly stands to reason that some are. And as long as that's true, capital punishment serves its purpose—saving innocent lives."

    COUNTERPOINT: "Regardless of what your common sense tells you, the statistics offer no support. There just isn't any conclusive evidence that the death penalty is a more powerful deterrent than prison. Besides, my common sense doesn't agree with yours. Mine tells me that very few murderers follow any kind of rational weighing of pros and cons. And in the rare cases when they do, the murderer isn't thinking that a life sentence won't be too high a price to pay. It's far more likely that the murderer doesn't expect to get caught in the first place."

2. *Capital punishment keeps the convicted murderer from killing again.*

    POINT: "Capital punishment guarantees at least one thing. We don't have to worry that an executed murderer will kill again. Even if every murderer sentenced to imprisonment for life without possibility of parole never leaves prison alive, which is highly doubtful, we still have to worry about murders committed in prison. The rest of society may be protected from these killers, but prison guards and fellow inmates aren't. Don't forget: Since they're already serving the maximum sentence, they have nothing to fear from killing again."

    COUNTERPOINT: "The truth of the matter is that convicted murderers rarely do kill again, whether in prison or in society after release or parole. Since we can never know which ones will kill again, we'd have to execute hundreds who wouldn't just to prevent one who would. Clearly, that can't be just. We might as well execute everyone who might conceivably commit a murder."

3. *Capital punishment balances the scales of justice.*

POINT: "Murder being the ultimate crime, simple justice requires that the murderer pay the ultimate penalty. After all, deterrence and prevention aren't the only purposes of punishing criminals. An equally important purpose is to see that justice is done, that moral retribution is taken. That's why we insist that the punishment must fit the crime. Furthermore, society has both the right and the obligation to express its moral outrage over the most heinous crimes committed against it. And both purposes are best served by capital punishment. Prison is just too weak a punishment for many murderers, and a prison term cannot satisfy society's moral outrage over vicious murders."

COUNTERPOINT: "You call it retribution and the expression of moral outrage, but I call it revenge. Certainly, justice requires that the guilty be punished for their crimes. It also requires that more severe crimes be met by more severe penalties. But there are moral limits to what we can inflict on even the cruelest criminals. We don't torture murderers who tortured their victims. We don't rape murderers who raped their victims. To do either wouldn't be justice but a gross perversion of justice. It would be blood-thirsty revenge, pure and simple. And that's what the death penalty is."

4. *Society shouldn't have to pay the economic costs of life sentences for murders.*

POINT: "When you put murderers away for life, you give up all hope of reforming them. That leaves society with the heavy cost of supporting the worst criminals in maximum security prisons until they die. Why should innocent taxpayers have to foot the bill for the care of depraved criminals who've demonstrated that they have no respect for society's laws or human life?"

COUNTERPOINT: "Because the rest of us do have—or at least should have—respect for human life. But if we continue to execute our fellow human beings because it's cheaper than keeping them alive, we demonstrate that our respect for human life isn't much stronger than theirs. Besides, don't be so sure that capital punishment is cheaper than life imprisonment. The costs of executing a convict, including the costs of the lengthy appeals process and the high costs of keeping a convict on death row, are enormous."

Speech in Favor of Capital Punishment

JOHN STUART MILL

The English philosopher John Stuart Mill (1806–1873) is best known for his development of utilitarianism, as well as his sweeping defense of the importance of free speech in the development of democracies. Routinely characterized as a "liberal," he supported capital punishment on what he perceived to be humanitarian grounds drawn from his theory of utilitarianism. He delivered this speech to the English Parliament in 1868 in opposition to a bill introduced by Mr. Gilpin that would ban capital punishment.

... It would be a great satisfaction to me if I were able to support this Motion. It is always a matter of regret to me to find myself, on a public question, opposed to those who are called—sometimes in the way of honour, and sometimes in what is intended for ridicule—the philanthropists. Of all persons who take part in public affairs, they are those for whom, on the whole, I feel the greatest amount of respect; for their characteristic is, that they devote their time, their labour, and much of their money to objects purely public, with a less admixture of either personal or class selfishness, than any other class of politicians whatever.

On almost all the great questions, scarcely any politicians are so steadily and almost uniformly to be found on the side of right; and they seldom err, but by an exaggerated application of some just and highly important principle. On the very subject that is now occupying us we all know what signal service they have rendered. It is through their efforts that our criminal laws—which within my memory hanged people for stealing in a dwelling house to the value of 40s.—laws by virtue of which rows of human beings might be seen suspended in front of Newgate by those who ascended or descended Ludgate Hill—have so greatly relaxed their most revolting and most impolitic ferocity, that aggravated murder is now practically the only crime which is punished with death by any of our lawful tribunals; and we are even now deliberating whether the extreme penalty should be retained in that solitary case. This vast gain, not only to humanity, but to the ends of penal justice, we owe to the philanthropists; and if they are mistaken, as I cannot but think they are, in the present instance, it is only in not perceiving the right time and place for stopping in a career hitherto so eminently beneficial.

Sir, there is a point at which, I conceive, that career ought to stop. When there has been brought home to any one, by conclusive evidence, the greatest crime known to the law; and when the attendant circumstances suggest no palliation of the guilt, no hope that the culprit may even yet not be unworthy to live among mankind, nothing to make it probable that the crime was an exception to his general character rather than a consequence of it, then I confess it appears to me that to deprive the criminal of the life of which he has proved himself to be unworthy—solemnly to blot him out from the fellowship of mankind and from the catalogue of the living—is the most appropriate as it is certainly the most impressive, mode in which society can attach to so great a crime the penal consequences which for the security of life it is indispensable to annex to it.

I defend this penalty, when confined to atrocious cases, on the very ground on which it is commonly attacked—on that of humanity to the criminal; as beyond comparison the least cruel mode in which it is possible adequately to deter from the crime. If, in our horror of inflicting death, we endeavour to devise some punishment for the living criminal which shall act on the human mind with a deterrent force at all comparable to that of death, we are driven to inflictions less severe indeed in appearance, and therefore less efficacious, but far more cruel in reality. Few, I think, would venture to propose, as a punishment for aggravated murder, less than imprisonment with hard labor for life; that is the fate to which a murderer would be consigned by the mercy which shrinks from putting him to death.

But has it been sufficiently considered what sort of a mercy this is, and what kind of life it leaves to him? If, indeed, the punishment is not really inflicted—if it becomes the sham which a few years ago such punishments were rapidly becoming—then, indeed, its adoption would be almost tantamount to giving up the attempt to repress murder altogether. But if it really is what it professes to be, and if it is realized in all its rigour by the popular imagination, as it very probably would not be, but as it must be if it is to be efficacious, it will be so shocking that when the memory of the crime is no longer fresh, there will be almost insuperable difficulty in executing it.

What comparison can there really be, in point of severity, between consigning a man to the short pang of a rapid death, and immuring him in a living tomb, there to linger out what may be a long life in the hardest and most monotonous toil, without any of its alleviations or rewards—debarred from all pleasant sights and sounds, and cut off from all earthly hope, except a slight mitigation of bodily restraint, or a small improvement of diet? Yet even such a lot as this, because there is no one moment at which the suffering is of terrifying intensity, and, above all, because it does not contain the element, so imposing to the imagination, of the unknown, is universally reputed a milder punishment than death—stands in all codes as a mitigation of the capital penalty, and is thankfully accepted as such. For it is characteristic of all punishments which depend on duration for their efficacy—all, therefore, which are not corporal or pecuniary—that they are more rigorous than they seem; while it is, on the contrary, one of the strongest recommendations a punishment can have, that it should seem more rigorous than it is; for its practical power depends far less on what it is than on what it seems.

There is not, I should think, any human infliction which makes an impression on the imagination so entirely out of proportion to its real severity as the punishment of death. The punishment must be mild indeed which does not add more to the sum of human misery than is necessarily or directly added by the execution of a criminal. As my hon. Friend the Member for Northampton (Mr. Gilpin) has himself remarked, the most that human laws can do to anyone in the matter of death is to hasten it; the man would have died at any rate; not so very much later, and on the average, I fear, with a considerably greater amount of bodily suffering. Society is asked, then, to denude itself of an instrument of punishment which, in the grave cases to which alone it is suitable, effects its purposes at a less cost of human suffering than any other; which, while it inspires more terror, is less cruel in actual fact than any punishment that we should think of substituting for it.

My hon. Friend says that it does not inspire terror, and that experience proves it to be a failure. But the influence of a punishment is not to be estimated by its effect on hardened criminals. Those whose habitual way of life keeps them, so to speak, at all times within sight of the gallows, do grow to care less about it; as, to compare good things with bad, an old soldier is not much affected by the chance of dying in battle. I can afford to admit all that is often said about the indifference of professional criminals to the gallows. Though of that indifference one-third is probably bravado and another third confidence

that they shall have the luck to escape, it is quite probable that the remaining third is real. But the efficacy of a punishment which acts principally through the imagination, is chiefly to be measured by the impression it makes on those who are still innocent; by the horror with which it surrounds the first promptings of guilt; the restraining influence it exercises over the beginning of the thought which, if indulged, would become a temptation; the check which it exerts over the graded declension towards the state—never suddenly attained—in which crime no longer revolts, and punishment no longer terrifies.

As for what is called the failure of death punishment, who is able to judge of that? We partly know who those are whom it has not deterred; but who is there who knows whom it has deterred, or how many human beings it has saved who would have lived to be murderers if that awful association had not been thrown round the idea of murder from their earliest infancy? Let us not forget that the most imposing fact loses its power over the imagination if it is made too cheap. When a punishment fit only for the most atrocious crimes is lavished on small offences until human feeling recoils from it, then, indeed, it ceases to intimidate, because it ceases to be believed in.

The failure of capital punishment in cases of theft is easily accounted for; the thief did not believe that it would be inflicted. He had learnt by experience that jurors would perjure themselves rather than find him guilty; that Judges would seize any excuse for not sentencing him to death, or for recommending him to mercy; and that if neither jurors nor Judges were merciful, there were still hopes from an authority above both. When things had come to this pass it was high time to give up the vain attempt.

When it is impossible to inflict a punishment, or when its infliction becomes a public scandal, the idle threat cannot too soon disappear from the statute book. And in the case of the host of offences which were formerly capital, I heartily rejoice that it did become impracticable to execute the law. If the same state of public feeling comes to exist in the case of murder; if the time comes when jurors refuse to find a murderer guilty; when Judges will not sentence him to death, or will recommend him to mercy; or when, if juries and Judges do not flinch from their duty, Home Secretaries, under pressure of deputations and memorials, shrink from theirs, and the threat becomes, as it became in the other cases, a mere *brutum fulmen*;[1] then, indeed, it may become necessary to do in this case what has been done in those—to abrogate the penalty.

That time may come—my hon. Friend thinks that it has nearly come. I hardly know whether he lamented it or boasted of it; but he and his Friends are entitled to the boast; for if it comes it will be their doing, and they will have gained what I cannot but call a fatal victory, for they will have achieved it by bringing about, if they will forgive me for saying so, an enervation, an effeminancy, in the general mind of the country. For what else than effeminancy is it to be so much more shocked by taking a man's life than by depriving him of all that makes life desirable or valuable? Is death, then, the greatest of all earthly ills? *Usque adeone mori miserum est?*[2] Is it, indeed, so dreadful a thing to die? Has it not been from of old one chief part of a manly education to make us despise death— teaching us to account it, if an evil at all, by no means high in the list of evils; at all events, as an inevitable one, and to hold, as it were, our lives in our hands, ready to be given or risked at any moment, for a sufficiently worthy object?

I am sure that my hon. Friends know all this as well, and have as much of all these feelings as any of the rest of us; possibly more. But I cannot think that this is likely to be the effect of their teaching on the general mind. I cannot think that the culti- vating of a peculiar sensitiveness of conscience on this one point, over and above what results from the general cultivation of the moral sentiments, is permanently consistent with assigning in our own minds to the fact of death no more than the degree of relative importance which belongs to it among the other incidents of our humanity.

The men of old cared too little about death, and gave their own lives or took those of oth- ers with equal recklessness. Our danger is of the opposite kind, lest we should be so much shocked by death, in general and in the abstract, as to care too much about it in individual cases, both those of other people and our own, which call for its being risked. And I am not putting things at the

worst, for it is proved by the experience of other countries that horror of the executioner by no means necessarily implies horror of the assassin. The stronghold, as we all know, of hired assassina- tion in the 18th century was Italy; yet it is said that in some of the Italian populations the infliction of death by sentence of law was in the highest degree offensive and revolting to popular feeling.

Much has been said of the sanctity of human life, and the absurdity of supposing that we can teach respect for life by ourselves destroying it. But I am surprised at the employment of this argument, for it is one which might be brought against any punishment whatever. It is not human life only, not human life as such, that ought to be sacred to us, but human feelings. The human capacity of suffering is what we should cause to be respected, not the mere capacity of existing.

And we may imagine somebody asking how we can teach people not to inflict suffering by our- selves inflicting it? But to this I should answer— all of us would answer—that to deter by suffer- ing from inflicting suffering is not only possible, but the very purpose of penal justice. Does fining a criminal show want of respect for property, or imprisoning him, for personal freedom? Just as unreasonable is it to think that to take the life of a man who has taken that of another is to show want of regard for human life. We show, on the con- trary, most emphatically our regard for it, by the adoption of a rule that he who violates that right in another forfeits it for himself, and that while no other crime that he can commit deprives him of his right to live, this shall.

There is one argument against capital punish- ment, even in extreme cases, which I cannot deny to have weight—on which my hon. Friend justly laid great stress, and which never can be entirely got rid of. It is this—that if by an error of justice an inno- cent person is put to death, the mistake can never be corrected; all compensation, all reparation for the wrong is impossible. This would be indeed a seri- ous objection if these miserable mistakes—among the most tragical occurrences in the whole round of human affairs—could not be made extremely rare.

The argument is invincible where the mode of criminal procedure is dangerous to the innocent, or where the Courts of Justice are not trusted.

And this probably is the reason why the objection to an irreparable punishment began (as I believe it did) earlier, and is more intense and more widely diffused, in some parts of the Continent of Europe than it is here. There are on the Continent great and enlightened countries, in which the criminal procedure is not so favorable to innocence, does not afford the same security against erroneous conviction, as it does among us; countries where the Courts of Justice seem to think they fail in their duty unless they find somebody guilty; and in their really laudable desire to hunt guilt from its hiding places, expose themselves to a serious danger of condemning the innocent.

If our own procedure and Courts of Justice afforded ground for similar apprehension, I should be the first to join in withdrawing the power of inflicting irreparable punishment from such tribunals. But we all know that the defects of our procedure are the very opposite. Our rules of evidence are even too favorable to the prisoner; and juries and Judges carry out the maxim, "It is better that ten guilty should escape than that one innocent person should suffer," not only to the letter, but beyond the letter. Judges are most anxious to point out, and juries to allow for, the barest possibility of the prisoner's innocence. No human judgment is infallible; such sad cases as my hon. Friend cited will sometimes occur; but in so grave a case as that of murder, the accused, in our system, has always the benefit of the merest shadow of a doubt.

And this suggests another consideration very germane to the question. The very fact that death punishment is more shocking than any other to the imagination, necessarily renders the Courts of Justice more scrupulous in requiring the fullest evidence of guilt. Even that which is the greatest objection to capital punishment, the impossibility of correcting an error once committed, must make, and does make, juries and Judges more careful in forming their opinion, and more jealous in their scrutiny of the evidence. If the substitution of penal servitude for death in cases of murder should cause any declaration in this conscientious scrupulosity, there would be a great evil to set against the real, but I hope rare, advantage of being able to make reparation to a condemned person who was afterwards discovered to be innocent.

In order that the possibility of correction may be kept open wherever the chance of this sad contingency is more than infinitesimal, it is quite right that the Judge should recommend to the Crown a commutation of the sentence, not solely when the proof of guilt is open to the smallest suspicion, but whenever there remains anything unexplained and mysterious in the case, raising a desire for more light, or making it likely that further information may at some future time be obtained. I would also suggest that whenever the sentence is commuted the grounds of the commutation should, in some authentic form, be made known to the public.

Thus much I willingly concede to my hon. Friend; but on the question of total abolition I am inclined to hope that the feeling of the country is not with him, and that the limitation of death punishment to the cases referred to in the Bill of last year will be generally considered sufficient. The mania which existed a short time ago for paring down all our punishments seems to have reached its limits, and not before it was time. We were in danger of being left without any effectual punishment, except for small of offences.

What was formerly our chief secondary punishment—transportation—before it was abolished, had become almost a reward. Penal servitude, the substitute for it, was becoming, to the classes who were principally subject to it, almost nominal, so comfortable did we make our prisons, and so easy had it become to get quickly out of them. Flogging—a most objectionable punishment in ordinary cases, but a particularly appropriate one for crimes of brutality, especially crimes against women—we would not hear of, except, to be sure, in the case of garotters, for whose peculiar benefit we reestablished it in a hurry, immediately after a Member of Parliament had been garrotted. With this exception, offences, even of an atrocious kind, against the person, as my hon. and learned Friend the Member for Oxford (Mr. Neate) well remarked, not only were, but still are, visited with penalties so ludicrously inadequate, as to be almost an encouragement to the crime.

I think, Sir, that in the case of most offences, except those against property, there is more need of strengthening our punishments than of weakening them; and that severer sentences, with an apportionment of them to the different kinds of offences which shall approve itself better than at present to the moral sentiments of the community, are the kind of reform of which our penal system now stands in need. I shall therefore vote against the Amendment.

NOTES

1. A display of force.
2. Is it so hard a thing to die?

༻ QUESTIONS FOR ANALYSIS

1. Mill defends capital punishment as the "most humane" punishment available for those who deserve severe punishment compared to the alternatives. Considering the options he weighs, is execution really the most humane? Given the punishments we typically use today, would Mill likely reach the same conclusion if he were alive now?
2. How does Mill rely on his principles of utilitarian reasoning in his consideration of capital punishment?
3. How are Mill's arguments similar to and different from contemporary debates?
4. How does he respond to concerns that innocent people might be executed? Does his answer adequately address concerns today, now that DNA testing is showing that many on death row are innocent?

A Life for a Life

IGOR PRIMORATZ

A professor emeritus of philosophy at the Hebrew University of Jerusalem, Igor Primoratz (1945–) has published extensively on ethics, political philosophy, and philosophy of law. He is now a Professorial Fellow at the Centre for Applied Philosophy and Public Ethics, Charles Sturt University, Canberra, Australia, where he is conducting research on contemporary terrorism. He received his Ph.D. from the University of Belgrade, in the capital of Serbia, before emigrating to Jerusalem in 1983.

In this excerpt from his book *Justifying Legal Punishment*, he argues in favor of capital punishment using retributivism (an "eye-for-an-eye"), in contrast with the consequentialist approach of deterrence. He concludes, however, that moral constraints prevent us from inflicting terrorism as a form of punishment on terrorists, however much they themselves might deserve it.

... According to the retributive theory, consequences of punishment, however important from the practical point of view, are irrelevant when it comes to its justification; *the* moral consideration is its justice. Punishment is morally justified insofar as it is meted out as retribution for the offense committed. When someone has committed an offense, he deserves to be punished: it is just, and consequently justified, that he be punished. The offense is the sole ground of the state's right and duty to punish. It is also the measure of legitimate punishment: the two ought to be proportionate. So the issue of

---

Reprinted from Igor Primoratz, *Justifying Legal Punishment*. (Amherst, NY: Humanity Books, 1989). pp. 158–59, 161–66. Copyright © 1989 Igor Primoratz. All rights reserved. Reprinted with permission of the publisher; www.prometheusbooks.com.

capital punishment within the retributive approach comes down to the question, Is this punishment ever proportionate retribution for the offense committed, and thus deserved, just, and justified?

The classic representatives of retributivism believed that it was, and that it was the only proportionate and hence appropriate punishment, if the offense was *murder*—that is, criminal homicide perpetrated voluntarily and intentionally or in wanton disregard of human life. In other cases, the demand for proportionality between offense and punishment can be satisfied by fines or prison terms; the crime of murder, however, is an exception in this respect, and calls for the literal interpretation of the *lex talionis*. The uniqueness of this crime has to do with the uniqueness of the value which has been deliberately or recklessly destroyed. We come across this idea as early as the original formulation of the retributive view— the biblical teaching on punishment: "You shall accept no ransom for the life of a murderer who is guilty of death; but he shall be put to death."[1] The rationale of this command—one that clearly distinguishes the biblical conception of the criminal law from contemporaneous criminal law systems in the Middle East—is that man was not only created *by* God, like every other creature, but also, alone among all the creatures, *in the image of God*:

> That man was made in the image of God ... is expressive of the peculiar and supreme worth of man. Of all creatures, Genesis 1 relates, he alone possesses this attribute, bringing him into closer relation to God than all the rest and conferring upon him the highest value.... This view of the uniqueness and supremacy of human life ... places life beyond the reach of other values. The idea that life may be measured in terms of money or other property ... is excluded. Compensation of any kind is ruled out. The guilt of the murderer is infinite because the murdered life is invaluable; the kinsmen of the slain man are not competent to say when he has been paid for. An absolute wrong has been committed, a sin against God which is not subject to human discussion.... Because human life is invaluable, to take it entails the death penalty.[2]

This view that the value of human life is not commensurable with other values, and that

consequently there is only one truly equivalent punishment for murder, namely death, does not necessarily presuppose a theistic outlook. It can be claimed that, simply because we have to be alive if we are to experience and realize any other value at all, there is nothing equivalent to the murderous destruction of a human life except the destruction of the life of the murderer. Any other retribution, no matter how severe, would still be less than what is proportionate, deserved, and just. As long as the murderer is alive, no matter how bad the conditions of his life may be, there are always at least *some* values he can experience and realize. This provides a plausible interpretation of what the classical representatives of retributivism as a philosophical theory of punishment, such as Kant and Hegel, had to say on the subject.

It seems to me that this is essentially correct. With respect to the larger question of the justification of punishment in general, it is the retributive theory that gives the right answer. Accordingly, capital punishment ought to be retained where it obtains, and reintroduced in those jurisdictions that have abolished it, although we have no reason to believe that, as a means of deterrence, it is any better than a very long prison term. It ought to be retained, or reintroduced, for one simple reason: that justice be done in cases of murder, that murderers be punished according to their deserts.

There are a number of arguments that have been advanced against this rationale of capital punishment.

... [One] abolitionist argument makes use of the idea of a right to life in a more straightforward manner: it simply says that capital punishment is illegitimate because it violates the right to life, which is a fundamental, absolute, sacred right belonging to each and every human being, and therefore ought to be respected even in a murderer.[3]

If any rights are fundamental, the right to life is certainly one of them; but to claim that it is absolute, inviolable under any circumstances and for any reason, is a different matter. If an abolitionist wants to argue his case by asserting an absolute right to life, she will also have to deny moral legitimacy to taking human life in war, revolution, and self-defense. This kind of pacifism is a consistent but farfetched and hence implausible position.

I do not believe that the right to life (nor, for that matter, any other right) is absolute. I have no general theory of rights to fall back upon here; instead, let me pose a question. Would we take seriously the claim to an absolute, sacred, inviolable right to life—coming from the mouth of a *confessed murderer?* I submit that we would not, for the obvious reason that it is being put forward by the person who confessedly denied another human being this very right. But if the murderer cannot plausibly claim such a right for himself, neither can *anyone else* do that in his behalf. This suggests that there is an element of reciprocity in our general rights, such as the right to life or property. I can convincingly claim these rights only so long as I acknowledge and respect the same rights of others. If I violate the rights of others, I thereby lose the same rights. If I am a murderer, I have no *right* to live.

Some opponents of capital punishment claim that a criminal law system which includes this punishment is contradictory, in that it prohibits murder and at the same time provides for its perpetration: "It is one and the same legal regulation which prohibits the individual from murdering, while allowing the state to murder.... This is obviously a terrible irony, an abnormal and immoral logic, against which everything in us revolts."[4]

This seems to be one of the more popular arguments against the death penalty, but it is not a good one. If it were valid, it would prove too much. Exactly the same might be claimed of other kinds of punishment: of prison terms, that they are "contradictory" to the legal protection of liberty; of fines, that they are "contradictory" to the legal protection of property. Fortunately enough, it is not valid, for it begs the question at issue. In order to be able to talk of the state as "murdering" the person it executes, and to claim that there is "an abnormal and immoral logic" at work here, which thrives on a "contradiction," one has to use the word "murder" in the very same sense—that is, in the usual sense, which implies the idea of the *wrongful* taking the life of another—both when speaking of what the murderer has done to the victim and of what the state is doing to him by way of punishment. But this is precisely the question at issue: whether capital punishment *is* "murder," whether it is wrongful or morally justified and right.

The next two arguments attack the retributive rationale of capital punishment by questioning the claim that it is only this punishment that satisfies the demand for proportion between offense and punishment in the case of murder. The first points out that any two human lives are different in many important respects, such as age, health, physical and mental capability, so that it does not make much sense to consider them equally valuable. What if the murdered person was very old, practically at the very end of her natural life, while the murderer is young, with most of his life still ahead of him, for instance? Or if the victim was gravely and incurably ill, and thus doomed to live her life in suffering and hopelessness, without being able to experience almost anything that makes a human life worth living, while the murderer is in every respect capable of experiencing and enjoying things life has to offer? Or the other way round? Would not the death penalty in such cases amount either to taking a more valuable life as a punishment for destroying a less valuable one, or *vice versa?* Would it not be either too much, or too little, and in both cases disproportionate, and thus unjust and wrong, from the standpoint of the retributive theory itself?[5]

Any plausibility this argument might appear to have is the result of a conflation of differences between, and value of, human lives. No doubt, any two human lives are *different* in innumerable ways, but this does not entail that they are not *equally valuable.* I have no worked-out general theory of equality to refer to here, but I do not think that one is necessary in order to do away with this argument. The modern humanistic and democratic tradition in ethical, social, and political thought is based on the idea that all human beings are equal. This finds its legal expression in the principle of equality of people under the law. If we are not willing to give up this principle, we have to stick to the assumption that, all differences notwithstanding, any two human lives, *qua* human lives, are equally valuable. If, on the other hand, we allow that, on the basis of such criteria as age, health, or mental or physical ability, it can be claimed that the life of one person is more or less valuable than the life of another, and we admit such claims in the sphere of law, including criminal law, we shall thereby give up the principle of equality of people under the law. In all consistency, we shall not be able to demand that property, physical and personal integrity, and all other rights and interests of individuals be given equal consideration in courts of law either—that is, we shall have to accept systematic discrimination between individuals on the basis of the same criteria across the whole field. I do not think anyone would seriously contemplate an overhaul of the whole legal system along these lines.

The second argument having to do with the issue of proportionality between murder and capital punishment draws our attention to the fact that the law normally provides for a certain period of time to elapse between the passing of a death sentence and its execution. It is a period of several weeks or months; in some cases it extends to years. This period is bound to be one of constant mental anguish for the condemned. And thus, all things considered, what is inflicted on him is disproportionately hard and hence unjust. It would be proportionate and just only in the case of "a criminal who had warned his victim of the date at which he would inflict a horrible death on him and who, from that moment onward, had confined him at his mercy for months."[6]

The first thing to note about this argument is that it does not support a full-fledged abolitionist stand; if it were valid, it would not show that capital punishment is *never* proportionate and just, but only that it is *very rarely* so. Consequently, the conclusion would not be that it ought to be abolished outright, but only that it ought to be restricted to those cases that would satisfy the condition cited above. Such cases do happen, although, to be sure, not very often; the murder of Aldo Moro, for instance, was of this kind. But this is not the main point. The main point is that the argument actually does not hit at capital punishment itself, although it is presented with that aim in view. It hits at something else: a particular way of carrying out this punishment, which is widely adopted in our time. Some hundred years ago and more, in the Wild West, they frequently hanged the man convicted to die almost immediately after pronouncing the sentence. I am not arguing here that we should follow this example today; I mention this piece of historical fact only in order to show that the interval between sentencing someone to death and carrying out the sentence is not a *part* of capital punishment itself. However unpalatable we might find those Wild West hangings, whatever objections we might want to voice against the speed with which they followed the sentencing, surely we shall not deny them the *description* of "executions." So the implication of the argument is not that we ought to do away with capital punishment altogether, nor that we ought to restrict it to those cases of murder where the murderer had warned the victim weeks or months in advance of what he was going to do to her, but that we ought to reexamine the procedure of carrying out this kind of punishment. We ought to weigh the reasons for having this interval between the sentencing and executing, against the moral and human significance of the repercussions such an interval inevitably carries with it.

These reasons, in part, have to do with the possibility of miscarriages of justice and the need to rectify them. Thus we come to the argument against capital punishment which, historically, has been the most effective of all: many advances of the abolitionist movement have been connected with discoveries of cases of judicial errors. Judges and jurors are only human, and consequently some of their beliefs and decisions are bound to be mistaken. Some of their mistakes can be corrected upon discovery; but precisely those with most disastrous repercussions—those which result in innocent people being executed—can never be rectified. In all other cases of mistaken sentencing we can revoke the punishment, either completely or in part, or at least extend compensation. In addition, by exonerating the accused we give moral satisfaction. None of this is possible after an innocent person has been executed; capital punishment is essentially different from all other penalties by being completely irrevocable and irreparable.[7] Therefore, it ought to be abolished.

A part of my reply to this argument goes along the same lines as what I had to say on the previous one. It is not so far-reaching as abolitionists assume; for it would be quite implausible, even fanciful, to claim that there have *never* been cases of murder which left no room whatever for reasonable doubt as to the guilt and full responsibility of the accused. Such cases may not be more frequent than those others, but they do happen. Why not retain the death penalty at least for them?

Actually, this argument, just as the preceding one, does not speak out against capital punishment itself, but against the existing procedures for trying capital cases. Miscarriages of justice result in innocent people being sentenced to death and executed, even in the criminal-law systems in which greatest care is taken to ensure that it never comes to that. But this does not stem from the intrinsic nature of the institution of capital punishment; it results from deficiencies, limitations, and imperfections of the criminal law procedures in which this punishment is meted out. Errors of justice do not demonstrate the need to do away with capital punishment; they simply make it incumbent on us to do everything possible to improve even further procedures of meting it out.

To be sure, this conclusion will not find favor with a diehard abolitionist. "I shall ask for the abolition of Capital Punishment until I have the infallibility of human judgement demonstrated to me," that is, as long as there is even the slightest possibility that innocent people may be executed because of judicial errors, Lafayette said in his day.[8] Many an opponent of this kind of punishment will say the same today. The demand to do away with capital punishment altogether, so as to eliminate even the smallest chance of that ever happening— the chance which, admittedly, would remain even after everything humanly possible has been done to perfect the procedure, although then it would be very slight indeed—is actually a demand to give a privileged position to murderers as against all other offenders, big and small. For if we acted on this demand, we would bring about a situation in which proportionate penalties would be meted out for all offenses, *except* for murder. Murderers would not be receiving the only punishment truly proportionate to their crimes, the punishment of

death, but some other, lighter, and thus disproportionate penalty. All other offenders would be punished according to their deserts; only murderers would be receiving less than *they* deserve. In all other cases justice would be done in full; only in cases of the gravest of offenses, the crime of murder, justice would not be carried out in full measure. It is a great and tragic miscarriage of justice when an innocent person is mistakenly sentenced to death and executed, but systematically giving murderers advantage over all other offenders would also be a grave injustice. Is the fact that, as long as capital punishment is retained, there is a possibility that over a number of years, or even decades, an injustice of the first kind may be committed, unintentionally and unconsciously, reason enough to abolish it altogether, and thus end up with a system of punishments in which injustices of the second kind are perpetrated daily, consciously, and inevitably?[9]

There is still another abolitionist argument that actually does not hit out against capital punishment itself, but against something else. Figures are sometimes quoted which show that this punishment is much more often meted out to the uneducated and poor than to the educated, rich, and influential people; in the United States, much more often to blacks than to whites. These figures are adduced as a proof of the inherent injustice of this kind of punishment. On account of them, it is claimed that capital punishment is not a way of doing justice by meting out deserved punishment to murderers, but rather a means of social discrimination and perpetuation of social injustice.

I shall not question these findings, which are quite convincing, and anyway, there is no need to do that in order to defend the institution of capital punishment. For there seems to be a certain amount of discrimination and injustice not only in sentencing people to death and executing them, but also in meting out other penalties. The social structure of the death rows in American prisons, for instance, does not seem to be basically different from the general social structure of American penitentiaries. If this argument were valid, it would call not only for abolition of the penalty of death, but for doing away with other penalties as well.

But it is not valid; as Burton Leiser has pointed out, ... this is not an argument, either against the death penalty or against any other form of punishment. It is an argument against the unjust and inequitable distribution of penalties. If the trials of wealthy men are less likely to result in convictions than those of poor men, then something must be done to reform the procedure in criminal courts. If those who have money and standing in the community are less likely to be charged with serious offenses than their less affluent fellow citizens, then there should be a major overhaul of the entire system of criminal justice... But the maldistribution of penalties is no argument against any particular form of penalty.[10]

... I have attempted to show that none of the standard arguments against the death penalty, which would be relevant within the retributive approach to punishment in general, are really convincing. But I shall end on a conciliatory note. I can envisage a way for a retributivist to take an abolitionist stand, without thereby being inconsistent. Let me explain this in just a few words.

The Eighth Amendment to the Constitution of the United States says that "excessive bail shall not be required, nor excessive fines imposed, nor cruel and unusual punishments inflicted."[11] I do not find the idea of a "usual" or "unusual" punishment very helpful. But I do think that punishments ought not to be *cruel*. They ought not to be cruel in the relative sense, by being considerably more severe than what is proportionate to the offense committed, what is deserved and just; but they also ought not to be cruel in an absolute sense—that is, severe beyond a certain threshold.

Admittedly, it would be very difficult to determine that threshold precisely, but it is not necessary for my purpose here. It will be enough to provide a paradigmatic case of something that is surely beyond that threshold: torture. I do not believe that a torturer has a *right* not to be tortured. If we could bring ourselves to torture him, as a punishment for what he has done to the victim, I do not think that it could be plausibly claimed that what we were doing to him was something undeserved and unjust. But I also do not think that we should try to bring ourselves to do that, in pursuit of proportion between offense and punishment and in striving to execute justice. Justice is one of

the most important moral principles—perhaps the most important one—but it is not *absolute*. On the other hand, I feel that torture is something *absolutely wrong* from the moral point of view: something indecent and inhuman, something immensely and unredeemably degrading both to the man tortured and to the torturer himself, something that is morally "beyond the pale." So to sentence a torturer to be tortured would not mean to give him a punishment which is undeserved and unjust, and hence cruel in the relative sense of the word; but it *would* mean to punish him in a way that is cruel in this second, absolute sense. On account of this, I would say that, when punishing a torturer, we ought to desist from giving him the full measure of what he has deserved by his deed, that we ought to settle for less than what in his case would be the full measure of justice. One of the moral principles limiting the striving to do justice is this prohibition of cruelty in the absolute sense of the word. We ought not to execute justice to the full, if that means that we shall have to be cruel.

I do not feel about executing a person in a swift and relatively painless manner the same way I feel about torturing him. But a person, or a society, could come to feel the same way about both. A person or a society that adhered to the retributive view of punishment, but at the same time felt this way about executing a human being, could decide that capital punishment is cruel and therefore unacceptable without being in any way inconsistent.

NOTES

1. Numbers 35.31 (R.S.V.).
2. M. Greenberg, "Some Postulates of Biblical Criminal Law," in J. Goldin (ed.), *The Jewish Expression* (New York: Bantam, 1970), pp. 25–6. (Post-biblical Jewish law evolved toward the virtual abolition of the death penalty, but that is of no concern here.)
3. For an example of this view, see L.N. Tolstoy, *Smertnaya kazn i hristianstvo* (Berlin: I.P. Ladizhnikov, n.d.), pp. 40–41.
4. S.V. Vulović, *Problem smrtne kazne* (Belgrade: Geca Kon, 1925), pp. 23–24.
5. Cf. W. Blackstone, *Commentaries on the Laws of England*, 4th ed., ed. J. DeWitt Andrews (Chicago: Callaghan & Co., 1899), p. 1224.

6. A. Camus, "Reflections on the Guillotine," *Resistance, Rebellion and Death*, trans. J. O'Brien (London: Hamish Hamilton, 1961), p. 143.

7. For an interesting critical discussion of this point, see M. Davis, "Is the Death Penalty Irrevocable?," *Social Theory and Practice* 10 (1984).

8. Quoted in E.R. Calvert, *Capital Punishment in the Twentieth Century* (London: G.P. Putnam's Sons, 1927), p. 132.

9. For a criticism of this argument, see L. Sebba, "On Capital Punishment—A Comment," *Israel Law Review* 17 (1982), pp. 392–395.

10. B.M. Leiser, *Liberty, Justice and Morals: Contemporary Value Conflicts* (New York: Macmillan, 1973), p. 225.

11. On the question whether the death penalty is cruel and unusual within the meaning of the Eighth Amendment, see M.J. Radin, "The Jurisprudence of Death: Evolving Standards for the Cruel and Unusual Clause," *University of Pennsylvania Law Review* 126 (1978); H.A. Bedau, "Thinking of the Death Penalty as a Cruel and Unusual Punishment," *U.C. Davis Law Review* 18 (1985).

👑 QUESTIONS FOR ANALYSIS

1. Why is retributivism the only way to justify punishment, according to Primoratz?

2. What is unique about the offense of murder that justifies capital punishment?

3. How does Primoratz answer the objection to the death penalty that such punishment violates the right to life?

4. How does he answer the objection that the death penalty is not always appropriately proportional to the crime?

5. What is the relevance of the delay between sentencing and the actual execution? Why does Primoratz think this does not support the claims of abolitionists?

6. How does he respond to objections that people are sometimes wrongly convicted and, once executed, cannot be compensated for the mistake?

7. How does Primoratz respond to objections that capital punishment is disproportionately imposed on the uneducated and the poor?

8. How does he suggest that a retributivist might become an abolitionist?

9. Should a consistent retributivist insist that someone convicted of torture be tortured as punishment?

10. Does a torturer have a right not to be tortured?

11. Is imposition of torture as punishment for a convicted torturer undeserved? unjust? cruel?

12. Is execution in a swift and relatively painless manner consistent with the prohibition on "cruel and unusual" punishment in the U.S. Constitution?

On Deterrence and the Death Penalty

ERNEST VAN DEN HAAG

Ernest van den Haag (1914–2002) was a professor of jurisprudence and social philosophy at several universities. Until 1988, he was the John M. Olin Professor of Jurisprudence and Public Policy at Fordham University. He begins his essay by conceding that capital punishment cannot be defended on grounds of rehabilitation or protection of society from unrehabilitated offenders. But he does believe that the ultimate punishment can be justified on grounds of deterrence.

To make his point, van den Haag at some length provides a psychological basis for deterrence. He associates deterrence with human responses to danger. Law functions to change

Reprinted by special permission of the *Journal of Criminal Law, Criminology, and Police Science*, © 1969 by Northwestern University School of Law, vol. 60, no. 2.

social dangers into individual ones: Legal threats are designed to deter individuals from actions that threaten society. Most of us, van den Haag argues, transfer these external penalty dangers into internal ones; that is, we each develop a conscience that threatens us if we do wrong. But this conscience is and needs to be reinforced by external authority, which imposes penalties for antisocial behavior.

Van den Haag then critically examines the reason punishment has fallen into disrepute as a deterrent to crime: the claim that slums, ghettos, and personality disorders are the real causes of crime. He dismisses these as spurious explanations and insists that only punishment can deter crime. In van den Haag's view, whether individuals will commit crimes depends exclusively on whether they perceive the penalty risks as worth it.

While he concedes that the death penalty cannot be proven to deter crime, van den Haag observes that this in no way means capital punishment lacks a deterrent value. Indeed, it is this very uncertainty about its deterrence that impels van den Haag to argue for its retention. In the last analysis, he believes that retaining capital punishment leads to a net gain for society, notwithstanding the occasional abuse of it. In arguing for capital punishment, then, van den Haag takes a utilitarian viewpoint.

I

If rehabilitation and the protection of society from unrehabilitated offenders were the only purposes of legal punishment, the death penalty could be abolished: It cannot attain the first end, and is not needed for the second. No case for the death penalty can be made unless "doing justice" or "deterring others" is among our penal aims.[1] Each of these purposes can justify capital punishment by itself; opponents, therefore, must show that neither actually does, while proponents can rest their case on either.

Although the argument from justice is intellectually more interesting, and, in my view, decisive enough, utilitarian arguments have more appeal: The claim that capital punishment is useless because it does not deter others is most persuasive. I shall, therefore, focus on this claim. Lest the argument be thought to be unduly narrow, I shall show, nonetheless, that some claims of injustice rest on premises which the claimants reject when arguments for capital punishment are derived there from; while other claims of injustice have independent standing: Their weight depends on the weight given to deterrence.

II

Capital punishment is regarded as unjust because it may lead to the execution of innocents, or because

the guilty poor (or disadvantaged) are more likely to be executed than the guilty rich.

Regardless of merit, these claims are relevant only if "doing justice" is one purpose of punishment. Unless one regards it as good, or, at least, better, that the guilty be punished rather than the innocent, and that the equally guilty be punished equally,[2] unless, that is, one wants penalties to be just, one cannot object to them because they are not. However, if one does include justice among the purposes of punishment, it becomes possible to justify any one punishment—even death—on grounds of justice. Yet, those who object to the death penalty because of its alleged injustice usually deny not only the merits, or the sufficiency, of specific arguments based on justice, but the propriety of justice as an argument: They exclude "doing justice" as a purpose of legal punishment. If justice is not a purpose of penalties, injustice cannot be an objection to the death penalty, or to any other; if it is, justice cannot be ruled out as an argument for any penalty.

Consider the claim of injustice on its merits now. A convicted man may be found to have been innocent; if he was executed, the penalty cannot be reversed. Except for fines, penalties never can be reversed. Time spent in prison cannot be returned. However, a prison sentence may be remitted once the prisoner serving it is found innocent; and he can be compensated for the time served (although compensation ordinarily cannot repair the harm). Thus, though (nearly) all penalties are irreversible, the death penalty, unlike others, is irrevocable as well.

Despite all precautions, errors will occur in judicial proceedings: The innocent may be found guilty,[3] or the guilty rich may more easily escape conviction, or receive lesser penalties than the guilty poor. However, these injustices do not reside in the penalties inflicted but in their maldistribution. It is not the penalty—whether death or prison—which is unjust when inflicted on the innocent, but its imposition on the innocent. Inequity between poor and rich also involves distribution, not the penalty distributed.[4] Thus injustice is not an objection to the death penalty but to the distributive process—the trial. Trials are more likely to be fair when life is at stake—the death penalty is probably less often unjustly inflicted than others. It requires special consideration not because it is more, or more often, unjust than other penalties, but because it is always irrevocable.

Can any amount of deterrence justify the possibility of irrevocable injustice? Surely injustice is unjustifiable in each actual individual case; it must be objected to whenever it occurs. But we are concerned here with the process that may produce injustice, and with the penalty that would make it irrevocable—not with the actual individual cases produced, but with the general rules which may produce them. To consider objections to a general rule (the provision of any penalties by law) we must compare the likely net result of alternative rules and select the rule (or penalty) likely to produce the least injustice. For however one defines justice, to support it cannot mean less than to favor the least injustice. If the death of innocents because of judicial error is unjust, so is the death of innocents by murder. If some murders could be avoided by a penalty conceivably more deterrent than others—such as the death penalty—then the question becomes: Which penalty will minimize the number of innocents killed (by crime and by punishment)? It follows that the irrevocable injustice sometimes inflicted by the death penalty would not significantly militate against it, if capital punishment deters enough murders to reduce the total number of innocents killed so that fewer are lost than would be lost without it.

In general, the possibility of injustice argues against penalization of any kind only if the expected usefulness of penalization is less important than the probable harm (particularly to innocents) and the probable inequities. The possibility of injustice argues against the death penalty only inasmuch as the added usefulness (deterrence) expected from irrevocability is thought less important than the added harm. (Were my argument specifically concerned with justice, I could compare the injustice inflicted by the courts with the injustice—outside the courts—avoided by the judicial process. "Important" here may be used to include everything to which importance is attached.)

We must briefly examine now the general use and effectiveness of deterrence to decide whether the death penalty could add enough deterrence to be warranted.

III

Does any punishment "deter others" at all? Doubts have been thrown on this effect because it is thought to depend on the incorrect rationalistic psychology of some of its 18th- and 19th-century proponents. Actually deterrence does not depend on rational calculation, on rationality or even on capacity for it; nor do arguments for it depend on rationalistic psychology. Deterrence depends on the likelihood and on the regularity—not on the rationality—of human responses to danger; and further on the possibility of reinforcing internal controls by vicarious external experiences.

Responsiveness to danger is generally found in human behavior; the danger can, but need not, come from the law or from society; nor need it be explicitly verbalized. Unless intent on suicide, people do not jump from high mountain cliffs, however tempted to fly through the air; and they take precautions against falling. The mere risk of injury often restrains us from doing what is otherwise attractive; we refrain even when we have no direct experience, and usually without explicit computation of probabilities, let alone conscious weighing of expected pleasure against possible pain. One abstains from dangerous acts because of vague, inchoate, habitual and, above all, pre-conscious fears. Risks and rewards are more often felt than calculated; one abstains without accounting to oneself, because "it isn't done," or because one literally does not conceive of the action one refrains from. Animals as well refrain from painful or injurious experiences presumably without calculation; and the threat of punishment can be used to regulate their conduct.

Unlike natural dangers, legal threats are constructed deliberately by legislators to restrain actions which may impair the social order. Thus legislation transforms social into individual dangers. Most people further transform external into internal danger: They acquire a sense of moral obligation, a conscience, which threatens them, should they do what is wrong. Arising originally from the external authority of rulers and rules, conscience is internalized and becomes independent of external forces. However, conscience is constantly reinforced in those whom it controls by the coercive imposition of external authority on recalcitrants and on those who have not acquired it. Most people refrain from offenses because they feel an obligation to behave lawfully. But this obligation would scarcely be felt if those who do not feel or follow it were not to suffer punishment.

Although the legislators may calculate their threats and the responses to be produced, the effectiveness of the threats neither requires nor depends on calculations by those responding. The predictor (or producer) of effects must calculate; those whose responses are predicted (or produced) need not. Hence, although legislation (and legislators) should be rational, subjects, to be deterred as intended, need not be: They need only be responsive.

Punishments deter those who have not violated the law for the same reasons—and in the same degrees (apart from internalization: moral obligation) as do natural dangers. Often natural dangers—all dangers not deliberately created by legislation (*e.g.*, injury of the criminal inflicted by the crime victim) are insufficient. Thus, the fear of injury (natural danger) does not suffice to control city traffic; it must be reinforced by the legal punishment meted out to those who violate the rules. These punishments keep most people observing the regulations. However, where (in the absence of natural danger) the threatened punishment is so light that the advantage of violating rules tends to exceed the disadvantage of being punished (divided by the

risk), the rule is violated (*i.e.*, parking fines are too light). In this case the feeling of obligation tends to vanish as well. Elsewhere punishment deters.

To be sure, not everybody responds to threatened punishment. Non-responsive persons may be (a) self-destructive or (b) incapable of responding to threats, or even of grasping them. Increases in the size, or certainty, of penalties would not affect these two groups. A third group (c) might respond to more certain or more severe penalties.[5] If the punishment threatened for burglary, robbery, or rape were a $5 fine in North Carolina, and 5 years in prison in South Carolina, I have no doubt that the North Carolina treasury would become quite opulent until vigilante justice would provide the deterrence not provided by law. Whether to increase penalties (or improve enforcement) depends on the importance of the rule to society, the size and likely reaction of the group that did not respond before, and the acceptance of the added punishment and enforcement required to deter it. Observation would have to locate the points—likely to differ in different times and places—at which diminishing, zero, and negative returns set in. There is no reason to believe that all present and future offenders belong to the *a priori* non-responsive groups, or that all penalties have reached the point of diminishing, let alone zero returns.

IV

Even though its effectiveness seems obvious, punishment as a deterrent has fallen into disrepute. Some ideas which help explain this progressive heedlessness were uttered by Lester Pearson, then Prime Minister of Canada, when, in opposing the death penalty, he proposed that instead "the state seek to eradicate the causes of crime—slums, ghettos and personality disorders."[6]

"Slums, ghettos, and personality disorders" have not been shown, singly or collectively, to be "the causes" of crime.

(1) The crime rate in the slums is indeed higher than elsewhere; but so is the death rate in hospitals. Slums are no more "causes" of crime than hospitals are of death; they are locations of crime, as hospitals are of death. Slums and hospitals attract people selectively; neither is the

"cause" of the condition (disease in hospitals, poverty in slums) that leads to the selective attraction.

As for poverty which draws people into slums, and, sometimes, into crime, any relative disadvantage may lead to ambition, frustration, resentment and, if insufficiently restrained, to crime. Not all relative disadvantages can be eliminated; indeed very few can be, and their elimination increases the resentment generated by the remaining ones; not even relative poverty can be removed altogether. (Absolute poverty—whatever that may be—hardly affects crime.) However, though contributory, relative disadvantages are not a necessary or sufficient cause of crime: Most poor people do not commit crimes, and some rich people do. Hence, "eradication of poverty" would, at most, remove one (doubtful) cause of crime.

In the United States, the decline of poverty has not been associated with a reduction of crime. Poverty measured in dollars of constant purchasing power, according to present government standards and statistics, was the condition of ½ of all our families in 1920; of ⅕ in 1962; and of less than ⅙ in 1966. In 1967, 5.3 million families out of 49.8 million were poor—⅑ of all families in the United States. If crime has been reduced in a similar manner, it is a well-kept secret.

Those who regard poverty as a cause of crime often draw a wrong inference from a true proposition: The rich will not commit certain crimes—Rockefeller never riots; nor does he steal. (He mugs, but only on T.V.) Yet while wealth may be the cause of not committing (certain) crimes, it does not follow that poverty (absence of wealth) is the cause of committing them. Water extinguishes or prevents fire; but its absence is not the cause of fire. Thus, if poverty could be abolished, if everybody had all "necessities" (I don't pretend to know what this would mean), crime would remain, for, in the words of Aristotle, "the greatest crimes are committed not for the sake of basic necessities but for the sake of superfluities." Superfluities cannot be provided by the government; they would be what the government does not provide.

(2) Negro ghettos have a high, Chinese ghettos have a low crime rate. Ethnic separation, voluntary or forced, obviously has little to do with crime; I can think of no reason why it should.[7]

(3) I cannot see how the state could "eradicate" personality disorders even if all causes and cures were known and available. (They are not.) Further, the known incidence of personality disorders within the prison population does not exceed the known incidence outside—though our knowledge of both is tenuous. Nor are personality disorders necessary or sufficient causes for criminal offenses, unless these be identified by means of (moral, not clinical) definition with personality disorders. In this case, Mr. Pearson would have proposed to "eradicate" crime by eradicating crime—certainly a sound, but not a helpful idea.

Mr. Pearson's views are part as well of the mental furniture of the former U.S. Attorney General Ramsey Clark, who told a congressional committee that "... only the elimination of the causes of crime can make a significant and lasting difference in the incidence of crime." Uncharitably interpreted, Mr. Clark revealed that only the elimination of causes eliminates effects—a sleazy cliché and wrong to boot. Given the benefit of the doubt, Mr. Clark probably meant that the causes of crime are social; and that therefore crime can be reduced "only" by non-penal (social) measures.

This view suggests a fireman who declines firefighting apparatus by pointing out that "in the long run only the elimination of the causes" of fire "can make a significant and lasting difference in the incidence" of fire, and that fire-fighting equipment does not eliminate "the causes"—except that such a fireman would probably not rise to fire chief. Actually, whether fires are checked depends on equipment and on the efforts of the firemen using it no less than on the presence of "the causes": inflammable materials. So with crimes. Laws, courts and police actions are no less important in restraining them than "the causes" are in impelling them. If firemen (or attorneys general) pass the buck and refuse to use the means available, we may all be burned while waiting for "the long run" and "the elimination of the causes."

Whether any activity—be it lawful or unlawful—takes place depends on whether the desire for it, or for whatever is to be secured by it, is stronger than the desire to avoid the costs involved. Accordingly people work, attend college, commit crimes, go to the movies—or refrain from any of these activities. Attendance at a theatre may be high because the show is entertaining and because the price of admission is low. Obviously the attendance depends on both—on the combination of expected gratification and cost. The wish, motive or impulse for doing anything—the experienced, or expected, gratification—is the cause of doing it; the wish to avoid the cost is the cause of not doing it. One is no more and no less "cause" than the other. (Common speech supports this use of "cause" no less than logic: "Why did you go to Jamaica?" *Because* it is such a beautiful place." "Why didn't you go to Jamaica?" "*Because* it is too expensive."—"Why do you buy this?" "*Because* it is so cheap." "Why don't you buy that?" "*Because* it is too expensive.") Penalties (costs) are causes of lawfulness, or (if too low or uncertain) of unlawfulness, of crime. People do commit crimes because, given their conditions, the desire for the satisfaction sought prevails. They refrain if the desire to avoid the cost prevails. Given the desire, low cost (penalty) causes the action, and high cost restraint. Given the cost, desire becomes the causal variable. Neither is intrinsically more causal than the other. The crime rate increases if the cost is reduced or the desire raised. It can be decreased by raising the cost or by reducing the desire.

The cost of crime is more easily and swiftly changed than the conditions producing the inclination to it. Further, the costs are very largely within the power of the government to change, whereas the conditions producing propensity to crime are often only indirectly affected by government action, and some are altogether beyond the control of the government. Our unilateral emphasis on these conditions and our undue neglect of costs may contribute to an unnecessarily high crime rate.

V

The foregoing suggests the question posed by the death penalty: Is the deterrence added (return) sufficiently above zero to warrant irrevocability (or other, less clear, disadvantages)? The question is not only whether the penalty deters, but whether it deters more than alternatives and whether the difference exceeds the cost of irrevocability. (I shall assume that the alternative is actual life imprisonment so as to exclude the complication produced by the release of the unrehabilitated.)

In some fairly infrequent but important circumstances the death penalty is the only possible deterrent. Thus, in case of acute *coups d'état*, or of acute substantial attempts to overthrow the government, prospective rebels would altogether discount the threat of any prison sentence. They would not be deterred because they believe the swift victory of the revolution will invalidate a prison sentence and turn it into an advantage. Execution would be the only deterrent because, unlike prison sentences, it cannot be revoked by victorious rebels. The same reasoning applies to deterring spies or traitors in wartime. Finally, men who, by virtue of past acts, are already serving, or are threatened, by a life sentence could be deterred from further offenses only by the threat of the death penalty.[8]

What about criminals who do not fall into any of these (often ignored) classes? Prof. Thorsten Sellin has made a careful study of the available statistics: He concluded that they do not yield evidence for the deterring effect of the death penalty.[9] Somewhat surprisingly, Prof. Sellin seems to think that this lack of evidence for deterrence is evidence for the lack of deterrence. It is not. It means that deterrence has not been demonstrated statistically—not that non-deterrence has been.

It is entirely possible, indeed likely (as Prof. Sellin appears willing to concede), that the statistics used, though the best available, are nonetheless too slender a reed to rest conclusions on. They indicate that the homicide rate does not vary greatly between similar areas with or without the death penalty, and in the same area before and after abolition. However, the similar areas are not similar enough; the periods are not long enough; many social differences and changes, other than the abolition of the death penalty, may account for the variation (or lack of it) in homicide rates with and without, before and after abolition; some of these social differences and changes are likely to have affected homicide rates. I am unaware of any statistical analysis which adjusts for such changes and differences. And logically, it is quite consistent with the postulated deterrent effect of capital punishment that there be less homicide after abolition: With retention there might have been still less.

Homicide rates do not depend exclusively on penalties any more than do other crime rates. A number of conditions which influence the propensity to crime, demographic, economic or generally social changes or differences—even such matters as changes of the divorce laws or of the cotton price—may influence the homicide rate. Therefore variation or constancy cannot be attributed to variations or constancy of the penalties, unless we know that no other factor influencing the homicide rate has changed. Usually we don't. To believe the death penalty deterrent does not require one to believe that the death penalty, or any other, is the only or the decisive causal variable; this would be as absurd as the converse mistake that "social causes" are the only or always the decisive factor. To favor capital punishment, the efficacy of neither variable need be denied. It is enough to affirm that the severity of the penalty may influence some potential criminals, and that the added severity of the death penalty adds to deterrence, or may do so. It is quite possible that such a deterrent effect may be offset (or intensified) by nonpenal factors which affect propensity; its presence or absence therefore may be hard, and perhaps impossible to demonstrate.

Contrary to what Prof. Sellin *et al.* seem to presume, I doubt that offenders are aware of the absence or presence of the death penalty state by state or period by period. Such unawareness argues against the assumption of a calculating murderer. However, unawareness does not argue against the death penalty if by deterrence we mean a preconscious, general response to a severe, but not necessarily specifically and explicitly apprehended, or calculated threat. A constant homicide rate, despite abolition, may occur because of unawareness and not because of lack of deterrence: People remain deterred for a lengthy interval by the severity of the penalty in the past, or by the severity of penalties used in similar circumstances nearby.

I do not argue for a version of deterrence which would require me to believe that an individual shuns murder while in North Dakota, because

of the death penalty, and merrily goes to it in South Dakota since it has been abolished there; or that he will start the murderous career from which he had hitherto refrained, after abolition. I hold that the generalized threat of the death penalty may be a deterrent, and the more so, the more generally applied. Deterrence will not cease in the particular areas of abolition or at the particular times of abolition. Rather, general deterrence will be somewhat weakened, through local (partial) abolition. Even such weakening will be hard to detect owing to changes in many offsetting, or reinforcing, factors.

For all of these reasons, I doubt that the presence or absence of a deterrent effect of the death penalty is likely to be demonstrable by statistical means. The statistics presented by Prof. Sellin *et al.* show only that there is no statistical proof for the deterrent effect of the death penalty. But they do not show that there is no deterrent effect. Not to demonstrate presence of the effect is not the same as to demonstrate its absence; certainly not when there are plausible explanations for the nondemonstrability of the effect.

It is on our uncertainty that the case for deterrence must rest.[10]

VI

If we do not know whether the death penalty will deter others, we are confronted with two uncertainties. If we impose the death penalty, and achieve no deterrent effect thereby, the life of a convicted murderer has been expended in vain (from a deterrent viewpoint). There is a net loss. If we impose the death sentence and thereby deter some future murderers, we spared the lives of some future victims (the prospective murderers gain too; they are spared punishment because they were deterred). In this case, the death penalty has led to a net gain, unless the life of a convicted murderer is valued more highly than that of the unknown victim, or victims (and the non-imprisonment of the deterred non-murderer).

The calculation can be turned around, of course. The absence of the death penalty may harm no one and therefore produce a gain—the life of the convicted murderer. Or it may kill future victims of murderers who could have been deterred, and thus produce a loss—their life.

To be sure, we must risk something certain—the death (or life) of the convicted man, for something uncertain—the death (or life) of the victims of murderers who may be deterred. This is in the nature of uncertainty—when we invest, or gamble, we risk the money we have for an uncertain gain. Many human actions, most commitments—including marriage and crime—share this characteristic with the deterrent purpose of any penalization, and with its rehabilitative purpose (and even with the protective).

More proof is demanded for the deterrent effect of the death penalty than is demanded for the deterrent effect of other penalties. This is not justified by the absence of other utilitarian purposes such as protection and rehabilitation; they involve no less uncertainty than deterrence.[11]

Irrevocability may support a demand for some reason to expect more deterrence than revocable penalties might produce, but not a demand for more proof of deterrence, as has been pointed out above. The reason for expecting more deterrence lies in the greater severity, the terrifying effect inherent in finality. Since it seems more important to spare victims than to spare murderers, the burden of proving that the greater severity inherent in irrevocability adds nothing to deterrence lies on those who oppose capital punishment. Proponents of the death penalty need show only that there is no more uncertainty about it than about greater severity in general.

The demand that the death penalty be proved more deterrent than alternatives cannot be satisfied any more than the demand that six years in prison be proved to be more deterrent than three. But the uncertainty which confronts us favors the death penalty as long as by imposing it we might save future victims of murder. This effect is as plausible as the general idea that penalties have deterrents which increase with their severity. Though we have no proof of the positive deterrence of the penalty, we also have no proof of zero or negative effectiveness. I believe we have no right to risk additional future victims of murder for the sake of sparing convicted murderers; on

the contrary, our moral obligation is to risk the possible ineffectiveness of executions. However rationalized, the opposite view appears to be motivated by the simple fact that executions are more subjected to social control than murder. However, this applies to all penalties and does not argue for the abolition of any.

NOTES

1. Social solidarity of "community feeling" (here to be ignored) might be dealt with as a form of deterrence.
2. Certainly a major meaning of *suum cuique tribue*.
3. I am not concerned here with the converse injustice, *which I regard as no less grave*.
4. Such inequity, though likely, has not been demonstrated. Note that, since there are more poor than rich, there are likely to be more guilty poor; and, if poverty contributes to crime, the proportion of the poor who are criminals also should be higher than of the rich.
5. I neglect those motivated by civil disobedience or, generally, moral or political passion. Deterring them depends less on penalties than on the moral support they receive, though penalties play a role. I also neglect those who may belong to all three groups listed, some successively, some even simultaneously, such as drug addicts. Finally, I must altogether omit the far-from-negligible role that problems of apprehension and conviction play in deterrence—beyond saying that, by reducing the government's ability to apprehend and convict, courts are able to reduce the risks of offenders.
6. I quote from the *New York Times* (November 24, 1967, p. 22). The actual psychological and other factors which bear on the disrepute—as distinguished from the rationalizations—cannot be examined here.
7. Mixed areas, incidentally, have higher crime rates than segregated ones. See, e.g., R. Ross and E. van den Haag, *The Fabric of Society* (New York: Harcourt, Brace & Co., 1957), pp. 102–4. Because slums are bad (morally) and crime is, many people seem to reason that "slums spawn crime"—which confuses some sort of moral with a causal relation.
8. Cautious revolutionaries, uncertain of final victory, might be impressed by prison sentences—but not in the acute stage, when faith in victory is high. And one can increase even the severity of a life sentence in prison. Finally, harsh punishment of rebels

can intensify rebellious impulses. These points, though they qualify it, hardly impair the force of the argument.

9. Sellin considered mainly homicide statistics. His work may be found in his *Capital Punishment* (New York: Harper & Row, 1967); or, most conveniently, in H. A. Bedau, *The Death Penalty in America* (Garden City, N.Y.: Doubleday & Co., 1964), which also offers other material, mainly against the death penalty.

10. In view of the strong emotions aroused (itself an indication of effectiveness to me: Might not murderers be as upset over the death penalty as those who wish to spare them?) and because I believe penalties must reflect community feeling to be effective, I oppose mandatory death sentences and favor optional, and perhaps binding, recommendations by juries after their finding of guilt. The opposite course risks the non-conviction of guilty defendants by juries who do not want to see them executed.

11. Rehabilitation or protection are of minor importance in our actual penal system (though not in our theory). We confine many people who do not need rehabilitation and against whom we do not need protection (e.g., the exasperated husband who killed his wife); we release many unrehabilitated offenders against whom protection is needed. Certainly rehabilitation and protection are not, and deterrence is, the main actual function of legal punishment if we disregard non-utilitarian ones.

♔ QUESTIONS FOR ANALYSIS

1. Van den Haag claims that injustice is an objection not to the death penalty but to the distributive process. What does he mean? Is his distinction between penalty and distribution germane?

2. What does deterrence depend on, in van den Haag's view?

3. How does punishment differ from natural dangers?

4. What kinds of people do not respond to threatened punishment? Would you be persuaded by the anti–capital punishment argument that insists the death penalty simply does not deter certain people?

5. What determines whether penalties ought to be increased? Explain how this is a utilitarian argument.

6. Does van den Haag convince you that slums and ghettos are "no more 'causes' of crimes than hospitals are of death"?

7. In van den Haag's view, what is the sole determinant of whether people will or will not commit crimes? Do you agree?

8. Why does van den Haag not believe that the presence or absence of a deterrent effect of the death penalty is likely to be proved statistically? Does this weaken, strengthen, or have no effect on his own retentionist position?

9. Explain why van den Haag believes there is more to be gained by retaining the death penalty than by abolishing it.

Capital Punishment and Social Defense

HUGO ADAM BEDAU

In this selection from a longer essay, abolitionist Hugo Adam Bedau (1926–2012), discusses the death penalty as a means of preventing convicted murderers from murdering again and as a means of deterring others from murdering. Neither, he concludes, justifies capital punishment. Bedau taught for most of his career at Tufts University in Massachusetts as the Austin B. Fletcher Professor of Philosophy until he retired in 1999.

When it comes to prevention, Bedau argues that few convicted murderers will murder again, and we cannot predict which ones will. Therefore, we would have to execute all convicted murderers, which is unacceptable. As for deterrence, the evidence does not show that capital punishment is a stronger deterrent than long prison terms. There are, however, significant social costs to the death penalty, including the executions of innocent people.

Bedau also argues that the courts do not apply the death penalty equitably. We do not execute the "worst of the bad," he says. Instead, we execute defendants who are put at a disadvantage by race, sex, poverty, and other unjust factors.

THE ANALOGY WITH SELF-DEFENSE

Capital punishment, it is sometimes said, is to the body politic what self-defense is to the individual. If the latter is not morally wrong, how can the former be morally wrong? In order to assess the strength of this analogy, we need first to inspect the morality of self-defense.

Except for absolute pacifists, who believe it is morally wrong to use violence even to defend themselves or others from unprovoked and undeserved aggression, most of us believe that it is not morally wrong and may even be our moral duty to use violence to prevent aggression directed either against ourselves or against innocent third parties. The law has long granted persons the right to defend themselves against the unjust aggressions of others, even to the extent of using lethal force to kill a would-be assailant. It is very difficult to think of any convincing argument that would show it is never rational to risk the death of another in order to prevent death or grave injury to oneself. Certainly self-interest dictates the legitimacy of self defense. So does concern for the well-being of others. So also does justice. If it is unfair for one person to inflict violence on another, then it is hard to see how morality could require the victim to acquiesce in the attempt by another to hurt him or her, rather than to resist it, even if that resistance involves or risks injury to the assailant.

The foregoing account assumes that the person acting in self-defense is innocent of any provocation of the assailant. It also assumes that there is no alternative to victimization except resistance. In actual life, both assumptions—especially the second—are often false, because there may be a third alternative: escape, or removing oneself from the scene of danger and imminent aggression. Hence, the law imposes on us the "duty to retreat." Before we use violence to resist aggression, must try to get out of the way, lest unnecessary violence be used to resist aggression. Now suppose that unjust aggression is imminent, and there is no path open for escape. How much violence may justifiably be used to ward off aggression? The answer is: No more violence than is necessary to prevent the aggressive assault. Violence beyond that is unnecessary and therefore unjustified. We may restate the principle governing the use of violence in self-defense in terms of the use of "deadly force" by the police in the discharge of their duties. The rule is this: Use of deadly force is justified only to prevent loss of life in immediate jeopardy where a lesser use of force cannot reasonably be expected to save the life that is threatened.

In real life, violence in self-defense in excess of the minimum necessary to prevent aggression, even though it is not justifiable, is often excusable. One cannot always tell what will suffice to deter or prevent becoming a victim, and so the law looks with a certain tolerance upon the frightened and innocent would-be victim who in self-protection turns upon a vicious assailant and inflicts a fatal injury even though a lesser injury would have been sufficient. What is not justified is deliberately using far more violence than is necessary to prevent becoming a victim. It is the deliberate, not the impulsive or the unintentional use of violence that is relevant to the death-penalty controversy, since the death penalty is enacted into law and carried out in each case only after ample time to weigh alternatives. Notice that we are assuming that the act of self-defense is to protect one's person or that of a third party. The reasoning outlined here does not extend to the defense of one's property.

Shooting a thief to prevent one's automobile from being stolen cannot be excused or justified in the way that shooting an assailant charging with a knife pointed at one's face can be. In terms of the concept of "deadly force," our criterion is that deadly force is never justified to prevent crimes against property or other violent crimes not immediately threatening the life of an innocent person.

The rationale for self-defense as set out above illustrates two moral principles of great importance to our discussion.... One is that if a life is to be risked, then it is better that it be the life of someone who is guilty (in our context, the initial assailant) rather than the life of someone who is not (the innocent potential victim). It is not fair to expect the innocent prospective victim to run the added risk of severe injury or death in order to avoid using violence in self-defense to the extent of possibly killing his assailant. It is only fair that the guilty aggressor run the risk.

The other principle is that taking life deliberately is not justified so long as there is any feasible alternative. One does not expect miracles, of course, but in theory, if shooting a burglar through the foot will stop the burglary and enable one to call the police for help, then there is no reason to shoot to kill. Likewise, if the burglar is unarmed, there is no reason to shoot at all. In actual life, of course, burglars are likely to be shot at by aroused householders because one does not know whether they are armed, and prudence may dictate the assumption that they are. Even so, although the burglar has no right to commit a felony against a person or a person's property, the attempt to do so does not give the chosen victim the right to respond in whatever way one pleases, and then to excuse or justify such conduct on the ground that one was "only acting in self-defense." In these ways the law shows a tacit regard for the life of even a felon and discourages the use of unnecessary violence even by the innocent; morality can hardly do less.

PREVENTING VERSUS DETERRING CRIME

The analogy between capital punishment and self-defense requires us to face squarely the empirical questions surrounding the preventive and deterrent effects of the death penalty. Executing a murderer in the name of punishment can be seen as a crime-*preventive* measure just to the extent it is reasonable to believe that if the murderer had not been executed he or she would have committed other crimes (including, but not necessarily confined to, murder). Executing a murderer can be seen as a crime *deterrent* just to the extent it is reasonable to believe that by the example of the execution other persons would be frightened off from committing murder. Any punishment can be a crime preventive without being a crime deterrent, just as it can be a deterrent without being a preventive. It can also be both or neither. Prevention and deterrence are theoretically independent because they operate by different methods. Crimes can be prevented by taking guns out of the hands of criminals, by putting criminals behind bars, by alerting the public to be less careless and less prone to victimization, and so forth. Crimes can be deterred only by making would-be criminals frightened of being arrested, convicted, and punished for crimes—that is, making persons overcome their desire to commit crimes by a stronger desire to avoid the risk of being caught and punished.

THE DEATH PENALTY AS A CRIME PREVENTIVE

Capital punishment is unusual among penalties because its preventive effects limit its deterrent effects. The death penalty can never deter the executed person from further crimes. At most, it can prevent a person from committing them. Popular discussions of the death penalty are frequently confused because they so often assume that the death penalty is a perfect and infallible deterrent so far as the executed criminal is concerned, whereas nothing of the sort is true. What is even more important, it is also wrong to think that in every execution the death penalty has proved to be an infallible crime preventive. What is obviously true is that once an offender has been executed, it is physically impossible for that person to commit any further crimes, since the punishment is totally incapacitative. But incapacitation is not identical with prevention. Prevention by means of incapacitation occurs only if the executed criminal would have committed other crimes if he or she had not been executed and had been punished only in some less incapacitative way (e.g., by imprisonment).

What evidence is there that the incapacitative effects of the death penalty are an effective crime preventive? From the study of imprisonment, parole, release records, this much is clear: If the murderers and other criminals who have been executed are like the murderers who were convicted but not executed, then (1) executing all convicted murderers would have prevented many crimes, but not many murders (less than one convicted murderer in five hundred commits another murder); and (2) convicted murderers, whether inside prison or outside after release, have at least as good a record of no further criminal activity as any other class of convicted felon.

These facts show that the general public tends to overrate the danger and threat to public safety constituted by the failure to execute every murderer who is caught and convicted. While it would be quite wrong to say that there is no risk such criminals will repeat their crimes—or similar ones—if they are not executed, it would be equally erroneous to say that by executing every convicted murderer many horrible crimes will be prevented. All we know is that a few such crimes will never be committed; we do not know how many or by whom they would have been committed. (Obviously, if we did know we would have tried to prevent them!) This is the nub of the problem. There is no way to know in advance which if any of the incarcerated or released murderers will kill again. It is useful in this connection to remember that the only way to guarantee that no horrible crimes ever occur is to execute *everyone* who might conceivably commit such a crime. Similarly, the only way to guarantee that no convicted murderer ever commits another murder is to execute them all. No modern society has ever done this, and for two hundred years ours has been moving steadily in the opposite direction.

These considerations show that our society has implicitly adopted an attitude toward the risk of murder rather like the attitude it has adopted toward the risk of fatality from other sources, such as automobile accidents, lung cancer, or drowning.

Since no one knows when or where or upon whom any of these lethal events will fall, it would be too great an invasion of freedom to undertake the severe restrictions that alone would suffice to prevent any such deaths from occurring. It is better to take the risks and keep our freedom than to try to eliminate the risks altogether and lose our freedom in the process. Hence, we have lifeguards at the beach, but swimming is not totally prohibited; smokers are warned, but cigarettes are still legally sold; pedestrians may be given the right of way in a crosswalk, but marginally competent drivers are still allowed to operate motor vehicles. Some risk is therefore imposed on the innocent; in the name of our right to freedom, our other rights are not protected by society at all costs.

THE DEATH PENALTY AS A CRIME DETERRENT

Determining whether the death penalty is an effective deterrent is even more difficult than determining its effectiveness as a crime preventive. In general, our knowledge about how penalties deter crimes and whether in fact they do—whom they deter, from which crimes, and under what conditions—is distressingly inexact. Most people nevertheless are convinced that punishments do deter, and that the more severe a punishment is the better it will deter. For half a century, social scientists have studied the questions whether the death penalty is a deterrent and whether it is a better deterrent than the alternative of imprisonment. Their verdict, while not unanimous, is nearly so. Whatever may be true about the deterrence of lesser crimes by other penalties, the deterrence achieved by the death penalty for murder is not measurably any greater than the deterrence achieved by long-term imprisonment. In the nature of the case, the evidence is quite indirect. No one can identify for certain any crimes that did not occur because the would-be offender was deterred by the threat of the death penalty and could not have been deterred by a less severe threat. Likewise, no one can identify any crimes that did occur because the offender was not deterred by the threat of prison even though he would have been deterred by the threat of death. Nevertheless, such evidence as we have fails to show that the more severe penalty (death) is really a better deterrent than the less severe penalty (imprisonment) for such crimes as murder.

If the conclusion stated above is correct, and the death penalty and long-term imprisonment are equally effective (or ineffective) as deterrents to murder, then the argument for the death penalty on grounds of deterrence is seriously weakened. One of the moral principles identified earlier now comes into play. It is the principle that unless there is a good reason for choosing a more rather than a less severe punishment for a crime, the less severe penalty is to be preferred. This principle obviously commends itself to anyone who values human life and who concedes that, all other things being equal, less pain and suffering is always better than more. Human life is valued in part to the degree that it is free of pain, suffering, misery, and frustration, and in particular to the extent that it is free of such experiences when they serve no purpose. If the death penalty is not a more effective deterrent than imprisonment, then its greater severity is gratuitous, purposeless suffering and deprivation. Accordingly, we must reject it in favor of some less severe alternative, unless we can identify some more weighty moral principle that the death penalty protects better than any less severe mode of punishment does. Whether there is any such principle is unclear.

A COST/BENEFIT ANALYSIS OF THE DEATH PENALTY

A full study of the costs and benefits involved in the practice of capital punishment would not be confined solely to the question of whether it is a better deterrent or preventive of murder than imprisonment. Any thoroughgoing utilitarian approach to the death-penalty controversy would need to examine carefully other costs and benefits as well, because maximizing the balance of all the social benefits over all the social costs is the sole criterion of right and wrong according to utilitarianism.... Let us consider, therefore, some of the other costs and benefits to be calculated. Clinical psychologists have presented evidence to suggest that the death penalty actually incites some persons of unstable mind to murder others, either because they are afraid to take their own lives and hope that society

will punish them for murder by putting them to death, or because they fancy that they, too, are killing with justification analogously to the lawful and presumably justified killing involved in capital punishment. If such evidence is sound, capital punishment can serve as a counter-preventive or even an incitement to murder; such incited murders become part of its social cost. Imprisonment, however, has not been known to incite any murders or other crimes of violence in a comparable fashion. (A possible exception might be found in the imprisonment of terrorists, which has inspired other terrorists to take hostages as part of a scheme to force the authorities to release their imprisoned comrades.) The risks of executing the innocent are also part of the social cost. The historical record is replete with innocent persons arrested, indicted, convicted, sentenced, and occasionally legally executed for crimes they did not commit. This is quite apart from the guilty persons unfairly convicted, sentenced to death, and executed on the strength of perjured testimony, fraudulent evidence, subernation of jurors, and other violations of the civil rights and liberties of the accused. Nor is this all. The high costs of a capital trial and of the inevitable appeals, the costly methods of custody most prisons adopt for convicts on "death row," are among the straightforward economic costs that the death penalty incurs. Conducting a valid cost/benefit analysis of capital punishment is extremely difficult, and it is impossible to predict exactly what such a study would show. Nevertheless, based on such evidence as we do have, it is quite possible that a study of this sort would favor abolition of all death penalties rather than their retention.

WHAT IF EXECUTIONS DID DETER?

From the moral point of view, it is quite important to determine what one should think about capital punishment if the evidence were clearly to show that the death penalty is a distinctly superior method of social defense by comparison with less severe alternatives. Kantian moralists ... would have no use for such knowledge, because their entire case for the morality of the death penalty rests on the way it is thought to provide just retribution, not on the way it is thought to provide social defense. For a utilitarian, however, such knowledge would be conclusive. Those who follow Locke's reasoning would also be gratified, because they defend the morality of the death penalty both on the ground that it is retributively just and on the ground that it provides needed social defense.

What about the opponents of the death penalty, however? To oppose the death penalty in the face of incontestable evidence that it is an effective method of social defense violates the moral principle that where grave risks are to be run, it is better that they be run by the guilty than by the innocent. Consider in this connection an imaginary world in which by executing the murderer his victim is invariably restored to life, whole and intact, as though the murder had never occurred. In such a miraculous world, it is hard to see how anyone could oppose the death penalty on moral grounds. Why shouldn't a murderer die if that will infallibly bring the victim back to life? What could possibly be morally wrong with taking the murderer's life under such conditions? The death penalty would now be an instrument of perfect restitution, and it would give a new and better meaning to *lex talionis*, "a life for a life." The whole idea is fanciful, of course, but it shows as nothing else can how opposition to the death penalty cannot be both moral and wholly unconditional. If opposition to the death penalty is to be morally responsible, then it must be conceded that there are conditions (however unlikely) under which that opposition should cease.

But even if the death penalty were known to be a uniquely effective social defense, we could still imagine conditions under which it would be reasonable to oppose it. Suppose that in addition to being a slightly better preventive and deterrent than imprisonment, executions also have a slight incitive effect (so that for every ten murders an execution prevents or deters, it also incites another murder). Suppose also that the administration of criminal justice in capital cases is inefficient, unequal, and tends to secure convictions and death sentences only for murderers who least "deserve" to be sentenced to death (including some death sentences and a few executions of the innocent). Under such conditions, it would still be reasonable to oppose the death

penalty, because on the facts supposed more (or not fewer) innocent lives are being threatened and lost by using the death penalty than would be risked by abolishing it. It is important to remember throughout our evaluation of the deterrence controversy that we cannot ever apply the principle ... that advises us to risk the lives of the guilty in order to save the lives of the innocent. Instead, the most we can do is weigh the risk for the general public against the execution of those who are *found* guilty by an imperfect system of criminal justice. These hypothetical factual assumptions illustrate the contingencies upon which the morality of opposition to the death penalty rests. And not only the morality of opposition; the morality of any defense of the death penalty rests on the same contingencies. This should help us understand why, in resolving the morality of capital punishment one way or the other, it is so important to know, as well as we can, whether the death penalty really does deter, prevent, or incite crime, whether the innocent really are ever executed, and how likely is the occurrence of these things in the future.

HOW MANY GUILTY LIVES IS ONE INNOCENT LIFE WORTH?

The great unanswered question that utilitarians must face concerns the level of social defense that executions should be expected to achieve before it is justifiable to carry them out. Consider three possible situations: (1) At the level of a hundred executions per year, each additional execution of a convicted murderer reduces the number of murder victims by ten. (2) Executing every convicted murderer reduces the number of murders to 5,000 victims annually, whereas executing only one out of ten reduces the number to 5,001. (3) Executing every convicted murderer reduces the murder rate no more than does executing one in a hundred and no more than does a random pattern of executions.

Many people contemplating situation (1) would regard this as a reasonable trade-off: The execution of each further guilty person saves the lives of ten innocent ones. (In fact, situation [1] or something like it may be taken as a description of what most of those who defend the death penalty on grounds of social defense believe is true.) But suppose that, instead of saving 10 lives, the number dropped to 0.5, i.e., one victim avoided for each two additional executions. Would that be a reasonable price to pay? We are on the road toward the situation described in situation (2), where a drastic 90 percent reduction in the number of persons executed causes the level of social defense to drop by only 0.0002 percent. Would it be worth it to execute so many more murderers at the cost of such a slight decrease in social defense? How many guilty lives is one innocent life worth? (Only those who think that guilty lives are *worthless* can avoid facing this problem.) In situation (3), of course, there is no basis for executing all convicted murderers, since there is no gain in social defense to show for each additional execution after the first out of each hundred has been executed. How, then, should we determine which out of each hundred convicted murderers is the unlucky one to be put to death?

It may be possible, under a complete and thoroughgoing cost/benefit analysis of the death penalty, to answer such questions. But an appeal merely to the moral principle that if lives are to be risked then let it be the lives of the guilty rather than of the innocent will not suffice. (We have already noticed ... that this abstract principle is of little use in the actual administration of criminal justice, because the police and the courts do not deal with the guilty as such but only with those *judged* guilty.) Nor will it suffice to agree that society deserves all the crime prevention and deterrence it can get as a result of inflicting severe punishments. These principles are consistent with too many different policies. They are too vague by themselves to resolve the choice on grounds of social defense when confronted with hypothetical situations like those proposed above.

Since no adequate cost/benefit analysis of the death penalty exists, there is no way to resolve these questions from that standpoint at this time. Moreover, it can be argued that we cannot have such an analysis without already establishing in some way or other the relative value of innocent lives versus guilty lives. Far from being a product of cost/benefit analysis, a comparative evaluation of lives would have to be available to us before we undertook any such analysis. Without it, no cost/benefit analysis can get off the ground. Finally, it must be noted that our knowledge at present does not approximate to anything like the situation described above in (1). On the contrary, from the evidence we do have it seems we achieve about the same deterrent and preventive effects whether we punish murder by death or by imprisonment.... Therefore, something like the situation in (2) or in (3) may be correct. If so, this shows that the choice between the two policies of capital punishment and life imprisonment for murder will probably have to be made on some basis other than social defense; on that basis alone, the two policies are equivalent and therefore equally acceptable....

EQUAL JUSTICE AND CAPITAL PUNISHMENT

During the past generation, the strongest practical objection to the death penalty has been the inequities with which it has been applied. As the late Supreme Court Justice William O. Douglas once observed, "One searches our chronicles in vain for the execution of any member of the affluent strata of this society."[1] One does not search our chronicles in vain for the crime of murder committed by the affluent. All the sociological evidence points to the conclusion that the death penalty is the poor man's justice; hence the slogan, "Those without the capital get the punishment." The death penalty is also racially sensitive. Every study of the death penalty for rape (unconstitutional only since 1977) has confirmed that black male rapists (especially where the victim is a white female) are far more likely to be sentenced to death and executed than white male rapists. Convicted black murderers are more likely to end up on "death row" than are others, and the killers of whites (whether white or non-white) are more likely to be sentenced to death than are the killers of nonwhites.

Let us suppose that the factual basis for such a criticism is sound. What follows for the morality of capital punishment? Many defenders of the death penalty have been quick to point out that since there is nothing intrinsic about the crime of murder or rape dictating that only the poor or only racial-minority males will commit it, and since there is nothing overtly racist about the statutes that authorize the death penalty for murder or rape, capital punishment itself is hardly at fault if in practice it falls with unfair impact on the poor and the black. There is, in short, nothing in the death penalty that requires it to be applied unfairly and with arbitrary or discriminatory results. It is at worst a fault in the system of administering criminal justice. (Some, who dispute the facts cited above, would deny even this.) There is an adequate remedy—execute more whites, women, and affluent murderers.

Presumably, both proponents and opponents of capital punishment would concede that it is a fundamental dictate of justice that a punishment should not be unfairly—inequitably or unevenly—enforced and applied. They should also be able to agree that when the punishment in question is the extremely severe one of death, then the requirement to be fair in using such a punishment becomes even more stringent. There should be no dispute in the death penalty controversy over these principles of justice. The dispute begins as soon as one attempts to connect the principles with the actual use of this punishment.

In this country, many critics of the death penalty have argued, we would long ago have got rid of it entirely if it had been a condition of its use that it be applied equally and fairly. In the words of the attorneys who argued against the death penalty in the Supreme Court during 1972, "It is a freakish aberration, a random extreme act of violence, visibly arbitrary and discriminatory—a penalty reserved for unusual application because, if it were usually used, it would affront universally shared standards of public decency."[2] It is difficult to dispute this judgment, when one considers that there have been in the United States during the past fifty years about half a million criminal homicides but only about 3,900 executions (all but 33 of which were of men).

We can look at these statistics in another way to illustrate the same point. If we could be assured

that the nearly 4,000 persons executed were the worst of the bad, repeated offenders incapable of safe incarceration, much less of rehabilitation, the most dangerous murderers in captivity—the ones who had killed more than once and were likely to kill again, and the least likely to be confined in prison without chronic danger to other inmates and the staff—then one might accept half a million murders and a few thousand executions with a sense that rough justice had been done. But the truth is otherwise. Persons are sentenced to death and executed not because they have been found to be uncontrollably violent or hopelessly poor confinement and release risks. Instead, they are executed because they have a poor defense (inexperienced or overworked counsel) at trial; they have no funds to bring sympathetic witnesses to court; they are transients or strangers in the community where they are tried; the prosecuting attorney wants the publicity that goes with "sending a killer to the chair"; there are no funds for an appeal or for a transcript of the trial record; they are members of a despised racial or political minority. In short, the actual study of why particular persons have been sentenced to death and executed does not show any careful winnowing of the worst from the bad. It shows that the executed were usually the unlucky victims of prejudice and discrimination, the losers in an arbitrary lottery that could just as well have spared them, the victims of the disadvantages that almost always go with poverty. A system like this does not enhance human life; it cheapens and degrades it. However heinous murder and other crimes are, the system of capital punishment does not compensate for or erase those crimes. It only tends to add new injuries of its own to the catalogue of human brutality.

NOTES

1. *Furman v. Georgia*, 408 U.S. 238 (1972), at pp. 251–252.
2. NAACP Legal Defense and Educational Fund, Brief for Petitioner in *Aikens v. California*, O.T. 1971, No. 68–5027, reprinted in Philip English Mackey, ed., *Voices Against Death: American Opposition to Capital Punishment, 1787–1975* (1975), p. 288.

1. According to Bedau, our attitude toward the risks of murder is like our attitude toward the risks of swimming. We do not outlaw swimming even though some swimmers will drown. Similarly, we do not execute all murderers even though some will murder again. In both cases, he says, the reasoning is the same: We allow some risk to the innocent in order to protect our freedoms. Do you agree with this analogy? Why or why not?

2. Bedau argues that a cost-benefit analysis of the death penalty would show that the costs outweigh the benefits. Why? What assumptions does he make? Do you accept these assumptions?

3. Even if the death penalty did deter some would-be murderers, Bedau says, there would still be good reasons to oppose it in some conditions. What conditions? Do they obtain today?

4. According to van den Haag, it is better to risk the lives of the guilty than the lives of the innocent. Bedau says that this principle will "not suffice" to justify the death penalty. Why not?

5. Bedau argues that "the strongest practical objection to the death penalty has been the inequities with which it has been applied." What inequities? How strong do you think the objection is?

6. Does Bedau provide a convincing refutation of van den Haag? Why or why not?

CASE PRESENTATION

Karla Faye Tucker and Stanley "Tookie" Williams: Rehabilitation on Death Row?

They were only two of 556 homicides recorded in Houston that year and received little initial attention, but they were surely two of the most sensational slayings in the city's history. One the night of June 14, 1983, Karla Faye Tucker and David Garrett climaxed a three-day drug binge by hacking to death Jerry Lynn Dean and Deborah Thornton. They had broken into Dean's apartment to steal motorcycle parts. Upon finding Dean at home, Garrett attacked him with a hammer. Tucker joined in with a pickax that belonged to Dean. Then she used it to kill Thornton, Dean's overnight visitor, who lay shivering in his bed. Far from feeling regret over the murders, the twenty-three-year-old former teenage prostitute boasted to friends that she felt a surge of sexual gratification with every thrust of the pickax. A year later, Tucker and Garrett were sentenced to death.

Garrett, who was Tucker's boyfriend at the time of the murders, died in prison before he could be executed. Tucker's case went on to become a worldwide controversy. While awaiting trial at the Harris County Jail, she claimed to have found God; she was now, she said, a born-again Christian who repented her crimes. At their trials, she confessed to the murders and then testified against Garrett; while on death row, she counseled her fellow inmates and married her own spiritual counselor.

Following the customary appeals through the courts, her execution was set for February 3, 1998. As the date neared, she attracted numerous supporters, including Pope John Paul II, television evangelist Pat Robertson, Jesse Jackson, the National Council of Churches, the European Parliament, and Ronald Carlson, Deborah Thornton's brother. Nearly 2,400 others sent letters to Texas Governor George W. Bush asking that her sentence be commuted to life. For many of her supporters, the issue was her religious conversion. She was not, they argued, the same woman who had committed the lurid murders. Nor was she a threat to society. Tucker argued the same point in her appeal for clemency before the Texas Board of Pardons and Parole, saying "If you decide you must carry out this execution, do it based solely on the brutality and heinousness of my crime. But please don't do it based on me being a future threat to our society, because I am definitely no longer a threat to our society, and in fact I believe I am a positive contributor to our society and helping others." Still, the board voted 16 to 0, with two abstentions, to deny her appeal.

Compounding the controversy was the fact that Tucker was a woman. Texas had not executed a woman since 1863, and the last U.S. execution of a woman—the only execution of a woman since 1976, when the Supreme Court allowed the states to resume capital punishment—had occurred in 1984 in North Carolina.

On February 3, the Supreme Court refused Tucker's last-minute appeal for a stay of execution. Governor Bush, who had the option to grant a one-time-only thirty-day stay, refused to do so, and the execution was carried out that evening by lethal injection. In her final statement, Tucker said, "I would like to say to all of you, the Thornton family and Jerry Dean's family, that I am sorry. I hope God will give you peace with this."

In 1979, four years before Tucker's crimes, Stanley "Tookie" Williams, one of the founders of the notorious Crips gang in Los Angeles, murdered a clerk at a convenience store and three people at a family-owned motel in California. He was sentenced to death but was on death row for twenty-four years while he pursued numerous appeals. He appealed for clemency from Governor Arnold Schwarzenegger, claiming that he had been transformed while in prison. He had published several books urging gang avoidance and peacemaking. But Williams, unlike Tucker, never admitted his crimes, let alone apologized for them. Prosecutors and the governor detailed the extensive evidence that he was guilty and had received a fair trial, as confirmed repeatedly during his appeals.

His case gained extensive press attention and the support of television star Mike Farrell, civil rights leader Jesse Jackson, and Sister Helen Prejean, a prominent death-penalty opponent who was the inspiration for the film *Dead Man Walking*. The governor denied his last-minute petition for clemency, and Williams was executed on December 13, 2005.

👑 QUESTIONS FOR ANALYSIS

1. Many death row prisoners claim they have found God and been rehabilitated. If true, should their sentences be commuted? How can we decide if the claims are true?

2. Between 1976 (when the Supreme Court permitted the resumption of executions) and June 2013, thirteen hundred men have been executed nationwide, while only thirteen women have been executed. Does the enormous disparity in the numbers of executed men and women show bias in favor of women? If so, what should be done about it?

3. Given their heinous, brutal crimes, did Tucker and Williams deserve the death penalty, regardless of their later behavior on death row? Can you imagine any situations where guilty murderers on death row should have their sentences commuted because of their conduct while on death row?

CASE PRESENTATION

A Failed Experiment?

Callins v. Collins was a routine decision for the U.S. Supreme Court. With no written opinion, the Court declined to review the death sentence of Bruce Edwin Callins, who had been convicted of murder by a Texas jury. What was not routine was Justice Harry A. Blackmun's headline-making dissent. When he first joined the Court more than twenty years earlier, he had been a supporter of the death penalty. But on February 22, 1994, during his final term, Justice Blackmun announced in a lone dissent that "the death penalty experiment has failed."

In arguing that it had failed, he claimed that two constitutional requirements for imposing the death penalty are incompatible. The requirement that it must be imposed consistently (from *Furman v. Georgia*), he wrote, clashes with other precedents that require individualized sentencing. Excerpts follow:

> … Twenty years have passed since this Court declared that the death penalty must be imposed fairly and with reasonable consistency or not at all (see *Furman v. Georgia*, 1972), and, despite the effort of the states and courts to devise legal formulas and procedural rules to meet this daunting challenge, the death penalty remains fraught with arbitrariness, discrimination, caprice and mistakes.…
>
> Experience has taught us that the constitutional goal of eliminating arbitrariness and discrimination from the

administration of death … can never be achieved without compromising an equally essential component of fundamental fairness: individualized sentencing. (See *Lockett v. Ohio*, 1978.)

It is tempting, when faced with conflicting constitutional commands, to sacrifice one for the other, or to assume that an acceptable balance between them already has been struck. In the context of the death penalty, however, such jurisprudential maneuvers are wholly inappropriate. The death penalty must be imposed "fairly, and with reasonable consistency, or not at all." (*Eddings v. Oklahoma*, 1982.)

To be fair, capital sentencing schemes must treat each person convicted of a capital offense with that "degree of respect for the uniqueness of the individual…." That means affording the sentencer the power and discretion to grant mercy in a particular case, and providing avenues for the consideration of any and all relevant mitigating evidence that would justify a sentence less than death.

Reasonable consistency, on the other hand, requires that the death penalty be inflicted evenhandedly, in accordance with reason and objective standards, rather than by whim, caprice or prejudice.

… [T]his Court, in my opinion, has engaged in a futile effort to balance these constitutional demands, and now is retreating not only from the *Furman* promise of consistency and rationality, but from the requirement of individualized sentencing as well….

From this day forward, I no longer shall tinker with the machinery of death. Rather than continue to coddle the Court's delusion that the desired level of fairness be achieved and the need for regulation eviscerated, I feel morally and intellectually obligated to concede that the death penalty experiment has failed.

It seems that the decision whether a human being should live or die is so inherently subjective, rife with all of life's understandings, experiences, prejudices, and passions, that it inevitably defies the rationality and consistency required by the Constitution.

Justice Antonin Scalia, in a rebutting opinion, responded as follows:

As Justice Blackmun describes … this court has attached to the imposition of the death penalty two quite incompatible sets of commands: the sentencer's discretion to impose death must be closely confined (see *Furman vs. Georgia*, 1972) but the sentencer's discretion not to impose death (to extend mercy) must be unlimited (*Eddings v. Oklahoma*, 1982; *Lockett v. Ohio*, 1978). These commands were invented without benefit of any textual support; they are the product of just such "intellectual, moral and personal" perceptions as Justice Blackmun expressed today….

Though Justice Blackmun joins those of us who have acknowledged the incompatibility of the Court's *Furman* and *Lockett-Eddings* lines of jurisprudence … he unfortunately draws the wrong conclusion from the acknowledgment….

Surely a different conclusion commends itself to wit, that at least one of the judicially announced irreconcilable commands which cause the Constitution to prohibit what its text [the Fifth Amendment] explicitly permits must be wrong….

♔ QUESTIONS FOR ANALYSIS

1. Justices Blackmun and Scalia agree that past Supreme Court decisions regarding the death penalty are incompatible. To the former, the incompatibility shows that the death penalty cannot be imposed constitutionally. To the latter, it shows that the Court has erred. With which justice do you agree?

2. Along with Justice Scalia, many critics have accused Justice Blackmun of reading his personal views into the Constitution. Do you agree?

3. Regardless of the constitutional issue, does Justice Blackmun have a strong moral position? That is, does justice require both evenhandedness and consideration for the uniqueness of the individual when we impose the death penalty? If so, are the two really incompatible?

4. Is the decision to impose the death penalty "inherently subjective"?

CASE PRESENTATION

Warren McClesky

Warren McClesky was black. The fatally wounded police officer was white. Their paths crossed in the Dixie Furniture Store near downtown Atlanta on May 13, 1978. McClesky was robbing the store at gunpoint; officer Frank Schlatt had responded to a silent alarm. Whether McClesky or one of his accomplices fired the bullet that killed Officer Schlatt is unknown, but in Georgia, as in many other states, McClesky could be charged with the murder nonetheless. He was tried, convicted, and sentenced to death.

On appeal, McClesky argued that his sentence was the result of racial bias. To back up the claim, the defense offered two studies by University of Iowa Professor David Baldus. These studies examined racial factors in the imposition of the death penalty in Georgia between 1973, when the state's capital punishment law took effect, and 1979. Among the results were the following:[1]

1. Although whites were victims of fewer than 40 percent of all homicides studied, they were victims in 87 percent that resulted in the death penalty for the killer.
2. Twenty-two percent of blacks convicted of killing whites received the death penalty, compared to only 8 percent of white defendants convicted of killing whites.
3. The racial disparities were greatest in cases that fell between the most heinous and least heinous

murders. The death penalty was imposed in 34 percent of such cases when the victim was white, but only 14 percent when the victim was black.
4. The disparities cannot be explained by nonracial factors.

In 1987, *McClesky v. Kemp* reached the Supreme Court, which upheld the sentence. The Court accepted the studies' findings, but it ruled that they did not prove discrimination in McClesky's case. Only proof that the jury, the prosecutor, or some other decision maker in his case was influenced by racial bias could do so. Wrote Justice Lewis F. Powell in his majority opinion, "Because discretion is essential to the criminal justice process, we would demand exceptionally clear proof before we infer that the discretion has been abused."

[1]Cited in Anthony G. Amsterdam, "*Race and the Death Penalty*," *Criminal Justice Ethics*, Vol. 7, No 1 (1988), pp. 84–86.

⚜ QUESTIONS FOR ANALYSIS

1. One of the studies' significant implications is that a white life counts for more than a black life when it comes to imposing the death penalty. If the implication is correct, does it taint the way capital punishment is imposed in Georgia?
2. Between 1973 and 1980, seventeen defendants were charged with killing police officers in Fulton County. In only two cases did the prosecution seek the death penalty. One was McClesky's. In the other case, the slain officer was black, and his killer was sentenced to life. Is it reasonable to suspect that racial bias played a role in the decision to seek the death penalty in McClesky's case? In his being sentenced to death?

3. In 1994, the U.S. Congress passed a massive anti-crime package that increased the number of federal crimes punishable by death. The Congressional Black Caucus had proposed a bill known as the Racial Justice Act, allowing convicts on death row to use statistical evidence to argue that race played a role in their sentencing. The bill was not part of the final package. Should it have been?
4. Suppose similar disparities could be found throughout the country. Would that justify the abolition of capital punishment?

CASE PRESENTATION

Punishing Child Rapists

In 1977, the U.S. Supreme Court in *Coker vs. Georgia* (433 U.S. 584) held that the death penalty was unconstitutional for persons convicted of raping an adult woman. At the time, Georgia was the only state which provided for execution in these circumstances. The Court noted that rape is a very serious crime, reprehensible both in a moral and legal sense, due to its

contempt for the personal integrity and autonomy of the female victim, concepts drawing from our ethical as well as legal traditions. However, the Court concluded that the death penalty was "grossly disproportionate and excessive punishment" for the crime of rape and thus a violation of the Eighth Amendment to the Constitution. The decision left open the issue of execution when the crime was rape of a child, a penalty allowed in a few other states.

In 2008, in a 5–4 decision, the U.S. Supreme Court held in *Kennedy v. Louisiana* that the death penalty was also unconstitutional as "cruel and unusual punishment" for the rape of a child. The defendant had been convicted of the aggravated rape of his then-eight-year-old stepdaughter. The Louisiana state law, which had been passed in 1995, provided for execution for rape of a child under twelve. The U.S. Supreme Court noted that several other states had passed similar laws in the 1990s, bringing to six the number of states providing for such executions. The Court thought this trend, as an effort to protect children from rape, was significant, even though few states had such laws in effect. Even so, the court concluded that the death penalty was disproportionate to the crime itself where the crime did not result in the victim's death. The Court also noted that no one in the U.S. had been executed for rape of an adult or a child since 1964, more than a decade before the *Coker* decision.

As in *Coker*, the Court cited compelling moral concerns in its deliberations, recognizing the heinous violation of the child's dignity and autonomy. The Court was also concerned about the special risk of wrongful conviction and execution, given documented problems of unreliable and even imagined child testimony. Nor was the Court persuaded that the death penalty would be a more effective deterrent to the rape of children, noting that it might actually add to the risk of nonreporting of child rape out of fear of negative consequences for the perpetrator, especially when that person was a family member. The Court also worried that the threat of execution might actually make a child rapist more likely to kill the victim, as the possible punishment would be the same.

♕ QUESTIONS FOR ANALYSIS

1. All agree that child rape is a horrible crime that deserves severe punishment. Do you agree with the U.S. Supreme Court that execution is excessive for this crime? What do you believe is the most appropriate punishment?

2. If we did not have to take the Eighth Amendment into account, could the death penalty be justified strictly on moral grounds for child rapists?

3. What consequentialist concerns does the Court raise about use of the death penalty in these circumstances?

4. Are there any crimes, other than murder, that warrant execution?

CHAPTER EIGHT

War, Terrorism, and Civil Liberties

- "Just War" Theory
- Preemptive Wars
- Violence and Terrorism
- Jihadism
- Pacifism
- Civil Liberties
- Arguments for Trading Civil Liberties for Safety
- Arguments against Trading Civil Liberties for Safety

MICHAEL WALZER **The Triumph of Just War Theory (and the Dangers of Success)**

R. G. FREY AND CHRISTOPHER W. MORRIS **Violence, Terrorism, and Justice**

ALAN M. DERSHOWITZ **Make Torture an Option**

DAVID LUBAN **Torture and the Ticking Bomb**

CASE PRESENTATIONS: • *Preemptive War* • *Driving While Veiled* • *Fear of Flying* • *The Geneva Conventions and Guantanamo Bay*

DID THE TRAGIC events of 9/11 "change everything," as many have said in the years since? At a minimum, the attacks and our national response to them have led us to reexamine our views of terrorism, violence, war, and when, if ever, they can be justified. America had experienced terrorist attacks before, including the bombing of the Federal Building in Oklahoma City. But most people in this country seemed to feel largely immune from the random attacks on civilians that are all too familiar in countries such as England, which has experienced years of terrorist attacks from the Irish Republican Army over issues in Northern Ireland. The ease of international travel reminded us that broad expanses of oceans on our borders do not insulate us from violent attacks by outsiders.

Historically, we often have had to address the justifiability of military action by the nation. Few seem to doubt that the attack on American naval installations in Pearl Harbor in 1941 justified a declaration of war against Japan, but the decision to drop nuclear bombs on two Japanese cities a few years later, killing or maiming many civilians, remains controversial. The decision to intervene on the side of the Allies in Europe during World War II was controversial at the time to many Americans who thought we should remain neutral. The American role in the Vietnam War remains perennially controversial, as do attempts by some to compare the invasion of Iraq to Vietnam.

In this chapter, we consider traditional and recent views on what counts as a "just war" in an age of often-frightening terrorism. We also consider a pervasive concern in our responses to terrorism, namely, the balancing of our safety and security with our tradition of freedom and civil liberties. In a well-known quotation, Benjamin Franklin said, "Those who would give up essential Liberty, to purchase a little temporary Safety, deserve neither Liberty nor Safety." Is this as true today as it was in the eighteenth century?

"JUST WAR" THEORY

Throughout history, people have developed justifications for their participation in war, and recent developments raise anew these issues for the American role in Afghanistan and Iraq. These theories of "just war" are often described as **jus ad bellum**, proposals to justify the use of force in a particular type of situation. Another theory, **jus in bello**, considers the justice of particular types of actions within a war, whether or not that war itself was justified. For example, a theory of *jus ad bellum* would ask whether the United States invasion of Iraq was justified. A theory of *jus in bello* would address whether it was justifiable to drop bombs on civilian areas during that war.

In the thirteenth century, St. Thomas Aquinas developed one of the most influential theories of just war in his work *Summa Theologica,* an approach which remains much debated even today. Much of Aquinas's work is rooted in that of the classic Greek philosopher Aristotle and is devoted to reconciling Aristotelian insights with Christian theology. Aquinas asked whether it is always sinful to wage war. In response, he argued, in part:

> In order for a war to be just, three things are necessary. First, the authority of the sovereign by whose command the war is to be waged. For it is not the business of a private individual to declare war, because he can seek for redress of his rights from the tribunal of his superior. Moreover it is not the business of a private individual to summon together the people, which has to be done in wartime. And as the care of the common weal is committed to those who are in authority, it is their business to watch over the common weal of the city, kingdom or province subject to them. And just as it is lawful for them to have recourse to the sword in defending that common weal against internal disturbances, when they punish evil-doers, ... so too, it is their business to have recourse to the sword of war in defending the common weal against external enemies....
>
> Secondly, a just cause is required, namely that those who are attacked, should be attacked because they deserve it on account of some fault....
>
> Thirdly, it is necessary that the belligerents should have a rightful intention, so that they intend the advancement of good, or the avoidance of evil.... For it may happen that the war is declared by the legitimate authority, and for a just cause, and yet be rendered unlawful through a wicked intention.[1]

---

[1]Literal translation by Fathers of the English Dominican Province, 1920. The complete text of the *Summa* can be found online: http://www.newadvent.org/summa/.

In summary, Aquinas believes we should first ask whether the entity declaring war is a legitimate sovereign. We might ask whether these sovereigns should include all recognized nations, regardless of how their leaders came to power, or whether we should also consider the legitimacy of those governments and perhaps limit recognized sovereigns to democratically elected governments. Should we be troubled that the United Nations recognizes many nations whose leaders came to power in violent and perhaps illegitimate ways? Should those nations not benefit from the defense of just war theory?

Second, Aquinas says that the people we attack should deserve it because of "some fault" of theirs, and we can ask what faults would legitimately support war against that country. Should we limit those faults to aggression against another nation? What if that aggression was an attempt to reclaim land that the aggressor believes was wrongfully seized centuries earlier? In the 1991 Gulf War, Iraq claimed that it was simply retaking land in Kuwait that was rightfully Iraq's anyway. In the wars in the Balkans, combatants have said they were merely reclaiming land wrongfully taken from their ancestors long ago. Who should decide who properly deserves to have this land? Should there be a statute of limitations or time limit against reclaiming land?

Are there other faults that would justify initiating war against another nation? Would knowledge of the concentration camps and the extermination of six million Jews in Nazi Germany have justified initiating war against that nation? If Timothy McVeigh, the Oklahoma City bomber, had been a citizen of Canada, would that alone have justified American initiation of war against Canada? If we had indisputable evidence that the Canadian government had provided McVeigh with financial assistance to carry out the bombing, would that have justified initiation of war against Canada? McVeigh, of course, was an American citizen, and there is not a shred of evidence of Canadian involvement. But it can be helpful in reasoning about a just war to imagine different hypothetical situations to test our views on the applicability of these theories.

Aquinas's third requirement for a just war is a "rightful intention," either "the advancement of good, or the avoidance of evil." How should we determine what a rightful intention is? By whose standards should we judge the advancement of "good"? Can we use the utilitarian theories of Mill or the human rights views of Kant to make these assessments? What other considerations should be brought to bear in making these decisions?

In the debates over the American invasion of Iraq, some argued that a well-founded belief that Saddam Hussein possessed weapons of mass destruction (WMD), which posed an imminent threat to the safety of Americans, was adequate justification for this war, even if it was later determined that those weapons did not exist. Another argument in support of the Iraq war noted that Hussein had committed genocide against his own Iraqi citizens and thus deserved to be deposed by a nation with the military power to accomplish that. How would you assess these claims using Aquinas's three requirements for a just war? Some critics of the war claim that it had a hidden agenda of gaining control over the Iraq oil fields to meet America's needs for oil. If that were true, would it constitute a violation of Aquinas's third condition?

PREEMPTIVE WARS

In 2002, President George W. Bush articulated a new theory of the justifiability of war, which has come to be known as "preemptive" war. (Excerpts from his announcement of this policy can be found in the Case Presentations.) He observed that the United States had traditionally engaged in war only in defense of aggression by other nations against us. Otherwise (or so it is claimed), we pursued a policy of deterrence from war, efforts to discourage other nations from attacking us with threats, for example, of "mutually assured destruction" from the dropping of nuclear bombs.

Critics of this analysis, however, claim that the United States was an aggressor nation in several earlier wars, including the U.S.–Mexican War (1846–48), the Spanish-American War (1898), and various incursions in Central America.

At the heart of the justification of preemptive war is the claim that changes in warfare and the character of our enemies throughout the world make preemption necessary in some circumstances. We can no longer wait for our adversaries to attack us, if those attacks might be nuclear bombs and other devastating attacks by terrorists that would make it impossible for us to even respond. Instead, we must strike first, the theory goes, to destroy those adversaries who pose a serious risk of attacking us first with weapons of mass destruction.

Supporters of President Bush's approach emphasize that the nature of warfare has changed, especially since the attacks of 9/11. The unpredictability of rogue states and the proliferation of nuclear arsenals, as well as biological weapons with enormous destructive potential, they argue, dictate that we take steps to protect ourselves that we might have found inappropriate in an earlier time. Critics are troubled by this change in longstanding national policy to become an aggressor nation. They wonder if this theory of preemptive wars will encourage other nations to initiate aggression, perhaps against us, if they suspect that we present an imminent threat to them.

Another criticism of the policy of preemptive war articulated by President Bush is that it overlooks the distinction between "preemptive" and "preventive." "Preventive" war is reserved for situations where an attack seems inevitable someday, while "preemptive" war addresses situations where an attack is imminent or likely to happen in the immediate future.

In President Barack Obama's book *The Audacity of Hope*, published in 2006, almost three years before he became president, he seemed to support preemptive war, but claimed that the conditions of imminent threat were not met before the U.S. invasion of Iraq in 2003.

> I would also argue that we have the right to take unilateral military action to eliminate an imminent threat to our security—so long as an imminent threat is understood to be a nation, group, or individual that is actively preparing to strike U.S. targets … and has or will have the means to do so in the immediate future. Al Qaeda qualifies under this standard, and we can and should carry out preemptive strikes against them wherever we can. Iraq under Saddam Hussein did not meet this standard, which is why our invasion was such a strategic blunder. If we are going to act unilaterally, then we had better have the goods on our targets.[2]

President Obama's critics note that this was written with the benefit of three years of hindsight after the invasion. Whether the U.S. invasion of Iraq was based on a truly

---

[2]Barack Obama. *The Audacity of Hope: Thoughts on Reclaiming the American Dream*. New York: Three Rivers Press, 2006, pp. 308–9.

"imminent" attack or merely one that seemed inevitable someday will be debated endlessly, and it must be acknowledged that no country embarks on war with perfect intelligence. Critics have also claimed that President Obama's decision to participate in the United Nations coalition to bomb Libya in 2011 to prevent "slaughter and mass graves before taking action" amounted to preemptive war.

President Obama addressed many of these concerns in a major address on May 23, 2013 (available on the White House web site: http://www.whitehouse.gov/). With regard to the use of drones against al Qaeda, he said,

> ... these strikes have saved lives. Moreover, America's actions are legal. We were attacked on 9/11. Within a week, Congress overwhelmingly authorized the use of force. Under domestic law, and international law, the United States is at war with al Qaeda, the Taliban, and their associated forces. We are at war with an organization that right now would kill as many Americans as they could if we did not stop them first. So this is a just war—a war waged proportionally, in last resort, and in self-defense.

Although the president said this is "a just war," we can still ask whether it would meet the classic tests of "just war" as articulated by Aquinas. The president also distinguished between law and morality when he said, "To say a military tactic is legal, or even effective, is not to say it is wise or moral in every instance." In explaining his decision to use drones to kill an American citizen, Anwar Awlaki, in Yemen, he notes:

> ... the high threshold that we have set for taking lethal action applies to all potential terrorist targets, regardless of whether or not they are American citizens. This threshold respects the inherent dignity of every human life.

But, he continued, these drone strikes were necessary, on balance, to protect American lives. In the coming years, all Americans, along with the courts and the U.S. Congress, will continue to assess whether the president has struck the right balance among civil liberties, human rights, and the safety of Americans.

VIOLENCE AND TERRORISM

Violence in the world is nothing new, and neither is terrorism. In considering these concepts, it is important to carefully scrutinize what we mean by these terms, an essential first step in good reasoning about when, if ever, they might be justifiable. Although everyone has an intuitive sense of how they understand these terms, under close scrutiny we might find that one person's justifiable aggression is another person's unjustifiable terrorism.

War itself seems necessarily to involve violence, but most people consider such violence justified, at least against military combatants, if the war itself was justified. Violence would include physical death and injury, but we also sometimes speak of "violence" to intellectual and conceptual ideas of cultural identity, economic well-being, and state of mind. Further, not all situations where physical injury might be involved seem appropriately labeled "violence."

R. G. Frey and Christopher W. Morris consider different definitions of "terrorism" in their essay in this chapter. They suggest that terrorism is included within violence but that not all violence is terrorism. One characteristic of terrorism, they suggest, is randomness or surprise. But modern warfare also depends on an element of surprise, yet that does not necessarily seem to make it terrorism. Another characteristic of terrorism is attack on nonmilitary personnel, innocent civilians, yet in war, innocent civilians often die as so-called "collateral damage," even if their deaths were not the intention of the military action. The attack of 9/11 on the Pentagon was typically called terrorism, even though most of the people killed were members or employees of the military.

If an act of violence can also be called terrorism, should this justify a change in our response to the behavior? Should we assess punishment or blame based on other factors, such as the claimed justification for the attack or the supposed involvement of the persons attacked in causing hardship to the attackers? Even if some violence can be justified—for example, violence in self-defense or violence in a justified war—can any terrorism be justified? Has the United States ever engaged in activities that others believe constituted terrorism? Are the attacks by the United States using unmanned aircraft (drones) against suspected enemies who have never been tried in the U.S. courts examples of terrorism, as some critics claim? Are historic attacks on the United States that we considered war more appropriately reconsidered now as terrorism?

JIHADISM

Since 9/11, a concept called *jihadism* has been the source of much controversy. Some use it to describe a campaign of violence against the West by a militant, extremist form of Islam, noting that all nineteen hijackers claimed Islam as their religion. However, many scholars of Islamic religion, especially practitioners living in the West, have insisted that this is a perversion of the Islamic faith. Some people seem to use jihadism as synonymous with terrorism, even though much of the terrorism in the world has been committed by persons who had no affiliation with any version of Islam and made no claim of engaging in a religious war against the West.

A passage in the Qur'an, the sacred text of Islam, has caused special concern and debate:

> Against them make ready your strength to the utmost of your power, including steeds of war, to strike terror into (the hearts of) the enemies, of God and your enemies, and others besides, whom ye may not know, but whom God doth know.
>
> —Holy Qur'an, Sura 8:60

Taken literally, this passage might seem to authorize—indeed, to order—physical violence against anyone who does not support the Muslim religion. This might mean violence against one's own government if it does not support Islam or perhaps violence against other nations that are a threat to Islam. But many adherents of Islam insist that this passage should be considered only metaphorically and not as an authorization for physical terror against non-Muslims. They suggest that Islam cannot be forced on people and that war would be justified only in self-defense. They also cite passages in the Qur'an that prohibit suicide and the harming of innocent civilians. After 9/11, dozens of prominent Islamic world leaders and scholars criticized the attacks as contrary to the teachings of Islam. Some noted that, under Islamic law, the 9/11 terrorism constituted the crime of *hirabah* (waging war against society).

In popular literature since 9/11, the word *jihadism* has taken on a pervasive meaning of aggressive terrorism against innocent civilians for religious purposes, especially for purportedly Islamic interests. As with so many other important concepts in our understanding of these contemporary challenges, care in clarifying our understanding of terms in such a way that our dialogue is clear and not laced with fallacies of reasoning is paramount.

PACIFISM

The tradition of pacifism can be traced back thousands of years, often with religious underpinnings and sometimes as a result of philosophical and ethical views. In general, pacifists believe that violence is always wrong, although adherents might emphasize their interests in different settings. Pacifism in war promotes an absolute ban on violence among nations and urges instead peaceful, nonviolent resolution of political and social differences. A consistent pacifist would also urge that all violence is wrong, such as the killing of a human being in any setting, whether as individuals, in self-defense, or as capital punishment.

Absolutist pacifism can result in other ethical dilemmas, however. If pacifists refuse to fight to defend their country in war, are they relying instead on others to fight those wars, likely benefitting the pacifists in the end? If pacifists urge a national policy that we should never respond to any aggression against us—whether Pearl Harbor or 9/11—are they actually encouraging aggressor nations to attack us on the belief that we will not respond? Is pacifism "unilateral disarmament" that makes us vulnerable to attack by nations that do not adhere to pacifism?

Self-defense in individual situations also presents ethical dilemmas for consistent pacifists. It is one thing to believe that you should never respond to an attack on your own life in self-defense and that it is better to die consistently with your moral views than to live in violation of your pacifist convictions. But what about situations where the pacifist is in a good position to intervene to protect someone else's innocent life? If a young child is being beaten to death by an insane person and the pacifist could easily kill the attacker with a club and save the life of the child, which is the more ethical conduct—to be consistent with pacifism and watch the child murdered or to murder the wrongdoer and save the child's life? It is one thing to sacrifice your own life in the name of ethical principles, but is it equally justifiable to sacrifice the life of another in the name of those principles?

Is pacifism a viable ethical alternative to "just war" theory and political realism?

In our deliberations, clarity in our understanding of these concepts is paramount, as is the avoidance of slippery language that distorts and blurs our fair consideration of these issues. One can object to preemptive war without necessarily being a pacifist. One can support preemptive war without necessarily being a terrorist. As in all areas of public dialogue, name-calling and *ad hominem*s accomplish nothing.

CIVIL LIBERTIES

"The Constitution is not a suicide pact." This somewhat sarcastic remark about the role of the liberties accorded to us under the Constitution (attributed to two U.S. Supreme Court Justices, Robert Jackson and, later, Arthur Goldberg) has become a familiar refrain since 9/11. And the statistics about the terrorist dangers in the United States can be frightening. Some 300,000 foreign nationals are in this country, even though they have already been ordered deported, according to the attorney general. Even just a small number of persons could cause massive destruction in our country. The Department of Justice claims to have broken up terrorist cells in Buffalo, Detroit, Seattle, and Portland that could have caused disastrous harm to American citizens on our own soil. The popular press buzzes with accounts of thousands of "sleeper cells" in the United States, preparing to launch attacks on everything from water supplies, bridges, and tunnels to oil pipelines, nuclear power plants, and shopping centers. Many acts of terrorism have been committed by American citizens, some native-born citizens (such as Timothy McVeigh, mastermind of the Oklahoma City bombings) and others naturalized (such as the surviving alleged bomber at the Boston Marathon in 2013). In the face of such uncertainty and fear, it is no wonder that many Americans have rushed to insist that everything possible be done to round up these potential terrorists, even at the expense of sacrificing their own civil liberties, guaranteed under the U.S. Constitution.

How much are people willing to give up to find the terrorists supposedly in our midst? Quite a bit it seems! In a *Newsweek* poll in November 2002, 72 percent said the restrictions on civil liberties by the Bush administration's war on terrorism were "about right."[3] In this poll 51 percent thought the Bill of Rights should apply only to U.S. citizens, excluding the many noncitizens who are in this country legally. In a poll taken two months after 9/11, Americans overwhelmingly favored restrictions on free speech if it would help the war on terrorism; 61 percent said that people who had expressed support for the terrorists should not be allowed to give a speech at a college; 40 percent would permit censorship of news reporting about war protests; and 36 percent approved of censorship of negative news reports about presidential conduct of the military[4]

Which civil liberties are at stake? The Bill of Rights, the first ten amendments to the U.S. Constitution, is a good starting point for review of provisions that are at issue in the new anti-terrorist measures. The First Amendment protects our right of free speech, freedom of association, and academic freedom. Efforts to censor public speeches, even if supportive of terrorism in the minds of some, would be protected under this constitutional right. If a college wants to sponsor a debate on the meaning of jihadism, should restrictions be placed on how wide-ranging the debate can be? If a local school raises money to donate to a charity and later learns that the charity has been linked with terrorist activities, should that school lose its right of freedom of association? Freedom of religion is also protected under the First Amendment. But in the interest of protecting us against terrorism, should the government be allowed to place special restrictions on religious schools that it suspects might promote anti-American views?

The Fourth Amendment protects us against "unreasonable searches and seizures" by the government. Yet the anti-terrorism provisions make it considerably easier for the government to conduct secret searches of homes and to tap cell phones with much greater ease if it asserts a "foreign intelligence" need.

---

[3]Jennifer Barrett, "*Newsweek* Poll: Public Backs Military Tribunals; Most Americans Support New Restrictions on Civil Liberties and Expanded Government Powers—Up to a Point," December 1, 2002, *Newsweek Web Exclusive.*

[4]The survey was conducted by National Public Radio News, the Kaiser Family Foundation, and the Harvard University Kennedy School of Government. http://www.npr.org/news/specials/civillibertiespoll/011130.poll.html.

The Sixth Amendment guarantees our right to "a speedy and public trial" yet the anti-terrorist measures ordered by President Bush after 9/11 allow secret military tribunals of persons who are not American citizens. The Seventh Amendment guarantees our right to a jury trial in a criminal proceeding, yet this is also denied in the secret military tribunals of persons who are not American citizens.

The Eighth Amendment guarantees that "Excessive bail shall not be required, nor excessive fines imposed, nor cruel and unusual punishments inflicted," yet thousands of immigrants, especially those of Middle Eastern descent, are being held in detention centers without formal charges being brought against them for months, even years, at a time.

The challenge ahead is to determine how best to protect the country and its residents from future terrorist attacks without jettisoning those liberties that our forefathers and so many generations of Americans fought to preserve.

ARGUMENTS FOR TRADING CIVIL LIBERTIES FOR SAFETY

1. *Only terrorists need to worry about searches by the government, not law-abiding citizens.*

   POINT: "People who have done nothing wrong have nothing to hide. If government officials want to search my house, let them. They won't find anything. If conducting a lot of searches means the government finds the terrorists and brings them to justice, then I say, let them search all of us."

   COUNTERPOINT: "We all have a right to privacy in our homes. I don't want the government searching my home on a fishing expedition. I'm not a terrorist, but I don't think my life should be an open book to government officials. And what if they find things that are perfectly innocent but might be taken out of context and make me look guilty of something I didn't do?"

2. *I'll never go on trial, as I follow the law, so the right to a public trial with a jury is irrelevant to me.*

   POINT: "Most people who are arrested are probably guilty anyway. And the terrorists who aren't even American citizens don't deserve the same rights citizens have under the Bill of Rights. Most countries in the world don't even have juries, so this is a luxury that people from those countries don't deserve if they do something wrong here."

   COUNTERPOINT: "Innocent people are arrested too, sometimes, and I want to know those rights will always be available to me to have a fair public trial with a jury. Further, our Bill of Rights is an important symbol we hold out to the world of our respect for human rights and human dignity. We should insist on upholding those rights, regardless of who commits a crime in our country, whether or not they are a citizen of this country."

3. *Good citizens should not speak ill of the president and the government in a time of war anyway.*

   POINT: "These are unusual times and we should all rally behind the president and the military. Publicly criticizing them is demoralizing to the nation and only encourages our enemies. Loyal Americans won't mind giving up some of their rights to free speech if it means we're more likely to defeat terrorism. Free speech is a luxury we can afford only during peacetime."

COUNTERPOINT: "Free speech is our best insurance that all viewpoints about the best way to proceed against terrorism are heard and discussed. We should never assume that one viewpoint from the government or the military is necessarily the right one. For centuries, the United States has stood for free speech and public debate on important issues, and in difficult times, we should not abandon that important belief."

4. *Those religious schools that teach Islam are a breeding ground for terrorists and should be closed down in this country.*
    POINT: "All nineteen of the hijackers on 9/11 were Muslims, and they thought they were carrying out the command of their religion. Religious schools in Saudi Arabia and Pakistan are teaching hatred of the West. I realize that most Muslims do not share those views, but while we are in danger from terrorism, we should be safe and close down the religious schools in this country that might be breeding more terrorism right here at home."
    COUNTERPOINT: "Islamic leaders in the United States and around the world have denounced the teachings espoused by the hijackers. Most Muslims love peace and condemn terrorism. We should encourage more of that. Closing down religious schools because they might have some terrorists working at them is a dangerous precedent. Timothy McVeigh was raised as a Christian, but nobody thought we should close down all the Christian schools in the country because of what he did."

ARGUMENTS AGAINST TRADING CIVIL LIBERTIES FOR SAFETY

1. *Our forefathers fought hard to give us precious civil liberties and we should value and protect them, even when times are frightening because of the threats of terrorism.*
    POINT: "Our Bill of Rights is over 200 years old and it provides a cornerstone for our country and its values. We should not so readily abandon it just because we are experiencing difficult times and fears of terrorism. Our forefathers would be disappointed to see us so readily agree to give up our liberties because we are afraid."
    COUNTERPOINT: "George Washington and the framers of the Constitution never could have envisioned a world in which we are threatened by terrorists, nuclear bombs, and hijacked airplanes flying into tall buildings. They would surely understand that we need to back away from some of their idealistic vision of liberty in the different and much more frightening world we live in today."

2. *Our protection of civil liberties and freedom is what sets us apart from other countries. We should set an example for the world and show how a free democracy really works.*
    POINT: "If we want the rest of the world to emulate our high standards of democracy, we must be vigilant to protect the liberties of a free and open society. If we start to curtail our own liberties because we are afraid, we encourage other countries to curtail what liberties they give their citizens

now or to continue to refuse to provide their citizens with any of the liberties we take for granted."

COUNTERPOINT: "No other country provides the degree of freedom and liberty to its citizens that we do in America. Cutting back a little to keep ourselves safe from terrorism won't discourage other countries from experimenting with democracy. And even if it does, it is more important to protect our nation from total devastation than to worry about setting an example for countries who don't like us anyway."

3. *We might think we're only hurting the terrorists and other criminals when we chip away at civil liberties, but we're putting ourselves at risk too.*

POINT: "Innocent people are sometimes arrested wrongly. Civil liberties in the Constitution protect us in ways that innocent people are not protected in other countries. If we look the other way at the diminishment of civil liberties for some people, it's a slippery slope before they start coming after the rest of us for no good reason."

COUNTERPOINT: "As long as you stay out of trouble, the government won't waste time searching your home or throwing you into jail for no good reason. Most people who are searched by the police or arrested are probably guilty anyway. Where there's smoke, there's fire!"

4. *Religious freedom is another hallmark of our nation, and we should continue to promote religious diversity and tolerance.*

POINT: "As a nation, we have always treasured our religious freedom, and this is no time to try to restrict some religions just because some of the terrorists belong to them. Many religions have promoted tolerance and understanding of each other, a message we desperately need in this day and age. If we have serious reason to believe terrorists plots are being developed anywhere, then go after them under the law, but don't assume an entire religion is plotting against us."

COUNTERPOINT: "Religious freedom is fine, but not when it preaches intolerance and breeds hatred against American values. We need to take whatever steps are necessary to protect us from the seething violence that is being fomented against us. Religion should not be a shield behind which terrorists can hide. Whether they are hiding in churches or charities or social groups, we need to go after them in any way we can."

The Triumph of Just War Theory (and the Dangers of Success)

MICHAEL WALZER

The distinguished political philosopher Michael Walzer is a Permanent Faculty Member Emeritus at the Institute for Advanced Study in Princeton, New Jersey. After receiving his Ph.D. from Harvard University, he taught at Princeton University and then Harvard University until 1980, when he joined the faculty at the Institute. He has published over two dozen books and numerous articles on just and unjust war, economic justice and the welfare state, nationalism and ethnicity, and political obligation. He takes a practical approach to political philosophy, applying theory to specific issues confronting us today.

In these excerpts from an essay he wrote in 2002, shortly after 9/11, he briefly surveys the "just war" theory promoted by Augustine in the fourth century, later developed by Aquinas in the thirteenth century. He then shows how its concepts have been used to justify and sometimes to rationalize wars throughout much of history. He does not advocate abandoning the theory but rather using it to constantly scrutinize and critique wars in our time.

Some political theories die and go to heaven; some, I hope, die and go to hell. But some have a long life in this world, a history most often of service to the powers-that-be, but also, sometimes, an oppositionist history. The theory of just war began in the service of the powers. At least that is how I interpret Augustine's achievement: he replaced the radical refusal of Christian pacifists with the active ministry of the Christian soldier. Now pious Christians could fight on behalf of the worldly city, for the sake of imperial peace (in this case, literally, *pax Romana*): but they had to fight justly, only for the sake of peace, and always, Augustine insisted, with a downcast demeanor, without anger or lust[1] Seen from the perspective of primitive Christianity, this account of just war was simply an excuse, a way of making war morally and religiously possible. And that was indeed the function of the theory. But its defenders would have said, and I am inclined to agree, that it made war possible in a world where war was, sometimes, necessary.

From the beginning, the theory had a critical edge: soldiers (or, at least, their officers) were supposed to refuse to fight in wars of conquest and to oppose or abstain from the standard military practices of rape and pillage after the battle was won. But just war was a worldly theory, in every sense of that term, and it continued to serve worldly interests against Christian radicalism. It is important to note, though, that Christian radicalism had more than one version: it could be expressed in a pacifist rejection of war, but it could also be expressed in war itself, in the religiously driven crusade. Augustine opposed the first of these; the medieval scholastics, following in Aquinas's footsteps, set themselves against the second. The classic statement is Vitoria's: "Difference of religion cannot be a cause of just war." For centuries, from the time of the Crusades to the religious wars of the Reformation years, many of the priests and preachers of Christian Europe, many lords and barons (and even a few kings), had been committed to the legitimacy of using military force against unbelievers: they had their own version of *jihad*. Vitoria claimed, by contrast, that "the sole and only just cause for waging war is when harm has been inflicted."[2] Just war was an argument of the religious center against pacifists, on the one side, and holy warriors, on the other, and because of its enemies (and even though its proponents were theologians), it took shape as a secular theory—which is simply another way of describing its worldliness.

So the rulers of this world embraced the theory, and did not fight a single war without describing it, or hiring intellectuals to describe it, as a war for peace and justice. Most often, of course, this description was hypocritical: the tribute that vice pays to virtue. But the need to pay the tribute opens those who pay it to the criticism of the virtuous—that is, of the brave and virtuous, of whom there have been only a few (but one could also say: at least a few). I will cite one heroic moment, from the history of the academic world: sometime around 1520, the faculty of the University of Salamanca met in solemn assembly and voted that the Spanish conquest of Central America was a violation of natural law and an unjust war.[3] I have not been able to learn anything about the subsequent fate of the good professors. Certainly, there were not many moments like that one, but what happened at Salamanca suggests that just war never lost its critical edge. The theory provided worldly reasons for going to war, but the reasons were limited—and they had to be worldly. Converting the Aztecs to Christianity was not a just cause; nor was seizing the gold of the Americas or enslaving its inhabitants.

Writers like Grotius and Pufendorf incorporated just war theory into international law, but the rise of the modern state and the legal (and philosophical) acceptance of state sovereignty pushed the theory into the background. Now the political foreground was occupied by people we can think of as Machiavellian princes, hard men (and sometimes women), driven by "reason of state," who did what (they said) they had to do. Worldly prudence triumphed over worldly justice; realism over what was increasingly disparaged as naive idealism. The princes of the world continued to defend their wars, using the language of international law, which was also, at least in part, the language of just war. But the defenses were marginal to the enterprise, and I suspect that it was the least important of the state's intellectuals who put them forward. States claimed a right to fight whenever their rulers deemed it necessary, and the rulers took sovereignty to mean that no one could judge their decisions. They not only fought when they wanted; they fought how they wanted, returning to the old Roman maxim that held war to be a lawless activity: *inter arma silent leges*—which, again, was taken to mean that there was no law above or beyond the decrees of the state; conventional restraints on the conduct of war could always be overridden for the sake of victory.[4] Arguments about justice were treated as a kind of moralizing, inappropriate to the anarchic conditions of international society. For this world, just war was not worldly enough.

In the 1950s and early 1960s, when I was in graduate school, realism was the reigning doctrine in the field of "international relations." The standard reference was not to justice but to interest. Moral argument was against the rules of the discipline as it was commonly practiced, although a few writers defended interest as the new morality.[5] There were many political scientists in those years

who preened themselves as modern Machiavellis and dreamed of whispering in the ear of the prince; and a certain number of them, enough to stimulate the ambition of the others, actually got to whisper. They practiced being cool and tough-minded; they taught the princes, who did not always need to be taught, how to get results through the calculated application of force. Results were understood in terms of "the national interest," which was the objectively determined sum of power and wealth here and now plus the probability of future power and wealth. More of both was almost always taken to be better; only a few writers argued for the acceptance of prudential limits; moral limits were, as I remember those years, never discussed. Just war theory was relegated to religion departments, theological seminaries, and a few Catholic universities. And even in those places, isolated as they were from the political world, the theory was pressed toward realist positions; perhaps for the sake of self-preservation, its advocates surrendered something of its critical edge.

Vietnam changed all this, although it took a while for the change to register at the theoretical level. What happened first occurred in the realm of practice. The war became a subject of political debate; it was widely opposed, mostly by people on the left. These were people heavily influenced by Marxism; they also spoke a language of interest; they shared with the princes and professors of American politics a disdain for moralizing. And yet the experience of the war pressed them toward moral argument. Of course, the war in their eyes was radically imprudent; it could not be won; its costs, even if Americans thought only of themselves, were much too high; it was an imperialist adventure unwise even for the imperialists; it set the United States against the cause of national liberation, which would alienate it from the Third World (and significant parts of the First). But these claims failed utterly to express the feelings of most of the war's opponents, feelings that had to do with the systematic exposure of Vietnamese civilians to the violence of American war-making. Almost against its will, the left fell into morality. All of us in the antiwar camp suddenly began talking the language of just war—though we did not know that that was what we were doing....

Once the war was over, just war became an academic subject; now political scientists and philosophers discovered the theory; it was written about in the journals and taught in the universities—and also in the (American) military academies and war colleges. A small group of Vietnam veterans played a major role in making the discipline of morality central to the military curriculum.[6] They had bad memories. They welcomed just war theory precisely because it was in their eyes a critical theory. It is, in fact, doubly critical—of war's occasions and its conduct. I suspect that the veterans were most concerned with the second of these. It is not only that they wanted to avoid anything like the My Lai massacre in future wars; they wanted, like professional soldiers everywhere, to distinguish their profession from mere butchery. And because of their Vietnam experience, they believed that this had to be done systematically; it required not only a code but also a theory. Once upon a time, I suppose, aristocratic honor had grounded the military code; in a more democratic and egalitarian age, the code had to be defended with arguments....

But there was another feature of Vietnam that gave the moral critique of the war special force: it was a war that we lost, and the brutality with which we fought the war almost certainly contributed to our defeat. In a war for "hearts and minds," rather than for land and resources, justice turns out to be a key to victory. So just war theory looked once again like the worldly doctrine that it is. And here, I think, is the deepest cause of the theory's contemporary triumph: there are now reasons of state for fighting justly. One might almost say that justice has become a military necessity.

There were probably earlier wars in which the deliberate killing of civilians, and also the common military carelessness about killing civilians, proved to be counterproductive. The Boer war is a likely example. But for us, Vietnam was the first war in which the practical value of *jus in bello* became apparent. To be sure, the "Vietnam syndrome" is generally taken to reflect a different lesson: that we should not fight wars that are unpopular at home and to which we are unwilling to commit the resources necessary for victory. But there was in fact another lesson, connected to but not the same as the "syndrome": that we should not fight wars about whose justice we are doubtful, and that once we are engaged we have to fight justly so as not to antagonize the civilian population, whose political support is necessary to a military victory. In Vietnam, the relevant civilians were the Vietnamese themselves; we lost the war when we lost their "hearts and minds." But this idea about the need for civilian support has turned out to be both variable and expansive: modern warfare requires the support of different civilian populations, extending beyond the population immediately at risk. Still, a moral regard for civilians at risk is critically important in winning wider support for the war ... for any modern war. I will call this the usefulness of morality. Its wide acknowledgement is something radically new in military history.

Hence the odd spectacle of George Bush (the elder), during the Persian Gulf war, talking like a just war theorist.[7] Well, not quite: for Bush's speeches and press conferences displayed an old American tendency, which his son has inherited, to confuse just wars and crusades, as if a war can be just only when the forces of good are arrayed against the forces of evil. But Bush also seemed to understand—and this was a constant theme of American military spokesmen—that war is properly a war of armies, a combat between combatants, from which the civilian population should be shielded. I do not believe that the bombing of Iraq in 1991 met just war standards; shielding civilians would certainly have excluded the destruction of electricity networks and water purification plants. Urban infrastructure, even if it is necessary to modern war-making, is also necessary to civilian existence in a modern city, and it is morally defined by this second feature.[8] Still, American strategy in the Gulf war was the result of a compromise between what justice would have required and the unrestrained bombing of previous wars; taken overall, targeting was far more limited and selective than it had been, for example, in Korea or Vietnam. The reasons for the limits were complicated: in part, they reflected a commitment to the Iraqi people (which turned out not to be very strong), in the hope that the Iraqis would repudiate the war and overthrow the regime that began it; in part, they reflected the political necessities of the coalition that made the war possible. Those necessities were shaped in turn by the media coverage of the war—that is, by the immediate access of the media to the battle and of people the world over to the media. Bush and his generals believed that these people would not tolerate a slaughter of civilians, and they were probably right (but what it might mean for them not to tolerate something was and is fairly unclear). Hence, although many of the countries whose support was crucial to the war's success were not democracies, bombing policy was dictated in important ways by the demos.

This will continue to be true: the media are omnipresent, and the whole world is watching. War has to be different in these circumstances. But does this mean that it has to be more just or only that it has to look most just, that it has to be described, a little more persuasively than in the past, in the language of justice? The triumph of just war theory is clear enough; it is amazing how readily military spokesmen during the Kosovo and Afghanistan wars used its categories, telling a causal story that justified the war and providing accounts of the battles that emphasized the restraint with which they were being fought. The arguments (and rationalizations) of the past were very different; they commonly came from outside the armed forces—from clerics, lawyers, and professors, not from generals—and they commonly lacked specificity and detail. But what does the use of these categories, these just and moral words, signify?

Perhaps naively, I am inclined to say that justice has become, in all Western countries, one of the tests that any proposed military strategy or tactic has to meet—only one of the tests and not the most important one, but this still gives just war theory a place and standing that it never had before. It is easier now than it ever was to imagine a general saying, "No, we can't do that; it would cause too many civilian deaths; we have to find another way." I am not sure that there are many generals who talk like that, but imagine for a moment that there are; imagine that strategies are evaluated morally as well as militarily; that civilian deaths are minimized; that new technologies are designed to avoid or limit collateral damage, and that these technologies are actually effective in achieving their intended purpose. Moral theory

has been incorporated into war-making as a real constraint on when and how wars are fought. This picture is, remember, imaginary, but it is also partly true; and it makes for a far more interesting argument than the more standard claim that the triumph of just war is pure hypocrisy. The triumph is real: what then is left for theorists and philosophers to do?

… [One] response is to take the moral need to recognize, condemn and oppose very seriously and then to raise the theoretical ante—that is, to strengthen the constraints that justice imposes on warfare. For theorists who pride themselves on living, so to speak, at the critical edge, this is an obvious and understandable response. For many years, we have used the theory of just war to criticize American military actions, and now it has been taken over by the generals and is being used to explain and justify those actions. Obviously, we must resist. The easiest way to resist is to make noncombatant immunity into a stronger and stronger rule, until it is something like an absolute rule: all killing of civilians is (something close to) murder; therefore any war that leads to the killing of civilians is unjust; therefore every war is unjust. So pacifism reemerges from the very heart of the theory that was originally meant to replace it. This is the strategy adopted, most recently, by many opponents of the Afghanistan war. The protest marches on American campuses featured banners proclaiming, "Stop the Bombing!" and the argument for stopping was very simple (and obviously true): bombing endangers and kills civilians. The marchers did not seem to feel that anything more had to be said.

Since I believe that war is still, sometimes, necessary, this seems to me a bad argument and, more generally, a bad response to the triumph of just war theory. It sustains the critical role of the theory vis-à-vis war generally, but it denies the theory the critical role it has always claimed, which is internal to the business of war and requires critics to attend closely to what soldiers try to do and what they try not to do. The refusal to make distinctions of this kind, to pay attention to strategic and tactical choices, suggests a doctrine of radical suspicion. This is the radicalism of people who do not expect to exercise power or use force, ever, and who are not prepared to make the judgments that this exercise and use require. By contrast, just war theory, even when it demands a strong critique of particular acts of war, is the doctrine of people who do expect to exercise power and use force. We might think of it as a doctrine of radical responsibility, because it holds political and military leaders responsible, first of all, for the well-being of their own people, but also for the well-being of innocent men and women on the other side. Its proponents set themselves against those who will not think realistically about the defense of the country they live in and also against those who refuse to recognize the humanity of their opponents. They insist that there are things that it is morally impermissible to do even to the enemy. They also insist, however, that fighting itself cannot be morally impermissible. A just war is meant to be, and has to be, a war that it is possible to fight.

But there is another danger posed by the triumph of just war theory—not the radical relativism and the near absolutism that I have just described, but rather a certain softening of the critical mind, a truce between theorists and soldiers. If intellectuals are often awed and silenced by political leaders who invite them to dinner, how much more so by generals who talk their language? And if the generals are actually fighting just wars, if *inter arma* the laws speak, what point is there in anything we can say? In fact, however, our role has not changed all that much. We still have to insist that war is a morally dubious and difficult activity. Even if we (in the West) have fought just wars in the Gulf, in Kosovo, and in Afghanistan, that is no guarantee, not even a useful indication, that our next war will be just. And even if the recognition of noncombatant immunity has become militarily necessary, it still conflicts with other, more pressing, necessities. Justice still needs to be defended; decisions about when and how to fight require constant scrutiny, exactly as they always have.

At the same time, we have to extend our account of "when and how" to cover the new strategies, the new technologies, and the new politics of a global age. Old ideas may not fit the emerging reality: the "war against terrorism," to take the most current example, requires a kind of international cooperation that is as radically undeveloped in theory as it is in practice. We should welcome military officers into the theoretical argument; they will make it a better argument than it would be if no one but professors took an interest. But we cannot leave the argument to them. As the old saying goes, war is too important to be left to the generals; just war even more so. The ongoing critique of war-making is a centrally important democratic activity.

Let me, then, suggest two issues, raised by our most recent wars, that require the critical edge of justice.

First, risk-free war-making. I have heard it said that this is a necessary feature of humanitarian interventions like the Kosovo war: soldiers defending humanity, in contrast to soldiers defending their own country and their fellow-citizens, will not risk their lives; or, their political leaders will not dare to ask them to risk their lives. Hence the rescue of people in desperate trouble, the objects of massacre or ethnic cleansing, is only possible if risk-free war is possible.[9] But, obviously, it is possible: wars can be fought from a great distance with bombs and missiles aimed very precisely (compared with the radical imprecision of such weapons only a few decades ago) at the forces carrying out the killings and deportations. And the soldier-technicians aiming these weapons are, in all the recent cases, largely invulnerable to counterattack. There is no principle of just war theory that bars this kind of warfare. So long as they can aim accurately at military targets, soldiers have every right to fight from a safe distance. And what commander, committed to his or her own soldiers, would not choose to fight in this way whenever it was possible? In his reflections on rebellion, Albert Camus argues that one cannot kill unless one is prepared to die.[10] But that argument does not seem to apply to soldiers in battle, where the whole point is to kill while avoiding getting killed. And yet there is a wider sense in which Camus is right.

Just war theorists have not, to my knowledge, discussed this question, but we obviously need to do so.... Massacre and ethnic cleansing commonly take place on the ground. The awful work might be done with bombs and poison gas delivered from the air, but in Bosnia, Kosovo, Rwanda, East Timor, and Sierra Leone, the weapons were rifles, machetes, and clubs; the killing and terrorizing of the population were carried out from close up. And a risk-free intervention undertaken from far away—especially if it promises to be effective in the long run—is likely to cause an immediate speed-up on the ground. This can be stopped only if the intervention itself shifts to the ground, and this shift seems to be morally necessary. The aim of the intervention, after all, is to rescue people in trouble, and fighting on the ground, in the case as I have described it, is what rescue requires. But then it is no longer risk-free. Why would anyone undertake it?

In fact, risks of this sort are a common feature of *jus in bello*, and while there are many examples of soldiers unwilling to accept them, there are also many examples of their acceptance. The principle is this: when it is our action that puts innocent people at risk, even if the action is justified, we are bound to do what we can to reduce those risks, even if this involves risks to our own soldiers. If we are bombing military targets in a just war, and there are civilians living near these targets, we have to adjust our bombing policy—by flying at lower altitudes, say—so as to minimize the risks we impose on civilians. Of course, it is legitimate to balance the risks; we cannot require our pilots to fly suicidal missions. They have to be, as Camus suggests, prepared to die, but that is consistent with taking measures to safeguard their lives. How the balance gets worked out is something that has to be debated in each case. But what is not permissible, it seems to me, is what NATO did in the Kosovo war, where its leaders declared in advance that they would not send ground forces into battle, whatever happened inside Kosovo once the air war began. Responsibility for the intensified Serbian campaign against Kosovar civilians, which was the immediate consequence of the air war, belongs no doubt to the Serbian government and army. They were to blame. But this was at the same time a foreseeable result of our action, and insofar as we did nothing to prepare for this result, or to deal with it, we were blameworthy too. We imposed risks on others and refused to accept them for ourselves, even when that acceptance was necessary to help the others.[11]

The second issue concerns war's endings. On the standard view, a just war (precisely because it is not a crusade) should end with the restoration of the status quo ante. The paradigm case is a war of aggression, which ends justly when the aggressor has been defeated, his attack repulsed, the old boundaries restored. Perhaps this is not quite enough for a just conclusion: the victim state might deserve reparations from the aggressor state, so that the damage the aggressor's forces inflicted can be repaired—a more extensive understanding of restoration, but restoration still. And perhaps the peace treaty should include new security arrangements, of a sort that did not exist before the war, so that the status quo will be more stable in the future. But that is as far as the rights of victims go; the theory as it was commonly understood did not extend to any radical reconstitution of the enemy state, and international law, with its assumptions about sovereignty, would have regarded any imposed change of regime as a new act of aggression. What happened after World War II in both Germany and Japan was something quite new in the history of war, and the legitimacy of occupation and political reconstitution is still debated, even by theorists and lawyers who regard the treatment of the Nazi regime, at least, as justified. Thus, as the Gulf war drew to a close in 1991, there was little readiness to march on Baghdad and replace the government of Saddam Hussein, despite the denunciation of that government in the lead-up to the war as Nazi-like in character. There were, of course, both military and geopolitical arguments against continuing the war once the attack on Kuwait had been repulsed, but there was also an argument from justice: that even if Iraq "needed" a new government, that need could only be met by the Iraqi people themselves. A government imposed by foreign armies would never be accepted as the product of, or the future agent of, self-determination.[12]

The World War II examples, however, argue against this last claim. If the imposed government is democratic and moves quickly to open up the political arena and to organize elections, it may erase the memory of its own imposition (hence the difference between the western and eastern regimes in post-war Germany). In any case, humanitarian intervention radically shifts the argument about endings, because now the war is from the beginning an effort to change the regime that is responsible for the inhumanity. This can be done by supporting secession, as the Indians did in what is now Bangladesh; or by expelling a dictator, as the Tanzanians did to Uganda's Idi Amin; or by creating a new government, as the Vietnamese did in Cambodia. In East Timor, more recently, the U.N. organized a referendum on secession and then worked to set up a new government. Had there been, as there should have been, an intervention in Rwanda, it would certainly have aimed at replacing the Hutu Power regime. Justice would have required the replacement. But what kind of justice is this? Who are its agents, and what rules govern their actions?

As the Rwandan example suggests, most states do not want to take on this kind of responsibility, and when they do take it on, for whatever political reasons, they do not want to submit themselves to a set of moral rules. In Cambodia, the Vietnamese shut down the killing fields, which was certainly a good thing to do, but they then went on to set up a satellite government, keyed to their own interests, which never won legitimacy either within or outside of Cambodia and brought no closure to the country's internal conflicts. Legitimacy and closure are the two criteria against which we can test war's endings. Both of them are likely to require, in almost all the humanitarian intervention cases, something more than the restoration of the status quo ante—which gave rise, after all, to the crisis that prompted the intervention. Legitimacy and closure, however, are hard tests to meet. The problems have to do in part with strategic interests, as in the Vietnamese–Cambodian case. But material interests also figure in a major way: remaking a government is an expensive business; it requires a significant commitment of resources—and the benefits are largely speculative and nonmaterial. Yet we can still point to the usefulness of morality in cases like these. A successful and extended intervention brings benefits of an important kind: not only gratitude and friendship, but an increment of peace and stability in a world where the insufficiency of both is costly—and not only to its immediate victims. Still, any particular country will always have good reasons to refuse to bear the costs of these benefits; or it will take

on the burden, and then find reasons to perform badly. So we still need justice's critical edge.

The argument about endings is similar to the argument about risk: once we have acted in ways that have significant negative consequences for other people (even if there are also positive consequences), we cannot just walk away. Imagine a humanitarian intervention that ends with the massacres stopped and the murderous regime overthrown; but the country is devastated, the economy in ruins, the people hungry and afraid; there is neither law nor order nor any effective authority. The forces that intervened did well, but they are not finished. How can this be? Is it the price of doing well that you acquire responsibilities to do well again … and again? The work of the virtuous is never finished. It does not seem fair. But in the real world, not only of international politics, but also of ordinary morality, this is the ways things work (though virtue, of course, is never so uncomplicated)….

This theory of justice-in-endings will have to include a description of legitimate occupations, regime changes, and protectorates—and also, obviously, a description of illegitimate and immoral activity in all these areas. This combination is what just war has always been about: it makes actions and operations that are morally problematic *possible* by constraining their occasions and regulating their conduct. When the constraints are accepted, the actions and operations are justified, and the theorist of just war has to say that, even if he sounds like an apologist for the powers-that-be. When they are not accepted, when the brutalities of war or its aftermath are unconstrained, he has to say that, even if he is called a traitor and an enemy of the people.

It is important not to get stuck in either mode—defense or critique. Indeed, just war theory requires that we maintain our commitment to both modes at the same time. In this sense, just war is like good government: there is a deep and permanent tension between the adjective and the noun, but no necessary contradiction between them. When reformers come to power and make government better (less corrupt, say), we have to be able to acknowledge the improvement. And when they hold on to power for too long, and imitate their predecessors, we have to be ready to criticize their behavior. Just war theory is not an apology for any particular war, and it is not a renunciation of war itself. It is designed to sustain a constant scrutiny and an immanent critique. We still need that, even when generals sound like theorists, and I am sure that we always will.

NOTES

1. Augustine's argument on just war can be found in *The Political Writings of St. Augustine*, ed. Henry Paolucci (Chicago: Henry Regnery, 1962), 162–83; modern readers will need a commentary: see Herbert A. Dean, *The Political and Social Ideas of St. Augustine* (New York: Columbia University Press, 1963), 134–71.

2. See Francisco deVitoria, *Political Writings*, ed. Anthony Pagden and Jeremy Lawrance (Cambridge: Cambridge University Press, 1991), 302–4, and for commentary, see James Turner Johnson, *Ideology, Reason, and the Limitation of War: Religious and Secular Concepts, 1200–1740* (Princeton: Princeton University Press, 1975), 150–71.

3. See James Boswell, *Life of Samuel Johnson LL.D.*, ed. Robert Maynard Hutchins, vol. 44 of *Great Books of the Western World* (Chicago: Encyclopedia Britannica, 1952), 129, quoting Dr. Johnson: "'I love the University of Salamanca, for when the Spaniards were in doubt as to the lawfulness of conquering America, the University of Salamanca gave it as their opinion that it was not lawful.' He spoke this with great emotion."

4. With some hesitation, I cite my own discussion of military necessity (and the references there to more sympathetic treatments): Michael Walzer, *Just and Unjust Wars* (New York: Basic Books, 1977), 144–51, 239–42, 251–55.

5. The best discussion of the realists is Michael Joseph Smith, *Realist Thought from Weber to Kissinger* (Baton Rouge: Louisiana State University Press, 1986); chapter 6, on Hans Morgenthau, is especially relevant to my argument here.

6. Anthony Hartle is one of those veterans, who eventually wrote his own book on the ethics of war: Anthony E. Hartle, *Moral Issues in Military Decision Making* (Lawrence: University Press of Kansas, 1989).

7. See the documents collected in *The Gulf War: History, Documents, Opinions*, ed. Micah L. Sifry and Christopher Cerf (New York: Times Books, 1991), 197–352, among them Bush's speeches and a wide range of other opinion papers.

8. I made the case against attacks on infrastructural targets immediately after the war (but others made it earlier) in *But Was It Just? Reflections on the Morality of the Persian Gulf War*, ed. David E. DeCosse (New York: Doubleday, 1992), 12–13.

9. This argument was made by several participants at a conference on humanitarian intervention held at the Zentrum für interdisziplinare Forschung, Bielefeld University, Germany, in January 2002.

10. "A life is paid for by another life, and from these two sacrifices springs the promise of a value." Albert Camus, *The Rebel*, trans. Anthony Bower (New York: Vintage, 1956), 169. See also the argument in act I of *The Just Assassins*, in Albert Camus, *Caligula and Three Other Plays*, trans. Stuart Gilbert (New York: Vintage, 1958), esp. 246–47.

11. For arguments in favor of using ground forces in Kosovo, see William Joseph Buckley, ed., *Kosovo: Contending Voices on Balkan Interventions* (Grand Rapids, Mich.: William B. Eerdmans, 2000), 293–94, 333–35, 342.

12. Bush's statement on stopping the American advance, and his declaration of victory, can be found in *The Gulf War: History, Documents, Opinions*, 449–51; arguments for and against stopping can be found in *But Was It Just?* 13–14, 29–32.

⚜ QUESTIONS FOR ANALYSIS

1. How did "just war" theory begin? How was it used in early wars in history?

2. What are traits of political figures Walzer descries as Machiavellian?

3. How did the rise of the modern state give rise to the view that war was a lawless activity?

4. How did the Vietnam War trigger a return to concerns about morality and just war?

5. What does Walzer mean when he says just war theory is a "worldly doctrine"?
6. How did the practical value of *jus in bello* become apparent in the Vietnam War? Why should we care about the impact of wars on civilians in the war zone?
7. Why does Walzer believe that the bombing of Iraq in 1991 failed to meet the standards of just war?

8. How has the triumph of just war theory become evident in recent wars in Kosovo and Afghanistan?
9. What is the appropriate use of just war theory now and for wars in our future?
10. How should a just war end? What should be included in justice-in-endings?

Violence, Terrorism, and Justice

R. G. FREY AND CHRISTOPHER W. MORRIS

R. G. Frey was Professor Emeritus of Philosophy at Bowling Green State University until his death in 2012. Christopher W. Morris is Professor of Philosophy at the University of Maryland. Each has written extensively on social and political theory, ethical theory, and applied ethics. This essay introduces discussions of violence and terrorism from a conference they organized in 1988.

Unless one is a pacifist, one is likely to find it relatively easy to think of scenarios in which the use of force and violence against others is justified. Killing other people in self-defense, for example, seems widely condoned, but so, too does defending our citizens abroad against attack from violent regimes. Violence in these cases appears reactive, employed to defeat aggression against or violence toward vital interests. Where violence comes to be seen as much more problematic, if not simply prohibited, is in its direct use for social/political ends. It then degenerates into terrorism, many people seem to think, and terrorism, they hold is quite wrong. But what exactly is terrorism? And why is it wrong?

Most of us today believe terrorism to be a serious problem, one that raises difficult and challenging questions. The urgency of the problem, especially to North Americans and Western Europeans, may appear to be that terrorism is an issue that we confront from outside—that, as

it were, it is an issue for us, not because violence for political ends is something approved of in our societies, but because we are the objects of such violence. The difficulty of the questions raised by contemporary terrorism has to do, we may suppose, with the complexity of issues having to do with the use of violence generally for political ends.

The first question, that of the proper characterization of terrorism, is difficult, in part because it is hard to separate from the second, evaluative question, that of the wrongness of terrorism. We may think of terrorism as a type of violence, that is, a kind of force that inflicts damage or harm on people and property. Terrorism thus broadly understood raises the same issues raised generally by the use of violence by individuals or groups. If we think of violence as being a kind of force, then the more general issues concern the evaluation of the use of force, coercion, and the like: When may we restrict people's options so that they have little or no choice but to do what we wish them to do? Violence may be used as one would use force, in order to obtain some end. But violence inflicts harm or damage and consequently adds a new element to the nonviolent use of force. When, then, if ever, may we inflict harm or damage on someone in the pursuit of some end? This question and the sets of issues it raises are familiar topics of moral and political philosophy.

Without preempting the varying characterizations of terrorism developed by the authors in this volume, however, we can think of it more narrowly; that is, we can think of it as a particular use of violence, typically for social/political ends, with several frequently conjoined characteristics. On this view, terrorism, as one would expect from the use of the term, usually involves creating terror or fear, even, perhaps, a sense of panic in a population. This common feature of terrorism is related to another characteristic, namely, the seemingly random or arbitrary use of violence. This in turn is related to a third feature, the targeting of the innocent of "noncombatants." This last, of course, is a more controversial feature than the others, since many terrorists attempt to justify their acts by arguing that their victims are not (wholly) innocent.

Thus characterized, terrorism raises specific questions that are at the center of contemporary philosophical debate. When, if ever, may one intentionally harm the innocent? Is the justification of terrorist violence to be based entirely on consequences, beneficial or other? Or are terrorist acts among those that are wrong independently of their consequences? What means may one use in combating people who use violence without justification? Other questions, perhaps less familiar, also arise. What does it mean for people to be innocent, that is, not responsible for the acts, say of their governments? May there not be some justification in terrorists' targeting some victims but not others? May terrorist acts be attributed to groups or to states? What sense, if any, does it make to think of a social system as terrorist?

Additionally, there are a variety of issues that specifically pertain to terrorists and their practices. What is the moral standing generally of terrorists? That is, what, if any duties do we have to them? How do their acts, and intentions, affect their standing? How does that standing affect our possible responses to them? May we, for instance, execute terrorists or inflict forms of punishment that would, in the words of the American Constitution, otherwise be "cruel and unusual"? What obligations might we, or officials of state, have in our dealings with terrorists? Is bargaining, of the sort practiced by virtually all Western governments, a justified response to terrorism? How, if at all, should our responses to terrorists be altered in the event that we admit or come to admit, to some degree, the justice of their cause?

Considered broadly, as a type of violence, or even more generally, as a type of force, terrorism is difficult to condemn out of hand. Force is a common feature of political life. We secure compliance with law by the use and threat of force. For many, this may be the sole reason for compliance. Force is used, for instance, to ensure that people pay their taxes, and force, even violence, is commonplace in the control of crime. In many such instances, there is not much controversy about the general justification of the use of force. The matter, say, of military conscription, though endorsed by many, is more controversial. In international contexts, however, the uses of force, and of violence, raise issues about which there is less agreement. Examples will come readily to mind.

More narrowly understood, involving some or all of the three elements mentioned earlier (the creation of terror, the seemingly random use of violence, and the targeting of the innocent or of noncombatants), the justification of terrorism is more problematic, as a brief glance at several competing moral theories will reveal.

Act-consequentialists, those who would have us evaluate actions solely in terms of their consequences, would presumably condone some terrorist acts. Were some such act to achieve a desirable goal, with minimal costs, the consequentialist might approve. Care, however, must be taken in characterizing the terrorists' goals and means. For contemporary consequentialists invariably are universalists; the welfare or ends of all people (and, on some accounts, all sentient beings) are to be included. Thus, terrorists cannot avail themselves of such theories to justify furthering the ends of some small group at the cost of greater damage to the interests of others. Merely to argue that the ends justify the means, without regard to the nature of the former, does not avail to one the resources of consequentialist moral theory.

Two factors will be further emphasized. First, consequentialist moral theory will focus upon effectiveness and efficiency, upon whether terrorist acts are an effective, efficient means to achieving desirable goals. The question naturally arises, then, whether there is an alternative means available, with equal or better likelihood of success in achieving the goals at a reduced cost. If resort to terrorism is a tactic, is there another tactic, just as likely to achieve the goal, at a cost more easy for us to bear? It is here, of course, that alternatives such as passive resistance and nonviolent civil disobedience will arise and need to be considered. It is here also that account must be taken of the obvious fact that terrorist acts seem often to harden the resistance of those the terrorists oppose. Indeed, the alleged justice of the terrorists' cause can easily slip into the background, as the killing and maiming come to preoccupy and outrage the target population. Second, consequentialist moral theory will focus upon the goal to be achieved: Is the goal that a specific use of terrorism is in aid of desirable enough for us to want to see it realized in society, at the terrible costs it exacts? It is no accident that terrorists usually portray their cause as concerned with the rectification and elimination of injustice; for *this* goal seems to be one the achievement of which we might just agree was desirable enough for us to tolerate significant cost. And it is here, of course, that doubts plague us, because we are often unsure where justice with respect to some issue falls. In the battle over Ireland, and the demand of the Irish Republican Army for justice, is there nothing to be said on the English side? Is the entire matter black and white? Here, too, a kind of proportionality rule may intrude itself. Is the reunification of Ireland worth all the suffering and loss the IRA inflicts? Is this a goal worth, not only members of the IRA's dying for, but also their making other people die for? For consequentialists, it typically will not be enough that members of the IRA think so; those affected by the acts of the IRA cannot be ignored.

Finally, consequentialist moral theory will stress how unsure we sometimes are about what counts as doing justice. On the one hand, we sometimes are genuinely unsure about what counts as rectifying an injustice. For instance, is allowing the Catholics of Northern Ireland greater and greater control over their lives part of the rectification process? For the fact remains that there are many more Protestants than Catholics in the North, so that *democratic* votes may well not materially change the condition of the latter, whatever their degree of participation in the process. On the other hand, we sometimes are genuinely unsure whether we can rectify or eliminate one injustice without perpetrating another. In the Arab–Israeli conflict, for example, can we remove one side's grievances without thereby causing additional grievances on the other side? Is there *any* way of rectifying an injustice in that conflict without producing another?

Thus, while consequentialist moral theory can produce a justification of terrorist acts, it typically will do so here, as in other areas, only under conditions that terrorists in the flesh will find it difficult to satisfy.

It is the seeming randomness of the violence emphasized by terrorism, understood in the narrower sense, that leads many moral theorists to question its legitimacy. Many moral traditions, especially nonconsequentialist ones, impose strict limits on the harm that may be done to the innocent. Indeed, some theories such as those associated with natural law and Kantian traditions, will impose an indefeasible prohibition on the intentional killing of the innocent, which "may not be overriden, whatever the consequences." Sometimes this prohibition is formulated in terms of the rights of the innocent not to be killed (e.g., the right to life), other times in terms merely of our duties not to take their lives. Either way the prohibition is often understood to be indefeasible.

If intentionally killing the innocent is indefeasibly wrong, that is, if it may never be done whatever the consequences, then many, if not most, contemporary terrorists stand condemned. Killing individuals who happen to find themselves in a targeted store, café, or train station may not be done, according to these traditions. Contemporary terrorists, who intend to bring about the deaths of innocent people by their acts, commit one of the most serious acts of injustice, unless, of course, they can show that these people are not innocent.

Much turns on their attempts, therefore, to attack the innocence claim.

Just as natural law and Kantian moral theories constrain our behavior and limit the means we may use in the pursuit of political ends, so they constrain our responses to terrorists. We may not, for instance, intentionally kill innocent people (e.g., bystanders, hostages) while combating those who attack us. Our hands may thus be tied in responding to terrorism. Many commentators have argued that a morally motivated reluctance to use the nondiscriminating means of terrorists makes us especially vulnerable to them.

Some natural law or Kantian thinking invoke the notions of natural or of human rights to understand moral standing, where these are rights which we possess simply by virtue of our natures or of our humanity. Now if our nature or our humanity is interpreted, as it commonly is in these traditions, as something we retain throughout our lives, at least to the extent that we retain those attributes and capacities that are characteristic of humans, then even those who violate the strictest prohibitions of justice will retain their moral standing. According to this view, a killer acts wrongly without thereby ceasing to be the sort of being that possesses moral standing. Terrorists, then, retain their moral standing, and consequently, there are limits to what we may do to them, by way either of resistance or of punishment. Conversely, though there is reason to think consequentialists, including those who reject theories of rights to understand moral standing, would not deny terrorists such standing, what may be done to terrorists may not be so easily constrained. For harming those who harm the innocent seems less likely to provoke outrage and opposition and so negative consequences.

Certainly, not every member of these consequentialist traditions will agree with this analysis. John Locke, for instance, believed that a murderer has "by the unjust Violence and Slaughter he hath committed upon one, declared War against all Mankind, and therefore may be destroyed as a *Lyon* or a *Tyger*, one of those wild Savage Beasts, with whom Men can have no Society nor Security."[1] It may, however, be argued that the analysis accords with many parts of these traditions, as well as with much of ordinary, commonsense morality.

Whether we follow these theories in understanding the prohibition on the intentional killing of the innocent to be indefeasible or not, this principle figures importantly in most moral traditions. Care, however, must be taken in its interpretation and application. Even if we understand terrorism narrowly, as involving attacks on the innocent, it may not be clear here as elsewhere exactly who is innocent. As made clear in the just war and abortion literature, the term "innocent" is ambiguous. The usual sense is to designate some individual who is not guilty of moral or legal wrongdoing, a sense usually called the moral or juridical sense of the term. By contrast, in discussing what are often called "innocent threats"—for instance, an approaching infant who unwittingly is booby-trapped with explosives, a fetus whose continued growth threatens the life of the woman—it is common to distinguish a "technical" or "causal" sense of "innocence." People lack innocence in this second sense insofar as they threaten, whatever their culpability.

Determining which sense of "innocence" is relevant (and this is not to prejudge the issue of still further, different senses) is controversial. In discussions of the ethics of war, it is often thought that "noncombatants" are not legitimate targets, because of their innocence. Noncombatants, however, may share some of the responsibility for the injustice of a war or the injustice of the means used to prosecute the war, or they may threaten the adversary in certain ways. In the first case, they would not be fully innocent in the moral or juridical sense; in the second, they would lack, to some degree, causal innocence.

This distinction is relevant to the moral evaluation of terrorist acts aimed at noncombatants. Sometimes attempts are made at justification by pointing to the victims' lack of innocence, in the first sense. Perhaps this is what Emile Henry meant when he famously said, in 1894, after exploding a bomb in a Paris café, "There are no innocents." Presumably in such cases, where the relevant notion of innocence is that of nonculpability, terrorists would strike only at members of certain national or political groups. Other times it might be argued that the victims in someway (for instance, by their financial, electoral, or tacit support for a repressive regime) posed a threat.

In these cases, terrorists would view themselves as justified in striking at anyone who, say, was present in a certain location. The distinction may also be of importance in discussions of the permissibility of various means that might be used in response to terrorist acts. If the relevant sense of innocence is causal, then certain means, those endangering the lives of victims, might be permissible.

Of course it is hard to understand how the victims of the Japanese Red Army attack at Israel's Lod airport in 1972 or of a bomb in a Paris department store in 1986 could be thought to lack innocence in either sense. In the first case, the victims were travelers (e.g., Puerto Rican Christians); in the second case, the store in question was frequented by indigent immigrants and, at that time of year, by mothers and children shopping for school supplies. It is this feature of some contemporary terrorism that has lead many commentators to distinguish it from earlier forms and from other political uses of violence.

The analogies here with another issue that has preoccupied moral theorists recently, that of the ethics of nuclear deterrence and conflict, are significant. The United States, of course, dropped atomic weapons on two Japanese cities at the end of the last world war. For several decades now, American policy has been to threaten the Soviet Union with a variety of kinds of nuclear strikes in the event that the latter attacked the United States or its Western allies with nuclear or, in the case of an invasion of Western Europe, merely with conventional weapons. These acts or practices involve killing or threatening to kill noncombatants in order to achieve certain ends: unconditional surrender in the case of Japan, deterrence of aggression in that of the Soviet Union. The possible analogies with terrorism have not gone unnoticed. Furthermore, just as some defenders of the atomic strikes against the Japanese have argued, those we attack, or threaten to attack, with nuclear weapons are themselves sufficiently similar to terrorists to justify our response.

A still different perspective on these issues may be obtained by turning from the usual consequentialist and natural law or Kantian theories to forms of contractarianism in ethics. Although this tradition has affinities with natural law and Kantian theories, especially with regard to the demands of justice or

the content of moral principles, there are differences that are especially noteworthy in connection with the issues that are raised by terrorist violence.

According to this tradition, justice may be thought of as a set of principles and dispositions that bind people insofar as those to whom they are obligated reciprocate. In the absence of constraint by others, one has little or no duty to refrain from acting toward them in ways that normally would be unjust. Justice may be thus thought, to borrow a phrase from John Rawls, to be a sort of "cooperative venture for mutual advantage." According to this view, justice is not binding in the absence of certain conditions, one of which would be others' cooperative behavior and dispositions.

Adherents to this tradition might argue that we would be in a "state of nature," that is, a situation where few if any constraints of justice would bind us, with regard to terrorists who attack those who are innocent (in the relevant sense). As Hume argues in the *Second Enquiry*, when in "the society of ruffians, remote from the protection of laws and government," or during the "rage and violence of public war," the conventions of justice are suspended:

> The laws of war, which then succeed to those of equity and justice, are rules calculated for the advantage and utility of that particular state, in which men are now placed. And were a civilized nation engaged with barbarians, who observed no rules even of war, the former must also suspend their observance of them, where they no longer serve to any purpose; and must render every action or rencounter as bloody and pernicious as possible to the first aggressors.[2]

Unlike the earlier views, then, this view holds that terrorists who, by act or by intent, forswear the rules of justice may thereby lose the protection of those rules, and so a major part of their moral standing.

Similarly, partisans of terrorism might argue that it is the acts of their victims or of their governments that make impossible cooperative relations of fair dealing between themselves and those they attack. The acts, or intentions, of the latter remove them from the protection of the rules of justice.

In either case, the acts of terrorists and our response to them take place in a world beyond, or prior to, justice. Students of international affairs and diplomacy will recognize here certain of the implications of a family of skeptical positions called "realism."

Consequentialists, it should be noted, are likely to find this exclusive focus on the virtue of justice to be misguided, and they are likely to be less enamored of certain distinctions involving kinds of innocence or types of violence that are incorporated into contractarianism. In general, they will argue, as noted earlier, that terrorism *can* be justified by its consequences, where these must include the effects not merely on the terrorists but also on their victims (and others). As terrorist acts appear often not to produce sufficient benefits to outweigh the considerable costs they inevitably exact, there will most likely be a moral presumption, albeit defeasible, against them. But wrongful terrorism will be condemned, not because of the existence of mutually advantageous conventions of justice, but because of the overall harm or suffering caused. Consequentialists, then, will doubtless stand out as much against contractarian views here as they do against natural law or Kantian ones.

The foregoing, then, is a sketch of different ways terrorism may be understood and of different types of moral theories in which its justification may be addressed. There is serious controversy on both counts, and this fact alone, whatever other differences may exist, makes the works of philosophers and political and social scientists on terrorism contentious even among themselves....

NOTES

1. John Locke, *Second Treatise of Government,* in *Two Treatises of Government,* ed. Peter Laslett (Cambridge: Cambridge University Press, 1988), p. 274 (chap. 2, sec. 11).
2. David Hume, *An Enquiry concerning the Principles of Morals,* in *Enquiries concerning Human Understanding and the Principles of Morals,* ed. L. A. Selby-Bigge, 3d ed., ed. P. H. Nidditch (Oxford: Clarendon, 1975), pp. 187–8 (sec. 3, pt. 1).

⚜ QUESTIONS FOR ANALYSIS

1. How would you define "terrorism" using ideas from Frey and Morris? Is it "violence against innocent civilians for social and political purposes"? Is it only a particular type of violence? How is violence different from force? Does terrorism include all social and political purposes or only some? During war, innocent civilians are often killed or injured, even if that is not the intent of the attacks. How is this different from terrorism?
2. Test your definition of terrorism by considering the attacks of 9/11 on the World Trade Center and the Pentagon, the attack on the Oklahoma City Federal Building, the spread of anthrax through the U.S. mail, the attack on the American ship the U.S.S. *Cole,* the truck bombings of the U.S. Embassy and the U.S. Marine Barracks in Beirut, and the Boston Marathon bombing. Does your definition explain everything that you consider terrorism? Does it cover things you do not ordinarily consider terrorism?
3. Can terrorism ever be justified using consequentialist or utilitarian ethical reasoning? Is this a weakness of consequentialist theories or a misuse of those theories?
4. What are the advantages and disadvantages of a Kantian or a natural law approach to terrorism, under which the taking of innocent life is always wrong, whether by a terrorist or in response to a terrorist attack?

Make Torture an Option

ALAN M. DERSHOWITZ

Alan M. Dershowitz is the Felix Frankfurter Professor of Law at Harvard Law School. He has published numerous books and articles, especially on civil liberties and criminal law. In this controversial essay, he argues that torture is justified in some circumstances, but it should be authorized by judges who would issue "torture warrants."

The FBI's frustration over its inability to get material witnesses to talk has raised a disturbing question rarely debated in this country: When, if ever, is it justified to resort to unconventional techniques such as truth serum, moderate physical pressure and outright torture?

The constitutional answer to this question may surprise people who are not familiar with the current U.S. Supreme Court interpretation of the Fifth Amendment privilege against self-incrimination: Any interrogation technique, including the use of truth serum or even torture, is not prohibited. All that is prohibited is the introduction into evidence of the fruits of such techniques in a criminal trial against the person on whom the techniques were used. But the evidence could be used against that suspect in a non-criminal case—such as a deportation hearing—or against someone else.

If a suspect is given "use immunity"—a judicial decree announcing in advance that nothing the defendant says (or its fruits) can be used against him in a criminal case—he can be compelled to answer all proper questions. The issue then becomes what sorts of pressures can constitutionally be used to implement that compulsion. We know that he can be imprisoned until he talks. But what if imprisonment is insufficient to compel him to do what he has a legal obligation to do? Can other techniques of compulsion be attempted?

Let's start with truth serum. What right would be violated if an immunized suspect who refused to comply with his legal obligation to answer questions truthfully were compelled to submit to an injection that made him do so? Not his privilege against self-incrimination, since he has no such privilege now that he has been given immunity.

What about his right of bodily integrity? The involuntariness of the injection itself does not pose a constitutional barrier. No less a civil libertarian than Justice William J. Brennan rendered a decision that permitted an allegedly drunken driver

to be involuntarily injected to remove blood for alcohol testing. Certainly there can be no constitutional distinction between an injection that removes a liquid and one that injects a liquid.

What about the nature of the substance injected? If it is relatively benign and creates no significant health risk, the only issue would be that it compels the recipient to do something he doesn't want to do. But he has a legal obligation to do precisely what the serum compels him to do: answer all questions truthfully.

What if the truth serum doesn't work? Could the judge issue a "torture warrant," authorizing the FBI to employ specified forms of non-lethal physical pressure to compel the immunized suspect to talk?

Here we run into another provision of the Constitution—the due process clause, which may include a general "shock the conscience" test. And torture in general certainly shocks the conscience of most civilized nations.

But what if it were limited to the rare "ticking bomb" case—the situation in which a captured terrorist who knows of an imminent large-scale threat refuses to disclose it?

Would torturing one guilty terrorist to prevent the deaths of a thousand innocent civilians shock the conscience of all decent people?

To prove that it would not, consider a situation in which a kidnapped child had been buried in a box with two hours of oxygen. The kidnapper refuses to disclose its location. Should we not consider torture in that situation?

All of that said, the argument for allowing torture as an approved technique, even in a narrowly specified range of cases, is very troubling.

We know from experience that law enforcement personnel who are given limited authority to torture will expand its use. The cases that have generated the current debate over torture illustrate this problem. And, concerning the arrests

Alan M. Dershowitz, "Make Torture an Option," *Los Angeles Times* (November 8, 2001). Reprinted by permission of the author.

made following the September 11 attacks, there is no reason to believe that the detainees know about specific future terrorist targets. Yet there have been calls to torture these detainees.

I have no doubt that if an actual ticking bomb situation were to arise, our law enforcement authorities would torture. The real debate is whether such torture should take place outside of our legal system or within it. The answer to this seems clear: If we are to have torture, it should be authorized by the law.

Judges should have to issue a "torture warrant" in each case. Thus we would not be winking an eye of quiet approval at torture while publicly condemning it.

Democracy requires accountability and transparency, especially when extraordinary steps are taken. Most important, it requires compliance with the rule of law. And such compliance is impossible when an extraordinary technique, such as torture, operates outside of the law.

♔ QUESTIONS FOR ANALYSIS

1. Are you satisfied with Dershowitz's argument that torture is consistent with the right against self-incrimination and can be justified in certain situations, so long as a judge issues a "torture warrant"?
2. Dershowitz seems to rely on utilitarian reasoning to support his analysis justifying torture. Restate his arguments to make this utilitarianism more explicit and consider whether they sufficiently outweigh the human rights concerns.
3. Even if torture is not prohibited by the U.S. Constitution, as Dershowitz suggests, does it violate ethical standards to which we should adhere?

Torture and the Ticking Bomb

DAVID LUBAN

David J. Luban, University Professor and Professor of Law and Philosophy at Georgetown University, has written extensively on international law, social justice, legal ethics, and jurisprudence. In this article, he argues that the "ticking bomb" scenario to justify torture is an intellectual fraud.

Ludwig Wittgenstein once wrote that confusion arises when we become bewitched by a picture. He meant that it's easy to be seduced by simplistic examples that look compelling but actually misrepresent the world we live in.

More than a year after Abu Ghraib, we continue to confront the issues of abusive interrogation, torture, and legal positions purporting to vindicate harsh tactics in the name of national security. In this confrontation, the picture that bewitches us is the "ticking bomb" scenario.

Suppose a bomb is planted somewhere in the crowded heart of an American city, and we have custody of the man who planted it. He won't talk. Surely, the scenario suggests, we shouldn't be too squeamish to torture the information out of him and save hundreds of lives. After all, abstract moral prohibitions must yield to the calculus of consequences.

To take a real-life example: in 1995, an al Qaeda plot to bomb 11 U.S. airliners was thwarted by information tortured out of a Pakistani suspect

David Luban, "Torture and the Ticking Bomb," *Georgetown Law* (Spring/Summer 2005), 48–51. Reprinted by permission of *Georgetown Law* and the author.

by the Philippine police. According to a report by journalists Marites Vitug and Glenda Gloria, "For weeks, agents hit him with a chair and a long piece of wood, forced water into his mouth, and crushed lighted cigarettes into his private parts. His ribs were almost totally broken and his captors were surprised he survived." Grisly, to be sure—and yet if they hadn't done it, thousands of innocent travelers might have died horrible deaths.

But look at the example again. The Philippine police were surprised he survived—in other words, they came close to torturing him to death before he talked. And they tortured him for weeks, during which time they presumably didn't know any of the details they wanted about the al Qaeda plot. What if he too hadn't known? Or what if there had been no such plot? Then they would have tortured him for weeks, possibly tortured him to death, for naught. For all they knew at the time, that is precisely what they were doing. We can't use the argument that preventing the al Qaeda attack justified the decision to torture, because at the moment the decision was made no one knew about the al Qaeda attack.

The ticking bomb scenario cheats its way around these difficulties by stipulating that the bomb is there, ticking away, and that officials know they have the man who planted it. Those conditions will seldom be met. Let's look at some more realistic scenarios and ask the questions they raise:

- The authorities know there may be a bomb plot in the offing, and they've captured a man who may know something about it, but may not. Should they torture him? How severely? For how long? For weeks? Months? The chances are considerable that they are torturing a man with nothing to tell. If he doesn't talk, is that a signal to stop, or to up the level of torture? How likely must it be that he knows something important? Fifty-fifty? Thirty-seventy? Will one out of a hundred suffice to land him on the water board?

- Do we really want to make the torture decision by running the numbers? A 1 percent chance of saving a thousand lives yields 10 statistical lives saved. Does that mean that we will torture up to nine people on a 1 percent chance of finding crucial information?

- Suppose authorities believed that one out of a group of 50 captives at Camp X-Ray in Guantanamo Bay, Cuba might know where Osama bin Laden is hiding—but they didn't know which captive. Torture them all? That is: torture 49 captives with nothing to tell you on the uncertain chance of capturing bin Laden? For that matter, would capturing bin Laden demonstrably save a single human life? Months ago, the Bush administration stated that bin Laden had been marginalized. Maybe capturing him would save lives somehow—but how do you demonstrate it? Or doesn't it matter whether the torture was intended to save lives, as long as it furthered some goal in the War on Terror? And if the answer is that it doesn't matter, why limit the efficacy of torture to the War on Terror? Why not torture in pursuit of any worthwhile goal?

- Indeed, if we're willing to torture 49 innocent people to get information from the one person who has it, why stop there? If suspects won't break under torture, why not torture their loved ones in front of them? A moral consequentialist should be willing to accept the torture of one innocent child to save hundreds of lives. Of course, until you try, you won't know whether torturing a child will break the suspect. But that just affects the odds, not the argument.

The point of these examples is that in a world of uncertainty and imperfect knowledge, the ticking bomb scenario should not form the point of reference in the torture debate. The ticking bomb is the picture that bewitches us. The actual choice is not between one guilty man's pain and hundreds of innocent lives. It is the choice between the certainty of that anguish and the mere possibility of learning something vital and saving lives.

There is a second insidious error built into the ticking bomb hypothetical. It assumes a single ad hoc decision about whether to torture, by officials who ordinarily would do no such thing except in a desperate emergency. But in the real world of interrogations, decisions are not made that way. They are based on policies, guidelines, and directives. Officials inhabit a world of practices, not of ad hoc emergency measures. Any responsible discussion of torture therefore must address the practice of torture, not the ticking bomb hypothetical.

That means discussing other, different questions. For instance, should we create a professional cadre of torturers, of interrogators who have been trained in the techniques and who have learned to overcome their instinctive revulsion against causing pain? Medieval executioners were schooled in the arts of agony. In Louis XIV's Paris, torture was a family trade whose tricks were passed on from father to son.

Of course, in our era, higher education has replaced inheritance of family trades. Should universities create an undergraduate major in torture? Or should the major be offered only in police and military academies? Would we want federal grants for research to devise new and better torture techniques? Patents issued on high-tech torture devices? Companies competing to manufacture them? Trade conventions in Las Vegas? Should there be a medical subspecialty of torture doctors, who ensure that gasping captives don't die before they talk? Recall the chilling words of Sgt. Ivan Fredericks, one of the abusers at Abu Ghraib, who saw the body of a detainee after the interrogation went awry: "They stressed the man out so much that he passed away." Real pros wouldn't let that happen; it wastes a good source. Who should teach torture-doctoring in medical school?

The basic question is this one: Do we really want to create a torture culture and the kind of people who inhabit it? The ticking time bomb distracts us from the real issue, which is not about emergencies but about the normalization of torture. Some might argue that keeping the practice of torture secret avoids the moral corruption that might arise from creating a public culture of torture. But concealment does not reject the normalization of torture. It accepts it but layers on top of it the normalization of state secrecy. The result would be a shadow culture of torturers and those who train and support them, operating outside the public eye and accountable only to other insiders of the torture culture.

Yet a further question arises: Who can guarantee that case-hardened torturers, inured to levels of violence and pain that would sicken ordinary people, will know where to draw the line? They never have in the past. In the Argentinian Dirty War, tortures began because terrorist cells had a policy of fleeing when any of their members had disappeared for 48 hours. Authorities had just two days to wring the information out of a captive. University of Iowa law professor Mark Osiel, who has studied the Dirty War, reports that at first many in the Argentinian military had qualms about what they were doing, until their priests assured them that they were fighting God's fight. By the end of the Dirty War, the qualms were gone, and, as John Simpson and Jana Bennett have reported, hardened young officers were placing bets on who could kidnap the prettiest girl to rape and torture. Escalation is the rule, not the aberration. Abu Ghraib is the fully predictable image of what a torture culture looks like. Abu Ghraib is not a few bad apples. It is the apple tree.

That is why Harvard law professor Alan Dershowitz has argued that judges, not torturers, should oversee the permission to torture by means of warrants. The irony is that former Assistant Attorney General Jay S. Bybee, who signed a notorious, highly permissive torture memo for the Justice Department in 2002, is now a federal judge. Politicians pick judges, and if the politicians accept torture, the judges will too. Judges don't fight their culture. They reflect it. Once we create a torture culture, only the naive would suppose that judges will provide a safeguard.

The ticking bomb scenario is an intellectual fraud. In its place, we must address the real questions about torture—questions about uncertainty, questions about the morality of consequences, questions about what it does to a culture to introduce the practice of torture, questions about what torturers are like and whether we really want them walking among us.

QUESTIONS FOR ANALYSIS

1. Luban objects to consequentialist reasoning—the idea that torturing one person is justifiable if it saves the lives of hundreds. What assumptions seem to underlie his objection? Does he object to all consequentialist reasoning or only to some arguments? Can a consequentialist

consistently respect a human right not to be tortured?

2. Are there any situations where Luban would find torture justifiable? Are there situations where you find torture justifiable? How might Luban object to your position and how would you respond?

3. Should we train a group of professional torturers to increase the chances of getting good information? If you find this an objectionable use of your tax money, explain why.

4. How does Luban respond to Dershowitz's proposal to have judges issue warrants to permit torture so there will be judicial oversight of this process?

CASE PRESENTATION

Preemptive War

President George W. Bush articulated a new strategy of "preemptive war," a marked change from the previous U.S. policy of deterrence to war and the use of force only in self-defense. *The National Security Strategy of the United States of America*, issued by President Bush on September 17, 2002, explains preemptive war as a way to "Prevent Our Enemies from Threatening Us, Our Allies, and Our Friends with Weapons of Mass Destruction":

The nature of the Cold War threat required the United States—with our allies and friends—to emphasize deterrence of the enemy's use of force, producing a grim strategy of mutual assured destruction. With the collapse of the Soviet Union and the end of the Cold War, our security environment has undergone profound transformation....

But new deadly challenges have emerged from rogue states and terrorists. None of these contemporary threats rival the sheer destructive power that was arrayed against us by the Soviet Union. However, the nature and motivations of these new adversaries, their determination to obtain destructive powers hitherto available only to the world's strongest states, and the greater likelihood that they will use weapons of mass destruction against us, make today's security environment more complex and dangerous.

In the 1990s we witnessed the emergence of a small number of rogue states that, while different in important ways, share a number of attributes. These states:

- brutalize their own people and squander their national resources for the personal gain of the rulers;
- display no regard for international law, threaten their neighbors, and callously violate international treaties to which they are party;
- are determined to acquire weapons of mass destruction, along with other advanced military technology, to be used as threats or offensively to achieve the aggressive designs of these regimes;

- sponsor terrorism around the globe; and
- reject basic human values and hate the United States and everything for which it stands.

At the time of the Gulf War, we acquired irrefutable proof that Iraq's designs were not limited to the chemical weapons it had used against Iran and its own people, but also extended to the acquisition of nuclear weapons and biological agents. In the past decade North Korea has become the world's principal purveyor of ballistic missiles, and has tested increasingly capable missiles while developing its own WMD arsenal. Other rogue regimes seek nuclear, biological, and chemical weapons as well. These states' pursuit of, and global trade in, such weapons has become a looming threat to all nations.

We must be prepared to stop rogue states and their terrorist clients before they are able to threaten or use weapons of mass destruction against the United States and our allies and friends. Our response must take full advantage of strengthened alliances, the establishment of new partnerships with former adversaries, innovation in the use of military forces, modern technologies, including the development of an effective missile defense system, and increased emphasis on intelligence collection and analysis....

It has taken almost a decade for us to comprehend the true nature of this new threat. Given the goals of rogue states and terrorists, the United States can no longer solely rely on a reactive posture as we have in the past. The inability to deter a potential attacker, the immediacy of today's threats, and the magnitude of potential harm that could be caused by our adversaries' choice of weapons, do not permit that option. We cannot let our enemies strike first.

In the Cold War, especially following the Cuban missile crisis, we faced a generally status quo, risk-averse adversary. Deterrence was an effective defense. But deterrence based only upon the threat of retaliation is less likely to work against leaders of rogue states more willing to take risks, gambling with the lives of their people, and the wealth of their nations.

- In the Cold War, weapons of mass destruction were considered weapons of last resort whose use risked the destruction of those who used them. Today, our enemies see weapons of mass destruction as weapons of choice. For rogue states these weapons are tools of intimidation and military aggression against their neighbors. These weapons may also allow these states to attempt to blackmail the United States and our allies to prevent us from deterring or repelling the aggressive behavior of rogue states. Such states also see these weapons as their best means of overcoming the conventional superiority of the United States.
- Traditional concepts of deterrence will not work against a terrorist enemy whose avowed tactics are wanton destruction and the targeting of innocents; whose so-called soldiers seek martyrdom in death and whose most potent protection is statelessness. The overlap between states that sponsor terror and those that pursue WMD compels us to action.

For centuries, international law recognized that nations need not suffer an attack before they can lawfully take action to defend themselves against forces that present an imminent danger of attack. Legal scholars and international jurists often conditioned the legitimacy of preemption on the existence of an imminent threat—most often a visible mobilization of armies, navies, and air forces preparing to attack.

We must adapt the concept of imminent threat to the capabilities and objectives of today's adversaries. Rogue states and terrorists do not seek to attack us using conventional means. They know such attacks would fail. Instead, they rely on acts of terror and, potentially, the use of weapons of mass destruction—weapons that can be easily concealed, delivered covertly, and used without warning.

The targets of these attacks are our military forces and our civilian population, in direct violation of one of the principal norms of the law of warfare. As was demonstrated by the losses on September 11, 2001, mass civilian casualties is the specific objective of terrorists and these losses would be exponentially more severe if terrorists acquired and used weapons of mass destruction.

The United States has long maintained the option of preemptive actions to counter a sufficient threat to our national security. The greater the threat, the greater is the risk of inaction—and the more compelling the case for taking anticipatory action to defend ourselves, even if uncertainty remains as to the time and place of the enemy's attack. To forestall or prevent such hostile acts by our adversaries, the United States will, if necessary, act preemptively.

The United States will not use force in all cases to preempt emerging threats, nor should nations use preemption as a pretext for aggression. Yet in an age where the enemies of civilization openly and actively seek the world's most destructive technologies, the United States cannot remain idle while dangers gather. We will always proceed deliberately, weighing the consequences of our actions. To support preemptive options, we will:

- build better, more integrated intelligence capabilities to provide timely, accurate information on threats, wherever they may emerge;
- coordinate closely with allies to form a common assessment of the most dangerous threats; and
- continue to transform our military forces to ensure our ability to conduct rapid and precise operations to achieve decisive results.

The purpose of our actions will always be to eliminate a specific threat to the United States or our allies and friends. The reasons for our actions will be clear, the force measured, and the cause just.

⚜ QUESTIONS FOR ANALYSIS

1. President Bush states that preemptive war will be used only for a cause that is "just." How does he understand "just cause" from his statements here? Do his tests for when he would initiate preemptive war meet the traditional standards for just war?
2. On March 16, 2006, the president officially reaffirmed his commitment to preemptive war, even though he had previously acknowledged that no WMD were found and no real connection had been identified between Sadaam Hussein and the attacks of 9/11. Does the policy seen in light of recent events, seem to justify invasion of such countries as Iran and North Korea if the United States credibly believes they possess nuclear warheads? After our experience in invading Iraq, does the preemption doctrine today seem sound?
3. Can you think of other circumstances in our nation's history when a preemptive war would have been justified but was not initiated?
4. Are there circumstances in the world today in which preemptive war would be justified under the president's rationale? What arguments could be raised against engaging in such war?

CASE PRESENTATION

Driving While Veiled

In March 2002, an ultraorthodox Muslim woman, Sultaana Lakiana Myke Freeman, a U.S. citizen, filed suit in Florida, claiming that the state's requirement that her photograph for her driver's license must be taken without her veil violated her "religious belief that her religion requires her to wear her veil in front of strangers and unrelated males." She argued that the state's revocation and cancellation of her driver's license because of her refusal to have her photograph taken without a veil violated her "religious freedom, freedom of speech, due process, equal protection and right to privacy."

After a trial in May 2003, a Florida court rejected her claim that the photographic requirement was an undue burden on the exercise of her religion: "... the State apparently has a practice of accommodating Muslim women holding similar beliefs on veiling. A DHSMV [Department of Highway Safety and Motor Vehicles] manager testified that in several instances, upon appointment, DHSMV employees have escorted women to a private room, with only a female license examiner present. No males were allowed, and the room had no windows through which anyone could see. The State argued that the 'momentary' lifting of the veil in order to complete the digitalized image or photo, done in 'private circumstances' as described, does not constitute a substantial burden on Plaintiff's right to free exercise of religion. The State asserted that Plaintiff would be free to place the photo license in her pocket and never show it to anyone, except perhaps to law enforcement officers in specific situations. The Court agrees, and finds that given Plaintiff's own testimony plus the State's willingness to accommodate Plaintiff to the degree stated, the momentary raising of her veil for the purpose of the ID photo does not constitute a 'substantial burden' on her right to exercise her religion."

The court agreed with the argument of the state of Florida "... that when religious practices collide with public safety, public safety must prevail.... The State called an expert witness who has been employed in law enforcement for almost 40 years and is currently a consultant to DHSMV on security matters. He stated that a facial image is 'absolutely essential' to law enforcement officers, because without it, officers conducting traffic stops are at risk during the extra time needed to check identities to 'make sure that's the person standing in front of them.' He emphasized that it is crucial to both criminal and intelligence investigators to be able to identify possible suspects (and victims of crimes or accidents) as quickly as possible, and that this ability has a significant impact on public safety."

The court also rejected her argument "... that photo IDs are largely flawed and can easily be thwarted by people who change their hair, cover their foreheads and ears, wear large glasses, shave their heads, grow their beards, or alter their appearance by other means, including contact lenses and plastic surgery. She stressed that some people have aged years since their license photo was taken and for that reason alone look different from the image on the license. Plaintiff also claimed that religious hairstyles and headwear are permitted for persons of other faiths, and suggested that she is being singled out because she is Muslim." The state responded, "... some facial features do not change, despite changes in the individual's style or age, and that photographic images of drivers evidencing some differences are still of greater value than an image with facial features completely blocked by a mask or a veil."

The Court acknowledged "... that today it is a different world than it was 20–25 years ago. It would be foolish not to recognize that there are new threats to public safety, including both foreign and domestic terrorism, and increased potential for 'widespread abuse' that did not exist ..." before. But, the Court insisted, "Plaintiff is not being singled out because she is Muslim. This Court would rule the same way for anyone—Christian, Jew, Buddhist, Atheist—who wished to have his or her driver's license identification photo taken while wearing anything—ski mask, costume mask, religious veil, hood—which cloaks all facial features except the eyes. Plaintiff's veiling practices must be subordinated to society's need to identify people as quickly as possible in situations in which safety and security of others could be at risk."

⚜ QUESTIONS FOR ANALYSIS

1. The judge rejected an argument by the state of Florida that most Muslim women do not wear veils and that she was part of a very small minority. Would you agree that this should be irrelevant in this case? If the vast majority of women in Florida wanted to wear veils when obtaining their driver's licenses, do you think the state of Florida would change its position on the issues here?

2. Before 9/11, Illinois, and later Florida, had issued her a driver's license showing her wearing the veil. Only after 9/11 did the state of Florida send her a notice that if she did not agree to have her photograph taken without the veil, her license would be revoked. Does this sequence of events suggest that Florida was singling her out for discriminatory treatment because of terrorist fears? If Florida's concern was "public safety" and effective law enforcement, why wasn't it concerned before 9/11?

3. In her arguments to the court, plaintiff noted a precedent, a 1984 decision, *Quaring v. Peterson*, in which a Pentecostal Christian woman refused to have her picture taken for a Nebraska driver's license because she believed that it would constitute making a graven image. The court found that denying the woman her license did not serve a compelling state interest. How, if at all, is this case different, and should the Florida court have followed the same reasoning?

4. Can you think of other religious or cultural forms of dress that might interfere with the full facial photograph required by Florida? Should those be allowed?

5. Using the reasoning of this Florida decision, should she also be required to provide a full facial photograph, without her veil, if she applies for a passport? An employee ID for a job? A photo ID for medical insurance coverage? If she flies on an airplane and airport security needs to compare her photo ID with her actual face, should she have to comply before boarding the airplane? How can her religious beliefs be balanced against these other societal interests in security?

CASE PRESENTATION

Fear of Flying

On the evening of September 11, 2001, then-Secretary of Transportation Norman Y. Mineta issued a statement that "In a democracy, there is always a balance between freedom and security. Our transportation systems, reflecting the values of our society, have always operated in an open and accessible manner. And, they will again." Two months later, Congress established the Transportation Security Administration (TSA) to take over all security at the nation's airports. While many members of the flying public seem to think professionalism and security have improved at the airports, others complain of what they perceive to be silly random searches of elderly grandmothers and very young children with plastic toy guns. The TSA continually announces new security problems, including ballpoint pens that hide sharp weapons and bombs made of plastic materials that are difficult to detect. Newspaper reports tell of continuing security breaches with potentially lethal weapons somehow brought past security checks onto the planes.

Despite continuing security breaches, Mineta insisted that airport screeners should not use any kind of racial profiling in identifying persons for special searches, including persons who might "appear to be of Arab, Middle Eastern or south Asian descent and/or Muslim." Mineta himself was one of the 120,000 Americans interned by the U.S. government during World War II, and he has been adamant in his public statements that this nation should not ever again practice such discrimination against anyone solely because of nationality, ancestry, or appearance. Critics of airport security complain that limited resources should be focused on the persons most likely to be 9/11 hijackers and point out that all nineteen were men of Middle Eastern descent.

☙ QUESTIONS FOR ANALYSIS

1. If you were designing an appropriate security system for the nation's airports, how would you focus limited resources to make it most likely that you would catch persons who planned terrorist attacks on airports and airplanes? Would you single out any particular type of person for special searches to protect the flying public? On what basis would you justify these special searches? Can your security plan be criticized for engaging in such fallacies as hasty generalization or faulty analogy? What criticisms could be raised of your security plan?

2. No terrorist attacks have occurred in the United States using airplanes since 9/11. Air travel has increased after dropping off dramatically right after 9/11. Fear of flying because of concerns over terrorism has steadily declined. Do these consequences show that the current airport security system is the best approach for the nation? Are the inconveniences to ordinary citizens and the element of risk with continued security breaches outweighed by the respect for human rights in the current approach that rejects singling out men of Middle Eastern descent during security searches at airports?

3. Some of Mineta's critics charged that his personal experiences during World War II made him unable to render objective decisions on airport security after 9/11. Is this an example of an *ad hominem* argument? Is this a justifiable criticism of Mineta's approach to airport security?

4. In 2007, the TSA started a new program called Screening of Passengers by Observation Techniques (SPOT), in which agents were trained in identifying potential terrorists from behavioral clues. A training program in Boston drew complaints from TSA officers that they were being told to focus on traits they considered racial profiling, such as Middle Eastern origins, African-Americans wearing expensive jewelry, and Latinos flying to Miami. The Inspector General of the TSA severely criticized the program in June 2013 for failing to be objective in its screening or cost-effective. After a decade of struggling to identify potential terrorists without simplistic racial profiling, what should the TSA do to safeguard the flying public? Are there ways to identify potential terrorists attempting to board aircraft without racial and ethnic profiling?

CASE PRESENTATION

The Geneva Conventions and Guantanamo Bay

In late 2001 the United States military invaded Afghanistan to root out the organizations and persons responsible for the attacks on September 11. A Yemeni national named Salim Ahmed Hamdan was captured by local militias, which turned him over to the U.S. military for transfer to its prison in Guantanamo Bay, Cuba. Over a year later, the president ruled that Hamdan was eligible for trial for unspecified crimes in a military commission. After another year passed, he was charged with "conspiracy … to commit … offenses triable by military commission." Hamdan sued in Federal court for, among other things, being tried in the absence of authority under the international law of war, the Geneva Conventions, or Congress.

President Bush had insisted that the persons held at Guantanamo Bay and in other prisons outside the United States were not entitled to the protections of the Geneva Conventions, because they were not from a "recognized nation," had not been wearing uniforms, and did not observe "traditional rules of war." Instead, the administration said, these "detainees" could be tried under military commissions that did not necessarily conform either to the Geneva Conventions or to requirements for justice in the United States. According to the administration, there are about 1,000 suspected terrorists being held in prisons by the United States around the world, with about 450 at Guantanamo Bay.

The Geneva Conventions do not recognize "conspiracy" as a crime in international law, nor had "conspiracy" been recognized at the Nuremberg Trials of Nazi war criminals after World War II. The Conventions also set requirements for authorized trials.

The U.S. Supreme Court held on June 29, 2006, in *Hamdan v. Rumsfeld*, that the Geneva Conventions do apply to the detainees at Guantanamo, including Hamdan. They ordered that Hamdan be tried by a "regularly constituted court affording all the judicial guarantees which are recognized as indispensable by civilized peoples." The majority opinion concluded with these words:

> Congress has not issued the Executive a "blank check." … Indeed, Congress has denied the President the legislative authority to create military commissions of the kind at issue here. Nothing prevents the President from returning to Congress to seek the authority he believes necessary. Where, as here, no emergency prevents consultation with Congress, judicial insistence upon that consultation does not weaken our Nation's ability to deal with danger. To the contrary, that insistence strengthens the Nation's ability to determine—through democratic means—how best to do so. The Constitution places its faith in those democratic means. Our Court today simply does the same.

A few weeks later, President Bush announced that the administration would henceforth comply with the

Geneva Conventions and asked Congress to establish trial procedures that would meet those requirements. The Defense Department issued an order to all branches of the armed forces to review their detention procedures, including methods of interrogation, to ensure that they were in compliance with the Conventions.

⚜ QUESTIONS FOR ANALYSIS

1. Do you agree with the Court that the rights of the Geneva Conventions should be granted to persons the military suspects might be involved with terrorism, even if they have never had a trial or been charged with a specific offense recognized in international law?

2. How far should we go in granting civil liberties to possible terrorists who are being held in prisons abroad? How should they be treated?

3. Do you believe that the way we treat terrorists reflects unfavorably on our nation in the "court of world opinion"?

CHAPTER NINE

Globalization and Social Justice

AMERICANS HAVE LONG had a generous spirit toward immigrants from around the world, who helped build this country and gave it such unusual diversity and strength. Internationally, the United States has a long history of generous financial aid to other countries in need. This country also has been generous in helping its own citizens, from Social Security and Medicare for the elderly to food stamps and unemployment insurance for others who have fallen on hard times.

Globalization and difficult economic realities have put enormous stress on this history of generosity in recent decades. The health care system in the United States has reached a crisis situation, with health care unavailable or prohibitively expensive for too many Americans. Immigration, both legal and illegal, has become a contentious issue. The 1986 immigration reform passed during the term of President Ronald Reagan was billed as a solution to illegal immigration, but decades later the issues seem to be even more contentious. Public debates on improving access to health care and education are complicated by the presence of an estimated 11 million undocumented immigrants, not just from Mexico but from countries all over the world. Dramatic improvements in international travel also have resulted in persons seeking asylum in the United States, as they flee political persecution and violence in their home countries.

New trade agreements since the 1990s promised improving economic conditions for all countries. Critics complain that they have led to exploitation of poor workers in third-world countries who work in sweatshop conditions for very cheap wages, making it difficult for American workers to compete fairly in this new environment. Defenders of these trade agreements note that many consumer goods are available much more cheaply if imported from other countries. Long-term, the best way to end global poverty is to build up the economic capacities of all countries, not to just give them hand-outs in foreign aid.

In this chapter, we will explore recent work by philosophers in understanding these urgent issues using the insights of philosophical reasoning.

GLOBALIZATION

The term "globalization" has come into common usage just in the past few decades. It typically refers to the rapid development of the technology, trade, and culture that has brought nations together physically as well as symbolically. Improvements in high-speed transportation and communication have accelerated our awareness of our fellow inhabitants on Earth. Globalization includes economic policies relying on the increased interdependence of national economies. Some see globalization as the "Americanization" of popular culture around the world, for good or ill.

International jet travel, available since the 1950s, has made rapid travel possible at ever lower prices. Jet travel enables business people, students, and educators to visit other countries with ease and improve international understanding and trade. But it also has enabled terrorists to invade other countries in ways unimaginable in the not-too-distant past, as they did on 9/11.

The Internet has made instantaneous communication around the planet readily available. In turn, this has made it easier for many companies in the U.S. to out-source important work to other countries, whether customer-service functions for companies of all sorts or back office paperwork for banks and other financial services. New technologies, from e-mail to Twitter and social networking sites, have played an important role in bringing news to the world such as of recent uprisings in Iran, an instantaneous source of information that was unimaginable just a few years ago.

Linguists have traced the word "globalization" back just a few decades, although the concept of an interconnected world long predates the jargon. In the 1960s, Marshall McLuhan made us aware of what he called a "global village," brought together by technology. And philosophers such as John Dewey in the early twentieth century worried about the impact of technology and rapid change on our social and political structures.

In considering our ethical challenges in this rapidly changing world, we should continue to worry about our ethical obligations to citizens of our own country. What obligations, if any, do we have to the elderly, the poor, the disabled, the down-and-out? Is health care and good education a right or a privilege in our own country? But we also increasingly focus on our ethical obligations to the world. Do we owe anything to the poor in other countries? Should we continue to welcome immigrants, the founding life-blood of this nation, or should we close our borders to focus in these difficult times on our own citizens? Should we continue to grant political asylum to people suffering per-secution in other countries or should we limit our concerns for human rights to pressur-ing those other governments to do a better job of respecting the rights we value here?

In this country, it was only in the twentieth century that we came to see government assistance as necessary and appropriate. Before that, help for the needy was expected to come from such private sources as charities, churches, and families. The turning point was the Great Depression in the 1930s, and two of the most important reasons advanced were compassion and social stability. With the economy unable to produce enough jobs, a great number of willing and able workers found themselves unemployed through no fault of their own, and private sources could not provide sufficient aid. To many Americans, the situation was intolerable. Something had to be done, both to help the victims of the Depression and to prevent unprecedented social upheaval. The only place to look to, they felt, was the federal government. In this era, the government started Social Security, unemployment insurance, public works projects to put people to work, and a variety of other public programs that we take for granted today.

Despite the widely shared sense of emergency, President Franklin Roosevelt's New Deal legislation produced considerable debate. With its regulations on industry and banking as well as its social welfare programs, it greatly expanded the role of government. Critics charged that individual rights were being violated, property rights in particular, and that the New Deal amounted to "creeping socialism." Helping people at the expense of individual rights, these critics argued, was unjust. New Deal proponents, on the other hand, argued that failing to provide the needed measures was unjust.

Today we are still recovering from what many refer to as the worst economic environment since the Great Depression. Once again we face serious public policy debates over how best to solve these problems and help our fellow Americans. Some urge that cutting taxes and allowing private enterprise to flourish is the key to improving the economy. Others point to the urgent needs of many citizens and support extensions of unemployment benefits, public works employment, assistance with foreclosures on homes, and many other measures that they hope will bring us to a good economy again where people can find work and take care of themselves. Today's debate, however, is complicated even more by the elements of globalization that had not yet emerged in the 1930s, making these debates ever more challenging.

As with many issues in this book, the competing views turn on differing conceptions of justice. In the case of transfer payments, it is a matter of economic justice, also called **distributive justice.** How should the wealth of society be distributed?

DISTRIBUTIVE JUSTICE

In Part 1, we looked at various principles of social justice, many of which bear on the question of distributive justice. In this section and those that follow, we will see how.

The Entitlement Conception of Justice

When discussing individual rights in Part 1, we noted the influence of the English philosopher John Locke on the U.S. Founding Fathers. According to Locke, we are born with the natural rights to life, liberty, and property, which we are free to exercise as long as we do not interfere with the natural rights of others. We are also born with the natural right to protect those three rights. In joining together to create a government, we transfer certain powers to society as a whole. That is, the government acts as our agent in exercising those powers. Because we cannot transfer to the government any powers that are not rightfully ours, the role of government is severely limited. We can transfer powers of protection—police and judicial powers, most notably—but not the power to interfere with the individual property rights of others.

How does this bear on distributive justice? According to Robert Nozick, whom we also considered in Part 1, the answer is simple: Transfer payments, whether to our own citizens or those of other nations, are beyond the rightful powers of government. Since no one has a natural right to force others to give to charity, we cannot transfer that power to society as a whole. However well intentioned, transfer payments are no different from ordinary theft. To demand on threat of imprisonment that individuals pay taxes to support such programs is equivalent to holding a gun to their heads and demanding that they give to our favorite charities.

On this view, then, government should not be in the business of distributing wealth at all. Wealth is not, as Nozick puts it, "manna from heaven." It does not magically appear from the sky, belonging to no one. Instead, society's wealth already belongs to particular individuals who came by it either honestly or dishonestly, through either the legitimate exercise of their natural rights or the violation of the natural rights of others. If they came by it dishonestly, they should be punished and their ill-gotten gains returned to the rightful owners. Otherwise, it is rightfully theirs. They alone are *entitled* to it, and no one, including the government, has the right to take it away from them without their consent. Thus, Nozick calls his view the **entitlement** conception of justice.

Justice as Fairness

We also looked at the views of John Rawls in Part 1. Rawls rejects the notion of natural rights. To him, social justice is a matter of fairness, in which case the just distribution of wealth is the fairest distribution. How do we decide on the fairest distribution?

Rawls's answer goes like this: Societies operate according to certain fundamental rules, and it is up to the members of society to set those rules. One such fundamental rule governs the distribution of wealth. If the rule is to be fair, it must give no member of society unfair advantage over any other members. And we can guarantee that outcome by requiring that the rule be acceptable to all members of society without knowing how the rule will work out for them. That is, they will know how wealth will be distributed among different segments of the population but not which segment they will belong to. In that case, they must be willing to accept the rule no matter what segment they will belong to.

Would an entitlement rule like Nozick's pass that test? Rawls says no because it allows for unacceptably large gaps between rich and poor. We would not know whether we will have the high-paying jobs that will make us wealthy or the low-paying jobs that will leave us unable to support our families. Nor would we know whether we will find ourselves impoverished due to a sudden loss of work or some other catastrophe. As long as we don't know where we will end up, we will demand a rule that allows every member of society a sufficient share of the wealth.

One way to accomplish this goal (Rawls's preferred way) is through transfer payments. Those nearer to the top will be taxed to supplement the incomes of the poor.

EQUALITY, NEED, AND MERIT

If we accept the justice of transfer payments, we still have to determine how generous to make the payments and under what circumstances to pay them out. That is, we will need to select a *principle* of distribution. The three most commonly cited are the principles of equality, need, and merit.

Equality

According to the **equality principle** of distribution, everyone in society ought to end up with an equal share of the wealth. Why choose this principle? Because, proponents say, when it comes to sharing the wealth, all humans deserve to be treated equally. The fact that someone is better looking than the norm (or a better athlete or musician), or lucky enough to be born into a wealthy family (or marry into one), does not make that person more deserving of wealth than others less fortunate. In that case, taxes and transfer payments should be set at rates that guarantee an equal distribution of wealth for all.

Whatever initial appeal this principle may have, at least one problem is readily apparent for those who advocate it. An equal distribution of wealth can lead to significant inequalities among individual lives. Consider healthcare, for example. To achieve real equality between a healthy person and a person with kidney failure, say, the second will need far greater benefits than the first to cover the cost of dialysis. The same consideration also applies to many other areas of life, such as education. It costs far more to educate a child with serious learning disabilities than a child without them. That's why many transfers come in the form of services rather than cash benefits, to accommodate the differing needs of different individuals. It is also why people who lean toward equal distribution usually adopt a different but related principle as well—the principle of need.

Need

According to the principle of need, everyone has an equal right to have his or her economic needs satisfied, and wealth should therefore be distributed according to the economic needs of society's members. Advocates of this principle often combine it with the principle of equality. *Basic* needs like food, housing, education, and medical care are to be taken care of according to individual need, and the remaining wealth is to be distributed equally. Other advocates demand only that everyone's basic needs be met without asking for further redistribution. In both cases, the justification of the principle of need is the same. When it comes to basic needs, everyone deserves to be treated equally. No one's basic needs should go unmet.

Opponents of both principles—need and equality—cite a variety of objections. First, of course, there are Nozick's moral arguments that government should not be in the business of redistributing wealth at all. Other objections are more practical. Rawls, for example, argues that certain inequalities ought to be allowed because they are to everyone's advantage, even those at the bottom. If we are to have an adequate supply of surgeons, for example, we must compensate them for their years spent in medical school. Many critics also argue that distribution according to need and equality discourages hard work. Why put in extra hours if we will earn no extra compensation? Indeed, why work at all if the government will take care of our basic needs and guarantee us an income equal to the income of those who do work? And even if the government guarantees our basic needs only, won't many people see that as sufficient reason not to work?

What's missing, these objectors say, is recognition of individual *merit*. Those who deserve more wealth than others—those who have earned it—should have it.

Merit

The appeal of merit as a principle of distributing wealth is more than merely practical. To many people, it is a matter of simple justice. Why should Mary, who works to support herself and her family, pay taxes on her hard-earned income so that John, a total stranger who refuses to work at all, can enjoy a standard of living equal to her own? To ask this question is to distinguish between the deserving poor and the undeserving poor, between those who can't work and those who simply won't work, between those who work hard at low wages and those who choose to freeload. To people who make this distinction, the deserving poor should be helped by transfer payments but not the undeserving poor.

Although it may be difficult to sort out the deserving poor from the undeserving poor in particular cases, at least the underlying principle seems quite clear: Freeloaders don't merit our help. But many advocates of the merit principle want to extend it to cover all members of society. In that case, matters grow far less clear. The question now becomes: How are we to rank individual merit? To see how hard it is to answer this question, ask yourself who are the most meritorious among us. Those who work the hardest? Put in the most hours every week? Shoulder the heaviest responsibility? Those who perform the most difficult tasks? The least desirable tasks? The tasks most needed by society? Or is it the best educated? The most skilled? Or those who fill the most seats at a football stadium for a concert? Or create the greatest number of jobs? Depending on how we answer these questions, the most meritorious can be a laborer, a traveling salesperson, an airline mechanic, a school bus driver, a sanitation worker, the nation's president, the founders of such enterprises as Microsoft and McDonald's, a college professor, or U2's Bono.

As matters stand in the United States, we generally let economic forces sort out such questions. The law of supply and demand is supposed to set prices and wages throughout the economy, and those who command the highest pay on the open market are said to merit it. But even if we allow that the best ballplayers, for example, make the most money in their respective sports, we might still ask if they deserve on their merits to be paid a hundred times more money than the best elementary schoolteachers. We might also ask if a nonworking mother married to a millionaire merits a standard of living considerably higher than a nonworking mother.

The answer to both questions, many would argue, is no. But if the market doesn't always reward merit, we are faced with still another question: Can society do a better job of determining the relative merits of its members? On the answer to this question, there is no clear agreement.

LIBERTARIANISM, WELFARE LIBERALISM, AND SOCIALISM

Robert Nozick's view of economic justice is often called **libertarianism** because it seeks to maximize individual liberty. In general, the libertarian view is that all forms of coercion—except to prevent harm to life, liberty, and property—are wrong, whether they come from other individuals or from the government. Because we need a police force to protect life, liberty, and property, we may be coerced into paying taxes to support one. Because transfer payments are a matter of charity, not protection, we may not be coerced into paying taxes to support them.

John Rawls's view is often called *welfare liberalism* or **welfare capitalism**. Like Nozick, Rawls recognizes many property rights—the right to own a business, the right to hire and fire workers, and the right to make economic decisions according to market forces. In other words, he supports a *capitalist* economy. But he also supports transfer payments to rectify what he considers the economic injustices of capitalism.

One way of expressing the differences between the two positions goes like this: Are we to think of the wealth in society as merely the sum of individual wealth or as society's wealth as well. Nozick gives the former answer because of his belief in natural rights. Rawls gives the latter answer because of his belief that all members of society cooperate in the creation of that wealth. Why? Because what makes it possible for individuals to earn the wealth they do are the mutually agreed upon fundamental rules of society.

There is another possible reason for giving the same answer as Rawls. This reason comes from proponents of **socialism**. Socialists ask us to consider who creates the wealth in any society. Their answer is the workers, those who turn raw materials into commodities that are sold for profit. Then they ask us to consider who, in a capitalist society, gets rich off those profits. Their answer to this question is the owners, the top executives, the bankers, the landlords, and so forth—those who don't create any wealth. The real producers of wealth, in other words, don't own the wealth they produce. They receive only a small portion of it in the form of wages. Nor do they even own a guaranteed stake in their own jobs. After investing as many as twenty years or more of their lives to create enormous wealth for others, they can be laid off or fired by the bosses they made rich.

The socialist way of achieving economic justice is to replace a capitalist economy with a socialist economy. "Socialism" takes various forms. In western European countries, private ownership of property and the means of production are preserved, but shared responsibilities are recognized and paid through the taxation system. These shared responsibilities include education, health care, and child care. In a true "communist" system, such as that of the former Soviet Union and the satellite countries of the former Warsaw Pact in eastern Europe, the government took ownership of the means of production. Communism in Russia and eastern Europe started to fall in 1989 and was replaced with a capitalistic economic system, although it retained some elements of socialism as understood in western Europe.

Why adopt such sweeping measures? First, proponents argue, socialism provides true economic justice and full social equality. Second, it maximizes freedom for everyone, not just the rich. The right to liberty, they claim, like the rights to life and property, is meaningless to people who can't afford a decent standard of living. Third, socialism extends democracy from the political realm to the economic realm. Not only does everyone have an equal say in how political decisions are made, but everyone has say in how major economic decisions are made as well. Fourth, it replaces the indignity of welfare with the dignity of work.

Socialism's critics raise a number of objections, many of which we have already discussed. The objections include the libertarian arguments based on liberty and natural rights, plus the moral and practical objections to the need and equality principles of distribution. Another important criticism concerns the relative merits of planned economies and market economies. Planned economies, critics say, do not work as well as market economies. As evidence, they point to the failures of eastern Europe's planned economies, which are now being converted to market economies. They also point to the many socialist parties in Western Europe that have shifted policies in favor of a market-oriented approach.

ARGUMENTS FOR GLOBAL AID

1. *You can't let people starve.*

   POINT: "You can't just let people starve; it's as simple as that. And you can't leave them homeless, either, or make them go without adequate healthcare and clothing. Food, housing, healthcare, and clothing are the very basics of human existence. Without them, the promise of life, liberty, and the pursuit of happiness is empty."

   COUNTERPOINT: "Of course our basic needs are important, but that's not the real issue. The real issue is: Who's responsible for making sure that their needs are met? And the answer is obvious. We're all responsible for ourselves. It's up to every one of us to see that our basic needs are met. If you're out of work, get yourself a job—any job. If you can't afford children, don't have them. And most important, if you're young, stay in school."

2. *Society is responsible for helping the unfortunate.*

   POINT: "You make it sound as though it's the fault of the poor that they're poor, as though they all deserve their poverty. Maybe that's true in some cases, but look around you. If you do, you'll see people struggling to get by on inadequate incomes, people thrown out of work through no fault of their own, and people struck by disabling injuries and illnesses. And you'll also see people who never had a fair chance to begin with because they grew up in hopeless poverty or because they went to schools that couldn't give them a decent education. These unfortunates were let down by society, and it's up to all of us to give them a helping hand."

   COUNTERPOINT: "Look, I'm not in favor of cutting off all kinds of help to every person who needs it. I'm not saying we should do away with unemployment compensation for people who are laid off. And I'm not saying we should cut off Social Security disability payments, either. Those programs are insurance, not welfare, and the only thing I'm talking about is welfare. If *you* want to help those 'unfortunates' who 'grew up in hopeless poverty,' go right ahead. That's what private charities are for. But don't force everyone else to help them out, especially when we see how many other people there are who grew up in poverty and turned out to be productive members of society."

3. *Refusing to help people in need hurts innocent children.*

   POINT: "One thing you're forgetting is the children of the poor, whether in this country or others. When you talk about cutting off aid, you're not just hurting adults who might be able to help themselves with hard work. You're also helping millions of innocent children. You can't blame children for their predicament, can you?"

   COUNTERPOINT: "Of course not, but the answer to that problem is to stop encouraging people to have children they can't afford, and that's exactly what aid payments do. Whether they are in our country or somebody else's, people should stop breeding children they can't afford to support."

4. *Poverty breeds other social problems.*

   POINT: "Poverty is everybody's problem, not just the poor's. Where you find poverty, you find crime. Where you find poverty, you find contagious diseases. You also find drug use, fear, despair, and a terrible waste of human resources.

Poverty is ruining our great cities, and the problems associated with it—street gangs, for instance—are spreading into small towns throughout the country. It's in everyone's interest to eradicate poverty."

COUNTERPOINT: "I couldn't agree with you more. It's your next step I disagree with, that welfare is the solution to all those problems. With decades of evidence staring us in the face, anyone can see that it isn't."

ARGUMENTS AGAINST GLOBAL AID

1. *Global aid is unjust.*

POINT: "The first thing to point out about aid is that it's a violation of individual freedom and individual rights, pure and simple. What's mine is mine, and no one has the right to take it away from me. Don't get me wrong. I'm not in favor of selfishness. I think everyone should give to charity. I certainly do. But like everyone else, I have the right to give to the charities of my own choosing. I even have the right not to give at all if I don't want to. Selfishness may be immoral, but so are a lot of other things, like cheating at tennis. It's not government's job to outlaw either one of them. Government's job is to protect my rights, not to interfere with them."

COUNTERPOINT: "Don't we also have the right to live in dignity? The right to a decent standard of living? And don't those rights count at least as much as your property rights? Besides, where do these property rights come from? Where is it written that you're entitled to *everything* you make? After all, where would you be without the cooperation of society as a whole—without our public roads and airports, for instance, or our legal systems at the federal, state, and municipal levels, or our federal banking system? Society contributes in any number of ways. Asking you to help people who haven't benefited as much as you have isn't asking too much."

2. *Aid is bad social policy.*

POINT: "How much does global aid really help? There was a time when countries were self-sufficient and didn't depend on hand-outs from wealthier nations to survive. They raised their own food, sustained their own economies, and seemed to manage just fine without asking for other nations to help. International aid has turned them into dependent nations, unable to stand on their own feet, and nobody wins in that kind of world."

COUNTERPOINT: "I don't deny that dependence on aid from wealthy nations can be a problem. But many of these countries were treated unfairly over the years and need help rebuilding their economies. Some had valuable natural resources which were extracted by corporations from other countries for a pittance. Others suffered the ravages of wars others started. And, with international travel so much easier, isn't it better to help people in their own countries, rather than encouraging a flood of refugees we can't afford in the more developed countries?"

3. *Aid removes stigmas that uphold important values.*

POINT: "We both agree that it's better to be self-sufficient than to depend on hand-outs, whether from our own government or somebody else's. Endless payments to aid others, whether in the form of welfare checks to our own citizens or transfers to other governments, only removes those old stigmas against depending on others. We should be encouraging everybody to stand on their own, work hard, solve their own problems, and not depend on others."

COUNTERPOINT: "That old cliche, 'Pull yourself up by your own bootstraps," doesn't work if you have no boots in the first place. By giving people appropriate help, we help them learn how to help themselves, and we all should be winners in the end. We can focus on things that help people flourish, whether it's improving education or health care or training for a new job. That kind of help is best and shouldn't have to go on forever."

4. *Aid rewards fraud and freeloading.*

POINT: "Hand-outs, whether to people in our own country or governments elsewhere, just encourages everybody to figure out how to cheat. They skim the money, save it in hidden accounts somewhere, and don't use it for the goals we had in mind. We can't afford to keep passing out money that just gets stolen by the cheaters."

COUNTERPOINT: "We definitely need to do a better job cracking down on the cheats, whether foreign governments or Wall Street titans or cheaters in our own country collecting welfare of some sort. Of course, it will cost us money to hire investigators to do that kind of oversight, so I hope you won't complain about those new government employees down the road! We won't be able to completely eliminate fraud, but we should be able to get it down to a reasonable level that is outweighed by the other benefits of helping people and governments who deserve it."

Global Poverty: What Are Our Obligations?

PETER SINGER

Peter Singer is the Ira W. DeCamp Professor of Bioethics at the University Center for Human Values, Princeton University, and the Laureate Professor at the Centre for Applied Philosophy and Public Ethics (CAPPE) at the University of Melbourne.

In 1972, he published an essay called "Famine, Affluence, and Morality," which argued that affluent persons and nations had a moral obligation to help alleviate the widespread starvation and malnourishment in much of the world. Failure to help someone in need is "gross moral negligence," he argued, whether that person is a child drowning in a swimming pool or a child starving on another continent. That essay has triggered extensive discussion and criticism concerning our moral obligations to the poor, wherever they are located. For example, philosopher John Arthur argued that, while our moral code might encourage benevolence to friends and neighbors, it need not require obligations to strangers elsewhere in the world.

The essay reprinted here in full was written almost four decades later. It urges that our common eating patterns waste food and contribute to greenhouse gases and climate change

Presented at the Harriet L. and Paul M. Weissman Center for Leadership and the Liberal Arts, Mount Holyoke College, South Hadley, MA, November 11, 2010. Published in *Spoken Words*, Mount Holyoke College, 2010–2011, pp. 26–34. Copyright 2010 Peter Singer.

that endanger the planet. He continues to argue, as he did in 1972, that more affluent nations and individuals have a moral obligation to help address world poverty. He is now concerned with what he calls the diffusion of responsibility and urges that we think more for ourselves and our individual responsibilities.

The world's food supply is affected by many different things, but some significant ones start with the lifestyle of affluent people in industrialized countries. This lifestyle produces greenhouse gases, as a result both of our very high levels of energy consumption compared to most places in the world, and because of our high levels of meat and dairy consumption. Another factor is the quantity of food that we actually absorb, not only directly but indirectly through the grains that have to be produced in order to be fed to the animals we eat. This adds to the strain we put on the environment. The world currently feeds about 750 million tons of grain to animals. From those animals, we get back only a small fraction of the food value of that amount of grain. It isn't hard to do the arithmetic on just how serious this waste is. Put the 750 million tons of grain together with the fact that there are about 1.4 billion people living in extreme poverty, according to the World Bank's definition, and it turns out that we could give all of those 1.4 billion people about three pounds of grain a day, which is significantly more than anybody needs to meet their basic caloric needs. I'm not saying that this would be a wise thing to do, or the best solution to global poverty, but it does show that the world is currently producing enough food. (And note that I haven't even mentioned the vast quantities of soybeans that are also fed to animals, nor the more than 100 million tons of grain that is used to make ethanol to put in our cars.)

So it is literally true that we produce plenty of food to feed all of the world. But that doesn't mean that if we stop feeding this grain to animals, the people who need it would get it. We don't have that sort of distributive mechanism. The grain is grown, because there's a market for it. There's a market for it because the agricultural producers can sell at certain prices because people want to buy meat, and the economics of producing that meat indicate that, if grain and soybeans are not too expensive, it pays to feed them to animals. If that stopped, then we would need at least different forms of distribution,

of incentives to produce and distribution. It might simply be that the world would produce less grain and fewer soybeans than it produces now. Still that would mean that there was a lot more agricultural land, it would mean that there was less market competition, and it would presumably mean that overall grain prices would fall because the possibility of producing it would still be there and the demand would be lower. So that is part of the solution to the problem of high food prices, which are causing hundreds of millions of people to go to bed hungry.

Somebody might say, "Well, if we have the resources to produce food, and if we enjoy eating meat or dairy products, then don't we have the right to spend our money as we choose? Don't we have the right to buy those animal products, and don't the people who want to produce them have the right to buy the grain or soybeans? And what's wrong with this? How are we actually doing something wrong to those who have less?"

I've already mentioned one way in which we are doing something wrong to the world's poor. We are harming them through our emissions of greenhouse gases, which, in turn, make it probable that at least some of them will not have the reliable rainfall that they need to produce their food. There's a variety of other consequences, of global warming, including rising sea levels. which will cause coastal inundation, especially in the fertile delta regions of poor countries like Bangladesh and Egypt. So, on the grounds of climate change alone, you can make out a good case that we are harming the world's poorest people. On any kind of defensible moral view, there's a serious social justice question there.

But I want to go beyond that. I want to argue not only that we should not harm the world's poor, but also that we have an obligation to help. The obligation that we have to help is, to put it briefly, that if we're in a position to help somebody in great need, at a relatively modest cost to ourselves, that's something that we ought to do. So, to illustrate this argument, in the first article I wrote on this topic many years ago, I asked you to imagine that you're walking across a park and you pass a shallow pond—shallow enough, to wade across, should you want to do that. You don't, of course, but as you pass this pond, which is normally quiet, you notice some splashing going on, and when you look more closely you're shocked to see that the splashing is small child, just a toddler, who's fallen into the pond. Although the pond is shallow, it's not shallow enough for a toddler to stand, and so this child appears to be in danger of drowning. You think. "Who's looking after this child? There must be somebody there must be parents, a babysitter, somebody must be responsible for this child." But you can't see anybody. There's nobody else there, there's just you and the child. So your next thought is, "Well, I'd better wade into that pond, maybe it's going to be cold, maybe the bottom is muddy, but I'd better wade into that pond and pull out that child." Then a slightly less noble thought occurs to you. "Damn, I just put on a new pair of shoes and a new pair of trousers, relatively expensive for what I spend on clothes, and they're probably going to get ruined, they're not built to take immersion in muddy water, it's definitely not going to be good for them, but I don't really have to time to get them off. The child could be drowning any minute. " So the thought occurs to you. "Well, what if I just didn't really notice the child and just went on my way to what I was doing? After all, I didn't push the child in the pond. The child's not my business, is it? "

So suppose that somebody did think that and just went on their way. How many of you think that person would be doing something wrong? That looks like all of you. Does anybody think that that person wouldn't be doing something wrong? No? I'm glad to say that your responses are in line with what always happens when I put that question to an audience. Overwhelmingly, people think that that is wrong, and quite seriously wrong, to walk on past the pond because you don't want to ruin your shoes. If I were to structure this as a formal argument, I would say that if we can prevent something bad happening at very small cost to ourselves, we ought to do it. In this case, the bad thing is the death of a child. We would all assume that the death of a toddler is a bad thing. We can prevent it happening. We can rescue the child. There is a cost

to ourselves, but it's a fairly small one. How can you compare the damage to your shoes or clothes with the value of a child's life? I think we'd all agree, they're not on the same scale; you shouldn't weigh them. So, that's an instance where we can fairly easily make a difference.

Now, if I've persuaded you to accept that premise, then we need to look at the situation that we're all in with regard to the world's poor. As I said earlier, according to the World Bank, there are about 1.4 billion people living in extreme poverty. Extreme poverty, in the World Bank's definition, means that they do not have enough income to reliably meet their basic needs: food, safe drinking water, some kind of shelter, to be able to give their children at least an elementary school education, and some basic health care, just at a very minimal level. That is, that if your child falls ill with something simple, like diarrhea, which is easily treatable, there is a health clinic you can go to and you can get the treatment that your child needs. We don't think of diarrhea in this country as something that kills children, but worldwide, it kills large numbers of children. Somewhere probably between one and two million children under live die from diarrhea each year. Of course, more of them get it because the poor often don't have safe drinking water; but in addition they don't have treatment for it because they don't have a health clinic that they can go to. Either there isn't one that they can reach, or there is one, but it charges money for its services, and they can't afford it. So just minimal health care like that, or like immunization against measles, another major killer of children in developing countries. It's those things that the 1.4 billion in extreme poverty can't afford.

The World Bank also calculates how much income it takes to be able to afford these basics. The figure it comes up with is the purchasing power equivalent of $1.25 U.S. Now, what does purchasing power equivalent mean? Some of you may have traveled in developing countries, and you may have noticed that when you go to the local bank and you exchange your U.S. dollars for whatever the local currency is the money that you've now got seems to go a lot further than it did here. You can get a meal, it might be lentils and rice, but it's an adequate meal that will fill your stomach and nourish you for maybe 50 cents. So you might think. "Oh well, $1.25 is not too bad; 50 cents for my dinner, and maybe I can find somewhere to sleep for not very much more than that." You can imagine living on that. But, that amount of money that your $1.25 turned into when you went to the bank in this country is not what the World Bank is talking about. The World Bank, as I said, is talking about the purchasing power equivalent, not the foreign exchange equivalent. The purchasing power equivalent is whatever it is in the local currency that buys as much as $1.25 buys in the U.S. So now we're thinking about something quite different. Could you survive on $1.25 per day in the U.S.? (I've cheated slightly because it's actually $1.25 in 1993 dollars, which would be worth approximately $2.00 in today's dollars.) But it's still an amount that you would have extreme difficulty in living on here, and people in developing countries are facing that extreme difficulty.

In terms of the premises of the argument I gave you, it's clearly a bad thing that there are people in extreme poverty. One indication of why it's a bad thing is that many children die because they're living iri extreme poverty. UNICEF estimates that about 8.1 million children under five die every year from avoidable, poverty-related causes. That is something like 22,000 children dying every day. That figure, though it's far too many deaths, of course, has been dropping. If you pick up the 2010 paperback edition of my book, *The Life You Can Save,* the figure it gives is 8.8 million. In the 2009 hardcover edition, the figure was almost a million more. In fact, going right back to the 1960s, it was as many as 20 million children a year. When you consider that the world's population in the 1960s was only about half of what it is today, that's encouraging progress. As a percentage of the world's population, the number of children who die before they reach the age of five from poverty-related causes is below a quarter of what it was 50 years ago. So this is not an insoluble problem: it's not a black hole that we just pour money into without seeing any results. We do see results, but we are still in a situation where more than 20,000 children are dying each day because of this preventable poverty. This is something that we could do something about. We know what, to

do and, as I say, we are doing it, and we're making progress. We're immunizing more children against measles. We're providing safe drinking water for more villages. We're providing local health, clinics with very simple treatments for diarrhea. Were providing more people with bed nets so their children don't get malaria, another major killer of children.

So there is something bad happening, and we can prevent those bad things going on. Therefore that is something that we ought to do. Some people may say. "Well aren't we already doing quite a lot? Maybe not me personally, but isn't the United States government doing it? I pay through my taxes or my parents pay through their taxes to do this already." But unfortunately, while the U.S. does do something in this area, it really does very little in comparison to the amount of wealth we have. Many Americans are under illusions about how much foreign aid the country actually gives. There've been surveys where people have been asked. "Do you think the country gives enough foreign aid, or too much foreign aid, or too little foreign aid?" Typically, about half the people say too much. So you might say. "Well there just isn't popular support for the government to give more foreign aid." Then you ask the people, "As a percentage of what the government spends, how much of that do you think should be foreign aid?" The answers people give tend to be in the range of between 5 and 10 percent of government spending. Remember, they think we give too much, or at least half of them do. So they presumably think we're giving significantly more than 5 to 10 percent of all government spending as foreign aid. In fact, we're giving less than 1 percent of government spending as foreign aid. So on the one hand, Americans are saying we're giving too much, and on the other hand they have a hugely inflated view of how much we do give.

We also don't do too well by comparison with comparable wealthy countries. The figure that's usually quoted for how much countries give as foreign aid is not as a percentage of government spending, but as a percentage of gross national income—that is, how much the nation earns as a whole. The United Nations, many years ago, back in the 1970s, suggested that an acceptable standard would be 0.7 percent of gross national income. That means that for every $100 that the nation earns, 70 cents—not even $1.00. but only 70 cents—would be given as foreign aid. At present, only five countries meet or exceed that goal. They are Sweden. Norway. Denmark, the Netherlands, and Luxembourg. The United States doesn't get near it. The United States gives, as government aid, around 20 cents in every $100 that we earn. So it's way down by comparison with those European nations that are leaders. In fact, we are pretty much on a par with some of the poorer European nations like Portugal and Greece. They're around the same level as a percentage of gross national income as we are. It's true, of course, that people in the U.S. also give privately. That's not counted in the government aid statistics. Privately we give rather more than, say, the Swedes, who feel that their government is doing more and they're taxed more for that. Swedes, incidentally, don't get a tax deduction for charitable donations so that's probably another reason why they don't give as much as Americans do. But even if you add in the private donations, we still don't get even to half as much as the Swedes do. We don't even get to half of that 70 cents in every $100 level. So the private donations don't make enough difference to enable us to think of ourselves as a generous nation.

If we really are interested in trying to calculate how much the U.S. gives to the world's poor, we'd have to take account of the fact that of that 20 cents of official aid we give for each $100 we earn, a large portion is directed towards furthering our geopolitical interests rather than towards helping the poor. So what nation gets the largest amount of U.S. official development assistance? I'm not talking about military aid now, I'm talking about what is classified as official development assistance that counts toward this percentage of our foreign aid. Does anyone know? Does anyone want to guess? [Audience member: "Saudi Arabia?"] No. [Audience member: "Iraq?"] Iraq is right. Iraq currently gets about four times as much as the next nation. So now that you know that Iraq is number one, can you guess what's number two? Afghanistan, you're right. OK, so in other words, the two nations in which we have the greatest involvement as part of the war against terror, are the top aid nations. While Afghanistan certainly is a poor country that should get some aid, Iraq is not all that poor. It's a lower-middle-income country, and it has vast oil reserves. If you look at the poorest countries of sub-Saharan Africa, which are of no great geopolitical interest to us, they tend to rank quite well down on our list. The result is, that we are not really doing very much about our responsibilities to the global poor. Even President Obama said, In a speech not that long ago, that we are one of the leaders in helping the world's poor. It's not true. There is a lot more that we could be doing, and I would say there's a lot more that we should be doing.

You might say, "Why aren't we doing that much more? " There are many reasons for that, and it's an interesting issue. Some of these are psychological reasons rather than ethical issues. But a lot of the things that people think of as somehow making a difference, I would say only make a psychological difference, not a real ethical difference. So, for instance, you all agreed that we should help the child in the pond, and probably you all would help the child in the pond if you were to find yourself in that situation. Why don't you all then help people elsewhere in the world? Part of the psychological problem is that they're not here in front of you, and you're not in a one-to-one situation where you can see that you can make a difference. Psychologists have studied a variety of different phenomena that are relevant to when a person will help a stranger. I've come to realize in looking at this literature that, when I came up with that example of the child drowning in the pond. I had unconsciously produced an example that is really well suited to drawing emotional responses, much better suited in fact than the global poverty issue is. So, for example, there is an identifiable victim that you're helping. So this makes a huge difference. Here's an example of the kind of study that shows it does. Psychologists ask students to come in for an experiment and offer them $15. Sound familiar? I don't know whether your psychology department here does it, but it happens on lots of campuses. So the students come in for this experiment; they're told, "Here's a questionnaire. Please fill it in. Hand it in. We'll pay you your $15." So they fill in the questionnaire, which of course has nothing to do with the experiment. They hand in the questionnaire at the end, and they're given $15 in cash in small bills, and they're told, "By the way, each month our department supports a charity. Here's some information about the charity we're supporting this month. I wonder if you'd like to give some of your earnings to the charity." Then, randomly selected, half of the students get a piece of information which has a picture of a seven-year-old African girl, and it says, "This is Rokia; she's seven years old; she lives in Malawi; she goes to bed hungry at night because her family can't provide enough food for her. You can help her." The other half are given a piece of information that has no photo, and says, "In Malawi, thousands of children go to bed hungry at night. You can help them." Sounds like pretty similar information, you're being given, isn't it? Except that in one case there's an identifiable person. But surely nobody thinks, "Oh, yes, the money that I give and that, everybody else here this month gives, is all going to Rokia." That would be a bit odd, wouldn't it, for the department just to collect for Rokia this month. That would mean that she would become quite wealthy by Malawian standards. So the students can't really think that. Yet, by quite a significant amount, more people give when they're given the information about Rokia than when they're given the general information.

So the fact that we're talking about anonymous masses of people, millions of people even, as I said, makes us less likely to respond. That's one important factor. Another factor is, in the example of the pond there was only you, remember; it was up to you to save the child. It's not up to you to save even Rokia, even if you're given a name, it's not up to you alone. Everybody's being given this information. We know there are other people in the world who could help at least as well as we could. In fact, obviously there are some people who could help much better than we could. What about Bill Gates? Why isn't he helping? Actually he is helping. No doubt there are other very wealthy people who aren't helping that much. So that's another phenomenon that psychologists have studied, the diffusion of responsibility Again, you can show quite easily, if you stage an accident in which there's a victim who needs help, and there's only one person there who can help the accident victim, that person's very likely to help. On the other hand, if that person is only one of half a dozen,

and the other half dozen are all the experimenter's stooges who have been told not to go and help the accident victim then the person who is the naïve subject, as psychologists call them, the one who doesn't know that this has all been rigged, is much less likely to go and help. In other words, basically we're sheep. We follow the leader: we don't often stand up and think for ourselves.

We need to try and change these variables. We need to change the cultural standard so that giving becomes more normal. That's one of the things I'm trying to do on a website I've set up, *www. thelifeyoucansave.com*. In my book and on the website, I've invited people to pledge to give a certain percentage of their income to help the global poor. (For most of you it is quite a modest percentage, you'll be pleased to know.) You can do that publicly; currently about 7,500 people have pledged. I hope that that makes it easier for others to go on and pledge, because you can see you're not alone in doing this. Some of them also have contributed photos of themselves and a line or two as to why this is significant and why it makes a difference. That's an attempt to change our culture so that instead of thinking that all you have to do to live a good life, an ethical life, is to obey the "thou shalt not" types of commandment—not cheat, steal, lie, attack others, and so on—we come to see that we have some positive obligations to help those in need where we can relatively easily do so. That would be a really important change in our world today. That would make a really significant difference.

I'm going to close with one last point. We're very much focused on thinking about our interests in terms of how much money we have. But when we stop and think about it, none of us would really say that the most important thing in life is to have a big bank balance. We would probably say, "Well, yes, you know it's nice to have a big bank balance, but that's because then you can do a variety of things and you'll be happier." But what has become clear is that people who are involved in causes larger than themselves, and who contribute to charity of various kinds, say that they are more satisfied with their lives than people who don't. That finding comes out again and again in the general well-being surveys that have been taken for many years in the U.S. and other countries. We're even now starting to get a little bit closer to the mechanisms of this because we now have the ability to take real-time images of what happens in people's brains when they do various kinds of things. This has been done (admittedly the study I am about to cite was a small one, and it would be good to have it replicated) with people who have been given some money and asked if they want to make a donation to a charity. Now, whether they say "yes" or "no" to that is not something the experimenter knows: it's done anonymously. So the reaction that I'm about to talk about is not related to the subjects knowing that they are enhancing their public reputation, as some cynics might say. Yet, with those people who do decide to give, we can see a spike in activity in the reward centers of the brain, the same areas of the brain that are active when we're doing things that we enjoy, whether it's a particular kind of food that we find delicious or sexual activity that we're enjoying or whatever else it might be. It seems that they

reward us for being generous as well as doing those other pleasant things. Exactly why is an interesting question. No doubt it has something to do with the circumstance in which we evolved in societies where giving was something that enhanced our survival value in a community that required some sort of cooperation. I'm arguing that we should extend that, beyond the immediate face-to-face community to the world as a whole. It seems that the same mechanisms are there. In terms of the way we live our lives, we are likely to find involvement in these larger causes something that is actually rewarding and fulfilling, something that enables us to feel that our lives are more meaningful than they are if we are simply living for ourselves and thinking only about our own narrower self interest. So while giving to help the global poor may involve some financial sacrifice, we should not think of it as involving any sacrifice of our real interests, properly understood.

⚜ QUESTIONS FOR ANALYSIS

1. Although global poverty persists, Singer argues that enough food is produced to feed everybody. What changes would be necessary to make it possible to actually feed everyone on the planet? How do Singer's proposals rely on changes in current beliefs and practices regarding environmental and animal ethics?

2. Singer argues that we have an obligation not to harm the poor, but also an obligation to help them. How does he make this argument? Is his analogy with the drowning toddler we see in a pond persuasive?

3. How does human psychology factor into our generosity in helping others, according to Singer?

4. What does Singer mean by "diffusion of responsibility"? How does this lessen our generosity in helping others?

5. What does Singer propose to alter the cultural standard for accepting responsibility for others we do not know?

6. What are "our real interests" in life, as Singer understands them?

7. Has Singer answered his critics from decades ago that he has not made the case that we have moral obligations to strangers elsewhere on the planet?

Sweatshops and Respect for Persons

DENIS G. ARNOLD AND NORMAN E. BOWIE

Denis G. Arnold is Associate Professor of Management and the Surtman Distinguished Scholar in Business Ethics at the Belk College of Business at the University of North Carolina at Charlotte. Norman E. Bowie is Professor Emeritus at the University of Minnesota. Until he retired in 2009, he held the Elmer L. Anderson Chair in Corporate Responsibility at the University of Minnesota, where he had joint appointments in the departments of philosophy and of strategic management and organization. Both have published extensively on business ethics.

In these excerpts from their 2003 essay, they use Kant's doctrine of respect for persons to analyze sweatshops around the globe. They argue that multinational corporations have a variety of duties in their off-shore manufacturing facilities and that they are responsible for the practices of their subcontractors and suppliers.

In recent years labor and human rights activists have been successful at raising public awareness regarding labor practices in both American and off-shore manufacturing facilities. Organizations such as Human Rights Watch, United Students Against Sweatshops, the National Labor Coalition, Sweatshop Watch, and the Interfaith Center on Corporate Responsibility have accused multinational enterprises (MNEs), such as Nike, WalMart, and Disney, of the pernicious exploitation of workers. Recent violations of American and European labor laws have received considerable attention.[1] However, it is the off-shore labor practices of North American and European based MNEs and their contractors that have been most controversial. This is partly due to the fact that many of the labor practices in question are legal outside North America and Europe, or are tolerated by corrupt or repressive political regimes. Unlike the recent immigrants who toil in the illegal sweatshops of North America and Europe, workers in developing nations typically have no recourse to the law or social service agencies. Activists have sought to enhance the welfare of these workers by pressuring MNEs to comply with labor laws, prohibit coercion, improve health and safety standards, and pay a living wage in their global sourcing operations. Meanwhile, prominent economists wage a campaign of their own in the opinion pages of leading newspapers, arguing that because workers for MNEs are often paid better when compared with local wages, they are fortunate to have such work. Furthermore, they argue that higher wages and improved working conditions will raise unemployment levels.

One test of a robust ethical theory is its ability to shed light on ethical problems. One of the standard criticisms of Immanuel Kant's ethical philosophy is that it is too abstract and formal to be of any use in practical decision making. We contend that this criticism is mistaken and that

Kantian theory has much to say about the ethics of sweatshops.[2] We argue that Kant's conception of human dignity provides a clear basis for grounding the obligations of employers to employees. In particular, we argue that respecting the dignity of workers requires that MNEs and their contractors adhere to local labor laws, refrain from coercion, meet minimum safety standards, and provide a living wage for employees....

I. RESPECT FOR PERSONS

Critics of sweatshops frequently ground their protests in appeals to human dignity and human rights. Arguably, Kantian ethics provides a philosophical basis for such moral pronouncements. The key principle here is Kant's second formulation of the categorical imperative: "Act so that you treat humanity, whether in your own person or in that of another, always as an end and never as a means only."[3] The popular expression of this principle is that morality requires that we respect people. One significant feature of the idea of respect for persons is that its derivation and application can be assessed independently of other elements of Kantian moral philosophy. Sympathetic readers need not embrace all aspects of Kant's system of ethics in order to grant the merit of Kant's arguments for the second formulation of the categorical imperative.[4] This is because Kant's defense of respect for persons is grounded in the uncontroversial claim that humans are capable of rational, self-governing activity. We believe that individuals with a wide range of theoretical commitments can and should recognize the force of Kant's arguments concerning respect for persons.

Kant did not simply assert that persons are entitled to respect, he provided an elaborate argument for that conclusion. Persons ought to be respected because persons have dignity. For Kant, an object

Denis G. Arnold and Norman E. Bowie, "Sweatshops and Respect for Persons," *Business Ethics Quarterly* 13:2 (April 2003), 221–242. Reprinted with permission from Philosophy Documentation Center.

that has dignity is beyond price. Employees have a dignity that machines and capital do not have. They have dignity because they are capable of moral activity. As free beings capable of self-governance they are responsible beings, since freedom and self-governance are the conditions for responsibility. Autonomous responsible beings are capable of making and following their own laws; they are not simply subject to the causal laws of nature. Anyone who recognizes that he or she is free should recognize that he or she is responsible (that he or she is a moral being). As Kant argues, the fact that one is a moral being entails that one possesses dignity.

> Morality is the condition under which alone a rational being can be an end in himself because only through it is it possible to be a lawgiving member in the realm of ends. Thus morality, and humanity insofar as it is capable of morality, alone have dignity.[5]

As a matter of consistency, a person who recognizes that he or she is a moral being should ascribe dignity to anyone who, like him or herself, is a moral being.

Although it is the capacity to behave morally that gives persons their dignity, freedom is required if a person is to act morally. For Kant, being free is more than freedom from causal necessity. This is negative freedom. Freedom in its fullest realization is the ability to guide one's actions from laws that are of one's own making. Freedom is not simply a spontaneous event. Free actions are caused, but they are caused by persons acting from laws they themselves have made. This is positive freedom.... When we act autonomously we have the capacity to act with dignity. We do so when we act on principles that are grounded in morality rather than in mere inclination. Reason requires that any moral principle that is freely derived must be rational in the sense that it is universal. To be universal in this sense means that the principle can be willed to be universally binding on all subjects in relevantly similar circumstances without contradiction. The fact that persons have this capability means that they possess dignity. And it is as a consequence of this dignity that a person "exacts respect for himself from all other rational beings in the world."[6]

As such, one can and should "measure himself with every other being of this kind and value himself on a footing of equality with them."[7]

Respecting people requires honoring their humanity; which is to say it requires treating them as ends in themselves. In Kant's words,

> Humanity itself is a dignity; for a man cannot be used merely as a means by any man ... but must always be used at the same time as an end. It is just in this that his dignity ... consists, by which he raises himself above all other beings in the world that are not men and yet can be used, and so over all *things*.[8]

Thomas Hill Jr. has discussed the implication of Kant's arguments concerning human dignity at length.[9] Hill argues that treating persons as ends in themselves requires supporting and developing certain human capacities, including the capacity to act on reason; the capacity to act on the basis of prudence or efficiency; the capacity to set goals; the capacity to accept categorical imperatives; and the capacity to understand the world and reason abstractly.[10] Based on Kant's writings in the *Metaphysics of Morals*, we would make several additions to the list. There Kant argues that respecting people means that we cannot be indifferent to them. Indifference is a denial of respect.[11] He also argues that we have an obligation to be concerned with the physical welfare of people and their moral well-being. Adversity, pain, and want are temptations to vice and inhibit the ability of individuals to develop their rational and moral capacities.[12] It is these rational and moral capacities that distinguish people from mere animals. People who are not free to develop these capacities may end up leading lives that are closer to animals than to moral beings. Freedom from externally imposed adversity, pain, and want facilitate the cultivation of one's rational capacities and virtuous character. Thus, treating people as ends in themselves means ensuring their physical well-being and supporting and developing their rational and moral capacities.

With respect to the task at hand, what does treating the humanity of persons as ends in themselves require in a business context—specifically in the context of global manufacturing facilities? In an earlier work Bowie has spelled out the implications of the Kantian view for businesses operating in developed countries.[13] Here we apply the same strategy in order to derive basic duties for MNEs operating in developing countries. Specifically, we derive duties that apply to MNEs that are utilizing the vast supplies of inexpensive labor currently available in developing economies. To fully respect a person one must actively treat his or her humanity as an end. This is an obligation that holds on every person *qua* person, whether in the personal realm or in the marketplace. As Kant writes, "Every man has a legitimate claim to respect from his fellow men and is *in turn* bound to respect every other."[14] There are, of course, limits to what managers of MNEs can accomplish. Nonetheless, we believe that the analysis we have provided entails that MNEs operating in developing nations have an obligation to respect the humanity of their employees. We discuss the implications of this conclusion below....

II. OUTSOURCING AND THE DUTIES OF MNEs

One significant feature of globalization that is of particular relevance to our analysis is the increase in outsourcing by MNEs. Prior to the 1970s most foreign production by MNEs was intended for local markets. In the 1970s new financial incentives led MNEs to begin outsourcing the production of goods for North American, European, and Japanese markets to manufacturing facilities in developing countries. Encouraged by international organizations such as The World Bank and the International Monetary Fund, developing nations established "free trade zones" to encourage foreign investment via tax incentives and a minimal regulatory environment. In the 1980s the availability of international financing allowed entrepreneurs to set up production facilities in developing economies in order to meet the growing demand by MNEs for offshore production.[15] Outsourcing production has many distinct advantages from the perspective of MNEs. These include the following:

Capacity. Companies can expand their business more rapidly by focusing on marketing their products rather than investing in plant capacity,

employees, and upgrading capital equipment. Companies can also accept special orders they would not be able to offer to large volume customers if their production capacity were fixed.

Specialization. Companies can market products requiring specialized skills or equipment that the firm does not have in-house.

Reduced Production Costs. In competitive industries where firms compete largely on the basis of price, outsourcing permits companies to reduce the size of their payroll and profit sharing obligations and shop around for lower and lower cost producers all across the globe.

Cycle Time. Outsourcing gives companies the flexibility to turn products around quickly in order to meet consumer demand and also avoid inventory build-ups.

Flexibility. The outsourcing model of production offers unique flexibility to firms that seek to cut costs in production or increase their capacity in that it offers opportunities to experiment with product lines and supplier relationships with minimal financial risk. The expense of developing new samples, for example, is borne by the factory that hopes to receive the order.[16]

Outsourcing has been especially popular in consumer products industries, and in particular in the apparel industry. Nike, for example, outsources all of its production.

Are MNEs responsible for the practices of their subcontractors and suppliers? We believe that they are....

We ... offer the following two-fold justification for the view that MNEs have a duty to ensure that the dignity of workers is respected in the factories of subcontractors. First, an MNE, like any other organization, is composed of individual persons and, since persons are moral creatures, the actions of employees in an MNE are constrained by the categorical imperative. This means MNE managers have a duty to ensure that those with whom they conduct business are properly respected.[17] Second, as Kant acknowledges, individuals have unique duties as a result of their unique circumstances. One key feature in determining an individual's duties is the power they have to render assistance. For example, Kant famously argues that a wealthy person has a duty of charity that an impoverished person lacks. Corollary duties apply to organizations. Researchers have noted that the relationship of power between MNEs and their subcontractors and suppliers is significantly imbalanced in favor of MNEs:

> [A]s more and more developing countries have sought to establish export sectors, local manufacturers are locked in fierce competitive battles with one another. The resulting oversupply of export factories allows U.S. companies to move from one supplier to another in search of the lowest prices, quickest turnaround, highest quality and best delivery terms, weighted according to the priorities of the company. In this context, large U.S. manufacturer-merchandisers and retailers wield enormous power to dictate the price at which they will purchase goods.[18]

MNEs are well positioned to help ensure that the employees of its business partners are respected because of this imbalance of power. In addition, MNEs can draw upon substantial economic resources, management expertise, and technical knowledge to assist their business partners in creating a respectful work environment.

III. THE RULE OF LAW

Lawlessness contributes to poverty[19] and is deeply interconnected with human and labor rights violations. One important role that MNEs can play to help ensure that the dignity of workers is properly respected is encouraging respect for the rule of law. The United Nations has emphasized the importance of ensuring that citizens in all nations are not subject to violations of the rule of law.

> The rule of law means that a country's formal rules are made publicly known and enforced in a predictable way through transparent mechanisms. Two conditions are essential: the rules apply equally to all citizens, and the state is subject to the rules. How state institutions comply with the rule of law greatly affects the daily lives of poor people, who are very vulnerable to abuses of their rights.[20]

It is commonplace for employers in developing nations to violate worker rights in the interest of economic efficiency and with the support of state institutions. Violations of laws relating to wages and benefits, forced overtime, health and safety, child labor, sexual harassment, discrimination, and environmental protection are legion....

Furthermore, in many nations in which MNEs operate those responsible for administering justice are violators of the law. Factory workers frequently have no legal recourse when their legal rights are violated.

The intentional violation of the legal rights of workers in the interest of economic efficiency is fundamentally incompatible with the duty of MNEs to respect workers. Indifference to the plight of workers whose legal rights are systematically violated is a denial of respect. At a minimum, MNEs have a duty to ensure that their offshore factories, and those of their suppliers and subcontractors, are in full compliance with local laws. Failure to honor the dignity of workers by violating their legal rights—or tolerating the violation of those rights—is also hypocritical. In Kantian terms, it constitutes a pragmatic contradiction. A pragmatic contradiction occurs when one acts on a principle that promotes an action that would be inconsistent with one's purpose if everyone were to act upon that principle. In this case, the principle would be something like the following: "It is permissible to violate the legal rights of others when doing so is economically efficient." MNEs rely on the rule of law to ensure, among other things, that their contracts are fulfilled, their property is secure, and their copyrights are protected. When violations of the legal rights of MNEs take place, MNEs and business organizations protest vociferously. Thus, MNEs rely on the rule of law to ensure the protection of their own interests. Without the rule of law, MNEs would cease to exist. Therefore, it is inconsistent for an MNE to permit the violation of the legal rights of workers while at the same time it demands that its own rights be protected.

IV. COERCION

We have shown why it is reasonable to believe that all persons possess dignity and that this dignity must be respected. The obligation that we respect others requires that we not use people as a means only, but instead that we treat other people as capable of autonomous law guided action. The requirement not to use people can be met passively, by not treating them in certain ways. However, the requirement to treat them as ends-in-themselves entails positive obligations. We will explore these positive obligations as they relate to sweatshops in Section VI. In this section and the next we explore the requirement that we not use people as a means only. One common way of doing so recognized by Kant is coercion. Coercion violates a person's negative freedom. Coercion is prima facie wrong because it treats the subjects of coercion as mere tools, as objects lacking the rational capacity to choose for themselves how they shall act.

Are sweatshops in violation of the no coercion requirement? An answer to this question depends both on the definition of the concepts in question and on the facts of the particular case. Elsewhere Arnold has provided accounts of physical and psychological coercion.[21] Physical coercion occurs when one's bodily movements are physically forced. In cases where one person (*P*) physically coerces another person (*Q*), *Q*'s body is used as an object or instrument for the purpose of fulfilling *P*'s desires. We assume that readers of this essay will agree that using physical coercion to keep people working in sweatshops against their will is disrespectful and morally wrong. While comparatively rare, physical coercion, or the threat of physical coercion, does take place. For example, at a shoe factory in Guangdong, China, it is reported that 2,700 workers were prevented from leaving the factory by 100 live-in security guards that patrolled the walled factory grounds.[22]

For psychological coercion to take place, three conditions most hold. First, the coercer must have a desire about the will of his or her victim. However, this is a desire of a particular kind because it can only be fulfilled through the will of another person. Second, the coercer must have an effective desire to compel his or her victim to act in a manner that makes efficacious the coercer's other regarding desire. The distinction between an other regarding desire and a coercive will is important because it provides a basis for delineating between cases of coercion and, for example, cases of rational persuasion. In both instances a person may have an other regarding desire, but in the case of coercion that desire will be supplemented by an effective first-order desire that seeks to enforce that desire on the person, and in cases of rational persuasion it will not. What is of most importance in such cases is that *P* intentionally attempts to compel *Q* to comply with an other regarding desire of *P*'s own. These are necessary, but not sufficient conditions of coercion. In order for coercion to take place, the coercer must be successful in getting his or her victim to conform to his or her other regarding desire. In all cases of coercion *P* attempts to violate the autonomy of *Q*. When *Q* successfully resists *P*'s attempted coercion, *Q* retains his or her autonomy. In such cases *P* retains a coercive will.

In typical cases, people work in sweatshops because they believe they can earn more money working there than they can in alternative employment, or they work in sweatshops because it is better than being unemployed. In many developing countries, people are moving to large cities from rural areas because agriculture in those areas can no longer support the population base. When people make a choice that seems highly undesirable because there are no better alternatives available, are those people coerced? On the definition of coercion employed here, having to make a choice among undesirable options is not sufficient for coercion. We therefore assume that such persons are not coerced even though they have no better alternative than working in a sweatshop.

Nonetheless, the use of psychological coercion in sweatshops appears widespread. For example, coercion is frequently used by supervisors to improve worker productivity. Workers throughout the world report that they are forced to work long overtime hours or lose their jobs....

We do not claim that production quotas are inherently coercive. Given a reasonable quota, employees can choose whether or not to work diligently to fill that quota. Employees who choose idleness over industriousness and are terminated as a result are not coerced. However, when a supervisor threatens workers who are ill or injured with termination unless they meet a production quota that either cannot physically be achieved by the employee, or can only be achieved at the cost of further injury to the employee, the threat is properly understood as coercive. In such cases the employee will inevitably feel compelled to meet the quota. Still other factory workers report being threatened with termination if they seek medical attention....

According to the analysis provided here, workers choose to work in sweatshops because the alternatives available to them are worse. However, once they are employed, coercion is often used to ensure that they will work long overtime hours and meet production quotas. Respecting workers requires that they be free to decline overtime work without fear of being fired. It also requires that if they are injured or ill—especially as a result of work related activities—they should be allowed to consult healthcare workers and be given work that does not exacerbate their illnesses or injuries. Using coercion as a means of compelling employees to work overtime, to meet production quotas despite injury, or to remain at work while in need of medical attention, is incompatible with respect for persons because the coercers treat their victims as mere tools. It is important to note that even if the victim of coercion successfully resisted in some way, the attempted coercion would remain morally objectionable. This is because the coercer acts as if it is permissible to use the employees as mere tools.

V. WORKING CONDITIONS

Critics of MNEs argue that many workers are vulnerable to workplace hazards such as repetitive motion injuries, exposure to toxic chemicals, exposure to airborne pollutants such as fabric particles, and malfunctioning machinery. One of the most common workplace hazards concerns fire safety. In factories throughout the world workers are locked in to keep them from leaving the factory. When fires break out workers are trapped.... Workers are also exposed to dangerous toxic chemicals and airborne pollutants.

If our analysis is correct, then those MNEs that tolerate such health and safety risks have a duty to improve those conditions. Lax health and safety standards violate the moral requirement that employers be concerned with the physical safety of their employees. A failure to implement appropriate safeguards means that employers are treating their employees as disposable tools rather than as beings with unique dignity.

We cannot provide industry specific health and safety guidelines in the space of this essay. However, we believe that the International Labour Organization's carefully worked out Conventions and Recommendations on safety and health provide an excellent template for minimum safety standards.[23]...

Ethicists, business people, and labor leaders with widely divergent views on a number of issues can agree on a minimum set of health and safety standards that should be in place in factories in the developing world....

VI. WAGES

One of the most controversial issues concerning sweatshops is the demand that employers raise the wages of employees in order to provide a "living wage." Workers from all over the world complain about low wages....

While a living wage is difficult to define with precision, one useful approach is to use a method similar to that used by the U.S. government to define poverty. This method involves calculating the cost of a market basket of food needed to meet minimum dietary requirements and then adding the cost of other basic needs. The Council on Economic Priorities uses this approach to define a wage that meets basic needs in different countries. Their formula is as follows:

1. Establish the local cost of a basic food basket needed to provide 2,100 calories per person.
2. Determine the share of the local household income spent on food. Divide into 1 to get total budget multiplier.
3. Multiply that by food spending to get the total per person budget for living expenses.
4. Multiply by half the average number of household members in the area. (Use a higher share if there are many single-parent households.)
5. Add at least 10% for discretionary income.[24]...

It is our contention that, at a minimum, respect for employees entails that MNEs and their suppliers have a moral obligation to ensure that employees do not live under conditions of overall poverty by providing adequate wages for a 48 hour work week to satisfy both basic food needs and basic non-food needs. Doing so helps to ensure the physical well-being and independence of employees, contributes to the development of their rational capacities, and provides them with opportunities for moral development. This in turn allows for the cultivation of self-esteem.[25] It is difficult to specify with precision the minimum number of hours per week that employees should work in order to receive a living wage. However, we believe that a 48 hour work week is a reasonable compromise that allows employees sufficient time for the cultivation of their rational capacities while providing employers with sufficient productivity. In addition, MNEs and their suppliers have an obligation to pay appropriate host nation taxes and meet appropriate codes and regulations to ensure that they contribute in appropriate ways to the creation and maintenance of the goods, services, and infrastructure necessary for the fulfillment of human capabilities. Anything less than this means that MNEs, or their suppliers, are not respecting employees as ends in themselves.

VII. ECONOMIC CONSIDERATIONS

The failure of many MNEs to meet the standards required by the application of the doctrine of respect for persons has not gone unnoticed. Through consumer boycotts, letter writing campaigns, opinion columns, and shareholder resolutions, activists have been successful in persuading some MNEs to implement changes. For example, Nike recently created the position of Vice President for Corporate Social Responsibility, hired a public affairs specialist to fill the position, and began to aggressively respond to activist complaints. In a recent open letter to its critics Nike concedes that "Several years ago, in our earlier expansion into certain countries, we had lots to learn about manufacturing practices and how to improve them.[26] However, Nike reports that it has fully embraced the goals of higher wages,

the elimination of child labor, and the creation of better working conditions. In short, Nike's response to its critics is "... guess what? You've already succeeded!"[27] Asked whether or not Nike would have made improvements without public pressure, a Nike official responded "Probably not as quickly, probably not to the degree."[28] Thus, ethical theory and a significant number of citizens of good will stand as one on this issue....

Put simply, workers whose minimum daily caloric intakes are met, and who have basic non-food needs met, will have more energy and better attitudes at work; will be less likely to come to work ill; and will be absent with less frequency. Workers are thus likely to be more productive and loyal. Economists refer to a wage that if reduced would make the firm worse off because of a decrease in worker productivity as the efficiency wage. Empirical evidence supports the view that increased productivity resulting from better nutrition offsets the cost of higher wages.[29] Thus, if workers are being paid less than the efficiency wage in a particular market there are good economic reasons, in addition to moral reasons, for raising wages. Higher productivity per hour could also help alleviate the need for overtime work and facilitate a 48 hour work week....

Two points concerning wages should be distinguished. First, conclusions concerning the impact of U.S. minimum wage legislation on unemployment cannot automatically be assumed to apply to developing nations. Careful study of the unique conditions of those labor markets is necessary before corollary claims can be assessed. Nonetheless, the textbook view rests significantly on studies concerning the U.S. labor market. As such, we believe that the burden of proof remains with those who maintain that increased labor costs must inevitably result in higher unemployment. Second, we wish to emphasize that we are not taking a position in this essay on increasing federally mandated minimum wages in developing nations. Rather, our contention is that it is economically feasible for MNEs to voluntarily raise wages in factories in developing economies without causing increases in unemployment. MNEs may choose to raise wages while maintaining existing employment levels. Increased labor costs that are not offset by greater productivity may be passed on to consumers, or, if necessary, absorbed through internal cost-cutting measures such as reductions in executive compensation.

VIII. CONCLUSION

As Kant argues, it is by acting in a manner consistent with human dignity that persons raise themselves above all things. Insofar as we recognize the dignity of humanity, we have an obligation to respect both ourselves and others.[30] We have argued that MNE managers who encourage or tolerate violations of the rule of law; use coercion; allow unsafe working conditions; and provide below subsistence wages, disavow their own dignity and that of their workers. In so doing, they disrespect themselves and their workers. Further, we have argued that this moral analysis is not undermined by economic considerations. Significantly, MNEs are in many ways more readily able to honor the humanity of workers. This is because MNEs typically have well defined internal decision structures that, unlike individual moral agents, are not susceptible to weakness of the will.[31] For this reason, MNE managers who recognize a duty to respect their employees, and those of their subcontractors, are well positioned to play a constructive role in ensuring that the dignity of humanity is respected.

NOTES

1. See, for example, Susan Chandler, "Look Who's Sweating Now," *BusinessWeek*, October 16, 1995; Steven Greenhouse, "Sweatshop Raids Cast Doubt on an Effort By Garment Makers to Police the Factories," *New York Times*, July 18, 1997; and Gail Edmondson et al., "Workers in Bondage," *BusinessWeek*, November 27, 2000.

2. For the purposes of this paper we define the term as any workplace in which workers are typically subject to two or more of the following conditions: income for a 48 hour work week less than the overall poverty rate for that country; systematic forced overtime; systematic health and safety risks that stem from negligence or the willful disregard of employee welfare; coercion; systematic deception that places workers at risk; and underpayment of earnings.

3. Immanuel Kant, *Foundations of the Metaphysics of Morals*, Lewis White Beck, trans. (New York: Macmillan, 1990), 46.

4. In making this claim we explicitly reject the conclusion reached by Andrew Wicks that one must

either "fully embrace Kant's metaphysics" or "break from the abstract universalism of Kant." See Andrew Wicks, "How Kantian A Theory of Capitalism," *Business Ethics Quarterly*, The Ruffin Series: Special Issue 1 (1998): 65.

5. Kant, *Foundations of the Metaphysics of Morals*, 52.

6. Immanuel Kant, *The Metaphysics of Morals*, Mary Gregor, trans., (Cambridge: Cambridge University Press, 1991), 230.

7. Ibid.

8. Ibid., 255.

9. Thomas Hill Jr., *Dignity and Practical Reason in Kant's Moral Theory* (Ithaca: Cornell University Press, 1992).

10. Ibid., 40–41.

11. Kant, *Metaphysics of Morals*, 245.

12. Ibid., 192–193 and 196–197.

13. Norman E. Bowie, *Business Ethics: A Kantian Perspective* (Malden, Mass.: Blackwell, 1999). See 41–81 for further discussion of the second categorical imperative.

14. Kant, *Metaphysics of Morals*, 255.

15. Pamela Varley, ed., *The Sweatshop Quandary: Corporate Responsibility on the Global Frontier* (Washington D.C., Investor Responsibility Research Center, 1998), 185–186.

16. Ibid., 85.

17. For a fuller discussion of this matter see Bowie, *Business Ethics: A Kantian Perspective*, esp. chap. 2.

18. Varley, ed., *The Sweatshop Quandary*. 95.

19. Better rule of law is associated with higher per capita income. See *World Development Report 2000/2001: Attacking Poverty* (New York: Oxford University Press, 2000), 103.

20. Ibid., 102. See also the United National Development Programme's *Human Development Report 2000* (New York: Oxford University Press, 2000), esp. 37–38.

21. Denis G. Arnold, "Coercion and Moral Responsibility," *American Philosophical Quarterly* 38 (2001): 53–67. The view of psychological coercion employed here is a slightly revised version of the view defended in that essay. In particular, the condition that cases of psychological coercion always involve psychological compulsion has been replaced with the condition that cases of psychological coercion always involve the victim's compliance with the threat.

22. Varley, ed., *The Sweatshop Quandary*. 72.

23. International Labour Organization, "SafeWork: ILO Standards on Safety and Health." Available at http://www.ilo.org/public/english/protection/safework/standard.htm.

24. Aaron Bernstein, "Sweatshop Reform: How to Solve the Standoff," *BusinessWeek,* May 3, 1999.
25. Self-esteem is grounded in the conscious recognition of one's dignity as a rational being.
26. Nike, "An Open Letter Response to USAS Regarding Their National Protest of Nike Through August 16, 2000." Available at http://nikebiz.com/labor/usas_let.shtml.
27. Ibid.
28. Frank Denton, "Close Look at Factory for Nikes," *Wisconsin State Journal,* July 30, 2000.
29. C. J. Bliss and N. H. Stern, "Productivity, Wages, and Nutrition, 2: Some Observations. *Journal of Development Economics* 5 (1978): 363–398. For theoretical discussion see C. J. Bliss and N. H. Stern, "Productivity, Wages, and Nutrition, 1: The Theory," *Journal of Development Economics* 5 (1978): 331–362.
30. Kant, *Foundations of the Metaphysics of Morals,* 255.
31. For a fuller defense of this position see Peter A. French, *Corporate Ethics* (Fort Worth, Tex.: Hartcourt Brace, 1995), 79–87.

✧ QUESTIONS FOR ANALYSIS

1. What steps have human rights activists taken in recent years to pressure multinational enterprises (MNEs) to improve the conditions of workers in foreign sweatshops?
2. What objections have many economists raised to this pressure from human rights activists?
3. How do Arnold and Bowie use Kant's ethical philosophy to address sweatshop issues? How do they understand Kant's second formulation of the categorical imperative?
4. What does treating the humanity of persons as ends in themselves require in a business context?
5. What were the advantages of outsourcing to other nations for the MNEs?
6. Why do Arnold and Bowie believe that MNEs have a duty to ensure that the dignity of workers is respected in the factories of subcontractors doing work for the MNEs?
7. Why should MNEs encourage respect for the rule of law in countries where they do business?
8. What are examples of coercion in outsourcing? Why is coercion wrong?
9. Why do MNEs have a moral obligation to ensure decent working conditions for workers, whether or not required under the laws of that country?
10. How should "living wage" be defined? Why do MNEs have a moral obligation to provide adequate wages?

Illegal Immigrants, Health Care, and Social Responsibility

JAMES F. DWYER

James F. Dwyer is an Associate Professor of Bioethics and Humanities at the Upstate Medical University, State University of New York, in Syracuse. He specializes in ethical research on health, justice and democracy; global health and ethics; and personal, professional, and social responsibility. He received his Ph.D. in philosophy from the University of California, Irvine, and previously taught at New York University.

This essay argues that the issue of health care for undocumented immigrants is inappropriately conceptualized in the public and scholarly debates. He urges that the issues be considered in terms of social justice and social responsibility. He rejects the views of "nationalists" who claim that people who have no right to be in a country have no rights to any benefits in that country, including health care. He also rejects, as inadequate, arguments that access to health care is a basic human right that should be provided to everyone, regardless of their status in a country.

"Illegal Immigrants, Health Care, and Social Responsibility," *Hastings Center Report* 34:5 (2004), 34–41. Reprinted with permission from John Wiley & Sons, Inc.

Illegal immigrants form a large and disputed group in many countries. Indeed, even the name is in dispute. People in this group are referred to as illegal immigrants, illegal aliens, irregular migrants, undocumented workers, or, in French, as *sans papiers*. Whatever they are called, their existence raises an important ethical question: Do societies have an ethical responsibility to provide health care for them and to promote their health?

This question often elicits two different answers. Some people—call them nationalists—say that the answer is obviously no. They argue that people who have no right to be in a country should not have rights to benefits in that country. Other people—call them humanists—say that the answer is obviously yes. They argue that all people should have access to health care. It's a basic human right.

I think both these answers are off the mark. The first focuses too narrowly on what we owe people based on legal rules and formal citizenship. The other answer focuses too broadly, on what we owe people qua human beings. We need a perspective that is in between, that adequately responds to the phenomenon of illegal immigration and adequately reflects the complexity of moral thought. There may be important ethical distinctions, for example, among the following groups: U.S. citizens who lack health insurance, undocumented workers who lack health insurance in spite of working full time, medical visitors who fly to the United States as tourists in order to obtain care at public hospitals, foreign citizens who work abroad for subcontractors of American firms, and foreign citizens who live in impoverished countries. I believe that we—U.S. citizens—have ethical duties in all of these situations, but I see important differences in what these duties demand and how they are to be explained.

In this paper, I want to focus on the situation of illegal immigrants. I will discuss several different answers to the question about what ethical responsibility we have to provide health care to illegal immigrants. (I shall simply assume that societies have an ethical obligation to provide their own citizens with a reasonably comprehensive package of health benefits.) The answers that I shall discuss tend to conceptualize the ethical issues in terms of individual desert, professional ethics, or human rights. I want to discuss the limitations of each of these approaches and to offer an alternative. I shall approach the issues in terms of social responsibility and discuss the moral relevance of work. In doing so, I tend to pull bioethics in the direction of social ethics and political philosophy. That's the direction I think it should be heading. But before I begin the ethical discussion, I need to say more about the phenomenon of illegal immigration.

HUMAN MIGRATION

People have always moved around. They have moved for political, environmental, economic, and familial reasons. They have tried to escape war, persecution, discrimination, famine, environmental degradation, poverty, and a variety of other problems. They have tried to find places to build better lives, earn more money, and provide better support for their families. A strong sense of family responsibility has always been an important factor behind migration.[1]

But while human migration is not new, *illegal* immigration is, since only recently have nation-states tried to control and regulate the flow of immigration. Societies have always tried to exclude people they viewed as undesirable: criminals, people unable to support themselves, people with contagious diseases, and certain ethnic or racial groups. But only in the last hundred years or so have states tried in a systematic way to control the number and kinds of immigrants.

In contrast, what the Athenian polis tried to control was not immigration, but citizenship. Workers, merchants, and scholars came to Athens from all over the Mediterranean world. They were free to work, trade, and study in Athens, although they were excluded from the rich political life that citizens enjoyed. Today, political states try to control both citizenship and residency.

Modern attempts to control residency are not remarkably effective. There are illegal immigrants residing and working all over the globe. When people think about illegal immigrants, they tend to focus on Mexicans in the United States or North Africans in France. But the phenomenon is really much more diverse and complex. Illegal immigrants come from hundreds of countries and go wherever they can get work. There are undocumented workers from Indonesia in Malaysia, undocumented workers from Haiti in the Dominican Republic, and undocumented workers from Myanmar in Thailand. Thailand is an interesting example because it is both a source of and a destination for undocumented workers: while many people from poorer countries have gone to work in Thailand, many Thais have gone to work in richer countries.

Since illegal activities are difficult to measure, and people are difficult to count, we do not know exactly how many people are illegal immigrants. The following estimates provide a rough idea. The total number of illegal immigrants in the U.S. is probably between five and eight million. About 30–40 percent of these people entered the country legally, but overstayed their visas. Of all the immigrants in Europe, about one third are probably illegal immigrants. A small country like Israel has about 125,000 foreign workers (not counting Palestinians). About 50,000 of these are in the country illegally.[2]

I believe that a sound ethical response to the question of illegal immigration requires some understanding of the work that illegal immigrants do. Most undocumented workers do the jobs that citizens often eschew. They do difficult and disagreeable work at low wages for small firms in the informal sector of the economy. In general, they have the worst jobs and work in the worst conditions in such sectors of the economy as agriculture, construction, manufacturing, and the food industry. They pick fruit, wash dishes, move dirt, sew clothes, clean toilets....

In the global economy, in which a company can shift its manufacturing base with relative ease to a country with cheaper labor, illegal immigrants often perform work that cannot be shifted overseas. Toilets have to be cleaned, dishes have to be washed, and children have to be watched *locally*. This local demand may help to explain a relatively new trend: the feminization of migration. Migrants used to be predominantly young men, seeking work in areas such as agriculture and construction. But that pattern is changing. More and more women migrants are employed in the service sector as, for example, maids, nannies, and health care aides.

Women migrants are also employed as sex workers. The connection between commercial sex and illegal immigration is quite striking. As women in some societies have more money, choices, schooling, and power, they are unwilling to work as prostitutes. These societies seem to be supplying their demands for commercial sex by using undocumented workers from poorer countries. Before brothels were legalized in the Netherlands, about 40 to 75 percent of the prostitutes who worked in Amsterdam were undocumented workers....

Some of the worst moral offenses occur in the trafficking of human beings, but even here it is important to see a continuum of activities. Sometimes traffickers simply provide transportation in exchange for payment. Sometimes, they recruit people with deceptive promises and false accounts of jobs, then transport them under horrible and dangerous conditions. If and when the immigrants arrive in the destination country, they are controlled by debt, threat, and force. Some become indentured servants, working without pay for a period of time. Others are controlled by physical threats or threats to expose their illegal status. A few are enslaved and held as property.

Not all illegal immigrants are victims, however, and an accurate account of illegal immigration, even if only sketched, must capture some of its complexity. My task is to consider how well different ethical frameworks deal with that complexity.

A MATTER OF DESERT

The abstract ethical question of whether societies have a responsibility to provide health care for illegal immigrants sometimes becomes a concrete political issue. Rising health care costs, budget reduction programs, and feelings of resentment sometimes transform the ethical question into a political debate. This has happened several times in the United States. In 1996, the Congress debated and passed the "Illegal Immigration Reform and Immigrant Responsibility Act." This law made all immigrants ineligible for Medicaid, although it did allow the federal government to reimburse states for emergency treatment of illegal immigrants.

In 1994, the citizens of California debated Proposition 187, an even more restrictive measure. This ballot initiative proposed to deny publicly funded health care, social services, and education to illegal immigrants. This law would have required publicly funded health care facilities to deny care, except in medical emergencies, to people who could not prove that they were U.S. citizens or legal residents.

This proposition was approved by 59 percent of the voters. It was never implemented because courts found that parts of it conflicted with other laws, but the deepest arguments for and against it remain very much alive. Because they will probably surface again, at a different time or in different place, it is worthwhile evaluating the ethical frameworks that they assume.

The first argument put forward is that illegal aliens should be denied public benefits because they are in the country illegally. Although it is true that illegal aliens have violated a law by entering or remaining in the country, it is not clear what the moral implication of this point is. Nothing about access to health care follows from the mere fact that illegal aliens have violated a law. Many people break many different laws. Whether a violation of a law should disqualify people from public services probably depends on the nature and purpose of the services, the nature and the gravity of the violation, and many other matters.

Consider one example of a violation of the law. People sometimes break tax laws by working off the books. They do certain jobs for cash in order to avoid paying taxes or losing benefits. Moreover, this practice is probably quite common. I recently asked students in two of my classes if they or anyone in their extended family had earned money that was not reported as taxable income. In one class, all but two students raised their hands. In the other class, every hand went up.

No one has suggested that health care facilities deny care to people suspected of working off the books. But undocumented work is also a violation of the law. Furthermore, it involves an issue of fairness because it shifts burdens onto others and diminishes funding for important purposes. Of course, working off the books and working without a visa are not alike in all respects. But without further argument, nothing much follows about whether it is right to deny benefits to people who have violated a law.

Proponents of restrictive measures also appeal to an argument that combines a particular conception of desert with the need to make trade-offs. Proponents of California's Proposition 187 stated that, "while our own citizens and legal residents go wanting, those who chose to enter our country ILLEGALLY get royal treatment at the expense of the California taxpayer."[3] Proponents noted that the legislature maintained programs that included free prenatal care for illegal aliens but increased the amount that senior citizens must pay for prescription drugs. They then asked, "Why should we give more comfort and consideration to illegal aliens than to *our* own needy American citizens?"

The rhetorical question is part of the argument. I would restate the argument in the following way: Given the limited public budget for health care, U.S. citizens and legal residents are more deserving of benefits than are illegal aliens. This argument frames the issue as a choice between competing goods in a situation of limited resources.

There is something right and something wrong about this way of framing the issue. What is right is the idea that in all of life, individual and political, we have to choose between competing goods. A society cannot have everything: comprehensive and universal health care, good public schools, extensive public parks and beaches, public services, and very low taxes. What is false is the idea that we have to choose between basic health care for illegal aliens and basic health care for citizens. Many other trade-offs are possible, including an increase in public funding.

The narrow framework of the debate pits poor citizens against illegal aliens in a battle for health care resources. Within this framework, the issue is posed as one of desert. Avoiding the idea of desert is impossible. After all, justice is a matter of giving people their due—giving them what they deserve. But a narrow conception of desert seems most at home in allocating particular goods that go beyond basic needs, in situations where the criteria of achievement and effort are very clear. For example, if we are asked to give an award for the best student in chemistry, a narrow notion of desert is appropriate and useful. But publicly funded health care is different and requires a broader view of desert.

The discussion of restrictive measures often focuses on desert, taxation, and benefits. Proponents tend to picture illegal immigrants as free riders who are taking advantage of public services without contributing to public funding. Opponents are quick to note that illegal immigrants do pay taxes. They pay sales tax, gas tax, and value-added tax. They often pay income tax and property tax. But do they pay enough tax to cover the cost of the services they use? Or more generally, are illegal immigrants a net economic gain or a net economic loss for society?

Instead of trying to answer the economic question, I want to point out a problem with the question itself. The question about taxation and benefits tends to portray society as a private business venture. On the business model, investors should benefit in proportion to the funds they put into the venture. This may be an appropriate model for some business ventures, but it is not an adequate model for all social institutions and benefits. The business model is not an adequate model for thinking about voting, legal defense, library services, minimum wages, occupational safety, and many other social benefits.

Consider my favorite social institution: the public library. The important question here is not whether some people use more library services than they pay for through taxation, which is obviously true. Some people pay relatively high taxes but never use the library, while others pay relatively low taxes but use the library quite often. In thinking about the public library, we should consider questions such as the following. What purposes does the library serve? Does it promote education, provide opportunity, and foster public life? Does it tend to ameliorate or exacerbate social injustice? Given the library's purposes, who should count as its constituents or members? And what are the rights and responsibilities of the library users? In the following sections, I shall consider analogous questions about illegal immigrants and the social institutions that promote health.

A MATTER OF PROFESSIONAL ETHICS

Some of the most vigorous responses to restrictive measures have come from those who consider the issue within the framework of professional ethics.

Tal Ann Ziv and Bernard Lo, for example, argue that "cooperating with Proposition 187 would undermine professional ethics."[4] In particular, they argue that cooperating with this kind of restrictive measure is inconsistent with physicians' "ethical responsibilities to protect the public health, care for persons in medical need, and respect patient confidentiality."[5]

Restrictive measures may indeed have adverse effects on the public health. For example, measures that deny care to illegal aliens, or make them afraid to seek care, could lead to an increase in tuberculosis. And physicians do have a professional obligation to oppose measures that would significantly harm the public health. But the public health argument has a serious failing, if taken by itself. It avoids the big issue of whether illegal immigrants should be considered part of the public and whether public institutions should serve their health needs. Instead of appealing to an inclusive notion of social justice, the argument suggests how the health of illegal immigrants may influence citizens' health, and then appeals to citizens' sense of prudence. The appeal to prudence is not wrong, but it avoids the larger ethical issues.

The second argument against Proposition 187 is that it restricts confidentiality in ways that are not justified. It requires health care facilities to report people suspected of being in the country illegally and to disclose additional information to authorities. Ziv and Lo argue that "Proposition 187 fails to provide the usual ethical justifications for overriding patient confidentiality."[6] Reporting a patient's "immigration status serves no medical or public health purpose, involves no medical expertise, and is not a routine part of medical care."[7] Thus this restriction on confidentiality is a serious violation of professional ethics.

But if restrictive measures work as designed, issues of confidentiality may not even arise. Illegal aliens will be deterred from seeking medical care or will be screened out before they see a doctor. Thus the issue of screening may be more important than the issue of confidentiality. First, if the screening is carried out, it should not be by physicians, because it is not their role to act as agents for the police or the immigration service. Professional ethics requires some separation of social roles, and terrible things have happened when physicians have become agents of political regimes. The bigger issue, though, is not who should do the screening, but whether it should be done at all.

Ziv and Lo note that "clerks will probably screen patients for their immigration status, just as they currently screen them for their insurance status."[8] They object to this arrangement, and they argue that physicians bear some responsibility for arrangements that conflict with professional ethics. In their view, screening out illegal aliens conflicts with physicians' ethical responsibility to "care for persons in medical need."[9]

This claim is important, but ambiguous. It could mean simply that physicians have an obligation to attend to anyone who presents to them in need of emergency care. That seems right. It would be wrong not to stabilize and save someone in a medical emergency. It would be inhumane, even morally absurd, to let someone die because her visa had expired. But a claim that physicians have an enduring obligation to provide emergency care is consistent with measures like Proposition 187 and the 1996 federal law.

The claim might also mean that the selection of patients should be based only on medical need, never on such factors as nationality, residency, immigration status, or ability to pay. This is a very strong claim. It means that all private practice is morally wrong. It means that most national health care systems are too restrictive. It means that transplant lists for organs donated in a particular country should be open to everyone in the world. It might even mean that physicians have an ethical responsibility to relocate to places where the medical need is the greatest. I shall say more about the strong claim in the next section. Here I just want to note one point. This claim goes well beyond professional ethics. It is an ethical claim that seems to be based on a belief about the nature of human needs and human rights.

Finally, Ziv and Lo's claim about physicians' responsibility to care for people in medical need might be stronger than the claim about emergency care but weaker than the universal claim. Perhaps we should interpret it to mean that it is wrong to turn patients away when society has no other provisions and institutions to provide them with basic care. The idea then is that society should provide all

members with basic health care and that physicians have some responsibility to work to realize this idea.

There is something appealing and plausible about this interpretation, but it too goes beyond professional ethics. It has more to do with the nature of social justice and social institutions than with the nature of medical practice. It makes an ethical claim based on a belief about social responsibility and an assumption that illegal aliens are to be counted as members of society. I shall try to elaborate this belief and assumption later.

Let me sum up my main points so far. Political measures that restrict medical care for illegal immigrants often involve violations of professional ethics, and health care professionals should oppose such measures. But the framework of professional ethics is not adequate for thinking about the larger ethical issues. It fails to illuminate the obligation to provide medical care. Furthermore, it fails to consider factors such as work and housing that may have a profound impact on health. In the next two sections I shall consider broader frameworks and discourses.

A MATTER OF HUMAN RIGHTS

To deal with the issue of health care and illegal immigrants, some adopt a humanistic framework and employ a discourse of human rights. They tend to emphasize the right of all human beings to medical treatment, as well as the common humanity of aliens and citizens, pointing to the arbitrary nature of national borders.

National borders can seem arbitrary. Distinctions based on national borders seem even more arbitrary when one studies how borders were established and the disparities in wealth and health that exist between countries. Since it doesn't seem just that some people should be disadvantaged by arbitrary boundaries, it may also seem that people should have the right to emigrate from wherever they are and to immigrate to wherever they wish. But does this follow from the fact that national borders can be seen as arbitrary?

John Rawls thinks not. He writes:

> It does not follow from the fact that boundaries are historically arbitrary that their role in the Law of Peoples cannot be justified. On the contrary,

to fix on their arbitrariness is to fix on the wrong thing. In the absence of a world state, there *must* be boundaries of some kind, which when viewed in isolation will seem arbitrary, and depend to some degree on historical circumstances.[10]

Even if boundaries depend on historical circumstances, a defined territory may allow a people to form a government that acts as their agent in a fair and effective way. A defined territory may allow a people to form a government that enables them to take responsibility for the natural environment, promote the well-being of the human population, deal with social problems, and cultivate just political institutions.[11]

From functions like these, governments derive a qualified right to regulate immigration. This right is not an unlimited right of communal self-determination. Societies do not have a right to protect institutions and ways of life that are deeply unjust. Furthermore, even when a society has a right to regulate immigration, there are ethical questions about whether and how the society should exercise that right. And there are ethical questions about how immigrants should be treated in that society.

The committed humanist, who begins with reflections on the arbitrary nature of national boundaries, sometimes reaches the same conclusion as the global capitalist: that all restrictions on labor mobility are unjustified. In their different ways, both the humanist and the capitalist devalue distinctions based on political community. To be sure, there is much to criticize about existing political communities, but we need to be cautious about some of the alternatives. Michael Walzer warns us about two possibilities. He says that to "tear down the walls of the state is not ... to create a world without walls, but rather to create a thousand petty fortresses."[12] Without state regulation of immigration, local communities may become more exclusionary, parochial, and xenophobic. Walzer also notes another possibility: "The fortresses, too, could be torn down: all that is necessary is a global state sufficiently powerful to overwhelm the local communities. Then the result would be ... a world of radically deracinated men and women."[13]

Of course, the humanist need not be committed to an abstract position about open borders. The humanist might accept that states have a qualified right to regulate immigration, but insist that all states must respect the human rights of all immigrants—legal and illegal. That idea makes a lot of sense, although much depends on how we specify the content of human rights.

The idea that all human beings should have equal access to all beneficial health care is often used to critique both national and international arrangements. In an editorial in the *New England Journal of Medicine,* Paul Farmer reflects on the number of people who go untreated for diseases such as tuberculosis and HIV. He writes:

> Prevention is, of course, always preferable to treatment. But epidemics of treatable infectious diseases should remind us that although science has revolutionized medicine, we still need a plan for ensuring equal access to care. As study after study shows the power of effective therapies to alter the course of infectious disease, we should be increasingly reluctant to reserve these therapies for the affluent, low-incidence regions of the world where most medical resources are concentrated. Excellence without equity looms as the chief human-rights dilemma of health care in the 21st century.[14]

I too am critical of the gross inequalities in health within countries and between countries, but here I only want to make explicit the framework and discourse of Farmer's critique. His critique appeals to two ideas: that there is a lack of proportion between the medical resources and the burden of disease and that there is a human right to equal access.

What is wrong with the claim that equal access to health care is a human right? First, to claim something as a right is more of a conclusion than an argument. Such claims function more to summarize a position than to further moral discussion. A quick and simple appeal to a comprehensive right avoids all the hard questions about duties and priorities. When faced with grave injustices and huge inequalities, claiming that all human beings have a right to health care is easy. Specifying the kind of care to which people are entitled is harder. Specifying duties is harder yet. And getting those duties institutionalized is hardest of all.

In addition to the general problems with claims about rights, a problem more specific to the issue of illegal immigration exists. Since a claim based on a human right is a claim based on people's common humanity, it tends to collapse distinctions between people. Yet for certain purposes, it may be important to make distinctions and emphasize different responsibilities. We may owe different things to, for example, the poor undocumented worker in our country, the middle-class visitor who needs dialysis, the prince who wants a transplant, people enmeshed in the global economy, and the most marginalized people in poor countries.

Rather than claiming an essentially limitless right, it makes more sense to recognize a modest core of human rights and to supplement those rights with a robust account of social responsibility, social justice, and international justice. I do not know if there is a principled way to delineate exactly what should be included in the core of human rights.[15] But even a short list of circumscribed rights would have important consequences if societies took responsibility for trying to protect everyone from violations of these rights. Illegal immigrants are sometimes killed in transport, physically or sexually abused, held as slaves, kept in indentured servitude, forced to work in occupations, and denied personal property. These are clear violations of what should be recognized as human rights. But this core of recognized rights should be supplemented with an account of social justice and responsibility.

A MATTER OF SOCIAL RESPONSIBILITY

Framing the issue in terms of social responsibility helps to highlight one of the most striking features of illegal immigration: the employment pattern within society. As I noted before, illegal immigrants often perform the worst work for the lowest wages. Illegal immigrants are part of a pattern that is older and deeper than the recent globalization of the economy. Societies have often used the most powerless and marginalized people to do the most disagreeable and difficult work. Societies have used slaves, indentured servants, castes, minorities, orphans, poor children, internal migrants, and foreign migrants. Of course, the pattern is not exactly the same in every society, nor even in every industry within a society, but the similarities are striking.

I see the use of illegal immigrants as the contemporary form of the old pattern. But it is not a natural phenomenon beyond human control. It is the result of laws, norms, institutions, habits, and conditions in society, and of the conditions in the world at large. It is a social construction that we could try to reconstruct.

Some might object that no one forces illegal immigrants to take unsavory jobs and that they can return home if they wish. This objection is too simple. Although most undocumented workers made a voluntary choice to go to another country, they often had inadequate information and dismal alternatives, and voluntary return is not an attractive option when they have substantial debts and poor earning potential at home. More importantly, even a fully informed and voluntary choice does not settle the question of social justice and responsibility. We have gone through this debate before. As the industrial revolution developed, many people agreed to work under horrible conditions in shops, factories, and mines. Yet most societies eventually saw that freedom of contract was a limited part of a larger social ethic. They accepted a responsibility to address conditions of work and to empower workers, at least in basic ways. Decent societies now try to regulate child labor, workplace safety, minimum rates of pay, workers' rights to unionize, background conditions, and much more. But because of their illegal status, undocumented workers are often unable to challenge or report employers who violate even the basic standards of a decent society.

We need to take responsibility for preventing the old pattern from continuing, and the key idea is that of "taking responsibility." It is not the same as legal accountability, which leads one to think about determining causation, proving intention or negligence, examining excuses, apportioning blame, and assigning costs. Taking responsibility is more about seeing patterns and problems, examining background conditions, not passing the buck, and responding in appropriate ways. A society need not bear full causal responsibility in order to assume social responsibility.

Why should society take responsibility for people it tried to keep out of its territory, for people who are not social members? Because in many respects illegal immigrants are social members. Although they are not citizens or legal residents, they may be diligent workers, good neighbors, concerned parents, and active participants in community life. They are workers, involved in complex schemes of social co-operation. Many of the most exploited workers in the industrial revolution—children, women, men without property—were also not full citizens, but they were vulnerable people, doing often undesirable work, for whom society needed to take some responsibility. Undocumented workers' similar role in society is one reason that the social responsibility to care for them is different from the responsibility to care for medical visitors.

If a given society had the ethical conviction and political will, it could develop practical measures to transform the worst aspects of some work, empower the most disadvantaged workers, and shape the background conditions in which the labor market operates. The interests of the worst-off citizens and the interests of illegal immigrants need not be opposed. Practical measures may raise labor costs and increase the price of goods and services, as they should. We should not rely on undocumented workers to keep down prices on everything from strawberries to sex.

I can already hear the objection. "What you propose is a perfect recipe for increasing illegal immigration. All the practical measures that you suggest would encourage more illegal immigration." Whether improving the situation of the worst-off workers will increase illegal immigration is a complex empirical question. The answer probably depends on many factors. But even if transforming the worst work and empowering the worst-off workers leads to an increase in illegal immigration, countries should take those steps. Although we have a right to regulate immigration, considerations of justice constrain the ways we can pursue that aim. A society might also decrease illegal immigration by decriminalizing the killing of illegal immigrants, but no one thinks that would be a reasonable and ethical social policy. Nor do I think that the old pattern of using marginalized people is a reasonable and ethical way to regulate immigration.

I have left out of my account the very point with which I began, namely, health and health care, and I ended up talking about work and social responsibility. Surely work and social responsibility are at the heart of the matter. Where then does health care fit in?

Good health care can, among other things, prevent death and suffering, promote health and well-being, respond to basic needs and vulnerabilities, express care and solidarity, contribute to equality of opportunity, monitor social problems (such as child abuse or pesticide exposure), and accomplish other important aims. But health care is just one means, and not always the most effective means, to these ends. To focus on access to and payment of health care is to focus our ethical concern too narrowly.

I believe that societies that attract illegal immigrants should pursue policies and practices that (1) improve the pay for and conditions of the worst forms of work; (2) structure and organize work so as to give workers more voice, power, and opportunity to develop their capacities; and (3) connect labor to unions, associations, and communities in ways that increase social respect for all workers. I cannot justify these claims in this paper, but I want to note how they are connected to health care. Providing health care for all workers and their families is a very good way to improve the benefit that workers receive for the worst forms of work, to render workers less vulnerable, and to express social and communal respect for them. These are good reasons for providing health care for all workers, documented and undocumented alike. And they express ethical concerns that are not captured by talking about human rights, public health, or the rights of citizens....

NOTES

1. See P. Warshall, "Human Flow," *Whole Earth* 108 (2002): 39–43.
2. These statistics are taken from the following sources: U.S. Immigration and Naturalization Service, "Illegal Alien Resident Population," available at http://www.ins.gov/graphics/aboutins/statistics/illegalalien/illegal.pdf, accessed October 1, 2002; B. Ghosh, *Huddled Masses and Uncertain Shores* (The Hague: Matinus Nijhoff Publishers, 1998); L. Platt, "The Working Caste," *The American Prospect* 13, Part 8 (2001): 32–36.
3. This and the following quotations are from the California Ballot Pamphlet, 1994, available at

http://www.holmes.uchastings.edu/cgi-bin/starfinder/5640/calprop/txt, accessed September 30, 2002.

4. T.A. Ziv and B. Lo, "Denial of Care to Illegal Immigrants," *NEJM* 332 (1995): 1095–1098.

5. Ibid., 1096.

6. Ibid., 1097.

7. Ibid.

8. Ibid., 1096.

9. Ibid.

10. J. Rawls, *The Law of Peoples* (Cambridge, Mass.: Harvard University Press, 1999), 39.

11. Compare Rawls, *The Law of Peoples*, 8.

12. M. Walzer, *Spheres of Justice* (New York: Basic Books, 1983), 39.

13. Ibid.

14. P. Farmer, "The Major Infectious Diseases in the World—To Treat or Not to Treat?" *NEJM* 345 (2001): 208–210.

15. Compare Rawls, *The Law of Peoples*, 79–80.

⚜ QUESTIONS FOR ANALYSIS

1. How does Dwyer understand "nationalists"? How does he understand "humanists" for the purposes of this essay? Why does Dwyer believe both are "off the mark" in analyzing the issue of health care for illegal immigrants?

2. How does Dwyer explain the prevalence around the globe of illegal immigration? What kind of work do they do?

3. How have the abstract ethical issues of health care for undocumented immigrants become a concrete political issue?

4. What was the goal of Proposition 187 in California? What arguments were put forth in its support?

5. Dwyer acknowledges that we must make choices among competing goods in a situation of limited resources. How does he claim this idea has been misused in the debate over medical care for illegal immigrants?

6. How would Proposition 187 and measures like it undermine the professional ethics of health professionals?

7. Do all human beings have a right to medical treatment? Does that right depend on whether or not they are in a country legally?

8. Why does Dwyer criticize the claim that health care is a human right? What does he suggest as a more modest alternative? Do you believe it is a human right?

9. Why does Dwyer believe the realities of illegal immigration mean that we as a society must take some social responsibility for their basic rights? Do you agree?

Female Genital Circumcision and Conventionalist Ethical Relativism

LORETTA M. KOPELMAN

Loretta M. Kopelman is Professor Emerita of Medical Humanities at the Brody School of Medicine, East Carolina University, in Greenville, North Carolina. She received her Ph.D. in philosophy from the University of Rochester, and has published extensively on medical ethics, the rights of women and children, and bias in allocating health care and making diagnoses.

She argues against tolerating the rites of female genital mutilalation around the world, even if they have cultural approval in some communities. Her analysis considers several different approaches to relativism that have been used to counsel tolerance of this mutilation.

Traditionally Masai girls from Kenya are circumcised at seven or eight in order to be eligible for marriage at fourteen or fifteen. Their fathers, however, are now arranging marriages for them at increasingly early ages, sometimes when they are only nine years old. A Kenya news account offers an economic explanation for this social change, saying that "fathers are motivated by greed and the desire to get their hands on the dowries they receive in exchange for their daughters as early as possible." They seek a top bride price, such as "two cows, several crates of beer and some money" before the girls are old enough to resist.[1] Masai girls want to go to school and escape marriages to men often as old as their fathers. Sometimes they run away and find sanctuary at a boarding school about an hour south of Nairobi, headed by Priscilla Nankurrai. She helps them get schooling, avoid arranged marriages, and obtain medical attention for their all-too-frequent emotional and physical scars. The girls' mothers may help them escape, although they risk beatings if discovered. A developmental consultant who is herself Masai, Naomi Kipury, says conservatives fiercely oppose schooling for girls because they believe "the girls will reject the traditions of Masai culture if they are allowed to go to school. I think some parents are trying to get their children out of school to marry them quickly and regain control. Education opens up a whole other world and they fear the girls will get lost from the community."[2]

This news account reminds us that what some of us view as child abuse, neglect, or exploitation is viewed by others as traditional family and cultural values. In many parts of the world female genital cutting, child marriages, and denying girls the same opportunities for schooling that boys receive are regarded as violations of the law. Female genital cutting … is viewed as mutilation and abuse in many parts of the world, including the United Kingdom, France, Canada, and the United States.[3] National medical societies such as the American Medical Association and influential international agencies including UNICEF, the International Federation of Gynecology and Obstetrics, and the World Health Organization (WHO) openly condemn and try to stop these practices. Around the world, women's groups protest the practice of female genital cutting and infibulation, denying that it is just a cultural issue and arguing that these rites should be treated with the same vigor as other human rights violations.[4]

These procedures involve the removal of some, or all, of the external female genitalia, denying women orgasms and causing disease, disability, and death in women, girls, and infants in these regions. These surgical rites, usually performed on girls between infancy and puberty, are intended to promote chastity, religion, group identity, cleanliness, health, family values, and marriage. Most of the people practicing this ritual are Muslim, but it is neither required by the Koran nor practiced in the spiritual center of Islam, Saudi Arabia.[5] These rites predate the introduction of Islam into these regions.

At least 80 million living women have had some form of this mutilation, and each year 4–5 million girls have it done.[6] It is hard to collect data, however, since these rites are technically illegal in many of these countries, the unenforced remnants of colonial days. The United Nations has a special ambassador on female genital mutilation; fashion model Waris Dirie, who, like some of the little Masai girls, ran away from her home in Somalia after undergoing a form of ritual circumcision making it impossible for her to have orgasms. She believes that these practices are wrong and should be stopped but warns that well-meaning Westerners may do more harm than good by attacking African practices. She urges them to use their energies to stop these rites in their own countries.[7] The Center for Disease Control estimates that around 48,000 girls currently living in the United States are likely to undergo these rites, over half of them living in the New York City area. Parents sometimes believe it is especially important to have these procedures done in the United States, since they view it as a sex-obsessed society where it is especially necessary to control female sexuality. Like the Masai fathers, these parents fear they will lose control of their daughters if they go uncircumcised. Immigrants generally get around laws prohibiting these rites by taking their girls back home or going to practitioners within their communities.

The U.S. federal laws are relatively new, however, and immigrants may not even know about them. Senator Pat Schroeder helped frame and pass the federal law upon hearing of the plight of Fauziy Kasinga.[8] In 1994, with the help of her female relatives, she fled Togo after learning she was about to be mutilated. She was imprisoned in the United States for illegal immigration but ultimately was allowed to stay. Her case set a precedent that female genital mutilation is a form of persecution.[9] In what follows, I argue against tolerating these rites as having cultural approval in these communities. I begin by defining some terms and clarifying the problem, since "female circumcision" and "relativism" have many different meanings.

DEFINING TERMS AND SETTING THE PROBLEM

Female genital cutting or circumcision is commonly classified according to three types. Type 1 circumcision is the removal of the clitoral hood or prepuce (skin around the clitoris). Type 2, or intermediary circumcision, is the removal of the entire clitoris and most or all of the labia minora. Type 3, or pharaonic circumcision, is the removal of the clitoris, labia minora, and parts of the labia majora. Infibulation refers to stitching shut the wound to the vulva from genital cutting, leaving a tiny opening so that the woman can pass urine and menstrual flow.

People who want to continue these practices resent crosscultural criticisms, seeing them as assaults on their social traditions and identity. A version of ethical relativism supports their judgment, holding that people from other cultures have no legitimate basis for such condemnation. Anthony Flew defines ethical relativism as follows: "To be a relativist about values is to maintain that there are no universal standards of good and bad, right and wrong."[10] To avoid confusion with other definitions of "ethical relativism," I will, following Louis P. Pojam,[11] call this position *conventionalist ethical relativism*. It denies the existence of any underlying universal moral principles among cultures, asserting that moral principles depend entirely on cultural notions and acceptances. It rejects all forms of objectivism (a view that social differences can have underlying similarities with universal validity).[12] David Hume disavowed

conventionalist ethical relativism when he wrote, "Many of the forms of breeding are arbitrary and casual; but the thing expressed by them is still the same. A Spaniard goes out of his own house before his guest, to signify that he leaves him master of all. In other countries, the landlord walks out last, as a common mark of deference and regard."[13]

Conventionalist ethical relativism is different from, although sometimes confused with, certain noncontroversial views.[14] For example, descriptive relativism holds that notions of moral right and wrong vary among cultures (sometimes called the diversity thesis). Conventionalist ethical relativism, however, goes beyond this to claim that no crosscultural moral judgments have moral force, since something is wrong or right only by the standards of some cultural group.[15] Conventionalist ethical relativism does not stop at asserting that different rankings and interpretations of moral values or rules by different groups exist but goes on to maintain that we have no basis for saying that one is better than another. Anthropologists sometimes use the locution "ethical relativism" differently, to mean what philosophers would call "descriptive relativism." Some simply use "ethical relativism" to signal that we should be very careful about making crosscultural judgments or that it is very hard to discern underlying similarities. To add to the confusion, both philosophers and anthropologists have used the locution "cultural relativism" to refer to normative as well as descriptive views.[16]

In addition, some philosophers and anthropologists seem to advocate a weaker version of "ethical relativism," especially those attracted to postmodern views. They hold that some crosscultural judgments have moral force but show disdain for substantive and fully articulated moral theories clothed as purely rational, abstract, and universal. For example, Susan Sherwin maintains that traditional moral theorists generally support the subservience of women and concludes, "Feminist moral relativism remains absolutist on the question of the moral wrong of oppression but is relativist on other moral matters."[17] She argues that female circumcision is wrong. By maintaining that some judgments have crosscultural moral authority, however, Sherwin is not defending conventionalist ethical relativism in the sense defined.

Female genital cutting and infibulation serve as a test case for conventionalist ethical relativism because these rites have widespread approval within the cultures that practice them and thus on this theory are right. Yet they have widespread disapproval outside their cultures for reasons that seem compelling but on this theory lack any moral authority. Thus many discussions in ethics about female genital mutilation examine which forms of ethical relativism entail that genital cutting is a justifiable practice in societies that approve it.[18]

Despite its popularity, there is a substantial logical problem with conventionalist ethical relativism.[19] From the fact that different cultures have different moral codes or norms, it does not follow that there is no objective moral truth or standards of *any sort* underlying our different behavior. The relativists' conclusion about what is the case (there are no universal moral codes or standards or any sort) does not follow from premises about what people believe is true.[20]

In response to this logical problem the conventionalist ethical relativists might argue that our different social lives and codes offer the best evidence that there are no objective moral standards and that what is right or good is determined by social approval. Therefore, I propose to consider the evidence and argue that it does not support the plausibility of conventionalist ethical relativism or a justification for tolerance of female genital circumcision or infibulation....

REASONS FOR FEMALE GENITAL CUTTING

Investigators have identified five primary reasons for these rites: (1) religious requirement, (2) group identity, (3) cleanliness and health, (4) virginity, family honor, and morality, and (5) marriage goals, including greater sexual pleasure for men.[21] These investigators, who are members of cultures practicing female genital mutilation, report many factual errors and inconsistent beliefs about the procedure and the goals they believe these rites serve.[22] They therefore argue that the real reasons for continuing this practice in their respective

countries rest on ignorance about reproduction and sexuality and, furthermore, that these rites fail as means to fulfill established community goals.

Meets a Religious Requirement

According to these studies, the main reason given for performing female genital cutting and infibulation is that it is a religious requirement. Most of the people practicing this ritual are Muslims, but it is not a practice required by the Koran.[23] El Dareer writes that "there is nothing in the Koran to suggest that the Prophet [Mohammed] commanded that women be circumcised."[24] Female genital cutting and infibulation, moreover, is not practiced in the spiritual center of Islam, Saudi Arabia. Another reason for questioning this as a Muslim practice is that clitoridectomy and infibulation predate Islam, going back to the time of the pharaohs.[25]

Preserves Group Identity

According to the anthropologist Scheper-Hughes,[26] when Christian colonialists in Kenya introduced laws opposing the practice of female circumcision in the 1930s, African leader Kenyatta expressed a view still popular today:

> This operation is still regarded as the very essence of an institution which has enormous educational, social, moral, and religious implications, quite apart from the operation itself. For the present, it is impossible for a member of the [Kikuyu] tribe to imagine an initiation without clitoridectomy.... the abolition of *IRUA* [the ritual operation] will destroy the tribal symbol which identifies the age group and prevents the Kikuyu from perpetuating that spirit of collectivism and national solidarity which they have been able to maintain from time immemorial.[27]

In addition, the practice is of social and economic importance to many women who are paid for performing the rituals.[28]...

Helps to Maintain Cleanliness and Health

The belief that the practice advances health and hygiene is incompatible with stable data from surveys done in these cultures, where female genital mutilation has been linked to mortality or morbidity such as shock, infertility, infections, incontinence, maternal-fetal complications, and protracted labor. The tiny hole generally left to allow for the passage of blood and urine is a constant source of infection.[29]...

Although promoting health is given as a reason for female genital mutilation, many parents seem aware of its risks and try to reduce the morbidity and mortality by seeking good medical facilities. Some doctors and nurses perform the procedures for high fees or because they are concerned about the unhygienic techniques that traditional practitioners may use. In many parts of the world, however, these practices are illegal, and medical societies prohibit doctors and nurses from engaging in them even if it might reduce morbidity and mortality.[30]

Preserves Virginity and Family Honor and Prevents Immorality

Type 3 circumcision and infibulation is used to control women's sexual behavior by trying to keep women from having sexual intercourse before marriage or conceiving illegitimate children. In addition, many believe that types 2 and 3 circumcision are essential because uncircumcised women have excessive or even uncontrollable sexual drives. El Dareer, however, believes that this view is not consistently held in her culture, the Sudan, where women are respected and men would be shocked to apply this cultural view to members of their own families....

Furthers Marriage Goals, Including Greater Beauty for Women and Sexual Pleasure for Men

Those practicing female genital cutting not only believe that it promotes marriage goals, including greater sexual pleasure for men, but that it deprives women of nothing important, according to investigator Koso-Thomas. El Dareer and Abdalla also found widespread misconceptions that women cannot have orgasms and that sex cannot be directly pleasing to women coexisting with beliefs that these rites are needed to control women's libido and keep them from becoming "man-crazy."[31]

To survive economically, women in these cultures must marry, and they will not be acceptable marriage partners unless they have undergone this ritual surgery.[32] It is a curse, for example, to say that someone is the child of an uncircumcised woman.[33]

The widely held belief that infibulation enhances women's beauty and men's sexual pleasure makes it difficult for women who wish to marry to resist this practice.[34] They view uncut female genitals as ugly.[35]

For those outside these cultures, beliefs that these rites make women more beautiful are difficult to understand, especially when surveys show that many women in these cultures attribute keloid scars, urine retention, pelvic infections, puerperal sepsis, and obstetrical problems to infibulation.[36]...

DEBATES OVER CONVENTIONALIST ETHICAL RELATIVISM

Do moral judgments made by outsiders concerning these rites simply reflect their own moral codes, which carry no moral authority in another culture? For example, when international agencies such as UNICEF or WHO condemn female genital mutilation, do they just express a cluster of particular societal opinions having no moral standing in other cultures? Consider some key points of this debate over how to answer these questions.

How Do You Count Cultures?

Debates over female genital cutting and infibulation illustrate a difficulty for defenders of conventionalist ethical relativism concerning the problem of differentiating cultures. People who take the practice of female circumcision with them when they move to another nation claim that they continue to make up a distinct cultural group. Some who moved to Canada, the United States, France, and Britain, for example, resent laws that condemn the practice as child abuse, claiming interference in their culture. If ethical relativists are to appeal to cultural approval in making the final determination of what is good or bad and right or wrong, they must tell us how to distinguish one culture from another.

How exactly do we count or separate cultures? A society is not a nation-state because some social groups have distinctive identities within nations. If we do not define societies as nations, however, how do we distinguish among cultural groups, for example, well enough to say that an action is child abuse in one culture but not in another? Subcultures in nations typically overlap and have many variations. Even if we could count cultural groups well enough to say exactly how to distinguish one culture from another, how and when would this be relevant? How big or old or vital must a culture, subculture, or cult be in order to be recognized as a society whose moral distinctions are self-contained and self-justifying?

A related problem is that there can be passionate disagreement, ambivalence, or rapid changes within a culture or group over what is approved or disapproved, as illustrated in the Masai people of Kenya. According to conventionalist ethical relativism, where there is significant disagreement within a culture there is no way to determine what is right or wrong. But what disagreement is significant? As we saw, some people in these cultures, often those with higher education, strongly disapprove of female genital cutting and infibulation and work to stop it.[37] Are they in the same culture as their friends and relatives who approve of these rituals?

It seems more accurate to say that people may belong to distinct groups that overlap and have many variations. Members of the same family may belong to different professional groups and religions, or marry into families of different racial or ethnic origins. To say that we belong to overlapping cultures, however, makes it difficult to see conventionalist ethical relativism as a helpful theory for determining what is right or wrong. To say that something is right when it has cultural approval is useless if we cannot identify distinct cultures.

Do We Share Any Methods of Assessing False Beliefs and Inconsistencies in Moral Judgments?

Critics of conventionalist ethical relativism argue that a culture's moral and religious views are often intertwined with beliefs that are open to rational and empirical evaluation, and this can be a basis of crosscultural examination and intercultural moral criticism. Defenders of female genital cutting and infibulation do not claim that this practice is a moral or religious requirement and end the discussion; they are willing to give and defend reasons for their views. For example, advocates of female genital cutting and infibulation claim that it is a means of enhancing women's health and well-being.

Such claims are open to crosscultural examination because facts can be weighed to determine whether these practices promote the ends of health or really cause morbidity or mortality. Beliefs that the practice enhances fertility and promotes health, that women cannot have orgasms, and that allowing the baby's head to touch the clitoris during delivery causes death to the baby are incompatible with stable medical data.[38] Thus shared medical information and values offer an opening for genuine crosscultural discussion or criticism of the practice.

As we saw in the section discussing the morbidity and mortality associated with these rites, some moral claims can be evaluated in terms of their consistency with one another or as means to goals. These rituals are incompatible with goals to promote maternal-fetal health because they imperil mothers and infants. We need not rank values similarly with people in another culture (or our own) to have coherent discussions about casual relationships, such as what means are useful to promote the ends of maternal-fetal safety. Even if some moral or ethical (I use these terms interchangeably) judgments express unique cultural norms, then critics argue they may still be morally evaluated by another culture on the basis of their logical consistency and their coherence with stable and crossculturally accepted empirical information.

Defenders of conventionalist ethical relativism could respond that we do not *really understand* their views at all, and certainly not well enough to pick them apart. The alleged inconsistencies and mistaken beliefs we find do not have the same meaning to people raised in the culture in question. In short, some defenders of conventionalist ethical relativism argue that we cannot know enough about another culture to make any crosscultural moral judgments. We cannot really understand another society well enough to criticize it, they claim, because our feelings, concepts, or ways of reasoning are too different; our so-called ordinary moral views about what is permissible are determined by our upbringing and environments to such a degree that they cannot be transferred to other cultures.

Philosophers point out that there are two ways to understand this objection.[39] The first is that nothing counts as understanding another culture except being raised in it. If that is what is meant, then the objection is valid in a trivial way. But it does not address the important issue of whether we can comprehend well enough to make relevant moral distinctions or engage in critical ethical discussions about the universal human right to be free of oppression.

The second, and nontrivial, way to view this objection is that we cannot understand another society well enough to justify claiming to know what is right or wrong in that society or even to raise moral questions about what enhances or diminishes life, promotes opportunities, and so on. Yet we think we can do this very well. We ordinarily view international criticism and international responses concerning human rights violations, aggression, torture, and exploitation as important ways to show that we care about the rights and welfare of other people and, in some cases, think these responses have moral authority. Travelers to other countries, moreover, quickly understand that approved practices in their own country are widely condemned elsewhere, sometimes for good reasons.

People who deny the possibility of genuine crosscultural moral judgments must account for why we think we can and should make them, or why we sometimes agree more with people from other cultures than with our own neighbors about the moral assessments of aggression, oppression, capital punishment, abortion, euthanasia, rights to health care, and so on. International meetings also seem to employ genuinely crosscultural moral judgments when they seek to distinguish good from bad uses of technology and promote better environmental safety, health policies, and so on.

Do We Share Any Goals or Values?

Although we may implement them differently, *some* common goals are shared by people from different parts of the world, for example, the desirability of promoting people's health, happiness, opportunities, and cooperation, and the wisdom of stopping war, pollution, disease, oppression, torture, and exploitation. These common values help to make us a world community. By using shared methods of reasoning and evaluation, critics argue we can discuss how these goals should be implemented. We use these shared goals, critics

argue, to assess whether genital cutting is more like respect or oppression, more like enhancement or diminishment of opportunities, or more like pleasure or torture. Genuine differences among citizens of the world exist, but arguably we could not pick them out except against a background of similarities. Highlighting our differences presupposes that we share ways to do this.

Defenders of conventionalist ethical relativism argue that cross cultural moral judgments lack genuine moral authority and perpetuate the evils of absolutism, dogmatism, and cultural imperialism. People rarely admit to such transgressions, often enlisting medicine, religion, or science to arrive at an allegedly impartial, disinterested, and justified conclusion that they should "enlighten" and "educate" the "natives," "savages," or "infidels." Anthropologist Scheper-Hughes[40] and others assume that if we claim we can make moral judgments across cultures, we thereby claim that a particular culture knows best and has the right to impose its allegedly superior knowledge on other cultures.

This presupposition is incorrect because being able on some occasions to judge aspects of other cultures in a way that has moral force does not entail that one culture is always right, absolutism is legitimate, or we can impose our beliefs on others. Relativists sometimes respond that even if this is not a strict logical consequence, it is a practical result. Philosopher Susan Sherwin writes, "Many social scientists have endorsed versions of relativism precisely out of their sense that the alternative promotes cultural dominance. They may be making a philosophical error in drawing that conclusion, but I do not think that they are making an empirical one."[41] I find even this more modest conclusion problematic, as I explain in the next section.

Does Conventionalist Ethical Relativism Promote or Avoid Oppression or Cultural Imperialism?

Defenders of ethical relativism such as Scheper-Hughes often argue that their theoretical stance is an important way to avoid cultural imperialism. I argue, in contrast, that it causes rather than avoids oppression and cultural imperialism. Conventionalist ethical relativism entails not only the affirmation that female genital cutting is right in cultures that approve it but that anything with wide social approval is right, including slavery, war, discrimination, oppression, recism, and torture. That is, if saying that an act is right means that it has cultural approval, then it follows that culturally endorsed acts of war, oppression, enslavement, aggression, exploitation, racism, or torture are right. The disapproval of other cultures, on this view, is irrelevant in determining whether acts are right or wrong. Accordingly, the disapproval of people in other cultures, even victims of war, oppression, enslavement, aggression, exploitation, racism, or torture, does not count in deciding what is right or wrong except in their own culture.

Consequently, conventionalist ethical relativism instructs us to regard as morally irrelevant the approval or objections by people in other cultures; the approval and complaints are merely an expression of their own cultural preferences and have no moral standing whatsoever in the society that is engaging in the acts in question. I have argued that this leads to abhorrent conclusions.[42] If this theoretical stance is consistently held, it leads to the conclusion that we cannot make intercultural judgments with moral force about *any* socially approved form of oppression, including wars, torture, or exploitation of other groups. As long as these activities are approved in the society that does them, they are right. Yet the world community believed that it was making important crosscultural judgments with moral force when it criticized the Communist Chinese government for crushing prodemocracy student protest rallies, apartheid in South Africa, the Soviets for using psychiatry to suppress dissent, and the slaughter of ethnic groups in the former Yugoslavia and Rwanda. In each case, representatives from the criticized society usually said something like, "You don't understand why this is morally justified in our culture even if it would not be in your society." If conventionalist ethical relativism is plausible, these responses should be as well.

Defenders of conventionalist ethical relativism may respond that cultures sometimes overlap and hence the victims' protests within or between cultures ought to count. But this response raises two further difficulties. If it means that the views of people in other cultures have moral standing and oppressors *ought* to consider the views of victims, such judgments are incompatible with conventionalist ethical relativism. They are inconsistent with this theory because they are crosscultural judgments with moral authority. Second, as we noted, unless cultures are distinct, conventionalist ethical relativism is not a useful theory for establishing what is right or wrong.

Conventionalist ethical relativists who want to defend sound social, crosscultural, and moral judgments about the value of freedom, equality of opportunity, or human rights in other cultures seem to have two choices. On the one hand, if they agree that some crosscultural norms have moral authority, they should also agree that some intercultural judgments about female genital cutting and infibulation also may have moral authority. Sherwin is a relativist taking this route, thereby rejecting the conventionalist ethical relativism being criticized here.[43] On the other hand, if they defend this version of conventionalist ethical relativism yet make crosscultural moral judgments about the importance of values like tolerance, group benefits, and the survival of cultures, they will have to admit to an inconsistency in their arguments. For example, Scheper-Hughes advocates tolerance of other cultural value systems but fails to see that claim as being inconsistent.[44] She is saying that tolerance between cultures is *right,* yet this is a crosscultural moral judgment using a moral norm (tolerance). Similarly, relativists who say it is *wrong* to eliminate rituals that give meaning to other cultures are also inconsistent in making a judgment that presumes to have genuine crosscultural moral authority. Even the sayings sometimes used by defenders of ethical relativism (e.g., "When in Rome do as the Romans") mean that it is *morally permissible* to adopt all the cultural norms of whatever culture one finds oneself in.[45] Thus it is not consistent for defenders of conventionalist ethical relativism to make intercultural moral judgments about tolerance, group benefit, intersocietal respect, or cultural diversity.

I have argued that, given these difficulties, the burden of proof is on defenders of conventionalist ethical relativism. They must show why we cannot do something we think we sometimes ought to do and can do very well, namely, engage in intercultural moral discussion, cooperation, or criticism and give support to people whose welfare or rights are in jeopardy in other cultures. Defenders of conventionalist ethical relativism need to account for what seems to be the genuine moral authority of international professional societies that take moral stands, for example, about fighting pandemics, stopping wars, halting oppression, promoting health education, or eliminating poverty. Responses that our professional groups are themselves cultures of a sort seem plausible but are incompatible with conventionalist ethical relativism, as already discussed.

Some defenders of conventionalist ethical relativism object that eliminating important rituals from a culture risks destroying the society. Scheper-Hughes insists that these cultures cannot survive if they change such a central practice as female circumcision. This counterargument, however, is not decisive. Slavery, oppression, and exploitation are also necessary to some ways of life, yet few would defend these actions in order to preserve a society. El Dareer responds to this objection, moreover, by questioning the assumption that these cultures can survive only by continuing clitoridectomy or infibulation. These cultures, she argues, are more likely to be transformed by war, famine, disease, urbanization, and industrialization than by the cessation of this ancient ritual surgery. Further, if slavery, oppression, and exploitation are wrong, whether or not there are group benefits, then a decision to eliminate female genital mutilation should not depend on a process of weighing its benefits to the group.

It is also inconsistent to hold that group benefit is so important that other cultures should not interfere with local practices. This view elevates group benefit as an overriding crosscultural value, something that these ethical relativists claim cannot be justified. If there are no crosscultural values about what is wrong or right, a defender of conventionalist ethical relativism cannot consistently make statements such as,

one culture ought not interfere with others, we ought to be tolerant of other social views, every culture is equally valuable, or it is wrong to interfere with another culture.

Each claim is an intercultural moral judgment presupposing authority based on something other than a particular culture's approval.

CONCLUSION

Female genital cutting and infibulation cause disability, death, and disease among mothers, infants, and children. It leads to difficulty in consummating marriage, infertility, prolonged and obstructed labor, and increased morbidity and mortality. It strains the overburdened health care systems in developing countries where it is practiced with impunity. Investigators who have documented these health hazards come from these cultures but draw upon interculturally shared methods of discovery, evaluation, and explanation in concluding that female genital mutilation fails as a means to fulfill many of the cultural goals for which it is intended, other than control of female sexuality. Although many values are culturally determined and we should not impose moral judgments across cultures hastily, we sometimes seem to know enough to condemn practices such as female genital mutilation, war, pollution, oppression, injustice, and aggression. Conventionalist ethical relativism challenges this view, but a substantial burden of proof falls on upholders of this moral theory to show why criticisms of other cultures *always* lack moral authority. Because of the hazards of even type 1 circumcision, especially on children, many groups, including WHO and the AMA, want to stop all forms of ritual genital surgery on women. Unenforced bans have proven ineffective, however, since this still popular practice has been illegal in most countries for many decades.[46] Other proposals by activists in these regions focus on fines and enforcement of meaningful legislation, but education of the harms of genital cutting and infibulation may be the most important route to stop these practices.[47] Thus an effective means to stopping these practices may be to promote education.

NOTES

1. Rosalind Russel, "Child Brides Rescued by Shoestring School: Masai Fathers Sell Daughters for Cows, Beer, Money," *Saturday Argus*, January 30–31, 1999, p. 13.
2. Ibid.
3. June Thompson, "Torture by Tradition," *Nursing Times* 85, no. 15 (1989): 17–18; Patricia Schroeder, "Female Genital Mutilation—A Form of Child Abuse," *New England Journal of Medicine* 331 (1994): 739–740.
4. Nah Toubia, "Female Circumcision As a Public Health Issue," *New England Journal of Medicine* 331 (1994): 712–716.
5. Asthma El Dareer, *Woman, Why Do You Weep? Circumcision and Its Consequences* (London: Zed, 1982); Daphne Williams Ntiri, "Circumcision and Health Among Rural Women of Southern Somalia as Part of a Family Life Survey," *Health Care for Women International* 14, no. 3 (1993): 215–216.
6. Ntiri, "Circumcision and Health," pp. 215–216.
7. Amy Finnerty, "The Body Politic," *New York Times Magazine*, May 9, 1999, p. 22.
8. Schroeder, "Female Genital Mutilation" pp. 739–740.
9. Sharon Lerner, "Rite or Wrong: As the U.S. Law Against Female Genital Mutilation Goes into Effect, African Immigrants Debate an Ancient Custom," *Village Voice Worldwide;* on-line http://www/villagevoice.com./inl/lerner.html. Accessed March 3, 1997.
10. Anthony Flew, "Relativism," *Dictionary of Philosophy* (New York: St. Martin's, 1979), p. 281.
11. Louis P. Pojman, "Relativism," in Robert Audi, ed., *The Cambridge Dictionary of Philosophy* (Cambridge: Cambridge University Press, 1995), pp. 690–691.
12. Edward Craig, "Relativism," in Edward Craig, ed., *Routledge Encyclopedia of Philosophy* (London: Routledge, 1998), 8:189–190.
13. David Hume, *An Enquiry Concerning the Principles of Morals*, 1777. References are to section and paragraph 8:2.
14. The definition of ethical relativism used here is similar to that found in the most recent and important encyclopedias of philosophy (Craig) and two influential dictionaries of philosophy (Flew and Pojman).
15. To add to the confusion, some call ethical relativism "cultural relativism."
16. Richard Shweder, "Ethical Relativism: Is There a Defensible Version?" *Ethos* 18 (1990): 205–218.
17. Susan Sherwin, *No Longer Patient: Feminist Ethics and Health Care* (Philadelphia: Temple University Press, 1992), pp. 58, 75.
18. Sherwin, *No Longer Patient;* Loretta M. Kopelman, "Female Circumcision and Genital Mutilation," in *Encyclopedia of Applied Ethics* (1998), 2:249–259. Portions of this article were used or adapted in writing this chapter.
19. Craig, "Relativism," pp. 189–190; Flew, "Relativism," p. 281; James Rachels, *The Elements of Moral Philosophy*, 2d ed. (New York: McGraw-Hill, 1993).
20. Rachels, *Elements of Moral Philosophy*.
21. El Dareer conducted her studies in the Sudan, Koso-Thomas in and around Sierra Leone, and Abdalla in Somalia.
22. El Dareer, *Woman;* Koso-Thomas, *Circumcision of Women;* Abdalla, *Sisters in Affliction;* Ntiri, "Circumcision and Health," pp. 215–216.
23. El Dareer, *Woman;* Ntiri, "Circumcision and Health," pp. 215–216.
24. El Dareer, *Woman*.
25. Ibid.; Abdalla, *Sisters in Affliction*.
26. Nancy Scheper-Hughes, "Virgin Territory: The Male Discovery of the Clitoris," *Medical Anthropology Quarterly* 5, no. 1 (1991): 25–28.
27. Ibid.
28. El Dareer, *Women:* Koso-Thomas, *Circumcision of Women;* Abdalla, *Sisters in Affliction;* Faye Ginsberg, "What Do Women Want? Feminist Anthropology Confronts Clitoridectomy," *Medical Anthropology Quarterly* 5, no. 1. (1991): 17–19.
29. Ibid.; Koso-Thomas, *Circumcision of Women;* Abdalla, *Sisters in Affliction;* Ntiri, "Circumcision and Health," pp. 215–216.
30. Thompson, "Torture by Tradition," pp. 17–18.
31. Lerner, "Rite or Wrong."
32. Abdalla, *Sisters in Affliction*.
33. Koso-Thomas, *Circumcision of Women*.
34. Ibid.; El Dareer, *Woman*.
35. Lerner, "Rite or Wrong."
36. Ntiri, "Circumcision and Health," pp. 215–216; Abdalla, *Sisters in Affliction*.
37. El Dareer, *Woman;* Koso-Thomas, *Circumcision of Women;* Abdalla, *Sisters in Affliction*.
38. Koso-Thomas, *Circumcision of Women*.
39. Elliott Sober, *Core Questions in Philosophy* (New York: Macmillan, 1991); Kopelman, "Medicine's Challenge to Relativism," pp. 221–238; Kopelman, "Female Circumcision," pp. 249–259.
40. Scheper-Hughes, "Virgin Territory," pp. 25–28.
41. Sherwin, *No Longer Patient*, pp. 63–64.

42. Kopelman, "Medicine's Challenge to Relativism," pp. 221–238; Kopelman, "Female Circumcision," pp. 249–259.
43. Sherwin, *No Longer Patient.*
44. Scheper-Hughes, "Virgin Territory," pp. 25–28.

45. Ibid.
46. El Dareer, *Woman.*
47. Ibid.; Abdalla, *Sisters in Affliction;* Dirie and Lindmark, "The Risk of Medical Complication" pp. 479–482; Toubia, "Female Circumcision," pp. 712–716.

⚜ QUESTIONS FOR ANALYSIS

1. How widespread is female genital mutilation in the world today? On what basis do cultures where it is practiced justify it?
2. Why is this practice outlawed in so many countries, including the United Kingdom, France, Canada, and the United States?
3. How does Kopelman understand "conventionalist ethical relativism"? How is this different from descriptive relativism?
4. What are different senses used by philosophers and anthropologists for "cultural relativism"?
5. What is the weaker version of "ethical relativism" sometimes used by postmodern theorists?
6. What is the logical problem with conventionalist ethical relativism?
7. What reasons are given for female genital cutting? What is problematic with these reasons?
8. What is the problem in "counting cultures"?
9. Should immigrant cultures that support female genital mutilation be allowed to continue this practice when they reside in Western countries that condemn and outlaw the practice? With what justification do you reach this conclusion?
10. How can conventionalist ethical relativism defend this mutilation? What objections can be raised to this defense?
11. In order to avoid cultural imperialism, is it necessary to adopt ethical relativism?
12. Are there cultural practices in other countries which should be tolerated, even if we might find them morally abhorrent? In our own country?
13. What does Kopelman believe is the most effective means for stopping this practice of female mutilation worldwide? What other means could be used? Are we justified in interfering with other cultural practices to pursue this goal?

CASE PRESENTATION

Stopping the Sweatshops

Nike, which controls over 40 percent of the international sporting goods industry, has been the target of human rights activists for over a decade. The public information campaign has sought to educate the American public about Nike's reliance on sweatshops in other countries which pay minimal wages and do not respect the most basic human rights in the workplace. Child labor, harassment in the workplace, and other inhumane working conditions have been cited. Nike has fought back by publicizing its efforts to improve the working conditions in those countries, even though they work mainly with contractors over which they say they have less control than in factories operated by Nike itself. Many other major manufacturers use contractors in impoverished countries in Asia, Central America, India, and elsewhere, but have not drawn the high-profile campaigns targeted at Nike.

Efforts in the U.S. Congress to clamp down on these sweatshop activities through trade agreements have had limited effect. In 2006, then-Congressman (now Senator) Sherrod Brown of Ohio and Senator Byron Dorgan of North Dakota introduced the Decent Working Conditions and Fair Competition Act to end "sweatshop profiteering" by prohibiting the importation, the exportation, or the sale of goods made with prisoner sweatshop labor, child labor, and abusive guest worker systems. The Senators argued that in addition to the flagrant violations of human rights in those other countries tolerating these practices, "sweatshop imports are economic suicide for our country." By this they mean that workers in America, where working conditions are regulated to prohibit such abuses, cannot compete on price and lose their jobs. Critics of these proposals charge that American consumers benefit considerably by being able to import economic goods manufactured around the world, from sports shoes to electronic manufactured goods to clothing. The bill was reintroduced in Congress in 2007. Despite dozens of cosponsors, it has never been passed.

☙ QUESTIONS FOR ANALYSIS

1. Do ordinary American consumers have any ethical obligation to take action to stop sweatshop working conditions in other countries? What actions can consumers take to stop these practices?
2. Do citizens of highly developed industrialized nations in North America and Europe have an ethical obligation to promote the human rights of citizens in less-developed countries?
3. Promoters of unregulated international trade often cite the good consequences for American consumers, especially much lower prices on goods that they might otherwise not be able to afford. Are these the only relevant consequences in the ethical equation? What other consequences seem relevant? How do you balance them against low prices when you go shopping?
4. Have you ever participated in actions to stop sweatshops abroad, such as boycotting the purchase of certain products or writing letters to those manufacturers or participating in public demonstrations outside their headquarters? If so, what were your motivations in taking these steps? Do you feel you have made progress toward the goal of stopping those abusive labor practices around the world? What other steps might be taken?
5. How should we balance the push for decent working conditions for all workers around the world with the demand for economical goods that consumers want to buy?

CASE PRESENTATION

Is There a Right to Health Care?

In 1948, the newly formed United Nations proclaimed The Universal Declaration of Human Rights, which included the following provision:

> Article 25. (1) Everyone has the right to a standard of living adequate for the health and well-being of himself and of his family, including food, clothing, housing and medical care and necessary social services, and the right to security in the event of unemployment, sickness, disability, widowhood, old age or other lack of livelihood in circumstances beyond his control.

(The full text of the Declaration is available on the United Nations website: http://www.un.org/en/documents/udhr/.)

During the 2008 Presidential campaign debate on October 7, 2008, then-Senators Barack Obama and John McCain, the Democratic and Republican candidates, respectively, were asked: "Is health care in America a privilege, a right, or a responsibility?" Senator Obama answered: "I think it should be a right for every American." Senator McCain answered: "I think it's a responsibility [...] it is certainly my responsibility. It is certainly small-business people and others, and they understand that responsibility". During the 2012 presidential campaign, the Republican candidate, Mitt Romney, did not say that health care was a right for all in the nation but proposed having individual states develop their own approaches to the provision of health care.

As of 2009, the United States was the only industrialized country which did not provide universal health care to all its residents, even considering only citizens and legal residents. The Affordable Care Act ("Obamacare"), passed in 2010 and upheld by the U.S. Supreme Court as constitutional in 2012, extends health care to many more Americans, but it does not guarantee it to everyone.

☙ QUESTIONS FOR ANALYSIS

1. Do you believe health care is a privilege, a right, or a responsibility? With regard to U.S. citizens? legal residents? undocumented residents? citizens of other countries?
2. The U.S. Constitution does not mention health care. If health care is a right, on what basis do persons have that right? Who has the obligation to provide that health care, if it is a right?

3. The U.N. Declaration lists many rights in addition to medical care. On what basis, if any, do we have such rights? Is it realistic to provide these basic rights to everyone on Earth? On what basis should we decide who gets these things and who does not?

4. Are these rights implicit in Kant's view that all persons are entitled to respect and dignity?

5. Could these claims of rights be justified on a utilitarian theory that recognizing them will result in the greatest happiness for the greatest number?

CASE PRESENTATION

Do Undocumented Immigrants Have a Right to Education?

In 1975 the Texas legislature passed a law authorizing local school districts to deny enrollment in their public schools to children who were not legally admitted to the country. This law also withheld state funds from local school districts to educate those children. In 1977, a class action law suit was filed in Federal court on behalf of school-age children of Mexican origin in Texas who had been denied admission to the public school of Tyler, Texas, because they could not prove that they had entered the U.S. legally.

The state argued that it had adopted this law merely to save money, even though data showed that the biggest drain on the education budget was from rapid increases in the enrollment of students legally in this country. The U.S. Supreme Court sided with the Mexican children in a 5–4 opinion in 1982, *Plyler v. Doe* (457 U.S. 202). The majority relied on the clause in the Fourteenth Amendment to the U.S. Constitution which says that no state may "deny to any person within its jurisdiction the equal protection of the laws." This Amendment applies, the Court said, to everyone physically present in the state, regardless of their immigration status. Its protection is not limited to citizens and legal residents.

The discrimination by Texas had no "rational basis," the Court said. Although the state might save some funds by denying this education, this was not an effective way to discourage illegal immigration,

especially in contrast with alternative means, such as enforcing laws denying employment to persons not in the country legally. The parents, not the children, had made the decision to come to this country illegally, so it was not fair to penalize the children for their parents' decisions. Further, the social costs of creating an uneducated underclass of children would benefit no one.

The Court was explicit in saying that public education is not a "right" in this country guaranteed by the Constitution, but nor is it a minor social benefit which states dispense. "The American people," the Court said, "have always regarded education and [the] acquisition of knowledge as matters of supreme importance."

The four dissenters in this case said that it was not the role of the courts to act as "Platonic Guardians" who set social policy for the nation, even though the dissenters believed that "it is senseless for an enlightened society to deprive any children—including illegal aliens—of an elementary education." The dissenters believed this decision on education should be left to the states, which paid for most of the costs of public education and would also bear the costs in the future of having an uneducated underclass. The dissenters also noted that they agreed that the Equal Protection Clause does apply to everyone physically in the country, but that does not mandate "identical treatment" for all those persons.

⚜ QUESTIONS FOR ANALYSIS

1. The Court considers many utilitarian or consequentialist factors in this analysis, especially the costs of educating and not educating this group of children. Identify consequences which seem relevant today in this analysis, including the economic and social costs. Have circumstances changed substantially in the quarter century since this case was decided?

2. The rights of the children in this case are also relevant. What is the source of those rights? Are they sufficiently strong to convince you that children

should be educated in the U.S. once their parents have made the decision to come here?

3. The U.S. Constitution does not recognize public education as a "right" for anyone. Should this right be added to the U.S. Constitution? the constitutions of the 50 states? Should it be recognized as a universal right?

4. This decision addressed only K–12 education. Should the analysis also be extended to college education?

CASE PRESENTATION

Yearning to Breathe Free

For over a decade the United States has been wrestling with the issue of whether to grant asylum to women who were the victims of abusive practices in their home countries, such as female genital mutilation or domestic violence.

In 1996, Fauziya Kassindja, a 19-year-old woman from Togo, sought and received political asylum in the U.S. to escape the genital mutilation practiced in her home country. This was the first time that a women who fled genital cutting was found by the courts to be eligible for asylum and her case set a precedent for women in later years. In 2007, however, three women from Guinea and one from Mali, were denied asylum on the grounds that they had already been mutilated. Although the Board of Immigration Appeals said they found the practice "reprehensible," it was a one-time event and no further harm could be expected when they returned to their home countries. Attorneys for the women argued that mutilation was part of a culture that deprived women of their rights in all their lives, a so-called "constellation of harm." Women from these cultures suffer continued domestic violence, rape, and other degrading treatment, even after that mutilation.

Defenders of these women in this country have urged that even if these few were granted asylum, it would not "open the floodgates" to millions of other asylum seekers from around the world, as they do not have the sophistication or the resources to escape to the United States to request asylum.

The United Nations High Commissioner for Refugees (UNHCR) issued guidance in May 2009 urging that genital mutilation should form the basis for granting asylum to women and also to parents who wanted to avoid mutilation for their young daughters in their home countries. (The full report is available here: http://www.unhcr.org/refworld/pdfid/4a0c28492.pdf.)

In June 2009, the U.S. Department of Homeland Security argued before immigration authorities that repeated domestic abuse, including imprisonment, beatings, and repeated rape should be accepted as grounds for political asylum. This new standard was applauded by human rights activists as clarifying the fundamental human rights at issue for women. An editorial in the *New York Times* on July 19, 2009, concluded: "Advocates who have fought for years to advance women's rights are celebrating the department's action, which brings reasoned compassion, and an overdue dose of clarity, to an issue of anguish and difficulty." In what appears to be the first case under the new standard, a woman from Mexico was granted asylum in August 2010. She had suffered decades of abuse, including rape at gunpoint and threats with machetes. The immigration judge concluded that the Mexican government refused to help her.

⚜ QUESTIONS FOR ANALYSIS

1. Do you believe the reassurances from human rights advocates that only a few women would actually come to this country seeking asylum from domestic violence? Is there a risk that once word got out and the means of international travel became easier and cheaper that advanced nations like the United States could be overwhelmed with asylum seekers?

2. Do you agree that freedom from domestic violence, including female genital mutilation, is an international human right? Or do you see it as an individual cultural practice with which we should not interfere by granting asylum to these women?

3. The United States recognizes asylum for people escaping political repression and violence, but not economic hardship. Many of the women seeking asylum from domestic abuse also suffer economic hardship. How should we distinguish these claims? Should we be more or less generous in granting asylum? On what basis?

4. A famous poem by Emma Lazarus, inscribed on the Statue of Liberty, includes these lines: "Give me your tired, your poor, your huddled masses yearning to breathe free." Should the United States welcome these immigrants as generously as it did a century ago? What limits should be set on immigration, and why?

CHAPTER TEN

Discrimination

- **Discrimination: Its Nature and Forms**
- **Evidence of Discrimination**
- **Affirmative Action: Preferential Treatment?**
- **Arguments against Affirmative Action**
- **Arguments for Affirmative Action**

TOM L. BEAUCHAMP **Affirmative Action and Diversity Goals in Hiring and Promotion**

ELIZABETH ANDERSON **Affirmative Action Is About Helping All of Us**

LISA NEWTON **Reverse Discrimination as Unjustified**

RICHARD D. KAHLENBERG **Class, Not Race**

CASE PRESENTATIONS: • *Proposition 209* • *Fisher v. University of Texas: Taking Race into Account* • *Reparations: An Overdue Debt to African Slaves in America?* • *Friendly Sexual Harassment?*

ON DECEMBER 10, 1970, the Equal Employment Opportunity Commission (EEOC) petitioned the Federal Communications Commission not to back a request by American Telephone and Telegraph (AT&T) for a rate increase on the grounds that AT&T was engaging in pervasive, systemwide, and blatantly unlawful discrimination against women, blacks, Spanish-surnamed Americans, and other minorities. After nearly two years of negotiation with the EEOC, AT&T finally reached an agreement with the government on December 28, 1972, whereby it agreed, among other things, not to discriminate in the future and to set up goals and timetables for hiring women and minorities into all nonmanagement job classifications where they were underrepresented. For its part, the EEOC agreed to drop all outstanding equal-employment actions against AT&T.

Three years later, on December 8, 1975, AT&T was sued by Dan McAleer, an AT&T service representative. McAleer claimed he had lost out on a promotion to a less qualified female employee as a result of AT&T's implementation of its agreement with the EEOC. McAleer had worked for AT&T for five years and had scored thirty-four of thirty-five on the company's performance rating. Sharon Hullery, the woman who beat McAleer for the promotion, had worked at AT&T for less than five years and had scored thirty points.

On June 9, 1976, the U.S. District Court in Washington, D.C., ruled that AT&T owed McAleer monetary compensation but not the promotion. AT&T owed McAleer the money, said the court, because he was an innocent victim of an agreement intended to remedy the company's wrongdoing. But the court didn't think AT&T owed McAleer the promotion because, in the court's view, that might help perpetuate and prolong the effects of the discrimination that the AT&T–EEOC agreement was designed to eliminate.

On January 18, 1979, the agreement between AT&T and the EEOC expired. AT&T had reached 99.7 percent of the female-hiring goals it had set up in 1973.

In recent years, laws have been passed and programs formulated to ensure fair and equal treatment of all people in employment practices. Nevertheless, unequal practices still exist. To help remedy these, the federal government in the early 1970s instituted an affirmative-action program.

Before affirmative action, many institutions already followed nondiscriminatory as well as merit-hiring employment practices to equalize employment opportunities. In proposing affirmative action, the government recognized the worth of such endeavors, but said that it did not think they were enough. *Affirmative action*, therefore, refers to positive measures beyond neutral nondiscriminatory and merit-hiring employment practices. It is an aggressive program intended to identify and remedy unfair discrimination practiced against many people who are qualified for jobs. Although most of our discussion focuses on discrimination in employment, closely analogous arguments apply in debates over admission to competitive colleges and universities, especially when racial minorities or women have been admitted historically in much smaller number than their presence in the applicant pool or the general population.

Among the most controversial versions of affirmative action are preferential-and quota-hiring systems. *Preferential hiring* is an employment practice designed to give special consideration to people from groups that traditionally have been victimized by racism, sexism, or other forms of discrimination. *Quota hiring* was sometimes ordered by the courts for a specific organization that had expressly refused to hire certain groups, until some appropriate balance could be achieved. For example, companies and unions were required to provide apprentice and reapprentice training to hire, promote, and train minorities and women in specified numerical ratios, in specified job categories, until specified remedial goals were achieved. But in other situations, a less rigid "goal" is established to assess whether hiring has indeed been nondiscriminatory over a period of time. For example, if a company has hired 20 percent women for a certain type of job over a number of years, but the labor pool of persons qualified and available to work in that job was 50 percent women, then this disparity raises a presumption that discrimination against women occurred in the hiring. Although not a "quota," this use of statistical analysis has also sometimes been called "quota hiring," though supporters object that this is a misleading label for the use of statistics to analyze discrimination.

But critics charge that, at least in some instances, implementing affirmative-action guidelines has led to *reverse discrimination—that is, the unfair treatment of a majority member (usually a white male)*. Presumably, this was the basis for McAleer's complaint. Was he treated unfairly? Was AT&T's action moral? Would it have been fairer had the employees names been thrown into a hat from which one was drawn? Obviously, such preferential programs raise questions of social justice.

Affirmative action also has meanings other than "preferential hiring." In its mildest form, it means simply an aggressive program of recruitment of candidates to ensure that qualified women and racial minorities are appropriately represented in the applicant pool. In a somewhat stronger form, it involves a conclusion that traditional hiring criteria have masked hidden biases against certain groups, requiring a modification of those criteria to more appropriately match the actual qualifications needed for the position in a way as free of bias as possible. Ferreting out qualifications that might seem on the surface to be appropriate distinguishing criteria is a long process upon which this version of affirmative action has focused.

Undoubtedly, some will wonder: Why not focus directly on the morality of sexism? By *sexism*, we mean the unfair treatment of a person exclusively on the basis of sex. Perhaps we should focus on it, but consider that in all our discussions so far, we have made reasonable cases for at least two sides of an issue. True, perhaps one side was more flawed than another, but in all cases, reasonable people could disagree. But the fact is that few seriously argue any more that sexism, as defined, is moral. So if we focused on sexism, we would be inviting a most lopsided discussion. This would be unfortunate in the light of so many aspects of sexism that genuinely deserve moral debate. One of these aspects involves such proposed remedies as preferential treatment.

Another reason for not considering sexism exclusively is that this chapter naturally raises questions of social justice. Many discussions of social justice founder because they remain abstract, content to theorize while scrupulously avoiding practice. For example, it is easy and safe to argue that a government must remedy racial injustice. It is far more controversial to argue that a government must implement forced busing to do so. The same applies to sexism. Most would agree that the government has an obligation to correct the social injustice of sexism, but how?

It is one thing to recognize, deplore, and want to correct any injustice. It is entirely another thing to remedy the injustice fairly. Sadly, too many discussions of social justice ignore means entirely, often offering the defense that the means vary from situation to situation. This is undoubtedly true, but the debate flying around so many social justice questions today concerns proposed means. We should learn to examine every situation's means and also the common but agonizing predicament of applauding the intention and even the probable consequences of an action, but deploring the action itself. For many people, preferential treatment is just such a problem.

Although we focus on issues of race and sex discrimination in this chapter, it is worth noting the emergence in recent years of very similar issues for people with disabilities, especially in the workplace. The Americans with Disabilities Act of 1990 requires that employers and educational institutions make "reasonable accommodation" so that individuals with disabilities can compete to the best of their abilities in employment and education. While everyone would agree that we should not discriminate *against* people with disabilities simply because of a disability, the controversy emerges over what some consider favoritism or special treatment of individuals with disabilities. In a 2001 decision, the U.S. Supreme Court held that the PGA tour must allow disabled golfer Casey Martin to use a golf cart in professional tournaments, even though the other players must all walk the course. The PGA had argued that his request would "fundamentally alter the nature" of the game, but this was rejected by the Court. By considering whether this is fair to other players, we confront many of the same issues concerning justice in society that we face with discrimination by race and sex. Is society obligated to do whatever it takes to create a truly "level playing field" for everyone? Do these programs give unfair advantages to some groups but not others? Or is society obligated only to make sure we do not discriminate *against* people based on race, sex, or disability, but otherwise let people fend for themselves?

Another area of employment discrimination that warrants mention here is by sexual orientation or gender identity. As of 2013, 29 states have no legislation prohibiting this discrimination, nor does the Federal government. In both the

Senate and the House of Representatives of the U.S. Congress, the Employment Non-Discrimination Act (ENDA) has been introduced that would extend these protections. It would not apply to religious organizations or small businesses, nor would it allow any preferential treatment or apply retroactively.

Another recent development is the first-ever election and then the reelection of an African-American as President of the United States, Barack Obama. This has generated a public dialogue on whether any affirmative action is needed or whether all the nation's problems, at least with regard to race, have been solved. By any number of measures, however, serious problems remain, such as the much higher unemployment rate for African-American males than Caucasians, especially in the difficult recession the country experienced in the final years of the George W. Bush presidency and the first term of President Obama.

President Obama himself has elevated another element of the debate over discrimination, namely, whether disadvantage by economic class should be addressed along with historic discrimination by race and gender. During the 2008 campaign, then-Senator Obama told a group of minority journalists in Chicago,

> We have to think about affirmative action and craft it in such a way where some of our children who are advantaged aren't getting more favorable treatment than a poor white kid who has struggled more.

This was discussed by Clarence Page, himself an African-American journalist for the *Chicago Tribune*, in his column on April 19, 2009. Page said he has been "struck by how much America's persistent problems with race have changed, while so many of our leading affirmative action proponents have not."

In the coming years, the nation will see how the dialogue over race, class, and gender will advance in this markedly different political climate. As President Obama said in his speech on race on March 18, 2008, during the campaign: "I have asserted a firm conviction … that working together we can move beyond some of our old racial wounds, and that in fact we have no choice if we are to continue on the path of a more perfect union."

DISCRIMINATION: ITS NATURE AND FORMS

To discriminate in employment is to make an adverse decision against employees based on their membership in a certain class. Included in the preceding definition of discrimination in employment are three basic elements: (1) The decision is against employees solely because of their membership in a certain group. (2) The decision is based on the assumption that the group is in some way inferior to some other group and thus deserving of unequal treatment. (3) The decision in some way harms those it's aimed at. Since, traditionally, most of the discrimination in the American workplace has been aimed at women and minorities such as blacks and Hispanics, the following discussion focuses on these groups.[1]

On-the-job discrimination can be intentional or unintentional, practiced by a single individual or individuals in a company or by the institution itself. *Intentional* here means knowingly or consciously; *unintentional* means unthinkingly or not consciously. *Institution* refers to the business, company, corporation, profession, or even the

---

[1]Manuel G. Velasquez, Business Ethics: Concepts and Cases (Englewood Cliffs, N.J.: Prentice-Hall, 1982), p. 266.

system within which the discrimination operates. These distinctions provide a basis for identifying four forms of discrimination: (1) intentional individual, (2) unintentional individual, (3) intentional institutional, and (4) unintentional institutional.

1. *Intentional individual* discrimination is an isolated act of discrimination *knowingly* performed by some individual out of personal prejudice. Example: A male personnel director routinely passes over females for supervisory jobs because he believes and knowingly acts on the belief that "lady bosses mean trouble."

2. *Unintentional individual* discrimination is an isolated act of discrimination performed by some individual who *unthinkingly* or *unconsciously* adopts traditional practices and stereotypes. Example: If the male in the preceding case acted without being aware of the bias underlying his decisions, his action would fall into this category.

3. *Intentional institutional* discrimination is an act of discrimination that is part of the reactive behavior of a company or profession which knowingly discriminates out of the personal prejudices of its members. Example: The male personnel director passes over women for supervisory jobs because "the boys in the company don't like to take orders from females."

4. *Unintentional institutional* discrimination is an act of discrimination that is part of the routine behavior of a company or profession that has unknowingly incorporated sexually or racially prejudicial practices into its operating procedures. Example: An engineering firm routinely avoids hiring women because of the stereotypical assumption that women don't make good engineers or that its clients won't do business with women.

In recent years, discussions of discrimination have focused on institutional forms, with special emphasis on the unintentional institutional. In fact, it's been this kind of discrimination that some believe only affirmative-action programs can root out. Others consider programs like this inherently unjust or counterproductive. They say that workplace discrimination can be corrected through strict enforcement of anti-discrimination law without resorting to preferential-treatment programs. The force of these positions depends in part on whether the body of anti-discriminatory legislation that has developed over the past forty years has, in fact, tended to reduce discrimination in the workplace. If it has, then it would lend weight to the anti-affirmative-action positions. If it hasn't, then the pro-affirmative-action position would be strengthened. So before inspecting the two positions, let's briefly examine the relative positions of whites and minorities and of males and females in the American workplace to see if they say anything about ongoing discrimination.

EVIDENCE OF DISCRIMINATION

Determining the presence of discrimination isn't easy because many factors could possibly account for the relative positions of various groups in the work world. But generally speaking, there are reasonable grounds for thinking that an institution is practicing discrimination (intentional or unintentional) when (1) statistics indicate that members of a group are being treated unequally in comparison with other groups, and (2) endemic attitudes, and formal and informal practices and policies, seem to account for the skewed statistics.

Statistical Evidence

Compelling statistical evidence points to the fact that a disproportionate number of women and minority members hold the less desirable jobs and get paid less than their white male counterparts. For example, at all occupational levels, women make less money than men—even for the same work—despite legislation forbidding discrimination on the basis of sex. According to Census Bureau statistics from 1999, women working full time earned only 75.1 percent as much as full-time male workers. Moreover, the disparity cut across all occupational categories from salaried administrators and officials (the highest paid) to farming, forestry, and fishing (the lowest paid). In the former category, the median income for men in 1998 was $55,664, while the median for women was $36,389; in the latter, the respective median incomes were $18,855 and $15,865. Even though much of the gap between men and women reflects differences among older workers, the 1999 average yearly earnings for female full-time workers under thirty years old remained lower than the average for men under thirty at every education level. For instance, the average income for male high school graduates between twenty-five and twenty-nine was $25,559 compared to $20,669 for women; among college graduates with only a bachelor's degree, the respective figures were $40,098 and $35,295; among those with a master's degree, $54,777 and $42,834.

Similar disparities show up between non-Hispanic white males and black and Hispanic males. The 1999 median income for full-time workers over twenty-five of the first group was $41,555 compared to $30,926 for their black counterparts and $25,242 for their Hispanic counterparts. Once again, the disparities applied to all educational levels. Among high school graduates, for example, the respective figures were $34,839, $27,408, and $25,291; among college graduates with only a bachelor's degree, $51,884, $40,805, and $41,467; among those with a master's degree, $61,904, $52,308, and $50,410.[2] These and other statistics indicate that women and minorities are still not treated as equals of white men.

Additional Evidence

Although some would disagree, the statistics alone don't establish discrimination, for one could always argue that other factors account for these disparities. But there are indications of widespread attitudes and formal and informal institutional practices and policies which, taken collectively, point to discrimination as the cause of these statistical differences.

One such indication is the number of job requirements that are not related to job performance but discriminate against minorities and women. Standardized intelligence tests, for example, are thought by many people to be culturally biased against blacks. Yet in many cases, standardized intelligence tests are required, and applicants scoring the highest are given the available jobs, even though lower scores do not correlate with poor job performance. Similarly, weight requirements often rule out women from jobs involving physical work even though they have the physical ability to perform well.

Then there's the commonplace practice in many trades and industries of filling positions by word-of-mouth recruitment policies. In jobs dominated by white males,

---

[2]These figures come from the Census Bureau's website at Historical Income Tables—People, table P-48, and Money Income in the United States: 1999, tables 9 and 10. For more detailed information, visit the Census Bureau's website (http://www.census.gov/) or the American FactFinder site, maintained by the Census Bureau (http://factfinder.census.gov/).

the word of a job vacancy tends to reach other white males. And even when others do learn of the vacancy, they may not be in any position to be hired to fill it. The problem is particularly acute at the executive level, where many women and minorities hit "an invisible ceiling" beyond which they have difficulty rising. Part of the problem, many claim, is the existence of private white male clubs, where important business contacts are made and developed. Another, they claim, is the resistance of people at the level to those who are "not like us."

Taken together, the statistics, personal and institutional attitudes, assumptions, and practices provide powerful evidence of intractable discrimination against women and minorities in the American workplace. Recognizing the existence of such discrimination and believing that, for a variety of reasons, it's wrong, we have as a nation passed laws expressly forbidding discrimination in recruitment, screening, promotion, compensation, and firing practices. In short, specific laws have been enacted to ensure equal opportunity in employment. The aim of these policies is to prevent further discrimination, and they probably have prevented egregious instances of discrimination. But the evidence indicates that they have not had the effect of providing equal opportunity to women and minorities as groups. Furthermore, anti-discrimination laws do not address the present-day effects of past discrimination. They ignore, for example, the fact that because of past discrimination women and minorities in general lack the skills of white males and are disproportionately underrepresented in more prestigious and better paying jobs. To remedy the effects of past discrimination and seeing no other way to counteract apparently visceral racism and sexism, many people today call for specific affirmative-action programs.

AFFIRMATIVE ACTION: PREFERENTIAL TREATMENT?

As amended by the Equal Employment Opportunity Act of 1972, the Civil Rights Act of 1964 requires businesses that have substantial dealings with the federal government to undertake affirmative-action programs. *Affirmative-action programs are plans designed to correct imbalances in employment that exist directly as a result of past discrimination.* Even though these acts do not technically require companies to undertake affirmative-action programs, courts responded to acts of job discrimination by ordering the offending firms to implement such programs to combat the effects of past discrimination. In effect, then, all business institutions must adopt affirmative-action programs either in theory or in fact. They must be able to prove that they have not been practicing institutional sexism or racism, and if they cannot prove this, they must undertake programs to ensure against racism or sexism.

What do affirmative-action programs involve? The EEOC lists general guidelines as steps to affirmative action. Under these steps, firms must issue a written equal-employment policy and an affirmative-action commitment. They must appoint a top official with responsibility and authority to direct and implement their program and to publicize their policy and affirmative-action commitment. In addition, firms must survey current female and minority employment by department and job classification. Where underrepresentation of these groups is evident, firms must develop goals and timetables to improve in each area of underrepresentation. They then must develop specific programs to achieve these goals, establish an internal audit system to monitor them, and evaluate progress in each aspect of the program. Finally, companies must develop supportive in-house and community programs to combat discrimination.

In implementing such programs, some companies have adopted a policy of preferential treatment for women and minorities. *Preferential treatment refers to the practice of giving individuals favored consideration in hiring or promotions for other than job-related reasons* (such as the person is female or black). Those espousing preferential treatment argue that such a policy is the only way to remedy traditional sexism and racism or at least that it is the most expeditious and fairest way to do it. In some instances, preferential treatment for women and minorities takes the form of a quota system—that is, *an employment policy of representing women and minorities in the firm in direct proportion to their numbers in society or in the community at large.* Thus, a firm operating in a community which has a 20 percent black population might try to ensure that 20 percent of its work force be black.[3]

To unravel some of the complex moral issues affirmative-action programs can raise, let's look at a specific instance of preferential hiring. Suppose an equally qualified man and woman are applying for a job. The employer, conscious of affirmative-action guidelines and realizing that the company has historically discriminated against women in its employment policies, adopts a preferential hiring system. Since males are already disproportionately well represented and females underrepresented, the preferential system gives the female applicant a decided advantage. As a result, the employer hires the female. Is this action moral? Are affirmative-action programs that operate in the preferential way moral?

Many people argue that affirmative-action programs are inherently discriminatory and therefore unjust. In this context, *discriminatory* should be understood to refer to policies that favor individuals on non-job-related grounds (for example, on the basis of sex, color, or ethnic heritage). It has been argued that preferential hiring is unjust because it involves giving preferential treatment to women and minorities over equally qualified white males, a practice that is clearly discriminatory, albeit in reverse.

Some in favor of affirmative action, however, attempt to rebut this objection by appealing to principles of *compensatory justice. Since women and minorities clearly continue to be victimized directly and indirectly by traditional discrimination in the workplace, they are entitled to some compensation.* This is one basis for preferential treatment. The soundness of this contention seems to rely on at least two factors: (1) that affirmative-action programs involving preferential treatment will in fact provide adequate compensation and (2) that they will provide compensation more fairly than any other alternative.[4] Since the justice and the morality of affirmative-action programs depend to a large degree on these assumptions, we should examine them.

The question that comes to mind in regard to the first assumption is: adequate compensation for whom? The answer seems obvious: for women and minorities. But does this mean *individual* women and minority-group members or women and minorities taken *collectively*? University of Tampa Professor Herman J. Saatkamp, Jr.,

---

[3]Some institutions simply reserved a number of places for women and minority members. The University of California at Davis, for example, had such a policy in its medical school when it denied Alan Bakke admission. Bakke appealed to the Supreme Court, which—in a 5 to 4 decision in 1978—ordered that he be admitted to the medical school and struck down the set-aside quota for racial minorities that Davis had in place at the time. However, the Court also said the university may take race into account in admissions as long as it did not establish rigid quotas for any particular group.
[4]Albert W. Flores, "Reverse Discrimination: Towards a Just Society," in Business & Professional Ethics, a quarterly newsletter/report (Troy, N.Y.: Center for the Study of the Human Dimensions of Science & Technology, Rensselaer Polytechnic Institute, Jan. 1978), p. 4.

has demonstrated that this question, far from being merely a technical one, bears directly on the morality of affirmative-action programs and how they are implemented.[5]

Saatkamp points out that the question of the conflict between individual and collective merit typifies the debate between government agencies and business over employment policies. On the one hand, business is ordinarily concerned with the individual merit and deserts of its employees. On the other hand, government agencies primarily focus on the relative status of groups within the population at large. To put the conflict in perspective, employment policies based solely on individual merit would try to ensure that only those individuals who could prove they deserved compensation would benefit and only those proved to be the source of discrimination would suffer. Of course, such a focus places an almost unbearable burden on the resources of an individual to provide sufficient, precise data to document employment discrimination, which is commonly acknowledged to exist at times in subtle, perhaps even imperceptible, forms at various organizational levels. Indeed, social policies recognize this difficulty by focusing on discrimination on an aggregate level. Individuals, then, need not prove they themselves were discriminated against but only that they are members of groups that have traditionally suffered because of discrimination.

Taking the collective approach to remedying job discrimination is not without its own disadvantages.

1. Policies based on collective merit tend to pit one social group against another. White males face off against all nonwhite males; women find themselves jockeying with other disadvantaged groups for priority employment status; black females can end up competing with Hispanic males for preferential treatment. This factionalizing aspect of policies based on collective merit can prove detrimental to society.
2. Policies based on collective merit victimize some individuals. The individual white male who loses out on a job because of preferential treatment given a woman or a minority-group member is penalized.
3. In some cases, the women and minority members selected under preferential treatment are in fact less deserving of compensation than those women and minorities who are not selected. In short, those most in need may not benefit at all when preference by group membership is divorced from individual need.
4. Some members of majority groups may be just as deserving or more deserving of compensation than some women or members of minority groups. Many white males, for example, are more seriously limited in seeking employment than some women and minority-group members are due to economic and class differences.
5. Policies based on collective merit can be prohibitively expensive for business. To enforce such programs, businesses must hire people to collect data, process forms, deal with government agencies, and handle legal procedures. From business's viewpoint, this additional time, energy, and expense could have been channeled into more commercially productive directions.

In sum, those who argue that affirmative-action programs will provide adequate compensation for the victims of discrimination must grapple with the problems of determining the focus of the compensation: on the individual or on the group. While both focuses have merit, neither is without disadvantages. Furthermore, it seems neither approach can be implemented without first resolving a complex chain of moral concerns.

---

[5]Flores, "Reverse Discrimination," pp. 5–6.

But even if we assume that affirmative-action programs will provide adequate compensation, it is still difficult to demonstrate the validity of the second assumption of those who endorse affirmative action by appealing to principles of compensatory justice: that such programs will provide compensation more fairly than any other alternative. By nature, affirmative-action programs provide compensation at the expense of the white males' right to fair and equal employment treatment. In other words, affirmative-action programs in the form of preferential treatment undermine the fundamental principle of just employment practice: that a person should be hired or promoted only on job-related grounds. Apparently, then, it is an awesome undertaking to defend the proposition that affirmative action will provide compensation more fairly than any other alternative when such a proposition makes a non-job-related factor (membership in a group) a relevant employment criterion.

Although it would appear that reverse discrimination may not be justified on grounds of compensation, we should not conclude that it cannot be justified. In fact, some people contend that a more careful examination of the principles of justice suggests an alternative defense. As we have mentioned, those who argue against affirmative-action programs do so because such programs allegedly involve unequal treatment and are therefore unjust. The clear assumption here is that whatever involves unequal treatment is in and of itself unjust. But as Professor Albert W. Flores points out, while justice would demand that equals receive equal treatment, it is likewise true that unequals should receive treatment appropriate to their differences. Hence, he concludes that "unfair or differential treatment may be required by the principles of justice."[6] In other words, unequal treatment is unfair in the absence of any characteristic difference between applicants which, from the viewpoint of justice, would constitute relevant differences. Following this line of reasoning, we must wonder whether being a female or a minority member would constitute a "relevant difference" that would justify unequal treatment.

To illustrate, let's ask how one could justify giving preferential consideration to a female job applicant over an equally qualified white male. Flores contends that while sex may be irrelevant to the job, it may be a relevant consideration as to who should be selected. In effect, he distinguishes between criteria relevant to a job and those relevant to candidate selection. He clearly bases this distinction on a concept of business's social responsibilities. As has been amply demonstrated elsewhere, business does not exist in a commercial vacuum. It is part of a social system and, as such, has obligations that relate to the welfare and integrity of society at large. Thus, Flores argues that when a firm must decide between two equally qualified applicants, say a white male and a female, it is altogether justified in introducing as a selection criterion some concept of social justice, which in this case takes cognizance of a fair distribution of society's resources amid scarcities among competing groups. From the viewpoint of justice, business may be correct in hiring the qualified female or minority member. Notice, however, that this contention is based primarily not on principles of compensatory justice but on a careful examination of the nature of justice.

The moral issues that affirmative-action programs raise in regard to justice are profound and complex. In this brief overview, we have been able to raise only a few, but these demonstrate that the morality of preferential treatment through affirmative action cuts to our basic assumptions about the nature of human beings and the

---

[6]Flores, "Reverse Discrimination," p. 4.

principles of justice. Any moral resolution of the problem of discrimination in the workplace will not only reflect these assumptions but must justify them.

ARGUMENTS AGAINST AFFIRMATIVE ACTION

1. *All discrimination on the basis of race and sex is inherently unfair.*
   POINT: "All human beings deserve equal treatment. No one should be denied a job because of sex or skin color. It's a simple matter of fairness that all people of good will should be able to agree on. Isn't that what the civil rights movement was originally all about? Isn't that what the feminist movement was originally all about? To discriminate against anyone on the basis of race or sex, white males included, is inherently unfair."

   COUNTERPOINT: "You can't equate affirmative action with racism and sexism. The purpose of racism and sexism is to deny equal opportunity. The purpose of affirmative action is to provide it, first by ensuring that employers don't discriminate against groups that have traditionally suffered from discrimination and, second, by compensating these groups for past discrimination. Certainly, a color-blind society is the ideal, but affirmative action is necessary in today's society if we're going to achieve it someday."

2. *Affirmative action leads to resentment and social tensions.*
   POINT: "Whatever the purpose of affirmative action, the result is racial tension and increased sexism. A lot of white males justifiably feel cheated by affirmative action. Denied jobs and promotions they're qualified for because they're white males, they naturally come to resent women and minorities. Just look at the rise of racial tensions in our cities. Or look at the prevalence of racism and sexism in recent popular music and comedy acts. Affirmative action isn't bringing us to a color-blind society but to an increasingly polarized one."

   COUNTERPOINT: "You could say the same thing about the original civil rights and feminist movements. Remember the name calling and rock throwing when blacks first tried to integrate public schools, buses, and lunch counters? Or all the bra-burning women's libber jokes when women began demanding equal pay for equal work? What the resentment and tensions show is pervasive racism and sexism, not the wrongness of affirmative action."

3. *Affirmative action stigmatizes minorities and women.*
   POINT: "It's not only white males who suffer from affirmative action. Minorities and women who rise to the top on their own merits also suffer. Instead of being respected for their accomplishments, they're objects of suspicion. There will always be people who believe women and minorities got where they are through preferential treatment. Not only that, but affirmative action can actually harm their careers. Given the choice between a doctor who got into medical school on his or her own merits and one who may have got in through an affirmative-action system, which would you pick? That's the stigma of affirmative action, and talented minorities and women will always have to live with it."

   COUNTERPOINT: "The stigma you talk about is nothing but prejudice. Whether hired through affirmative action or not, whether admitted into medical school through affirmative action or not, people still have to prove themselves afterward. After all, the idea behind affirmative action isn't to give women and minorities a leg up through their entire careers but to give them an opportunity to prove themselves on a level playing field. And anyone who accomplishes that deserves as much respect as anyone else."

4. *Affirmative action wastes the best human resources.*

POINT: "The real idea behind affirmative action is to make sure that the best people for the job don't get it. Places in professional schools are taken from superior students who happen to be white males. More qualified applicants who happen to be white males are denied important jobs in business and industry. No society can afford to waste its best resources like that, especially in a world as competitive as ours has become."

COUNTERPOINT: "You could just as easily say that no society can afford to waste over half its human resources by denying them the opportunity to prove themselves in areas traditionally closed to them. Remember, affirmative-action guidelines aren't designed to result in the hiring of unqualified applicants. They're designed to help less qualified applicants whose relative lack of qualifications are the product of institutional racism and sexism. By giving them that help, we give them the opportunity to overcome impediments in their background and improve their qualifications. Though there are unfortunate abuses in affirmative-action programs, in the end we still have a much larger pool of qualified workers to choose from."

ARGUMENTS FOR AFFIRMATIVE ACTION

1. *Justice requires that we compensate for the results of past discrimination.*

POINT: "No one can deny the United States's history of racism and sexism. If the effects of that history were behind us, affirmative action would be unnecessary. But they're not behind us. Walk into any inner city neighborhood and try to tell me the children playing in the streets have the same opportunities as their white suburban counterparts. If we really believe in justice and equal opportunity, we have to compensate for the effects of our history."

COUNTERPOINT: "Compensatory justice is certainly a noble ideal, but there are two serious flaws in your argument. First, compensatory justice for one group brings harm to another, and when the harmed group isn't responsible for the plight of the others, you're punishing the innocent for the sins of their ancestors. To tell a young white male to forget about his share of the American Dream because of what happened before he was born is no kind of justice at all. Second, not all women and minorities suffer from the effects of past discrimination, whereas many white males have led truly disadvantaged lives. Take a middle-class black man or white woman who went to good schools and was always encouraged to aspire to great success. Why is that person entitled to preferential treatment over a white male from the most depressed area of Appalachia or a severely distressed manufacturing community?"

2. *Affirmative action is the only way to overcome current racism and sexism.*

POINT: "Despite the passage of numerous civil rights laws, bias in the workplace is still with us. Women remain subject to sexual harassment. Racial and sexual stereotypes continue to take their toll. You don't even need statistics to know how bad it is. You can hear it in casual conversation and you can see it in a seemingly never-ending stream of lawsuits won by women and minorities who were denied promotions. Employers can always find a way to justify hiring or promoting a white male over a black or a woman. The only way to overcome such discrimination is through affirmative-action guidelines."

COUNTERPOINT: "The fact that women and minorities are winning their discrimination suits shows that we don't need affirmative action. The Civil Rights Act and the Equal Employment Opportunity Act give them all the legal teeth they need to fight bias, on the job or anywhere else. The just way to fight discrimination is to take the discriminators to court, not to institutionalize affirmative action."

3. *Women and minorities need role models in all walks of life.*
   POINT: "One of the most unfortunate effects of past discrimination is the lack of role models for young women and minorities. Before Sandra Day O'Connor, how many young women could aspire to be an associate justice of the U.S. Supreme Court? Before Colin Powell, how many young black men could aspire to be secretary of state? We need women and minority physics professors, architects, welders, electricians, bank presidents, and anything else you can think of to let *all* young people know that all possibilities are open to them if they have the talent and perseverance."

   COUNTERPOINT: "Certainly, role models are important, but unfair discrimination against white males is too high a price to pay, especially when adequate enforcement of anti-discrimination legislation will provide them anyway. After all, Colin Powell wasn't selected for his position *because* of his race. Nor were many other talented blacks in many other kinds of work. Nor were many talented women selected for their positions because of their gender. Furthermore, many of them got where they are without any role models at all. As important as role models may be, they can't replace encouragement from parents and teachers, and they can't replace hard work."

4. *It's just not true that all decisions in employment and education are made on the basis of pure objective merit, even leaving aside affirmative-action programs.*
   POINT: "It's hypocritical to say that if it were not for affirmative action, everyone would have a fair chance to compete based strictly on merit. Many decisions are made on factors that have little to do with so-called objective merit. Many universities give preference to the children of alumni, even if they don't meet normal admissions standards. Universities seek a wide range of abilities and talents, whether athletes or musicians or artists, even if they don't meet the narrowly defined standards of grade point and SAT scores. Many corporations are notorious for hiring relatives and cronies for jobs for which those persons are less qualified. As long as we allow these other forms of unfair discrimination, we shouldn't complain about giving a break to underrepresented minorities and women."

   COUNTERPOINT: "Perhaps we should insist that those other forms of discrimination be abolished too. But even if they are allowed to continue, race and gender go to core constitutional values, while those other factors don't. If you own a business, there's nothing wrong with showing favoritism to your relatives. And universities rely on their alumni for financial contributions, so why not reward them by showing a little favoritism to admissions for their children?"

Affirmative Action and Diversity Goals in Hiring and Promotion

TOM L. BEAUCHAMP

Tom L. Beauchamp is a professor of philosophy and a senior research scholar in Georgetown University's Kennedy Institute of Ethics. In this essay, he assumes that affirmative action might sometimes include preferential treatment by race or gender, but that it can be morally justified. He observes that corporate goals for "diversity" are well served by corporate policies for "affirmative action." He is also concerned that unintentional discrimination remains pervasive in many environments, necessitating the setting of goals or targets that some might consider "quotas."

Since the 1960s, government and corporate policies that set goals for hiring women and minorities have encountered many criticisms. Opponents maintain that these policies establish indefensible quotas and discriminate in reverse against sometimes more qualified white males. Although some policies undoubtedly do violate rules of fair and equal treatment, I will argue that well-constructed policies that have specific, targeted goals are morally justified. These goals may be fixed in affirmative action policies, but increasingly they are fixed through diversity policies.

TWO POLAR POSITIONS ON AFFIRMATIVE ACTION

I start with the relevant historical background. In 1965, President Lyndon Johnson issued an executive order that announced a toughened federal initiative requiring that employers with a history of discrimination in employment supply goals and timetables for the achievement of equal employment opportunity.[1] Since this order, several U.S. government policies and laws have encouraged or required corporations and other institutions to advertise jobs fairly and to promote members of groups formerly discriminated against, most notably women, minority ethnic groups, and the handicapped. The stated goals were to eradicate overt discrimination, redress the results of past discrimination, and smooth the course of equal opportunity in employment and admission to educational institutions. Today race and ethnicity have become the main focus of affirmative action policies, and often the exclusive focus.

These laws and related policies and reforms of practices were quickly labeled "affirmative action." Today the term "affirmative action" most commonly refers to positive steps to rank, admit, hire, or promote persons who are members of groups previously or presently discriminated against, but historically it has been used to refer to many types of practice and policy, from open advertisement of positions to quotas in employment and promotion. The term has widely, though controversially, been interpreted as synonymous with "preferential treatment."

The following introductory statement by the University of California Berkeley for its affirmative action policy for staff employment is a good example of the kind of general commitments found in many affirmative action policies as they now exist:

From Tom L. Beauchamp, "Affirmative Action and Diversity Goals in Hiring and Promotion," *Ethical Theory and Business*, 9th ed., pp. 211–216. Pearson Education, Inc., 2013. Copyright 1987, 1992, 1996, 2003, 2007, 2013 by the author. Reprinted by permission of the author.

The 2010–2011 Staff Affirmative Action Plan

This Plan sets annual placement goals when the percentage of minorities or women employed in a particular job group is less than would be reasonably expected given their availability percentage in that particular job group. Placement goals are set for the period October 1, 2010—September 30, 2011....

> The University commits itself to apply every good faith effort to achieve prompt and full utilization of minorities and women in all segments of its workforce where deficiencies exist. These efforts conform to all current legal and regulatory requirements, and are consistent with University standards of quality and excellence.[2]

The placement goals are adjusted annually, and the results published in some detail.

The practice of using such goals in policies has from the beginning come into sharp conflict with a school of thought that is critical of affirmative action. Its proponents denounced preferential policies as themselves discriminatory and argued that all persons are equally entitled to a fair employment opportunity and to constitutional guarantees of equal protection in a color-blind, nonsexist society. They have argued – and still do so today – that affirmative action is partial and preferential, and therefore violates impartial principles of fair treatment and equal opportunity. Civil rights laws, from this perspective, should offer protection only to individuals who have themselves been explicitly victimized by forms of discrimination, not to groups. Corporate hiring goals and timetables therefore may function to create a reverse discrimination that decreases opportunities for populations such as nonminority males. That is, the properties of race and sex used in affirmative action policies discriminate against those who are not members of the designated race, ethnicity, or sex.

These two schools of thought often do not agree on the core meaning of the term "affirmative action," which has been defined in different ways by different parties. The original meaning of "affirmative action" was minimalist. It referred to plans to safeguard equal opportunity, to protect against discrimination, to advertise positions openly, and to create scholarship programs to ensure recruitment from specific groups.[3] If this were all that "affirmative action" meant, few would oppose it. However, "affirmative action" has both expanded and contracted in meaning over the last quarter century. Today it is typically associated with preferential policies that target specific groups, especially women and minority groups, in order to promote the interests of members of those groups and to raise their status. Here "affirmative action" refers to positive steps to rank, admit, hire, or promote persons.

Although the meaning of "affirmative action" is still contested, I will, for present purposes, stipulate the meaning as functionally equivalent to the elements in the following policy of the IBM Company (in a 2005 statement):

> To provide equal opportunity and affirmative action for applicants and employees, IBM carries out programs on behalf of women, minorities, people with disabilities, special disabled veterans and other veterans covered by the Vietnam Era Veterans Readjustment Act. ... This includes outreach as well as human resource programs that ensure equity in compensation and opportunity for growth and development.

Affirmative action here, as with many American corporations, means that the company extends its commitment beyond mere equal opportunity (a negative condition of nondiscrimination) to proactively recruit, hire, develop and promote qualified women, minorities, people with disabilities, and veterans (a positive condition requiring organized action).[4] I too will use "affirmative action" to refer to both equal opportunity provisions and positive steps taken to hire persons from groups previously and presently discriminated against, leaving open what will count as a "positive step" to remove discrimination and also leaving open precisely what "equal opportunity" means.

The two schools of thought identified thus far may not be as far apart morally as they at first appear. If legal enforcement of civil rights law could efficiently and comprehensively identify discriminatory treatment and could protect its victims, both schools would agree on the centrality of the principle of equal opportunity and would agree that the legal-enforcement strategy is preferable. However, there are at least two reasons why this solution will not be accepted, at the present time, by proponents of affirmative action. First, there is an unresolved issue about whether those in contemporary society who have been advantaged by *past* discrimination, such as wealthy owners of decades-old family businesses, deserve their advantages. Second, there is the issue of whether *present*, ongoing discrimination can be successfully and comprehensively overcome in a timely fashion by identifying and prosecuting violators and without resorting to the outreach programs involved in affirmative action. Many believe that it takes constant vigilance to protect against discriminatory actions and ensure fair hiring and promotion.

Diversity

In many corporations the language of "diversity policy" has been either substituted for or merged with "affirmative action policy." For example General Motors now states its commitment to "Diversity Management" as follows:

> We believe that diversity is the collective mixture of similarities and differences. This recognizes that managing diversity includes race and gender as well as the broader aspects of age, education level, family status, language, military status, physical abilities, religion, sexual orientation, union representation, and years of service.... We remain committed to Affirmative Action as required by the Federal law. As such, we monitor our programs to determine whether recruitment, hiring and other personnel practices are operating in a nondiscriminatory manner. This process includes outreach programs designed to identify qualified individuals of any race or gender who are not fully represented in the talent pools from which we select and promote employees.... We recognize that it is essential that our work force structure reflects both the marketplace and our customers.[5]

General Motors also states that workplace diversity is of sufficient importance that it may be achieved by means of affirmative action.

Another example is the Coca-Cola Company, which worked with a task force from 2002–2006 to implement a diversity strategy "with quantifiable outcomes, timelines, and plans." The design has been to integrate diversity into the "business plan" of the company, which maintains a Diversity & Workplace Fairness Department in Human Resources. This department is "responsible for centralized strategy and monitoring of EEO issues

and affirmative action plans (AAPs)." A policy initiated in 2004 was a particularly venturesome approach (later reduced and intentionally made less "aggressive"):

> Under the Diversity Goals program, all senior managers based in North America will have a portion of their incentive tied to the achievement of the Company's diversity goals. This program tracks progress on an annual basis and was implemented in January 2004. For calendar year 2004, the program tied executive and senior manager compensation to a 2% net increase in representation of women and minorities at salary grades 10 and above, very ambitious goals for the first year of this program.[6]

Achieving diversity in a workforce or educational institution can be viewed as a means to the end of eradicating discrimination and therefore as an arm of affirmative action. However, diversity has often functioned as a goal that is independent of anti-discrimination goals, and reasons for diversity policies can be notably different from reasons for affirmative action policies. The two kinds of policy share parts of the same history and they often have overlapping goals, but they are neither synonymous in meaning nor identical in policy.

Diversity first burst into prominence because of 1970s affirmative action programs initiated in American colleges and universities that sought to bring to campus higher levels of representation of Hispanic and African-American students as well as women and minorities on the staff and faculty. Many universities altered their criteria of admission to achieve these goals, and diversity was prominently mentioned as a major goal.

In cases heard over a period of years, the United States Supreme Court has determined (as a matter of law rather than ethics, of course) that a racial or ethnic classification scheme by itself is too narrow to express a proper understanding of the goal of diversity. The desired objective of obtaining educational benefits requires consideration of properties beyond race and ethnic origin. A diversity goal for an educational environment could include many abilities, experiences, and endowments in the student body. The Court has found that diversity policies can lawfully include criteria of race and ethnicity, but only in the context of a larger set of criteria of diversity.

In a controversial 2003 case about a University of Michigan Law School policy, the Court stated that race can be considered along with other factors, but only if quotas and weighted points are not parts of the admissions structure. Twenty Fortune 500 companies had filed a legal brief in support of the University of Michigan's admissions policies in the case, and Justice O'Connor in the majority opinion frequently mentioned and quoted from the brief, noting the significance of affirmative action policies well beyond higher education.[7]

The Supreme Court has brought U.S. law to the conclusion that a diversity of abilities, backgrounds, nationalities, experiences, aptitudes, and gifts—along with ethnic and racial diversity—create a mixture that is legal and that reasonably contributes to the educational experience in an institution of higher learning. Still undecided, however, is the precise mixture of criteria of diversity that may legitimately be used. Currently what often happens in one institution in the way of a mixture does not closely resemble what happens in another, because they use disparate criteria. Corporations include a wide array of criteria when stating their diversity policies, including race, gender, ethnicity, age, conditions of disability, sexual orientation, cultural background, religion, economic status, education, and prior types of experience. These criteria are proudly mentioned in many corporate policies, but rarely are they spelled out or linked to historical discrimination. American institutions clearly are struggling with how to understand and implement criteria of diversity and with the reasons why certain criteria should or should not be adopted.

We may currently be experiencing a historical period in which diversity is gradually displacing affirmative action as the centerpiece of policies regarding underrepresented groups. More strongly put, it can be argued that, as a social matter in the United States, the demise of affirmative action began with the presidency of Ronald Reagan and was effectively transformed into diversity policy by recent social change, court cases, and new state legislation. It is too early to tell, but if affirmative action is now in its death throes, the same cannot be said about diversity policies. One way to frame the current situation is to say that many American corporations are swinging from a powerful commitment to affirmative action to a powerful commitment to affirmative diversity.

THE OBJECTIVES OF CORPORATE POLICIES

Many writings about corporate affirmative action programs suggest that *legal* requirements determine the *moral* obligations of corporations, but this assumption confuses ethics with law, and most forward-looking corporations have not been confused about their extra-legal moral commitments. In 1995, shortly after the United States Department of Labor gave an award to Proctor & Gamble for its commitment to pursuing equal employment opportunities, Edwin L. Artzt, then chairman of the board and CEO of Proctor & Gamble, said, "Affirmative action has been a positive force in our company. What's more, we have always thought of affirmative action as a starting point. We have never limited our standards for providing opportunities to women and minorities to levels mandated by law.... Regardless of what government may do, we believe we have a moral contract with all of the women and minorities in our company—a moral contract to provide equal opportunity for employment, equal opportunity for advancement, and equal opportunity for financial reward."[8] Starting from this perspective, many corporations make positive commitments, in voluntary programs, of hiring and promotions that build significantly on and move well beyond what laws and federal agencies determine to be basic responsibilities.

Another moral objective of a corporate policy can be diversity itself (a goal I will here simply assume to be morally worthy). Corporations that fail to seek broadly for diversity will recruit narrowly and will fail to look at the full range of qualified persons in the market. This will be a moral unfairness of narrow recruiting, as well as a failure to act in the best interest of the company. Many corporations have reported that promoting diversity in the workforce by recruiting widely is correlated with higher-quality employees, reductions in the costs of discrimination claims, a lowering of absenteeism, less turnover, and increased customer satisfaction. While the desire to achieve these goals, so stated, comes more from corporate self-interest rather than moral commitment, these reports suggest that the claim made by opponents of affirmative action that corporations lower standards and hire weaker employees under affirmative action plans have turned out not to be supported.[9]

An example is found in the Dell Computer Corporation, which announced in 2003 that, by design, it had substantially increased its diversity recruiting and global diversity. Dell noted that "companies that diversify workforce and supply bases are more successful in gaining access to multicultural markets. Mutually beneficial relationships with minority suppliers open doors for Dell to market its products and services to women and minority customers, provide growth opportunities for our suppliers, and benefit our communities."[10] If many companies were today to withdraw their carefully developed affirmative-action and/or diversity plans, they would violate moral commitments that have been set in place after direct negotiations with and promises made to minority groups, unions, and others. Many corporations report that they have, for moral as well as business reasons, invested heavily in eliminating managerial biases and stereotypes by training managers to hire through outreach programs.

UNINTENTIONAL DISCRIMINATION AND PROBLEMS OF PROOF

Affirmative action, and arguably diversity too, have a history in racial and sexual discrimination. In some cases there existed *intentional* forms of favoritism and exclusion, but intent to discriminate is not a necessary condition of discrimination and not a necessary condition of having a justified affirmative action or diversity policy. Institutional patterns and networks can unintentionally hold back persons. Employees are frequently hired through a network that, without design, excludes women, minority groups, or other groups. For example, hiring may occur through personal connections or by word of mouth; and layoffs may be governed by a seniority system rather than by considerations of merit and performance.[11]

The U.S. Supreme Court has reasonably held that persons may be guilty of discriminating against the handicapped (in this particular case) where there is no "invidious animus, but rather [a discriminatory effect] of thoughtlessness and indifference—of benign neglect." The Court found that discrimination would be difficult and perhaps impossible to prove or to prevent if intentional discrimination alone qualified as discrimination.[12] The Court has also noted that discrimination is often invisible to those who discriminate as well as invisible to the public. This, in my judgment, is the main reason why reasonable target goals in affirmative action and diversity policies can be (but are not always) justifiable: They may be the only way to break down patterns of discrimination, intentional or unintentional, and bring meaningful diversity to the workplace.

Courts in the United States have on a few occasions either required or endorsed specific numerical targets on grounds that an employer had an intractable history and a bullheaded resistance to change that necessitated strong measures. The Supreme Court has never directly supported quotas using the term "quota"[13] (a term now largely displaced by "target goals," "diversity objectives," and the like), but it did at one point in its history uphold affirmative action programs that contain numerically expressed hiring formulas that are intended to reverse the patterns of both intentional and unintentional discrimination.[14] However, the Supreme Court has also clearly stated that some affirmative action programs using numerical formulas have gone too far and are not justified.[15]

THE IMPORTANCE OF CONTEXT AND EMPIRICAL STUDIES

Factual questions about the actual breadth and depth of discrimination at work in hiring and promotion policies (as well as in college admissions, home mortgage lending, etc.) may divide us as a society more than any other issue about the role of diversity and affirmative action. Many believe that there is a narrow sliver of discrimination that is controllable by presently available laws, whereas others believe that discrimination is deeply, and often invisibly, entrenched in society. Based on available empirical studies, discriminatory attitudes and practices are deep-seated in some institutions, while there are no such attitudes in others. In some institutions and corporations affirmative action programs are not needed today. They have achieved their goals. In others, only modest good faith programs are in order; and in still others targeted goals will continue to be necessary to break down discriminatory patterns.

Empirical studies help us understand the scope discrimination in many American institutions and sectors. Although much has been learned through these studies about patterns of discrimination, much remains to be discovered. The hidden and subtle character of discrimination often makes it particularly difficult to study.

CONCLUSION

Issues of social discrimination and equality of opportunity affect all societies, and, from this perspective, problems of affirmative action could be interpreted as universal moral problems—not merely moral problems in the U.S., as I have largely treated them. No well-informed person would deny that there are serious problems of discrimination in virtually every nation, in every part of the world. Both diversity and fair hiring and promotion are global problems, rising to deeply offensive levels in some countries. However, the notion of *affirmative action* has throughout its history been so closely tied to issues, laws, policies, and judicial decisions in the United States that it would be ill-advised to try to reinvent this particular concept as a global problem of social justice.

If the social circumstances of discrimination change in the future, various of my suggestions and conclusions in this paper will need to be modified, perhaps substantially. I agree with critics of affirmative action that the introduction of programs of preferential treatment on a large scale runs the risk of producing economic advantages to individuals who do not deserve them, protracted court battles, a lowering of admission and work standards, increased racial and minority hostility, and the continued suspicion that well-placed minorities received their positions purely on the

basis of preferential and unfair treatment. These reasons constitute a strong case *against* some affirmative action policies that set specific goals. However, this powerful case is not sufficient to overcome the still strong arguments in favor of specifically targeted affirmative action and diversity policies for those contexts in which they are still needed.

NOTES

1. University of California Berkeley, 2010–2011 Staff Affirmative Action Plan, avaviable at http://hrweb.berkeley.edu/sites/hrweb.berkeley .edu/files/attachments/StaffAAP.pdf (accessed August 1, 2011).

2. For historical and definitional issues, see Carl Cohen and James P. Sterba, *Affirmative Action and Racial Preference* (New York: Oxford University Press, 2003), 14, 18–20, 25, 40, 101, 200–201, 253, 279, 296.

3. IBM, "Equal Opportunity," www-03.ibm.com/employment/us/diverse/equal_opportunity.shtml (accessed January 15, 2007).

4. IBM, "Equal Opportunity," www-03.ibm.com/employment/us/diverse/equal_opportunity.shtml (accessed January 15, 2007).

5. General Motors, "Diversity Management," www.gm.com/.../sustainability/reports/01/social_and_community_info/socialmanagement/diversity_manage.html (January 13, 2007).

6. Coca-Cola Company, "Fifth Annual Report of the Task Force: December 1, 2006," pp. 36–41; available at http://www.thecoca-colacompany.com/ourcompany/task_force_report_2006.pdf (accessed August 7, 2011).

7. *Grutter v. Bollinger*, 539 U.S. 306 (2003); and see also *Gratz v. Bollinger*, 539 U.S. 244 (2003).

8. American Council on Education, Washington, DC, "Making the Case for Affirmative Action," www.acenet.edu/bookstore/descriptions/makingthecase/works/business.cfm (accessed January 13, 2007).

9. John Yinger, *Closed Doors, Opportunities Lost* (New York: Russell Sage Foundation, 1995); Jerry T. Ferguson and Wallace R. Johnston, "Managing Diversity," *Mortgage Banking* 55 (1995): 3236L.

10. Dell Computer Corporation, at http://www.dell.com/us/en/gen/corporate/visiondiversity.htm (Accessed May 15, 2007).

11. See Laura Purdy, "Why Do We Need Affirmative Action?" *Journal of Social Philosophy* 25

(1994): 133–43; Farrell Bloch, *Antidiscrimination Law and Minority Employment: Recruitment Practices and Regulatory Constraints* (Chicago: University of Chicago Press, 1994); Joseph Sartorelli, "Gay Rightsand Affirmative Action" in *Gay Ethics*, ed. Timothy F. Murphy (New York: Haworth Press, 1994).

12. *Alexander v. Choate,* 469 U.S. 287, at 295.
13. But the Court comes very close in *Local 28 of the Sheet Metal Workers' International Association v. Equal Employment Opportunity Commission,* 478 U.S. 421 (1986).

14. *Fullilove v. Klutznick,* 448 U.S. 448 (1980); *United Steelworkers v. Weber,* 443 U.S. 193 (1979); *United States v. Paradise,* 480 U.S. 149 (1987); *Johnson v. Transportation Agency,* 480 U.S. 616 (1987).
15. *Firefighters v. Stotts,* 467 U.S. 561 (1984); *City of Richmond v. J. A. Croson Co.,* 109 S.Ct. 706 (1989); *Adarand Constructors Inc. v. Federico Pena,* 63 LW 4523 (1995); *Wygant v. Jackson Bd. of Education,* 476 U.S. 267 (1986); *Wards Cove Packing v. Atonio,* 490 U.S. 642.

♛ QUESTIONS FOR ANALYSIS

1. What are the two reasons why legal enforcement of equal protection is inadequate for proponents of affirmative action?
2. What is the relationship of "diversity policy" and "affirmative action policy" in corporations today? In what ways are they similar and different? How do those policies interact?
3. Although the Supreme Court has recognized the legitimacy of diversity as a goal in education, what remains to be decided? How would you decide those remaining issues?
4. What is the relationship of ethics and law in corporations today? What are example of appropriate moral obligations for corporations?
5. How does unintentional discrimination occur in a company? What are some examples of such unintentional discrimination? What steps are appropriate to eradicate this type of discrimination?
6. What empirical studies are still needed to better understand and eradicate discrimination?

Affirmative Action Is About Helping All of Us

ELIZABETH ANDERSON

Elizabeth Anderson is the Arthur F. Thurnau Professor and John Rawls Collegiate Professor of Philosophy and Women's Studies at the University of Michigan at Ann Arbor. Her most recent book, *The Imperative of Integration*, was published in 2010 by Princeton University Press.

She challenges the common appeal to "diversity" by asking precisely which kinds of diversity matter and why. Her strategy is to focus on the profound impact of race on American life, even today, and the fundamental goals of higher education. According to Anderson, diversity in higher education improves the understanding of all students of the social and economic realities of all races and classes.

It's no secret that race-based affirmative action in higher education faces a crisis of legitimacy. It has been banned in California, Florida, Michigan, Washington, Arizona, and Nebraska. Even as the U.S. Supreme Court upheld the constitutionality of affirmative action in 2003 in *Grutter v. Bollinger,*

"Affirmative Action Is About Helping All of Us," *The Chronicle Review,* May 29, 2011, pp. B11–B13. Reprinted by permission of the author.

the justices expressed an expectation that the policy would soon no longer be needed, practically inviting relitigation....

One might expect colleges to rise to the challenge of forcefully articulating a clear case for their policies. Instead we find the same tired arguments on the left, and critiques of affirmative action on the right that reflect ignorance of the realities of race in America.

We need new arguments for affirmative action. We can find them by resurrecting the ideal of integration from the grave of the civil-rights movement.

Colleges defend their policies by vaguely appealing to the educational benefits of diversity, while failing to present a frank discussion of how racial identities matter. That leaves the public wondering how diversity in skin color or ancestry could have any educational relevance.

Or are institutions suggesting with their multiculturalist rhetoric that racial diversity is a form of cultural diversity? That raises more questions than it answers. Why, uniquely among "diversity" factors, like having lived abroad or practiced an unusual religion, is racial diversity so important? If the diversity that affirmative-action beneficiaries bring is cultural, why don't colleges prefer to admit students from Africa and Latin America over African-Americans, Puerto Ricans, and Chicanos, given that the former would bring even more cultural diversity to campus than the latter? If race is a proxy for diverse ideas, why not admit students directly on the basis of their ideas? If diversity of ideas is important, why can't course materials represent it just as well? If institutions are free to practice "reverse" racial discrimination in the name of educational goals, why can't institutions practice segregation if they judge that students learn better in more comfortable, racially homogeneous surroundings?

Outside the ranks of university administrators, advocates are more attracted to the argument that racial minorities are entitled to compensation for past discrimination. At least that defense has the merit of tying affirmative action to a compelling interest in justice. Moreover, it highlights the weakness of what many observers feel is the strongest objection to affirmative action—that the policy burdens innocent whites. Wherever there is wrongdoing, innocents suffer. The only question

is whether the costs of wrongdoing should be concentrated on the victims or shared more widely. That the costs should be shared is the premise of all systems of justice administered by public agencies and financed by general taxation.

The real weaknesses of the compensatory defense lie elsewhere. When the injustices to be compensated for are located in the past, the case for compensation fades as those injustices recede from memory. People wonder why affirmative action's beneficiaries don't overcome adversity on their own, as they imagine that previous victims of discrimination, like Jews and Irish-Americans, did. Absent a frank discussion of continuing racial injustices, the image of the undeserving black or Latino beneficiary of affirmative action looms large. The compensatory rationale also represents affirmative action's beneficiaries as passive consumers of a benefit rather than as actively contributing to the educational mission of colleges—and thereby earning their places on their merits.

Higher education needs a rationale for affirmative action that fits the weight institutions assign to it, a rationale that clearly explains the contributions racially diverse students (not just their ideas) make to education and thereby represents its beneficiaries as meritorious, and that ties educational goals to urgent requirements of justice rather than to past events or optional educational goals.

To forge such a rationale, we need a clear understanding of how profoundly race still structures life in America, especially in the ways it continues to determine access to advantage, and how that affects people's ideas. And we need to tie such an understanding to the fundamental mission of higher education.

That requires a shift of focus: from the good that higher education does for the people who receive it, to the good that those who receive it are supposed to do for everyone else. One of the fundamental missions of higher education is to train leaders—an elite who will occupy professional, managerial, and political positions—to effectively serve people from all walks of life. A competent elite needs to be so constituted that it is systematically responsive to the interests and problems of people in all sectors of society, to be disposed to serve those interests, and to be able to respectfully interact with people across all sectors.

Most opponents of race-based affirmative action grant that sectors of society are defined in part by class and region. We hear virtually no complaints about affirmative-action preferences for the poor, or about the preferences that public institutions extend to in-state applicants. The point of those preferences is not simply to offer educational benefits to the poor and to the taxpayers who finance state colleges. We rightly accept that the poor bring firsthand knowledge of the challenges of poverty that is vital for elites to know. We rightly grant that states have an interest in training leaders who will serve their residents, and that their colleges should select students whose geographical origins make them more likely to stay in the region—an argument that gains strength the more regions are underserved.

Now consider the core reality about race in America today: We live in a profoundly racially segregated society. When I was looking for housing in the Detroit area some years ago, I was struck by the stark racial segregation of neighborhoods. Landlords repeatedly assured me that they were collectively holding the line against black entry into "their" neighborhoods. One showed me a home with a pile of cockroaches in the kitchen. He was confident that a white woman like me would rather live with cockroaches as housemates than with blacks as neighbors.

So blacks and whites overwhelmingly grow up in different neighborhoods. Latinos, too, are moderately segregated from blacks and whites. Different regions are delineated by race—black Detroit, white suburbs. Moreover, racially segregated regions differ sharply in the socioeconomic advantages and disadvantages they deliver to their residents. Most Americans know about inner-city ghettos. Opponents of affirmative action imagine that blacks and Latinos, upon attaining a middle-class occupation and income, escape the disadvantages of segregated neighborhoods. In reality, as the sociologists Douglas S. Massey and Nancy A. Denton have documented in *American Apartheid: Segregation and the Making of the Underclass* (Harvard University Press, 1993), levels of black segregation hardly decline as income rises.

That means that blacks are far less able to convert a middle-class education, occupation, and income into socioeconomic advantages for themselves and their children than are whites. In numerous metropolitan areas, middle-class blacks live in neighborhoods with lower housing values than whites, making less than half their income. Thus they suffer from worse city services and schools, and higher poverty, crime, and tax rates than lower-income whites. Massey and his colleagues have shown in *The Source of the River: The Social Origins of Freshmen at America's Selective Colleges and Universities* (Princeton University Press, 2003) that even among the most privileged minority students—those attending an elite university practicing affirmative action—half grew up in segregated or racially mixed neighborhoods, a condition that gave them starkly different experiences than those of their white peers. Those largely middle-class black students, along with their similarly segregated Latino peers, are vastly more likely to have witnessed gunshots, muggings, and other social disorders, and to have known homeless people, prostitutes, and gang members than their white peers.

My point is not that because even middle-class blacks and Latinos suffer socioeconomic disadvantages as a result of their race, they are entitled to compensation in the form of affirmative-action preferences. It is that they bring firsthand knowledge of racial conditions that is essential for elites to know if they are to be able to competently serve disadvantaged, racially segregated sectors of society. Growing up in closer contact with disadvantaged people than many whites do, many minority students bring practical competence in establishing rapport and respectful interaction with the less privileged. And, as Miriam Komaromy and colleagues have shown for minority physicians, and Timothy Bates has shown for black business owners, they are far more likely to serve racially segregated, grievously underserved communities, and to employ their residents, than are their white peers. All of that makes a vital contribution to higher education.

From Glenn Loury to Gary Orfield and Xavier de Sousa Briggs, most scholars who study segregation emphasize how it deprives the less advantaged of the knowledge and skills, including social and cultural capital, they need to advance. It is high time to consider how segregation also deprives the more advantaged of knowledge. They are less likely to understand the problems faced by those from whom they are segregated. They are more likely to form stigmatizing stereotypes of the latter, less likely to feel at ease interacting with them, more likely to perpetuate segregation by avoidance. A largely homogeneous elite constituted by those advantaged by racial segregation thus suffers from cognitive deficits.

If segregation is a cause of ignorance, incompetence, and unresponsiveness on the part of an elite, then integration is a remedy. The presence in higher education of groups disadvantaged by segregation, and not just their ideas, is needed— not only to foster respectful interaction among groups, but because there is nothing like the presence of members of other groups standing on equal terms with everyone else to inspire a vivid sense of accountability in those others.

An integrated elite is a smarter, more responsible elite. Justice Sandra Day O'Connor understood that when she wrote in *Grutter v. Bollinger,* "Effective participation by members of all racial and ethnic groups in the civic life of our Nation is essential if the dream of one Nation, indivisible, is to be realized." Let's not kid ourselves. We live in a nation deeply divided by race. Integration is needed to create "one Nation, indivisible."

☙ QUESTIONS FOR ANALYSIS

1. What kinds of "diversity" does Anderson consider and which are most important in higher education?
2. What is "compensatory justice" as a rationale for affirmative action? What are the problems with this approach?
3. What evidence does Anderson cite for her claim that "we live in a profoundly racially segregated society"? How relevant is this evidence for your own community? Is there evidence that your own community is racially segregated that is consistent with hers? Is there evidence that challenges her view?
4. What do middle-class blacks and Latinos bring to higher education? Does this support continuation of affirmative action by race, even for those not economically deprived?
5. What is the importance of integration by race, according to Anderson?

Reverse Discrimination as Unjustified

LISA NEWTON

Lisa Newton, a professor of philosophy at Fairfield University, delivered a version of the following essay at a meeting of the Society for Women in Philosophy in 1972. She argues that reverse discrimination cannot be justified by an appeal to the ideal of equality. Indeed, according to Newton, reverse discrimination does not advance but actually undermines equality because it violates the concept of equal justice under law for all citizens.

Specifically, Newton attacks the defense for reverse discrimination on grounds of equality. She contends that no violation of justice can be justified by an appeal to the ideal of equality, for the idea of equality is logically dependent on the notion of justice.

In addition to this theoretical objection to reverse discrimination, Newton opposes it because she believes it raises insoluble problems. Among them are determining what groups have been sufficiently discriminated against in the past to deserve preferred treatment in the present and determining the degree of reverse discrimination that will be compensatory. Newton concludes that reverse discrimination destroys justice, law, equality, and citizenship itself.

From Lisa H. Newton, "Reverse Discrimination as Unjustified," *Ethics* 83 (1973): 308–12. Copyright © 1973 by The University of Chicago Press. Reprinted by permission of the publisher.

I have heard it argued that "simple justice" requires that we favor women and blacks in employment and educational opportunities, since women and blacks were "unjustly" excluded from such opportunities for so many years in the not so distant past. It is a strange argument, an example of a possible implication of a true proposition advanced to dispute the proposition itself, like an octopus absentmindedly slicing off his head with a stray tentacle. A fatal confusion underlies this argument, a confusion fundamentally relevant to our understanding of the notion of the rule of law.

Two senses of justice and equality are involved in this confusion. The root notion of justice, progenitor of the other, is the one that Aristotle (*Nicomachean Ethics* 5.6; *Politics* 1.2; 3.1) assumes to be the foundation and proper virtue of the political association. It is the conclusion which free men establish among themselves when they "share a common life in order that their association bring them self-sufficiency"—the regulation of their relationship by law, and the establishment, by law, of equality before the law. Rule of law is the name and pattern of this justice; its equality stands against the inequalities—of wealth, talent, etc.—otherwise obtaining among its participants, who by virtue of that equality are called "citizens." It is an achievement—complete, or, more frequently, partial—of certain people in certain concrete situations. It is fragile and easily disrupted by powerful individuals who discover that the blind equality of rule of law is inconvenient for their interests. Despite its obvious instability, Aristotle assumed that the establishment of justice in this sense, the creation of citizenship, was a permanent possibility for men and that the resultant association of citizens was the natural home of the species. At levels below the political association, this rule-governed equality is easily found; it is exemplified by any group of children agreeing together to play a game. At the level of the political association, the attainment of this justice is more difficult, simply because the stakes are so much higher for each participant. The equality of citizenship is not something that happens of its own accord, and without the expenditure of a fair amount of effort it will collapse into the rule of a powerful few over an apathetic many. But at least it has been achieved, at some times in some places; it is always worth trying to achieve, and eminently worth

trying to maintain, wherever and to whatever degree it has been brought into being.

Aristotle's parochialism is notorious; he really did not imagine that persons other than Greeks could associate freely in justice, and the only form of association he had in mind was the Greek *polis*. With the decline of the *polis* and the shift in the center of political thought, his notion of justice underwent a sea change. To be exact, it ceased to represent a political type and became a moral ideal: the ideal of equality as we know it. This ideal demands that all men be included in citizenship—that one Law govern all equally, that all men regard all other men as fellow citizens, with the same guarantees, rights, and protections. Briefly, it demands that the circle of citizenship achieved by any group be extended to include the entire human race. Properly understood, its effect on our associations can be excellent: It congratulates us on our achievement of rule of law as a process of government but refuses to let us remain complacent until we have expanded the associations to include others within the ambit of the rules, as often and as far as possible. While one man is a slave, none of us may feel truly free. We are constantly prodded by this ideal to look for possible unjustifiable discrimination, for inequalities not absolutely required for the functioning of the society and advantageous to all. And after twenty centuries of pressure, not at all constant, from this ideal, it might be said that some progress has been made. To take the cases in point for this problem, we are now prepared to assert, as Aristotle would never have been, the equality of sexes and of persons of different colors. The ambit of American citizenship, once restricted to white males of property, has been extended to include all adult free men, then all adult males including ex-slaves, then all women. The process of acquisition of full citizenship was for these groups a sporadic trail of half-measures, even now not complete; the steps on the road to full equality are marked by legislation and judicial decisions which are only recently concluded and still often not enforced. But the fact that we can now discuss the possibility of favoring such groups in hiring shows that over the area that concerns us, at least, full equality is presupposed as a basis for discussion. To that extent, they are full citizens, fully protected by the law of the land.

It is important for my argument that the moral ideal of equality be recognized as logically distinct from the condition (or virtue) of justice in the political sense. Justice in this sense exists *among* a citizenry, irrespective of the number of the populace included in that citizenry. Further, the moral ideal is parasitic upon the political virtue, for "equality" is unspecified—it means nothing until we are told in what respect that equality is to be realized. In a political context, "equality" is specified as "equal rights"—equal access to the public realm, public goods and offices, equal treatment under the law—in brief, the equality of citizenship. If citizenship is not a possibility, political equality is unintelligible. The ideal emerges as a generalization of the real condition and refers back to that condition for its content.

Now, if justice (Aristotle's justice in the political sense) is equal treatment under law for all citizens, what is injustice? Clearly, injustice is the violation of that equality, discrimination for or against a group of citizens, favoring them with special immunities and privileges or depriving them of those guaranteed to the others. When the southern employer refuses to hire blacks in white-collar jobs, when Wall Street will only hire women as secretaries with new titles, when Mississippi high schools routinely flunk all the black boys above ninth grade, we have examples of injustice, and we work to restore the equality of the public realm by ensuring that equal opportunity will be provided in such cases in the future. But of course, when the employers and the schools *favor* women and blacks, the same injustice is done. Just as the previous discrimination did, this reverse discrimination violates the public equality which defines citizenship and destroys the rule of law for the areas in which these favors are granted. To the extent that we adopt a program of discrimination, reverse or otherwise, justice in the political sense is destroyed, and none of us, specifically affected or not, is a citizen, a bearer of rights—we are all petitioners for favors. And to the same extent, the ideal of equality is undermined, for it has content only where justice obtains, and by destroying justice we render the ideal meaningless. It is, then, an ironic paradox, if not a contradiction in terms, to assert that the ideal of equality justifies the violation of justice; it is as if one should argue, with William

Buckley, that an ideal of humanity can justify the destruction of the human race.

Logically, the conclusion is simple enough: All discrimination is wrong prima facie because it violates justice, and that goes for reverse discrimination too. No violation of justice among the citizens may be justified (may overcome the prima facie objection) by appeal to the ideal of equality, for that ideal is logically dependent upon the notion of justice. Reverse discrimination, then, which attempts no other justification than an appeal to equality, is wrong. But let us try to make the conclusion more plausible by suggesting some of the implications of the suggested practice of reverse discrimination in employment and education. My argument will be that the problems raised there are insoluble, not only in practice but in principle.

We may argue, if we like, about what "discrimination" consists of. Do I discriminate against blacks if I admit none to my school when none of the black applicants are qualified by the tests I always give? How far must I go to root out cultural bias from my application forms and tests before I can say that I have not discriminated against those of different cultures? Can I assume that women are not strong enough to be roughnecks on my oil rigs, or must I test them individually? But this controversy, the most popular and well-argued aspect of the issue, is not as fatal as two others which cannot be avoided: If we are regarding the blacks as a "minority" victimized by discrimination, what is a "minority"? And for any group—blacks, women, whatever—that has been discriminated against, what amount of reverse discrimination wipes out the initial discrimination? Let us grant as true that women and blacks were discriminated against, even where laws forbade such discrimination, and grant for the sake of argument that a history of discrimination must be wiped out by reverse discrimination. What follows?

First, are there other groups which have been, discriminated against? For they should have the same right of restitution. What about American Indians, Chicanos, Appalachian Mountain whites, Puerto Ricans, Jews, Cajuns, and Orientals? And if these are to be included, the principle according to which we specify a "minority" is simply the criterion of "ethnic (sub) group," and we're stuck with every hyphenated American in the lower middle class clamoring for special privileges for *his* group—and with equal justification. For be it noted, when we run down the Harvard roster, we find not only a scarcity of blacks (in comparison with the proportion in the population) but an even more striking scarcity of those second-, third-, and fourth-generation ethnics who make up the loudest voice of Middle America. Shouldn't they demand *their* share? And eventually, the WASPs will have to form their own lobby; for they too are a minority. The point is simply this: There is no "majority" in America who will not mind giving up just a bit of their rights to make room for a favored minority. There are only other minorities, each of which is discriminated against by the favoring. The initial injustice is then repeated dozens of times, and if each minority is granted the same right of restitution as the others, an entire area of rule governance is dissolved into a pushing and shoving match between self-interested groups. Each works to catch the public eye and political popularity by whatever means of advertising and power politics lend themselves to the effort, to capitalize as much as possible on temporary popularity until the restless mob picks another group to feel sorry for. Hardly an edifying spectacle, and in the long run no one can benefit: The pie is no larger—it just that instead of setting up and enforcing rules for getting a piece, we've turned the contest into a free-for-all, requiring much more effort for no larger a reward. It would be in the interests of all the participants to reestablish an objective rule to govern the process, carefully enforced and the same for all.

Second, supposing that we do manage to agree in general that women and blacks (and all the others) have some right of restitution, some right to a privileged place in the structure of opportunities for a while, how will we know when that while is up? How much privilege is enough? When will the guilt be gone, the price paid, the balance restored? What recompense is right for centuries of exclusion? What criterion tells us when we are done? Our experience with the Civil Rights movement shows us that agreement on these terms cannot be presupposed: A process that appears to some to be going at a mad gallop into a black takeover appears to the rest of us to be at a standstill. Should a

practice of reverse discrimination be adopted, we may safely predict that just as some of us begin to see "a satisfactory start toward righting the balance," others of us will see that we "have already gone too far in the other direction" and will suggest that the discrimination ought to be reversed again. And such disagreement is inevitable, for the point is that we could not *possibly* have any criteria for evaluating the kind of recompense we have in mind. The context presumed by any discussion of restitution is the context of the rule of law: Law sets the rights of men and simultaneously sets the method for remedying the violation of those rights. You may exact suffering from others and/ or damage payments for yourself if and only if the others have violated your rights; the suffering you have endured is not sufficient reason for them to suffer. And remedial rights exist only where there is law: Primary human rights are useful guides to legislation but cannot stand as reasons for awarding remedies for injuries sustained. But then, the context presupposed by any discussion of restitution is the context of preexistent full citizenship. No remedial rights could exist for the excluded; neither in law nor in logic does there exist a right to *sue* for a standing to sue.

From these two considerations, then, the difficulties with reverse discrimination become evident. Restitution for a disadvantaged group whose rights under the law have been violated is possible by legal means, but restitution for a disadvantaged group whose grievance is that there was no law to protect them simply is not. First, outside of the area of justice defined by the law, no sense can be made of "the group's rights," for no law recognizes that group or the individuals in it, qua members, as bearers of rights (hence *any* group can constitute itself as a disadvantaged minority in some sense and demand similar restitution). Second, outside of the area of protection of law, no sense can be made of the violation of rights (hence the amount of the recompense cannot be decided by any objective criterion). For both reasons, the practice of reverse discrimination undermines the foundation of the very ideal in whose name it is advocated; it destroys justice, law, equality, and citizenship itself, and replaces them with power struggles and popularity contests.

QUESTIONS FOR ANALYSIS

1. What is the "fatal confusion" underlying the argument that "simple justice" requires preferential treatment?
2. Can you describe how justice under Aristotle moved from a "political type" to a "moral ideal"?
3. Why is it important for Newton's argument that she distinguish the moral ideal of equality from the condition of justice in the political sense?
4. Central to Newton's argument is her definition of justice and her assumptions about the relationship between justice and equality. Do you agree with her?
5. Do you think Rawls would agree with Newton's analysis? Explain.
6. Would you agree that in part Newton objects to reverse discrimination on utilitarian grounds? Explain.
7. Do you agree that the problems Newton says surround reverse discrimination really are "insoluble"?

Class, Not Race

RICHARD D. KAHLENBERG

Richard Kahlenberg is a Senior Fellow at The Century Foundation in Washington, D.C. He received his B.A. from Harvard University and his J.D. from Harvard Law School. He spent a year at the University of Nairobi School of Journalism as a Rotary Scholar and worked as a legislative assistant to Senator Charles S. Robb of Virginia.

In this essay, he argues that granting preferences by class, not race, would promote the original goals of the Civil Rights Act more effectively than current practices. He explores possible definitions of class or disadvantage, depending on context. He also considers several significant objections to this approach that he believes need to be answered.

In an act that reflected panic as much as cool reflection, Bill Clinton said recently that he is reviewing all federal affirmative action programs to see "whether there is some other way we can reach [our] objective without giving a preference by race or gender." As the country's mood swings violently against affirmative action, and as Republicans gear up to use the issue to bludgeon the Democratic coalition yet again in 1996, the whole project of legislating racial equality seems suddenly in doubt. The Democrats, terrified of the issue, are now hoping it will just go away. It won't. But at every political impasse, there is a political opportunity. Bill Clinton now has a chance, as no other Democrat has had since 1968, to turn a glaring liability for his party into an advantage—without betraying basic Democratic principles.

There is, as Clinton said, a way "we can work this out." But it isn't the "*Bakke* straddle," which says yes to affirmative action (race as a factor) but no to quotas. It isn't William Julius Wilson's call to "emphasize" race-neutral social programs, while downplaying affirmative action. The days of downplaying are gone; we can count on the Republicans for that. The way out—an idea Clinton hinted at—is to introduce the principle of race neutrality and the goal of aiding the disadvantaged into affirmative action preference programs themselves: to base preferences, in education, entry-level employment and public contracting, on class, not race.

Richard Kahlenberg, "Class, Not Race," *The New Republic* (April 3, 1995), pp. 212, 214. Reprinted with permission of the author.

Were Clinton to propose this move, the media would charge him with lurching to the right. Jesse Jackson's presidential campaign would surely soon follow. But despite its association with conservatives such as Clarence Thomas, Antonin Scalia and Dinesh D'Souza, the idea of class-bassed affirmative action should in fact appeal to the left as well. After all, its message of addressing class unfairness and its political potential for building cross-racial coalitions are traditional liberal staples.

For many years, the left argued not only that class was important, but also that it was more important than race. This argument was practical, ideological and politic. An emphasis on class inequality meant Robert Kennedy riding in a motorcade through cheering white and black sections of racially torn Gary, Indiana, in 1968, with black Mayor Richard Hatcher on one side, and white working-class boxing hero Tony Zale on the other.

Ideologically, it was clear that with the passage of the Civil Rights Act of 1964, class replaced caste as the central impediment to equal opportunity. Martin Luther King Jr. moved from the Montgomery Boycott to the Poor People's Campaign, which he described as "his last, greatest dream," and "something bigger than just a civil rights movement for Negroes," RFK told David Halberstam that "it was pointless to talk about the real problem in America being black and white, it was really rich and poor, which was a much more complex subject."

Finally, the left emphasized class because to confuse class and race was seen not only as wrong but as dangerous. This notion was at the heart of the protest over Daniel Patrick Moynihan's 1965 report, *The Negro Family: The Case for National Action*, in which Moynihan depicted the rising rates of illegitimacy among poor blacks. While Moynihan's critics were wrong to silence discussion of illegitimacy among blacks, they rightly noted that the title of the report, which implicated all blacks, was misleading, and that fairly high rates of illegitimacy also were present among poor whites—a point which Moynihan readily endorses today. (In the wake of the second set of L.A. riots in 1992, Moynihan rose on the Senate floor to reaffirm that family structure "is not an issue of race but of class. … It is class behavior.")

The irony is that affirmative action based on race violates these three liberal insights. It provides the ultimate wedge to destroy Robert Kennedy's coalition. It says that despite civil rights protections, the wealthiest African American is more deserving of preference than the poorest white. It relentlessly focuses all attention on race.

In contrast, Lyndon Johnson's June 1965 address to Howard University, in which the concept of affirmative action was first unveiled, did not ignore class. In a speech drafted by Moynihan, Johnson spoke of the bifurcation of the black community, and, in his celebrated metaphor, said we needed to aid those "hobbled" in life's race by past discrimination. This suggested special help for disadvantaged blacks, not all blacks; for the young Clarence Thomas, but not for Clarence Thomas's son. Johnson balked at implementing the thematic language of his speech. His Executive Order 11246, calling for "affirmative action" among federal contractors, initially meant greater outreach and required hiring without respect to race. In fact, LBJ rescinded his Labor Department's proposal to provide for racial quotas in the construction industry in Philadelphia. It fell to Richard Nixon to implement the "Philadelphia Plan," in what Nixon's aides say was a conscious effort to drive a wedge between blacks and labor. (Once he placed racial preferences on the table, Nixon adroitly extricated himself, and by 1972 was campaigning against racial quotas.)

The ironies were compounded by the Supreme Court. In the 1974 case *De Funis v. Odegaard*, in which a system of racial preferences in law school admissions was at issue, it was the Court's liberal giant, William O. Douglas, who argued that racial preferences were unconstitutional, and suggested instead that preferences be based on disadvantage. Four years later, in the *Bakke* case, the great proponent of affirmative action as a means to achieve "diversity" was Nixon appointee Lewis F. Powell Jr. Somewhere along the line, the right wing embraced Douglas and Critical Race Theory embraced Powell.

Today, the left pushes racial preferences, even for the most advantaged minorities, in order to promote diversity and provide role models for disadvantaged blacks—an argument which, if it came from Ronald Reagan, the left would rightly dismiss as trickle-down social theory. Today, when William

Julius Wilson argues the opposite of the Moynihan report—that the problems facing the black community are rooted more in class than race—it is Wilson who is excoriated by civil rights groups. The left can barely utter the word "class", instead resorting to euphemisms such as "income groups," "wage earners" and "people who play by the rules."

For all of this, the left has paid a tremendous price. On a political level, with a few notable exceptions, the history of the past twenty-five years is a history of white, working-class Robert Kennedy Democrats turning first into Wallace Democrats, then into Nixon and Reagan Democrats and ultimately into today's Angry White Males. Time and again, the white working class votes its race rather than its class, and Republicans win. The failure of the left to embrace class also helps turn poor blacks, for whom racial preferences are, in Stephen Carter's words, "stunningly irrelevant," toward Louis Farrakhan.

On the merits, the left has committed itself to a goal—equality of group results—which seems highly radical, when it is in fact rather unambitious. To the extent that affirmative action, at its ultimate moment of success, merely creates a self-perpetuating black elite along with a white one, its goal is modest—certainly more conservative than real equality of opportunity, which gives blacks and whites and other Americans of all economic strata a fair chance at success.

The priority given to race over class has inevitably exacerbated white racism. Today, both liberals and conservatives conflate race and class because it serves both of their purposes to do so. Every year, when SAT scores are released, the breakdown by race shows enormous gaps between blacks on the one hand and whites and Asians on the other. The NAACP cites these figures as evidence that we need to do more. Charles Murray cites the same statistics as evidence of intractable racial differences. We rarely see a breakdown of scores by class, which would show enormous gaps between rich and poor, gaps that would help explain the differences in scores by race.

On the legal front, it once made some strategic sense to emphasize race over class. But when states moved to the remedial phrase—and began trying to address past discrimination—the racial focus became a liability. The strict scrutiny that struck down Jim Crow is now used, to varying degrees, to curtail racial preferences. Class, on the other hand, is not one of the suspect categories under the Fourteenth Amendment, which leaves class-based remedies much less assailable.

If class-based affirmative action is a theory that liberals should take seriously, how would it work in practice? … Michael Kinsley has asked, "Does Clarence Thomas, the sharecropper's kid, get more or fewer preference points than the unemployed miner's son from Appalachia?" Most conservative proponents of class-based affirmative action have failed to explain their idea with any degree of specificity. Either they're insincere—offering the alternative only for tactical reasons—or they're stumped.

The former is more likely. While the questions of implementation are serious and difficult, they are not impossible to answer. At the university level, admissions committees deal every day with precisely the type of apples-and-oranges question that Kinsley poses. Should a law school admit an applicant with a 3.2 GPA from Yale or a 3.3 from Georgetown? How do you compare those two if one applicant worked for the Peace Corps but the other had slightly higher LSATs?

In fact, a number of universities already give preferences for disadvantaged students in addition to racial minorities. Since 1989 Berkeley has granted special consideration to applicants "from socioeconomically disadvantaged backgrounds … regardless of race or ethnicity." Temple University Law School has, since the 1970s, given preference to "applicants who have overcome exceptional and continuous economic deprivation." And at Hastings College of Law, 20 percent of the class is set aside for disadvantaged students through the Legal Equal Opportunity Program. Even the U.C. Davis medical program challenged by Allan Bakke was limited to "disadvantaged" minorities, a system which Davis apparently did not find impossible to administer.

Similar class-based preference programs could be provided by public employers and federal contractors for high school graduates not pursuing college, on the theory that at that age their class-based handicaps hide their true potential and are not at all of their own making. In public contracting, government agencies could follow the model of New York City's old class-based program, which provided preferences based not on the ethnicity or gender of the contractor, but to small firms located in New York City which did part of their business in depressed areas or employed economically disadvantaged workers.

The definition of class or disadvantage may vary according to context, but if, for example, the government chose to require class-based affirmative action from universities receiving federal funds, it is possible to devise an enforceable set of objective standards for deprivation. If the aim of class-based affirmative action is to provide a system of genuine equality of opportunity, a leg up to promising students who have done well despite the odds, we have a wealth of sociological data to devise an obstacles test. While some might balk at the very idea of reducing disadvantage to a number, we currently reduce intellectual promise to number—SATs and GPAs—and adding a number for disadvantage into the calculus just makes deciding who gets ahead and who does not a little fairer.

There are three basic ways to proceed: with a simple, moderate or complex definition. The simple method is to ask college applicants their family's income and measure disadvantage by that factor alone, on the theory that income is a good proxy for a whole host of economic disadvantages (such as bad schools or a difficult learning environment). This oversimplified approach is essentially the tack we've taken with respect to compensatory race-based affirmative action. For example, most affirmative action programs ask applicants to check a racial box and sweep all the ambiguities under the rug. Even though African Americans have, as Justice Thurgood Marshall said in *Bakke*, suffered a history "different in kind, not just degree, from that of other ethnic groups," universities don't calibrate preferences based on comparative group disadvantage (and, in the Davis system challenged by Bakke, two-thirds of the preferences went to Mexican-Americans and Asians, not blacks). We also ignore the question of when an individual's family immigrated in order to determine whether the family was even theoretically subject to the official discrimination in this country on which preferences are predicated.

"Diversity" was supposed to solve all this by saying we don't care about compensation, only

viewpoint. But, again, if universities are genuinely seeking diversity of viewpoints, they should inquire whether a minority applicant really does have the "minority viewpoint" being sought. Derrick Bell's famous statement—"the ends of diversity are not served by people who look black and think white"—is at once repellent and a relevant critique of the assumption that all minority members think alike. In theory, we need some assurance from the applicant that he or she will in fact interact with students of different backgrounds, lest the cosmetic diversity of the freshman yearbook be lost to the reality of ethnic theme houses.

The second way to proceed, the moderately complicated calculus of class, would look at what sociologists believe to be the Big Three determinants of life chances: parental income, education and occupation. Parents' education, which is highly correlated with a child's academic achievement, can be measured in number of years. And while ranking occupations might seem hopelessly complex, various attempts to do so objectively have yielded remarkably consistent results—from the Barr Scale of the early 1920s to Alba Edwards' Census rankings of the 1940s to a Duncan Scores of the 1960s.

The third alternative, the complex calculus of disadvantage, would count all the factors mentioned, but might also look at net worth, the quality of secondary education, neighborhood influences and family structure. An applicant's family wealth is readily available from financial aid forms, and provides a long-term view of relative disadvantage, to supplement the "snapshot" picture that income provides. We also know that schooling opportunities are crucial to a student's life chances, even controlling for home environment. Some data suggest that a disadvantaged student at a middle-class school does better on average than a middle-class student at a school with high concentrations of poverty. Objective figures are available to measure secondary school quality—from per student expenditure, to the percentage of students receiving free or reduced-price lunches, to a school's median score on standardized achievement tests. Neighborhood influences, measured by the concentration of poverty within Census tracts or zip codes, could also be factored in, since numerous studies have found that living in a low-income community can adversely affect an individual's life chances above and beyond family income. Finally, everyone from Dan Quayle to Donna Shalala agrees that children growing up in single-parent homes have a tougher time. This factor could be taken into account as well.

The point is not that this list is the perfect one, but that it *is* possible to devise a series of fairly objective and verifiable factors that measure the degree to which a teenager's true potential has been hidden. (As it happens, the complex definition is the one that disproportionately benefits African Americans. Even among similar income groups, blacks are more likely than whites to live in concentrated poverty, go to bad schools and live in single-parent homes.) It's just not true that a system of class preferences is inherently harder to administer than a system based on race. Race only seems simpler because we have ignored the ambiguities. And racial preferences are just as easy to ridicule. To paraphrase Kinsley, does a new Indian immigrant get fewer or more points than a third-generation Latino whose mother is Anglo?

Who should benefit? Mickey Kaus, in "Class Is In" (TRB, March 27), argued that class preferences should be reserved for the underclass. But the injuries of class extend beyond the poorest. The offspring of the working poor and the working class lack advantages, too, and indeed SAT scores correlate lockstep with income at every increment. Unless you believe in genetic inferiority, these statistics suggest unfairness is not confined to the underclass. As a practical matter, a teenager who emerges from the underclass has little chance of surviving at an elite college. At Berkeley, administrators found that using a definition of disadvantaged, under which neither parent attended a four-year college and the family could not afford to pay $1,000 in education expenses, failed to bring in enough students who were likely to pass.

Still, there are several serious objections to class-based preferences that must be addressed.

1. *We're not ready to be color-blind because racial discrimination continues to afflict our society.* Ron Brown says affirmative action "continues to be needed not to redress grievances of the past, but the current discrimination that continues to exist." This is a relatively new theory, which

conveniently elides the fact that preferences were supposed to be temporary. It also stands logic on its head. While racial discrimination undoubtedly still exists, the Civil Rights Act of 1964 was meant to address prospective discrimination. Affirmative action—discrimination in itself—makes sense only to the extent that there is a current-day legacy of *past* discrimination which new prospective laws cannot reach back and remedy.

In the contexts of education and employment, the Civil Rights Act already contains powerful tools to address intentional and unintentional discrimination. The Civil Rights Act of 1991 reaffirmed the need to address unintentional discrimination—by requiring employers to justify employment practices that are statistically more likely to hurt minorities—but it did so without crossing the line to required preferences. This principle also applies to Title VI of the Civil Rights Act, so that if, for example, it can be shown that the SAT produces an unjustified disparate impact, a university can be barred from using it. In addition, "soft" forms of affirmative action, which require employers and universities to broaden the net and interview people from all races are good ways of ensuring positions are not filled by word of mouth, through wealthy white networks.

We have weaker tools to deal with discrimination in other areas of life—say, taxi drivers who refuse to pick up black businessmen—but how does a preference in education or employment remedy that wrong? By contrast, there is nothing illegal about bad schools, bad housing and grossly stunted opportunities for the poor. A class preference is perfectly appropriate.

2. *Class preferences will be just as stigmatizing as racial preferences.* Kinsley argues that "any debilitating self-doubt that exists because of affirmative action is not going to be mitigated by being told you got into Harvard because of your 'socioeconomic disadvantage' rather than your race."

But class preferences are different from racial preferences in at least two important respects. First, stigma—in one's own eyes and the eyes of others—is bound up with the question of whether an admissions criterion is accepted as legitimate. Students with good grades aren't seen as getting in "just because they're smart." And there appears to be a societal consensus—from Douglas to

Scalia—that kids from poor backgrounds deserve a leg up. Such a consensus has never existed for class-blind racial preferences.

Second, there is no myth of inferiority in this country about the abilities of poor people comparable to that about African Americans. Now, if racial preferences are purely a matter of compensatory justice, then the question of whether preferences exacerbate white racism is not relevant. But today racial preferences are often justified by social utility (bringing different racial groups together helps dispel stereotypes) in which case the social consequences are highly relevant. The general argument made by proponents of racial preferences—that policies need to be grounded in social reality, not ahistorical theory—cuts in favor of the class category. Why? Precisely because there is no stubborn historical myth for it to reinforce.

Kaus makes a related argument when he says that class preferences "will still reward those who play the victim." But if objective criteria are used to define the disadvantaged, there is no way to "play" the victim. Poor and working-class teenagers are the victims of class inequality not of their own making. Preferences, unlike, say, a welfare check, tell poor teenagers not that they are helpless victims, but that we think their long-run potential is great, and we're going to give them a chance—if they work their tails off—to prove themselves.

3. *Class preferences continue to treat people as members of groups as opposed to individuals.* Yes. But so do university admissions policies that summarily reject students below a certain SAT level. It's hard to know what treating people as individuals means. (Perhaps if university admissions committees interviewed the teachers of each applicant back to kindergarten to get a better picture of their academic potential, we'd be treating them more as individuals.) The question is not whether we treat people as members of groups—that's inevitable—but whether the group is a relevant one. And in measuring disadvantage (and hidden potential) class is surely a much better proxy than race.

4. *Class-based affirmative action will not yield a diverse student body in elite colleges.* Actually, there is reason to believe that class preferences will disproportionately benefit people of color in most contexts—since minorities are disproportionately

poor. In the university context, however, class-based preferences were rejected during the 1970s in part because of fear that they would produce inadequate numbers of minority students. The problem is that when you control for income, African American students do worse than white and Asian students on the SAT—due in part to differences in culture and linguistic patterns, and in part to the way income alone as a measurement hides other class-based differences among ethnic groups.

The concern is a serious and complicated one. Briefly, there are four responses. First, even Murray and Richard Herrnstein agree that the residual racial gap in scores has declined significantly in the past two decades, so the concern, though real, is not as great as it once was. Second, if we use the sophisticated definition of class discussed earlier—which reflects the relative disadvantage of blacks vis-à-vis whites of the same income level—the racial gap should close further. Third, we can improve racial diversity by getting rid of unjustified preferences—for alumni kids or students from underrepresented geographic regions—which disproportionately hurt people of color. Finally, if the goal is to provide genuine equal opportunity, not equality of group result, and if we are satisfied that a meritocratic system which corrects for class inequality is the best possible approximation of that equality, then we have achieved our goal.

5. *Class-based affirmative action will cause as much resentment among those left out as race-based affirmative action.* Kinsley argues that the rejected applicant in the infamous Jesse Helms commercial from 1990 would feel just as angry for losing out on a class-based as a race-based preference, since both involve "making up for past injustice." The difference, of course, is that class preferences go to the actual victims of class injury, mooting the whole question of intergenerational justice. In the racial context, this was called "victim specificity." Even the Reagan administration was in favor of compensating actual victims of racial discrimination.

The larger point implicit in Kinsley's question is a more serious one: that any preference system, whether race- or class-based, is "still a form of zero-sum social engineering." Why should liberals push for class preferences at all? Why not just provide more funding for education, safer schools, better nutrition? The answer is that liberals should do these things; but we cannot hold our breath for it to happen. In 1993, when all the planets were aligned—a populist Democratic president, Democratic control of both Houses of Congress—they produced what *The New York Times* called "A BUDGET WORTHY OF MR. BUSH." Cheaper alternatives, such as preferences, must supplement more expensive strategies of social spending. Besides, to the extent that class preferences help change the focus of public discourse from race to class, they help reforge the coalition needed to sustain the social programs liberals want.

Class preferences could restore the successful formula on which the early civil rights movement rested: morally unassailable underpinnings and a relatively inexpensive agenda. It's crucial to remember that Martin Luther King Jr. called for special consideration based on class, not race. After laying out a forceful argument for the special debt owed to blacks, King rejected the call for a Negro Bill or Rights in favor of a Bill of Rights for

the Disadvantaged. It was King's insight that there were nonracial ways to remedy racial wrongs, and that the injuries of class deserve attention along with the injuries of race.

None of this is to argue that King would have opposed affirmative action if the alternative were to do nothing. For Jesse Helms to invoke King's color-blind rhetoric now that it is in the interests of white people to do so is the worst kind of hypocrisy. Some form of compensation is necessary, and I think affirmative action, though deeply flawed, is better than nothing.

But the opportunity to save affirmative action of any kind may soon pass. If the Supreme Court continues to narrow the instances in which racial preferences are justified, if California voters put an end to affirmative action in their state and if Congress begins to roll back racial preferences in legislation which President Clinton finds hard to veto—or President Phil Gramm signs with gusto—conservatives will have less and less reason to bargain. Now is the time to call their bluff.

⚜ QUESTIONS FOR ANALYSIS

1. Why does the political environment of the last two decades suggest that a new strategy of class-based affirmative action is needed, instead of the traditional race-based programs?
2. Focussing on class, not just race, is not a new idea, as Kahlenberg explains. How were these views demonstrated in the words of President Lyndon Johnson, Senator Daniel Patrick Moynihan, and Justice William O. Douglas?
3. How would a class-based affirmative action approach work in practice in education? in public employment and contracting?

4. How should "class-based disadvantage" be defined? What does Kahlenberg propose as a simple, moderate, or complex definition? Do his proposals demonstrate that it is possible to devise a series of objective and verifiable factors, as he claims?
5. What objections to this approach does Kahlenberg identify? How successfully does he answer them?
6. Do you agree with Kahlenberg in thinking that class-based preferences offer more promise for addressing historic wrongs than race-based preferences?

CASE PRESENTATION

Proposition 209

Over the years, California voters have passed many controversial ballot initiatives that proved to be bellwethers for the rest of the nation. Among the most controversial is Proposition 209, an amendment to the state constitution that appeared on the 1996 ballot and passed by a margin of 54 percent to 45 percent. According to that measure, "The state shall not discriminate against, or grant preferential treatment to, any individual or group

on the basis of race, sex, color, ethnicity, or national origin in the operation of public employment, public education, or public contracting."

These words may seem innocuous at first. In fact, they are modeled on the Civil Rights Act of 1964. But they sparked a lawsuit in federal court seeking to have the amendment declared unconstitutional. The problem, the plaintiffs argued, is that the measure puts an end to all state-sponsored affirmative-action programs, and in doing so, it places an unconstitutional hardship on minorities and women. A district court judge agreed and blocked the law with a preliminary injunction, but the Ninth Circuit Court of Appeals overruled him, and the law went into effect in August 1997. Still, the legal battle did not end until November 3 of that year, when the U.S. Supreme Court unanimously declined to hear the plaintiffs' challenge to the law.

California Governor Pete Wilson hailed the ruling. The *Los Angeles Times* quoted him as saying, "It is time for those who have resisted Prop. 209 to acknowledge that equal rights under law, not special preferences, is the law of the land. A measure that eliminates any form of discrimination based on race and gender violates no one's constitutional rights." The paper also quoted Mark Rosenbaum of the American Civil Liberties Union, the plaintiffs' chief attorney, who called the measure "mean-spirited and unjust" and "1990s-style discrimination against minorities and women, more insidious than any state-wide measure since the era of Southern resistance to *Brown v. Board of Education*."

In the fall of 2006, only 2 percent of the incoming freshmen at UCLA were African-American, a 57 percent drop in the ten years since adoption of Prop. 209. In the ten-campus University of California system, only 3.4 percent of all freshmen offered admission for fall 2006 were African-American.

A coalition of civil rights groups challenged the constitutionality of Prop 209 again in 2010. They argued that statistics on minority admissions since passage of 209 in 1996 showed that it had an adverse impact on minority enrollment at the University of California. The Federal courts, however, refused to overturn Prop 209, saying that they had set a precedent in the earlier legal challenges that this type of proposition does not violate the Federal constitution.

The same group that won passage of Prop. 209 in California has promoted very similar measures in other states. The state of Washington adopted one in 1998, Michigan in 2006, Nebraska in 2008, and Arizona in 2010, but Colorado narrowly defeated the measure in 2008.

The U.S. Supreme Court has agreed to hear a challenge to the proposition in Michigan in 2013, in a case called *Schuette v. Coalition to Defend Affirmative Action*. A Federal appeals court had struck down the proposition on equal protection grounds.

♛ QUESTIONS FOR ANALYSIS

1. Opponents of Proposition 209 charge that it targets minorities and women. Does it?
2. Proponents of Proposition 209 hail the Supreme Court decision as a major step toward a color-blind society. Do you agree?
3. According to one perspective, affirmative action leads to greater racial discord. According to another, measures like Proposition 209 do. Which view do you think is right?
4. Voters in several other states have begun movements to repeal affirmative-action laws. Is this activity a sign that affirmative action is on the way out? Should it be on the way out?

CASE PRESENTATION

Fisher v. University of Texas: *Taking Race into Account*

In June 2003, the U.S. Supreme Court announced the *Grutter v. Bollinger* decision, reaffirming a controversial element of the 1978 *Bakke* decision. In *Bakke*, the Court had said that universities may not set aside a rigid quota of places in its entering class limited to particular racial minorities but that they may "take race into account." They reasoned that diversity in college classrooms was a legitimate goal in college admissions. Just as colleges seek a diversity of athletes, musicians, artists, scholars, and scientists, so too can they legitimately pursue cultural and racial diversity in their classes of students.

The *Grutter* case challenged the policy for admission to the highly competitive University of Michigan Law School. Admissions were based on a student's academic abilities along with an assessment of a range of talents, experiences, and potential. Among the factors considered were each student's contribution to the diversity of the law school. While not limited to racial diversity, the Law School said that it was committed to including a "critical mass" of under-represented minorities, especially African American, Hispanic, and Native American students. The majority decision, written by Justice Sandra Day O'Conner, said in part:

> ... Today, we hold that the Law School has a compelling interest in attaining a diverse student body. The Law School's educational judgment that such diversity is essential to its educational mission is one to which we defer....

In 2013, the U.S. Supreme Court issued an opinion examining university admissions programs that had been designed to comply with the 2003 *Grutter* decision. In the new decision, *Fisher v. University of Texas at Austin*, the circumstances under which race may constitutionally be taken into account have been narrowed even further. Although diversity remains a legitimate goal, the University must clearly demonstrate that it has examined all other options to attain that diversity before it will be permitted to take race into account. As Justice Kennedy said, writing for the 7-1 majority,

> A university is not permitted to define diversity as "some specified percentage of a particular group merely because of its race or ethnic origin." "That would amount to outright racial ... balancing, which is patently unconstitutional."... "Racial balancing is not transformed from 'patently unconstitutional' to a compelling state interest simply by relabeling it 'racial diversity.' " ...
>
> Once the University has established that its goal of diversity is consistent with strict scrutiny, however, there must still be a further judicial determination that the admissions process meets strict scrutiny in its implementation. The University must prove that the means chosen by the University to attain diversity are narrowly tailored to that goal. On this point, the University receives no deference.... True, a court can take account of a university's experience and expertise in adopting or rejecting certain admissions processes. But, ... it remains at all times the University's obligation to demonstrate, and the Judiciary's obligation to determine, that admissions processes "ensure that each applicant is evaluated as an individual and not in a way that makes an applicant's race or ethnicity the defining feature of his or her application." ...
>
> Narrow tailoring also requires that the reviewing court verify that it is "necessary" for a university

to use race to achieve the educational benefits of diversity.... This involves a careful judicial inquiry into whether a university could achieve sufficient diversity without using racial classifications. Although "[n]arrow tailoring does not require exhaustion of every conceivable race-neutral alternative," strict scrutiny does require a court to examine with care, and not defer to, a university's "serious, good faith consideration of workable race-neutral alternatives."

Justice Clarence Thomas, the only African-American member of the Court, agreed with the majority to this extent, but wrote a separate opinion indicating that he does not believe diversity is a worthy goal.

> Unfortunately for the University, the educational benefits flowing from student body diversity—assuming they exist—hardly qualify as a compelling state interest. Indeed, the argument that educational benefits justify racial discrimination was advanced in support of racial segregation in the 1950's, but emphatically rejected by this Court. And just as the alleged educational benefits of segregation were insufficient to justify racial discrimination then, ... the alleged educational benefits of diversity cannot justify racial discrimination today.

Justice Thomas also complains that minorities admitted under these diversity programs are forever stamped with "a badge of inferiority":

> It taints the accomplishments of all those who are admitted as a result of racial discrimination.... And, it taints the accomplishments of all those who are the same race as those admitted as a result of racial discrimination.... "When blacks [and Hispanics] take positions in the highest places of government, industry, or academia, it is an open question ... whether their skin color played a part in their advancement." ... "The question itself is the stigma—because either racial discrimination did play a role, in which case the person may be deemed 'otherwise unqualified,' or it did not, in which case asking the question itself unfairly marks those ... who would succeed without discrimination." ... Although cloaked in good intentions, the University's racial tinkering harms the very people it claims to be helping.

♛ QUESTIONS FOR ANALYSIS

1. Critics of the *Bakke* and *Grutter* decision had hoped that the Court in *Fisher* would overturn the principle that it was constitutional for colleges and universities to take race into account in admission decisions, especially after more than a quarter of a century of continued efforts to improve opportunities for racial minorities in this country. Has the time come for a truly color-blind society in which admission decisions based solely on scholarly

measures will result in a diverse student body without having to consider race during the admission process? Will such a time ever come?

2. Explain the use of consequentialist reasoning in the appeal to diversity in justifying these race-conscious admissions decisions. Is this persuasive? Is any consideration given to the human rights of all applicants in this approach? Does the Court reason appropriately in defending its decision? Do

you believe there are additional considerations that should be taken into account?

3. Can arguments about the importance of universities as a training ground for the nation's leaders be extended to all levels of education? Are there alternative ways of meeting that societal goal that would not involve taking race into account in university admissions?

4. Some critics of the *Fisher* decision have claimed that admitting students not as well qualified academically as most entering students actually backfires because as they do not graduate at the top of the class, as they might at a less prestigious institution where their academic work would be more comparable to the other students. Is this a persuasive argument against the Texas admissions program?

5. In California, public universities are prohibited under Proposition 209 from taking race into account, despite these Supreme Court decisions. Instead, those universities now emphasize a variety of additional factors in their admissions, such as overcoming adversity in completing college. Does this approach achieve appropriate diversity in ways that do not unfairly disadvantage white applicants?

6. What are alternative ways of achieving diverse student bodies without taking race into account? How effective are these, in your experience?

7. Consider Justice Thomas's concern about the consequences of race-conscious admissions policies. Do the adverse consequences outweigh the benefits of these admissions programs?

CASE PRESENTATION

Reparations: An Overdue Debt to African Slaves in America?

Charles J. Ogletree, Jr., the Jesse Climenko Professor of Law at Harvard University, is a leading activist for the payment of reparations for the institution of slavery in the United States and co-chair and counsel for the Reparations Coordinating Committee. The RCC seeks reparations for the "contemporary victims of slavery and the century-long practice of *de jure* racial discrimination which followed slavery." The reparations movement gained recognition and momentum with the 1999 book *The Debt: What America Owes to Blacks*, by Randall Robinson, a graduate of Harvard Law School and founder of Trans-Africa, which promotes human rights in the Caribbean and Africa.

Ogletree points out that the U.S. Congress paid reparations of $20,000 each to the Japanese-Americans who had been interred during World War II. He also notes that the United Nations Conference Against Racism has defined slavery as "a crime against humanity." The call for reparations for the descendants of African slaves in America is based in part on the promise made in 1865 to give all newly freed slaves "forty acres of tillable ground," among other things. But the order was rescinded by President Andrew Johnson a few months later, after the assassination of President Abraham Lincoln, and the government seized the land that had already been allocated to 40,000 blacks in the South. The continuing discrimination against blacks, much of it mandated in the notorious "Jim Crow" laws, provides further justification of reparations.

Ogletree is not seeking payments to the individual descendants of slaves. Rather, he wants the money to go into a trust fund that would assist the poorest members of the black community to escape the grinding poverty that is one legacy of slavery and Jim Crow. His law suits are being filed against the federal government, as well as American institutions and businesses that benefitted from slavery.

Reparations also have also been sought in recent years for destruction of the property and lives of African-Americans after the abolition of slavery. In 1898, a group of white supremacists in Wilmington, North Carolina, killed 60 African-American residents and drove thousands more from the city. A North Carolina commission has urged the state government to pay damages to the descendants of that violence. A race riot in the Greenwood district of Tulsa, Oklahoma, in 1921 killed as many as 300 black residents and burned over a thousand homes, businesses, a library, and a hospital in the once-thriving black community. A lengthy report commissioned by the state legislature demonstrated in 2001 that white mob violence, assisted by the Tulsa police, was to blame. Ogletree filed suit for damages, but the case was thrown out on the grounds that the statute of limitations had expired.

In 1989, Representative John Conyers, Jr. of Michigan introduced, in the U.S. Congress, legislation

To acknowledge the fundamental injustice, cruelty, brutality, and inhumanity of slavery in the United States and the 13 American colonies between 1619 and 1865 and to establish a commission to examine the institution of slavery, subsequently de jure and de facto racial and economic discrimination against African-Americans, and the impact of these forces on living African-Americans, to make recommendations to the Congress on appropriate remedies, and for other purposes.

Conyers has reintroduced this legislation repeatedly, but it has never been adopted or even brought up for a vote.

On June 19, 2009, the U.S. Senate passed on a voice vote, without objection, a resolution apologizing on behalf of the nation to African-Americans for the legacy of slavery and the enforced segregation system of Jim Crow. The measure was introduced by Senators Tom Harkin of Iowa and Sam Brownback of Kansas. This resolution included a disclaimer that nothing in the resolution supported reparations for the descendants of slaves nor served as a settlement of any claim again the U.S., leaving open the reparations issue.

In the previous Congress, a similar resolution had been approved on a voice vote in the House of Representatives, introduced by Representative Steve Cohen of Tennessee and with the support of Representative Conyers.

Critics of reparations, including such African-Americans as John H. McWhorter, a Senior Fellow at the Manhattan Institute, and Glen C. Loury, Professor of Economics at Boston University, argue that reparations have already been paid, in effect, by the government's affirmative-action programs and numerous social welfare programs, which have disproportionately benefitted persons of African descent. McWhorter complains about what he perceives as the misguided notions "that serious black achievement is impossible except under ideal conditions, that white neglect must be at the root of any black–white disparity, and that only the actions of whites can significantly improve the conditions of blacks."[1]

---

[1]The Reparations Racket: America Has Already Made Amends for Slavery," *City Journal* (March 29, 2002) (http://www.city-journal.org/).

⚜ QUESTIONS FOR ANALYSIS

1. Given that all persons who were slaves and all persons who were slave-owners when President Lincoln signed the Emancipation Proclamation in 1863 are deceased, who should now have to pay reparations and who should benefit? Is it feasible to accurately identify the descendants of those slaves and slave-owners?

2. Have the government services and affirmative-action programs of the last century adequately compensated the descendants of slaves, as the critics of reparations argue? Does the government have an obligation to do more as long as significant disparities persist in the economic status of African-Americans?

3. Other immigrant groups have suffered from discrimination in this country. Should their descendants be paid reparations, too? Are there significant differences between the descendants of slaves and the descendants of other minority groups?

CASE PRESENTATION

Friendly Sexual Harassment?

In 1976, the federal courts recognized for the first time that sexual harassment in the workplace is a form of discrimination prohibited under the U.S. Civil Rights Act. The rationale was that serious and pervasive harassment makes it impossible for a woman to carry out her job responsibilities and compete fairly in the employment workplace. In the years since, additional court decisions have recognized the problem of sexual harassment of men by women and sexual harassment by men against other men perceived to be homosexual.

In 1999, Amaani Lyle was working as a comedy writers' assistant on the television show "Friends."

She was fired after four months and filed suit for discrimination. Lyle complained that three male comedy writers had used sexually coarse and vulgar language and conduct, including a simulation of masturbation, during writing sessions. This, she argued, constituted sexual harassment in the workplace, making it impossible for her to carry out her job responsibilities of typing and transcribing jokes for the scripts for the show.

Warner Brothers Television argued that Lyle had been warned about the working conditions beforehand but accepted the job anyway. *Amicus curiae* (friend of the court) briefs were filed by several organizations supporting the writers on the grounds of creative freedom and freedom of speech.

The case was decided in favor of Warner Brothers by the Supreme Court of California in April 2006. The Court noted that the vulgar language was not directed specifically at Lyle, or at any other women in the workplace, and thus did not constitute illegal harassment. Nor, the Court said, were the comments "severe enough or sufficiently pervasive to create a work environment that was hostile or abusive to" Lyle.

Supporters of the writers hailed this as a victory for free speech and creative freedom. Critics expressed concern that employers now would simply warn new employees that vulgar language might be used in the workplace and thus escape future harassment charges.

⚜ QUESTIONS FOR ANALYSIS

1. The U.S. Supreme Court has recognized that a "hostile work environment" can constitute discriminatory sexual harassment, even if there is no specific *quid pro quo* demanding sexual favors in exchange for a job or promotion. In the 1993 decision *Harris v. Forklift*, the Court found that pervasive and severe sexual innuendos and insults directed at Teresa Harris detracted from her job performance, discouraged her from remaining on the job, and kept her from advancing in her career. How should we draw the line between a discriminatory hostile work environment and one in which workers are simply exercising their right of free speech and should not be liable for harassment?

2. Should television writers for a popular show filled with sexual innuendo be held to different standards for workplace conduct than workers in other professions? How should we balance freedom of expression with a right to freedom from harassment?

3. The Supreme Court does not require proof of psychological damage or emotional distress to demonstrate a hostile work environment, although such evidence is very relevant if it exists. Should this proof be required to help draw a workable line between innocent office joking and kidding and illegal sexual harassment?

CHAPTER ELEVEN

Animal Rights and Environmental Ethics

- **What Do We Owe Nonhuman Animals?**
- **What's Wrong with Speciesism?**
- **Environmental Ethics**
- **Environmental Problems**
- **The Moral Issue**
- **Why Environmental Ethics?**
- **Arguments for Ethical Treatment of Animals and the Environment**
- **Arguments Against Ethical Treatment of Animals and the Environment**

PETER SINGER **All Animals Are Equal ... or Why Supporters of Liberation for Blacks and Women Should Support Animal Liberation Too**

TOM REGAN **The Case for Animal Rights**

CARL COHEN **Do Animals Have Rights?**

PAUL W. TAYLOR **The Ethics of Respect for Nature**

CASE PRESENTATIONS: • *Animal Liberators* • *Religious Sacrifice* • *A Metaphor for the Energy Debate* • *The Spotted Owl*

MOST OF THE ISSUES we consider in this volume involve the ethical obligations and rights of persons, but important ethical issues also arise with regard to our relationships with nonhuman animals and the entire environment itself. Whether or not it makes sense to attribute ethical rights to entities that are not persons is one issue we take up in this unit. We are used to thinking about ethics in terms of relationships among persons. We have obligations to other persons, and they have the right to expect us to treat them in certain ways. Do we have an obligation to provide a right-to-die to seriously ill patients? Do we have a right to pursue our sexual private lives in ways we choose? Does capital punishment meet our obligation to treat people convicted of serious crimes in ways that are not cruel and unusual? Do we have a right to our civil liberties, even in a time of war? These important questions all involve ethical relationships among persons.

But does it make sense to think about ethical relationships with things that are not persons and that have no ethical obligation to us in any meaningful sense? Do we have ethical obligations to lower animals, plants, trees, rocks, air, and water? Does it make sense to say those things have ethical obligations to us or even ethical rights to claim against us? Do any supposed ethical obligations of this nature really amount to obligations to other persons and concern about the impact our treatment of animals and the environment has on other persons?

In the late 1960s, the nation was preoccupied with enormous disagreements over the Vietnam war, the draft, and the burgeoning civil rights movement. By the early 1970s, attention became focused on both environmental issues and animal rights, to which we turn here.

WHAT DO WE OWE NONHUMAN ANIMALS?

In 1975, Australian philosopher Peter Singer published his landmark book, *Animal Liberation*. The title of the first chapter, like the title of the book itself, clearly announced the author's basic moral message: "All Animals Are Equal." Succeeding chapters documented another message: All animals are not treated equally. Singer's point is simple. Nonhuman animals, like human animals, can experience both pleasure and pain. And that is a morally important fact. If it is wrong to cause human suffering to achieve a good that does not outweigh that suffering, Singer argues, it is wrong to cause nonhuman suffering to achieve such a good. Given the variety of nutritious and tasty vegetarian recipes available, the suffering caused by factory farms is not justified by the human desire for meat. Given the availability of canvas shoes and leather substitutes for belts and such, human demand for leather is not worth the suffering it brings to nonhuman animals.

Historically, the weight of Western opinion has not been on Singer's side. Both our religious and philosophical traditions have been inhospitable to the notion that we have moral obligations to other animals. Let's take a brief look at both.

The Judeo-Christian Tradition

Beginning with the creation story of Genesis, Judeo-Christian thought has told us that other animals were put here for our purposes. According to that story, we are to "fill the earth and subdue it; and have dominion over the fish of the sea and over the birds of the air and over every living thing that moves upon the earth." And later in Genesis, after the flood, we are told, "Every moving thing that lives shall be food for you; and as I gave you the green plants, I give you everything."

Of course, not all Jewish and Christian thought has viewed animals as merely there for our use. St. Francis of Assisi, for example, who once preached to sparrows, is as well known for his love of animals as for founding the Franciscan order. This tradition recognizes that animals have value (as does all of nature) because everything that exists is a good, and also that it is wrong to cause unnecessary suffering to animals. Still, these biblical injunctions have been supported by centuries of Christian theology. Humans are created in the image of God; other animals are not. Humans have immortal souls; other animals do not. Humans belong to both the spiritual and the material worlds; other animals belong only to the material. Given these differences, plus the influence of Christian thought on Western culture, no one should be surprised by our treatment of nonhuman animals.

The Philosophical Tradition

Secular philosophers have, in the main, given nonhuman animals no greater consideration. Writing at a time when such scientists as Galileo were ushering in the era of modern science, the great French philosopher René Descartes (1596–1650) argued that nonhuman animals are no better than biological robots, incapable of feeling any sensations, even pain. The nonphysical mind is the seat of sensation, he argued, and only creatures capable of reason have nonphysical minds. Since nonhuman animals cannot reason, they are simply physical creatures. Therefore, they cannot feel pain.

Immanuel Kant had other reasons for excluding nonhuman animals from moral consideration. As we saw in Part 1, Kant put respect for *persons* at the center of morality; we are not to treat other *persons* merely as a means to our own ends. Although Kant did not deny that animals can suffer, he did deny that they are persons. To be a person, he said, is to be an autonomous being, one that has the capacity to act for reasons and to reason about its reasons. And that capacity does not belong to nonhuman animals. They are, then, beyond the pale of morality. (Kant did recommend that we be nice to animals, though—not out of moral obligation, of course, but for another reason. If we treat animals cruelly, he felt, we run the risk of developing insensitive characters.)

Another strain in moral philosophy—**social contract theory**—is equally exclusive of nonhuman animals. According to this view, morality is the product of an informal agreement among the members of society. Each of us agrees to follow certain rules on the condition that others do the same. The purpose of the agreement is to ensure that all of us act in dependable ways, providing the mutual trust necessary for social cooperation. An important aspect of social contract theory is that this informal agreement is the source of all moral obligation. We have moral obligations to others who have entered into the agreement with us. We have no such obligations to those who are not part of the agreement. Nonhuman animals, who are incapable of entering into contracts, are not part of the agreement. Therefore, we have no moral obligations to them.

In traditional Western views, then, we owe nonhuman animals nothing. We have no moral obligations to them. We may have moral obligations *concerning* them, but those obligations are *to* other people. We ought not, for example, poison somebody else's pet for the same reason that we ought not destroy somebody else's sofa. The pet and the sofa are another person's property, and our obligations to that person forbid us to destroy his or her property. The pet itself is due no more moral consideration than the sofa—none.

Utility vs. Rights

The basis of Singer's moral appeal is the principle of utility: Since we morally ought to maximize happiness and minimize suffering, and since nonhuman animals are just as capable of happiness and suffering as human animals, our calculations ought to include them as well. Against our own pleasure in eating veal, we ought to balance the suffering of veal calves. Against the benefits of research on animals, we ought to balance the suffering of laboratory animals. Their pain should matter just as much as ours.

Other animal advocates make a different moral appeal. As they see it, the principle of utility does not guarantee fit treatment of nonhuman animals. Suppose, for example, that the elimination of factory farms would create such havoc in our economy that utility is maximized by keeping them. Would that justify keeping them? If our answer is yes, we should ask ourselves an analogous question: Suppose we could maximize utility by reintroducing slavery. Would that justify doing so? Presumably, our answer to that question is no. Humans have certain rights that we morally cannot violate, regardless of utility. If we do not feel the same about at least some animals, aren't we guilty of speciesism?

Thus, philosophers like Tom Regan focus their attention on animal rights. He argues that just as respect for persons requires that we not treat other humans in certain ways, regardless of utility, so should respect for at least some nonhuman animals require that we not treat them in certain ways, regardless of utility.

Which animals? At the very least, those that, like us, are experiencing subjects of their own lives. By that phrase, Regan means the following: conscious creatures that are aware of their environment, that have desires, feelings, emotions, memories, beliefs, preferences, goals, and a sense of their own identity and future. Although we cannot be sure precisely where we can draw the line between animals that meet these criteria and animals that do not, we can be sure of one thing, he says. Adult mammals do. And because they do, their lives, like ours, have inherent value—value independent of any use they may be to us. In that case, we ought not use them merely as a means to our own ends.

WHAT'S WRONG WITH SPECIESISM?

Most of us are, undeniably, speciesists. But what, you may be wondering, is wrong with that? Most of us agree that pointless cruelty to animals should not be tolerated, but that is a far cry from agreeing that animals are our moral equals. Why should they be? Shouldn't human beings matter more than other animals?

The Conventional View Defended

Certainly, speciesism doesn't *seem* to be as bad as racism or sexism. To deny full moral equality to other people on the basis of skin color is totally arbitrary, since skin color is of no moral importance whatever. But for species? Can we really say that the differences between rabbits and humans are as trivial, morally speaking, as the differences between blacks and whites, women and men? The common-sense answer to these questions is, of course, no. The conventional view is that morality is our own—humankind's—institution, developed and maintained and improved for our own purposes, for our own individual and social good. To the extent that the good of other animals contributes to our own good, it should be of concern to us. Because our pets play unique and rewarding roles in our lives, we should treat them as more than mere things. Because sympathy, compassion, and kindness contribute in crucial ways to the human good, we should not accept needless cruelty to nonhuman animals. But we have no obligation to promote the good of nonhuman animals at humankind's own expense. To do that would be to undercut the whole purpose of morality.

The Conventional View Criticized

However reasonable the conventional view may seem, animal rights advocates attack it on two fronts. First, they claim, we do not apply the conventional view consistently. Humans who are not fully persons are protected by our morality; humans who cannot fully participate in our moral community are granted moral rights. We do not test new cosmetics on people who are severely retarded. We do not run cruel psychological experiments on infants. We do not conduct medical experiments on irreversibly comatose humans. Why not? Because they are human. Why do we test cosmetics on rabbits, experiment on dogs, raise veal calves for food? Because they are not human. And that, animal rights activists say, *is* discrimination purely on the basis of species.

Second, even if the conventional view were applied consistently, they claim, it would still be inadequate. Granted, difference of species is not the only difference between normal adult humans and farm animals, but the differences stressed by the conventional view are not morally crucial ones. What is so morally important about the fact that steers cannot enter into our social contract? Why should it matter so much that pigs can't have all the aspirations that humans have or that sheep can't develop the same virtues and talents? What the conventional view boils down to, they say, is this: Only moral *agents* can have rights.

What are moral agents? Creatures that have two closely related abilities. The first is the ability to take on moral duties toward others, to understand that they have obligations toward others that they ought to fulfill. The second is the ability to make moral claims against others, to understand that they have moral rights that others can violate. But why, critics of the conventional view ask, should those abilities be crucial?

The Conventional View Reconsidered

The foregoing criticisms show that the acceptability of our treatment of other animals turns on two points. The first is consistency. Do we apply the conventional view consistently? And if not, can we justify our inconsistency? The second strikes at the heart of the conventional view. Does it draw a morally defensible line between human and nonhuman animals? And if so, is there an even better place to draw the line between creatures with rights (or as Singer would put it, creatures whose interests matter as much as our own) and creatures without rights (or creatures whose interests do not matter as much as our own)?

Regarding the first point, defenders of current treatment of other animals can say this: If we do apply the conventional view inconsistently, we do so in a *principled* way. Moral agents—persons—stand at the center of our morality. They are the primary holders of moral rights. We grant rights to human infants because they will *become* moral agents and so deserve our respect. We grant rights to humans in comas because they *were* moral agents and so also deserve our respect. We grant rights to people who are severely retarded because they are so much like some other holders of rights that it seems almost incoherent not to.

As for second point, defenders of current practices can do little more than repeat the reasons for drawing the line where we now do and then throw the question back to their critics: Why is Singer's dividing line or Regan's any better than the one we now draw? The fact that nonhuman animals can suffer should certainly have some moral weight, but why should it lead us to put them on an equal footing with full members of our moral community? The fact that some of them are experiencing subjects of their own lives should also have some moral weight, but why should it have as much weight as other facts about ourselves?

Whether these answers are acceptable depends on two further questions. First, are at least some nonhuman animals so much like some humans that it seems almost incoherent to deny them rights? Second, assuming that morality did arise to advance the human good, should we now say that the time has come to recognize that other goods are of equal value? Critics of our treatment of other animals answer yes to both questions. Defenders answer no.

ENVIRONMENTAL ETHICS

The first Earth Day was celebrated on April 22, 1970, often considered the beginning of the modern environmental movement. Millions of Americans across the country gathered to listen to speeches and demonstrate their concern for the future of the planet. Two years later, during the presidency of Republican Richard M. Nixon, and with strong bipartisan support in Congress, the Federal government established the U.S. Environmental Protection Agency, underscoring the commitment of the nation to protecting the natural resources of air, water, and land from pollution.

ENVIRONMENTAL PROBLEMS

Despite expressions of concern for the environment, environmental problems continue to abound and, in many cases, worsen. Species are dying out on a daily basis; air quality is worsening in many cities; the earth's protective ozone layer is thinning; we are creating increasing amounts of trash with no place to put it; and, many scientists argue, emissions of carbon dioxide and methane gases are turning the earth's atmosphere into a greenhouse.

Ozone Depletion

Extending from approximately seven to thirty miles above the earth, the layer of the earth's atmosphere known as the stratosphere is an area of little temperature change above the earth's rain clouds. An important component of the stratosphere is ozone, which acts as a shield against the sun's ultraviolet rays. Without this shield, or even with a thinner shield, we would see a significant increase in skin cancer and diseases of the immune system. We would also see considerable damage to food crops and phytoplankton—marine plants that are a vital link in our ocean's food chain.

Although CFCs were banned in 1947 under an international agreement called the Montreal Protocol, they are very long-lived in the environment. NASA predicts that it will take fifty years for the Antarctica ozone hole to disappear.

Development of CFC alternatives has been very expensive, but the consequences to human health have been recognized as more important than these economic costs of product development, an example of consequentialist ethical reasoning.

Climate Change

Throughout the earth's history, average temperatures have changed as the atmosphere has changed, growing warmer with an increase in greenhouse gases—most notably carbon dioxide—and cooler with a decrease. The modern industrial world, chiefly through increased use of fossil fuels and through deforestation, has seen a sharp increase of greenhouse gases. Using computer models, scientists have predicted an increase in the earth's temperatures of from three to nine degrees by the middle of the twenty-first century. An increase that large would lead to severe inland droughts, resultant food shortages, coastal flooding, mass extinctions of species, and increased pollution in overheated cities.

Although most scientists agree on the dangers of climate change, the solutions are the subject of much debate. The Kyoto Protocol, an international proposal for emission reductions, was rejected by the U.S. Senate in 1997. The treaty imposed restrictions the Senate thought were unfairly burdensome on the most industrialized nations, including the United States, while allowing less well-developed nations to continue dangerous emissions. President George W. Bush repeatedly rejected the Kyoto Protocol and insisted that developing nations must also agree to emissions reductions.

President Barack Obama has repeatedly expressed his commitment to reducing global warming. On Earth Day, April 22, 2009, he said that "… no issue deserves more immediate attention than global warming." Along with steps that every individual can take to reduce carbon emissions, such as driving energy efficient cars and using energy efficient lightbulbs, major steps will be needed by government and business alike. The immediate cost to the economy is of concern to some, in the decisions that must be made to reduce climate change for the longer-term.

Much of the current debate centers on consequentialist arguments, such as the economic cost to industry and the possible loss of jobs resulting from the proposed measures to reduce climate change. But many environmentalists are now urging that climate change trumps all other environmental concerns. Hal Clifford quotes Henry David Thoreau: "What is the use of a house if you haven't got a tolerable planet to put it on?"

Acid Rain

Most scientists believe that acid rain is caused primarily by pollutants from the burning of fossil fuels—carbon dioxide, sulfur dioxide, and nitrogen oxides. These pollutants, which can be carried thousands of miles by the wind, mix with other chemicals in the atmosphere to form corrosive and poisonous compounds that are washed back to earth by rainfall.

The effects of acid rain are believed to be wide ranging. They include damage to rives and lakes, ground water, soil, forests, and buildings. But because there have been relatively few studies on the subject, the extent of damage due to acid rain is difficult to gauge.

Trash

The problem of what to do with the trash of a society that throws away 16 billion disposable diapers and 2 billion disposable razors annually, yet recycles only 10 percent of its trash, is a serious one. The most common solution to the trash problem is sanitary landfills, where 80 percent of the country's solid waste ends up. But this solution is far from ideal. First, since much of our trash is non biodegradable plastic, we are quickly running out of space. Second, landfills pose risks to surface and ground water. For combustible waste, the chief alternative is incineration, which has its own problems. The ash must be treated and then disposed of, and the gases released during incineration contribute to air pollution.

Extinction of Species

Though the problems of species extinction is most acute in the Amazon, development of land by humans throughout the world is causing the loss of species at a rate estimated to be as high as one a day.

The threat of extinction is most highly publicized in cases like the tiger, blue whale, giant panda, and other animal species that humans have a particularly high regard for. But the loss of many other species—plant species as well as animal species, many of which are still unidentified—should also concern us. Species in tropical rain forests, for instance, are valuable in the development of cancer drugs and antibiotics. They also give us valuable genetic information that contributes to the raising of domestic animals and the growing of food crops.

THE MORAL ISSUE

A loss of the ozone layer and significant climate change would be disastrous for human beings. And it is because of our shared sense of impending disaster that most people now claim to be environmentalists.

In other cases of environmental damage, however, the issue is not serious danger to human life but diminishing quality of human life. We view nature as a valuable resource for recreation as well as economic development.

All such concerns are **anthropocentric** at heart; that is, they center on human well-being. We should care about the environment because it is *our* environment. We should care about the survival of various plant and animal species because they matter to *us*.

But other things matter to us as well. We want a strong economy that will produce the goods, jobs, and tax revenues we desire. We like our cars and the highways we drive them on. We like air-conditioning. We like to hold down the costs of producing consumer goods in order to hold down prices.

So when acting both as individuals and as a society, we weigh our concern for the environment against these other concerns. The result is often a compromise, such as auto emission controls that are not as strong as they otherwise might be. Because of these compromises, the most committed environmentalists have begun arguing for radical changes in our moral and legal reasoning, changes that give nature a special place in our thinking. Two proposed changes have received the most attention. Both have one thing in common. They are nonanthropocentric.

The Land Ethic

In his much discussed book, *A Sand County Almanac*, environmentalist Aldo Leopold proposed what he called the land ethic. According to Leopold's land ethic, humans are to begin thinking of themselves as part of a wider community, the biotic community, which includes not only all living things but also all members of the ecological system, including water, soil, and air. To think of ourselves in that way is to reject the view that we are masters of nature and that nature is there to be exploited by us. It is to think of ourselves as members of a team, living and working harmoniously with our teammates. It is also to recognize that the crucial moral question is not what benefits individual human beings or the human community as a whole, but what benefits the biotic community as a whole.

According to Leopold, "A thing is right when it tends to preserve the integrity, stability, and beauty of the biotic community. It is wrong when it tends otherwise."

Two things are notable about this point of view. First, of course, it is nonanthropocentric. But equally important, it is not individualistic. What is to be considered as morally fundamental is not the good of individual members of the biotic community but the good of the community itself. Thus, the land ethic is often considered to be a **holistic ethic**; that is, we have duties not just to individuals but to the whole—in this case, the biotic community.

Environmental Individualism

Others forms of environmental ethics tend to be **biocentric** but nonholistic. They stress duties to individual members of the biotic community but not to the community itself. According to this view, the good of individual plants, animals, and streams—not just the good of individual humans—must be taken into account in moral and legal reasoning.

In the moral realm, this involves balancing the interests of nonhuman members of the environment against human interests Chopping down a tree, for instance, would become a morally significant act independent of damage to its owner.

In the legal realm, it would involve giving trees, lakes, and animals standing in the courts. To give them standing would be to make them interested parties in lawsuits and allow lawyers to bring suit on their behalf, not just on behalf of humans who are affected by their treatment. As matters now stand, the interests of nature are irrelevant in legal matters, unless human interests are also affected.

Holism and Individualism Compared

Although both views promote the interests of plants, animals, water, air, and soil as independent goods, their practical payoffs may be far different. To see how, we can consider the problem of endangered species.

According to the holistic point of view, a threat to an entire species is more significant than the sum total of the threats to be individual members of the species because what is morally most important is the species' contribution to the biotic community. Because species diversity contributes to ecological stability, the loss of a member of an endangered species counts more than the loss of a member of a nonendangered one. According to the nonholistic point of view, on the other hand, a threat to a species is not in itself more significant than the sum total of the threats to individual members. All other things being equal, the loss of a member of a nonendangered species is morally equivalent to the loss of a member of an endangered one.

Holists and individualists may differ on other points as well. The holistic view contains no grounds to reject hunting, for instance, unless it damages the environment. There is nothing *inherently* immoral about hunting, and when hunting contributes to the well-being of the biotic community, it is morally good. The individualistic view, however, naturally leans toward an anti-hunting position. The life of an individual deer is not to be sacrificed for the sake of the whole.

WHY ENVIRONMENTAL ETHICS?

Why, then, do environmentalists call for a radical change in our ethical thinking? The impetus toward environmental ethics has two sources. The first, as we saw, is the belief that anthropocentric ethics and law are inadequate to deal with the vast array of environmental problems that face us. The second is the belief that nature, wilderness areas, and nonhuman life have their own inherent value and therefore deserve moral consideration.

Anthropocentric Ethics

Proponents of this view deny that we need a land ethic or legal standing for trees. What we need instead, they say, are better cost-benefit analyses of decisions that affect the environment. We need to make sure that these analyses take adequate account of the harm to human interests that environmental damage can cause. In considering what limit to place on auto emissions, for example, we should take into account not only the added costs to automakers and consumers but also the costs in human disease and death from pollutants and greenhouse gases.

Critics of this approach argue that cost-benefit analyses in such cases are inadequate. The basic problem, they claim, is that cost-benefit analyses calculate only *economic* costs and benefits. But certain goods cannot be given an economic value. How much is a human life worth, for instance? How much is a beautiful view worth? How much is it worth to be able to swim or fish in a river?

Furthermore, even if we could assign economic value to such goods, is it possible to identify all the relevant costs and benefits? And even if we could identify them, why should economic costs and benefits be the only deciding factors?

Respect for Nature

A key point of environmental ethics is that nature itself or individual natural objects have their own interests and goods, which are omitted from cost-benefit analyses. We should value nature not because of its value to us but because of its inherent value.

According to this view, even if we minimize human costs and maximize human benefits, we do not act morally if we significantly harm nature. To some extent, arguments over this point can parallel animal rights disputes.

Various arguments for or against animal rights can be used as arguments for or against rights or standing for streams, species, trees, and so forth. But for many environmentalists, the issue is different. We don't have to grant nature *rights* to ensure adequate moral treatment. We only have to treat it in accordance with an attitude of proper *respect*.

ARGUMENTS FOR ETHICAL TREATMENT OF ANIMALS AND THE ENVIRONMENT

1. *Human beings hold no special place in nature.*

   POINT: "What's so special about humans, anyway? From Mother Nature's point of view, *all* animals are equal. We all evolved from the same beginnings, we're all made of the same stuff, and we all belong to the same biosphere. The world wasn't made for any one species. It's here for all of us. And it's nothing but pure arrogance for humans to think that *we're* the pinnacle of creation, that we have the right to treat the rest of the animal kingdom any way we want. It's time we recognize that we're part of nature, not lords over it, and we ought to act accordingly."

   COUNTERPOINT: "Of course, we're part of nature. But what does that prove? Tigers, eagles, and other predators are also part of nature. What can be more natural than eating other animals? Besides, why stop at animals? Plants are part of nature too. So are rocks, rivers, and dirt. From Mother Nature's point of view, they must matter just as much as animals. Should we treat them equally too? Finally, why should we even care about Mother Nature's point of view (whatever *that* might be)? We have our own point of view—the human point of view—and if that point of view is no better than any other, it's no worse either. It's ours, and we're entitled to live our lives according to it."

2. *Human good is not the only good.*

   POINT: "You make it sound as though human good is the only good that counts for anything. But what about the good of a species, a forest, a river, or a lake? Or even a single redwood tree? What right do we have to cut down something that's been alive for thousands of years just to make a picnic table? After all, human interests aren't the only interests. Why must our interests always come first?"

COUNTERPOINT: "To hear you tell it, someone might think a redwood tree actually cares what happens to it. But a tree has no interest in its own survival. It can't have an interest in anything. Don't get me wrong. I'm not saying we should destroy entire redwood forests just to make picnic tables. No one's saying that. I'm just as impressed by the beauty of a redwood forest as you are, and I'm just as concerned about saving that beauty for my children and grandchildren. But it's preposterous to say that our concerns don't matter more than a tree's."

3. *The biotic community is like a human community.*

POINT: "The first principle of any community is cooperation. We have to cooperate with our family members, we have to cooperate with our fellow workers, and we have to cooperate with our fellow citizens. Not only do we have to cooperate with one another, but we also have to treat one another with respect. The same holds for the biotic community as well. Ecology has taught us that each part of an ecosystem is a member of a community, with all members working together to maintain the good of the whole. It's time that humans recognized that we're also part of the biotic community. It's time for us to work together with our fellow members and show them the respect they deserve."

COUNTERPOINT: "This notion of a biotic community is nothing but a metaphor at best. Do predators cooperate with their prey? Do members of different species resolve their differences the way people of varying interests do? Are insects and the soil members of the same team the way a pitcher and catcher are? What we've learned from ecology is certainly important, and we ignore its lessons at our own risk. But we gain nothing by sentimentalizing nature to the extent that we work against our own interests."

4. *Nature isn't here just for human purposes.*

POINT: "Too often when humans look at nature, all they see is something to be exploited. They look at forests and they see timber. They look at rivers and oceans and they see places to dump their waste. As far as they're concerned, nature is there for us, period. What they can use they take, and what they can't use they're willing to sacrifice because it's of no importance to them. But nature was here long before we were, with its own majesty and its own integrity. We're just a part of it, not its master, and we have no right to upset that integrity. To think of ourselves as nature's master is nothing but hubris."

COUNTERPOINT: "Of course we're part of nature. And like everything else in nature, we use what's useful to us. The problem isn't our tendency to look on nature as something that's there to be used by us—nothing could be more natural than that—but our tendency to use it unwisely. As long as we keep our own long-term interests clearly in mind, as long as we remember that we need trees for oxygen as well as timber, for instance, and that species of no direct use to us now can be important to us in ways we don't recognize yet, we and nature will be fine."

ARGUMENTS AGAINST ETHICAL TREATMENT OF ANIMALS AND THE ENVIRONMENT

1. *Giving animals rights would lead to absurd interference with nature.*

    POINT: "Humans aren't the only animals that eat other animals, you know. What about wolves, eagles, tigers, and other predators? If we grant rights to their prey, then we'll have to protect animals from each other, not least from ourselves. After all, if we don't have the right to violate another animal's rights, neither does a wolf. But if we do protect the prey, what happens to the predator? What, for that matter, happens to all of nature? If you follow your position to its logical conclusion, the results are absurd."

    COUNTERPOINT: "The kind of interference that worries you is *not* a logical consequence of my position. What you're forgetting is that tigers and wolves aren't moral *agents*. They don't have any obligations to other animals, so there's nothing immoral about their preying on other animals. Humans are moral agents, though, so there is something immoral about our preying on other animals."

2. *Putting our own species first is the natural thing to do.*

    POINT: "It's only natural that we care more about other humans than we care about nonhumans. After all, being members of the same species is an important relationship, like being members of the same family. We care more about our parents than we do about strangers, so why shouldn't we care more about our fellow humans than we do about sheep? And just take a look at the rest of the animal kingdom. A lot of animals cooperate with members of their own species but not with other animals, and in some cases, animals will even lay down their lives for other members of their species. As the old saying goes, birds of a feather flock together. Why should humans be any different?"

    COUNTERPOINT: "Humans are different. We can rise above our natural inclinations. That's what civilization and culture are all about. It's why we have laws and morality. And since you're so fond of old sayings, it's why a tiger can't change its stripes but a human can. We know the difference between right and wrong, and the point of teaching that difference is to get people to put a check on some of their natural inclinations. Selfishness is just as natural as altruism, you know—maybe even more natural—but I don't hear you saying that we shouldn't try to curb our selfishness. So even if speciesism is natural, if it's wrong we should stamp it out."

3. *People count more than trees.*

    POINT: "What environmental ethicists fail to see is that the environment matters because it's *our* environment—our water, our air, our forests. No one denies that we have to protect the environment to protect ourselves and advance our own interests. But you want to go further than that. You want to protect the environment *against* our own interests. You want to sacrifice logging jobs, wreck entire economies, to protect owls. You want to deny us badly needed power plants to protect fish. And that's just crazy. Any way you look at it, people matter more than trees, owls, and fish."

COUNTERPOINT: "As of matter of fact, people don't matter more than trees, owls, and fish any way you look at it. To nature, all species are equal. That doesn't mean human interests *never* come first, of course, but it does mean they don't *always* come first. Job losses are unfortunate, but economies and individuals rebound. And as for your badly needed power plants, Americans rely too much on electricity as it is. Giving up some of our electric appliances is a small enough sacrifice, not only to protect an entire species but also to protect the environment as a whole."

4. *Environmental ethics is elitist.*
   POINT: "The 'small' sacrifices you call for aren't all that small to most people. When a mining, manufacturing, or logging region dies, the human costs are enormous, whether the region eventually bounces back or not. And many of them don't. Even added costs to consumer goods can be a major burden for many people. The problem with environmental ethics is that it's elitist. The well-off can easily afford the costs of putting nature on an equal footing with humans, but the rest of us can't."

   COUNTERPOINT: "Nature is everyone's home, and there's nothing elitist about trying to save our home. I realize that the costs of environmentalism fall heavier on some people than others, but the answer isn't to reject environmental ethics. The answer is to adopt social policies that will compensate them for their loss— retraining, public investment, tax breaks, and other measures to help them out. If we all share the burden, it can be a small one for each of us."

All Animals Are Equal ... or Why Supporters of Liberation for Blacks and Women Should Support Animal Liberation Too

PETER SINGER

In this selection from the first chapter of *Animal Liberation*, Peter Singer, the Ira W. DeCamp Professor of Bioethics, University Center for Human Values, Princeton Unversity, and the Laureate Professor at the Centre for Applied Philosophy and Public Ethics (CAPPE) at the University of Melbourne compares speciesism to sexism and racism. He argues that the same considerations that make sexism and racism morally unjustifiable make speciesism morally unjustifiable. He bases his argument on the *principle of equal consideration*, according to which the pain that nonhuman animals feel is of equal moral importance to the pain that humans feel.

While supporting the principle of equal consideration, Singer stresses that it does not always require equal treatment of all animals, since the same treatment can cause unequal amounts of suffering to different animals. He also points out that the principle does not require

From Peter Singer, *Animal Liberation* (New York: New York Review, 1975), pp. 1–23. Reprinted with permission of the author.

us to say that all lives are equal. Often, a human life is morally more important than the life of a nonhuman animal. Sometimes, though, it is not. When forced to choose between a human and nonhuman animal's life, we should base our decision on the mental capacities of the individuals involved, not on species.

"Animal Liberation" may sound more like a parody of other liberation movements than a serious objective. The idea of "The Rights of Animals" actually was once used to parody the case for women's rights. When Mary Wollstonecraft, a forerunner of today's feminists, published her *Vindication of the Rights of Women* in 1792, her views were widely regarded as absurd, and before long an anonymous publication appeared entitled *A Vindication of the Rights of Brutes*. The author of this satirical work (now known to have been Thomas Taylor, a distinguished Cambridge philosopher) tried to refute Mary Wollstonecraft's arguments by showing that they could be carried one stage further. If the argument for equality was sound when applied to women, why should it not be applied to dogs, cats, and horses? The reasoning seemed to hold for these "brutes" too; yet to hold that brutes had rights was manifestly absurd; therefore the reasoning by which this conclusion had been reached must be unsound, and if unsound when applied to brutes, it must also be unsound when applied to women, since the very same arguments had been used in each case.

In order to explain the basis of the case for the equality of animals, it will be helpful to start with an examination of the case for the equality of women. Let us assume that we wish to defend the case for women's rights against the attack by Thomas Taylor. How should we reply?

One way in which we might reply is by saying that the case for equality between men and women cannot validly be extended to nonhuman animals. Women have a right to vote, for instance, because they are just as capable of making rational decisions about the future as men are; dogs, on the other hand, are incapable of understanding the significance of voting, so they cannot have the right to vote. There are many other obvious ways in which men and women resemble each other closely, while humans and animals differ greatly. So, it might be said, men and women are

similar beings and should have similar rights, while humans and nonhumans are different and should not have equal rights.

The reasoning behind this reply to Taylor's analogy is correct up to a point, but it does not go far enough. There *are* important differences between humans and other animals, and these differences must give rise to *some* differences in the rights that each have. Recognizing this obvious fact, however, is no barrier to the case for extending the basic principle of equality to nonhuman animals. The differences that exist between men and women are equally undeniable, and the supporters of Women's Liberation are aware that these differences may give rise to different rights. Many feminists hold that women have the right to an abortion on request. It does not follow that since these same feminists are campaigning for equality between men and women they must support the right of men to have abortions too. Since a man cannot have an abortion, it is meaningless to talk of his right to have one. Since a dog can't vote, it is meaningless to talk of its right to vote. There is no reason why either Women's Liberation or Animal Liberation should get involved in such nonsense. The extension of the basic principle of equality from one group to another does not imply that we must treat both groups in exactly the same way, or grant exactly the same rights to both groups. Whether we should do so will depend on the nature of the members of the two groups. The basic principle of equality does not require equal or identical *treatment*; it requires equal *consideration*. Equal consideration for different beings may lead to different treatment and different rights.

So there is a different way of replying to Taylor's attempt to parody the case for women's rights, a way that does not deny the obvious differences between humans and nonhumans but goes more deeply into the question of equality and concludes by finding nothing absurd in the idea that the basic principle of equality applies to so-called "brutes." At this point such a conclusion may appear odd; but if we examine more deeply the basis on which our opposition to discrimination on grounds of race or sex ultimately rests, we will see that we would be on shaky ground if we were to demand equality for blacks, women, and other groups of oppressed humans while denying equal consideration to nonhumans. To make this clear we need to see, first, exactly why racism and sexism are wrong.

When we say that all human beings, whatever their race, creed, or sex, are equal, what is it that we are asserting? Those who wish to defend hierarchical, inegalitarian societies have often pointed out that by whatever test we choose it simply is not true that all humans are equal. Like it or not we must face the fact that humans come in different shapes and sizes; they come with different moral capacities, different intellectual abilities, different amounts of benevolent feeling and sensitivity to the needs of others, different abilities to communicate effectively, and different capacities to experience pleasure and pain. In short, if the demand for equality were based on the actual equality of all human beings, we would have to stop demanding equality.

Still, one might cling to the view that the demand for equality among human beings is based on the actual equality of the different races and sexes. Although, it may be said, humans differ as individuals there are no differences between the races and sexes *as such*. From the mere fact that a person is black or a woman we cannot infer anything about that person's intellectual or moral capacities. This, it may be said, is why racism and sexism are wrong. The white racist claims that whites are superior to blacks, but this is false—although there are differences among individuals, some blacks are superior to some whites in all of the capacities and abilities that could conceivably be relevant. The opponent of sexism would say the same: a person's sex is no guide to his or her abilities, and this is why it is unjustifiable to discriminate on the basis of sex.

The existence of individual variations that cut across the lines of race or sex, however, provides us with no defense at all against a more sophisticated opponent of equality, one who proposes that, say,

the interests of all those with IQ scores below 100 be given less consideration than the interests of those with ratings over 100. Perhaps those scoring below the mark would, in this society, be made the slaves of those scoring higher. Would a hierarchical society of this sort really be so much better than one based on race or sex? I think not. But if we tie the moral principle of equality to the factual equality of the different races or sexes, taken as a whole, our opposition to racism and sexism does not provide us with any basis for objecting to this kind of inegalitarianism.

There is a second important reason why we ought not to base our opposition to racism and sexism on any kind of actual equality, even the limited kind that asserts that variations in capacities and abilities are spread evenly between the different races and sexes: we can have no absolute guarantee that these capacities and abilities really are distributed evenly, without regard to race or sex, among human beings. So far as actual abilities are concerned there do seem to be certain measurable differences between both races and sexes. These differences do not, of course, appear in each case, but only when averages are taken. More important still, we do not yet know how much of these differences is really due to the different genetic endowments of the different races and sexes, and how much is due to poor schools, poor housing, and other factors that are the result of past and continuing discrimination. Perhaps all of the important differences will eventually prove to be environmental rather than genetic. Anyone opposed to racism and sexism will certainly hope that this will be so, for it will make the task of ending discrimination a lot easier; nevertheless it would be dangerous to rest the case against racism and sexism on the belief that all significant differences are environmental in origin. The opponent of, say, racism who takes this line will be unable to avoid conceding that *if* differences in ability do after all prove to have some genetic connection with race, racism would in some way be defensible.

Fortunately there is no need to pin the case for equality to one particular outcome of a scientific investigation. The appropriate response to those who claim to have found evidence of genetically based differences in ability between the races or sexes is not to stick to the belief that the genetic explanation must be wrong, whatever evidence to the contrary may turn up: instead we should make it quite clear that the claim to equality does not depend on intelligence, moral capacity, physical strength, or similar matters of fact. Equality is a moral idea, not an assertion of fact. There is no logically compelling reason for assuming that a factual difference in ability between two people justifies any difference in the amount of consideration we give to their needs and interests. *The principle of the equality of human beings is not a description of an alleged actual equality among humans: it is a prescription of how we should treat humans.*

Jeremy Bentham, the founder of the reforming utilitarian school of moral philosophy, incorporated the essential basis of moral equality into his system of ethics by means of the formula: "Each to count for one and none for more than one." In other words, the interests of every being affected by an action are to be taken into account and given the same weight as the like interests of any other being. A later utilitarian, Henry Sidgwick, put the point in this way: "The good of any one individual is of no more importance, from the point of view (if I may say so) of the Universe, than the good of any other." More recently the leading figures in contemporary moral philosophy have shown a great deal of agreement in specifying as a fundamental presupposition of their moral theories some similar requirement which operates so as to give everyone's interests equal consideration—although these writers generally cannot agree on how this requirement is best formulated.[1]

It is an implication of this principle of equality that our concern for others and our readiness to consider their interests ought not to depend on what they are like or on what abilities they may possess. Precisely what this concern or consideration requires us to do may vary according to the characteristics of those affected by what we do: concern for the well-being of a child growing up in America would require that we teach him to read; concern for the well-being of a pig may require no more than that we leave him alone with other pigs in a place where there is adequate food and room to run freely. But the basic element—the taking into account of the interests of the being, whatever those interests may be—must, according to the principle of equality, be extended to all beings, black or white, masculine or feminine, human or nonhuman.

Thomas Jefferson, who was responsible for writing the principle of the equality of men into the American Declaration of Independence, saw this point. It led him to oppose slavery even though he was unable to free himself fully from his slaveholding background. He wrote in a letter to the author of a book that emphasized the notable intellectual achievements of Negroes in order to refute the then common view that they had limited intellectual capacities:

> Be assured that no person living wishes more sincerely than I do, to see a complete refutation of the doubts I have myself entertained and expressed on the grade of understanding allotted to them by nature, and to find that they are on a par with ourselves … but whatever be their degree of talent it is no measure of their rights. Because Sir Isaac Newton was superior to others in understanding, he was not therefore lord of the property or person of others.[2]

Similarly when in the 1850s the call for women's rights was raised in the United States a remarkable black feminist named Sojourner Truth made the same point in more robust terms at a feminist convention:

> … they talk about this thing in the head; what do they call it? ["Intellect," whispered someone near by.] That's it. What's that got to do with women's rights or Negroes' rights? If my cup won't hold but a pint and yours holds a quart, wouldn't you be mean not to let me have my little half-measure full?[3]

It is on this basis that the case against racism and the case against sexism must both ultimately rest; and it is in accordance with this principle that the attitude that we may call "speciesism," by analogy with racism, must also be condemned. Speciesism—the word is not an attractive one, but I can think of no better term—is a prejudice or attitude of bias toward the interests of members of one's own species and against those of members of other species. It should be obvious that the fundamental objections to racism and sexism made by Thomas Jefferson and Sojourner Truth apply equally to speciesism. If possessing a higher degree of intelligence does not entitle one human to use another for his own ends, how can it entitle humans to exploit nonhumans for the same purpose?[4]

Many philosophers and other writers have proposed the principle of equal consideration of interests, in some form or other, as a basic moral principle; but not many of them have recognized that this principle applies to members of other species as well as to our own. Jeremy Bentham was one of the few who did realize this. In a forward-looking passage written at a time when black slaves had been freed by the French but in the British dominions were still being treated in the way we now treat animals, Bentham wrote:

> The day *may* come when the rest of the animal creation may acquire those rights which never could have been withholden from them but by the hand of tyranny. The French have already discovered that the blackness of the skin is no reason why a human being should be abandoned without redress to the caprice of a tormentor. It may one day come to be recognized that the number of the legs, the villosity of the skin, or the termination of the *os sacrum* are reasons equally insufficient for abandoning a sensitive being to the same fate. What else is it that should trace the insuperable line? Is it the faculty of reason, or perhaps the faculty of discourse? But a full-grown horse or dog is beyond comparison a more rational, as well as a more conversable animal, than an infant of a day or a week or even a month, old. But suppose they were otherwise, what would it avail? The question is not, Can they *reason*? nor Can they *talk*? but, *Can they suffer?*[5]

In this passage Bentham points to the capacity for suffering as the vital characteristic that gives a being the right to equal consideration. The capacity for suffering—or more strictly, for suffering and/or enjoyment or happiness—is not just another characteristic like the capacity for language or higher mathematics. Bentham is not saying that those who try to mark "the insuperable line" that determines whether the interests of a being should be considered happen to have chosen the wrong characteristic. By saying that we must consider the interests of all beings with the capacity for suffering or enjoyment Bentham does not arbitrarily exclude from consideration any interests at all—as those who draw the line with reference to the possession of reason or language do. The capacity

for suffering and enjoyment is *a prerequisite for having interests at all*, a condition that must be satisfied before we can speak of interests in a meaningful way. It would be nonsense to say that it was not in the interests of a stone to be kicked along the road by a schoolboy. A stone does not have interests because it cannot suffer. Nothing that we can do to it could possibly make any difference to its welfare. A mouse, on the other hand, does have an interest in not being kicked along the road, because it will suffer if it is.

If a being suffers there can be no moral justification for refusing to take that suffering into consideration. No matter what the nature of the being, the principle of equality requires that its suffering be counted equally with the like suffering—insofar as rough comparisons can be made—of any other being. If a being is not capable of suffering, or of experiencing enjoyment or happiness, there is nothing to be taken into account. So the limit of sentience (using the term as a convenient if not strictly accurate shorthand for the capacity to suffer and/or experience enjoyment) is the only defensible boundary of concern for the interests of others. To mark this boundary by some other characteristic like intelligence or rationality would be to mark it in an arbitrary manner. Why not choose some other characteristic, like skin color?

The racist violates the principle of equality by giving greater weight to the interests of members of his own race when there is a clash between their interests and the interests of those of another race. The sexist violates the principle of equality by favoring the interests of his own sex. Similarly the speciesist allows the interests of his own species to override the greater interests of members of other species. The pattern is identical in each case.

Most human beings are speciesists. The following chapters show that ordinary human beings—not a few exceptionally cruel or heartless humans, but the overwhelming majority of humans—take an active part in, acquiesce in, and allow their taxes to pay for practices that require the sacrifice of the most important interests of members of other species in order to promote the most trivial interests of our own species.

There is, however, one general defense of the practices to be described in the next two chapters that needs to be disposed of before we discuss the practices themselves. It is a defense which, if true, would allow us to do anything at all to nonhumans for the slightest reason, or for no reason at all, without incurring any justifiable reproach. This defense claims that we are never guilty of neglecting the interests of other animals for one breathtakingly simple reason: they have no interests. Nonhuman animals have no interests, according to this view, because they are not capable of suffering. By this is not meant merely that they are not capable of suffering in all the ways that humans are—for instance, that a calf is not capable of suffering from the knowledge that it will be killed in six months time. That modest claim is, no doubt, true; but it does not clear humans of the charge of speciesism, since it allows that animals may suffer in other ways—for instance, by being given electric shocks, or being kept in small, cramped cages. The defense I am about to discuss is the much more sweeping, although correspondingly less plausible, claim that animals are incapable of suffering in any way at all; that they are, in fact, unconscious automata, possessing neither thoughts nor feelings nor a mental life of any kind.

Although, as we shall see in a later chapter, the view that animals are automata was proposed by the seventeenth-century French philosopher René Descartes, to most people, then and now, it is obvious that if, for example, we stick a sharp knife into the stomach of an unanesthetized dog, the dog will feel pain. That this is so is assumed by the laws in most civilized countries which prohibit wanton cruelty to animals. Readers whose common sense tells them that animals do suffer may prefer to skip the remainder of this section, moving straight on to page 466, since the pages in between do nothing but refute a position which they do not hold. Implausible as it is, though, for the sake of completeness this skeptical position must be discussed.

Do animals other than humans feel pain? How do we know? Well, how do we know if anyone, human or nonhuman, feels pain? We know that we ourselves can feel pain. We know this from the direct experiences of pain that we have when, for instance, somebody presses a lighted cigarette against the back of our hand. But how do we know that anyone else feels pain? We cannot directly experience anyone else's pain, whether that "anyone" is our best friend or a stray dog. Pain is a state of consciousness, a "mental event," and as such it can never be observed. Behavior like writhing, screaming, or drawing one's hand away from the lighted cigarette is not pain itself; nor are the recordings a neurologist might make of activity within the brain observations of pain itself. Pain is something that we feel, and we can only infer that others are feeling it from various external indications.

In theory, we *could* always be mistaken when we assume that other human beings feel pain. It is conceivable that our best friend is really a very cleverly constructed robot, controlled by a brilliant scientist so as to give all the signs of feeling pain, but really no more sensitive than any other machine. We can never know, with absolute certainty, that this is not the case. But while this might present a puzzle for philosophers, none of us has the slightest real doubt that our best friends feel pain just as we do. This is an inference, but a perfectly reasonable one, based on observations of their behavior in situations in which we would feel pain, and on the fact that we have every reason to assume that our friends are beings like us, with nervous systems like ours that can be assumed to function as ours do, and to produce similar feelings in similar circumstances.

If it is justifiable to assume that other humans feel pain as we do, is there any reason why a similar inference should be unjustifiable in the case of other animals?

Nearly all the external signs which lead us to infer pain in other humans can be seen in other species, especially the species most closely related to us—other species of mammals, and birds. Behavioral signs—writhing, facial contortions, moaning, yelping or other forms of calling, attempts to avoid the source of pain, appearance of fear at the prospect of its repetition, and so on—are present. In addition, we know that these animals have nervous systems very like ours, which respond physiologically as ours do when the animal is in circumstances in which we would feel pain: an initial rise of blood pressure, dilated pupils, perspiration, an increased pulse rate, and, if the stimulus continues, a fall in blood pressure. Although humans have a more developed cerebral cortex than other animals, this part of the brain is concerned with thinking functions rather than with basic impulses, emotions, and feelings. These impulses, emotions, and feelings are located in the diencephalon, which is well developed in many other species of animals, especially mammals and birds.[6]

We also know that the nervous systems of other animals were not artificially constructed to mimic the pain behavior of humans, as a robot might be artificially constructed. The nervous systems of animals evolved as our own did, and in fact the evolutionary history of humans and other animals, especially mammals, did not diverge until the central features of our nervous systems were already in existence. A capacity to feel pain obviously enhances a species' prospects of survival, since it causes members of the species to avoid sources of injury. It is surely unreasonable to suppose that nervous systems which are virtually identical physiologically have a common origin and a common evolutionary function, and result in similar forms of behavior in similar circumstances should actually operate in an entirely different manner on the level of subjective feelings.

It has long been accepted as sound policy in science to search for the simplest possible explanation of whatever it is we are trying to explain. Occasionally it has been claimed that it is for this reason "unscientific" to explain the behavior of animals by theories that refer to the animal's conscious feelings, desires, and so on—the idea being that if the behavior in question can be explained without invoking consciousness or feelings, that will be the simpler theory. Yet we can now see that such explanations, when placed in the overall context of the behavior of both human and nonhuman animals, are actually far more complex than their rivals. For we know from our own experience that explanations of our own behavior that did not refer to consciousness and the feeling of pain would be incomplete; and it is simpler to assume that the similar behavior of animals with similar nervous systems is to be explained in the same way than to try to invent some other explanation for the behavior of nonhuman animals as well as an explanation for the divergence between humans and nonhumans in this respect.

The overwhelming majority of scientists who have addressed themselves to this question agree.

Lord Brain, one of the most eminent neurologists of our time, has said:

> I personally can see no reason for conceding mind to my fellow men and denying it to animals.... I at least cannot doubt that the interests and activities of animals are correlated with awareness and feeling in the same way as my own, and which may be, for aught I know, just as vivid.[7]

While the author of a recent book on pain writes:

> Every particle of factual evidence supports the contention that the higher mammalian vertebrates experience pain sensations at least as acute as our own. To say that they feel less because they are lower animals is an absurdity; it can easily be shown that many of their senses are far more acute than ours—visual acuity in certain birds, hearing in most wild animals, and touch in others; these animals depend more than we do today on the sharpest possible awareness of a hostile environment. Apart from the complexity of the cerebral cortex (which does not directly perceive pain) their nervous systems are almost identical to ours and their reactions to pain remarkably similar, though lacking (so far as we know) the philosophical and moral overtones. The emotional element is all too evident, mainly in the form of fear and anger.[8]

In Britain, three separate expert government committees on matters relating to animals have accepted the conclusion that animals feel pain. After noting the obvious behavioral evidence for this view, the Committee on Cruelty to Wild Animals said:

> … we believe that the physiological, and more particularly the anatomical, evidence fully justifies and reinforces the common sense belief that animals feel pain.

And after discussing the evolutionary value of pain they concluded that pain is "of clear-cut biological usefulness" and this is "a third type of evidence that animals feel pain." They then went on to consider forms of suffering other than mere physical pain, and added that they were "satisfied that animals do suffer from acute fear and terror." In 1965, reports by British government committees on experiments on animals, and on the welfare of animals under intensive farming methods, agreed with this view, concluding that animals are capable of suffering both from straightforward physical injuries and from fear, anxiety, stress, and so on.[9]

That might well be thought enough to settle the matter; but there is one more objection that needs to be considered. There is, after all, one behavioral sign that humans have when in pain which nonhumans do not have. This is a developed language. Other animals may communicate with each other, but not, it seems, in the complicated way we do. Some philosophers, including Descartes, have thought it important that while humans can tell each other about their experience of pain in great detail, other animals cannot. (Interestingly, this once neat dividing line between humans and other species has now been threatened by the discovery that chimpanzees can be taught a language.)[10] But as Bentham pointed out long ago, the ability to use language is not relevant to the question of how a being ought to be treated—unless that ability can be linked to the capacity to suffer, so that the absence of a language casts doubt on the existence of this capacity.

This link may be attempted in two ways. First, there is a hazy line of philosophical thought, stemming perhaps from some doctrines associated with the influential philosopher Ludwig Wittgenstein, which maintains that we cannot meaningfully attribute states of consciousness to beings without language. This position seems to me very implausible. Language may be necessary for abstract thought, at some level anyway; but states like pain are more primitive, and have nothing to do with language.

The second and more easily understood way of linking language and the existence of pain is to say that the best evidence that we can have that another creature is in pain is when he tells us that he is. This is a distinct line of argument, for it is not being denied that a non-language-user conceivably *could* suffer, but only that we could ever have sufficient reason to believe that he is suffering. Still, this line of argument fails too. As Jane Goodall has pointed out in her study of chimpanzees, *In the Shadow of Man*, when it comes to the expressions of feelings and emotions language is less important than in other areas. We tend to fall back on nonlinguistic modes of communication such as a cheering pat on the back, an exuberant embrace, a clasp of the hands, and so on. The basic signals we use to convey pain, fear, anger, love, joy, surprise, sexual arousal, and many other emotional states are not specific to our own species.[11]

Charles Darwin made an extensive study of this subject, and the book he wrote about it, *The Expression of the Emotions in Man and Animals*, notes countless nonlinguistic modes of expression. The statement "I am in pain" may be one piece of evidence for the conclusion that the speaker is in pain, but it is not the only possible evidence, and since people sometimes tell lies, not even the best possible evidence.

Even if there were stronger grounds for refusing to attribute pain to those who do not have a language, the consequences of this refusal might lead us to reject the conclusion. Human infants and young children are unable to use language. Are we to deny that a year-old child can suffer? If not, language cannot be crucial. Of course, most parents understand the responses of their children better than they understand the responses of other animals; but this is just a fact about the relatively greater knowledge that we have of our own species, and the greater contact we have with infants, as compared to animals. Those who have studied the behavior of other animals, and those who have pet animals, soon learn to understand their responses as well as we understand those of an infant, and sometimes better. Jane Goodall's account of the chimpanzees she watched is one instance of this, but the same can be said of those who have observed species less closely related to our own. Two among many possible examples are Konrad Lorenz's observations of geese and jackdaws, and N. Tinberger's extensive studies of herring gulls.[12] Just as we can understand infant human behavior in the light of adult human behavior, so we can understand the behavior of other species in the light of our own behavior—and sometimes we can understand our own behavior better in the light of the behavior of other species.

So to conclude: there are no good reasons, scientific or philosophical, for denying that animals feel pain. If we do not doubt that other humans feel pain we should not doubt that other animals do so too.

Animals can feel pain. As we saw earlier, there can be no moral justification for regarding the pain (or pleasure) that animals feel as less important than the same amount of pain (or pleasure) felt by humans. But what exactly does this mean, in practical terms? To prevent misunderstanding I shall spell out what I mean a little more fully.

If I give a horse a hard slap across its rump with my open hand, the horse may start, but it presumably feels little pain. Its skin is thick enough to protect it against a mere slap. If I slap a baby in the same way, however, the baby will cry and presumably does feel pain, for its skin is more sensitive. So it is worse to slap a baby than a horse, if both slaps are administered with equal force. But there must be some kind of blow—I don't know exactly what it would be, but perhaps a blow with a heavy stick—that would cause the horse as much pain as we cause a baby by slapping it with our hand. That is what I mean by "the same amount of pain" and if we consider it wrong to inflict that much pain on a baby for no good reason then we must, unless we are speciesists, consider it equally wrong to inflict the same amount of pain on a horse for no good reason.

There are other differences between humans and animals that cause other complications. Normal adult human beings have mental capacities which will, in certain circumstances, lead them to suffer more than animals would in the same circumstances. If, for instance, we decided to perform extremely painful or lethal scientific experiments on normal adult humans, kidnapped at random from public parks for this purpose, every adult who entered a park would become fearful that he would be kidnapped. The resultant terror would be a form of suffering additional to the pain of the experiment. The same experiments performed on nonhuman animals would cause less suffering since the animals would not have the anticipatory dread of being kidnapped and experimented upon. This does not mean, of course, that it would be right to perform the experiment on animals, but only that there is a reason, which is *not* speciesist, for preferring to use animals rather than normal adult humans, if the experiment is to be done at all. It should be noted, however, that this same argument gives us a reason for preferring to use human infants—orphans perhaps—or retarded humans for experiments, rather than adults, since infants and retarded humans would also have no idea of what was going to happen to them. So far as this argument is concerned

nonhuman animals and infants and retarded humans are in the same category; and if we use this argument to justify experiments on nonhuman animals we have to ask ourselves whether we are also prepared to allow experiments on human infants and retarded adults; and if we make a distinction between animals and these humans, on what basis can we do it, other than a barefaced—and morally indefensible—preference for members of our own species?

There are many areas in which the superior mental powers of normal adult humans make a difference: anticipation, more detailed memory, greater knowledge of what is happening, and so on. Yet these differences do not all point to greater suffering on the part of the normal human being. Sometimes an animal may suffer more because of his more limited understanding. If, for instance, we are taking prisoners in wartime we can explain to them that while they must submit to capture, search, and confinement they will not otherwise be harmed and will be set free at the conclusion of hostilities. If we capture a wild animal, however, we cannot explain that we are not threatening its life. A wild animal cannot distinguish an attempt to overpower and confine from an attempt to kill; the one causes as much terror as the other.

It may be objected that comparisons of the sufferings of different species are impossible to make, and that for this reason when the interests of animals and humans clash the principle of equality gives no guidance. It is probably true that comparisons of suffering between members of different species cannot be made precisely, but precision is not essential. Even if we were to prevent the infliction of suffering on animals only when it is quite certain that the interests of humans will not be affected to anything like the extent that animals are affected, we would be forced to make radical changes in our treatment of animals that would involve our diet, the farming methods we use, experimental procedures in many fields of science, our approach to wildlife and to hunting, trapping and the wearing of furs, and areas of entertainment like circuses, rodeos, and zoos. As a result, a vast amount of suffering would be avoided.

So far I have said a lot about the infliction of suffering on animals, but nothing about killing them.

This omission has been deliberate. The application of the principle of equality to the infliction of suffering is, in theory at least, fairly straightforward. Pain and suffering are bad and should be prevented or minimized, irrespective of the race, sex, or species of the being that suffers. How bad a pain is depends on how intense it is and how long it lasts, but pains of the same intensity and duration are equally bad, whether felt by humans or animals.

The wrongness of killing a being is more complicated. I have kept, and shall continue to keep, the question of killing in the background because in the present state of human tyranny over other species the more simple, straightforward principle of equal consideration of pain or pleasure is a sufficient basis for identifying and protesting against all the major abuses of animals that humans practice. Nevertheless, it is necessary to say something about killing.

Just as most humans are speciesists in their readiness to cause pain to animals when they would not cause a similar pain to humans for the same reason, so most humans are speciesists in their readiness to kill other animals when they would not kill humans. We need to proceed more cautiously here, however, because people hold widely differing views about when it is legitimate to kill humans, as the continuing debates over abortion and euthanasia attest. Nor have moral philosophers been able to agree on exactly what it is that makes it wrong to kill humans, and under what circumstances killing a human being may be justifiable.

Let us consider first the view that it is always wrong to take an innocent human life. We may call this the "sanctity of life" view. People who take this view oppose abortion and euthanasia. They do not usually, however, oppose the killing of nonhumans—so perhaps it would be more accurate to describe this view as the "sanctity of *human* life" view.

The belief that human life, and only human life, is sacrosanct is a form of speciesism. To see this, consider the following example.

Assume that, as sometimes happens, an infant has been born with massive and irreparable brain damage. The damage is so severe that the infant can never be any more than a "human vegetable," unable to talk, recognize other people, act independently of others, or develop a sense of self-awareness. The parents of the infant, realizing that they cannot hope for any improvement in their child's condition and being in any case unwilling to spend, or ask the state to spend, the thousands of dollars that would be needed annually for proper care of the infant, ask the doctor to kill the infant painlessly.

Should the doctor do what the parents ask? Legally, he should not, and in this respect the law reflects the sanctity of life view. The life of every human being is sacred. Yet people who would say this about the infant do not object to the killing of nonhuman animals. How can they justify their different judgments? Adult chimpanzees, dogs, pigs, and many other species far surpass the brain-damaged infant in their ability to relate to others, act independently, be self-aware, and any other capacity that could reasonably be said to give value to life. With the most intensive care possible, there are retarded infants who can never achieve the intelligence level of a dog. Nor can we appeal to the concern of the infant's parents, since they themselves, in this imaginary example (and in some actual cases), do not want the infant kept alive.

The only thing that distinguishes the infant from the animal, in the eyes of those who claim it has a "right to life," is that it is, biologically, a member of the species Homo sapiens, whereas chimpanzees, dogs, and pigs are not. But to use *this* difference as the basis for granting a right to life to the infant and not to the other animals is, of course, pure speciesism.* It is exactly the kind of arbitrary difference that the most crude and overt kind of racist uses in attempting to justify racial discrimination.

---

*I am here putting aside religious views, for example the doctrine that all and only humans have immortal souls, or are made in the image of God. Historically these views have been very important, and no doubt are partly responsible for the idea that human life has a special sanctity. Logically, however, these religious views are unsatisfactory, since a reasoned explanation of why it should be that all humans and no nonhumans have immortal souls is not offered. This belief too, therefore, comes under suspicion as a form of speciesism. In any case, defenders of the "sanctity of life" view are generally reluctant to base their position on purely religious doctrines, since these doctrines are no longer as widely accepted as they once were.

This does not mean that to avoid speciesism we must hold that it is as wrong to kill a dog as it is to kill a normal human being. The only position that is irredeemably speciesist is the one that tries to make the boundary of the right to life run exactly parallel to the boundary of our own species. Those who hold the sanctity of life view do this because while distinguishing sharply between humans and other animals they allow no distinctions to be made within our own species, objecting to the killing of the severely retarded and the hopelessly senile as strongly as they object to the killing of normal adults.

To avoid speciesism we must allow that beings which are similar in all relevant respects have a similar right to life—and mere membership in our own biological species cannot be a morally relevant criterion for this right. Within these limits we could still hold that, for instance, it is worse to kill a normal adult human, with a capacity for self-awareness, and the ability to plan for the future and have meaningful relations with others, than it is to kill a mouse, which presumably does not share all of these characteristics; or we might appeal to the close family and other personal ties which humans have but mice do not have to the same degree; or we might think that it is the consequences for other humans, who will be put in fear of their own lives, that makes the crucial difference; or we might think it is some combination of these factors, or other factors altogether.

Whatever criteria we choose, however, we will have to admit that they do not follow precisely the boundary of our own species. We may legitimately hold that there are some features of certain beings which make their lives more valuable than those of other beings; but there will surely be some nonhuman animals whose lives, by any standards, are more valuable than the lives of some humans. A chimpanzee, dog, or pig, for instance, will have a higher degree of self-awareness and a greater capacity for meaningful relations with others than a severely retarded infant or someone in a state of advanced senility. So if we base the right to life on these characteristics we must grant these animals a right to life as good as, or better than, such retarded or senile humans.

Now this argument cuts both ways. It could be taken as showing that chimpanzees, dogs, and pigs, along with some other species, have a right to life and we commit a grave moral offense whenever we kill them, even when they are old and suffering and our intention is to put them out of their misery. Alternatively one could take the argument as showing that the severely retarded and hopelessly senile have no right to life and may be killed for quite trivial reasons, as we now kill animals.

Since the focus of this book is on ethical questions concerning animals and not on the morality of euthanasia I shall not attempt to settle this issue finally. I think it is reasonably clear, though, that while both of the positions just described avoid speciesism, neither is entirely satisfactory. What we need is some middle position which would avoid speciesism but would not make the lives of the retarded and senile as cheap as the lives of pigs and dogs now are, nor make the lives of pigs and dogs so sacrosanct that we think it wrong to put them out of hopeless misery. What we must do is bring nonhuman animals within our sphere of moral concern and cease to treat their lives as expendable for whatever trivial purposes we may have. At the same time, once we realize that the fact that a being is a member of our own species is not in itself enough to make it always wrong to kill that being, we may come to reconsider our policy of preserving human lives at all costs, even when there is no prospect of a meaningful life or of existence without terrible pain.

I conclude, then, that a rejection of speciesism does not imply that all lives are of equal worth. While self-awareness, intelligence, the capacity for meaningful relations with others, and so on are not relevant to the question of inflicting pain—since pain is pain, whatever other capacities, beyond the capacity to feel pain, the being may have—these capacities may be relevant to the question of taking life. It is not arbitrary to hold that the life of a self-aware being, capable of abstract thought, of planning for the future, of complex acts of communication, and so on, is more valuable than the life of a being without these capacities. To see the difference between the issues of inflicting pain and taking life, consider how we would choose within our own species. If we had to choose to save the life of a normal human or a mentally defective human, we would probably choose to save the life of the normal human; but if we had to choose between preventing pain in the normal human or the mental defective—imagine that both have received painful but superficial injuries, and we only have enough painkiller for one of them—it is not nearly so clear how we ought to choose. The same is true when we consider other species. The evil of pain is, in itself, unaffected by the other characteristics of the being that feels the pain; the value of life is affected by these other characteristics.

Normally this will mean that if we have to choose between the life of a human being and the life of another animal we should choose to save the life of the human; but there may be special cases in which the reverse holds true, because the human being in question does not have the capacities of a normal human being. So this view is not speciesist, although it may appear to be at first glance. The preference, in normal cases, for saving a human life over the life of an animal when a choice *has* to be made is a preference based on the characteristics that normal humans have, and not on the mere fact that they are members of our own species. This is why when we consider members of our own species who lack the characteristics of normal humans we can no longer say that their lives are always to be preferred to those of other animals. This issue comes up in a practical way in the following chapter. In general, though, the question of when it is wrong to kill (painlessly) an animal is one to which we need give no precise answer. As long as we remember that we should give the same respect to the lives of animals as we give to the lives of those humans at a similar mental level, we shall not go far wrong.

In any case, the conclusions that are argued for in this book flow from the principle of minimizing suffering alone. The idea that it is also wrong to kill animals painlessly gives some of these conclusions additional support which is welcome, but strictly unnecessary. Interestingly enough, this is true even of the conclusion that we ought to

become vegetarians, a conclusion which in the popular mind is generally based on some kind of absolute prohibition on killing.

NOTES

1. For Bentham's moral philosophy, see his *Introduction to the Principles of Morals and Legislation*, and for Sidgwick's see *The Methods of Ethics* (the passage quoted is from the seventh edition, p. 382). As examples of leading contemporary moral philosophers who incorporate a requirement of equal consideration of interests, see R. M. Hare, *Freedom and Reason* (New York: Oxford University Press, 1963) and John Rawls, *A Theory of Justice* (Cambridge: Harvard University Press, Belknap Press, 1972). For a brief account of the essential agreement on this issue between these and other positions, see R. M. Hare, "Rules of War and Moral Reasoning," *Philosophy and Public Affairs*, vol. 1, no. 2 (1972).
2. Letter to Henri Gregoire, February 25, 1809.
3. Reminiscences by Francis D. Gage, from Susan B. Anthony, *The History of Woman Suffrage*, vol. 1; the passage is to be found in the extract in Leslie Tanner, ed., *Voices from Women's Liberation* (New York: Signet, 1970).
4. I owe the term "speciesism" to Richard Ryder.
5. *Introduction to the Principles of Morals and Legislation,* chapter 17.
6. Lord Brain, "Presidential Address" in C. A. Keele and R. Smith, eds., *The Assessment of Pain in Men and Animals* (London: Universities Federation for Animal Welfare, 1962).
7. Ibid., p. 11.
8. Richard Serjeant, *The Spectrum of Pain* (London: Hart-Davis London:, 1969), p. 72.
9. See the reports of the committee on Cruelty to Wild Animals (Command Paper 8266, 1951), paragraphs 36–42; the Departmental Committee on Experiments on Animals (Command Paper 2641, 1965), paragraphs 179–182; and the Technical Committee to Enquire into the Welfare of Animals Kept under Intensive Livestock Husbandry Systems (Command Paper 2836, 1965), paragraphs 26–28 (London: Her Majesty's Stationery Office).
10. One chimpanzee, Washoe, has been taught the sign language used by deaf people, and acquired a vocabulary of 350 signs. Another, Lana, communicates in structured sentences by pushing buttons on a special machine. For a brief account of Washoe's abilities, see Jane van Lawick-Goodall, *In the Shadow of Man*

(Boston: Houghton Mifflin, 1971), pp. 252–254; and for Lana, see *Newsweek*, 7 January 1974, and *New York Times*, 4 December 1974.

11. *In the Shadow of Man*, p. 225; Michael Peters makes a similar point in "Nature and Culture," in Stanley and Roslind Godlovitch and John Harris, eds., *Animals, Men and Morals* (New York: Taplinger Publishing Co., 1972).

12. Konrad Lorenz, *King Solomon's Ring* (New York: T.Y. Crowell, 1952); N. Tinbergen, *The Herring Gull's World*, rev. ed. (New York: Basic Books, 1974).

☙ QUESTIONS FOR ANALYSIS

1. What does Singer mean by his claim that the principle of human equality is not a description of actual equality but a prescription of how we should treat humans?
2. On what grounds does Singer equate speciesism with sexism and racism?
3. What reasons have been advanced in favor of the view that animals cannot suffer? How does Singer rebut them?
4. Singer notes certain differences between human and nonhuman capacities and the complications that follow from them. What are these differences, and what kinds of complications follow from them?
5. To reject speciesism, Singer says, is not to say that all lives are of equal worth. Why not?
6. Normally, Singer says, we should choose a human over a nonhuman life if forced to choose between them. Why? Under what circumstances should we choose the nonhuman one?
7. In what way is Singer's principle of equal consideration related to the principle of utility?

The Case for Animal Rights

TOM REGAN

In this essay, Tom Regan, a professor emeritus of philosophy at North Carolina State University, offers an alternative approach to Peter Singer's. Like Singer, he opposes speciesism. Unlike Singer, he does not offer a utilitarian moral theory. He argues that the focus of our moral concern should not be to minimize suffering and maximize pleasure but to avoid treating individual animals (human and nonhuman alike) in certain ways regardless of the consequences.

All animals that are the experiencing subjects of their own lives, he says, have inherent value. They, like humans, deserve what we called in Part 1 Kantian respect. They are not to be treated as mere things, even if we can maximize happiness by doing so. What makes eating meat or experimenting on animals wrong, then, is not that the human benefit does not outweigh the animal suffering, but that such practices deny the inherent value of the animals involved.

In defending his position, Regan criticizes *contractarian* views of morality, which deny that nonhuman animals can have rights. He also disagrees with Singer's view that some lives of creatures with the right to life are more valuable than others. All lives that have inherent value, he says, are equal.

From "The Case for Animal Rights," *In Defense of Animals* edited by Peter Singer (1985), pp. 13–26. Reprinted by permission of John Wiley & Sons, Inc.

I regard myself as an advocate of animal rights—as a part of the animal rights movement. That movement, as I conceive it, is committed to a number of goals, including:

the total abolition of the use of animals in science;

the total dissolution of commercial animal agriculture;

the total elimination of commercial and sport hunting and trapping.

There are, I know, people who profess to believe in animal rights but do not avow these goals. Factory farming, they say, is wrong—it violates animals' rights—but traditional animal agriculture is all right. Toxicity tests of cosmetics on animals violates their rights, but important medical research—cancer research, for example—does not. The clubbing of baby seals is abhorrent, but not the harvesting of adult seals. I used to think I understood this reasoning. Not any more. You don't change unjust institutions by tidying them up.

What's wrong—fundamentally wrong—with the way animals are treated isn't the details that vary from case to case. It's the whole system. The forlornness of the veal calf is pathetic, heart wrenching; the pulsing pain of the chimp with electrodes planted deep in her brain is repulsive; the slow, tortuous death of the raccoon caught in the leg-hold trap is agonizing. But what is wrong isn't the pain, isn't the suffering, isn't the deprivation. These compound what's wrong. Sometimes—often—they make it much, much worse. But they are not the fundamental wrong.

The fundamental wrong is the system that allows us to view animals as *our resources*, here for *us*—to be eaten, or surgically manipulated, or exploited for sport or money. Once we accept this view of animals as our resources—the rest is as predictable as it is regrettable. Why worry about their loneliness, their pain, their death? Since animals exist for us, to benefit us in one way or another, what harms them really doesn't matter—or matters only if it starts to bother us, makes us feel a trifle uneasy when we eat our veal escalope, for example. So, yes, let us get veal calves out of solitary confinement, give them more space, a little straw, a few companions. But let us keep our veal escalope.

But a little straw, more space and a few companions won't eliminate—won't even touch—the basic wrong that attaches to our viewing and treating these animals as our resources. A veal calf killed to be eaten after living in close confinement is viewed and treated in this way: but so, too, is another who is raised (as they say) "more humanely." To right the wrong of our treatment of farm animals requires more than making rearing methods "more humane"; it requires the total dissolution of commercial animal agriculture.

How we do this, whether we do it or, as in the case of animals in science, whether and how we abolish their use—these are to a large extent political questions. People must change their beliefs before they change their habits. Enough people, especially those elected to public office, must believe in change—must want it—before we will have laws that protect the rights of animals. This process of change is very complicated, very demanding, very exhausting, calling for the efforts of many hands in education, publicity, political organization and activity, down to the licking of envelopes and stamps. As a trained and practicing philosopher, the sort of contribution I can make is limited but, I like to think, important. The currency of philosophy is ideas—their meaning and rational foundation—not the nuts and bolts of the legislative process, say, or the mechanics of community organization. That's what I have been exploring over the past ten years or so in my essays and talks and, most recently, in my book, *The Case for Animal Rights*. I believe the major conclusions I reach in the book are true because they are supported by the weight of the best arguments. I believe the idea of animal rights has reason, not just emotion, on its side.

In the space I have at my disposal here I can only sketch, in the barest outline, some of the main features of the book. Its main themes—and we should not be surprised by this—involve asking and answering deep, foundational moral questions about what morality is, how it should be understood and what is the best moral theory, all considered. I hope I can convey something of the shape I think this theory takes. The attempt to do this will be (to use a word a friendly critic once used to describe my work) cerebral, perhaps too cerebral. But this is misleading. My feelings about how animals are sometimes treated run just as deep and just as strong as those of my more volatile compatriots. Philosophers do—to use the jargon of the day—have a right side to their brains. If it's the left side we contribute (or mainly should), that's because what talents we have reside there.

How to proceed? We begin by asking how the moral status of animals has been understood by thinkers who deny that animals have rights. Then we test the mettle of their ideas by seeing how well they stand up under the heat of fair criticism. If we start our thinking in this way, we soon find that some people believe that we have no duties directly to animals, that we owe nothing to them, that we can do nothing that wrongs them. Rather, we can do wrong acts that involve animals, and so we have duties regarding them, though none to them. Such views may be called indirect duty views. By way of illustration: suppose your neighbour kicks your dog. Then your neighbour has done something wrong. But not to your dog. The wrong that has been done is a wrong to you. After all, it is wrong to upset people, and your neighbour's kicking your dog upsets you. So you are the one who is wronged, not your dog. Or again: by kicking your dog your neighbour damages your property. And since it is wrong to damage another person's property, your neighbour has done something wrong—to you, of course, not to your dog. Your neighbour no more wrongs your dog than your car would be wronged if the windshield were smashed. Your neighbour's duties involving your dog are indirect duties to you. More generally, all of our duties regarding animals are indirect duties to one another—to humanity.

How could someone try to justify such a view? Someone might say that your dog doesn't feel anything and so isn't hurt by your neighbour's kick, doesn't care about the pain since none is felt, is as unaware of anything as is your windshield. Someone might say this, but no rational person

will, since, among other considerations, such a view will commit anyone who holds it to the position that no human being feels pain either—that human beings also don't care about what happens to them. A second possibility is that though both humans and your dog are hurt when kicked, it is only human pain that matters. But, again, no rational person can believe this. Pain is pain wherever it occurs. If your neighbour's causing you pain is wrong because of the pain that is caused, we cannot rationally ignore or dismiss the moral relevance of the pain that your dog feels.

Philosophers who hold indirect duty views—and many still do—have come to understand that they must avoid the two defects just noted: that is, both the view that animals don't feel anything as well as the idea that only human pain can be morally relevant. Among such thinkers the sort of view now favoured is one or other form of what is called *contractarianism*.

Here, very crudely, is the root idea: morality consists of a set of rules that individuals voluntarily agree to abide by, as we do when we sign a contract (hence the name contractarianism). Those who understand and accept the terms of the contract are covered directly; they have rights created and recognized by, and protected in, the contract. And these contractors can also have protection spelled out for others who, though they lack the ability to understand morality and so cannot sign the contract themselves, are loved or cherished by those who can. Thus young children, for example, are unable to sign contracts and lack rights. But they are protected by the contract none the less because of the sentimental interests of others, most notably their parents. So we have, then, duties involving these children, duties regarding them, but no duties to them. Our duties in their case are indirect duties to other human beings, usually their parents.

As for animals, since they cannot understand contracts, they obviously cannot sign; and since they cannot sign, they have no rights. Like children, however, some animals are the objects of the sentimental interest of others. You, for example, love your dog or cat. So those animals that enough people care about (companion animals, whales, baby seals, the American bald eagle), though they lack rights themselves, will be protected because of the sentimental interests of people. I have, then, according to contractarianism, no duty directly to your dog or any other animal, not even the duty not to cause them pain or suffering; my duty not to hurt them is a duty I have to those people who care about what happens to them. As for other animals, where no or little sentimental interest is present—in the case of farm animals, for example, or laboratory rats—what duties we have grow weaker and weaker, perhaps to vanishing point. The pain and death they endure, though real, are not wrong if no one cares about them.

When it comes to the moral status of animals, contractarianism could be a hard view to refute if it were an adequate theoretical approach to the moral status of human beings. It is not adequate in this latter respect, however, which makes the question of its adequacy in the former case, regarding animals, utterly moot. For consider: morality, according to the (crude) contractarian position before us, consists of rules that people agree to abide by. What people? Well, enough to make a difference—enough, that is, *collectively* to have the power to enforce the rules that are drawn up in the contract. That is very well and good for the signatories but not so good for anyone who is not asked to sign. And there is nothing in contractarianism of the sort we are discussing that guarantees or requires that everyone will have a chance to participate equally in framing the rules of morality. The result is that this approach to ethics could sanction the most blatant forms of social, economic, moral and political injustice, ranging from a repressive caste system to systematic racial or sexual discrimination. Might, according to this theory, does make right. Let those who are the victims of injustice suffer as they will. It matters not so long as no one else—no contractor, or too few of them—cares about it. Such a theory takes one's moral breath away … as if, for example, there would be nothing wrong with apartheid in South Africa if few white South Africans were upset by it. A theory with so little to recommend it at the level of the ethics of our treatment of our fellow humans cannot have anything more to

recommend it when it comes to the ethics of how we treat our fellow animals.

The version of contractarianism just examined is, as I have noted, a crude variety, and in fairness to those of a contractarian persuasion it must be noted that much more refined, subtle and ingenious varieties are possible. For example, John Rawls, in his *A Theory of Justice*, sets forth a version of contractarianism that forces contractors to ignore the accidental features of being a human being—for example, whether one is white or black, male or female, a genius or of modest intellect. Only by ignoring such features, Rawls believes, can we ensure that the principles of justice that contractors would agree upon are not based on bias or prejudice. Despite the improvement a view such as Rawls's represents over the cruder forms of contractarianism, it remains deficient: it systematically denies that we have direct duties to those human beings who do not have a sense of justice—young children, for instance, and many mentally retarded humans. And yet it seems reasonably certain that, were we to torture a young child or a retarded elder, we would be doing something that wronged him or her, not something that would be wrong if (and only if) other humans with a sense of justice were upset. And since this is true in the case of these humans, we cannot rationally deny the same in the case of animals.

Indirect duty views, then, including the best among them, fail to command our rational assent. Whatever ethical theory we should accept rationally, therefore, it must at least recognize that we have some duties directly to animals, just as we have some duties directly to each other. The next two theories I'll sketch attempt to meet this requirement.

The first I call the cruelty–kindness view. Simply stated, this says that we have a direct duty to be kind to animals and a direct duty not to be cruel to them. Despite the familiar, reassuring ring of these ideas, I do not believe that this view offers an adequate theory. To make this clearer, consider kindness. A kind person acts from a certain kind of motive—compassion or concern, for example. And that is a virtue. But there is no guarantee that a kind act is a right act. If I am a generous racist, for example, I will be inclined to act kindly towards members of my own race, favouring their interests above those of others. My kindness would be real and, so far as it goes, good. But I trust it is too obvious to require argument that my kind acts may not be above moral reproach—may, in fact, be positively wrong because rooted in injustice. So kindness, notwithstanding its status as a virtue to be encouraged, simply will not carry the weight of a theory of right action.

Cruelty fares no better. People or their acts are cruel if they display either a lack of sympathy for or, worse, the presence of enjoyment in another's suffering. Cruelty in all its guises is a bad thing, a tragic human failing. But just as a person's being motivated by kindness does not guarantee that he or she does what is right, so the absence of cruelty does not ensure that he or she avoids doing what is wrong. Many people who perform abortions, for example, are not cruel, sadistic people. But that fact alone does not settle the terribly difficult question of the morality of abortion. The case is no different when we examine the ethics of our treatment of animals. So, yes, let us be for kindness and against cruelty. But let us not suppose that being for the one and against the other answers questions about moral right and wrong.

Some people think that the theory we are looking for is utilitarianism. A utilitarian accepts two moral principles. The first is that of equality: everyone's interests count, and similar interests must be counted as having similar weight or importance. White or black, American or Iranian, human or animal—everyone's pain or frustration matters, and matters just as much as the equivalent pain or frustration of anyone else. The second principle a utilitarian accepts is that of utility: do the act that will bring about the best balance between satisfaction and frustration for everyone affected by the outcome.

As a utilitarian, then, here is how I am to approach the task of deciding what I morally ought to do: I must ask who will be affected if I choose to do one thing rather than another, how much each individual will be affected, and where the best results are most likely to lie—which option, in other words, is most likely to bring about the best results, the best balance between satisfaction and frustration.

That option, whatever it may be, is the one I ought to choose. That is where my moral duty lies.

The great appeal of utilitarianism rests with its uncompromising *egalitarianism*: everyone's interests count and count as much as the like interests of everyone else. The kind of odious discrimination that some forms of contractarianism can justify—discrimination based on race or sex, for example—seems disallowed in principle by utilitarianism, as is speciesism, systematic discrimination based on species membership.

The equality we find in utilitarianism, however, is not the sort an advocate of animal or human rights should have in mind. Utilitarianism has no room for the equal moral rights of different individuals because it has no room for their equal inherent value or worth. What has value for the utilitarian is the satisfaction of an individual's interests, not the individual whose interests they are. A universe in which you satisfy your desire for water, food and warmth is, other things being equal, better than a universe in which these desires are frustrated. And the same is true in the case of an animal with similar desires. But neither you nor the animal has any value in your own right. Only your feelings do.

Here is an analogy to help make the philosophical point clearer: a cup contains different liquids, sometimes sweet, sometimes bitter, sometimes a mix of the two. What has value are the liquids: the sweeter the better, the bitterer the worse. The cup, the container, has no value. It is what goes into it, not what they go into, that has value. For the utilitarian you and I are like the cup; we have no value as individuals and thus no equal value. What has value is what goes into us, what we serve as receptacles for; our feelings of satisfaction have positive value, our feelings of frustration negative value.

Serious problems arise for utilitarianism when we remind ourselves that it enjoins us to bring about the best consequences. What does this mean? It doesn't mean the best consequences for me alone, or for my family or friends, or any other person taken individually. No, what we must do is, roughly, as follows: we must add up (somehow!) the separate satisfactions and frustrations of everyone likely to be affected by our choice, the satisfactions in one column, the frustrations in the other. We must total each column for each of the options before us. That is what it means to say the theory is aggregative. And then we must choose that option which is most likely to bring about the best balance of totaled satisfactions over totaled frustrations. Whatever act would lead to this outcome is the one we ought morally to perform—it is where our moral duty lies. And that act quite clearly might not be the same one that would bring about the best results for me personally, or for my family or friends, or for a lab animal. The best aggregated consequences for everyone concerned are not necessarily the best for each individual.

That utilitarianism is an aggregative theory—different individuals' satisfactions or frustrations are added, or summed, or totaled—is the key objection to this theory. My Aunt Bea is old, inactive, a cranky, sour person, though not physically ill. She prefers to go on living. She is also rather rich. I could make a fortune if I could get my hands on her money, money she intends to give me in any event, after she dies, but which she refuses to give me now. In order to avoid a huge tax bite, I plan to donate a handsome sum of my profits to a local children's hospital. Many, many children will benefit from my generosity, and much joy will be brought to their parents, relatives and friends. If I don't get the money rather soon, all these ambitions will come to naught. The once-in-a-lifetime opportunity to make a real killing will be gone. Why, then, not kill my Aunt Bea? Of course I *might* get caught. But I'm no fool and, besides, her doctor can be counted on to cooperate (he has an eye for the same investment and I happen to know a good deal about his shady past). The deed can be done … professionally, shall we say. There is *very* little chance of getting caught. And as for my conscience being guilt-ridden, I am a resourceful sort of fellow and will take more than sufficient comfort—as I lie on the beach at Acapulco—in contemplating the joy and health I have brought to so many others.

Suppose Aunt Bea is killed and the rest of the story comes out as told. Would I have done anything wrong? Anything immoral? One would have thought that I had. Not according to utilitarianism. Since what I have done has brought about the best balance between totaled satisfaction and frustration for all those affected by the outcome, my action is not wrong. Indeed, in killing Aunt Bea the physician and I did what duty required.

This same kind of argument can be repeated in all sorts of cases, illustrating, time after time, how the utilitarian's position leads to results that impartial people find morally callous. It is wrong to kill my Aunt Bea in the name of bringing about the best results for others. A good end does not justify an evil means. Any adequate moral theory will have to explain why this is so. Utilitarianism fails in this respect and so cannot be the theory we seek.

What to do? Where to begin anew? The place to begin, I think, is with the utilitarian's view of the value of the individual—or, rather, lack of value. In its place, suppose we consider that you and I, for example, do have value as individuals—what we'll call *inherent value*. To say we have such value is to say that we are something more than, something different from, mere receptacles. Moreover, to ensure that we do not pave the way for such injustices as slavery or sexual discrimination, we must believe that all who have inherent value have it equally, regardless of their sex, race, religion, birthplace and so on. Similarly to be discarded as irrelevant are one's talents or skills, intelligence and wealth, personality or pathology, whether one is loved and admired or despised and loathed. The genius and the retarded child, the prince and the pauper, the brain surgeon and the fruit vendor, Mother Teresa and the most unscrupulous used-car salesman—all have inherent value, all possess it equally, and all have an equal right to be treated with respect, to be treated in ways that do not reduce them to the status of things, as if they existed as resources for others. My value as an individual is independent of my usefulness to you. Yours is not dependent on your usefulness to me. For either of us to treat the other in ways that fail to show respect for the other's independent value is to act immorally, to violate the individual's rights.

Some of the rational virtues of this view—what I call the rights view—should be evident. Unlike (crude) contractarianism, for example, the rights view in *principle* denies the moral tolerability of any and all forms of racial, sexual or social discrimination; and unlike utilitarianism, this view *in principle* denies that we can justify good results by using evil means that violate an individual's rights—denies, for example, that it could be moral to kill my Aunt Bea to harvest beneficial consequences for others. That would be to sanction the disrespectful treatment of the individual in the name of the social good, something the rights view will not—categorically will not—ever allow.

The rights view, I believe, is rationally the most satisfactory moral theory. It surpasses all other theories in the degree to which it illuminates and explains the foundation of our duties to one another—the domain of human morality. On this score it has the best reasons, the best arguments, on its side. Of course, if it were possible to show that only human beings are included within its scope, then a person like myself, who believes in animal rights, would be obliged to look elsewhere.

But attempts to limit its scope to humans only can be shown to be rationally defective. Animals, it is true, lack many of the abilities humans possess. They can't read, do higher mathematics, build a bookcase or make *baba ghanoush*. Neither can many human beings, however, and yet we don't (and shouldn't) say that they (these humans) therefore have less inherent value, less of a right to be treated with respect, than do others. It is the *similarities* between those human beings who most clearly, most non-controversially have such value (the people reading this, for example), not our differences, that matter most. And the really crucial, the basic similarity is simply this: we are each of us the experiencing subject of a life, a conscious creature having an individual welfare that has importance to us whatever our usefulness to others. We want and prefer things, believe and feel things, recall and expect things. And all these dimensions of our life, including our pleasure and pain, our enjoyment and suffering, our satisfaction and frustration, our continued existence or our untimely death—all make a difference to the quality of our life as lived, as experienced, by us as individuals. As the same is true of those animals that concern us (the ones that are eaten and trapped, for example), they too must be viewed as the experiencing subjects of a life, with inherent value of their own.

Some there are who resist the idea that animals have inherent value. "Only humans have such value," they profess. How might this narrow view be defended? Shall we say that only humans have the requisite intelligence, or autonomy, or reason? But there are many, many humans who fail to meet these

standards and yet are reasonably viewed as having value above and beyond their usefulness to others. Shall we claim that only humans belong to the right species, the species *Homo sapiens*? But this is blatant speciesism. Will it be said, then, that all and only—humans have immortal souls? Then our opponents have their work cut out for them. I am myself not ill-disposed to the proposition that there are immortal souls. Personally, I profoundly hope I have one. But I would not want to rest my position on a controversial ethical issue on the even more controversial question about who or what has an immortal soul. That is to dig one's hole deeper, not to climb out.

Rationally, it is better to resolve moral issues without making more controversial assumptions than are needed. The question of who has inherent value is such a question, one that is resolved more rationally without the introduction of the idea of immortal souls than by its use.

Well, perhaps some will say that animals have some inherent value, only less than we have. Once again, however, attempts to defend this view can be shown to lack rational justification. What could be the basis of our having more inherent value than animals? Their lack of reason, or autonomy, or intellect? Only if we are willing to make the same judgment in the case of humans who are similarly deficient. But it is not true that such humans—the retarded child, for example, or the mentally deranged—have less inherent value than you or I. Neither, then, can we rationally sustain the view that animals like them in being the experiencing subjects of a life have less inherent value. All who have inherent value have it *equally*, whether they be human animals or not.

Inherent value, then, belongs equally to those who are the experiencing subjects of a life. Whether it belongs to others—to rocks and rivers, trees and glaciers, for example—we do not know and may never know. But neither do we need to know, if we are to make the case for animal rights. We do not need to know, for example, how many people are eligible to vote in the next presidential election before we can know whether I am. Similarly, we do not need to know how many individuals have inherent value before we can know that some do. When it comes to the case for animal rights, then, what we need to know is whether the animals that, in our culture, are routinely eaten, hunted and used in our laboratories, for example, are like us in being subjects of a life. And we do know this. We do know that many—literally, billions and billions—of these animals are the subjects of a life in the sense explained and so have inherent value if we do. And since, in order to arrive at the best theory of our duties to one another, we must recognize our equal inherent value as individuals, reason—not sentiment, not emotion—reason compels us to recognize the equal inherent value of these animals and, with this, their equal right to be treated with respect.

That, *very* roughly, is the shape and feel of the case for animal rights. Most of the details of the supporting argument are missing. They are to be found in the book to which I alluded earlier. Here, the details go begging, and I must, in closing, limit myself to four final points.

The first is how the theory that underlies the case for animal rights shows that the animal rights movement is a part of, not antagonistic to, the human rights movement. The theory that rationally grounds the rights of animals also grounds the rights of humans. Thus those involved in the animal rights movement are partners in the struggle to secure respect for human rights—the rights of women, for example, or minorities, or workers. The animal rights movement is cut from the same moral cloth as these.

Second, having set out the broad outlines of the rights view, I can now say why its implications for farming and science, among other fields, are both clear and uncompromising. In the case of the use of animals in science, the rights view is categorically abolitionist. Lab animals are not our tasters; we are not their kings. Because these animals are treated routinely, systematically as if their value were reducible to their usefulness to others, they are routinely, systematically treated with a lack of respect, and thus are their rights routinely, systematically violated. This is just as true when they are used in trivial, duplicative, unnecessary or unwise research as it is when they are used in studies that hold out real promise of human benefits. We can't justify harming or killing a human being (my Aunt Bea, for example) just for these sorts of reason. Neither can we do so even in the case of so lowly a creature as a laboratory rat. It is not just refinement or reduction that is called for, not just larger, cleaner cages, not just more generous use of anaesthetic or the elimination of multiple surgery, not just tidying up the system. It is complete replacement. The best we can do when it comes to using animals in science is—not to use them. That is where our duty lies, according to the rights view.

As for commercial animal agriculture, the rights view takes a similar abolitionist position. The fundamental moral wrong here is not that animals are kept in stressful close confinement or in isolation, or that their pain and suffering, their needs and preferences are ignored or discounted. All these *are* wrong, of course, but they are not the fundamental wrong. They are symptoms and effects of the deeper, systematic wrong that allows these animals to be viewed and treated as lacking independent value, as resources for us—as, indeed, a renewable resource. Giving farm animals more space, more natural environments, more companions does not right the fundamental wrong, any more than giving lab animals more anaesthesia or bigger, cleaner cages would right the fundamental wrong in their case. Nothing less than the total dissolution of commercial animal agriculture will do this, just as, for similar reasons I won't develop at length here, morality requires nothing less than the total elimination of hunting and trapping for commercial and sporting ends. The rights view's implications, then, as I have said, are clear and uncompromising.

My last two points are about philosophy, my profession. It is, most obviously, no substitute for political action. The words I have written here and in other places by themselves don't change a thing. It is what we do with the thoughts that the words express—our acts, our deeds—that changes things. All that philosophy can do, and all I have attempted, is to offer a vision of what our deeds should aim at. And the why. But not the how.

Finally, I am reminded of my thoughtful critic, the one I mentioned earlier, who chastised me for being too cerebral. Well, cerebral I have been: indirect duty views, utilitarianism, contractarianism—hardly the stuff deep passions are made of. I am also reminded, however, of the image another friend once set before me—the image of the ballerina as expressive of disciplined passion. Long hours of sweat and toil, of loneliness and practice, of doubt and fatigue: those are the discipline of her craft.

But the passion is there too, the fierce drive to excel, to speak through her body, to do it right, to pierce our minds. That is the image of philosophy I would leave with you, not "too cerebral" but *disciplined passion*. Of the discipline enough has been seen. As for the passion: there are times, and these not infre-quent, when tears come to my eyes when I see, or read, or hear of the wretched plight of animals in the hands of humans. Their pain, their suffering, their loneliness, their innocence, their death. Anger. Rage. Pity. Sorrow. Disgust. The whole creation groans under the weight of the evil we humans visit upon these mute, powerless creatures. It is our hearts, not just our heads, that call for an end to it all, that demand of us that we overcome, for them, the habits and forces behind their systematic oppression. All great movements, it is written, go through three stages: ridicule, discussion, adoption. It is the realization of this third stage, adoption, that requires both our passion and our discipline, our hearts and our heads. The fate of animals is in our hands. God grant we are equal to the task.

☙ QUESTIONS FOR ANALYSIS

1. What is the difference between direct and indirect duties? Why does Regan reject the view that we can have only indirect duties to nonhuman animals?
2. On what grounds does Regan reject contractarian views of moral obligations?
3. What is the cruelty–kindness view of morality? Why does Regan find it inadequate?
4. What does Regan find appealing about utilitarian thinking? What does he find objectionable about it?
5. What does Regan mean by inherent value? What traits must a creature possess to have it?
6. What objections to the view that some animals have inherent value does Regan consider? How does he rebut them?
7. What practical differences can you see between Regan's view and Singer's?

Do Animals Have Rights?

CARL COHEN

Carl Cohen is professor of philosophy at the University of Michigan, where he has taught since 1955. He has published extensively on issues of practical importance, from the moral status of animals and the protection of human subjects in medical experiments to race preference and affirmative action.

In this essay, he defends the right of humans to use animals in medical research and argues that defending animal rights is "a gigantic mistake." He argues against Tom Regan's view that animals, including the lowly lab rat used in most research, has a right not to be used in experiments, as animals simply do not have rights. Cohen does accept that we should treat animals humanely.

Whether animals have rights is a question of great importance because if they do, those rights must be respected, even at the cost of great burdens for human beings. A right (unlike an interest) is a valid claim, or potential claim, made by a moral agent, under principles that govern both the claimant and the target of the claim. Rights are precious; they are dispositive; they count.

You have a right to the return of money you lent me; we both understand that. It may be very

Carl Cohen "Do Animals Have Rights?" *Ethics and Behavior* 7:2 (1997), 91–102. Copyright 1997 Carl Cohen. Reprinted by permission of the author.

convenient for me to keep the money, and you may have no need of it whatever; but my convenience and your needs are not to the point. You have a *right* to it, and we have courts of law partly to ensure that such rights will be respected.

If you make me a promise, I have a moral right to its fulfillment—even though there may be no law to enforce my right. It may be very much in your interest to break that promise, but your great interests and the silence of the law cut no mustard when your solemn promise—which we both well understood—had been given. Likewise, those holding power may have a great and benevolent interest in denying my rights to travel or to speak freely—but their interests are overridden by my rights.

A great deal was learned about hypothermia by some Nazi doctors who advanced their learning by soaking Jews in cold water and putting them in refrigerators to learn how hypothermia proceeds. We have no difficulty in seeing that they may not advance medicine in that way; the subjects of those atrocious experiments had rights that demanded respect. For those who ignored their rights we have nothing but moral loathing.

Some persons believe that animals have rights as surely as those Jews had rights, and they therefore look on the uses of animals in medical investigations just as we look at the Nazi use of the Jews, with moral loathing. They are consistent in doing so. If animals have rights they certainly have the right not to be killed, even to advance our important interests.

Some may say, "Well, they have rights, but we have rights too, and our rights override theirs." That may be true in some cases, but it will not solve the problem because, although we may have a weighty *interest* in learning, say, how to vaccinate against polio or other diseases, we do not have a *right* to learn such things. Nor could we honestly claim that we kill research animals in self-defense; they did not attack us. If animals have rights, they certainly have the right not to be killed to advance the interests of others, whatever rights those others may have.

In 1952 there were about 58,000 cases of polio reported in the United States, and 3,000 polio deaths; my parents, parents everywhere, trembled in fear for their children at camp or away from home. Polio vaccination became routine in 1955, and cases dropped to about a dozen a year; today polio has been eradicated completely from the Western Hemisphere. The vaccine that achieved this, partly developed and tested only blocks from where I live in Ann Arbor, could have been developed *only* with the substantial use of animals. Polio vaccines had been tried many times earlier, but from those earlier vaccines children had contracted the disease; investigators had become, understandably, exceedingly cautious.

The killer disease for which a vaccine now is needed most desperately is malaria, which kills about 2 million people each year, most of them children. Many vaccines have been tried—not on children, thank God—and have failed. But very recently, after decades of effort, we learned how to make a vaccine that does, with complete success, inoculate mice against malaria. A safe vaccine for humans we do not yet have—but soon we will have it, thanks to the use of those mice, many of whom will have died in the process. To test that vaccine first on children would be an outrage, as it would have been an outrage to do so with the Salk and Sabin polio vaccines years ago. We use mice or monkeys *because there is no other way*. And there never will be another way because untested vaccines are very dangerous; their first use on a living organism is inescapably experimental; there is and will be no way to determine the reliability and safety of new vaccines without repeated tests on live organisms. Therefore, because we certainly may not use human children to test them, we will use mice (or as we develop an AIDS vaccine, primates) *or we will never have such vaccines.*

But if those animals we use in such tests have rights as human children do, what we did and are doing to them is as profoundly wrong as what the Nazis did to those Jews not long ago. Defenders of animal rights need not hold that medical scientists are vicious; they simply believe that what medical investigators are doing with animals is morally wrong. Most biomedical investigations involving animal subjects use rodents: mice and rats. The rat is the animal appropriately considered (and used by the critic) as the exemplar whose moral stature is in dispute here. Tom Regan is a leading defender of the view that rats do have such rights, and may not be used in biomedical investigations. He is an honest man. He sees the consequences of his view and accepts them forthrightly. In *The Case for Animal Rights* (Regan, 1983) he wrote,

> The harms others might face as a result of the dissolution of [some] practice or institution is no defense of allowing it to continue.... No one has a right to be protected against being harmed if the protection in question involves violating the rights of others.... No one has a right to be protected by the continuation of an unjust practice, one that violates the rights of others.... Justice *must* be done, though the ... heavens fall. (pp. 346–347)

That last line echoes Kant, who borrowed it from an older tradition. Believing that rats have rights as humans do, Regan (1983) was convinced that killing them in medical research was morally intolerable. He wrote,

> On the rights view, [he means, of course, the Regan rights view] we cannot justify harming a single rat *merely* by aggregating "the many human and humane benefits" that flow from doing it.... Not even a single rat is to be treated as if that animal's value were reducible to his *possible utility* relative to the interests of others. (p. 384)

If there are some things that we cannot learn because animals have rights, well, as Regan (1983) put it, so be it.

This is the conclusion to which one certainly is driven if one holds that animals have rights. If Regan is correct about the moral standing of rats, we humans can have no right, ever, to kill them—unless perchance a rat attacks a person or a human baby, as rats sometimes do; then our right of self-defense may enter, I suppose. But medical investigations cannot honestly be described as self-defense, and medical investigations commonly require that many mice and rats be killed. Therefore, all medical investigations relying on them, or any other animal subjects—which includes most studies and all the most important studies of certain kinds—will have to stop. Bear in mind that the replacement of animal subjects by computer simulations, or tissue samples, and so on, is in most research a phantasm, a fantasy. Biomedical investigations using animal subjects (and of course all uses of animals as food) will have to stop.

This extraordinary consequence has no argumentative force for Regan and his followers; they are not consequentialists. For Regan the *interests*

of humans, their desire to be freed of disease or relieved of pain, simply cannot outweigh the *rights* of a single rat. For him the issue is one of justice, and the use of animals in medical experiments (he believes) is simply not just. But the consequences of his view will give most of us, I submit, good reason to weigh very carefully the arguments he offers to support such far-reaching claims. Do you believe that the work of Drs. Salk and Sabin was morally right? Would you support it now, or support work just like it saving tens of thousands of human children from diphtheria, hepatitis, measles, rabies, rubella, and tetanus (all of which relied essentially on animal subjects)—as well as, now, AIDS, Lyme disease, and malaria? I surely do. If you would join me in this support we must conclude that the defense of animal rights is a gigantic mistake. I next aim to explain why animals *cannot* possess rights.

WHY ANIMALS DO NOT HAVE RIGHTS

Many obligations are owed by humans to animals; few will deny that. But it certainly does not follow from this that animals have rights because it is certainly not true that every obligation of ours arises from the rights of another. Not at all. We need to be clear and careful here. Rights entail obligations. If you have a right to the return of the money I borrowed, I have an obligation to repay it. No issue. If we have the right to speak freely on public policy matters, the community has the obligation to respect our right to do so. But the proposition *all rights entail obligations* does not convert simply, as the logicians say. From the true proposition that all trees are plants, it does not follow that all plants are trees. Similarly, not all obligations are entailed by rights. Some obligations, like mine to repay the money I borrowed from you, do arise out of rights. But many obligations are owed to persons or other beings who have no rights whatever in the matter.

Obligations may arise from commitments freely made: As a college professor I accept the obligation to comment at length on the papers my students submit, and I do so; but they have not the right to *demand* that I do so. Civil servants and elected officials surely ought to be courteous to members of the public, but that obligation certainly is not grounded in citizens' rights.

Special relations often give rise to obligations: Hosts have the obligation to be cordial to their guests, but the guest has not the right to demand cordiality. Shepherds have obligations to their dogs, and cowboys to their horses, which do not flow from the rights of those dogs or horses. My son, now 5, may someday wish to study veterinary medicine as my father did; I will then have the obligation to help him as I can, and with pride I shall—but he has not the authority to demand such help as a matter of right. My dog has no right to daily exercise and veterinary care, but I do have the obligation to provide those things for her.

One may be obliged to another for a special act of kindness done; one may be obliged to put an animal out of its misery in view of its condition—but neither the beneficiary of that kindness nor that dying animal may have had a claim of right.

Beauchamp and Childress (1994) addressed what they called the "correlativity of rights and obligations" and wrote that they would defend an "untidy" (pp. 73–75) variety of that principle. It would be very untidy indeed. Some of our most important obligations—to members of our family, to the needy, to neighbors, and to sentient creatures of every sort—have no foundation in rights at all. Correlativity appears critical from the perspective of one who holds a right; your right correlates with my obligation to respect it. But the claim that rights and obligations are *reciprocals*, that *every* obligation flows from another's right, is false, plainly inconsistent with our general understanding of the differences between what we think we *ought* to do, and what others can justly *demand* that we do.

I emphasize this because, although animals have no rights, it surely does not follow from this that one is free to treat them with callous disregard. Animals are not stones; they feel. A rat may suffer; surely we have the obligation not to torture it gratuitously, even though it be true that the concept of a right could not possibly apply to it. We humans are obliged to act humanely, that is, being aware of their sentience, to apply to animals the moral principles that govern us regarding the gratuitous imposition of pain and suffering; which is not, of course, to treat animals as the possessors of rights.

Animals cannot be the bearers of rights because the concept of rights is essentially *human*; it is rooted in, and has force within, a human moral world. Humans must deal with rats—all too frequently in some parts of the world—and must be moral in their dealing with them; but a rat can no more be said to have rights than a table can be said to have ambition. To say of a rat that it has rights is to confuse categories, to apply to its world a moral category that has content only in the human moral world.

Try this thought experiment. Imagine, on the Serengeti Plain in East Africa, a lioness hunting for her cubs. A baby zebra, momentarily left unattended by its mother, is the prey; the lioness snatches it, rips open its throat, tears out chunks of its flesh, and departs. The mother zebra is driven nearly out of her wits when she cannot locate her baby; finding its carcass she will not even leave the remains for days. The scene may be thought unpleasant, but it is entirely natural, of course, and extremely common. If the zebra has a right to live, if the prey is just but the predator unjust, we ought to intervene, if we can, on behalf of right. But we do not intervene, of course—as we surely would intervene if we saw the lioness about to attack an unprotected human baby or you. What accounts for the moral difference? We justify different responses to humans and to zebras on the ground (implicit or explicit) that their moral stature is very different. The human has a right not to be eaten alive; it is, after all, a human being. Do you believe the baby zebra has the *right* not to be slaughtered by that lioness? That the lioness has the *right* to kill that baby zebra for her cubs? If you are inclined to say, confronted by such natural rapacity—duplicated with untold variety millions of times each day on planet earth—that neither is right or wrong, that neither has a *right* against the other, I am on your side. Rights are of the highest moral consequence, yes; but zebras and lions and rats are totally amoral; there is no morality for them; they do no wrong, ever. In their world there are no rights.

A contemporary philosopher who has thought a good deal about animals, referring to them as "moral patients," put it this way:

> A moral patient lacks the ability to formulate, let alone bring to bear, moral principles in deliberating about which one among a number of possible

acts it would be right or proper to perform. Moral patients, in a word, cannot do what is right, nor can they do what is wrong.... Even when a moral patient causes significant harm to another, the moral patient has not done what is wrong. Only moral agents can do what is wrong. (Regan, 1983, pp. 152–153)

Just so. The concepts of wrong and right are totally foreign to animals, not conceivably within their ken or applicable to them, as the author of that passage clearly understands.

When using animals in our research, therefore, we ought indeed be humane—but we can never violate the rights of those animals because, to be blunt, they have none. Rights do not *apply* to them.

But humans do have rights. Where do our rights come from? Why are we not crudely natural creatures like rats and zebras? This question philosophers have struggled to answer from earliest times. A definitive account of the human moral condition I cannot here present, of course. But reflect for a moment on the kinds of answers that have been widely given:

- Some think our moral understanding, with its attendant duties, to be a divine gift. So St. Thomas said: The moral law is binding, and humans have the power, given by God, to grasp its binding character, and must therefore respect the rights that other humans possess. God makes us (Saint Augustine said before him) in his own image, and therefore with a will that is free, and gives us the power to recognize that, and therefore, unlike other creatures, we must choose between good and evil, between right and wrong.

- Many philosophers, distrusting theological justifications of rights and duties, sought the ground of human morality in the membership, by all humans, in a moral community. The English idealist, Bradley, called it an organic moral community; the German idealist, Hegel, called it an objective ethical order. These and like accounts commonly center on human interrelations, on a moral *fabric* within which human agents always act, and within which animals never act and never can possibly act.

- The highly abstract reasoning from which such views emerge has dissatisfied many; you may find more nearly true the convictions of

ethical intuitionists and realists who said, as H. A. Prichard, Sir David Ross, and my friend and teacher C. D. Broad, of happy memory, used to say, that there is a direct, underivative, intuitive cognition of rights as possessed by other humans, but not by animals.

- Or perhaps in the end we will return to Kant, and say with him that critical reason reveals at the core of human action a uniquely moral will, and the unique ability to grasp and to lay down moral laws for oneself and for others— an ability that is not conceivably within the capacity of any nonhuman animal whatever.

To be a moral agent (on this view) is to be able to grasp the generality of moral restrictions on our will. Humans understand that some things, which may be in our interest, *must not be willed*; we lay down moral laws for ourselves, and thus exhibit, as no other animal can exhibit, moral autonomy. My dog knows that there are certain things she must not do—but she knows this only as the outcome of her learning about her interests, the pains she may suffer if she does what had been taught forbidden. She does not know, cannot know (as Regan agrees) that any conduct is wrong. The proposition *It would be highly advantageous to act in such-and-such a way, but I may not because it would be wrong* is one that no dog or mouse or rabbit, however sweet and endearing, however loyal or attentive to its young, can ever entertain, or intend, or begin to grasp. Right is not in their world. But right and wrong are the very stuff of human moral life, the ever-present awareness of human beings who can do wrong, and who by seeking (often) to avoid wrong conduct prove themselves members of a moral community in which rights may be exercised and must be respected.

Some respond by saying, "This can't be correct, for human infants (and the comatose and senile, etc.) surely have rights, but they make no moral claims or judgments and can make none— and any view entailing that children can have no rights must be absurd." Objections of this kind miss the point badly. It is not individual persons who qualify (or are disqualified) for the possession of rights because of the presence or absence in them of some special capacity, thus resulting in the award of rights to some but not to others. Rights are universally human; they arise in a *human moral world*, in a moral *sphere*. In the human world moral judgments are pervasive; it is the fact that all humans including infants and the senile are members of that moral community—not the fact that as individuals they have or do not have certain special capacities, or merits—that makes humans bearers of rights. Therefore, it is beside the point to insist that animals have remarkable capacities, that they really have a consciousness of self, or of the future, or make plans, and so on. And the tired response that because infants plainly cannot make moral claims they must have no rights at all, or rats must have them too, we ought forever put aside. Responses like these arise out of a misconception of right itself. They mistakenly suppose that rights are tied to some identifiable individual abilities or sensibilities, and they fail to see that rights arise only in a community of moral beings, and that therefore there are spheres in which rights do apply and spheres in which they do not.

Rationality is not at issue; the capacity to communicate is not at issue. My dog can reason, if rather weakly, and she certainly can communicate. Cognitive criteria for the possession of rights, Beauchamp (this issue) said, are morally perilous. Indeed they are. Nor is the capacity to suffer here at issue. And, if *autonomy* be understood only as the capacity to choose this course rather than that, autonomy is not to the point either. But *moral autonomy*—that is, *moral self-legislation*—is to the point, because moral autonomy is uniquely human and is for animals out of the question, as we have seen, and as Regan and I agree. In talking about autonomy, therefore, we must be careful and precise.

Because humans do have rights, and these rights can be violated by other humans, we say that some humans commit *crimes*. But whether a crime has been committed depends utterly on the moral state of mind of the actor. If I take your coat, or your book, honestly thinking it was mine, I do not steal it. The *actus reus* (the guilty deed) must be accompanied, in a genuine crime, by a guilty mind, a *mens rea*. That recognition, not just of possible punishment for an act, but of moral duties that govern us, no rat or cow ever can possess. In primitive times humans did sometimes bring cows and horses to the bar of human justice. We chuckle at that practice now, realizing that accusing cows

of crimes marks the primitive moral view as inane. Animals never can be criminals because they have no moral state of mind.

Mistakes parallel to this in other spheres may be helpful to think about. In the Third Part of *The Critique of Pure Reason*, Immanuel Kant explained with care the metaphysical blunders into which we are led when we misapply concepts of great human import. In our human experience, for example, the concepts of time and space, the relations of cause and effect, of subject and attribute, and others, are essential, fundamental. But, forgetting that these are concepts arising only within the world of our human experience, we sometimes are misled into asking: Was the world caused, or is it uncaused? Did the world have a beginning in time, or did it not? Kant explained—in one of the most brilliant long passages in all philosophical literature—why *it makes no sense to ask such questions*. Cause applies to phenomena we humans encounter *in* the world, it is a category of our experience and cannot apply to the world as a whole. Time is the condition of our experience, not an absolute container in which the world could have begun. The antinomies of pure reason, and after those the paralogisms of pure reason, Kant patiently exhibited as confusions arising from the misapplication of the categories of experience. His lesson is powerful and deep. The misapplication of concepts leads to error and, sometimes, to nonsense. So it is with rights also. To say that rats have rights is to apply to the world of rats a concept that makes good sense when applied to humans, but which makes no sense at all when applied to rats.

WHY ANIMALS ARE MISTAKENLY BELIEVED TO HAVE RIGHTS

From the foregoing discussion it follows that, if some philosophers believe that they have proved that animals have rights, they must have erred in the alleged proof. Regan is a leader among those who claim to *argue* in defense of the rights of rats; he contends that the best arguments are on his side. I aim next to show how he and others with like views go astray. Bear in mind that Regan's book is long, its argument tortuous and at times convoluted. In what follows I must compress the report of his views, obviously; but I promise to be fair and to hold Regan responsible for nothing that he does not clearly say. We know—if we are agreed that rats are not the holders of rights—that Regan must have got off the track. Examining *The Case for Animal Rights*, let us see if we can find the faulty switch.

Much of Regan's (1983) book is devoted to a general treatment of the nature of ethical thinking and theory, to discussions of animal consciousness and animal awareness, and to detailed critiques of the views of others whom he thinks in error. Regan sought to show, patiently and laboriously, that the common belief that we do have obligations to animals, although they have no rights, has not been defended satisfactorily. That belief cannot be justified, he contended, by direct duty views of which he finds two categories: those depending on the obligation to be kind or not to be cruel, and those depending on any kind of utilitarian calculation.

None of this counterargument could possibly establish his conclusion that animals do have rights, unless Regan had proved that his listing of all alternative conflicting views was exhaustive, which it was not, and unless he had proved conclusively that every such candidate is untenable, which he did not do....

The case is built entirely on the principle that allegedly *carries over* almost everything earlier claimed about human rights to rats and other animals. What principle is that? It is the principle, put in italics but given no name, that equates moral agents with moral patients:

> *The validity of the claim to respectful treatment, and thus the case for the recognition of the right to such treatment, cannot be any stronger or weaker in the case of moral patients than it is in the case of moral agents.* (Regan, p. 279)

But hold on. Why in the world should anyone think this principle to be true? Back ... where Regan first recounted his view of moral patients, he allowed that some of them are, although capable of experiencing pleasure and pain, lacking in other capacities. But he is interested, he told us there, in those moral patients—those animals—that are like humans in having *inherent value*. This is the key to the argument for animal rights, the possession

of inherent value. How that concept functions in the argument becomes absolutely critical. I will say first briefly what will be shown more carefully later: *Inherent value* is an expression used by Regan (and many like him) with two very different senses—in one of which it is reasonable to conclude that those who have inherent value have rights, and in another sense in which that inference is wholly unwarranted. But the phrase, *inherent value* has some plausibility in both contexts, and thus by sliding from one sense of inherent value to the other Regan appears to succeed, in two pages, in making the case for animal rights.

The concept of inherent value first entered the discussion in the seventh chapter of Regan's (1983) book, at which point his principle object is to fault and defeat utilitarian arguments. It is not (he argued there) the pleasures or pains that go "into the cup" of humanity that give value, but the "cups" themselves; humans are equal in value because they are humans, having inherent value. So we are, all of us, equal—equal in being moral agents who have this inherent value. This approach to the moral stature of humans is likely to be found quite plausible. Regan called it the "postulate of inherent value"; all humans, "The lonely, forsaken, unwanted, and unloved are no more nor less inherently valuable than those who enjoy a more hospitable relationship with others" (p. 237). And Regan went on to argue for the proposition that all moral agents are "equal in inherent value." Holding some such views we are likely to say, with Kant, that all humans are beyond price. Their inherent value gives them moral dignity, a unique role in the moral world, as agents having the capacity to act morally and make moral judgments. This is inherent value in Sense 1.

The expression *inherent value* has another sense, however, also common and also plausible. My dog has inherent value, and so does every wild animal, every lion and zebra, which is why the senseless killing of animals is so repugnant. Each animal is unique, not replaceable in itself by another animal or by any rocks or clay. Animals, like humans, are not just things; they live, and as unique living creatures they have inherent value. This is an important point, and again likely to be thought plausible; but here, in Sense 2, the phrase *inherent value* means something quite distinct from what was meant in its earlier uses.

Inherent value in Sense 1, possessed by all humans but not by all animals, which warrants the claim of human rights, is very different from inherent value in Sense 2, which warrants no such claim. The uniqueness of animals, their intrinsic worthiness as individual living things, does not ground the possession of rights, has nothing to do with the moral condition in which rights arise. Regan's argument reached its critical objective with almost magical speed because, having argued that beings with inherent value (Sense 1) have rights that must be respected, he quickly asserted (putting it in italics lest the reader be inclined to express doubt) that rats and rabbits also have rights because they, too, have inherent value (Sense 2).

This is an egregious example of the fallacy of equivocation: the informal fallacy in which two or more meanings of the same word or phrase have been confused in the several premises of an argument (Cohen & Copi, 1994, pp. 143–144). Why is this slippage not seen at once? Partly because we know the phrase *inherent value* often is used loosely, so the reader is not prone to quibble about its introduction; partly because the two uses of the phrase relied on are both common, so neither signals danger; partly because inherent value in Sense 2 is indeed shared by those who have it in Sense 1; and partly because the phrase inherent value is woven into accounts of what Regan (1983) elsewhere called the *subject-of-a-life criterion,* a phrase of his own devising for which he can stipulate any meaning he pleases, of course, and which also slides back and forth between the sphere of genuine moral agency and the sphere of animal experience. But perhaps the chief reason the equivocation between these two uses of the phrase inherent value is obscured (from the author, I believe, as well as from the reader) is the fact that the assertion that animals have rights appears only indirectly, as the outcome of the application of the principle that moral patients are entitled to the same respect as moral agents—a principle introduced at a point in the book long after the important moral differences between moral patients and moral agents have been recognized, with a good deal of tangled philosophical argument having been injected in between.

I invite readers to trace out this equivocation in detail; my limited space here precludes more extended quotation. But this assurance I will give: there is no argument or set of arguments in *The Case for Animal Rights* that successfully makes the case for animal rights. Indeed, there *could* not be, any more than any book, however long and convoluted, could make the case for the emotions of oak trees, or the criminality of snakes.

Animals do not have rights. Right does not apply in their world. We do have many obligations to animals, of course, and I honor Regan's appreciation of their sensitivities. I also honor his seriousness of purpose, and his always civil and always rational spirit. But he is, I submit, profoundly mistaken. I conclude with the observation that, had his mistaken views about the rights of animals long been accepted, most successful medical therapies recently devised—antibiotics, vaccines, prosthetic devices, and other compounds and instruments on which we now rely for saving and improving human lives and for the protection of our children—could not have been developed; and were his views to become general now (an outcome that is unlikely but possible) the consequences for medical science and for human well-being in the years ahead would be nothing less than catastrophic.

Advances in medicine absolutely require experiments, many of which are dangerous. Dangerous experiments absolutely require living organisms as subjects. Those living organisms (we now agree) certainly may not be human beings. Therefore, most advances in medicine will continue to rely on the use of nonhuman animals, or they will stop. Regan is free to say in response, as he does, "so be it." The rest of us must ask if the argument he presents is so compelling as to force us to accept that dreadful result.

REFERENCES

Beauchamp, T. L., & Childress, J. F. (1994). *Principles of biomedical ethics* (4th ed.). New York: Oxford University Press.

Cohen, C., & Copi, I. M. (1994). *Introduction to logic* (9th ed.). New York: Macmillan.

Regan, T. (1983). *The case for animal rights.* Berkeley: University of California Press.

⚜ QUESTIONS FOR ANALYSIS

1. Does Cohen justify the use of animals in medical research on consequentialist or utilitarian grounds? What examples does he give which support this kind of reasoning?

2. What does Cohen mean when he says that "rights entail obligations"? How do obligations arise? Is it possible for us to have obligations to animals, without those animals having any rights?

3. Why does Cohen reject the claim that rights and obligations are always reciprocal, that every obligation flows from another's right?

4. Why does Cohen believe that animals cannot be the "bearers of rights"?

5. What reasons does Cohen give for saying that we should act humanely to animals, even though they have no rights?

6. How does he respond to the criticism that human infants have rights, even though they are not functioning as autonomous moral agents?

7. What, according to Cohen, does Regan understand as the "concept of inherent value"?

8. What is the fallacy of equivocation? Why does Cohen accuse Regan of relying on that fallacy?

The Ethics of Respect for Nature

PAUL W. TAYLOR

The following essay by Paul W. Taylor, professor emeritus of philosophy, Brooklyn College, presents an alternative theory of environmental ethics to Aldo Leopold's land ethic. Though nonanthropocentric and sensitive to ecological issues, it is individualistic rather than holistic. According to Taylor, the principal moral concern of environmental ethics is individual organisms, not the biotic community. Ecological relationships provide us with important knowledge that help us in our dealings with individual organisms, he says, but they do not provide us with moral norms.

In developing his view of respect for nature, Taylor emphasizes that the respect he means is an ultimate attitude, one that is not derived from some other moral norm but is fundamental, like Kantian respect for persons. We should adopt that attitude, he says, because of a recognition that all living things, not just humans, have inherent worth.

I. HUMAN-CENTERED AND LIFE-CENTERED SYSTEMS OF ENVIRONMENTAL ETHICS

In this paper I show how the taking of a certain ultimate moral attitude toward nature, which I call "respect for nature," has a central place in the foundations of a life-centered system of environmental ethics....

In designating the theory to be set forth as life-centered, I intend to contrast it with all anthropocentric views. According to the latter, human actions affecting the natural environment and its nonhuman inhabitants are right (or wrong) by either of two criteria: they have consequences which are favorable (or unfavorable) to human well-being, or they are consistent (or inconsistent) with the system of norms that protect and implement human rights. From this human-centered standpoint it is to humans and only to humans that all duties are ultimately owed. We may have responsibilities *with regard to* the natural ecosystems and biotic communities of our planet, but these responsibilities are in every case based on the contingent fact that our treatment of those ecosystems and communities of life can further the realization of human values and/or human rights. We have no obligation to promote or protect the good of nonhuman living things, independently of this contingent fact.

From *Environmental Ethics*, vol. 3 (Fall 1981), pp. 197–218. Reprinted by permission of the author.

A life-centered system of environmental ethics is opposed to human-centered ones precisely on this point. From the perspective of a life-centered theory, we have prima facie moral obligations that are owed to wild plants and animals themselves as members of the Earth's biotic community. We are morally bound (other things being equal) to protect or promote their good for *their* sake. Our duties to respect the integrity of natural ecosystems, to preserve endangered species, and to avoid environmental pollution stem from the fact that these are ways in which we can help make it possible for wild species populations to achieve and maintain a healthy existence in a natural state. Such obligations are due those living things out of recognition of their inherent worth. They are entirely additional to and independent of the obligations we owe to our fellow humans. Although many of the actions that fulfill one set of obligations will also fulfill the other, two different grounds of obligation are involved. Their well-being, as well as human well-being, is something to be realized *as an end in itself.*

If we were to accept a life-centered theory of environmental ethics, a profound reordering of our moral universe would take place. We would begin to look at the whole of the Earth's biosphere in a new light. Our duties with respect to the "world" of nature would be seen as making prima facie claims upon us to be balanced against our duties with respect to the "world" of human civilization. We could no longer simply take the human point of view and consider the effects of our actions exclusively from the perspective of our own good.

II. THE GOOD OF A BEING AND THE CONCEPT OF INHERENT WORTH

… Two concepts are essential to the taking of a moral attitude of the sort in question. A being which does not "have" these concepts, that is, which is unable to grasp their meaning and conditions of applicability, cannot be said to have the attitude as part of its moral outlook. These concepts are, first, that of the good (well-being, welfare) of a living thing, and second, the idea of an entity possessing inherent worth. I examine each concept in turn.

1. Every organism, species population, and community of life has a good of its own which moral agents can intentionally further or damage by their actions. To say that an entity has a good of its own is simply to say that, without reference to any other entity, it can be benefited or harmed. One can act in its overall interest or contrary to its overall interest, and environmental conditions can be good for it (advantageous to it) or bad for it (disadvantageous to it). What is good for an entity is what "does it good" in the sense of enhancing or preserving its life and well-being. What is bad for an entity is something that is detrimental to its life and well-being.[1]

We can think of the good of an individual nonhuman organism as consisting in the full development of its biological powers. Its good is realized to the extent that it is strong and healthy. It possesses whatever capacities it needs for successfully coping with its environment and so preserving its existence throughout the various stages of the normal life cycle of its species. The good of a population or community of such individuals consists in the population or community maintaining itself from generation to generation as a coherent system of genetically and ecologically related organisms whose average good is at an optimum level for the given environment. (Here *average good* means that the degree of realization of the good of *individual organisms* in the population or community is, on average, greater than would be the case under any other ecologically functioning order of interrelations among those species populations in the given ecosystem.)

The idea of a being having a good of its own, as I understand it, does not entail that the being must have interests or take an interest in what affects its life for better or for worse. We can act in a being's interest or contrary to its interest without its being interested in what we are doing to it in the sense of wanting or not wanting us to do it. It may, indeed, be wholly unaware that favorable and unfavorable events are taking place in its life. I take it that trees, for example, have no knowledge or desires or feelings. Yet it is undoubtedly the case that trees can be harmed or benefited by our actions. We can crush their roots by running a bulldozer too close to them. We can see to it that they get adequate nourishment and moisture by fertilizing and watering the soil around them. Thus we can help or hinder them in the realization of their good. It is the good of trees themselves that is thereby affected. We can similarly act so as to further the good of an entire tree population of a certain species (say, all the redwood trees in a California valley) or the good of a whole community of plant life in a given wilderness area, just as we can do harm to such a population or community....

2. The second concept essential to the moral attitude of respect for nature is the idea of inherent worth. We take that attitude toward wild living things (individuals, species populations, or whole biotic communities) when and only when we regard them as entities possessing inherent worth....

What does it mean to regard an entity that has a good of its own as possessing inherent worth? Two general principles are involved: the principle of moral consideration and the principle of intrinsic value.

According to the principle of moral consideration, wild living things are deserving of the concern and consideration of all moral agents simply in virtue of their being members of the Earth's community of life. From the moral point of view their good must be taken into account whenever it is affected for better or worse by the conduct of rational agents. This holds no matter what species the creature belongs to. The good of each is to be accorded some value and so acknowledged as having some weight in the deliberations of all rational agents. Of course, it may be necessary for such agents to act in ways contrary to the good of this or that particular organism or group of organisms in order to further the good of others, including the good of humans. But the principle of moral consideration prescribes that, with respect to each being an entity having its own good, every individual is deserving of consideration.

The principle of intrinsic value states that, regardless of what kind of entity it is in other respects, if it is a member of the Earth's community of life, the realization of its good is something *intrinsically* valuable. This means that its good is prima facie worthy of being preserved or promoted as an end in itself and for the sake of the entity whose good it is. Insofar as we regard any

organism, species population, or life community as an entity having inherent worth, we believe that it must never be treated as if it were a mere object or thing whose entire value lies in being instrumental to the good of some other entity. The well-being of each is judged to have value in and of itself.

Combining these two principles, we can now define what it means for a living thing or group of living things to possess inherent worth. To say that it possesses inherent worth is to say that its good is deserving of the concern and consideration of all moral agents, and that the realization of its good has intrinsic value, to be pursued as an end in itself and for the sake of the entity whose good it is....

III. THE ATTITUDE OF RESPECT FOR NATURE

Why should moral agents regard wild living things in the natural world as possessing inherent worth? To answer this question we must first take into account the fact that, when rational, autonomous agents subscribe to the principles of moral consideration and intrinsic value and so conceive of wild living things as having that kind of worth, such agents are *adopting a certain ultimate moral attitude toward the natural world*. This is the attitude I call "respect for nature." It parallels the attitude of respect for persons in human ethics. When we adopt the attitude of respect for persons as the proper (fitting, appropriate) attitude to take toward all persons as persons, we consider the fulfillment of the basic interests of each individual to have intrinsic value. We thereby make a moral commitment to live a certain kind of life in relation to other persons. We place ourselves under the direction of a system of standards and rules that we consider validly binding on all moral agents as such.[2]

Similarly, when we adopt the attitude of respect for nature as an ultimate moral attitude we make a commitment to live by certain normative principles. These principles constitute the rules of conduct and standards of character that are to govern our treatment of the natural world. This is, first, an *ultimate* commitment because it is not derived from any higher norm. The attitude of respect for nature is not grounded on some other, more general, or more fundamental attitude. It sets the total framework for our responsibilities toward the natural world. It can be justified, as I show below, but its justification cannot consist in referring to a more general attitude or a more basic normative principle.

Second, the commitment is a *moral* one because it is understood to be a disinterested matter of principle. It is this feature that distinguishes the attitude of respect for nature from the set of feelings and dispositions that comprise the love of nature. The latter stems from one's personal interest in and response to the natural world. Like the affectionate feelings we have toward certain individual human beings, one's love of nature is nothing more than the particular way one feels about the natural environment and its wild inhabitants. And just as our love for an individual person differs from our respect for all persons as such (whether we happen to love them or not), so love of nature differs from respect for nature. Respect for nature is an attitude we believe all moral agents ought to have simply as moral agents, regardless of whether or not they also love nature. Indeed, we have not truly taken the attitude of respect for nature ourselves unless we believe this....

Although the attitude of respect for nature is in this sense a disinterested and universalizable attitude, anyone who does adopt it has certain steady, more or less permanent dispositions. These dispositions, which are themselves to be considered disinterested and universalizable, comprise three interlocking sets: dispositions to seek certain ends, dispositions to carry on one's practical reasoning and deliberation in a certain way, and dispositions to have certain feelings. We may accordingly analyze the attitude of respect for nature into the following components. (a) The disposition to aim at, and to take steps to bring about, as final and disinterested ends, the promoting and protecting of the good of organisms, species populations, and life communities in natural ecosystems. (These ends are "final" in not being pursued as means to further ends. They are "disinterested" in being independent of the self-interest of the agent.) (b) The disposition to consider actions that tend to realize those ends to be prima facie obligatory *because* they have that tendency. (c) The disposition to experience positive and negative feelings toward states of affairs in the world *because* they are favorable or unfavorable to

the good of organisms, species populations, and life communities in natural ecosystems.

IV. THE JUSTIFIABILITY OF THE ATTITUDE OF RESPECT FOR NATURE

I return to the question posed earlier, which has not yet been answered: why *should* moral agents regard wild living things as possessing inherent worth?...

We must keep in mind that inherent worth is not some mysterious sort of objective property belonging to living things that can be discovered by empirical observation or scientific investigation. To ascribe inherent worth to an entity is not to describe it by citing some feature discernible by sense perception or inferable by inductive reasoning. Nor is there a logically necessary connection between the concept of a being having a good of its own and the concept of inherent worth. We do not contradict ourselves by asserting that an entity that has a good of its own lacks inherent worth. In order to show that such an entity "has" inherent worth we must give good reasons for ascribing that kind of value to it (placing that kind of value upon it, conceiving of it to be valuable in that way). Although it is humans (persons, valuers) who must do the valuing, for the ethics of respect for nature, the value so ascribed is not a human value. That is to say, it is not a value derived from considerations regarding human well-being or human rights. It is a value that is ascribed to nonhuman animals and plants themselves, independently of their relationship to what humans judge to be conducive to their own good.

Whatever reasons, then, justify our taking the attitude of respect for nature as defined above are also reasons that show why we *should* regard the living things of the natural world as possessing inherent worth. We saw earlier that, since the attitude is an ultimate one, it cannot be derived from a more fundamental attitude nor shown to be a special case of a more general one. On what sort of grounds, then, can it be established?

The attitude we take toward living things in the natural world depends on the way we look at them, on what kind of beings we conceive them to be, and on how we understand the relations we bear to them. Underlying and supporting our attitude is a certain *belief system* that constitutes a particular world view or outlook on nature and the place of human life in it. To give good reasons for adopting the attitude of respect for nature, then, we must first articulate the belief system which underlies and supports that attitude. If it appears that the belief system is internally coherent and well-ordered, and if, as far as we can now tell, it is consistent with all known scientific truths relevant to our knowledge of the object of the attitude (which in this case includes the whole set of the Earth's natural ecosystems and their communities of life), then there remains the task of indicating why scientifically informed and rational thinkers with a developed capacity of reality awareness can find it acceptable as a way of conceiving of the natural world and our place in it. To the extent we can do this we provide at least a reasonable argument for accepting the belief system and the ultimate moral attitude it supports.

I do not hold that such a belief system can be *proven* to be true, either inductively or deductively. As we shall see, not all of its components can be stated in the form of empirically verifiable propositions. Nor is its internal order governed by purely logical relationships. But the system as a whole, I contend, constitutes a coherent, unified, and rationally acceptable "picture" or "map" of a total world. By examining each of its main components and seeing how they fit together, we obtain a scientifically informed and well-ordered conception of nature and the place of humans in it.

This belief system underlying the attitude of respect for nature I call (for want of a better name) "the biocentric outlook on nature." ... It might best be described as a philosophical world view, to distinguish it from a scientific theory or explanatory system. However, one of its major tenets is the great lesson we have learned from the science of ecology: the interdependence of all living things in an organically unified order whose balance and stability are necessary conditions for the realization of the good of its constituent biotic communities.

Before turning to an account of the main components of the biocentric outlook, it is convenient here to set forth the overall structure of my theory of environmental ethics as it has now emerged. The ethics of respect for nature is made up of three basic elements: a belief system, an ultimate moral attitude, and a set of rules of duty and standards of character. These elements are connected with each other in the following manner. The belief system provides a certain outlook on nature which supports and makes intelligible an autonomous agent's adopting, as an ultimate moral attitude, the attitude of respect for nature. It supports and makes intelligible the attitude in the sense that, when an autonomous agent understands its moral relations to the natural world in terms of this outlook, it recognizes the attitude of respect to be the only *suitable* or *fitting* attitude to take toward all wild forms of life in the Earth's biosphere. Living things are now viewed as *the appropriate objects of the attitude of respect* and are accordingly regarded as entities possessing inherent worth. One then places intrinsic value on the promotion and protection of their good. As a consequence of this, one makes a moral commitment to abide by a set of rules of duty and to fulfill (as far as one can by one's own efforts) certain standards of good character. Given one's adoption of the attitude of respect, one makes that moral commitment because one considers those rules and standards to be validly binding on all moral agents. They are seen as embodying forms of conduct and character structures in which the attitude of respect for nature is manifested.

This three-part complex which internally orders the ethics of respect for nature is symmetrical with a theory of human ethics grounded on respect for persons. Such a theory includes, first, a conception of oneself and others as persons, that is, as centers of autonomous choice. Second, there is the attitude of respect for persons as persons. When this is adopted as an ultimate moral attitude it involves the disposition to treat every person as having inherent worth or "human dignity." Every human being, just in virtue of her or his humanity, is understood to be worthy of moral consideration, and intrinsic value is placed on the autonomy and well-being of each. This is what Kant meant by conceiving of persons as ends in themselves. Third, there is an ethical system of duties which are acknowledged to be owed by everyone to everyone. These duties are forms of conduct in which public recognition is given to each individual's inherent worth as a person....

V. THE BIOCENTRIC OUTLOOK ON NATURE

The biocentric outlook on nature has four main components. (1) Humans are thought of as members of the Earth's community of life, holding that membership on the same terms as apply to all the nonhuman members. (2) The Earth's natural ecosystems as a totality are seen as a complex web of interconnected elements, with the sound biological functioning of each being dependent on the sound biological functioning of the others. (This is the component referred to above as the great lesson that the science of ecology has taught us.) (3) Each individual organism is conceived of as a teleological center of life, pursuing its own good in its own way. (4) Whether we are concerned with standards of merit or with the concept of inherent worth, the claim that humans by their very nature are superior to other species is a groundless claim and, in the light of elements (1), (2), and (3) above, must be rejected as nothing more than an irrational bias in our own favor.

The conjunction of these four ideas constitutes the biocentric outlook on nature. In the remainder of this paper I give a brief account of the first three components, followed by a more detailed analysis of the fourth. I then conclude by indicating how this outlook provides a way of justifying the attitude of respect for nature.

VI. HUMANS AS MEMBERS OF THE EARTH'S COMMUNITY OF LIFE

We share with other species a common relationship to the Earth. In accepting the biocentric outlook we take the fact of our being an animal species to be a fundamental feature of our existence. We consider it an essential aspect of "the human condition." We do not deny the differences between ourselves and other species, but we keep in the forefront of our consciousness the fact that in relation to our planet's natural ecosystems we are but one species population among many. Thus we acknowledge our origin in the very same evolutionary process that gave rise to all other species and we recognize ourselves to be confronted with similar environmental challenges to

those that confront them. The laws of genetics, of natural selection, and of adaptation apply equally to all of us as biological creatures. In this light we consider ourselves as one with them, not set apart from them. We, as well as they, must face certain basic conditions of existence that impose requirements on us for our survival and well-being. Each animal and plant is like us in having a good of its own. Although our human good (what is of true value in human life, including the exercise of individual autonomy in choosing our own particular value systems) is not like the good of a nonhuman animal or plant, it can no more be realized than their good can without the biological necessities for survival and physical health.

When we look at ourselves from the evolutionary point of view, we see that not only are we very recent arrivals on Earth, but that our emergence as a new species on the planet was originally an event of no particular importance to the entire scheme of things. The Earth was teeming with life long before we appeared. Putting the point metaphorically, we are relative newcomers, entering a home that has been the residence of others for hundreds of millions of years, a home that must now be shared by all of us together.

The comparative brevity of human life on Earth may be vividly depicted by imagining the geological time scale in spatial terms. Suppose we start with algae, which have been around for at least 600 million years. (The earliest protozoa actually predated this by several *billion* years.) If the time that algae have been here were represented by the length of a football field (300 feet), then the period during which sharks have been swimming in the world's oceans and spiders have been spinning their webs would occupy three quarters of the length of the field; reptiles would show up at about the center of the field; mammals would cover the last third of the field; hominids (mammals of the family *Hominidae*) the last two feet; and the species *Homo sapiens* the last six inches.

Whether this newcomer is able to survive as long as other species remains to be seen. But there is surely something presumptuous about the way humans look down on the "lower" animals, especially those that have become extinct. We consider the dinosaurs, for example, to be biological failures, though they existed on our planet for 65 million years. One writer has made the point with beautiful simplicity:

> We sometimes speak of the dinosaurs as failures; there will be time enough for that judgment when we have lasted even for one tenth as long....[3]

The possibility of the extinction of the human species, a possibility which starkly confronts us in the contemporary world, makes us aware of another respect in which we should not consider ourselves privileged beings in relation to other species. This is the fact that the well-being of humans is dependent upon the ecological soundness and health of many plant and animal communities, while their soundness and health does not in the least depend upon human well-being. Indeed, from their standpoint the very existence of humans is quite unnecessary. Every last man, woman, and child could disappear from the face of the Earth without any significant detrimental consequence for the good of wild animals and plants. On the contrary, many of them would be greatly benefited. The destruction of their habitats by human "developments" would cease. The poisoning and polluting of their environment would come to an end. The Earth's land, air, and water would no longer be subject to the degradation they are now undergoing as the result of large- scale technology and uncontrolled population growth. Life communities in natural ecosystems would gradually return to their former healthy state. Tropical forests, for example, would again be able to make their full contribution to a life- sustaining atmosphere for the whole planet. The rivers, lakes, and oceans of the world would (perhaps) eventually become clean again. Spilled oil, plastic trash, and even radioactive waste might finally, after many centuries, cease doing their terrible work. Ecosystems would return to their proper balance, suffering only the disruptions of natural events such as volcanic eruptions and glaciation. From these the community of life could recover, as it has so often done in the past. But the ecological disasters now perpetrated on it by humans— disasters from which it might never recover—these it would no longer have to endure.

If, then, the total, final, absolute extermination of our species (by our own hands?) should take place and if we should not carry all the others with us into oblivion, not only would the Earth's community of life continue to exist, but in all probability its well-being would be enhanced. Our presence, in short, is not needed. If we were to take the standpoint of the community and give voice to its true interest, the ending of our six-inch epoch would most likely be greeted with a hearty "Good riddance!"

VII. THE NATURAL WORLD AS AN ORGANIC SYSTEM

To accept the biocentric outlook and regard ourselves and our place in the world from its perspective is to see the whole natural order of the Earth's biosphere as a complex but unified web of interconnected organisms, objects, and events. The ecological relationships between any community of living things and their environment form an organic whole of functionally interdependent parts. Each ecosystem is a small universe itself in which the interactions of its various species populations comprise an intricately woven network of cause–effect relations. Such dynamic but at the same time relatively stable structures as food chains, predator–prey relations, and plant succession in a forest are self-regulating, energy- recycling mechanisms that preserve the equilibrium of the whole.

As far as the well-being of wild animals and plants is concerned, this ecological equilibrium must not be destroyed. The same holds true of the well-being of humans. When one views the realm of nature from the perspective of the biocentric outlook, one never forgets that in the long run the integrity of the entire biosphere of our planet is essential to the realization of the good of its constituent communities of life, both human and nonhuman.

Although the importance of this idea cannot be overemphasized, it is by now so familiar and so widely acknowledged that I shall not further elaborate on it here. However, I do wish to point out that this "holistic" view of the Earth's ecological systems does not itself constitute a moral norm. It is a factual aspect of biological reality, to be understood as a set of causal connections in ordinary empirical terms. Its significance for humans is the same as its significance for nonhumans, namely, in setting basic conditions for the realization of the good of living things. Its ethical implications for our treatment of the natural environment lie entirely in the fact that our *knowledge* of these causal connections is an essential *means* to fulfilling the aims we set for ourselves in adopting the attitude of respect for nature. In addition, its theoretical implications for the ethics of respect for nature lie in the fact that it (along with the other elements of the biocentric outlook) makes the adopting of that attitude a rational and intelligible thing to do.

VIII. INDIVIDUAL ORGANISMS AS TELEOLOGICAL CENTERS OF LIFE

As our knowledge of living things increases, as we come to a deeper understanding of their life cycles, their interactions with other organisms, and the manifold ways in which they adjust to the environment, we become more fully aware of how each of them is carrying out its biological functions according to the laws of its species-specific nature. But besides this, our increasing knowledge and understanding also develop in us a sharpened awareness of the uniqueness of each individual organism. Scientists who have made careful studies of particular plants and animals, whether in the field or in laboratories, have often acquired a knowledge of their subjects as identifiable individuals. Close observation over extended periods of time has led them to an appreciation of the unique "personalities" of their subjects. Sometimes a scientist may come to take a special interest in a particular animal or plant, all the while remaining strictly objective in the gathering and recording of data. Nonscientists may likewise experience this development of interest when, as amateur naturalists, they make accurate observations over sustained periods of close acquaintance with an individual organism. As one becomes more and more familiar with the organism and its behavior, one becomes fully sensitive to the particular way it is living out its life cycle. One may become fascinated by it and even experience some involvement with its good and bad fortunes (that is, with the occurrence of environmental conditions favorable or unfavorable to the realization of its good). The organism comes to

mean something to one as a unique, irreplaceable individual. The final culmination of this process is the achievement of a genuine understanding of its point of view and, with that understanding, an ability to "take" that point of view. *Conceiving of it as a center of life, one is able to look at the world from its perspective.*

This development from objective knowledge to the recognition of individuality, and from the recognition of individuality to full awareness of an organism's standpoint, is a process of heightening our consciousness of what it means to be an individual living thing. We grasp the particularity of the organism as a teleological center of life, striving to preserve itself and to realize its own good in its own unique way.

It is to be noted that we need not be falsely anthropomorphizing when we conceive of individual plants and animals in this manner. Understanding them as teleological centers of life does not necessitate "reading into" them human characteristics. We need not, for example, consider them to have consciousness. Some of them may be aware of the world around them and others may not. Nor need we deny that different kinds and levels of awareness are exemplified when consciousness in some form is present. But conscious or not, all are equally teleological centers of life in the sense that each is a unified system of goal-oriented activities directed toward their preservation and well-being.

When considered from an ethical point of view, a teleological center of life is an entity whose "world" can be viewed from the perspective of *its* life. In looking at the world from that perspective we recognize objects and events occurring in its life as being beneficent, maleficent, or indifferent. The first are occurrences which increase its powers to preserve its existence and realize its good. The second decrease or destroy those powers. The third have neither of these effects on the entity. With regard to our human role as moral agents, we can conceive of a teleological center of life as a being whose standpoint we can take in making judgments about what events in the world are good or evil, desirable or undesirable. In making those judgments it is what promotes or protects the being's own good, not what benefits moral agents themselves, that sets the standard of evaluation. Such judgments can be made about anything that happens to the entity which is favorable or unfavorable in relation to its good. As was pointed out earlier, the entity itself need not have any (conscious) interest in what is happening to it for such judgments to be meaningful and true.

It is precisely judgments of this sort that we are disposed to make when we take the attitude of respect for nature. In adopting that attitude those judgments are given weight as reasons for action in our practical deliberation. They become morally relevant facts in the guidance of our conduct.

IX. THE DENIAL OF HUMAN SUPERIORITY

This fourth component of the biocentric outlook on nature is the single most important idea in establishing the justifiability of the attitude of respect for nature. Its central role is due to the special relationship it bears to the first three components of the outlook. This relationship will be brought out after the concept of human superiority is examined and analyzed.[4]

In what sense are humans alleged to be superior to other animals? We are different from them in having certain capacities that they lack. But why should these capacities be a mark of superiority? From what point of view are they judged to be signs of superiority and what sense of superiority is meant? After all, various nonhuman species have capacities that humans lack. There is the speed of a cheetah, the vision of an eagle, the agility of a monkey. Why should not these be taken as signs of *their* superiority over humans?

One answer that comes immediately to mind is that these capacities are not as *valuable* as the human capacities that are claimed to make us superior. Such uniquely human characteristics as rational thought, aesthetic creativity, autonomy and self-determination, and moral freedom, it might be held, have a higher value than the capacities found in other species. Yet we must ask: valuable to whom, and on what grounds?

The human characteristics mentioned are all valuable to humans. They are essential to the preservation and enrichment of our civilization and culture. Clearly it is from the human standpoint that they are being judged to be desirable and good. It is not difficult here to recognize a begging of the question. Humans are claiming human superiority from a strictly human point of view, that is, from a point of view in which the good of humans is taken as the standard of judgment. All we need to do is to look at the capacities of nonhuman animals (or plants, for that matter) from the standpoint of *their* good to find a contrary judgment of superiority. The speed of the cheetah, for example, is a sign of its superiority to humans when considered from the standpoint of the good of its species. If it were as slow a runner as a human, it would not be able to survive. And so for all the other abilities of nonhumans which further their good but which are lacking in humans. In each case the claim to human superiority would be rejected from a nonhuman standpoint.

… There is, however, another way of understanding the idea of human superiority. According to this interpretation, humans are superior to nonhumans not as regards their merits but as regards their inherent worth. Thus the claim of human superiority is to be understood as asserting that all humans, simply in virtue of their humanity, have *a greater inherent worth* than other living things.

The inherent worth of an entity does not depend on its merits.[5] To consider something as possessing inherent worth, we have seen, is to place intrinsic value on the realization of its good. This is done regardless of whatever particular merits it might have or might lack, as judged by a set of grading or ranking standards. In human affairs, we are all familiar with the principle that one's worth as a person does not vary with one's merits or lack of merits. The same can hold true of animals and plants. To regard such entities as possessing inherent worth entails disregarding their merits and deficiencies, whether they are being judged from a human standpoint or from the standpoint of their own species.

The idea of one entity having more merit than another, and so being superior to it in merit, makes perfectly good sense. Merit is a grading or ranking concept, and judgments of comparative merit are based on the different degrees to which things satisfy a given standard. But what can it mean to talk about one thing being superior to another in inherent worth? In order to get at what is being asserted in such a claim it is helpful first to look at the social origin of the concept of degrees of inherent worth.

The idea that humans can possess different degrees of inherent worth originated in societies having rigid class structures. Before the rise of modern democracies with their egalitarian outlook, one's membership in a hereditary class determined one's social status. People in the upper classes were looked up to, while those in the lower classes were looked down upon. In such a society, one's social superiors and social inferiors were clearly defined and easily recognized.

Two aspects of these class-structured societies are especially relevant to the idea of degrees of inherent worth. First, those born into the upper classes were deemed more worthy of respect than those born into the lower orders. Second, the superior worth of upper class people had nothing to do with their merits nor did the inferior worth of those in the lower classes rest on their lack of merits. One's superiority or inferiority entirely derived from a social position one was born into. The modern concept of a meritocracy simply did not apply. One could not advance into a higher class by any sort of moral or nonmoral achievement. Similarly, an aristocrat held his title and all the privileges that went with it just because he was the eldest son of a titled nobleman. Unlike the bestowing of knighthood in contemporary Great Britain, one did not earn membership in the nobility by meritorious conduct.

We who live in modern democracies no longer believe in such hereditary social distinctions. Indeed, we would wholeheartedly condemn them on moral grounds as being fundamentally unjust. We have come to think of class systems as a paradigm of social injustice, it being a central principle of the democratic way of life that among humans there are no superiors and no inferiors.... That idea is incompatible with our notion of human equality based on the doctrine that all humans, simply in virtue of their humanity, have the same inherent worth. (The belief in universal human rights is one form that this egalitarianism takes.)

The vast majority of people in modern democracies, however, do not maintain an egalitarian outlook when it comes to comparing human beings with other living things. Most people consider our own species to be superior to all other species and this superiority is understood to be a matter of inherent worth, not merit. There may exist thoroughly vicious and depraved humans who lack all merit. Yet because they are human they are thought to belong to a higher class of entities than any plant or animal. That one is born into the species *Homo sapiens* entitles one to have lordship over those who are one's inferiors, namely, those born into other species. The parallel with hereditary social classes is very close. Implicit in this view is a hierarchical conception of nature according to which an organism has a position of superiority or inferiority in the Earth's community of life simply on the basis of its genetic background. The "lower" orders of life are looked down upon and it is considered perfectly proper that they serve the interests of those belonging to the highest order, namely humans. The intrinsic value we place on the well-being of our fellow humans reflects our recognition of their rightful position as our equals. No such intrinsic value is to be placed on the good of other animals, unless we choose to do so out of fondness or affection for them. But their well-being imposes no moral requirement on us. In this respect there is an absolute difference in moral status between ourselves and them.

This is the structure of concepts and beliefs that people are committed to insofar as they regard humans to be superior in inherent worth to all other species.... This structure of concepts and beliefs is completely groundless. If we accept the first three components of the biocentric outlook and from that perspective look at the major philosophical traditions which have supported that structure, we find it to be at bottom nothing more than the expression of an irrational bias in our own favor.

... That [it] is nothing more than a deep-seated prejudice is brought home to us when we look at our relation to other species in the light of the first three elements of the biocentric outlook. Those elements taken conjointly give us a certain overall view of the natural world and of the place of humans in it. When we take this view we come to understand other living things, their environmental conditions, and their ecological relationships in such a way as to awake in us a deep sense of our kinship with them as fellow members of the Earth's community of life. Humans and nonhumans alike are viewed together as integral parts of one unified whole in which all living things are functionally interrelated. Finally, when our awareness focuses on the individual lives of plants and animals, each is seen to share with us the characteristic of being a teleological center of life striving to realize its own good in its own unique way.

… Rejecting the notion of human superiority entails its positive counterpart: the doctrine of species impartiality. One who accepts that doctrine regards all living things as possessing inherent worth—the *same* inherent worth, since no one species has been shown to be either "higher" or "lower" than any other. Now we saw earlier that, insofar as one thinks of a living thing as possessing inherent worth, one considers it to be the appropriate object of the attitude of respect and believes that attitude to be the only fitting or suitable one for all moral agents to take toward it.…

X. MORAL RIGHTS AND THE MATTER OF COMPETING CLAIMS

I have not asserted anywhere in the foregoing account that animals or plants have moral rights. This omission was deliberate. I do not think that the reference class of the concept, bearer of moral rights, should be extended to include nonhuman living things. My reasons for taking this position, however, go beyond the scope of this paper. I believe I have been able to accomplish many of the same ends which those who ascribe rights to animals or plants wish to accomplish. There is no reason, moreover, why plants and animals, including whole species populations and life communities, cannot be accorded *legal* rights under my theory. To grant them legal protection could be interpreted as giving them legal entitlement to be protected, and this, in fact, would be a means by which a society that subscribed to the ethics of respect for nature could give public recognition to their inherent worth.

There remains the problem of competing claims, even when wild plants and animals are not thought of as bearers of moral rights. If we accept the biocentric outlook and accordingly adopt the attitude of respect for nature as our ultimate moral attitude, how do we resolve conflicts that arise from our respect for persons in the domain of human ethics and our respect for nature in the domain of environmental ethics? This is a question that cannot adequately be dealt with here. My main purpose in this paper has been to try to establish a base point from which we can start working toward a solution to the problem. I have shown why we cannot just begin with an initial presumption in favor of the interests of our own species. It is after all within our power as moral beings to place limits on human population and technology with the deliberate intention of sharing the Earth's bounty with other species. That such sharing is an ideal difficult to realize even in an approximate way does not take away its claim to our deepest moral commitment.

NOTES

1. The conceptual links between an entity *having* a good, something being good *for* it, and events doing good to it are examined by G. H. Von Wright in *The Varieties of Goodness* (New York: Humanities Press, 1963), chaps. 3 and 5.
2. I have analyzed the nature of this commitment of human ethics in "On Taking the Moral Point of View," *Midwest Studies in Philosophy*, vol. 3, *Studies in Ethical Theory* (1978), pp. 35–61.
3. Stephen R. L. Clark, *The Moral Status of Animals* (Oxford: Clarendon Press, 1977), p. 112.
4. My criticisms of the dogma of human superiority gain independent support from a carefully reasoned essay by R. and V. Routley showing the many logical weaknesses in arguments for human-centered theories of environmental ethics. R. and V. Routley, "Against the Inevitability of Human Chauvinism," in K. E. Goodpaster and K. M. Sayre, eds., *Ethics and Problems of the 21st Century* (Notre Dame: University of Notre Dame Press, 1979), pp. 36–59.
5. For this way of distinguishing between merit and inherent worth, I am indebted to Gregory Vlastos, "Justice and Equality," in R. Brandt, ed., *Social Justice* (Englewood Cliffs, N.J.: Prentice-Hall, 1962), pp. 31–72.

☖ QUESTIONS FOR ANALYSIS

1. According to Taylor, every "organism, species population, and community of life has a good of its own." What does he mean by that claim? What importance does it have for environmental ethics?

2. Taylor says that inherent worth is not an objective property. He also says that the attitude of ultimate respect for nature is supported by a belief system that cannot be proven true. Why, then, should we adopt that attitude?

3. In discussing individual organisms as teleological centers of life, Taylor says that we can look at the world from a plant's point of view without engaging in "false anthropomorphizing." What does he mean by that? How is it possible?

4. Much of Taylor's argument against human superiority rests on the claim that inherent worth does not admit of degrees. Do you agree? Why or why not?

5. Although Taylor does not advocate giving non-human organisms moral rights, he does advocate giving them *legal* rights. What might his justification be for denying one but granting the other?

6. Is Taylor's individualistic view preferable to Leopold's holistic view?

CASE PRESENTATION

Animal Liberators

On May 24, 1984, five members of the Animal Liberation Front (ALF) raided the University of Pennsylvania's Experimental Head Injury Lab, located in the subbasement of the Anatomy-Chemistry Building. Although the purpose of most ALF raids is to liberate laboratory animals, this raid was different. This time, the goal was to "liberate" videotapes of the experiments being conducted in the lab, experiments that included using a hydraulic jack to compress the heads of monkeys. They found what they came for, and along the way, they ransacked the lab—destroying equipment and removing files.

What the videotapes showed was gruesome. There were images of pistons piercing the heads of baboons and of unanesthetized primates crawling in pain from operating tables. There were also images that showed clear violations of standard research procedures, such as operations performed without surgical masks while workers were smoking cigarettes.

A great controversy followed the release of the tapes. Dr. Thomas Gennarelli, head of the lab, defended his research and decried the raid. All animals were anesthetized and felt no pain, he insisted, and the raid had seriously set back important medical research. The university also defended Dr. Gennarelli's research, as did the National Institutes of Health (NIH), which, despite protests from People for the Ethical Treatment of Animals, gave the lab a new grant of $500,000.

The raiders, in an interview that appeared in the November 1986 issue of *Omni* ("Inhuman Bondage"

by Robert Well), likened the research to the cruel medical experiments that Nazi Dr. Josef Mengele conducted on humans. (Indeed, one of the raiders was himself a survivor of a Nazi concentration camp.)

As the controversy continued, protesters demonstrated at the Penn campus, and animal rights activists staged a sit-in at the NIH until Secretary of Health and Human Services Margaret Heckler ordered a halt to all federal funding of the Head Injury Lab. That was July 18, 1985. Four months later, Penn agreed to pay a $4,000 fine for violating the Animal Welfare Act. The university also agreed to improve its use of pain-relieving drugs, its care of injured animals, and its training of research workers who handle laboratory animals.

And the raiders? Despite a grand jury investigation, no indictments were handed down. ALF members, invoking their Fifth Amendment rights, refused to testify against themselves.

The ALF continues its underground efforts today in forty countries. PETA (People for the Ethical Treatment of Animals) has refused to criticize their activities, saying "… we realize that other groups have different methods and we try not to condemn any efforts in behalf of animals in which no one is harmed." PETA cites the Underground Railroad in the effort to end slavery as a laudable example of law-breaking that served a greater good.

👑 QUESTIONS FOR ANALYSIS

1. Is the comparison between Drs. Gennarelli and Mengele justified?
2. Dr. Gennarelli and the NIH obviously believed that his research would bring significant medical benefit. If his research workers had not violated standard research procedures, would that benefit have justified it?
3. Suppose that ALF and Tom Regan are right about such experiments violating animals' rights. Does that justify ALF's tactics?
4. Which is the more important moral issue—the research itself or the violations of the Animal Welfare Act? Why?
5. If similar research was done on mice, would your reaction to it be any different?

CASE PRESENTATION

Religious Sacrifice

Of the many Cubans who have come to southern Florida in recent decades, some 70,000 practice the religion of Santería. Santería is a distinctively Afro- Cuban religion. It combines the Roman Catholicism of Cuba's Spanish settlers and the traditional Yoruba religion of West Africa, which came to the Caribbean island on the slave ships. Among Santería's traditional Yoruba rituals is animal sacrifice. Turtles, pigeons, chickens, goats, and sheep are slaughtered to appease the Santería gods, after which they are usually eaten by adherents in attendance.

Like other cities in southern Florida, Hialeah has its share of Cuban immigrants. In 1987, the Church of Lukumi Babalu Aye announced its plans to build a Santería church and community center in Hialeah. The city responded with a series of ordinances banning the ritual sacrifice of animals, with one of the ordinances defining the outlawed practice this way: To perform a ritual animal sacrifice is to "unnecessarily kill, torment, torture or mutilate an animal in a public or private ritual or ceremony not for the primary purpose of food consumption."

The church went to court, charging that the ordinances violated the religious freedom of its members. Hialeah defended the ordinances as a public health measure. In a unanimous decision announced in June of 1993, the U.S. Supreme Court ruled in favor of the church. Santería's adherents were jubilant, but opponents of cruelty to animals worried about the fate of animal cruelty laws throughout the country.

Today, the Church in Hialeah is still open. It has a Facebook page on which it attempts to counteract what it considers misleading information about its practices, but the size of its membership is unclear.

👑 QUESTIONS FOR ANALYSIS

1. The Court saw the case as a matter of religious freedom, not as a matter of cruelty to animals. Hialeah claimed to see the case as a matter of public health rather than a matter of cruelty to animals. How do you think Singer and Regan would feel about that?
2. In an earlier case, Native Americans who use peyote in religious rituals sought exemption from drug laws that ban peyote's use. The Court ruled against them because the drug laws were not designed to interfere with religion. But the Hialeah ordinances were so designed, according to the Court, because they singled out only one reason for killing animals. Should Hialeah have broadened them to include other reasons? If so, how?
3. Should animal sacrifices be permitted? How would Singer and Regan answer?
4. If you agree that at least some animals have rights, how would you balance them against human rights to practice religion?

CASE PRESENTATION

A Metaphor for the Energy Debate

In the worst oil spill in U.S. history to that time, the *Exxon Valdez* tanker spilled 11 million gallons of crude oil into Alaska's Prince William Sound. The March 24, 1989, spill affected more than 1,000 miles of shoreline, including three national wildlife refuges, and left many thousands of animals dead, including an estimated 100,000 birds and 1,000 sea otters.

At the time of the spill, the oil industry had been hoping that the federal government would open the coastal plain of Alaska's Arctic National Wildlife Refuge (ANWR) to drilling. Two hundred and fifty miles north of the Arctic Circle, this tundra area is inhabited by caribou and musk oxen. Since only a few hundred Eskimos also live there, its 19 million acres are practically untouched by humans. The coastal plain area of the preserve, which covers 1.5 million acres, may also be home to the largest untapped oil reserve in the country. A five-year study by the Department of the Interior had reported in 1987 that the plain presented "the best single opportunity to increase significantly domestic oil production." But after the massive public outrage sparked by the *Exxon Valdez* spill, opening the plain to drilling was politically unthinkable.

A year and a half later, the unthinkable suddenly became thinkable when Iraq invaded Kuwait and the flow of oil from the two Persian Gulf countries was halted. Public attention quickly focused on U.S. dependence on foreign oil, and with the renewed attention came a renewal of the drilling debate. In the words of Alaska's Governor Steve Cowper, who noted that Alaska was both the country's wilderness and major source of energy, "This is a metaphor for the energy debate."

That debate, and the refuge's centrality to it, continues to this day, reaching another peak in the year 2000. After years of decline, energy prices suddenly soared to near record levels, and the Clinton administration, bowing to public pressure, released oil from the strategic oil reserve in an effort to lower fuel prices. Once again, concern grew over U.S. dependence on foreign oil, and the question of drilling in the refuge became a major issue in that year's presidential election campaign. George W. Bush, the eventual winner of the election in a very close race, campaigned in favor of drilling. Gale Norton, his selection to head the Department of the Interior, had also voiced support for it.

Since the election of President Barack Obama in 2008, ANWR has remained closed to drilling. On December 6, 2010, the fiftieth anniversary of ANWR, President Obama issued a proclamation that said, in part, "Today, the Arctic National Wildlife Refuse remains distinct in the American landscape, and we must remain committed to making responsible choices and ensuring the continued conservation of these wild lands." The Republican-controlled House voted to open it to drilling in February 2012, but the Democratic-controlled Senate refused to consider the measure.

To those who favor drilling, the plain is a frozen desert with significant potential to strengthen national security and improve the economy of the northern part of the state. To those who oppose drilling, the plain is a magnificent wilderness that must be protected from aesthetic and ecological damage.

⚜ QUESTIONS FOR ANALYSIS

1. Many people consider reliance on foreign oil a threat to national security. Options for reducing U.S. reliance include energy conservation, alternative fuels, and increased domestic drilling. Should drilling be allowed in areas currently protected by federal law?

2. Oil companies and the Department of the Interior claim that drilling in the coastal plain will not harm the environment. The environmentalists dispute the claim but also argue that aesthetic damage will occur in any case. How much weight should aesthetics be given when balanced against energy needs and economic concerns?

3. The Arctic National Wildlife Refuge is isolated, generally considered less attractive than many other protected areas, and rarely visited by outsiders. Do those factors improve the case of drilling proponents, or are they irrelevant to the dispute?

4. Debate also surrounds the issue of new drilling off the coasts of California and Florida. Especially since the explosion of the BP Deepwater Horizon oil rig in April 2010 in the Gulf of Mexico off Louisiana, the debate has recognized the serious risks of this drilling to human life, the environment, and the economy. An estimated 172 million gallons of oil were spilled in this explosion (compared with 11 million in the *Exxon Valdez* spill in 1989). Given our dependence on foreign oil, should offshore drilling be increased in those areas, despite these risks?

CASE PRESENTATION

The Spotted Owl

On June 22, 1990, the U.S. Fish and Wildlife Service declared the northern spotted owl a threatened species. Under the Endangered Species Act of 1973, the declaration made it illegal to harm the owl or its habitat, the Pacific Northwest forests.

Though environmentalists hailed the declaration, other groups, most notably the timber industry, objected. The Pacific Northwest forests are home to giant cedars, Douglas firs, and redwood trees, and the timber industry constituted a large portion of the economies of Washington, Oregon, and northern California. Of the seventeen national forests involved, the timber industry cleared 70,000 acres annually. Under a plan proposed by federal biologists, 4 million acres were to be added to the 1.5 million acres already off limits to logging.

Like many such disputes, this one pitted environmental concerns against economic ones. On the one side was not only the future of the spotted owls—which were down to 3,000 mating pairs—but the future of the forests, which had already lost 90 percent of their ancient trees. On the other side was the future of the area's economy. According to government estimates, 28,000 jobs would be lost over a ten-year period. According to industry officials' estimates, the number could be as high as 50,000.

Four days later, the administration of President George H. W. Bush, which initially said it would not interfere with plans to protect the owl's habitat, reversed itself. Instead of going ahead with the original plans, it decided to delay protection of the forests while it set up a commission to study ways of balancing the interests of the logging industry and the owls. It also decided to seek changes in the Endangered Species Act to make it easier to permit some species to diminish in order to avoid severe economic consequences. As the law stood at the time (and still does), such permission could be given only by a committee of federal agency heads, informally known as the "God Committee." Because of the difficulties involved in convening a meeting of the committee and the time involved in coming to a decision, the procedure is rarely used.

Neither side was pleased by the administration's plan to delay a solution to the problem. Environmentalists claimed that the administration was declaring war on the Endangered Species Act, while the timber industry argued that the delay would aggravate the region's economic uncertainty. Then, in 1991, a federal judge in Seattle ordered an end to the logging, ruling that the Bush administration was in violation of federal laws. Judge William Dryer also ordered the government to devise an environmental plan for the region. Until an acceptable plan was presented to him, the ban on logging would remain.

The issue wasn't settled until December 1994, when the same judge gave final approval to a plan proposed fifteen months earlier by the newly inaugurated Clinton administration. Under that plan, which the administration hailed as a way to protect the region's economy as well as its natural habitats, logging resumed at a reduced level. The plan also included restoration projects for damaged forests and streams in addition to other forms of economic aid to the region. Once again, neither side was satisfied, especially the timber industry, which vowed to continue its battle over the Endangered Species Act in Congress. Although minor changes have been made in the Act over the years and despite continuing efforts to curtail or even abolish it altogether, the Act remains largely in place as of 2013.

QUESTIONS FOR ANALYSIS

1. To what extent should economic impact be considered when seeking a plan to protect an endangered species or a forest area?
2. As most of the timber harvested in the seventeen northwestern forests is exported to other countries, closing an additional 4 million acres to foresting will not affect lumber supplies or building costs in the United States. Is that a relevant factor in deciding whether to close off the acres to logging?
3. Environmental groups had been trying to save the Pacific Northwest forests long before the spotted owl was declared a threatened species. What economic costs should we be willing to allow to protect our forests, even when diminishing them does not affect a threatened species?
4. Should it be easier or more difficult to allow a species to become extinct in order to prevent severe economic harm?

CHAPTER TWELVE

Computer Ethics and the Internet

- **What Is Computer Ethics?**
- **Issues in Computer Ethics**
- **Arguments in Favor of Ethical Conduct with Computers and the Internet**
- **Arguments Against Ethical Conduct with Computers and the Internet**

LAURENCE H. TRIBE   **The Constitution in Cyberspace: Law and Liberty Beyond the Electronic Frontier**

RICHARD A. SPINELLO   **Free Speech in Cyberspace**

EUGENE H. SPAFFORD   **Are Computer Hacker Break-ins Ethical?**

HERMAN T. TAVANI AND FRANCES S. GRODZINSKY   **Cyberstalking, Personal Privacy, and Moral Responsibility**

CASE PRESENTATIONS: • *Ticketed for Obscenity on the Information Superhighway* • *A Chill in Cyberspace* • *Censoring Political Speech* • *Pirates of the Campuses*

AUGUST 12, 2006 marked the twenty-fifth anniversary of the first IBM personal computers, which made the use of computing seem acceptable for ordinary people. Although the Apple II computer was introduced in 1977 and some small computer kits had been available before this for what we might now call "geeks," the PC brought computing into the mainstream and revolutionized the way we live, work, and play.

What we now call the Internet began as something called ARPAnet, which in 1969 linked computers at universities and the U.S. Defense Department. The goal at the time was to develop a communications system that could withstand military attack. Because there is no physical central switching location, bombing the location of one computer in the system would not disable the communications among the others. The earliest e-mail programs can be traced to 1971. But it was not until development of the international HTML protocols for the World Wide Web in the early 1990s and recognition of the enormous potential for commercial and private use of the web and e-mail that most people even heard about these electronic methods for communication and information exchange. Now, it is difficult to imagine a college or business or public library that is not connected to the Internet. As the prices of personal computers and laptops fell, they became increasingly ubiquitous in society, although the technological "divide" attributable to economic realities also became an issue.

With these new technologies, however, also came a burgeoning range of ethical issues. Do the rights we take for granted elsewhere also apply on the Internet? Should we be able to exercise the rights of free speech under the First Amendment online, especially when so many young children have easy access to the Internet? Should we be as respectful of the intellectual property rights of software owners and artists online as we are expected to be in the world of hard-copy books and paintings on canvas? Can we expect the same right to privacy in our e-mail communications as we demand in our telephone calls? With the rapid-fire communication possible online, has defamation of the character of persons become much more serious than when we merely utter some defamatory remarks in the physical presence of a few friends?

Computer ethics long predates personal computers, however. In 1950, Norbert Wiener, a mathematics professor at the Massachusetts Institute of Technology, published what many experts consider the first systematic consideration of computer ethics, *The Human Use of Human Beings*. In this chapter, we will consider some of these ethical problems, as we encounter them today in our use of computers and the Internet. We also will chart some things to consider in identifying and addressing ethical issues that present themselves as technologies evolve in ways we cannot yet imagine in these early years of the twenty-first century. Can we identify long-standing ethical principles from Kantian and utilitarian perspectives that will assist us in responding to these newly emerging ethical problems?

WHAT IS COMPUTER ETHICS?

In 1985, James H. Moor, a professor at Dartmouth College, published the seminal article "What Is Computer Ethics?"[1] that has defined the issues in recent decades. He proposed defining **computer ethics** as "the analysis of the nature and social impact of computer technology and the corresponding formulation and justification of policies for the ethical use of such technology." It seems consistent with his definition to recognize the Internet, which emerged into general use a decade later, as an element or application of that technology. Moor noted that we are provided with "new capabilities" and "new choices for action" because of computers, but no policies or guidelines for how to behave ethically in that environment.

We are faced with two challenges. First, studying computer ethics should help us identify specific issues in this area in such a way that we can clearly and systematically consider them. Second, we can then consider whether ethical-reasoning methods will help us chart a well-reasoned path to decision making in what Moor considers uncharted terrain.

ISSUES IN COMPUTER ETHICS

We here identify a sampling of the issues we face in computer ethics. This is intended not as a comprehensive or exhaustive list but, rather, as representative of the issues we face today.

---

[1]James H. Moor, "What Is Computer Ethics"? *Metaphilosophy* 16:4 (1985).

Freedom of Expression

Freedom of expression is guaranteed in the First Amendment to the U.S. Constitution and hence is one of the ten amendments known as the Bill of Rights. It is also guaranteed in Article 19 of the Universal Declaration of Human Rights of the United Nations:

> Everyone has the right to freedom of opinion and expression; this right includes freedom to hold opinions without interference and to seek, receive and impart information and ideas through any media and regardless of frontiers.

We recognize this right in our ability to speak freely in a public square or publish a newspaper or deliver a speech. But even though mass communication long predates computers and the Internet, the speed with which speech can be disseminated worldwide to untold millions of people renews our focus on these rights.

Defamation is one of several exceptions to our right of free speech, which is not absolute. It consists of a factual claim that is false and is damaging to someone's reputation. Spoken defamation is **slander**, and written defamation is **libel**. If a television reporter publicly claimed that a certain famous singer was a child molester, it would be defamation, but only if that statement were false, because truth is an absolute defense to defamation.

Although this legal wrong has been recognized for centuries in Anglo-American law, it can cause massive damage with the speed of communication of the Internet. A defamatory statement made in front of a few people in the same physical location might not cause too much damage, especially if it were followed by a sincere apology. But a defamatory statement posted on the Web or blasted out via a list-serv e-mail to thousands of people can cause irreparable harm to someone's career or financial investments or professional standing. And once something is out there in cyberspace, it never really disappears, magnifying the damage. Defaming another person's reputation is not just a legal issue. It also is an ethical problem, because one person can cause serious harm to another person—a wrong whether viewed from a Kantian respect for persons or from a utilitarian concern for maximizing pleasure and minimizing pain.

Another exception to freedom of expression is **obscenity**. Philosopher J. S. Mill, as he stated in his book *On Liberty* (1859), and many civil libertarians believe that obscenity should enjoy the same free-speech protections as all other speech. However, in the United States, the Supreme Court has never recognized this right. Defining obscenity is particularly difficult. In the landmark decision *Miller v. California,*[2] the Court said that something is obscene only if it meets all elements of this three-pronged test:

> (A) whether "the average person, applying contemporary community standards" would find that the work, taken as a whole, appeals to the prurient interest, (b) whether the work depicts or describes, in a patently offensive way, sexual conduct specifically defined by the applicable state law, and (c) whether the work, taken as a whole, lacks serious literary, artistic, political, or scientific value.

---

[2]413 U.S. 15 (1973).

But almost every word and phrase in this definition is fraught with interpretive difficulties and disagreement. What are "contemporary community standards," especially with the worldwide reach of the Internet? Should the standards be those of a rural community in the South or those of an urban neighborhood in New York or Los Angeles? What is a "prurient interest"? Who decides what is "patently offensive"? How do we determine whether a painting has serious "artistic" value?

But the new worldwide community isn't the only problem we face in making sense of the issue of sexually explicit material. It has long been recognized by the courts that material that is pornographic or offensive in any way *is* protected by the First Amendment, so long as it is not "obscene." But even then, it is legitimate to restrict access to this material to minors. Municipalities can legitimately enact zoning rules that restrict "adult bookstores" to certain neighborhoods and require that persons buying that material be at least eighteen years of age. Municipalities also can legitimately, without infringing on First Amendment protection, restrict public displays of pornography, as on billboards or outdoor stages. These restrictions balance the right of adults to see such materials, if they choose, against the right of others not to be forced to look at them, while denying minors access to them.

The Web complicates this long-standing balance enormously. Children who cannot gain admittance to an adult movie theater or bookstore can find it easy to access the same material on the Web. Rules that only those with credit cards can see such pages are difficult to enforce, if children know the credit card numbers of their parents. In the landmark 1997 case *Reno v. ACLU*,[3] the U.S. Supreme Court struck down, as excessively broad, federal legislation that attempted to ban all such material. The goal of blocking access to children resulted in a suppression of protected free-speech material to adults, the Court reasoned, and it encouraged better use of screening tools by parents to restrict access to content they found objectionable. It also is often noted that a substantial portion of the controversial content available on the Web is being sent from locations outside the United States, where U.S. laws could not be enforced anyway.

Privacy

The use of computers to gather and store information has been hailed as a huge achievement in most sectors of life. In just the last few years, our lives have been transformed by the ease with which we can access data online and perform tasks once limited to the U.S. mail or telephone calls or personal office visits. We can renew our driver's license, pay our taxes, buy books, and check whether a package was delivered by FedEx or UPS or the United States Postal Service, all on the Internet. We can search databases of newspapers, magazines, court cases, and even books in a matter of minutes to do research that used to require hours and days in a traditional print library. Some medical services, especially the Veterans Administration and some large HMOs (such as Kaiser Permanente in California and other states), now maintain all of our medical records on electronic databases, so doctors at any location can quickly and efficiently see our entire medical history.

But this massive data storage and access have created huge problems with violation of our privacy. Regular news reports in recent years reveal numerous breaches

---

[3]521 U.S. 844 (1997).

of security of these databases. Lost laptops containing confidential employment information, health data, and other records place thousands of private citizens at risk of identity theft. Hackers frequently find ways to access these confidential data and misuse them in many different ways.

Although some laws are in place to prosecute misuse of confidential data, it can be very difficult to identify the persons who found the data or to correct the damage. Identity theft can victimize innocent persons for many years while they try to clear their credit records.

As with so many issues involving computers and the Internet, these problems are not new. A clerk in a doctor's office might have misused confidential information in a private medical file in the past. A dishonest employee at a government agency might look at tax returns or driver's license records or other government documents and misuse that information. But computerized databases make that information far more accessible and easier to obtain and misuse by many more people.

The ethical obligations extend not only to those persons who might steal and misuse this private information, but also to the organizations that collect the data and fail to put in place appropriate security to protect our privacy.

Intellectual Property

Copyright protects the expression of ideas, whether in words, symbols, or other forms of expression. The founding fathers provided for copyright protection in the U.S. Constitution, because granting a limited monopoly on this work so it could be exploited financially was thought to be a good way to encourage creativity that would benefit the entire nation. Issues of intellectual property, which includes patent and trademark as well as copyright, have existed for centuries. Once again, though, computers and the Internet have magnified the potential abuse and the possibilities for theft of other people's work.

Stealing someone else's words and passing them off as your own has been possible as long as students have been in school. This is likely not only to violate someone's copyright but also to constitute plagiarism prohibited at schools, colleges, and universities. Computers and the Internet make this theft much easier, because so much material is available and easy to "copy and paste" into any document on any topic. But just as it is easy for students to steal other people's work, it is equally easy for professors to find the source, using such search tools as Google.com. Commercial products such as Turnitin.org, now widely used at colleges and universities, enable professors to submit an entire document in digitized form and have it compared in minutes with a massive database. This database includes not only the entire contents of the Web but also the contents of "term paper mills" where some students buy papers *and* all previous papers submitted by all instructors using the service around the country.

Plagiarism can have serious consequences for a student, including a failing grade or suspension from a university. It also raises serious ethical issues, because it consists of stealing someone else's work and falsifying its source by turning it in as one's own.

Intellectual-property violations of other kinds also are now rampant on the Internet. Words and images are easily retrieved and saved in digitized files. Graphics software can be used to modify images, violating yet another right of copyright owners. Posting the text of a copyrighted book can damage the commercial potential of that print book irretrievably.

Intellectual-property issues also arise with the sharing of copyrighted files for music and film. Although many Internet users seem to have a "Wild West" mentality, believing that everything should be free, that attitude overlooks the fact that most of this material is actually property owned by somebody who worked hard to produce it and wants a fair return in exchange. Copying copyrighted software in violation of the terms of the purchase of that software is another violation of intellectual property.

All of these violations raise legal issues. The copyright owners can sue for damages for misuse—and they often do. But these are also ethical issues. They involve behavior that we routinely recognize as unethical, even if we are never caught by legal officials: theft, violations of another person's autonomy, and dishonesty.

Computer Crime

Computers and the Internet have spawned all sorts of crimes that interfere with the peaceable enjoyment of those technologies by everyone. Hackers steal confidential data online. Sending "viruses" through e-mail interferes with the regular access of thousands of Internet users, destroying a valuable property interest in our computers and Internet services. Spam messages clog our e-mail, slow down services, and might constitute harassment that interferes with our daily lives and work.

All of this behavior is not only illegal but also unethical. These crimes existed in various forms before computers and the Internet. But, like the other issues we are considering, they are magnified exponentially by the capabilities of the technology.

Access to the Internet and the Technological "Divide"

For all the new opportunities presented by computers and the Internet, they depend on the economic capability of accessing these technologies. Many schools have tried to ensure that all students have access, regardless of their economic means. Public libraries provide free access to all residents, at least in industrialized nations. But access to these technologies in developing and impoverished nations can be very restricted, further exacerbating the divide in economic development between the "haves" and the "have-nots." If wealthy nations have an ethical obligation to help provide basic nourishment and healthcare to impoverished nations, do they also have an ethical obligation to assist those nations in gaining access to these increasingly vital technologies?

Moral and Legal Issues

Most of the issues here have a legal dimension and a moral dimension as well. One method for analysis is to identify the underlying ethical issue and ask how and whether it can be extended to the dimensions of computers and the Internet. Some of these ethical issues can be extended without difficulty. Others might demand fresh approaches, as the magnitude of the problems forces serious reconsideration.

Our right to protect our privacy is fundamental to our basic autonomy as persons. Not only is it a crime to violate that privacy by stealing confidential information from a computerized database, but it also violates our ethical rights to privacy and autonomy.

Our right to freedom of expression also might require re-examination, especially if our expression exposes minors to inappropriate material. We might want to protect our own rights, but don't we have an ethical obligation not to cause emotional harm to minors who have easy access to material we might be posting?

Our ethical obligation not to steal seems to extend not only to our neighbor's car or watch but also to the intellectual property we find on the Internet—the writing, visual images, software, and music files. Those who believe the ethical obligation not to steal does not apply on the Internet have the burden of coming up with a plausible justification for such a view.

ARGUMENTS IN FAVOR OF ETHICAL CONDUCT WITH COMPUTERS AND THE INTERNET

1. *I strive to be ethical whether or not other people know about it because it makes me a better person overall.*

    POINT: "Behaving ethically is something I strive for, regardless of whether anybody knows it. I just feel better about myself knowing that I am doing my best to be a better person. Although it might be easier to misbehave in the privacy of my study logged onto the Internet, I still know what I'm doing and it's important to me to respect myself. And there's always the chance that somebody will find out what I am doing anyway. With all the tracking systems on the Internet, I'm not confident that anything I do there will not someday become known to other people."

    COUNTERPOINT: "It's a tough world out there, and if you can get away with something in private, go for it. Everybody else is out for themselves, and that's the only way to get ahead in this cut-throat world we live in. Besides, if you're careful, you can stay anonymous on the Internet, at least for things you don't want others to know about. Your chances of getting caught doing something unethical are pretty slim, and most of your friends are probably doing the same thing anyway."

2. *I don't post pornography on the web or look at it because I consider it degrading to women.*

    POINT: "Every piece of pornography shares at least one thing with every other piece of pornography—it degrades human beings. By separating sex from love, by concentrating on impersonal lust at the expense of our more human emotions, by appealing to and arousing the lust of its readers and viewers, even the mildest pornography reduces humanity to the level of animals. And much of today's pornography goes even further, portraying the most disgusting and dehumanizing acts of sexual sadomasochism imaginable."

    COUNTERPOINT: "You might find pornography degrading, but many other people don't. In fact, they actually enjoy it. And there's no reason why they shouldn't. After all, lust is as human as any other emotion, and there isn't anything inherently immoral about being 'turned on' by erotic pictures and writings. Nor is there anything inherently immoral about portraying sex without love. Even if most people consider sex with love the ideal, why must everything we see and read portray ideal situations only, sexual or nonsexual? And even though much of today's pornography disgusts me as much as it disgusts you, the fact that we're disgusted by it doesn't make it immoral or dehumanizing, any more than the fact that we find certain foods or clothing styles disgusting makes them immoral or dehumanizing."

3. *I don't download music or movies or share files for those with my friends, because stealing is always wrong.*

    POINT: "I wouldn't dream of trying to shoplift in a record store or movie rental store, because if I got caught, having a criminal record would really wreck my career plans. In just the same way, I don't want to take a chance that I'd get caught illegally downloading music or movie files on the Internet. The entertainment industry is after college students nowadays, and my campus is also cracking down on these illegal downloads. Even if I don't get caught today, I'll always worry that they'll track me down in the future, with all the capabilities they have now for tracing computer records. And whether or not I get caught, I'll always know that I behaved unethically by stealing something that didn't belong to me."

COUNTERPOINT: "There are millions of college students in this country. What are the odds that the entertainment industry will come after me? I wouldn't shoplift either, but the changes of getting caught in illegal downloading from the Internet are just very slim to almost nonexistent. Besides, the industry is wealthy beyond belief. They've made plenty of money off me already when I buy CDs and DVDs, and it's only fair that I get a little free 'bonus' now and then from the Internet. Ordinarily, stealing is wrong, but it can be justified in circumstances like this."

4. *If I see something on the web that looks like a criminal might be threatening another person, I'll report it to the proper authorities.*

POINT: "We all have to watch out for each other in this world. If somebody were threatening me on the Web, I'd want to know about it and would want others to do what they could to tell the authorities. It takes a little time to do these things and get involved, but we'd all be in a better world if more people would take the time and effort to do this."

COUNTERPOINT: "Turning somebody else in could jeopardize my own life. And the authorities will insist that I testify and spend my own precious time pursuing whatever case they think they might have. It's risky to get involved. Everybody needs to watch out for themselves and not assume some do-gooders will get involved."

ARGUMENTS AGAINST ETHICAL CONDUCT WITH COMPUTERS AND THE INTERNET

1. *I can be anonymous on the Internet, so nobody will know if I spam or send out viruses or steal music off the web.*

POINT: "The great thing about the Internet is that it's so easy to do things I could never get away with in person. I can look up all kinds of confidential information about people I don't like. I can blast spam and viruses out to let the world know how much power ordinary people have, thanks to computers and the Internet. Huge multinational corporations need to be reminded that they don't control everything, and stealing music or sending out viruses or spam is a good way to protest."

COUNTERPOINT: "You're really not anonymous on the Internet. People who steal music or movies on the web are being sued by the big entertainment companies. The police and FBI are finding ways to track down spammers and those who send viruses. The consequences if you are caught at any of this stuff could be very severe, and a criminal record could ruin your future plans for education and career. If you want to protest the control of huge corporations, find a different way to do it that doesn't jeopardize your own future. It would be a brutish world if all we cared about in ethical decisions was whether or not we might get caught. We should be following good ethical standards regardless."

2. *Everybody cheats on the Internet and hardly anybody ever gets caught.*

   POINT: "I have lots of friends who find material on the Internet that they take without change and submit in their classes as their own work. I hear them brag all the time about how they got away with it, and the professors don't seem to notice. I'm working part-time to put myself through college and I don't have time to go to the library and write everything from scratch. Plagiarism is so rampant nowadays that I don't see how it could hurt me, even if I do get caught. Some famous authors, professors, and even university presidents have been found to be plagiarizing. If it's okay for them, it ought to be okay for students to do the same thing."

   COUNTERPOINT: "It's gotten very easy for professors to find plagiarism when you turn in your papers, especially with new search tools that can find it almost instantaneously. I don't hear my friends bragging when they get caught and flunk a course or get suspended from school, so I don't believe nobody gets caught nowadays. Computers make it easy to steal, but they also make it easy for professors to find plagiarism. It's just not worth the risk. My professors try to play fair with me, so I owe it to them to try my best in my work for class, idealistic as that might sound."

3. *The Internet is the new Wild West. I can say or do whatever I want and nobody has any grounds for complaining.*

   POINT: "At last, ordinary people like me have a place where we can speak our mind, whether by creating a website or posting comments to a chatroom or blasting out e-mail that speaks the truth about people or corporations I don't like. Isn't that what free speech is all about? If they don't like what I'm saying, they can post their own stuff on the web to respond, but at least I have a chance to vent in a public place where people can hear me."

   COUNTERPOINT: "We do have a lot of freedom of expression, but it's not absolute. Whether in person or on the web, we have to respect some limits. We should not defame innocent people by spreading falsehoods that hurt their reputations. We should not incite crime against other people. If we all respect a few reasonable limits on free speech, we as a society will all be better off."

4. *Posting pornography on the web or looking at pornography that others have posted is my right under the principle of free speech. Pornography can actually be beneficial.*

   POINT: "Despite all your talk of the harmful effects of pornography, it actually has many beneficial effects. It can aid normal sexual development, invigorate flagging sexual relationships, encourage openness about sex between sexual partners, and provide a release for people who, for one reason or another, are unable to find sexual fulfillment in other ways. It's even been used successfully in sex therapy to treat various sexual disorders. Finally, there's reason to believe that pornography prevents sex crimes by providing catharsis for people who would otherwise behave harmfully."

   COUNTERPOINT: "Reliable scientific studies refute your catharsis argument. Studies show that the group reporting the highest rate of excitation to masturbation by pornography were rapists. Obviously, pornography didn't provide these possible rapists with an adequate outlet. As for the rest, much of it is just speculation. And even if some of it is true, it hardly justifies pornography, which remains degrading to all humans, most of all to women. When something is inherently immoral, as pornography is, a few beneficial effects can't make it moral, especially when we have evidence that it has harmful effects as well."

The Constitution in Cyberspace: Law and Liberty Beyond the Electronic Frontier

LAURENCE H. TRIBE

Laurence H. Tribe is the Carl M. Loeb University Professor and Professor of Constitutional Law at Harvard Law School and a prominent expert on constitutional law. In these excerpts from his pioneering keynote address at the First Conference on Computers, Freedom and Privacy, March 26, 1991, he outlines a range of basic principles that frame not only our understanding of legal problems presented by the Internet, but also ethical issues of continuing concern.

His central focus is whether a document written in the eighteenth century to address the realities of the world at that point in history can appropriately be applied to the world of cyberspace and virtual reality that we now inhabit. He believes the core values of the Constitution will best endure if we recognize that it protects people, not places.

My topic is how to "map" the text and structure of our Constitution onto the texture and topology of "cyberspace." That's the term coined by cyberpunk novelist William Gibson, which many now use to describe the "place"—a place without physical walls or even physical dimensions—where ordinary telephone conversations "happen," where voice-mail and e-mail messages are stored and sent back and forth, and where computer-generated graphics are transmitted and transformed, all in the form of interactions, some real-time and some delayed, among countless users, and between users and the computer itself.

... My topic, broadly put, is the implications of that rapidly expanding array for our constitutional order.... When the lines along which our Constitution is drawn warp or vanish, what happens to the Constitution itself?

SETTING THE STAGE

To set the stage with a perhaps unfamiliar example, consider a decision handed down nine months

ago, *Maryland v. Craig*, where the U.S. Supreme Court upheld the power of a state to put an alleged child abuser on trial with the defendant's accuser testifying not in the defendant's presence but by one-way, closed-circuit television. The Sixth Amendment, which of course antedated television by a century and a half, says: "In all criminal prosecutions, the accused shall enjoy the right ... to be confronted with the witnesses against him." Justice O'Connor wrote for a bare majority of five Justices that the state's procedures nonetheless struck a fair balance between costs to the accused and benefits to the victim and to society as a whole....

But new technological possibilities for seeing your accuser clearly without having your accuser see you at all—possibilities for sparing the accuser any discomfort in ways that the accuser couldn't be spared before one-way mirrors [and] closed-circuit TVs were developed—*should* lead us at least to ask ourselves whether *two*-way confrontation, in which your accuser is supposed to be made uncomfortable, and thus less likely to lie, really *is* the core value of the Confrontation Clause. If so, "virtual" confrontation should be held constitutionally insufficient. If not—if the core value served by the Confrontation Clause is just the ability to *watch* your accuser say that you did it—then "virtual" confrontation should suffice. New technologies should lead us to look more closely at just *what values* the Constitution seeks to preserve. New technologies should *not* lead us to react reflexively *either way*—either by assuming that technologies the Framers didn't know about make their concerns and values obsolete, or by assuming that those new technologies couldn't possibly provide new ways out of old dilemmas and therefore should be ignored altogether.

… The world in which the Sixth Amendment's Confrontation Clause was written and ratified was a world in which "being confronted with" your accuser *necessarily* meant a simultaneous physical confrontation so that your accuser had to *perceive* you being accused by him. Closed-circuit television and one-way mirrors changed all that by *decoupling* those two dimensions of confrontation, marking a shift in the conditions of information-transfer that is in many ways typical of cyberspace.

What does that sort of shift mean for constitutional analysis? A common way to react is to treat the pattern as it existed *prior* to the new technology (the pattern in which doing "A" necessarily *included* doing "B") as essentially arbitrary or accidental. Taking this approach, once the technological change makes it possible to do "A" *without* "B"—to see your accuser without having him or her see you, or to read someone's mail without her knowing it, to switch examples—one concludes that the "old" Constitution's inclusion of "B" is irrelevant; one concludes that it is enough for the government to guarantee "A" alone. Sometimes that will be the case; but it's vital to understand that, sometimes, it won't be.

A characteristic feature of modernity is the subordination of purpose to accident—an acute appreciation of just how contingent and coincidental the connections we are taught to make often are. We understand, as moderns, that many of the ways we carve up and organize the world reflect what our social history and cultural heritage, and perhaps our neurological wiring,

bring to the world, and not some irreducible "way things are."…

The Constitution's core values, I'm convinced, need not be transmogrified, or metamorphosed into oblivion, in the dim recesses of cyberspace. But to say that they *need* not be lost there is hardly to predict that they *will* not be. On the contrary, without further thought and awareness of the kind this conference might provide, the danger is clear and present that they *will* be.

The "event horizon" against which this transformation might occur is already plainly visible. Electronic trespassers like Kevin Mitnik don't stop with cracking pay phones, but break into NORAD—the North American Defense Command computer in Colorado Springs—not in a *WarGames* movie, but in real life.

Less challenging to national security but more ubiquitously threatening, computer crackers download everyman's credit history from institutions like TRW; start charging phone calls (and more) to everyman's number; set loose "worm" programs that shut down thousands of linked computers; and spread "computer viruses" through everyman's work or home PC.

It is not only the government that feels threatened by "computer crime"; both the owners and the users of private information services, computer bulletin boards, gateways, and networks feel equally vulnerable to this new breed of invisible trespasser.…

THE PROBLEM

The Constitution's architecture can too easily come to seem quaintly irrelevant, or at least impossible to take very seriously, in the world as reconstituted by the microchip. I propose today to canvass five axioms of our constitutional law—five basic assumptions that I believe shape the way American constitutional scholars and judges view legal issues—and to examine how they can adapt to the cyberspace age. My conclusion (and I will try not to give away too much of the punch line here) is that the Framers of our Constitution were very wise indeed. They bequeathed us a framework for all seasons, a truly astonishing document whose principles are suitable for all times and all technological landscapes.

Axiom 1: There Is a Vital Difference Between Government and Private Action

The first axiom I will discuss is the proposition that the Constitution, with the sole exception of the Thirteenth Amendment prohibiting slavery, regulates action by the *government* rather than the conduct of *private* individuals and groups.

... [A]s a general proposition it is only what *governments* do, either through such rules or through the actions of public officials, that the United States Constitution constrains. And nothing about any new technology suddenly erases the Constitution's enduring value of restraining *government* above all else, and of protecting all private groups, large and small, from government.

It's true that certain technologies may become socially indispensable—so that equal or at least minimal access to basic computer power, for example, might be as significant a constitutional goal as equal or at least minimal access to the franchise, or to dispute resolution through the judicial system, or to elementary and secondary education. But all this means (or should mean) is that the Constitution's constraints on government must at times take the form of imposing *affirmative duties* to ensure access rather than merely enforcing *negative prohibitions* against designated sorts of invasion or intrusion.

Today, for example, the government is under an affirmative obligation to open up criminal trials to the press and the public, at least where there has not been a particularized finding that such openness would disrupt the proceedings. The government is also under an affirmative obligation to provide free legal assistance for indigent criminal defendants, to ensure speedy trials, to underwrite the cost of counting ballots at election time, and to desegregate previously segregated school systems. But these occasional affirmative obligations don't, or shouldn't, mean that the Constitution's axiomatic division between the realm of public power and the realm of private life should be jettisoned.

Nor would the "indispensability" of information technologies provide a license for government to impose strict content, access, pricing, and other types of regulation. *Books* are indispensable to most of us, for example—but it doesn't follow that government should therefore be able to regulate the content of what goes onto the shelves of *bookstores*. The right of a private bookstore owner to decide which books to stock and which to discard, which books to display openly and which to store in limited access areas, should remain inviolate. And note, incidentally, that this needn't make the bookstore owner a "publisher" who is liable for the words printed in the books on her shelves. It's a common fallacy to imagine that the moment a computer gateway or bulletin board begins to exercise powers of selection to control who may be on line, it must automatically assume the responsibilities of a newscaster, a broadcaster, or an author. For computer gateways and bulletin boards are really the "bookstores" of cyberspace; most of them organize and present information in a computer format, rather than generating more information content of their own.

Axiom 2: The Constitutional Boundaries of Private Property and Personality Depend on Variables Deeper Than Social Utility and Technological Feasibility

The second constitutional axiom, one closely related to the private–public distinction of the first axiom, is that a person's mind, body, and property belong *to that person* and not to the public as a whole. Some believe that cyberspace challenges that axiom because its entire premise lies in the existence of computers tied to electronic transmission networks that process digital information. Because such information can be easily replicated in series of "1"s and "0"s, anything that anyone has come up with in virtual reality can be infinitely reproduced. I can log on to a computer library, copy a "virtual book" to my computer disk, and send a copy to your computer without creating a gap on anyone's bookshelf. The same is true of valuable computer programs, costing hundreds of dollars, creating serious piracy problems. This feature leads some, like Richard Stallman of the Free Software Foundation, to argue that in cyberspace everything should be free—that information can't be owned. Others, of course, argue that copyright and patent protections of various kinds are needed in order for there to be incentives to create "cyberspace property" in the first place.

Needless to say, there are lively debates about what the optimal incentive package should be as a matter of legislative and social policy. But the only *constitutional issue*, at bottom, isn't the utilitarian or instrumental selection of an optimal policy. Social judgments about what ought to be subject to individual appropriation, in the sense used by John Locke and Robert Nozick, and what ought to remain in the open public domain, are first and foremost *political* decisions.

To be sure, there are some constitutional constraints on these political decisions. The Constitution does not permit anything and everything to be made into a *private commodity*. Votes, for example, theoretically cannot be bought and sold. Whether the Constitution itself should be read (or amended) so as to permit all basic medical care, shelter, nutrition, legal assistance and, indeed, computerized information services, to be treated as mere commodities, available only to the highest bidder, are all terribly hard questions—as the Eastern Europeans are now discovering as they attempt to draft their own constitutions. But these are not questions that should ever be confused with issues of what is technologically possible, about what is realistically enforceable, or about what is socially desirable.

Similarly, the Constitution does not permit anything and everything to be *socialized* and made into a public good available to whoever needs or "deserves" it most. I would hope, for example, that the government could not use its powers of eminent domain to "take" live body parts like eyes or kidneys or brain tissue for those who need transplants and would be expected to lead particularly productive lives. In any event, I feel certain that whatever constitutional right each of us has to inhabit his or her own body and to hold on to his or her own thoughts and creations should not depend solely on cost–benefit calculations, or on the availability of technological methods for painlessly effecting transfers or for creating good artificial substitutes.

Axiom 3: Government May Not Control Information Content

A third constitutional axiom, like the first two, reflects a deep respect for the integrity of each individual and a healthy skepticism toward government. The axiom is that, although information and ideas have real effects in the social world, it's not up to government to pick and choose for us in terms of the *content* of that information or the *value* of those ideas.

This notion is sometimes mistakenly reduced to the naive child's ditty that "sticks and stones may break my bones, but words can never hurt me." Anybody who's ever been called something awful by children in a schoolyard knows better than to believe any such thing. The real basis for First Amendment values isn't the false premise that information and ideas have no real impact, but the belief that information and ideas are *too important* to entrust to any government censor or overseer.

If we keep that in mind, and *only* if we keep that in mind, will we be able to see through the tempting argument that, in the Information Age, free speech is a luxury we can no longer afford. That argument becomes especially tempting in the context of cyberspace, where sequences of "0"s and "1"s may become virtual life forms. Computer "viruses" roam the information nets, attaching themselves to various programs and screwing up computer facilities. Creation of a computer virus involves writing a program; the program then replicates itself and mutates. The electronic code involved is very much like DNA. If information content is "speech," and if the First Amendment is to apply in cyberspace, then mustn't these viruses be "speech"—and mustn't their writing and dissemination be constitutionally protected? To avoid that nightmarish outcome, mustn't we say that the First Amendment is *inapplicable* to cyberspace?

The answer is no. Speech is protected, but deliberately yelling "Boo!" at a cardiac patient may still be prosecuted as murder. Free speech is a constitutional right, but handing a bank teller a hold-up note that says, "Your money or your life," may still be punished as robbery. Stealing someone's diary may be punished as theft—even if you intend to publish it in book form. And the Supreme Court, over the past fifteen years, has gradually brought advertising within the ambit of protected expression without preventing the government from protecting consumers from deceptive advertising. The lesson, in short, is that constitutional principles

512 CHAPTER 12 • Computer Ethics and the Internet

are subtle enough to bend to such concerns. They needn't be broken or tossed out.

Axiom 4: The Constitution Is Founded on Normative Conceptions of Humanity That Advances in Science and Technology Cannot "Disprove"

A fourth constitutional axiom is that the human spirit is something beyond a physical information processor. That axiom, which regards human thought processes as not fully reducible to the operations of a computer program, however complex, must not be confused with the silly view that, because computer operations involve nothing more than the manipulation of "on" and "off" states of myriad microchips, it somehow follows that government control or outright seizure of computers and computer programs threatens no First Amendment rights because human thought processes are not directly involved. To say that would be like saying that government confiscation of a newspaper's printing press and tomorrow morning's copy has nothing to do with speech but involves only a taking of metal, paper, and ink. Particularly if the seizure or the regulation is triggered by the content of the information being processed or transmitted, the First Amendment is of course fully involved. Yet this recognition that information processing by computer entails something far beyond the mere sequencing of mechanical or chemical steps still leaves a potential gap between what computers can do internally and in communication with one another—and what goes on within and between human minds. It is that gap to which this fourth axiom is addressed; the very existence of any such gap is, as I'm sure you know, a matter of considerable controversy.

What if people like the mathematician and physicist Roger Penrose, author of *The Emperor's New Mind*, are wrong about human minds? In that provocative recent book, Penrose disagrees with those Artificial Intelligence, or AI, gurus who insist that it's only a matter of time until human thought and feeling can be perfectly simulated or even replicated by a series of purely physical operations—that it's all just neurons firing and neurotransmitters flowing, all subject to perfect modeling in suitable computer systems. Would an adherent of that AI orthodoxy, someone whom Penrose fails to persuade, have to reject as irrelevant for cyberspace those constitutional protections that rest on the anti-AI premise that minds are *not* reducible to really fancy computers?

Consider, for example, the Fifth Amendment, which provides that "no person shall be … compelled in any criminal case to be a witness against himself." The Supreme Court has long held that suspects may be required, despite this protection, to provide evidence that is not "testimonial" in nature—blood samples, for instance, or even exemplars of one's handwriting or voice. Last year, in a case called *Pennsylvania v. Muniz*, the Supreme Court held that answers to even simple questions like "When was your sixth birthday?" are testimonial because such a question, however straightforward, nevertheless calls for the product of mental activity and therefore uses the suspect's mind against him. But what if science could eventually describe thinking as a process no more complex than, say, riding a bike or digesting a meal? Might the progress of neurobiology and computer science eventually overthrow the premises of the *Muniz* decision?

I would hope not. For the Constitution's premises, properly understood, are *normative* rather than *descriptive*. The philosopher David Hume was right in teaching that no "ought" can ever be logically derived from an "is." If we should ever abandon the Constitution's protection for the distinctively and universally human, it won't be because robotics or genetic engineering or computer science have led us to deeper truths, but rather because they have seduced us into more profound confusions. Science and technology open options, create possibilities, suggest incompatibilities, generate threats. They do not alter what is "right" or what is "wrong." The fact that those notions are elusive and subject to endless debate need not make them totally contingent on contemporary technology.

Axiom 5: Constitutional Principles Should Not Vary with Accidents of Technology

In a sense, that's the fifth and final constitutional axiom I would urge upon this gathering: that the Constitution's norms, at their deepest level, must be invariant under merely *technological* transformations. Our constitutional law evolves through judicial interpretation, case by case, in a process of reasoning by analogy from precedent. At its best, that process is ideally suited to seeing beneath the surface and extracting deeper principles from prior decisions. At its worst, though, the same process can get bogged down in superficial aspects of preexisting examples, fixating upon unessential features while overlooking underlying principles and values.

When the Supreme Court in 1928 first confronted wiretapping and held in *Olmstead v. United States* that such wiretapping involved no "search" or "seizure" within the meaning of the Fourth Amendment's prohibition of "unreasonable searches and seizures," the majority of the Court reasoned that the Fourth Amendment "itself shows that the search is to be of material things—the person, the house, his papers or his effects," and said that "there was no searching" when a suspect's phone was tapped because the Constitution's language "cannot be extended and expanded to include telephone wires reaching to the whole world from the defendant's house or office." After all, said the Court, the intervening wires "are not part of his house or office any more than are the highways along which they are stretched."...

It is easy to be pessimistic about the way in which the Supreme Court has reacted to technological change.... For example, when movies were invented, and for several decades thereafter, the Court held that movie exhibitions were not entitled to First Amendment protection. When community access cable TV was born, the Court hindered municipal attempts to provide it at low cost by holding that rules requiring landlords to install small cable boxes on their apartment buildings amounted to a compensable taking of property. And in *Red Lion v. FCC*, decided twenty-two years ago but still not repudiated today, the Court ratified government control of TV and radio broadcast content with the dubious logic that the scarcity of the electromagnetic spectrum justified not merely government policies to auction off, randomly allocate, or otherwise ration the spectrum according to neutral rules, but also much more intrusive and

content-based government regulation in the form of the so-called "fairness doctrine."

Although the Supreme Court and the lower federal courts have taken a somewhat more enlightened approach in dealing with cable television, these decisions for the most part reveal a curious judicial blindness, as if the Constitution had to be reinvented with the birth of each new technology. Judges interpreting a late 18th century Bill of Rights tend to forget that, unless its *terms* are read in an evolving and dynamic way, its *values* will lose even the *static* protection they once enjoyed. Ironically, *fidelity* to original values requires *flexibility* of textual interpretation....

Judicial error in this field tends to take the form of saying that, by using modern technology ranging from the telephone to the television to computers, we "assume the risk." But that typically begs the question. Justice Harlan, in a dissent penned two decades ago, wrote: "Since it is the task of the law to form and project, as well as mirror and reflect, we should not ... merely recite ... risks without examining the *desirability* of saddling them upon society." (*United States v. White*, 401 U.S. at 786). And, I would add, we should not merely recite risks without examining how imposing those risks comports with the Constitution's fundamental values of *freedom*, *privacy*, and *equality*.

Failing to examine just that issue is the basic error I believe federal courts and Congress have made:

- in regulating radio and TV broadcasting without adequate sensitivity to First Amendment values;
- in supposing that the selection and editing of video programs by cable operators might be less than a form of expression;
- in excluding telephone companies from cable and other information markets;
- in assuming that the processing of "0"s and "1"s by computers as they exchange data with one another is something less than "speech"; and
- in generally treating information processed electronically as though it were somehow less entitled to protection for that reason.

The lesson to be learned is that these choices and these mistakes are not dictated by the Constitution. They are decisions for us to make in interpreting that majestic charter, and in implementing the principles that the Constitution establishes.

CONCLUSION

If my own life as a lawyer and legal scholar could leave just one legacy, I'd like it to be the recognition that the Constitution *as a whole* "protects people, not places." If that is to come about, the Constitution as a whole must be read through a technologically transparent lens. That is, we must embrace, as a rule of construction or interpretation, a principle one might call the "cyber space corollary." It would make a suitable Twenty-seventh Amendment to the Constitution, one befitting the 200th anniversary of the Bill of Rights. Whether adopted all at once as a constitutional amendment, or accepted gradually as a principle of interpretation that I believe should obtain even without any formal change in the Constitution's language, the corollary I would propose would do for *technology* in 1991 what I believe the Constitution's Ninth Amendment, adopted in 1791, was meant to do for *text*.

The Ninth Amendment says: "The enumeration in the Constitution, of certain rights, shall not be construed to deny or disparage others retained by the people." That amendment provides added support for the long-debated, but now largely accepted, "right of privacy" that the Supreme Court recognized in such decisions as the famous birth control case of 1965, *Griswold v. Connecticut*. The Ninth Amendment's simple message is: The *text* used by the Constitution's authors and ratifiers does not exhaust the values our Constitution recognizes. Perhaps a Twenty-seventh Amendment could convey a parallel and equally simple message: The *technologies* familiar to the Constitution's authors and ratifiers similarly do not exhaust the *threats* against which the Constitution's core values must be protected.

The most recent amendment, the Twenty-sixth, adopted in 1971, extended the vote to 18-year-olds. It would be fitting, in a world where youth has been enfranchised, for a Twenty-seventh amendment to spell a kind of "childhood's end" for constitutional law. The Twenty-seventh Amendment, to be proposed for at least serious debate in 1991, would read simply:

This Constitution's protections for the freedoms of speech, press, petition, and assembly, and its protections against unreasonable searches and seizures and the deprivation of life, liberty, or property without due process of law, shall be construed as fully applicable without regard to the technological method or medium through which information content is generated, stored, altered, transmitted, or controlled.

♔ QUESTIONS FOR ANALYSIS

1. Tribe details several ways in which the courts have had difficulty grasping technological changes to adapt legal principles. Are there parallel problems in our development of ethical principles?

2. Tribe identifies several political decisions we face in society in the recognition of technological change, and he appeals to political philosophers we considered in Part I, especially John Locke and Robert Nozick. How should we proceed in developing those policies? Should we recognize a right of access to technology by all citizens in order to participate fully in our democracy? Should we expand the recognition of the public domain and fair use of intellectual property, so people would not have to pay so much money in royalties for the software, recordings, and writings of others?

3. In Axiom 4, Tribe appeals to the philosopher David Hume in arguing that new *descriptive* information, knowledge, or technology can never transform our *normative* standards. What does Tribe mean by that? Do you agree that new scientific or technological information does not force us to change our normative views, whether in the law or in ethics?

4. Assess Tribe's proposed Twenty-seventh Amendment to the Constitution. Is it written in such a way as to protect our core constitutional values, regardless of what technologies emerge in the future that we cannot today even imagine? Do you anticipate that some of those values will have to be relinquished in the face of new technologies?

Free Speech in Cyberspace

RICHARD A. SPINELLO

Richard A. Spinello, an associate research professor at the Carroll School of Management, Boston College, has published extensively on issues of ethics and law related to the Internet and cyberspace. In this excerpt from his book *Cyberethics: Morality and Law in Cyberspace*, he reviews a wide range of problematic free-speech issues, including pornography, filtering mechanisms to restrict content, hate speech, anonymous speech, and spam.

INTRODUCTION

The Internet has clearly expanded the potential for individuals to exercise their First Amendment right to freedom of expression. The 'net gives all of its users a vast expressive power if they choose to take advantage of it. For example, users can operate their own bulletin boards, public electronic newsletters, or establish a home page on the Web. According to Michael Godwin, the net "puts the full power of 'freedom of the press' into each individual's hands."[1] Or as the Supreme Court eloquently wrote in its *Reno v. ACLU* decision, the Internet enables an ordinary citizen to become "a pamphleteer, ... a town crier with a voice that resonates farther than it could from any soapbox."[2]

As a result, the issue of free speech and content control in cyberspace has emerged as arguably the most contentious moral problem of the nascent Information Age. Human rights such as free speech have taken a place of special prominence in this century. In some respects, these basic rights now collide with the state's inclination to reign in this revolutionary power enjoyed by Internet users. Although the United States has sought to suppress on-line pornography, the target of some European countries, such as France and Germany, has been hate speech.

In addition, speech is at the root of most other major ethical and public policy problems in cyberspace, including privacy, intellectual property, and security....

Those who pioneered Internet technology have consistently asserted that the right to free expression in cyberspace should have as broad a scope as possible. For many years, the government was reluctant to restrict or filter any form of information on the network for fear of stifling an atmosphere that thrives on the free and open exchange of ideas.

However, the increased use of the Internet, especially among more vulnerable segments of the population (such as young children), forced some public policy makers to rethink this laissez-faire approach. In the United States, the result has been several futile attempts to control Internet content through poorly crafted legislation. An unfortunate byproduct of this has been publicity and attention to this matter that is probably out of proportion to the depth or gravity of the problem.

Despite the calls for regulation, there is a powerful sentiment among many Internet stakeholders to maintain this status quo. The strongest voices continue to come from those who want to preserve the Internet's libertarian spirit and who insist that the surest way to endanger the vitality of this global network are onerous regulations and rules, which would stifle the creative impulses of its users and imperil this one last bastion of free, uninhibited expression....

PORNOGRAPHY IN CYBERSPACE

Before we discuss the U.S. Congress' recent efforts to regulate speech on the net we should be clear about what constitutes pornographic speech. There are two broad classes of such speech: (1) obscene speech, which is completely unprotected by the First Amendment, and (2) "indecent" speech, which is not obscene for adults but should be kept out of the hands of children under the age of seventeen. In *Miller v. California* (1973), the Supreme Court established a three-part test to determine whether or not speech fell in the first category and was obscene for everyone. To meet this test, speech had to satisfy the following conditions: (1) it depicts sexual (or excretory) acts explicitly prohibited by state law; (2) it appeals to prurient interests as judged by a reasonable person using community standards; and (3) it has no serious literary, artistic, social, political, or scientific value. Child pornography is an unambiguous example of obscene speech.

The second class of speech, often called *indecent* speech, is obscene for children but not for adults. The relevant legal case is *Ginsberg v. New York*, which upheld New York's law banning the sale of speech "harmful to minors" to anyone under the age of seventeen. The law in dispute in the Ginsberg case defined *harmful to minors* as follows: "that quality of any description or representation, in whatever from, of nudity, sexual conduct, sexual excitement, or sado-masochistic abuse, when it: (1) predominantly appeals to the prurient, shameful, or morbid interests of minors, and (2) is patently offensive to prevailing standards in the adult community as a whole with respect to what is suitable for minors, and (3) is utterly without redeeming social importance for minors." Although state legislatures have applied this case differently to their statutes prohibiting the sale of obscene material to minors, these criteria can serve as a general guide to what we classify as "Ginsberg" speech, which should be off limits to children under the age of seventeen.

PUBLIC POLICY OVERVIEW

The Communications Decency Act (or CDA I)

The ubiquity of both forms of pornography on the Internet is a challenge for lawmakers. As the quantity of communications grows in the realm of cyberspace, there is a much greater likelihood that people will become exposed to forms of speech or images that are offensive and potentially harmful. If you are seeking to send an e-mail to the President of the United States and accidentally retrieve the Web site www.whitehouse.com instead of www.whitehouse.gov, you will see what we mean. By some estimates, the Internet currently has about 280,000 sites that cater to various forms of pornography, and some sources report that there is an average of an additional 500 sites coming on-line everyday, hence the understandable temptation of governments to regulate and control free expression on the Internet to contain the negative effects of unfettered free speech on this medium. The Communications Decency Act (CDA), recently ruled unconstitutional by the U.S. Supreme Court, represented one such futile, and some say misguided, attempt at such regulation....

The CDA included several key provisions that restricted the distribution of sexually explicit material to children. It imposed criminal penalties on anyone who "initiates the transmission of any communication which is ... indecent, knowing that the recipient of the communication is under 18 years of age." It also criminalized the display of patently offensive sexual material "in a manner available to a person under 18 years of age"[3]...

A panel of federal judges in Philadelphia ruled unanimously that the CDA was a violation of the First and Fifth Amendments. The Justice Department appealed the case, which now became known as *Reno v. ACLU*, but to no avail. The Supreme Court agreed with the lower court's ruling, and in June 1997, it declared that this federal law was unconstitutional. The Court was especially concerned about the vagueness of this content-based regulation of speech. According to the majority opinion written by Justice Stevens, "We are persuaded that the CDA lacks the precision that the First Amendment requires when a statue regulates the content of speech. In order to deny minors access to potentially harmful speech, the CDA effectively suppresses a large amount of speech that adults have a constitutional right to receive and to address to one another."[4] Stevens also held that the free expression on the Internet is entitled to the highest level of First Amendment protection. This is in contrast to the more limited protections for other more pervasive media such as radio and broadcast and cable television, where the Court has allowed many government-imposed restrictions. In making this important distinction, the Court assumes that computer users have to actively seek offensive material, whereas they are more likely to encounter it accidentally on television or radio if it were so available.

CDA II

Most of those involved in the defeat of the CDA realized that the issue would not soon go away. Congress, still supported by public opinion, was sure to try again. In October 1998, they did try again, passing an omnibus budget package that included the Child Online Protection Act (COPA), a successor to the original CDA, which has become known as CDA II. The law was signed by President Clinton, and like its predecessor, it was immediately challenged by the ACLU. CDA II would make it illegal for the operators of commercial Web sites to make sexually explicit materials harmful to minors available to those younger than seventeen years of age. Commercial Web site operators would be required to collect an identification code, such as a credit card number, as proof of age before allowing viewers access to such material.

The ACLU and other opponents claimed that the law would lead to excessive self-censorship. CDA II would have a negative impact on the ability of these commercial Web sites to reach an adult audience. According to Max Hailperin, "There is no question that the COPA impairs commercial speakers' ability to cheaply, easily, and broadly communicate material to adults that is constitutionally protected as to the adults (non-obscene), though harmful to minors."[5] The law is more narrowly focused than CDA I because it attempts to define objectionable sexual content more carefully. Such content would lack "serious literary, artistic, political or scientific value" for those younger than seventeen years of age. However, the law's critics contend that it is still worded too broadly. Those critics also worry about what will happen if the law is arbitrarily or carelessly applied. For example, would some sites offering sexual education information violate the law?

In February 1999, a Philadelphia federal judge issued a preliminary injunction against CDA II, preventing it from going into effect. This judge accepted the argument that the law would lead to self-censorship and that "such a chilling effect could result in the censoring of constitutionally protected speech, which constitutes an irreparable harm to the plaintiffs." An appeal is considered likely, meaning that the ultimate resolution will have to await the Supreme Court's decision.

At the heart of the debate about the CDA and content regulation is the basic question … about how the Internet should be controlled. Should government impose the kind of central controls embodied in this legislation? Or should the Internet be managed and controlled through a more bottoms-up, user-oriented approach, with users empowered to develop their own solutions tailored to their own needs and value systems? One advantage of the latter approach is that such controls are more consistent with the Internet's decentralized network architecture. For many users, decentralism in the area of content control seems preferable to formal state regulations. It respects civil liberties and leaves the opportunity for content control in the hands of those most capable of exercising it.

However, reliance on a decentralized solution is certainly not without opposition and controversy. If we empower users to control Internet content in some ways, we are still left with many questions. If we assert that the purpose of censoring the Internet is the preservation of the community's values, how do we define *community*? Also, how do we ascertain what the community's values really are? Finally, can we trust technology to help solve the problem or will it make matters even worse?

AUTOMATING CONTENT CONTROLS

Nonetheless, thanks to the rulings against CDA I and II, the burden of content control is now shifting to parents and local organizations. This communal power has raised some concerns. To what extent should local communities and institutions (such as schools, prisons, libraries, and so on) assume direct responsibility for controlling content on the

Internet? Libraries, for example, must consider whether it is appropriate to use filtering software to protect young patrons from pornography on the Internet. Is this a useful and prudent way to uphold local community or institutional standards? Or does this sort of censorship compromise a library's traditional commitment to the free flow of ideas?

There are two broad areas of concern about the use of content controls that need elaboration. The first area concerns the ethical probity of censorship itself, even when it is directed at the young. There is a growing tendency to recognize a broad spectrum of rights, even for children, and to criticize parents, educators, and politicians who are more interested in imposing their value systems on others than in protecting vulnerable children....

Lurking in the background of this debate is the question of whether children have a First Amendment right to access indecent materials. Legal scholars have not reached a consensus about this, but if children do have such a right, it would be much more difficult to justify filtering out indecent materials in libraries or educational institutions. One school of thought about this issue is that a child's free speech rights should be proportionate to his or her age. The older the child, the more problematic are restrictions on indecent material.

The second area of concern pertains to the suitability of the blocking methods and other automated controls used to accomplish this censorship. Two basic problems arise with the use of blocking software. The first problem is the unreliability and lack of precision that typifies most of these products; there are no perfect or foolproof devices for filtering out obscene material. Programs like the popular SurfWatch operate by comparing Web site addresses to a list of prohibited sites that are known to contain pornographic material. SurfWatch currently prohibits more than 30,000 Web sites. However, this filtering program is less effective with Usenet newsgroups (electronic bulletin boards or chat rooms). SurfWatch depends on the name of the newsgroup to decide whether it should be banned; thus, an earlier version missed a chat room that displays pornographic material but goes under the name alt.kids-talk.penpals.

Another problem is that these blocking programs can be used to enforce a code of political correctness unbeknownst to parents or librarians who choose to install them. Sites that discuss AIDS, homosexuality, and related topics are routinely blocked by certain filtering programs. Often, these programs are not explicit or forthright about their blocking criteria, which greatly compounds this problem....

It is never easy to advocate censorship at any level of society precisely because the right to free expression is so valuable and cherished. However, proponents of automated content controls argue that all human rights, including the right to free expression, are limited by each other and by other aspects of the common good, which can be called *public morality*. According to this perspective, parents and schools are acting prudently when they choose to *responsibly* implement filtering technologies to help preserve and promote the values of respect for others and appropriate sexual conduct that are part of our public morality. Preserving free speech and dealing with sexually explicit material will always be a problem in a free and pluralistic society, and this is one way of achieving a proper balance when the psychological health of young children is at stake.

HATE SPEECH

The rapid expansion of hate speech on the Web raises similar problems and controversies. Many groups, such as white supremacists and anarchists, have Web sites that advocate their particular point of view. Some of these sites are blatantly anti-Semitic, whereas others are dominated by Holocaust revisionists who claim that the Holocaust never happened. On occasion, these sites can be especially virulent and outrageous, such as the Web site of the Charlemagne Hammerskins. The first scene reveals a man disguised in a ski mask who is bearing a gun and standing next to a swastika. The site has this ominous warning for its visitor: "Be assured, we still have one-way tickets to Auschwitz."

Some hate Web sites take the form of computer games, such as Doom and Castle Wolfenstein, which have been constructed to include African Americans, Jews, or homosexuals as targets of violence. In one animated game, the Dancing Baby, which became a popular television phenomenon, has been depicted as the "white power baby."

In the United States, the most widely publicized of these hate speech sites are those that attack doctors who perform abortions. Some of these sites are especially menacing and venomous, such as "The Nuremberg Files," which features a "Wanted" list of abortion doctors. The site's authors contend that they are not advocating violence but only expressing their opinion, albeit in a graphic format.

What can be done about this growing subculture of hate on the Internet? The great danger is that the message of hate and bigotry, once confined to reclusive, powerless groups, can now be spread more efficiently in cyberspace. Unlike obscenity and libel, hate speech is not illegal under U.S. federal law and is fully protected by the First Amendment. Even speech that incites hatred of a particular group is legally acceptable. The only exception to this is the use of "fighting words," which were declared beyond the purview of the First Amendment by the Supreme Court. Such speech, however, must threaten a clear and present danger. In the controversial case of the anti-abortion Web sites, a federal court recently ruled that the site's content was too intimidating and hence was not protected by the First Amendment. But in general, censorship of on-line hate speech is inconsistent with the First Amendment.

On the other hand, in European countries like Germany and France, anti-Semitic, Nazi-oriented Web sites are illegal. In Germany, the government has required ISPs to eliminate these sites under the threat of prosecution. Critics of this approach argue that it is beyond the capability of ISPs to control content in such a vast region as the World Wide Web. It is also illegal for Internet companies to ship Nazi materials into Germany. This means that Amazon.com should not be selling books like Hitler's *Mein Kampf* to its German customers, although this restriction too will be difficult to enforce.

Although government regulation and explicit laws about hate speech are suitable for some countries, an alternative to government regulation is once again reliance on user empowerment and *responsible* filtering that does not erroneously exclude legitimate political speech. Parents and certain private and religious institutions might want to seize the initiative to shield young children

and sensitive individuals from some of this material such as virulent anti-Semitism.

However, even more caution must be exercised in this case because the distinction between hate speech and unpopular or unorthodox political opinion is sometimes difficult to make. A rule of thumb is that hate speech Web sites are those that attack, insult, and demean whole segments of the population, such as Jews, Italians, African-Americans, whites, homosexuals, and so forth. Many sites will fall in a nebulous gray area, and this will call for conscientiousness and discretion on the part of those charged with labeling those sites.

ANONYMOUS SPEECH

Anonymous communication in cyberspace is enabled largely through the use of anonymous remailers, which strip off the identifying information on an e-mail message and substitute an anonymous code or a random number. By encrypting a message and then routing that message through a series of anonymous remailers, a user can rest assured that his or her message will remain anonymous and confidential. This process is called *chained remailing*. The process is effective because none of the remailers will have the key to read the encrypted message; neither the recipient nor any remailers (except the first) in the chain can identify the sender; the recipient cannot connect the sender to the message unless every single remailer in the chain cooperates. This would assume that each remailer kept a log of their incoming and outgoing mail, which is highly unlikely....

Do we really need to ensure that digital anonymity is preserved, especially since it is so often a shield for subversive activities? It would be difficult to argue convincingly that anonymity is a core human good, utterly indispensable for human flourishing and happiness. One can surely conceive of people and societies where anonymity is not a factor for their happiness. However, although anonymity may not be a primary good, it is surely a secondary one because *for some people in some circumstances*, a measure of anonymity is important for the exercise of their rational life plan and for human flourishing. The proper exercise of freedom, and especially free expression, requires the support of anonymity in some situations. Unless the speaker or author can choose to remain anonymous, opportunities for free expression become limited for various reasons and that individual may be forced to remain mute on critical matters. Thus, without the benefit of anonymity, the value of freedom is constrained.

We can point to many specific examples in support of the argument that *anonymous free expression* deserves protection. Social intolerance may require some individuals to rely on anonymity to communicate openly about an embarrassing medical condition or an awkward disability. Whistle-blowers may be understandably reluctant to come forward with valuable information unless they can remain anonymous. And political dissent even in a democratic society that prizes free speech may be impeded unless it can be done anonymously. Anonymity then has an incontestable value in the struggle against repression and even against more routine corporate and government abuses of power. In the conflict in Kosovo, for example, some individuals relied on anonymous programs (such as anonymizer.com) to describe atrocities perpetrated against ethnic Albanians. If the Serbians were able to trace the identity of these individuals, their lives would have been in grave danger.

Thus, although there is a cost to preserving anonymity, its central importance in human affairs is certainly beyond dispute. It is a positive good; that is, it possesses positive qualities that render it worthy to be valued. At a minimum, it is valued as an instrumental good, as a means of achieving the full actualization of free expression.

Anonymous communication, of course, whether facilitated by remailers or by other means, does have its drawbacks. It can be abused by criminals or terrorists seeking to communicate anonymously to plot their crimes. It also permits cowardly users to communicate without civility or to libel someone without accountability and with little likelihood of apprehension by law enforcement authorities. Anonymity can also be useful for revealing trade secrets or violating other intellectual property laws. In general, secrecy and anonymity are not beneficial for society if they are overused or used improperly.…

Although we admit that too much secrecy is problematic, the answer is not to eliminate all secrecy and make everything public and

transparent, which could be the inevitable result of this loss of digital anonymity. Nonetheless, it cannot be denied that anonymity has its disadvantages and that digital anonymity and an unfettered Internet can be exploited for many forms of mischief. Therefore, governments are tempted to sanction the deployment of architectures that will make Internet users more accountable and less able to hide behind the shield of anonymity.

Despite the potential for abuse, however, there are cogent reasons for eschewing the adoption of those architectures and protecting the right to anonymous free speech. A strong case can be put forth that the costs of banning anonymous speech in cyberspace are simply too high in an open and democratic society. The loss of anonymity may very well diminish the power of that voice that now resonates so loudly in cyberspace. As a result, regulators must proceed with great caution in this area.…

SPAM AS COMMERCIAL FREE SPEECH

Spam refers to unsolicited, promotional e-mail, usually sent in bulk to thousands or millions of Internet users. Quite simply, it is junk e-mail that is usually a significant annoyance to its recipients. The major difference between electronic junk mail and paper junk mail is that the per copy cost of sending the former is so much lower. There are paper, printing, and postage charges for each piece of regular junk mail, but the marginal cost of sending an additional piece of junk e-mail is negligible. For example, some direct marketers who specializes in spam charge their clients a fee as low as $400 to send out several million messages.

But spam is not cost free. The problem is that the lion's share of these costs are externalities, that is, they are costs borne involuntarily by others. As Robert Raisch has observed, spam is "postage-due marketing."[6] The biggest cost associated with spam is the consumption of computer resources. For example, when someone sends out spam the messages must sit on a disk somewhere, and this means that valuable disk space is being filled with unwanted mail. Also, many users must pay for each message received or for each disk block used. Others pay for the time they are connected to the

Internet, time that can be wasted downloading and deleting spam. As the volume of spam grows and commercial use of the Internet expands, these costs will continue their steady increase. Furthermore, when spam is sent through ISPs they must bear the costs of delivery. This amounts to wasted network bandwidth and the use of system resources such as disk storage space along with the servers and transfer networks involved in the transmission process....

Should all bulk e-mail, even noncommerical communications, be considered spam? If the Internet is to realize its full potential as a "democratizing force," shouldn't some forms of bulk e-mail be permitted, both morally and legally? What should be the decisive factors in determining when bulk e-mail is intrusive spam or a legitimate form of communication?...

POSTSCRIPT

Spam, pornography, libel, hate speech—all are problematic forms of free expression that pose formidable challenges to cyberspace jurisprudence, which seeks to balance individual rights with the public good. Ideally, of course, individuals and organizations should regulate their own expression by refraining from hate speech, refusing to disseminate pornography to children, and repressing the temptation to use spam as a means of advertising goods or services. In the absence of such self-restraint, Internet stakeholders must make difficult decisions about whether to shield themselves from unwanted speech, whether it be crude obscenities or irksome junk e-mail.

Top-down government regulations such as the CDA II or laws that ban junk e-mail represent one method for solving this problem. Sophisticated filtering devices, which will undoubtedly continue to improve in their precision and accuracy, offer a different, but more chaotic, alternative. As we have been at pains to insist here, whatever combination of constraints are used—code, law, market, or norms—full respect must be accorded to key moral values such as personal autonomy; hence the need for nuanced ethical reflection about how these universal moral standards can best be preserved as we develop effective constraints for aberrant behavior in cyberspace. Otherwise, our worst apprehensions about the tyranny of the code *or* the laws of cyberspace may be realized.

Another option, of course, is to refrain from the temptation to take *any* action against these controversial forms of speech in cyberspace. Some civil libertarians convincingly argue that Internet stakeholders should eschew regulations and filtering and leave the Internet as unfettered as possible. We should tolerate nuisance speech on the Internet just as we tolerate it in the physical world.

NOTES

1. Godwin, M. 1998. *CyberRights*. New York: Random House, p. 16.
2. *ACLU v. Reno*, 521 U.S. p. 870 (1997).
3. See *Communications Decency Act*, 47 U.S.C. p. 223 (d)(1)(B).
4. *ACLU v. Reno*, p. 882.
5. Halperin, M. 1999. The COPA BATTLE AND THE FUTURE OF FREE SPEECH. *Communications of the ACM* p. 42(1): 25.
6. Raisch, R. *Postage due marketing: An Internet company white paper*. Available http://www.internet.com:2010/marketing/postage.html

⚜ QUESTIONS FOR ANALYSIS

1. How would you propose to restrict access by children to pornography in cyberspace without interfering with the rights of adults to access this material? Do you support the approach taken by Congress or the emphasis on free speech upheld by the courts with regard to the Communications Decency Acts I and II? Or do you support unrestricted access by children to all material?
2. Should hate speech be protected by the First Amendment? If we can prove that it provokes illegal activity against certain groups, should we restrict or prohibit it?
3. Should anonymous speech be protected, especially if we learn that it is being used by terrorists and other criminals? Would prohibiting it for them infringe on the rights of others with legitimate noncriminal reasons for communicating anonymously?
4. Should spam be protected as commercial free speech?

Are Computer Hacker Break-ins Ethical?

EUGENE H. SPAFFORD

Eugene H. Spafford is a professor of computer science at Purdue University, where he has taught since 1987. He also has courtesy appointments at Purdue in philosophy, communication, electrical and computer engineering, and political science. Spafford has consulted extensively with numerous large corporations and government agencies on computer security and cybercrime. He is also the executive director of the Purdue University Center for Education and Research in Information Assurance and Security (CERIAS).

As a computer scientist, Spafford is concerned to promote ethical behavior in the profession. He examines several rationalizations offered by hackers for their behavior and challenges all of them.

Introduction

On November 2,1988, a program was run on the Internet that replicated itself on thousands of machines, often loading them to the point where they were unable to process normal requests (Seeley, 1989; Spafford, 1989a, 1989b). This Internet Worm program was stopped in a matter of hours, but the controversy engendered by its release raged for years. Other recent incidents, such as the "wily hackers"[1] tracked by Cliff Stoll (1989), the "Legion of Doom" members who are alleged to have stolen telephone company 911 software (Schwartz, 1990), and the growth of the computer virus problem (Denning, 1991; Hoffman, 1990; Spafford, Heaphy, and Ferbrache, 1989; Stang, 1990) have added to the discussion. What constitutes improper access to computers? Are some break-ins ethical? Is there such a thing as a "moral hacker" (Baird, Baird, and Ranauro, 1987).

It is important that we discuss these issues. The continuing evolution of our technological base and our increasing reliance on computers for critical tasks suggests that future incidents may well have more serious consequences than those we have seen to date. With human nature as varied and extreme as it is, and with the technology as available as it is, we must expect to experience more of these incidents.

In this [article], I introduce a few of the major issues that these incidents have raised, and present some related arguments. For clarification, I have separated a few issues that often have been combined when debated; it is possible that most people are in agreement on some of these points once they are viewed as individual issues.

What Is Ethical?

Webster's Collegiate Dictionary defines ethics as: "The discipline dealing with what is good and bad and with moral duty and obligation." More simply, it is the study of what is right to do in a given situation—what we ought to do. Alternatively, it is sometimes described as the study of what is good and how to achieve that good. To suggest whether an act is right or wrong, we need to agree on an ethical system that is easy to understand and apply as we consider the ethics of computer break-ins.

Reprinted from *Journal of Systems and Software*, 17(1), 41–47, Eugene H. Spafford, "Are Computer Hacker Break-ins Ethical?" © 1971, with permission from Elsevier.
[1]I realize that many law-abiding individuals consider themselves hackers—a term formerly used as a compliment. The press and general public have coopted the term, however, and it is now commonly viewed as a pejorative. Herein, I use the word as the general public now uses it.

Philosophers have been trying for thousands of years to define right and wrong, and I will not make yet another attempt at such a definition. Instead, I suggest that we make the simplifying assumption that we can judge the ethical nature of an act by applying a deontological assessment: Regardless of the effect, is the act itself ethical? Would we view that act as sensible and proper if everyone were to engage in it? Although this may be too simplistic a model (and it can certainly be argued that other ethical philosophies also may be applied), it is a good first approximation for purposes of discussion. If you are unfamiliar with any other formal ethical evaluation method, try applying this assessment to the points I raise later in this paper. If the results are obviously unpleasant or dangerous in the large, then they should be considered unethical as individual acts.

Note that this philosophy assumes that right is determined by actions and not by results. Some ethical philosophies assume that the ends justify the means; our current society does not operate by such a philosophy, although many individuals do. As a society, we profess to believe that "it isn't whether you win or lose, it's how you play the game." This is why we are concerned with issues of due process and civil rights, even for chose espousing repugnant views and committing heinous acts. The process is important no matter the outcome, although the outcome may help to resolve a choice between two almost equal courses of action.

Philosophies that consider the results of an act as the ultimate measure of good are often impossible to apply because of the difficulty in understanding exactly what results from any arbitrary activity. Consider an extreme example: The government orders a hundred cigarette smokers, chosen at random, to be beheaded on live nationwide television. The result might well be that many hundreds of thousands of other smokers would quit "cold turkey," thus prolonging their lives. It might also prevent hundreds of thousands of people from ever starting to smoke, thus improving the health and longevity of the general populace. The health of millions of other people would improve because they would no longer be subjected to secondary smoke. The overall impact on the environment would be very favorable; tons of air and ground pollutants would no longer be released by smokers or tobacco companies.

Yet, despite the great good this might hold for society, everyone, except for a few extremists, would condemn such an act as immoral. We would likely object even if only one person was executed. It would not matter what the law might be on such a matter; we would not feel that the act was morally correct, nor would we view the ends as justifying the means.

Note that we would be unable to judge the morality of such an action by evaluating the results, because we would not know the full scope of those results. Such an act might have effects, favorable or otherwise, on issues of law, public health, tobacco use, and TV shows for decades or centuries to follow. A system of ethics that considered primarily the results of our actions would not allow us to evaluate our current activities at the time when we would need such guidance; if we are unable to discern the appropriate course of action prior to its commission, then our system of ethics is of little or no value to us. To obtain ethical guidance, we must base our actions primarily on evaluations of the actions and not on the possible results.

More to the point of this [article], if we attempt to judge the morality of a computer break-in based on the sum total of all future effect, we would be unable to make such a judgement, either for a specific incident or for the general class of acts. In part, this is because it is so difficult to determine the long-term effects of various actions and to discern their causes. We cannot know, for instance, if increased security awareness and restrictions are better for society in the long term, or whether these additional restrictions will result in greater costs and annoyance when using computer systems. We also do not know how many of these changes are directly traceable to incidents of computer break-ins.

One other point should be made here: It is undoubtedly possible to imagine scenarios where a computer break-in would be considered to be the preferable course of action. For instance, if vital medical data were on a computer and necessary to save someone's life in an emergency, but the authorized users of the system could not be located, breaking into the system might well be considered the right thing to do. However, that action does not make the break-in ethical. Rather, such situations occur when a greater wrong would undoubtedly occur if the unethical act were not committed. Similar reasoning applies to situations such as killing in self-defense. In the following discussion, I assume that such conflicts are not the root cause of the break-ins; such situations should very rarely present themselves.

Motivations

Individuals who break into computer systems or who write vandalware usually use one of a few rationalizations for their actions. (See, for example, Landreth [1984] and the discussion in Adelaide et al. [1990].) Most of these individuals would never think to walk down a street, trying every door to find one unlocked, then search through the drawers of the furniture inside. Yet, these same people seem to give no second thought to making repeated attempts at guessing passwords to accounts they do not own, and once on to a system, browsing through the files on disk.

These computer burglars often present the same reasons for their actions in an attempt to rationalize their activities as morally justified. I present and refute some of the most commonly used justifications in what follows; motives involving theft and revenge are not uncommon, and their moral nature is simple to discern, so I do not include them here.

The Hacker Ethic

Many hackers argue that they follow an ethic that both guides their behavior and justifies their break-ins. This hacker ethic states, in part, that all information should be free (Baird et al., 1987). This view holds that information belongs to everyone, and there should be no boundaries or restraints to prevent anyone from examining information. Richard Stallman (1986) states much the same thing in his GNU Manifesto. He and others have further stated in various forums that if information is free, it logically follows that there should be no such thing as intellectual property, and no need for security.

What are the implications and consequences of such a philosophy? First and foremost, it raises some disturbing questions of privacy. If all information is (or should be) free, then privacy is no longer a possibility. For information to be free to everyone, and for individuals to no longer be able to claim it as property, means that anyone may access the information if they please. Furthermore, as it is no longer property of any individual, that means that anyone can alter the information. Items such as bank balances, medical records, credit histories, employment records, and defense information all cease to be controlled. If someone controls information and controls who may access it, the information is obviously not free. But without that control, we would no longer be able to trust the accuracy of the information.

In a perfect world, this lack of privacy and control might not be a cause for concern. However, if all information were to be freely available and modifiable, imagine how much damage and chaos would be caused in our real world by such a philosophy! Our whole society is based on information whose accuracy must be ensured. This includes information held by banks and other financial institutions, credit bureaus, medical agencies and professionals, government agencies such as the IRS, law enforcement agencies, and educational institutions. Clearly, treating all their information as "free" would be unethical in any world where there might be careless and unethical individuals.

Economic arguments can be made against this philosophy, too, in addition to the overwhelming need for privacy and control of information accuracy. Information is not universally free. It is held as property because of privacy concerns, and because it is often collected and developed at great expense. Development of a new algorithm, program, or collection of a specialized database may involve the expenditure of vast sums of time and effort. To claim that it is free or should be free is to express a naive and unrealistic view of the world. To use this as a justification for computer break-ins is clearly unethical. Although not all information currently treated as private or controlled as proprietary needs such protection, that does not justify unauthorized access to it or to any other data.

The Security Arguments

These arguments are the most common ones within the computer community. One common argument was the same one used most often by people attempting to defend the author of the Internet Worm program in 1988: Break-ins illustrate security problems to a community that will otherwise not note the problems.

In the Worm case, one of the first issues to be discussed widely in Internet mailing lists dealt with the intent of the perpetrator—exactly why the Worm program had been written and released. Explanations put forth by members of the community ranged from simple accident to the actions of a sociopath. A common explanation was that the Worm was designed to illustrate security defects to a community that would not otherwise pay attention. This was not supported by the testimony during the author's trial, nor is it supported by past experience of system administrators.

The Worm author, Robert T. Morris, appears to have been well-known at some universities and major companies, and his talents were generally respected. Had he merely explained the problems or offered a demonstration to these people, he would have been listened to with considerable attention. The month before he released the Worm program on the Internet, he discovered and disclosed a bug in the file transfer program ftp; news of the flaw spread rapidly, and an official fix was announced and available within a matter of weeks. The argument that no one would listen to his report of security weaknesses is clearly fallacious.

In the more general case, this security argument is also without merit. Although some system administrators might have been complacent about the security of their systems before the Worm incident, most computer vendors, managers of government computer installations, and system administrators at major colleges and universities have been attentive to reports of security problems. People wishing to report a problem with the security of a system need not exploit it to report it. By way of analogy, one does not set fire to the neighborhood shopping center to bring attention to a fire hazard in one of the stores, and then try to justify the act by claiming that firemen would otherwise never listen to reports of hazards.

The most general argument that some people make is that the individuals who break into system are performing a service by exposing security flaws, and thus should be encouraged or even rewarded. This argument is severely flawed in several ways. First, it assumes that there is some compelling need to force users to install security fixes on their systems, and thus computer burglars are justified in "breaking and entering" activities. Taken to extremes, it suggests that it would be perfectly acceptable to engage in such activities on a continuing basis, so long as they might expose security flaws. This completely loses sight of the purpose of the computers in the first place—to serve as tools and resources, not as exercises in security. The same reasoning implies that vigilantes have the right to attempt to break into the homes in my neighborhood on a continuing basis to demonstrate that they are susceptible to burglars.

Another flaw with this argument is that it completely ignores the technical and economic factors that prevent many sites from upgrading or correcting their software. Not every site has the resources to install new system software or to correct existing software. At many sites, the systems are run as turnkey systems, employed as tools and maintained by the vendor. The owners and users of these machines simply do not have the ability to correct or maintain their systems independently, and they are unable to afford custom software support from their vendors. To break into such systems, with or without damage, is effectively to trespass into places of business; to do so in a vigilante effort to force the owners to upgrade their security structure is presumptuous and reprehensible. A burglary is not justified, morally or legally, by an argument that the victim has poor locks and was therefore "asking for it."

A related argument has been made that vendors are responsible for the maintenance of their software, and that such security breaches should immediately require vendors to issue corrections to their customers, past, and present. The claim is made that without highly visible break-ins, vendors will not produce or distribute necessary fixes to software. This attitude is naive, and is neither economically feasible nor technically workable. Certainly, vendors should bear some responsibility for the adequacy of their software (Mcilroy, 1990), but they should not be responsible for fixing every possible flaw in every possible configuration.

Many sites customize their software or otherwise run systems incompatible with the latest vendor releases. For a vendor to be able to provide quick response to security problems, it would be necessary for each customer to run completely standardized software and hardware mixes to ensure the correctness of vendor-supplied updates. Not only would this be considerably less attractive for many customers and contrary to their usual practice, but the increased cost of such "instant" fix distribution would add to the price of such a system—greatly increasing the cost borne by the customer. It is unreasonable to expect the user community to sacrifice flexibility and pay a much higher cost per unit simply for faster corrections to the occasional security breach. That assumes it was even possible for the manufacturer to find those customers and supply them with fixes in a timely manner, something unlikely in a market where machines and software are often repackaged, traded, and resold.

The case of the Internet Worm is a good example of the security argument and its flaws. It further stands as a good example of the conflict between ends and means valuations of ethics. Various people have argued that the Worm's author did us a favor by exposing security flaws. At Mr. Morris's trial on federal charges stemming from the incident, the defense attorneys also argued that their client should not be punished because of the good the Worm did in exposing those flaws. Others, including the prosecuting attorneys for the government, argued that the act itself was wrong no matter what the outcome. Their contention has been that the result does not justify the act itself, nor does the defense's argument encompass all the consequences of the incident.

This is certainly true; the complete results of the incident are still not known. There have been many other break-ins and network worms since November 1988, perhaps inspired by the media coverage of that incident. More attempts will possibly be made, in part inspired by Mr. Morris's act.

Some sites on the Internet have restricted access to their machines, and others were removed from the network; I have heard of sites where a decision has been made not to pursue a connection, even though this will hinder research and operations. Combined with the many decades of person-hours devoted to cleaning up afterward, this seems to be a high price to pay for a claimed "favor".

The legal consequences of this act are also not yet known. For instance, many bills were introduced into Congress and state legislatures in subsequent years as a (partial) result of these incidents. One piece of legislation introduced into the House of Representatives, HR-5061, entitled "The Computer Virus Eradication Act of 1988," was the first in a series of legislative actions that had the potential to affect significantly the computer profession. In particular, HR-5061 was notable because its wording would have prevented it from being applied to true computer viruses.[2] The passage of similar well-intentioned but poorly defined legislation could have a major negative effect on the computing profession as a whole.

The Idle System Argument

Another argument put forth by system hackers is that they are simply making use of idle machines. They argue that because some systems are not used at any level near their capacity, the hacker is somehow entitled to use them.

This argument is also flawed. First of all, these systems usually are not in service to provide a general-purpose user environment. Instead, they are in use in commerce, medicine, public safety, research, and government functions. Unused capacity is present for future needs and sudden surges of activity, not for the support of outside individuals. Imagine if large numbers of people without a computer were to take advantage of a system with idle processor capacity. The system would quickly be overloaded and severely degraded or unavailable for the rightful, owners. Once on the system, it would be difficult (or impossible) to oust these

---

[2]It provided penalties only in cases where programs were introduced into computer systems; a computer virus is a segment of code attached to an existing program that modifies other programs to include a copy of itself (Spafford et al., 1989).

individuals if sudden extra capacity was needed by the rightful owners. Even the largest machines available today would not provide sufficient capacity to accommodate such activity on any large scale.

I am unable to think of any other item that someone may buy and maintain, only to have others claim a right to use it when it is idle. For instance, the thought of someone walking up to my expensive car and driving off in it simply because it is not currently being used is ludicrous. Likewise, because I am away at work, it is not proper to hold a party at my house because it is otherwise not being used. The related positions that unused computing capacity is a shared resource, and that my privately developed software belongs to everyone, are equally silly (and unethical) positions.

The Student Hacker Argument

Some trespassers claim that they are doing no harm and changing nothing—they are simply learning about how computer systems operate. They argue that computers are expensive, and that they are merely furthering their education in a cost-effective manner. Some authors of computer viruses claim that their creations are intended to be harmless, and that they are simply learning how to write complex programs.

There are many problems with these arguments. First, as an educator, I claim that writing vandalware or breaking into a computer and looking at the files has almost nothing to do with computer education. Proper education in computer science and engineering involves intensive exposure to fundamental aspects of theory, abstraction, and design techniques. Browsing through a system does not expose someone to the broad scope or theory and practice in computing, nor does it provide the critical feedback so important to a good education (see Denning et al., 1989; Tucker et al., 1991). Neither does writing a virus or worm program and releasing it into an unsupervised environment provide any proper educational experience. By analogy, stealing cars and joyriding does not provide one with an education in mechanical engineering, nor does pouring sugar in the gas tank.

Furthermore, individuals "learning" about a system cannot know how everything operates and what results from their activities. Many systems have been damaged accidentally by ignorant (or careless) intruders; most of the damage from computer viruses (and the Internet Worm) appears to be caused by unexpected interactions and program faults. Damage to medical systems, factory control, financial information, and other computer systems could have drastic and far-ranging effects that have nothing to do with education, and certainly could not be considered harmless.

A related refutation of the claim has to do with knowledge of the extent of the intrusion. If I am the person responsible for the security of a critical computer system, I cannot assume that any intrusion is motivated solely by curiosity and that nothing has been harmed. If I know that the system has been compromised, I must fear the worst and perform a complete system check for damages and changes. I cannot take the word of the intruder, for any intruder who actually caused damage would seek to hide it by claiming that he or she was "just looking." To regain confidence in the correct behavior of my system, I must expend considerable energy to examine and verify every aspect of it.

Apply our universal approach to this situation and imagine if this "educational" behavior was widespread and commonplace. The result would be that we would spend all our time verifying our systems and never would be able to trust the results fully, clearly, this is not good, and thus we must conclude that these "educational" motivations are also unethical.

The Social Protector Argument

One last argument, more often heard in Europe than in the United States, is that hackers break into systems to watch for instances of data abuse and to help keep "Big Brother" at bay. In this sense, the hackers are protectors rather than criminals. Again, this assumes that the ends justify the means. It also assumes that the hackers are actually able to achieve some good end.

Undeniably, there is some misuse of personal data by corporations and by the government. The increasing use of computer-based record systems and networks may lead to further abuses. However, it is not clear that breaking into these systems will aid in righting the wrongs. If anything, it will cause those agencies to become even more secretive and use the break-ins as an excuse for more restricted access. Break-ins and vandalism have not resulted in new open records laws, but they have resulted in the introduction and passage of new criminal statutes. Not only has such activity failed to deter "Big Brother," but it has also resulted in significant segments of the public urging more laws and more aggressive law enforcement—the direct opposite of the purported goal.

It is also not clear that these are the individuals we want "protecting" us. We need to have the designers and users of the systems—trained computer professionals—concerned about our rights and aware of the dangers involved with the inappropriate use of computer monitoring and record keeping. The threat is a relatively new one, as computers and networks have become widely used only in the last few decades. It will take some time for awareness of the dangers to spread throughout the profession. Clandestine efforts to breach the security of computer systems do nothing to raise the consciousness of the appropriate individuals. Worse, they associate that commendable goal (heightened concern) with criminal activity (computer break-ins), discouraging proactive behavior by the individuals in the best positions to act in our favor. Perhaps it is in this sense that computer break-ins and vandalism are most unethical and damaging.

Concluding Remarks

I have argued here that computer break-ins, even when no obvious damage results, are unethical. This must be the considered conclusion even if the result is an improvement in security, because the activity itself is disruptive and immoral. The results of the act should be considered separately from the act itself, especially when we consider how difficult it is to understand all the effects resulting from such an act.

Of course, I have not discussed every possible reason for a break-in There might well be an instance, where a break-in might be necessary to save a life or to preserve national security. In

such cases, to perform one wrong act to prevent a greater wrong may be the right thing to do. It is beyond the scope or intent of this chapter to discuss such cases, especially as no known hacker break-ins have been motivated by such instances.

Historically, computer professionals as a group have not been overly concerned with questions of ethics and propriety as they relate to computers. Individuals and some organizations have tried to address these issues, but the whole computing community needs to be involved to address the problems in any comprehensive manner. Too often, we view computers simply as machines and algorithms, and we do not perceive the, serious ethical questions inherent in their use.

When we consider, however, that these machines influence the quality of life of millions of individuals, both directly and indirectly, we understand that there are broader issues. Computers are used to design, analyze, support, and control applications that protect and guide the lives and finances of people. Our use (and misuse) of computing-systems may have effects beyond our wildest imagining. Thus, we must reconsider our attitudes about acts demonstrating a lack of respect for the rights and privacy of other people's computers and data.

We must also consider what our attitudes will be toward future security problems. In particular, we should consider the effect of widely publishing the source code for worms, viruses, and other threats to security. Although we need a process for rapidly disseminating corrections and security information as they become known, we should realize that widespread publication of details will imperil sites where users are unwilling or unable to install updates and fixes.[3] Publication should serve a useful purpose; endangering the security of other people's machines or attempting to force them into making changes they are unable to snake or afford is not ethical.

Finally, we must decide these issues of ethics as a community of professionals and then present them to society as a whole. No matter what laws are passed, and no matter how good security measures might become, they will not be enough for us to have completely secure systems. We also

---

[3]To anticipate the oft-used comment that the "bad guys" already have such information: Not every computer burglar knows or will know every system weakness, unless we provide them with detailed analyses.

need to develop and act according to some shared ethical values. The members of society need to be educated so that they understand the importance of respecting the privacy and ownership of data. If locks and laws were all that kept people from robbing houses, there would be many more burglars than there are now; the shared mores about the sanctity of personal property are an important influence in the prevention of burglary. It is our duty as informed professionals to help extend those mores into the realm of computing.

References

Adelaide, John Perry Barlow, Robert Jacobson Bluefire, Russell Brand, Clifford Stoll, Dave Hughes, Franck Drake, Eddie Joe Homeboy, Emmanuel Goldstein, Hank Roberts, Jim Gasperini JIMG, Jon Carroll JRC, Lee Felsenstein, Tom Mandel, Robert Horvitz RH, Richard Stallman RMS, Glenn Tenney, Acid Phreak, and Phiber Optik. (1990). "Is Computer Hacking a Crime?" *Harper's Magazine*, Vol. 280, No. 1678, pp. 45–57.

Baird, Bruce J., Lindsay L. Bard Jr., and Ronald P. Ranauro. (1987). "The Moral Cracker?" *Computers and Security*, Vol. 6, No. 6, pp. 471–478.

Denning, Peter J., ed. (1991). *Computers Under Attack: Intruders, Worms, and Viruses*. New York, ACM Books/Addison-Wesley.

Denning, P. J., D. E. Comer, D. Gries, M. C. Mulder, A. Tucker, A. J. Turner, and P. R. Young. (1989). "Computing as a Discipline." *Communications of the ACM*, Vol. 32, No. 1, pp. 9–23.

Hoffman, Lance, ed. (1990). *Rogue Programs: Viruses, Worms, and Trojan Horses*. New York, Van Nostrand Reinhold.

Landreth, Bill. (1984). *Out of the Inner Circle: A Hacker's Guide to Computer Security*. New York, Microsoft Press.

McIlroy, M. Douglas. (1990). "Unsafe at Any Price." *Information Technology Quarterly*, Vol. IX, No. 2, pp. 21–23.

Schwartz, John. (1990). "The Hacker Dragnet." *Newsweek*, Vol. 65, No. 18.

Seeley, Donn. (1989 January). "A tour of the worm." *In Proceedings of the Winter 1989 Usenix Conference*. The Usenix Association.

Spafford, Eugene H. (1989a). "An analysis of the Internet Worm." In C. Ghezzi and J. A. McDermid, eds. *Proceedings of the 2nd European Software Engineering Conference*, New York Springer-Verlag, pp. 446–468.

Spafford, Eugene H. (1989b). "The Internet Worm: Crisis and Aftermath." *Communications of the ACM*, Vol. 32, No. 6, pp. 678–698.

Spafford, Eugene H., Kathleen A. Heaphy, and David J. Ferbrache. (1989). *Computer Viruses: Dealing with Electronic Vandalism and Programmed Threats*. Arlington, VA, ADAPSO.

Stallman, Richard. (1986). "The GNU Manifesto." *In GNU EMacs Manual*, Free Software Foundation, pp. 233–248.

Stang, David J. (1990). *Computer Viruses*, 2nd ed. Washington, DC: National Computer Security Association.

Stoll, Clifford. (1989). *Cuckoo's Egg*. New York, Doubleday.

Tucker, Allen B., Bruce H. Barnes, Robert M. Aiken, Keith Barter, Kim B. Bruce, J. Thomas Cain, Susan E. Corny, Gerald L. Engel, Richard G. Epstein, Doris K, Lidtke, Michael C. Mulder, Jean B. Rogers, Eugene H. Spafford, and A. Joe Turner. (1991). *Computing Curriculo 1991*. IEEE Society.

♔ QUESTIONS FOR ANALYSIS

1. Why does Spafford, a computer scientist, think that it is important for the ethics of computer break-ins be discussed?

2. What does Spafford understand as ethics? Why does he emphasize actions rather than results Is his approach to ethics more like Kant's or Mill's?

3. What is the "hacker ethic"? What does Spafford find objectionable about it?

4. Some hackers try to justify their actions as a public service of testing computer security systems and exposing their flaws. Why does Spafford find this objectionable?

5. What is the "idle system" argument that hackers use to justify their actions? What are the objections to this?

6. What is the "student hacker" argument and what are the objections to it?

7. What is the "social protector" argument and what are the objections to it?

8. Can you think of additional arguments hackers use to justify their actions? How would Spafford assess the ethics of those arguments?

Cyberstalking, Personal Privacy, and Moral Responsibility[1]

HERMAN T. TAVANI AND FRANCES S. GRODZINSKY

In this excerpt from a longer article, some of the moral issues presented by the more dangerous aspects of cyberspace are explored. Herman T. Tavani is a professor emeritus of philosophy at Rivier College, and Frances S. Grodzinsky is a professor of computer science and information technology at Sacred Heart University. The easy availability of personal information about all of us on the Internet also makes it easier for criminals who stalk and sometimes murder their prey. Tavani and Grodzinsky ask whether so much private information should be available on the Internet and whether all Internet users have a moral obligation to assist victims of cyberstalking.

CYBERSTALKING: AN INTRODUCTION AND OVERVIEW

What exactly is cyberstalking, and how do stalking incidents in cyberspace raise concerns for ethics? In answering these questions, we begin with a definition of stalking in general. According to *Webster's New World Dictionary of the American Language*, to engage in stalking is 'to pursue or approach game, an enemy, etc. stealthily, as from cover.' In the context of criminal activities involving human beings, a stalking crime is generally considered to be one in which an individual ('the stalker') clandestinely tracks the movements of an another individual or individuals ('the stalkee[s]'). Cyberstalking can be understood as a form of behavior in which certain types of stalking related activities, which in the past have occurred in physical space, are extended to the on-line world. On the one hand, we do not claim that cyberstalking is a new kind of crime.[2] On the other hand, we believe that the Internet has made a relevant difference with respect to stalking-related crimes because of the ways in which stalking activities can now be carried out. For example, Internet stalkers can operate anonymously or pseudononymously while on-line. In addition, a cyberstalker can stalk one or more individuals from the comfort of his or her home,

and thus not have to venture out into the physical world to stalk someone. So Internet technology has provided stalkers with a certain mode of stalking that was not possible in the pre-Internet era.

Many people have become concerned about the kind of stalking-related activities that have recently occurred in cyberspace, and there are several reasons why these individuals would seem justified in their concern. Because stalking crimes in general are not fully understood in terms of their conceptual boundaries and their implications, it is that much more difficult to comprehend exactly what it would mean to commit a stalking crime in the cyber-realm....

SOME ETHICAL REFLECTIONS ON THE AMY BOYER CASE

On October 15, 1999, Amy Boyer, a twenty-year-old resident of Nashua, NH, was murdered by a young man who had stalked her via the Internet. Her stalker, Liam Youens, was able to carry out many of the stalking activities that eventually led to Boyer's death by using a variety of on-line tools available to him. Through the use of standard Internet search facilities, and related on-line tools, Youens was able to find out where Boyer lived, where she worked, what kind of vehicle she drove, and so forth. In addition to using Internet search-related tools to

With kind permission from Springer Science+Business Media: Ethics and Information Technology, "Cyberstalking, Personal Privacy, and Moral Responsibility," Herman T. Tavani and Frances S. Grodzinsky, 4 (2002): 123–132.

acquire personal information about Boyer, Youens was also able to take advantage of other kinds of online facilities, such as those provided by Internet service providers (ISPs), to construct two Web sites. On one site, he posted personal information about Boyer, including a picture of her; and on another site, Youens described, in explicit detail, his plans to murder Boyer.

The Amy Boyer case has raised some controversial questions, many of which would seem to have significant moral implications for cyberspace. But is there anything special about the Amy Boyer case from an ethical perspective? One might be inclined to answer *no*. For example, one could argue that 'murder is murder', and that whether a murderer uses a computing device that included Internet tools to assist in carrying out a particular murder is irrelevant from an ethical point of view. One could further argue that there is nothing special about cyberstalking incidents in general—irrespective of whether or not those incidents result in the death of the victims—since stalking activities have had a long history of occurrence in the 'off-line' world. According to this line of reasoning, the use of Internet technology could be seen simply as the latest in a series of tools or techniques that have become available to stalkers to assist them in carrying out their criminal activities. However, it could also be argued that certain aspects of cyberstalking raise special problems that challenge our conventional moral and legal frameworks. For example, one could point out that a cyberstalker can stalk multiple victims simultaneously through the use of multiple 'windows' on his or her computer. The stalker can also stalk victims who happen to live in states and countries that are geographically distant from the stalker. We leave open the question whether any of the ethical issues involving cyberstalking are new or unique.[3] Instead, we focus on some ways in which cyberstalking challenges our existing moral framework.

We have argued elsewhere (see Grodzinsky and Tavani, 2002) that cyberstalking activities have significant implications for a range of ethical and social issues, including security, free speech, and censorship. In this essay, we argue that cyberstalking also raises questions involving personal privacy, moral responsibility and legal liability. Our primary focus, however, is on some of the ways that these particular ethical

issues impact the Amy Boyer case. For example, was Boyer's right to (or at least her expectations about) privacy violated because of the personal information about her that was made available so easily to Internet users such as Liam Youens? Did Youens have a 'right' to set up a dedicated Web site about Amy Boyer without Boyer's knowledge and express consent; and did Youens have a right to post on that Web site any kind of information about Boyer—regardless of whether that information about her was psychologically harmful, offensive, or defamatory? If so, is such a right one that is—or ought to be—protected by free speech? Should the two ISPs that permitted Youens to post such information to Web sites that reside in their Internet 'space' be held legally liable, especially when information contained on those sites can easily lead to someone being physically harmed or, as in the case of Amy Boyer, murdered? Furthermore, do ordinary users who happen to come across a web site that contains a positing of a death threat directed at an individual or group of individuals have a moral responsibility to inform those individuals whose lives are threatened? …

INTERNET SEARCH ENGINES, PUBLIC RECORDS, AND PERSONAL PRIVACY

Consider the useful, and arguably important, function that Internet search engines provide in directing us to online resources involving academic research, commerce, recreation, and so forth. Hence, some might be surprised by the suggestion that search-engine technology itself could be controversial in some way. However, search engines can also be used to locate personal information about individuals. Sometimes that personal information resides in the form of public records that are available to Internet users, as in the case of information acquired about Amy Boyer by Liam Youens. Other types of personal information about individuals can also be acquired easily because of certain kinds of personal data that have been made accessible to Internet search engines without the knowledge and consent of the person or persons on whom an on-line search is conducted. But one might still ask why exactly the use of search-engine technology is controversial with respect to the privacy of individuals. Consider that an individual may be unaware that his or her name is among those included in one or more databases accessible to search engines. Because of this, individuals have little, if any, control over how information about them can be made available and be disseminated across the Internet.[4] This was certainly the case in the incident involving Amy Boyer, who had no knowledge about or control over the ways in which certain kinds of personal information about her was accessible to Youens through Internet search engines. It should be noted that Boyer neither placed any personal information about herself on the Internet, nor was she aware that such information about her had been so listed.

It could be argued that all information currently available on the Internet, including information about individual persons such as Amy Boyer, is, by virtue of the fact that it resides on the Internet, public information. Traditionally, information about persons that is available to the general public has not been protected by privacy laws and policies. We can, of course, question whether all of the information currently available on the Internet should be treated as 'public information' that deserves no normative protection.

Because of concerns related to the easy flow of personal information between and across databases, certain laws have been enacted to set limits on the ways in which electronic records containing *confidential* or *intimate* data can be exchanged. However, these laws and policies typically apply only to the exchange of electronic information such as that contained in medical records and financial records. Helen Nissenbaum (1998) has pointed out that such protection does not apply to personal information in the public sphere or in what she describes as 'spheres other than the intimate.'[5] Unfortunately for Amy Boyer, the kind of information that was gathered about her by Youens would be considered non-intimate and non-confidential in nature and thus would likely be viewed, by default, as information that does not warrant normative protection. Is this presumption about non-intimate personal information that is publicly available on the Internet one that it is either reasonable or fair? Was it fair to Amy Boyer?

The Commodification of Personal Information in Public Records

With respect to privacy policies and laws in the Internet age, what status should be accorded to personal information that resides in public sources, such as in public records? Consider that in the era preceding the Internet, information of this particular kind could be acquired by individuals who were willing to travel to municipal buildings and, where applicable, pay a small fee for a copy of the desired records. If this kind of information was already available to the general public before the advent of cyber-technology, why should its status necessarily change because of the new technology? Perhaps an equally important question is: Why were such records made public in the first place? For example, were they made public so that on-line entrepreneurs like Docusearch.com could collect this information, combine it with other kinds of personal information, and then sell it for a profit? Of course, it could be argued that entrepreneurs who were so motivated could have engaged in this activity—and some, no doubt, did—in the era preceding the Internet. But we could respond by asking how profitable and how practical such an enterprise would have been.

First, consider that 'information merchants' would have had to purchase copies of the physical records (that were publicly available). These merchants would then have had to hire legions of clerks to convert the purchased data into electronic form, sort the data according to some scheme, and finally prepare it for sale. This process, in addition to being highly impractical in terms of certain physical requirements, would hardly have been a profitable venture given the amount of labor and cost involved. So, most likely, it would not have occurred to entrepreneurs to engage in such a business venture prior to the advent of sophisticated information technology. But again, we should ask why public records were made 'public' in the first place.

In order for governmental agencies at the local, state, and federal levels to operate efficiently, records of certain kinds of personal information were needed to be readily available for access. For example, municipal governments needed certain information for tax-assessment purposes, such as assessing tax rates for houses and commercial real estate. State governments needed information about motor vehicles registered in a particular state as well as information about the residents of that state who are licensed to drive those vehicles. And federal governments needed relevant information as well. Those records had to be accessible to governmental agencies at various levels and had to be able to be transferred and exchanged relatively easily. Since the records in question contained personal information that was generally considered to be neither confidential nor intimate, there were good reasons to declare them 'public records.' It was assumed that no harm could come to individuals because of the availability of those public records, and it was believed that communities would be better served because of the access and flow of those records for purposes that seemed to be legitimate. But certain factors have changed significantly. Information-gathering companies now access those public records, manipulate the records in certain ways, and then sell that information to third parties.[6] Was this the original intent for making such information accessible to the public?

A Questionable Inference

Many information merchants seem to believe that because: (a) *public records have always been available in a public space*; and (b) *the Internet is a public space*; it follows that (c) *all public records ought to be made available online*. According to this line of reasoning, it is not only a good thing that many public records have, in fact, been placed on-line; rather it is assumed that municipal governments should be required to make *all* public records available online. Defenders of this view often proceed on the reasoning that, as citizens, we have a right to know what the government is up to (based on the notion of freedom of information). Placing public records on-line, they further assume, will ensure that such information flows freely. However, there have now been several cases in which operating on such a presumption has caused outrage on the part of many citizens,[7] as well as harm to some, which in the case of Amy Boyer resulted

in death. So perhaps we should rethink our policies regarding access toon-line public records. We should also perhaps develop specific policies and guidelines regarding which kinds of personal information should be made available to search engines.

If Youens [had] had to track down Amy Boyer without the aid of Internet search facilities, would it have made a difference? Would he have gone to the relevant municipal building to acquire information about Boyer (or would he possibly have hired a private detective to do so)? If Youens himself had gone to the municipal building, would it have been possible that someone, for example a clerk in one of the offices, might have noticed that Youens was behaving strangely? If so, would such an observation have promoted the clerk to notify his or her supervisor or possibly even the police? And would such an action, in turn, possibly have helped to avoid the tragic outcome of the Boyer case? Of course, each of these questions is speculative in nature.[8] And because we are focusing here on the Boyer incident, it is difficult do say what the answers to these questions would mean in a broader sense with regard to cybers talking and to the easy access of public records. But these questions do give us some pause, and they may force us to reconsider our current beliefs about the public vs. private realm of personal information. These questions also cause us to consider the need for implementing explicit policies with regard to use of Internet search engines in the retrieval of personal information.

What can we conclude so far with respect to Amy Boyer's rights and expectations regarding privacy? Was her privacy violated; and if so, in what sense? Amy Boyer's stepfather, Tim Remsberg, believes that his stepdaughter's privacy was indeed violated. He has appeared before congressional groups and has influenced those in the U.S. Congress to sponsor legislation that would make it illegal to sell the social security numbers of one or more individuals as a part of online commercial transactions. Remsberg has also sued Docusearch.com, the online company that provided Youens with information about where Boyer lived and worked. Additionally, Remsberg has filed a wrongful death suit against Tripod and Geocities, the two ISPs that hosted the Web sites that Youens set up about Boyer....

MORAL OBLIGATION AT THE LEVEL OF INDIVIDUALS

We now consider the question of individual moral obligation, by asking what kinds of responsibilities Internet users have to inform 'would-be victims' of their immanent danger to online stalkers. For example, if an Internet user had been aware of Boyer's situation, should that user have notified Boyer that she was being stalked? In other words, is that user under a moral obligation to do so? If we want to be responsible, or at least caring citizens, in cyberspace, the answer would seem to be *yes*. In this case, it would not be morally permissible to wait for stalking activities to move into physical space before we took any action.

Various proposals for controlling individual behavior in on-line society have resulted in a conflict between those who wish to regulate by law and those who wish to preserve the practice of self-regulation. Of course, this dispute is sometimes also at the base of arguments involving claims having to do with a 'safe' social space vs. 'restrictive' one. In the case of cyberstalking, should our duty, if we have one, to assist others be based on legal regulations or should it rest on grounds of individual moral obligation to assist others?

What exactly is meant by 'moral obligation'? Historically, philosophers have offered diverse, and sometimes competing, definitions of what is meant by this expression. An Internet user consulting a dictionary to locate a colloquial definition would likely discover one similar to the following: '[moral obligation is] founded on the fundamental principles of right conduct rather than on legalities enactment of custom' (*Random House Dictionary*). Of course, philosophers have attempted to give us far more rigorous definitions of 'moral obligation.' An interesting question is whether our notion of moral obligation is one that is derived from our concept of justice, or whether instead our sense of 'justice' derives from moral obligation. This, obviously, is a complex question and is one that cannot be satisfactorily discussed and answered in this paper. Of course, the question of which moral notion—obligation or justice—is more fundamental could help us to get a clearer sense of exactly what is at stake in disputes involving individual moral responsibility. Contemporary philosophers and ethicists as diverse as Josef Peiper (1966), Carol Gilligan (1982), and Anton Vedder (2001) have explored this question. Unfortunately, we are not able to examine the three positions in the depth that each deserves. Nonetheless, we sketch out some general themes in their respective arguments.

Three Views of Moral Obligation: The Peiper, Gilligan, and Vedder Models

Josef Peiper (1966) has argued that the concept of moral obligation is one that is not only 'personal' but also linked to one's community. For Peiper, 'doing good' is more than obeying some abstract norm (i.e., some Kantian abstract notion of duty and universality). Rather, it is about the individual's relationship to other individuals and to the community itself. Carol Gilligan (1982), in her work in feminist ethics, first proposed a position similar to Peiper's. Both Peiper and Gilligan suggest that moral obligation goes far beyond the notion of an individual simply obeying laws. For them, moral obligation is closely tied with a more complex concept of justice. As such, justice involves the *relationship* of individuals, including their individual moral obligations to one another. In the writings of both Peiper and Gilligan, despite their very different objectives, can be found the basis for the thesis that individuals are interconnected and that these individual relationships play a primary role in the development of the concept of moral responsibility.

The notion of moral obligation is seen as extending beyond the self to others, both in Pieper's concept of 'commutative justice' and Gilligan's 'ethic of care.' This 'ethic of care,' as it is labeled in feminist ethics, is more than a mere 'non-interference ethic.' Based on that belief that care and justice are part of the same moral framework, it has been argued that individuals have a moral obligation to assist others and to prevent harm. From this perspective, individuals would be compelled to act from a basis of moral obligation, even though there may be no specific laws or rules to prescribe such actions.[9]

Anton Vedder (2001) has recently put forth a theory of moral obligation that also has implications at the level of the individual. From Vedder's view, it would seem to follow that we cannot excuse ourselves from our moral responsibility to inform the victim of a threat to his/her life simply because there is no specific law obligating us to do so. Vedder asserts that 'the sheer ability and opportunity to act in order to avoid or prevent harm, danger, and offense from taking place' puts an obligation on the agent. We saw in the preceding section how Vedder's argument can be applied to issues of moral responsibility involving organisations. He also points out that in cases 'when harm, danger or offense would be considerable while the appropriate action would not present significant risks, costs or burdens to the agent,' the same notion of moral responsibility applies, regardless of whether the *agent* is a natural person or an organization (Vedder, 2001).

A Minimalist Notion of Moral Obligation

Some have argued that, while morality can demand of an agent that he or she 'do no harm' to others, it cannot *require* the agent to actively 'prevent harm' or 'do good.' In one sense, to do no harm is to act in accordance with moral obligation. But is doing so always sufficient for complying with what is required of us as moral agents? In other words, if it is in our power to prevent harm and to do good, *should* we always be required to do so? And, if the answer to this question is *yes*, what are the grounds for such a theory of obligation.

A number of theoretical perspectives support the view that individuals should prevent harm (and other wise do good) whenever it is in their power to do so. For example, if one believes, as some natural law theorists assert, that the purpose of morality is to alleviate human suffering and to promote human flourishing whenever possible, then clearly we would seem obligated to prevent harm in cyberspace. For an interesting account of this type of moral theory, see Louis

Pojman (2001). Unfortunately, we are not able to present Pojman's argument here in the detail that it deserves, since doing so would take us beyond the scope of this paper. But we can at least now see how, based on a model like Pojman's, one might develop a fuller theory in which individuals have an obligation to prevent harm or a 'duty to assist.' Of course, we recognize the difficulties of defending a natural law theory and we are not prepared to do so here. However, we also believe that the kind of limited or 'moderate' natural law theories that can be found in Pojman, and to some extent in James Moor (1988), can be very useful in making the case for individual moral obligation.

Expanding the Sphere of Moral Obligation: The Duty to Assist

Questions concerning whether individuals have a 'duty to assist' others often arise in the aftermath of highly publicized crimes, such as the one involving in the Kitty Genovese case in 1964. A young woman, Genovese was murdered on the street outside her apartment building in Queens, New York, as thirty-eight of her neighbors watched. None of her neighbors called the police during the 35-minute period of repeated stabbings. Some have since referred to this refusal to assist a neighbor in critical need as 'the Genovese syndrome.' Police involved in the Genovese case believe that the witnesses were morally obligated to notify the police, even though there may have been no formal law or specific statute requiring them to do so.

Drawing an analogy between the Genovese and Boyer cases, we can ask whether users who might have been able to assist Boyer should have done so (i.e., morally obligated to assist). We can also ask what kind of place cyberspace will become, if people refuse to assist users who may be at risk to predators and murderers. Is our obligation to our fellow users one in which we are required merely to do no harm? Peiper, Gilligan and Vedder would each answer *no*. Consider the potential harm that could come from doing nothing vs. the level of inconvenience caused to self, which would be minimal, by coming to the assistance of others who may be in danger in cyberspace. In the cyberstalking case involving Barber and Dellapenta, Barber's father, with the cooperation of the men who were soliciting her, provided evidence that led to Dellapenta's arrest. In the case of Amy Boyer, however, the sense of individual moral responsibility was not apparent, since certain online users had indeed viewed the Youens' Web site and did not inform Amy Boyer that she was being stalked. As in the case of Kitty Genovese, Boyer was also murdered. Was Boyer's death an on-line manifestation of the 'Genovese syndrome?'

In light of what happened to Amy Boyer, we suggest that on-line users adopt a notion of individual responsibility to assist others. Doing so would help to keep cyberspace a safer place for everyone, but especially for women and children who are particularly vulnerable groups. Some might be inclined to argue that the threat to Boyer was merely virtual, since the threat itself did not occur in physical space.[10] Such an argument, however, ignores the fact that threats in virtual space have, in fact, resulted in physical harm to individuals. In addition to the harm resulting in cyberstalking cases, consider the physical harm that has resulted to some victims of Internet pedophilia. In avoiding our individual duty to assist, individual users disconnect themselves from their responsibility towards fellow human beings. When they accept the duty to assist, they are acknowledging their moral obligation to help prevent others from being harmed.

CONCLUSION

We have examined some ethical aspects of cyberstalking in general, and the Amy Boyer case in particular. We saw that the cyberstalking case involving Boyer raised privacy concerns that cause us to reconsider the kinds of protections currently accorded to on-line public records. We also saw that cyberstalking issues have raised questions for ISPs having to do with legal liability and moral responsibility. It was argued that issues of moral responsibility involving cyberstalking span two spheres: the collective (e.g., ISPs) and the individual (i.e., ordinary Internet users). We believe

that both ISPs and individual users, each in different ways, should assume some moral responsibility for preventing harm from coming to individuals targeted by cyberstalkers. Although we recognise the difficulties inherent in defending arguments involving moral responsibility at both the collective and individual levels, we nonetheless offer some preliminary suggestions for why both organisations (such as ISPs) and individuals should act to prevent harm from coming to their fellow Internet users, whenever it is in their power to do so.

ACKNOWLEDGMENTS

We are grateful to Anton Vedder for some very helpful comments on an earlier version of this paper. We also wish to thank Detective Sergeant Frank Paison of the Nashua, NH Police Department, who was the chief investigator in the Amy Boyer cyberstalking case, for some helpful information that he provided during an interview with him.

BIBLIOGRAPHY

Alison Adam. Cyberstalking: Gender and Computer Ethics. In Eileen Green and Alison Adam, Editors, *Virtual Gender: Technology, Consumption, and Identity*, pages 209–234. Routledge, London, 2001.

Alison Adam. Cyberstalking and Internet Pornography: Gender and Gaze. *Ethics and Information Technology*, 4(2): 133–142, 2002.

Richard T. De George. Law and Ethics in the Information Age. A paper presented at River College, Nashua, NH, April 3, 2001.

Carol Gilligan. *In a Different Voice*. Harvard University Press, Cambridge, 1982.

Frances S. Grodzinsky and Herman. T. Tavani. Is Cyberstalking a Special Type of Computer Crime? In Terrell Ward Bynum, et al. editors. *Proceedings of ETHICPMP 2001: The Fifth International Conference on the Social and Ethical Impacts of Information and Communication Technology*, Vol. 2, pages 72–81. Wydawnicktwo Mikom Publishers, Gdańsk, Poland, 2001.

Frances S. Grodzinsky and Herman T. Tavani. Cyberstalking, Moral Responsibility, and Legal Liability Issues for Internet Service Providers. In Joseph Herkert, editor, *Proceedings of ISTAS 2002: The*

International Symposium on Technology and Society. pages 331–339. IEEE Computer Society Press, Los Alamitos, CA, 2002.

Deborah G. Johnson. *Computer Ethics*, 3rd ed. Prentice Hall, Upper Saddle River, NJ, 2001.

James H. Moor. Reason, Relativity, and Responsibility in Computer Ethics. *Computers and Society*, 28(1): 14–21, 1998.

James H. Moor. Just Consequentialism. A paper presented at the 2000–2001 River College Humanities Lecture Series, Nashua, NH, February 20, 2001.

Helen Nissenbaum. Computing and Accountability. In Deborah Y. Johnson and Helen Nissenbaum, Editors, *Computing, Ethics and Social Values*, pages 526–538. Englewood Cliffs, NJ, Prentice Hall, 1995.

Helen Nissenbaum. Toward an Approach to Privacy in Public: Challenges of Information Technology. *Ethics & Behavior*, 7(3): 207–219, 1997.

Helen Nissenbaum. Protecting Privacy in an Information Age: The Problem of Privacy in Public. *Law and Philosophy*, 17: 559–496. 1998.

Josef Peiper: *The Four Cardinal Virtues*. University of Notre Dame Press, Indiana, 1966.

Louis P. Pojman, *Ethics: Discovering Right and Wrong*, 4th ed. Wadsworth, Belmont, CA, 2001.

Michael Scanlan. Informational Privacy and Moral Values. *Ethics and Information Technology*, 3(1): 3–12, 2001.

Richard A. Spinello. Internet Service Providers and Defamation: New Standards of Liability. In Richard A. Spinello and Herman T. Tavanii, Editors, *Reading in CyberEthics*, pages 198–209. Sudbury, MA, Jones and Bartlett, 2001.

Herman T. Tavani. Internet Search Engines and Personal Privacy. In Jeroen van den Hoven, Editor, *Proceedings of CEPE '97: Conference on Computer Ethics—Philosophical Enquiry*, pages 214–223. Erasmus University Press, Rotterdam, The Netherlands, 1998.

Herman T. Tavani, Defining the Boundaries of Computer Crime: Piracy, Break-ins and Sabotage in Cyberspace. *Computers and Society*, 30(4): 3–9, 2000.

Herman T. Tavani. The Uniqueness Debate in Computer Ethics: What Exactly Is at Issue, and Why Does It Matter? *Ethics and Information Technology*, 4(1): 37–54, 2002.

Anton H. Vedder. Accountability of Internet Access and Service Providers: Strict Liability entering Ethics. *Ethics and Information Technology*, 3(1): 67–74, 2001.

NOTES

1. An earlier version of this paper was presented at the CEPE 2001 Conference, Lancaster University, UK, December 14–16, 2001. The present paper expands on two earlier works (Grodzinsky and Tavani, 2001, 2002). Portions of this article are extracted from H.T. Tavani, *Ethics in an Age of Information and Communication Technology* (forthcoming from John Wiley & Sons Publishers). We are grateful to Wiley for permission to use that material in this paper.

2. Nor do we argue that cyberstalking is a 'genuine computer crime.' See Tavani (2000) for some distinctions that can be drawn between genuine computer crimes and computer-related crimes.

3. For an in-depth discussion of the question whether cyberstalking has introduced any unique ethical issues, see Tavani (2002).

4. For a more detailed discussion of privacy problems that can arise from certain uses of Internet search engines, see Tavani (1998).

5. See also Nissenbaum (1997) for a discussion of some of the challenges that information technology poses for the 'problem of privacy in public.'

6. Richard De George (2001) has suggested that because Internet and computing technology has made it possible for organisations and individuals to gather information in ways that were not possible in the pre-Internet era, we need to reconsider why societies have public records and how those records should be protected.

7. For example, Michael Scanlan (2001) describes a controversial case involving the state of Oregon, which sold records in its Motor Vehicle Registry database to an on-line consulting business. The citizens of Oregon complained and the state eventually reversed its policy regarding the sale of information about its licensed drivers.

8. Richard De George (2001) points out that when public records were accessible only in public buildings, there was a much easier way of tracing the acquisition of those records in the event that some 'misuse' had been made of the information contained in them.

9. For a discussion of some ways in which Gilligan's system of ethics can be applied to issues involving cyberstalking, as well as to issues in computer ethics in general, see Alison Adam (2001, 2002).

10. This type of reasoning is a variation of what James Moor (2001) refers to as the 'virtuality fallacy.' According to this particular line of fallacious reasoning: X exists in cyberspace; cyberspace is not in the real world; therefore, X is exempt from the demands of the real world.

☙ QUESTIONS FOR ANALYSIS

1. Does the sad fact of cyberstalking and the murder of innocent victims like Amy Boyer justify more serious efforts to restrict access to our private data on the Internet? Has our demand for easy access to information gone too far, resulting in these crimes? What kind of legislation do you believe would be appropriate to curtail such activities, balancing freedom of expression of non-criminals with the threatening behavior of people like Boyer's murderer?

2. Should the freedom of expression to post threatening web sites, as Boyer's murderer did, be restricted? Who should police such sites? Should the Internet service providers be responsible for monitoring such web sites and taking them offline?

3. Would you, as a user of the Internet, feel a moral obligation to contact people like Amy Boyer if you saw something on the Web that seemed threatening? Or would you be reluctant to "get involved," as people were in the Kitty Genovese case many years ago in New York?

CASE PRESENTATION

Ticketed for Obscenity on the Information Superhighway

Robert and Carleen Thomas ran a computer bulletin board for members only from their home in Milpitas, California. What bound the members of Amateur Action Bulletin Board System was an interest in kinky pornography, which the married couple provided for a fee. The operation ran smoothly until a postal inspector in Memphis, Tennessee, joined the bulletin board under an assumed name and began receiving sexually explicit photographs on his computer. As a result, the Thomases were charged with violating federal obscenity laws. In July of 1994 they were tried and convicted of eleven counts of transmitting obscenity through interstate phone lines. They were sentenced to 37 and 30 months of incarceration, respectively.

Theirs was not the first case of a bulletin board operator being tried for violating federal obscenity laws, but in all previous cases the trials were held in the area where the material originated. The Thomas trial was held in Memphis, where the photographs were received. A federal appeals court in Cincinnati upheld their convictions and sentences in January 1996.

The U.S. Supreme Court, in 1997, declined to hear the case. The issue that free-speech supporters had hoped the Court would address was the obscenity test from *Miller v. California*, which appeals to "contemporary community standards," where *community* means "local community." Memphis is a very conservative community when it comes to pornography and censorship; its standards are stricter than California's. For the Thomases, it was a question of fairness. Did the prosecutors shop around for a trial venue that would guarantee a conviction? Should the defendants be judged by the standards of a community other than their own? For the nation's freedom of speech on the information superhighway, the questions are much broader: What constitutes a community on computer networks? Should the standards of the most conservative communities govern the free-speech rights of the rest of the country? The Appeals Court had rejected the arguments of the Thomases' lawyers that new technology had wiped out traditional concepts of community. Instead, it ruled that *Miller* applies to the Internet.

Civil libertarians consider the Thomas case an alarming reminder of the problems in applying traditional concepts of free speech to the Internet. Electronic Internet communications do not always have a clear counterpart in traditional print formats, and new principles are needed to guarantee traditional rights.

☙ QUESTIONS FOR ANALYSIS

1. How would you answer the four questions posed in the third paragraph?

2. Does the notion of a local community make sense in the context of a computer network available to individuals throughout the nation and much of the world?

3. *Miller v. California*'s obscenity test was designed in part to let residents control their own communities. Let the standards of New Yorkers determine what bookstores and movie theaters are acceptable in New York City, and let those of Memphis residents determine the

same for their city. Is that purpose applicable to international computer networks?

4. What kind of obscenity test do you think is appropriate for computer networks?

5. Should minors be protected from indecent material on the Internet? If so, how?

CASE PRESENTATION

A Chill in Cyberspace

When John Osborne and his roommate moved from Florida to Georgia in 1997, their U-Haul rental truck broke down repeatedly, and their trip turned into a 27-hour nightmare. After U-Haul seized their property and made them pay to fix the truck, Osborne filed complaints with U-Haul and the Better Business Bureau. When those approaches failed to resolve the matter to Osborne's satisfaction, he turned to the Internet, posting a site called "The U-Hell Website: Misadventures in Moving," and he encouraged disgruntled U-Haul customers to post their own stories.

U-Haul filed suit in Arizona for libel and trademark infringement, claiming that Arizona Internet users would be able to see the site, but also knowing that Osborne could not afford to defend himself in a distant state. The Electronic Frontier Foundation and the Arizona ACLU provided free legal assistance to Osborne and got the case dismissed. U-Haul then threatened to sue him in Georgia, where he lived, but there is no court record of any such suit.

♔ QUESTIONS FOR ANALYSIS

1. Osborne successfully argued that the Internet's availability in Arizona was not sufficient to warrant filing a lawsuit against him in that state. Yet the Thomases, in the previous case presentation, were not able to succeed with such an argument. Do the courts seem clear on the nature of the Internet in making what seem to be contradictory rulings about the "location" of the Internet? Where do you think "virtual reality" is located? Should wrong-doers be able to escape the reach of the law entirely?

2. Aggressive lawsuits by such companies as U-Haul have had a chilling effect on individual persons with complaints about those companies, creating a *David v. Goliath* scenario that most ordinary people cannot afford to fight. Defamation is not protected under the free-speech guarantees of the first amendment, but should the courts participate

in this apparent attempt by large corporations to suppress legitimate free speech by disgruntled consumers? Knowing Osborne's legal nightmare with U-Haul, would you be less likely to post angry web sites or comments to a chatroom criticizing a big company by name? Should the courts attempt to level the playing field by refusing to hear such defamation cases?

3. In the early years of the Internet, some supporters saw it as the Wild West, with no rules or laws, and reveled in this freedom. Should we try to return to that environment, or should all the laws and ethical principles that apply in non-cyberspace apply to our interactions online?

4. Have you ever posted comments that might be defamatory on a site like Ratemyprofessors.com? Should professors be able to sue for defamatory statements posted on such sites on the Internet?

CASE PRESENTATION

Censoring Political Speech

Although the Internet has been proclaimed an extraordinary mechanism for worldwide communication, free of government interference, political speech is encountering censorship after all, to the dismay of many Internet users.

The German government bans the publication and sale of Adolf Hitler's *Mein Kampf*, a ban originally ordered by the Allies at the end of World War II. That ban was easier to enforce when the book was available only at physical book stores and libraries in a physical form. The Allies and later the German government defended the ban as necessary to prevent the rise of neo-Nazism in the country responsible for the horrors of the Holocaust. With the easy availability of texts online, however, German Internet users can now access the banned book on several Internet sites. Amazon.com ran afoul of the German government when German patrons started ordering the book from the American site, even though the German version of Amazon.com refused to sell the book. Bans on the sale of *Mein Kampf* are widespread in other countries in Europe. It cannot be sold in France, except in scholarly editions with commentaries and discussions. The Netherlands prohibits sale of the book, but not owning or lending it. The state of Bavaria has attempted to prohibit sales on the grounds that it owns the copyright on the book, but the English version has not been copyrighted in Bavaria and is freely available in the United States and the United Kingdom.

A new variation of censorship of political speech is occurring on Twitter. In October 2012, the company agreed to block access in Germany to neo-Nazi accounts that violated German law. Days later, Twitter blocked all access to anti-Semitic posts that were originating in France, in response to demands by Jewish groups in that country. They cited French laws that ban discrimination based on race, ethnicity, or religion.

Another form of censorship of political speech on the Internet has emerged in China. The huge Internet search engine Google.com agreed to censor its search engine in the Chinese language, at the insistence of the Chinese government. Searches in that language do not report sites that present candid information about the democracy protests at Tiananmen Square in 1989 or the protest group Falun Gong, for example. In its defense, Google argues that it does not block access to the actual web sites, but only removes them from the search results. Some staunch supporters of free speech are trying to protest by refusing to use Google or dropping Google ads from their own web sites. Other well-known search engines, including Yahoo and MSN, also entered into censorship agreements with the Chinese government.

After a long struggle, Google has added a link to its site in Hong Kong, which is not censored but exempt from most Chinese laws. On mainland China, some Google services have been curtailed.

⚜ QUESTIONS FOR ANALYSIS

1. Do these attempts at government censorship reduce the value of the Internet as a medium for international education and free speech? Should world governments—or perhaps the United Nations—attempt to intervene and insist on free speech and unfettered access to information?

2. Do you agree with the European governments that fear that being able to read *Mein Kampf* might encourage a resurgence of neo-Nazism? Or would you agree with J. S. Mill and civil libertarians that the best way to learn what is wrong with those benighted ideas is to expose them to the light of day and encourage free and open debate?

3. Is there anything we can do to protest the censorship of the Google.com search engine in China? Or is this a matter of national autonomy that should not concern us? If the U.S. government demanded that Google.com censor its search engine to eliminate access to controversial political speech that the government deemed inappropriate, would you support this censorship?

CASE PRESENTATION

Pirates of the Campuses

In 2004, the Recording Industry Association of America filed lawsuits against 532 individuals for illegally swapping songs. Eighty-nine of those users were students using 21 different university networks across the country. For years, the RIAA had pressured university administrators to crack down on students who were using campus broadband Internet capabilities to swap music using technologies like Napster, in violation of copyright law.

Universities complain that they are trying to get students to behave in compliance with the law by running educational programs about the illegality of file-sharing of copyrighted music. The RIAA complains that these efforts have been ineffective and that they are losing huge revenues from the sale of CDs or legal downloads on the Internet, for which one must pay a fee.

Two much-publicized lawsuits have sided with the industry. In *A&M Records v. Napster*, the Federal Court of Appeals for the Ninth Circuit in 2001 sided with the recording industry in ruling that the Napster technology for sharing music files online encouraged users to violate copyright. The site for free downloads was essentially put out of business, but it has re-emerged along with several other sites to sell the downloads, with a portion of the royalties going to the record industry.

In 2005, the U.S. Supreme Court unanimously sided with Metro-Goldwyn-Mayer Studios in a lawsuit against Grokster Ltd., which developed and promoted a program that facilitated downloads on the Internet of movies, as well as songs. As Justice David Souter wrote in the court's opinion, "We hold that one who distributes a device with the object of promoting its use to infringe copyright … is liable for the resulting acts of infringement by third parties."

⚜ QUESTIONS FOR ANALYSIS

1. Many students believe that downloading free music and movies from the Internet is their best way of protesting what they consider excessively high prices charged by unfair monopolies in the entertainment industry. Do you believe this provides an ethical justification for downloading, in violation of copyright law and the property rights of the movie and recording industries? Are there additional considerations here that provide ethical support for this file-sharing?

2. Deterrence is one major theory of punishment in the criminal law. Now that the recording industry is aggressively filing suit against college students for these downloads, does this reduce the likelihood that you yourself will engage in this practice, whether or not you have in the past? What other considerations would make you less likely to continue to engage in illegal downloading?

3. Say you are a struggling artist, filmmaker, or musician hoping to earn income from your artistic work and support yourself in a career. Do you think it would be fair for future college students to download your work without paying you copyright royalties?

4. Say you are a computer software engineering student. Do you think it will be fair for you to be held responsible if someone misuses the software you design to violate the law? (This is essentially what the courts did in the *Napster* and *Grokster* decisions.)

AFTERWORD

MORE THAN ONE CYNIC has claimed that logical arguments are nothing but rationalizations of our prejudices. And there is, unfortunately, some truth to that claim, at least when it comes to people who spout reason but refuse to listen to reason. But when we are truly open to the arguments of others, the claim clearly misses, especially when we allow ourselves to be convinced by compelling arguments and consequently change our minds.

Now that your course in applied ethics is finished, it might be wise to ask yourself a few questions about it. Did the arguments you came across, either in class or in this book, cause you to reevaluate your positions on some topics? Did any one of them cause you to soften a given position? Cause you to change your mind completely? If you can answer yes to any or all of these questions, the course has served you well, regardless of your grade. If you cannot, you might want to ask yourself another question. Why can't you? And if your quick answer is that you were right all along, you might want to search for a not-so-quick one.

That's one point worth making at the end of your course. Another concerns all the topics you didn't cover, including some in this book (no single-semester course can cover them all) and those not in this book. (For reasons of space and format, we could not include every possible issue in applied ethics.) The latter include questions about "political correctness," for example; about violence, personal freedoms, medical and recreational use of marijuana, and gun safety; and about all the many issues that we can't anticipate but that are sure to arise over the years. Like the issues you did cover, each of them is difficult, involving complex matters of fact, morality, and often law. We hope that your experiences in this course have prepared you to deal with them in a thorough, dispassionate way and maybe to reevaluate your views on some of them.

Finally, we hope that the course has been a real eye-opener for you. Even if you changed your mind about nothing, we hope that you at least were struck by the complexities of the issues you studied, the many ingenious approaches to them you encountered, and the reasonableness of your opponents' positions.

Abolitionist Someone who advocates doing away with a particular practice, such as the death penalty.

Active euthanasia The act of painlessly putting to death persons suffering from incurable conditions or diseases.

***Ad hominem* argument** An argument that relies on attacking the opponent rather than the opponent's argument. When the attack is irrelevant to whether we should accept the opponent's argument, it is considered a fallacy.

Anthropocentric Centering on human beings, or regarding human beings as central to any larger group. In ethics, it means centering on human welfare, or regarding the environment as important only as it affects human welfare.

Argument A collection of statements containing a conclusion and supporting statements (also called evidence, reasons, grounds, or premises) whose purpose is to show that the conclusion is true or likely to be true.

Argument by analogy An argument that concludes that two different things are alike in some ways because they are alike in some other ways. When such an argument fails to make its case, it is considered both a faulty analogy and a fallacy.

Assisted suicide Suicide by a patient, with assistance from a physician, usually by prescribing a lethal dose of drugs.

Autonomy Independence, particularly from the control of outside forces. In philosophy, it refers to the capacity to act on our choices, where these choices are the product of our own goals, desires, and reasoning powers. To have this capacity is to be an autonomous being.

Biocentric Centering on the biosphere, or the earth's ecological system. In ethics, it means regarding the health of the ecological system as central rather than the welfare of humans.

Biotic community In the philosophy of Aldo Leopold and his followers, a community made up of all members of the ecological system, including water, soil, and air as well as living things.

Capitalism An economic system in which the means of production are in private hands and economic decisions are made by private individuals in response to market forces.

Casuistic Determining what is right and wrong by appeal to principles in ethics.

Categorical imperative In the philosophy of Kant, a command that applies to all rational beings independent of their desires, a command they ought to follow whether they want to or not.

Causal generalization The conclusion that one thing causes another because of observations that the first has been followed by the other.

Certiorari Agreement by an appeals court to review the decision of a lower court.

Charity, principle of Understanding the arguments of opponents in the most reasonable or plausible way possible, to give them a fair hearing.

Civil union A formal partnership between two people with some, but not necessarily all, of the rights of a married couple, as recognized by a governmental authority.

Clone An exact genetic copy of a cell, plant, or animal.

Consequentialist Ethical reasoning which looks to the consequences of alternative actions to determine which is right.

Contractarianism An ethical theory based on appeal to a social contract entered into voluntarily.

Counterexample An example that shows a generalization to be false or a rule of reasoning to be invalid.

Cultural relativism In ethics, the view that moral truths are not absolutely true but are relative to a particular society, that whether an act is right or wrong depends on the moral norms of society and not on an absolute standard.

Deductive argument An argument that claims to follow truth-preserving rules.

Deductive logic The area of logic that deals with deductive arguments.

Defamation Words communicating factual claims which are false and which damage the reputation of another person.

Deterrence The preventing or discouraging of an act, often by fear or doubt.

Difference principle In the philosophy of John Rawls, the principle that determines what kinds of inequalities can exist in a just society.

Distributive justice The area of justice that deals with how society's wealth should be distributed among its members.

Ecocentric Centering on the ecological health of the environment. See biocentric.

Egalitarianism The belief in equal rights for all people, including political economic, and social rights.

Entitlement A right or a claim to something.

Equality principle In the philosophy of John Rawls, the principle that every person has a right to the greatest basic freedom compatible with equal freedom for all.

Equivocation Implicitly relying on two or more meanings of the same word. When an argument relies on the premise to reach a conclusion, it is a fallacy.

Ethical relativism The view that moral truths are not absolutely true but true relative to some particular standards.

Eudaimonia Happiness, or total well-being.

Eugenics A movement to improve the genetic makeup of the human race

Euthanasia Literally, "good death." The term is usually applied to the act of ending the life of someone suffering from a fatal or incurable disease or, most commonly in the case of nonhuman animals, ending a life painlessly.

Ex parte Done for one party only; in the absence of the other party in a legal proceeding.

Ex post facto law A law passed after the fact; a retroactive law.

Fallacy An unreliable way of reasoning, one that does not provide good reason for accepting an argument's conclusion.

Faulty analogy An argument by analogy that fails to make its case.

Formal fallacy A rule of reasoning that appears to be truth preserving but isn't.

Germ cell A sperm or an egg.

Globalization The rapid development of the technology, trade, and culture that brings nations together physically as well as symbolically

Greatest happiness principle The moral principle that we should produce the greatest balance of happiness over unhappiness, giving equal consideration to the happiness and unhappiness of everyone who will be affected by our actions.

Hegemony Predominance, or predominant influence, of one state over others.

Holistic ethics Ethical views that focus on duties to some particular whole, such as the biotic community or the state.

Hypothetical imperative In the philosophy of Kant, a command we have reason to follow only if it serves a desire of ours.

Idealist Someone who has high ideals, even if unrealistic and visionary; a philosophical theory that ideas are more real than external objects of perception.

In camera In private; in the chambers of the judge in a legal proceeding.

Individual relativism In ethics, the view that moral truths are not absolute but relative to individuals, that whether an act is right or wrong depends on the convictions of the person performing it and not on an absolute standard.

Inductive argument An argument in which the supporting statements, or evidence, aim to show that it is reasonable to accept that the conclusion is true.

Informal fallacy A common but unreliable reasoning strategy that generally relies on hidden premises that are false, irrelevant, or otherwise suspect.

Involuntary euthanasia Termination of a life when decision is made by someone else, and the patient has never made preferences known to anyone.

Jus ad bellum The justice of war; the law on the use of force.

Jus cogens Overriding principles of general international law.

Jus in bello The law or justice within a war, regardless of the justifiability of the war itself.

Le peuple, c'est moi! I am the people.

Libel Written defamation.

Libertarianism In political thought, the view that all forms of coercion – except to prevent harm to life, liberty, and property – are wrong, whether they come from individuals or from the government.

Living will A document executed by a competent adult directing physicians not to use artificial or extraordinary measures to prolong the person's life.

Marriage A legally recognized relationship between two people

Maxim In the philosophy of Kant, a general principle of behavior: for example, whenever someone hurts me, I will hurt him back

Moral agent A being capable of making moral claims and accepting moral duties.

Moral intuition A moral conviction arrived at after careful consideration of the relevant facts.

Natural law Any law of nature, as opposed to a state law or federal law. In ethics, moral laws that are embedded in nature as scientific laws are.

Natural rights Rights that all persons are born with. Rights that all persons have by virtue of being persons.

Nonvoluntary euthanasia Ending the life of a person suffering a fatal or incurable disease, in which the decision is made by someone other than the patient.

Obscenity In U.S. law, pornography that is not protected by the First Amendment.

Ontological Relating to the theory and nature of being and existence.

Ontology The theory and nature of being and existence.

Passive euthanasia Any act of allowing a patient to die.

Paternalism The practice of treating others as a father would. In political thought, government policies that limit individual rights to protect individuals from harming themselves.

Person In ethics, either an autonomous being or a being who is a full-fledged member of the moral community.

Pluralism The existence of many independent centers of power within a society

Pornography Erotic material that is intended primarily to cause sexual arousal or in fact does have that primary effect.

Practical imperative In Kant's philosophy, respect for persons as ends, never as means.

Premise A supporting statement in an argument. A statement that aims to show that the conclusion is true or likely to be true.

Prima facie duty or obligation An obligation that may or may not be binding at a given time depending on whether some other obligation takes precedence at that time.

Principle of utility The moral principle that we should produce the greatest balance of happiness over unhappiness, giving equal consideration to the happiness and unhappiness of everyone who will be affected by our actions.

Procrustes' bed In Greek mythology, cutting off one's feet to fit the size of the bed; in reasoning, altering important facts to meet an arbitrary or inappropriate standard or rule.

Question-begging argument A form of fallacy in which you assume as a premise what you want to prove.

Realism A political theory favoring pragmatism and literal truth; a philosophical position that universal principles are more real than sensory objects.

Red herring A form of fallacy in which an irrelevant issue is introduced to distract attention from the issue at hand.

Respect for persons The moral principle that we should never use another person merely as a means to our own ends.

Retentionist Someone who advocates keeping in place a particular practice, such as the death penalty.

Retribution Punishment for wrongdoing.

Retributive Punishment that is justified as repayment for past wrongdoing.

Sexual libertarianism The view that sex is morally no different from any other activity; that there are no special moral rules that apply only to sexual behavior.

Si vis pacem, para bellum If you wish for peace, prepare for war

Sine qua non Without which not; something essential or indispensable.

Slander Spoken defamation.

Slippery slope argument Assuming that an action will lead to an unwanted outcome as a result of many small steps that will inevitably follow. If the assumption is not sufficiently justified, it is a fallacy.

Social contract theory Ethical or political thought that views morality or the state as the product of an agreement (a social contract) among individuals.

Socialism An economic system in which major economic issues are recognized as shared obligations of society, such as education, help for the poor and elderly, child care, and health care.

Somatic cell Any cell that is not a germ cell.

Sound deductive argument An argument that passes two tests: that it is valid and that all of its premises are true

Speciesism The position that it is ethically justifiable to give preference to members of the species homo sapiens over other animal species.

Stare decisis The tradition in English common law of following the precedent of previous decisions.

Straw man The form of fallacy in which the opponent's position is distorted.

Supererogatory Acts which are morally good, but are not morally required

Teleological Pertaining to design or ultimate purpose.

Thought experiment A mental exercise in which someone imagines a set of circumstances to try to discover what would follow from it. In ethics, the purpose is usually to test moral principles or rules.

Transfer payment A payment that involves the transfer of wealth from one segment of the population to another; for example, welfare payments.

Truth-preserving rule A valid rule of deductive logic, a rule of reasoning that guarantees that the conclusion is true if the premises are true.

Utilitarianism The consequentialist ethical theory that assesses the rightness of actions as that which produces the greatest good for the greatest number of people. The moral philosophy that considers the principle of utility to be the one basic moral principle.

Valid argument An argument that follows truth-preserving rules only.

Veil of ignorance In the philosophy of John Rawls, a condition for deciding if the basic structures of society are just. To decide from behind a veil of ignorance is to decide without knowing how any one individual will be affected by these structures.

Virtue A habit, tendency, or disposition that helps us to achieve our goals.

Voluntary euthanasia Ending the life of a person suffering a fatal or incurable disease, in which the decision is made by the patient.

Warranted argument An inductive argument in which the supporting statements, or evidence, show that it is reasonable to accept the conclusion.

Welfare capitalism An economic system that follows most tenets of capitalism but also includes transfer payments.

INDEX

CPSIA information can be obtained
at www.ICGtesting.com
Printed in the USA
BVHW011124270721
612974BV00015B/72